The History of Nap

by John Gibson Lockhart

INTRODUCTION

[LOCKHART, 1794-1854]

"Nations yet to come will look back upon his history as to some grand and supernatural romance. The fiery energy of his youthful career, and the magnificent progress of his irresistible ambition, have invested his character with the mysterious grandeur of some heavenly appearance; and when all the lesser tumults and lesser men of our age shall have passed away into the darkness of oblivion, history will still inscribe one mighty era with the majestic name of Napoleon."

These enthusiastic words, too, are Lockhart's, though they are not from this history, but from some "Remarks on the Periodical Criticism of England," which he published in Blackwood's Magazine. They serve, if they are taken in conjunction with his book, to mark his position in the long list of the historians, biographers and critics who have written in English, and from an English or a British point of view, upon "Napoleon the Great." Lockhart, that is to say, was neither of the idolaters, like Hazlitt, nor of the decriers and blasphemers.

One recalls at once what he said of "the lofty impartiality" with which Sir Walter Scott had written of Napoleon before him, and with which he appears to have faced his lesser task. As a biography, as a writing of history, as an example of historic style, Lockhart's comparatively modest essay must be called a better performance than Scott's. But "the real Napoleon" has not yet been painted.

Lord Rosebery, in his book on Napoleon: the Last Phase, asks if there will ever be an adequate portrait? The life is yet to be written that shall profit by all the new material that has come to light since Scott wrote his nine volumes in 1827, and Lockhart published his in 1829. But Lockhart's book has still the value of one written by a genuine man of letters, who was a born biographer, and one written while the world-commotion of Napoleon was a matter of personal report. It is tinged by some of the contemporary illusions, no doubt; but it is clearer in its record than Scott's, and while it is less picturesque, it is more direct.

His comparative brevity is a gain, since he has to tell how, in brief space, "the lean, hungry conqueror swells," as Lord Rosebery says, "into the sovereign, and then into the sovereign of sovereigns."

In view of the influence of the one book upon the other, and the one writer upon the other, it is worth note that Lockhart had a fit of enthusiasm over Scott's Napoleon when it first appeared, or rather when he first read the first six volumes of the work, before they were "out," in 1827. He thought Scott would make as great an effect by it as by any two of his novels. This proved a mistaken forecast, but Scott was paid an enormous price--some eighteen thousand pounds. When then John Murray, who had already co-opted Lockhart as his Quarterly editor, thought of inaugurating a "Family Library," and he proposed to his editor this other Napoleon book, it must have seemed in many ways a very attractive piece of work. But owing partly to Lockhart's relations with Scott, and partly to the need of avoiding any literary comparisons, these small, fat duodecimos appeared anonymously. That was, as it has been already mentioned, in 1829, two years after Scott's book.

To-day, it makes a capital starting-point for the long Napoleon adventure, whose end, so far as it is prolonged by fresh literary divigations, seems to be as remote as ever.

It is from the French side that one might chiefly draw those vivid and sometimes questionable glimpses at first-hand, that can best add to Lockhart's presentment. One must compare his retreat from Russia with Rapp's and other remembrancers' accounts, and be reminded by Rapp to go on to Jomini's Vie Militaire, and even turn for a single personal reminiscence to a flagrant hero-worshipper like Dumas, in his rapid and military biography.

"Only twice in his life," said Dumas, "had he who writes these lines seen Napoleon. The first time on the way to Ligny; the second, when he returned from Waterloo. The first time in the light of a lamp; the first time amid the acclamations of the multitude; the second, amid the silence of a populace. Each time Napoleon was seated in the same carriage, in the same seat, dressed in the same attire; each time, it was the same look, lost and vague; each time, the same head, calm and impassible, only his brow was a little more bent over his breast in returning than in going. Was it from weariness that he could not sleep, or from grief to have lost the world?"

This is the French postscript to many English books about the victor and loser of the world.

* * * * *

The following is a list of the works of John Gibson Lockhart (1794-1854):--

Peter's Letters to his Kinsfolk, by Peter Morris the Odontist (pseud.) 1819; Valerius, a Roman Story, 1821; Some Passages in the Life of Mr. Adam Blair, 1822; Reginald Dalton, a Story of English University Life, 1823; Ancient Spanish Ballads (trans.) 1823; Matthew Wald, a Novel, 1824; Life of Robert Burns, 1828; History of Napoleon Buonaparte, 1829; History of the late War, with Sketches of Nelson, Wellington and Napoleon, 1832; Memoirs of the Life of Sir Walter Scott, 7 vols. 1836-8; Theodore Hook, a Sketch, 1852.

Lockhart was a Contributor to "Blackwood," and Editor of the "Quarterly Review" from 1825 to 1853.

LIFE OF NAPOLEON BUONAPARTE

CHAPTER I

Birth and Parentage of Napoleon Buonaparte--His Education at Brienne and at Paris--His Character at this Period--His Political Predilections--He enters the Army as Second Lieutenant of Artillery--His First Military Service in Corsica in 1793.

Napoleon Buonaparte was born at Ajaccio on the 15th of August, 1769. The family had been of some distinction, during the middle ages, in Italy; whence his branch of it removed to Corsica, in the troubled times of the Guelphs and Gibellines. They were always considered as belonging to the gentry of the island. Charles, the father of Napoleon, an advocate of considerable reputation, married his mother, Letitia Ramolini, a young woman eminent for beauty and for strength of mind, during the civil war--when the Corsicans, under Paoli, were struggling to avoid the domination of the French. The advocate had espoused the popular side in that contest, and his lovely and high-spirited wife used to attend him through the toils and dangers of his mountain campaigns. Upon the termination of the war, he would have exiled himself along with Paoli; but his relations dissuaded him from this step, and he was afterwards reconciled to the conquering party, and protected and patronised by the French governor of Corsica, the Count de Marboeuff.

It is said that Letitia had attended mass on the morning of the 15th of August; and, being seized suddenly on her return, gave birth to the future hero of his age, on a temporary couch covered with tapestry, representing the heroes of the Iliad. He was her second child. Joseph, afterwards King of Spain, was older than he: he had three younger brothers, Lucien, Louis, and Jerome; and three sisters, Eliza, Caroline, and Pauline. These grew up. Five others must have died in infancy; for we are told that Letitia had given birth to thirteen children, when at the age of thirty she became a widow.

In after-days, when Napoleon had climbed to sovereign power, many flatterers were willing to give him a lofty pedigree. To the Emperor of Austria, who would fain have traced his unwelcome son-in-law to some petty princes of Treviso, he replied, "I am the Rodolph of my race,"[1] and silenced, on a similar occasion, a professional genealogist, with, "Friend, my patent dates from Monte Notte."[2]

Charles Buonaparte, by the French governor's kindness, received a legal appointment in Corsica--that of Procureur du Roi (answering nearly to Attorney-General); and scandal has often said that Marboeuff was his wife's lover. The story received no credence in Ajaccio.

Concerning the infancy of Napoleon we know nothing, except that he ever acknowledged with the warmest gratitude the obligations laid on him, at the threshold of life by the sagacity and wisdom of Letitia. He always avowed his belief that he owed his subsequent elevation principally to her early lessons; and indeed laid it down as a maxim that "the future good or bad conduct of a child depends entirely on the mother." Even of his boyish days few anecdotes have been preserved in Corsica. His chosen plaything, they say, was a small brass cannon; and, when at home in the school-vacations, his favourite retreat was a solitary summer-house among the rocks on the sea-shore, about a mile from Ajaccio, where his mother's brother (afterwards Cardinal Fesch) had a villa. The place is now in ruins, and overgrown with bushes, and the people call it "Napoleon's Grotto." He has himself said that he was remarkable only for obstinacy and curiosity: others add, that he was high-spirited, quarrelsome, imperious; fond of solitude; slovenly in his dress. Being detected stealing figs in an orchard, the proprietor threatened to tell his mother, and the boy pleaded for himself with so much eloquence, that the man suffered him to escape. His careless attire, and his partiality for a pretty little girl in the neighbourhood, were ridiculed together in a song which his playmates used to shout after him in the streets of Ajaccio:

"Napoleone di mezza calzetta Fa l'amore a Giacominetta."[3]

His superiority of character was early felt. An aged relation, Lucien Buonaparte, Archdeacon of Ajaccio, called the young people about his death-bed to take farewell and bless them: "You, Joseph," said the expiring man, "are the eldest; but Napoleon is the head of his family. Take care to remember my words." Napoleon took excellent care that they should not be forgotten. He began with beating his elder brother into subjection.

From his earliest youth he chose arms for his profession. When he was about seven years old (1776) his father was, through Marboeuff's patronage, sent to France as one of a deputation from the Corsican noblesse to King Louis XVI.; and Napoleon, for whom the count had also procured admission into the military school of Brienne, accompanied him. After seeing part of Italy, and crossing France, they reached Paris; and the boy was soon established in his school, where at first everything delighted him, though, forty years afterwards, he said he should never forget the bitter parting with his mother ere he set out on his travels. He spoke only Italian when he reached Brienne; but soon mastered French. His progress in Latin, and in literature generally, attracted no great praise; but in every study likely to be of service to the future soldier, he distinguished himself above his contemporaries. Of the mathematical tutors accordingly he was a great favourite. One of the other teachers having condemned him for some offence or neglect to wear a course woollen dress on a particular day, and dine on his knees at the door of the refectory, the boy's haughty spirit swelling under this dishonour, brought on a sudden vomiting, and a strong fit of hysterics. The mathematical master passing by, said they did not understand what they were dealing with, and released him. He cared little for common pastimes; but his love for such as mimicked war was extreme; and the skill of his fortifications, reared of turf, or of snow, according to the season, and the address and pertinacity with which he conducted their defence, attracted the admiration of all observers. Napoleon was poor and all but a foreigner[4] among the French youth, and underwent many mortifications from both causes. His temper was reserved and proud; he had few friends--no bosom-companion; he lived by himself, and among his books and maps. M. Bourienne, whose friendship for him commenced thus early, says-- "Buonaparte was noticeable at Brienne for his Italian complexion, the keenness of his look, and the tone of his conversation both with masters and comrades. There was almost always a dash of bitterness in what he said. He had very little of the disposition that leads to attachments, which I can only attribute to the misfortunes of his family every since his birth, and the impression which the conquest of his country had made on his early years." One day, at dinner, the principal of the school happened to say something slightingly of Paoli. "He was a great man," cried young Buonaparte, "he loved his country; and I shall never forgive my father, who had been his adjutant, for consenting to the union of Corsica with France. He ought to have followed the fortunes of Paoli."

There is reason to believe that the levity and haughtiness with which some of the young French gentlemen at this seminary conducted themselves towards this poor, solitary alien, had a strong effect on the first political feelings of the future Emperor of France. He particularly resented their jokes about his foreign name Napoleon. Bourienne says he often told him-- "Hereafter I will do the French what harm I can; as for you, you never make me your jest--you love me."

From the beginning of the revolutionary struggle, boy and youth, he espoused and kept by the side of those who desired the total change of government. It is a strange enough fact, that Pichegru, afterwards so eminent and ultimately so unfortunate, was for some time his monitor in the school of Brienne. Being consulted many years later as to the chance of enlisting Buonaparte in the cause of the exiled Bourbons, this man is known to have answered: "It will be lost time to attempt that--I knew him in his youth--he has taken his side, and he will not change it."

In 1783 Buonaparte was, on the recommendation of his masters, sent from Brienne to the Royal Military School at Paris; this being an extraordinary compliment to the genius and proficiency of a boy of fifteen.[5] Here he spent nearly two years, devoted to his studies. That he laboured hard, both at Brienne and at Paris, we may judge; for his after-life left scanty room for book-work, and of the vast quantity of information which his strong memory ever placed at his disposal, the far greater proportion must have been accumulated now. He made himself a first-rate mathematician; he devoured history--his chosen authors being Plutarch and Tacitus; the former the most simple painter that antiquity has left us of heroic characters--the latter the profoundest master of political wisdom. The poems of Ossian were then new to Europe, and generally received as authentic remains of another age and style of heroism. The dark and lofty genius which they display, their indistinct but solemn pictures of heroic passions, love, battle, victory, and death, were appropriate food for Napoleon's young imagination; and, his taste being little scrupulous as to minor particulars, Ossian continued to be through life his favourite poet. While at Paris, he attracted much notice among those who had access to compare him with his fellows; his acquirements, among other advantages, introduced him to the familiar society of the celebrated Abb?Raynal. Napoleon, shortly after entering the school at Paris, drew up a memorial, which he in person presented to the superintendents of the establishment. He complained that the mode of life was too expensive and delicate for "poor gentlemen," and could not prepare them either for returning to their "modest homes," or for the hardships of the camp. He proposed that, instead of a regular dinner of two courses daily, the students should have ammunition bread, and soldiers' rations, and that they should be compelled to mend and clean their own stockings and shoes. This memorial is said to have done him no service at the military school.

He had just completed his sixteenth year when (in August, 1785,) after being examined by the great Laplace, he obtained his first commission as second lieutenant in the artillery regiment La Fere. His corps was at Valance when he joined it; and he mingled, more largely than might have been expected from his previous habits, in the cultivated society of the place. His personal advantages were considerable; the outline of the countenance classically beautiful; the eye deep-set and dazzlingly brilliant; the figure short, but slim, active, and perfectly knit. Courtly grace and refinement of manners he never attained, nor perhaps coveted; but he early learned the art, not difficult probably to any person possessed of such genius and such accomplishments, of rendering himself eminently agreeable wherever it suited his purpose or inclination to be so.

On the 27th February in this year his father died of a cancer in the stomach, aged forty-five; the same disease which was destined, at a somewhat later period of life, to prove fatal to himself.

While at Valance Buonaparte competed anonymously for a prize offered by the Academy of Lyons for the best answer to Raynal's Question: "What are the principles and institutions by the application of which mankind can be raised to the highest happiness?" He gained the prize: what were the contents of his Essay we know not. Talleyrand, long afterwards, obtained the manuscript, and, thinking to please his sovereign, brought it to him. He threw his eye over two or three pages, and tossed it into the fire. The treatise of the Lieutenant probably abounded in opinions which the Emperor had found it convenient to forget.

Even at Brienne his political feelings had been determined. At Valance he found the officers of his regiment divided, as all the world then was, into two parties; the lovers of the French Monarchy, and those who desired its overthrow. He sided openly with the latter. "Had I been a general," said

Napoleon in the evening of his life, "I might have adhered to the king: being a subaltern, I joined the patriots."

 In the beginning of 1792 he became captain of artillery (unattached;) and, happening to be in Paris, witnessed the lamentable scenes of the 20th of June, when the revolutionary mob stormed the Tuileries, and the king and his family, after undergoing innumerable insults and degradations, with the utmost difficulty preserved their lives. He followed the crowd into the garden before the palace; and when Louis XVI. appeared on a balcony with the red cap on his head, could no longer suppress his contempt and indignation. "Poor driveller!" said Napoleon, loud enough to be heard by those near him, "how could he suffer this rabble to enter? If he had swept away five or six hundred with his cannon, the rest would be running yet." He was also a witness of the still more terrible 10th of August, when, the palace being once more invested, the National Guard assigned for its defence took part with the assailants; the royal family were obliged to take refuge in the National Assembly, and the brave Swiss Guards were massacred almost to a man in the courts of the Tuileries. Buonaparte was a firm friend to the Assembly, to the charge of a party of which, at least, these excesses must be laid; but the spectacle disgusted him. The yells, screams, and pikes with bloody heads upon them, formed a scene which he afterwards described as "hideous and revolting." At this time Napoleon was without employment and very poor; and De Bourienne describes him as wandering idly about Paris, living, chiefly at his (M. de B.'s) expense, at restaurateurs' shops, and, among other wild-enough schemes, proposing that he and his schoolfellow should take some houses on lease, and endeavour to get a little money by subletting them in apartments. Such were the views and occupations of Buonaparte--at the moment when the national tragedy was darkening to its catastrophe. As yet he had been but a spectator of the Revolution, destined to pave his own path to sovereign power; it was not long before circumstances called on him to play a part.

 General Paoli, who had lived in England ever since the termination of that civil war in which Charles Buonaparte served under his banner, was cheered, when the great French Revolution first broke out, with the hope that liberty was about to be restored to Corsica. He came to Paris, was received with applause as a tried friend of freedom, and appointed governor of his native island, which for some time he ruled wisely and happily. But as the revolution advanced, Paoli, like most other wise men, became satisfied that license was more likely to be established by its leaders, than law and rational liberty; and avowing his aversion to the growing principles of Jacobinism, and the scenes of tumult and bloodshed to which they gave rise, he was denounced in the National Assembly as the enemy of France. An expedition was sent to deprive him of his government, under the command of La Combe, Michel, and Salicetti, one of the Corsican deputies to the Convention; and Paoli called on his countrymen to take arms in his and their own defence.

Buonaparte happened at that time (1793) to have leave of absence from his regiment, and to be in Corsica on a visit to his mother. He had fitted up a little reading-room at the top of the house as the quietest part of it, and was spending his mornings in study, and his evenings among his family and old acquaintance, when the arrival of the expedition threw the island into convulsion. Paoli, who knew him well, did all he could to enlist him in his cause; he used, among other flatteries, to clap him on the back, and tell him he was "one of Plutarch's men." But Napoleon had satisfied himself that Corsica was too small a country to maintain independence,--that she must fall under the rule either of France or England; and that her interests would be best served by adhering to the former. He therefore resisted all Paoli's offers, and tendered his sword to the service of Salicetti. He was appointed provisionally to the command of a battalion of National Guards; and the first military service on which he was employed was the reduction of a small fortress, called the Torre di Capitello, near Ajaccio. He took it, but was soon besieged in it, and he and his garrison, after a gallant defence, and living for some time on horseflesh, were glad to evacuate the tower, and escape to the sea. The English government now began to reinforce Paoli, and the cause of the French party seemed for the moment to be desperate. The Buonapartes were banished from Corsica, and their mother and sisters took refuge first at Nice, and afterwards at Marseilles, where for some time they suffered all the inconveniences of exile and poverty. Napoleon rejoined his regiment. He had chosen France for his country; and seems, in truth, to have preserved little or no affection for his native soil.

After arriving at supreme power, he bestowed one small fountain on Ajaccio; and succeeded, by the death of a relation, to a petty olive garden near that town. In the sequel of his history the name of Corsica will scarcely recur.

[Footnote 1: Rodolph of Hapsburg was the founder of the Austrian family.]

[Footnote 2: His first battle.]

[Footnote 3: Napoleon, with his stockings about his heels, makes love to Giacominetta.]

[Footnote 4: Corsica became by law a French department only two months before Napoleon was born.]

[Footnote 5: The report, in consequence of which Buonaparte received this distinction, is in these words: "M. de Buonaparte (Napoleon), born the 15th August, 1769, height four feet ten inches ten lines; good constitution; health excellent; character docile, upright, grateful; conduct very regular: has always distinguished himself by his application to the mathematics. He is passably acquainted with history and geography: is weak enough as to his Latin diction and other elegant accomplishments: would make an excellent sea-officer: deserves to be transferred to the Military School at Paris."]

CHAPTER II

Buonaparte commands the Artillery at Toulon--Fall of Toulon--The Representatives of the People--Junot.

Buonaparte's first military service occurred, as we have seen, in the summer of 1793. The king of France had been put to death on the 21st of January in that year; and in less than a month afterwards the convention had declared war against England. The murder of the king, alike imprudent as atrocious, had in fact united the princes of Europe against the revolutionary cause; and within France itself a strong reaction took place. The people of Toulon, the great port and arsenal of France on the Mediterranean, partook these sentiments, and invited the English and Spanish fleets off their coast to come to their assistance, and garrison their city. The allied admirals took possession accordingly of Toulon, and a motley force of English, Spaniards, and Neapolitans, prepared to defend the place. In the harbour and roads there were twenty-five ships of the line, and the city contained immense naval and military stores of every description, so that the defection of Toulon was regarded as a calamity of the first order by the revolutionary government.

This event occurred in the midst of that period which has received the name of the reign of terror. The streets of Paris were streaming with innocent blood; Robespierre was glutting himself with murder; fear and rage were the passions that divided mankind, and their struggles produced on either side the likeness of some epidemic frenzy. Whatever else the government wanted, vigour to repel aggressions from without was displayed in abundance. Two armies immediately marched upon Toulon; and after a series of actions, in which the passes in the hills behind the town were forced, the place was at last invested, and a memorable siege commenced.

It was conducted with little skill, first by Cartaux, a vain coxcomb who had been a painter, and then by Doppet, an ex-physician, and a coward. To watch and report on the proceedings of these chiefs, there were present in the camp several Representatives of the People, as they were called--persons holding no military character or rank, but acting as honourable spies for the government at Paris. The interference of these personages on this, as on many other occasions, was productive of delays, blunders, and misfortunes; but the terror which their ready access to the despotic government inspired was often, on the other hand, useful in stimulating the exertions of the military. The younger Robespierre was one of the deputies at Toulon, and his name was enough to make his presence formidable.

Cartaux had not yet been superseded, when Napoleon Buonaparte made his appearance at headquarters, with a commission to assume the command of the artillery. It has been said that he owed his appointment to the private regard of Salicetti; but the high testimonials he had received from the Military Academy were more likely to have served him; nor is it possible to suppose that he had been so long in the regiment of La Fere without being appreciated by some of his superiors. He had, besides, shortly before this time, excited attention by a pamphlet, called the Supper of Beaucaire, in which the politics of the Jacobin party were spiritedly supported; and of which he was afterwards so ashamed, that he took great pains to suppress it. However this may have been, he was received almost with insolence by Cartaux, who, strutting about in an uniform covered with gold lace, told him his assistance was not wanted, but he was welcome to partake in his glory.

The commandant of the artillery, on examining the state of affairs, found much to complain of. They were still disputing which extremity of the town should be the chief object of attack; though at the one there were two strong and regular fortifications, and at the other only a small and imperfect fort called Malbosquet. On inspecting their batteries, he found that the guns were placed about two gunshots from the walls; and that it was the custom to heat the shot at a distance from the place where they were to be discharged; in other words, to heat them to no purpose. Choosing officers of his own acquaintance to act under him, and exerting himself to collect guns from all quarters, Buonaparte soon remedied these disorders, and found himself master of an efficient train of 200 pieces; and he then urged the general to adopt a wholly new plan of operations in the future conduct of the siege.

The plan of Buonaparte appears now the simplest and most obvious that could have been suggested; yet it was not without great difficulty that he could obtain the approbation of the doctor, who had by this time superseded the painter. "Your object," said he, "is to make the English evacuate Toulon. Instead of attacking them in the town, which must involve a long series of operations, endeavour to establish batteries so as to sweep the harbour and roadstead. If you can do this--the English ships must take their departure, and the English troops will certainly not remain behind them." He pointed out a promontory nearly opposite the town, by getting the command of which he was sure the desired effect must be accomplished. "Gain La Grasse" said he, "and in two days Toulon falls." His reasoning at length forced conviction, and he was permitted to follow his own plan.

A month before nothing could have been more easy; but within that time the enemy had perceived the importance of the promontory, which commands the narrow passage between the port and the Mediterranean, and fortified it so strongly, that it passed by the name of the Little Gibraltar. It was necessary, therefore, to form extensive batteries in the rear of La Grasse, before there could be a prospect of seizing it. Buonaparte laboured hard all day, and slept every night in his cloak by the guns, until his works approached perfection. He also formed a large battery behind Malbosquet; but this he carefully concealed from the enemy. It was covered by a plantation of olives, and he designed to distract their attention by opening its fire for the first time when he should be about to make his great effort against Little Gibraltar. But the Representatives of the People had nearly spoiled everything. These gentlemen, walking their rounds, discovered the battery behind the olives, and inquiring how long it had been ready, were told for eight days. Not guessing with what views so many guns had been kept so long idle, they ordered an immediate cannonade. The English made a vigorous sally, and spiked the guns before Buonaparte could reach the spot. On his arrival at the eminence behind, he perceived a long deep ditch, fringed with brambles and willows, which he thought might be turned to advantage. He ordered a regiment of foot to creep along the ditch, which they did without being discovered until they were close upon the enemy. General O'Hara, the English commander, mistook them for some of his own allies, and, rushing out to give them some direction, was wounded and made prisoner. The English were dispirited when they lost their general; they retreated, and the French were at liberty to set about the repair of their battery. In this affair much blood was shed. Napoleon himself received a bayonet-thrust in his thigh, and fell into the arms of Muiron, who carried him off the field. Such was the commencement of their brotherly friendship. His wound, however, did not prevent him from continuing his labours behind Little Gibraltar.

That fort had very nearly been seized, by a sort of accident, some time before his preparations were completed; a casual insult excited a sudden quarrel between the men in Buonaparte's trenches and the Spaniards in Little Gibraltar. The French soldiers, without waiting for orders, seized their arms, and rushed to the assault with fury. Napoleon coming up, perceived that the moment was favourable, and persuaded Doppet to support the troops with more regiments; but the doctor, marching at the head of his column, was seized with a panic, on seeing a man killed by his side, and ordered a retreat, before anything could be effected.

A few days after, this poltroon was in his turn superseded by a brave veteran, General Dugommier, and Napoleon could at last count on having his efforts backed. But, for the second time, the Representatives did their best to ruin his undertaking. The siege had now lasted four months, provisions were scarce in the camp, and these civilians, never being able to comprehend what was meant by bestowing all this care on a place so far below the city as Little Gibraltar, wrote to Paris that they saw no chance of success, and hoped the government would agree with them that the siege ought to be abandoned. Two days before this letter reached Paris, Toulon had fallen, and the Representatives gave out that the despatch was a forgery.

The moment had at last come when Buonaparte judged it right to make his grand attempt. During the night of the 17th of December he threw 8000 bombs and shells into Little Gibraltar, and the works being thus shattered, at daybreak Dugommier commanded the assault. The French, headed by the brave Muiron, rushed with impetuous valour through the embrasures, and put the whole garrison to the sword. The day was spent in arranging the batteries, so as to command the shipping; and next morning--so true had been Buonaparte's prophecy--when the French stood to their posts, the English fleet was discovered to be already under weigh.

Then followed a fearful scene. The English would not quit Toulon without destroying the French ships and arsenals that had fallen into their possession; nor could they refuse to carry with them the Antijacobin inhabitants, who knew that their lives would be instantly sacrificed if they should fall into the hands of the victorious Republicans, and who now flocked to the beach to the number of 14,000, praying for the means of escape. The burning of ships, the explosion of magazines, the roar of artillery, and the cries of these fugitives, filled up many hours. At last the men-of-war were followed by a flotilla bearing those miserable exiles; the walls were abandoned; and Dugommier took possession of the place.

The Republicans found that all persons of condition, who had taken part against them, had escaped; and their rage was to be contented with meaner victims. A day or two having been suffered to pass in quiet, a proclamation, apparently friendly, exhorted the workmen, who had been employed on the batteries of the besieged town, to muster at headquarters. One hundred and fifty poor men, who expected to be employed again in repairing the same fortifications obeyed this summons--were instantly marched into a field--and shot in cold blood; not less than a thousand persons were massacred under circumstances equally atrocious. Buonaparte himself repelled with indignation the charge of having had a hand in this butchery. Even if he had, he was not the chief in command, and durst not have disobeyed orders but at the sacrifice of his own life. It is on all sides admitted that a family of royalists, being shipwrecked on the coast near Toulon a few days after, were rescued from the hands of the ferocious Republicans, solely by his interference and address. Putting himself at the head of some of his gunners, he obtained possession of the unhappy prisoners; quieted the mob by assuring them that they should all be publicly executed the next morning; and meanwhile sent them off during the night in artillery waggons supposed to be conveying stores.

The recovery of Toulon was a service of the first importance to the government. It suppressed all insurrectionary spirit in the south of France; and placed a whole army at their disposal elsewhere. But he, to whose genius the success was due, did not at first obtain the credit of his important achievement at Paris. The Representatives of the People never made their appearance on the eventful morning at Little Gibraltar, until three hours after the troops were in possession of the best part of the fortifications. Then, indeed, they were seen sword in hand in the trenches, blustering and swaggering in safety. Yet these men did not blush to represent themselves as having headed the assault, while, in their account of the conflict, even the name of Buonaparte did not find a place. The truth could not, however, be concealed effectually; and he was appointed to survey and arrange the whole line of fortifications on the Mediterranean coast of France.

It was during the siege of Toulon that Napoleon, while constructing a battery under the enemy's fire, had occasion to prepare a despatch, and called out for some one who could use a pen. A young sergeant, named Junot, leapt out, and, leaning on the breastwork, wrote as he dictated. As he finished, a shot struck the ground by his side, scattering dust in abundance over him and everything near him. "Good," said the soldier, laughing, "this time we shall spare our sand." The cool gaiety of this pleased Buonaparte; he kept his eye on the man; and Junot came in the sequel to be Marshal of France and Duke of Abrantes.

CHAPTER III

Buonaparte Chief of Battalion at Nice--Fall of Robespierre--He is superseded--Buonaparte at Paris in 1795--The day of the Sections--Commands the Army of the Interior--Marries Josephine de Beauharnois--Appointed to the command of the Army of Italy.

From this time Napoleon advanced by rapid strides to greatness. His admirable skill was still further displayed in his survey of the fortifications above mentioned; and having completed this service, he was appointed to join the army of Italy, then stationed at Nice, with the rank of Chief of

Battalion.

Here his advice suggested a plan by which the Sardinians were driven from the Col di Tende on the 7th March, 1794; Saorgio, with all its stores, surrendered; and the French obtained possession of the maritime Alps, so that the difficulties of advancing into Italy were greatly diminished. Of these movements, however, his superior officers reaped as yet the honour. He was even superseded (Aug. 6, 1794) very shortly after their success. But this, which at the moment seemed a heavy misfortune, was, in truth, one of the luckiest circumstances that ever befell him.

It is not true that he was put under arrest in consequence of the downfall of Robespierre; although there is no doubt that he was supposed to belong to the party which that monster had made the instrument of his crimes, and known to have lived on terms of friendship with his younger brother. He incurred the suspicion of Laporte and the other "Representatives" attached to "the army of Italy," in consequence of a journey to the Gulf of Genoa, which he performed in obedience to secret orders from Paris; and, so soon as his absence from headquarters was thus explained, he regained his freedom. The officer, who came to release him, was surprised to find him busy in his dungeon over the map of Lombardy. The "Representatives," however, had certainly taken up a general prejudice against him; for he did not reassume his functions at Nice; and seems to have spent some time in obscurity with his own family, who were then in very distressed circumstances, at Marseilles. It was here that he fell in love with Mademoiselle Clery, whom, but for some accident, it appears he would have married. Her sister was shortly afterwards united to his brother Joseph, and she herself became in the sequel the wife of Bernadotte, now King of Sweden. It is supposed that Buonaparte found himself too poor to marry at this time; and circumstances interfered to prevent any renewal of his proposals.

Before the end of the year he came to Paris to solicit employment; but at first he met with nothing but repulses. The President of the Military Committee, Aubry, objected to his youth. "Presence in the field of battle," said Buonaparte, "might be reckoned in place of years." The President, who had not seen much actual service, thought he was insulted, and treated Napoleon very coldly. After a little while, however, he was asked to go to La Vend 閑, as commandant of a brigade of infantry. This he declined, alleging, that nothing could reconcile him to leave the artillery, but really, if we are to follow De Bourienne, considering the Vendean warfare as unworthy of him. His refusal was followed by the erasure of his name from the list of general officers in employment; and for a time his fortunes seemed to be in a desperate condition. He thought of settling in some way in Paris; and said to Bourienne, that, if he could afford to have a small house in the street where his school-fellow lived, and to keep a cabriolet, he would be contented. His elder brother had about this time married Mademoiselle Clery, whose father, the merchant of Marseilles, gave her a handsome dowry. "How fortunate," Napoleon would often exclaim, "is that fool Joseph!"[6]

Talma, the celebrated tragedian, was one of his chief associates at this time, and even then talked with confidence of the future fortunes of "little Buonaparte." This player's kindness and Aubry's opposition were both remembered. The Emperor always patronised Talma; and Aubry died in exile.

Napoleon, despairing of employment at home, now drew up a memorial to the government, requesting to be sent with a few other officers of artillery into Turkey, for the purpose of placing that branch of the Grand Seignior's service in a condition more suitable to the circumstances of the times--in which it seemed highly probable that the Porte might find itself in alliance with France, and assaulted by the combined armies of Russia and Austria. No answer was returned to this memorial, over which he dreamt for some weeks in great enthusiasm. "How strange," he said to his friends, "would it be if a little Corsican soldier should become King of Jerusalem!" Go where he might, he already contemplated greatness.

At length Napoleon was nominated to the command of a brigade of artillery in Holland. The long-deferred appointment was, no doubt, very welcome; but in the meantime his services were called for on a nearer and a more important field.

The French nation were now heartily tired of the National Convention: it had lost most of its distinguished members in the tumults and persecutions of the times; and above all it had lost respect by remaining for two years the slave and the tool of the Terrorists. The downfall of Robespierre, when it did take place, showed how easily the same blessed deliverance might have been effected long before, had this body possessed any sense of firmness or of dignity. Even the restoration of the members banished by the tyrant did not serve to replace the Convention in the confidence of the public. They themselves saw clearly that a new remodelling of the government was called for and must be; and their anxiety was to devise the means of securing for themselves as large a share as possible of substantial power, under some arrangement sufficiently novel in appearance to throw dust in the eyes of the people.

A great part of the nation, there is no doubt, were at this time anxious to see the royal family restored, and the government settled on the model of 1791. Among the more respectable citizens of Paris in particular such feelings were very prevalent. But many causes conspired to surround the adoption of this measure with difficulties, which none of the actually influential leaders had the courage, or perhaps the means, to encounter. The soldiery of the Republican armies had been accustomed to fight against the exiled princes and nobility, considered them as the worst enemies of France, and hated them personally. The estates of the church, the nobles, and the crown, had been divided and sold; and the purchasers foresaw that, were the monarchy restored at this period, the resumption of the forfeited property would be pressed with all the powers of government. And, lastly, the men who had earned for themselves most distinction and influence in public affairs, had excellent reasons for believing that the Bourbons and nobility, if restored, would visit on their own heads the atrocities of the Revolution, and above all the murder of the King.

The Conventionalists themselves, however, had learned by this time that neither peace nor security could be expected, unless some form of government were adopted, in which the legislative and the executive functions should at least appear to be separated; and they were also at length inclined to admit the excellence of that part of the British constitution, which, dividing the legislatorial power between two assemblies of senators, thus acquires the advantage of a constant revision of counsels, and regulates the political machine by a system of mutual checks and balances. They were desirous, therefore, of proposing some system which might, in a certain degree, satisfy those who had been endeavouring to bring about the restoration of the monarchy; and the new constitution of the year three of the Republic (1795) presented the following features. I. The executive power was to be lodged in Five Directors, chosen from time to time, who were to have no share in the legislation. II. There was to be a Council of Five Hundred, answering generally to our House of Commons: and III. A smaller assembly, called the Council of Ancients, intended to fulfil in some measure the purposes of a House of Peers.

The outline of this scheme might perhaps have been approved of; but the leading members of the Convention, from views personal to themselves, appended to it certain conditions which excited new disgust. They decreed, first, that the electoral bodies of France, in choosing representatives to the two new Councils, must elect at least two-thirds of the present members of Convention; and, secondly, that if full two-thirds were not returned, the Convention should have the right to supply the deficiency out of their own body. It was obvious that this machinery had no object but the continuance of the present legislators in power; and the nation, and especially the superior classes in Paris, were indignant at conduct which they considered as alike selfish and arbitrary. The royalist party gladly lent themselves to the diffusion of any discontents; and a formidable opposition to the measures of the existing government was organised.

The Convention meantime continued their sittings, and exerting all their skill and influence, procured from many districts of the country reports accepting of the New Constitution, with all its conditions. The Parisians, being nearer and sharper observers, and having abundance of speakers and writers to inform and animate them, assembled in the several sections of the city, and proclaimed their hostility to the Convention and its designs. The National Guard, consisting of armed citizens, almost unanimously sided with the enemies of the Convention; and it was openly proposed to march to the Tuileries, and compel a change of measures by force of arms.

The Convention, perceiving their unpopularity and danger, began to look about them anxiously for the means of defence. There were in and near Paris 5000 regular troops, on whom they thought they might rely, and who of course contemned the National Guard as only half-soldiers. They had besides some hundreds of artillerymen; and they now organized what they called "the Sacred Band," a body of 1500 ruffians, the most part of them old and tried instruments of Robespierre. With these means they prepared to arrange a plan of defence; and it was obvious that they did not want materials, provided they could find a skilful and determined head.

The Insurgent Sections placed themselves under the command of Danican, an old general of no great skill or reputation. The Convention opposed to him Menou; and he marched at the head of a column into the section Le Pelletier to disarm the National Guard of that district--one of the wealthiest of the capital. The National Guard were found drawn up in readiness to receive him at the end of the Rue Vivienne; and Menou, becoming alarmed, and hampered by the presence of some of the "Representatives of the People," entered into a parley, and retired without having struck a blow.

The Convention judged that Menou was not master of nerves for such a crisis; and consulted eagerly about a successor to his command. Barras, one of their number, had happened to be present at Toulon, and to have appreciated the character of Buonaparte. He had, probably, been applied to by Napoleon in his recent pursuit of employment. Deliberating with Tallien and Carnot, his colleagues, he suddenly said, "I have the man whom you want; it is a little Corsican officer, who will not stand upon ceremony."

These words decided the fate of Napoleon and of France. Buonaparte had been in the Od 闱 n Theatre when the affair of Le Pelletier occurred, had run out, and witnessed the result. He now happened to be in the gallery, and heard the discussion concerning the conduct of Menou. He was presently sent for, and asked his opinion as to that officer's retreat. He explained what had happened, and how the evil might have been avoided, in a manner which gave satisfaction. He was desired to assume the command, and arrange his plan of defence as well as the circumstances might permit; for it was already late at night, and the decisive assault on the Tuileries was expected to take place next morning. Buonaparte stated that the failure of the march of Menou had been chiefly owing to the presence of the "Representatives of the People," and refused to accept the command unless he received it free from all such interference. They yielded: Barras was named Commander-in-Chief; and Buonaparte second, with the virtual control. His first care was to dispatch Murat, then a major of Chasseurs, to Sablons, five miles off, where fifty great guns were posted. The Sectionaries sent a stronger detachment for these cannon immediately afterwards; and Murat, who passed them in the dark, would have gone in vain had he received his orders but a few minutes later.

On the 4th of October (called in the revolutionary almanack the 13th

Vendemaire) the affray accordingly occurred. Thirty thousand National Guards advanced, about two p.m., by different streets, to the siege of the palace: but its defence was now in far other hands than those of Louis XVI.

Buonaparte, having planted artillery on all the bridges, had effectually secured the command of the river, and the safety of the Tuileries on one side. He had placed cannon also at all the crossings of the streets by which the National Guard could advance towards the other front; and having posted his battalions in the garden of the Tuileries and Place du Carousel, he awaited the attack.

The insurgents had no cannon; and they came along the narrow streets of Paris in close and heavy columns. When one party reached the church of St. Roche, in the Rue St. Honor? they found a body of Buonaparte's troops drawn up there, with two cannons. It is disputed on which side the firing began; but in an instant the artillery swept the streets and lanes, scattering grape-shot among the National Guards, and producing such confusion that they were compelled to give way. The first shot was a signal for all the batteries which Buonaparte had established; the quays of the Seine, opposite to the Tuileries, were commanded by his guns below the Palace and on the bridges. In less than an hour the action was over. The insurgents fled in all directions, leaving the streets covered with dead and wounded: the troops of the Convention marched into the various sections, disarmed the terrified inhabitants, and before nightfall everything was quiet.

This eminent service secured the triumph of the Conventionalists, who now, assuming new names, continued in effect to discharge their old functions. Barras took his place at the head of the Directory, having Sieyes, Carnot, and other less celebrated persons, for his colleagues, and the First Director took care to reward the hand to which he owed his elevation. Within five days from the day of the Sections Buonaparte was named second in command of the army of the interior; and shortly afterwards, Barras, finding his duties as Director sufficient to occupy his time, gave up the command-in-chief of the same army to his "little Corsican officer."

He had no lack of duties to perform in this new character. The National Guard was to be re-organised; a separate guard for the representative body to be formed; the ordnance and military stores were all in a dilapidated condition. The want of bread, too, was continually producing popular riots, which could rarely be suppressed but by force of arms. On one of these last occasions, a huge sturdy fishwife exhorted the mob to keep to their places, when Buonaparte had almost persuaded them to disperse. "These coxcombs with their epaulettes and gorgets," said she, "care nothing for us; provided they feed well and fatten, we may starve." "Good woman," cried the general of the interior, who at this time was about the leanest of his race, "only look at me,--and decide yourself which of the two is the fatter." The woman could not help laughing: the joke pleased the multitude, and harmony was restored.

Buonaparte, holding the chief military command in the capital, and daily rising in importance from the zeal and firmness of his conduct in this high post, had now passed into the order of marked and distinguished men. He continued, nevertheless, to lead in private a quiet and modest life, studying as hard as ever, and but little seen in the circles of gaiety. An accident which occurred one morning at his military levee, gave at once a new turn to his mode of life, and a fresh impetus to the advance of his fortunes.

A fine boy, of ten or twelve years of age, presented himself; stated to the general that his name was Eugene Beauharnois, son of Viscount Beauharnois, who had served as a general officer in the Republican armies on the Rhine, and been murdered by Robespierre; and said his errand was to recover the sword of his father. Buonaparte caused the request to be complied with; and the tears of the boy, as he received and kissed the relic, excited his interest. He treated Eugene so kindly, that next day his mother, Josephine de Beauharnois, came to thank him; and her beauty and singular gracefulness of address made a strong impression.

This charming lady, the daughter of a planter, by name Tascher de la Pagerie, was born in the island of Martinico, 24th June, 1763. While yet an infant, according to a story which she afterwards repeated, a negro sorceress had prophesied that "she should one day be greater than a queen, and yet outlive her dignity."[7]

The widow of Beauharnois had been herself imprisoned until the downfall of Robespierre. In that confinement she had formed a strict friendship with another lady who was now married to Tallien, one of the most eminent of the leaders of the Convention. Madame Tallien had introduced Josephine to her husband's friends; and Barras, the First Director, having now begun to hold a sort of court at the Luxembourg, these two beautiful women were the chief ornaments of its society. It was commonly said--indeed it was universally believed--that Josephine, whose character was in some respects indifferent, possessed more than legitimate influence over the First Director. Buonaparte, however, offered her his hand; she, after some hesitation, accepted it; and the young general by this marriage (9th March, 1796) cemented his connection with the society of the Luxembourg, and in particular with Barras and Tallien, at that moment the most powerful men in France.

Napoleon had a strong tendency to the superstition of fatalism, and he always believed that his fortunes were bound up in some mysterious manner with those of this graceful woman. She loved him warmly, and served him well. Her influence over him was great, and it was always exerted on the side of humanity. She, and she alone, could overrule, by gentleness, the excesses of passion to which he was liable; and her subsequent fate will always form one of the darkest pages in the history of her lord.

Tranquillity was now restored in Paris; and the Directory had leisure to turn their attention to the affairs of the army of Italy, which were in a most confused and unsatisfactory condition. They determined to give it a new general; and Buonaparte was appointed to the splendid command. It is acknowledged, in one of Josephine's letters, that the First Director had promised to procure it for him before their marriage took place. "Advance this man," said Barras to his colleagues, "or he will advance himself without you."

Buonaparte quitted his wife ten days after their marriage; paid a short visit to his mother at Marseilles; and arrived, after a rapid journey, at the headquarters at Nice. From that moment opened the most brilliant scene of his existence; yet, during the months of victory and glory that composed it, his letters, full of love and home-sickness, attest the reluctance with which he had so soon abandoned his bride.

[Footnote 6: De Bourienne.]

[Footnote 7: According to some, the last clause ran "die in an hospital," and this was in the sequel interpreted to mean Malmaison--a palace which (like our own St. James's) had once been an hospital.]

CHAPTER IV

The Army of Italy--Tactics of Buonaparte--Battle of Monte Notte--Battle of Millesimo--Battle of Mondovi--Armistice of Cherasco--Close of the Campaign of Piedmont--Peace granted to Sardinia.

Buonaparte at the age of twenty-six assumed the command of the army of Italy; exulting in the knowledge that, if he should conquer, the honour would be all his own. He had worked for others at Toulon, at the Col di Tende, at Saorgio: even in the affair of the Sections the first command had been nominally in the hands of Barras. Henceforth he was to have no rivals within the camp. "In three months," said he, "I shall be either at Milan or at Paris." He had already expressed the same feeling in a still nobler form. "You are too young," said one of the Directors, hesitating about his appointment as general. "In a year," answered Napoleon, "I shall be either old or dead."

He found the army in numbers about 50,000; but wretchedly deficient in cavalry, in stores of every kind,[8] in clothing and even in food; and watched by an enemy greatly more numerous. It was under such circumstances that he at once avowed the daring scheme of forcing a passage to Italy, and converting the richest territory of the enemy himself into the theatre of the war. "Soldiers," said he, "you are hungry and naked; the Republic owes you much, but she has not the means to pay her debts. I am come to lead you into the most fertile plains that the sun beholds. Rich provinces, opulent towns, all shall be at your disposal. Soldiers! with such a prospect before you, can you fail in courage and constancy?" This was his first address to his army. The sinking hearts of the men beat high with hope and confidence when they heard the voice of the young and fearless leader; and Augereau, Massena, Serrurier, Joubert, Lannes--distinguished officers might themselves have aspired to the chief command--felt, from the moment they began to understand his character and system, that the true road to glory would be to follow the star of Napoleon.

He perceived that the time was come for turning a new leaf in the history of war. With such numbers of troops as the infant Republic could afford him, he saw that no considerable advantages could be obtained against the vast and highly-disciplined armies of Austria and her allies, unless the established rules and etiquettes of strategy were abandoned. It was only by such rapidity of motion as should utterly transcend the suspicion of his adversaries, that he could hope to concentrate the whole pith and energy of a small force upon some one point of a much greater force opposed to it, and thus rob them (according to his own favourite phrase) of the victory. To effect such rapid marches, it was necessary that the soldiery should make up their minds to consider tents and baggage as idle luxuries; and that, instead of a long and complicated chain of reserves and stores, they should dare to rely wholly for the means of subsistence on the resources of the countries into which their leader might conduct them. They must be contented to conquer at whatever hazard; to consider no sacrifices or hardships as worthy of a thought. The risk of destroying the character and discipline of the men, by accustoming them to pillage, was obvious. Buonaparte trusted to victory, the high natural spirit of the nation, and the influence of his own genius, for the means of avoiding this danger; and many years, it must be admitted, elapsed, before he found much reason personally to repent of the system which he adopted. Against the enemies of the Republic its success was splendid, even beyond his hopes.

The objects of the approaching expedition were three: first, to compel the King of Sardinia, who had already lost Savoy and Nice, but still maintained a powerful army on the frontiers of Piedmont, to abandon the alliance of Austria: secondly, to compel the Emperor, by a bold invasion of Lombardy, to make such exertions in that quarter as might weaken those armies which had so long hovered on the Rhine; and, if possible, to stir up the Italian subjects of that crown to adopt the revolutionary system and emancipate themselves for ever from its yoke. The third object, though more distant, was not less important. The influence of the Romish Church was considered by the Directory as the chief, though secret, support of the cause of royalism within their own territory; and to reduce the Vatican into insignificance, or at least force it to submission and quiescence, appeared indispensable to the internal tranquillity of France. The Revolutionary Government, besides this general cause of hatred and suspicion, had a distinct injury to avenge. Their agent, Basseville, had three years before been assassinated in a popular tumult at Rome: the Papal troops had not interfered to protect him, nor the Pope to punish his murderers; and the haughty Republic considered this as an insult which could only be washed out with a sea of blood.

Napoleon's plan for gaining access to the fair regions of Italy differed from that of all former conquerors: they had uniformly penetrated the Alps at some point or other of that mighty range of mountains: he judged that the same end might be accomplished more easily by advancing along the narrow strip of comparatively level country which intervenes between those enormous barriers and the Mediterranean Sea, and forcing a passage at the point where the last of the Alps melt, as it were, into the first and lowest of the Apennine range. No sooner did he begin to concentrate his troops towards this region, than the Austrian general, Beaulieu, took measures for protecting Genoa, and the entrance of Italy. He himself took post with one column of his army at Voltri, a town within ten miles of Genoa: he placed D'Argenteau with another Austrian column at Monte Notte, a strong height further to the westward; and the Sardinians, under Colli, occupied Ceva-- which thus formed the extreme right of the whole line of the allied army. The French could not advance towards Genoa but by confronting some one of the three armies thus strongly posted, and sufficiently, as Beaulieu supposed, in communication with each other.

It was now that Buonaparte made his first effort to baffle the science of those who fancied there was nothing new to be done in warfare. On the 10th of April, D'Argenteau came down upon Monte Notte, and attacked some French redoubts, in front of that mountain and the villages which bear its name, at Montelegino. At the same time General Cervoni and the French van were attacked by Beaulieu near Voltri, and compelled to retreat. The determined valour of Colonel Rampon, who commanded at Montelegino, held D'Argenteau at bay during the 10th and 11th: and Buonaparte, contenting himself with watching Beaulieu, determined to strike his effectual blow at the centre of the enemy's line. During the night of the 11th various columns were marched upon Montelegino, that of Cervoni and that of Laharpe from the van of the French line, those of Augereau and Massena from its rear. On the morning of the 12th, D'Argenteau, preparing to renew his attack on the redoubts of Montelegino, found he had no longer Rampon only and his brave band to deal with; that French columns were in his rear, on his flank, and drawn up also behind the works at Montelegino; in a word, that he was surrounded. He was compelled to retreat among the mountains; he left his colours and cannon behind him, 1000 killed, and 2000 prisoners. The centre of the allied army had been utterly routed, before either the Commander-in-Chief at the left, or General Colli at the right of the line, had any notion that a battle was going on.

Such was the battle of Monte Notte, the first of Napoleon's fields. Beaulieu, in order that he might re-establish his communication with Colli (much endangered by the defeat of D'Argenteau) was obliged to retreat upon Dego; the Sardinian, with the same purpose in view, fell back also, and took post at Millesimo; while D'Argenteau was striving to re-organise his dispirited troops in the difficult country between. It was their object to keep fast in these positions until succours could come up from Lombardy; but Napoleon had no mind to give them such respite.

The very next day after this victory he commanded a general assault on the Austrian line. Augereau, with a fresh division, marched at the left upon Millesimo; Massena led the centre towards Dego; and Laharpe, with the French right wing, manoeuvred to turn the left flank of Beaulieu.

Augereau rushed upon the outposts of Millesimo, seized and retained the gorge which defends that place, and cut off Provera with two thousand Austrians, who occupied an eminence called Cossaria, from the main body of Colli's army. Next morning Buonaparte himself arrived at that scene of the operations. He forced Colli to accept battle, utterly broke and scattered him, and Provera, thus abandoned, was obliged to yield at discretion.

Meanwhile Massena on the same day had assaulted the heights of Biastro, and carrying them at the point of the bayonet, cut off Beaulieu's communication with Colli; then Laparpe came in front and in flank also upon the village of Dego, and after a most desperate conflict, drove the Austrian commander-in-chief from his post. From this moment Colli and Beaulieu were entirely separated. After the affairs of Dego and Millesimo, the former retreated in disorder upon Ceva; the latter, hotly pursued, upon Aqui; Colli, of course, being eager to cover Turin, while the Austrian had his anxious thoughts already upon Milan. Colli was again defeated at Mondovi in his disastrous retreat; he there lost his cannon, his baggage, and the best part of his troops. The Sardinian army might be said to be annihilated. The conqueror took possession of Cherasco, within 10 miles of Turin, and there dictated the terms on which the King of Sardinia was to be permitted to retain any shadow of sovereign power.

Thus, in less than a month, did Napoleon lay the gates of Italy open before him. He had defeated in three battles forces much superior to his own; inflicted on them in killed, wounded and prisoners, a loss of 25,000 men; taken eighty guns and twenty-one standards; reduced the Austrians to inaction; utterly destroyed the Sardinian king's army; and lastly, wrested from his hands Coni and Tortona, the two great fortresses called "the keys of the Alps,"--and indeed, except Turin itself, every place of any consequence in his dominions. This unfortunate prince did not long survive such humiliation. He was father-in-law to both of the brothers of Louis XVI., and, considering their cause and his own dignity as equally at an end, died of a broken heart, within a few days after he had signed the treaty of Cherasco.

Buonaparte meanwhile had paused for a moment to consolidate his columns on the heights, from which the vast plain of Lombardy, rich and cultivated like a garden, and watered with innumerable fertilising streams, lay at length within the full view of his victorious soldiery. "Hannibal forced the Alps," said he gaily, as he now looked back on those stupendous barriers, "and we have turned them."

"Hitherto" (he thus addressed his troops) "you have been fighting for barren rocks, memorable for your valour, but useless to your country; but now your exploits equal those of the armies of Holland and the Rhine. You were utterly destitute, and you have supplied all your wants. You have gained battles without cannon, passed rivers without bridges, performed forced marches without shoes, bivouacked without strong liquors, and often without bread. None but republican phalanxes, soldiers of liberty, could have endured such things. Thanks for your perseverance! But, soldiers, you have done nothing-- for there remains much to do. Milan is not yet ours. The ashes of the conquerors of Tarquin are still trampled by the assassins of Basseville."

The consummate genius of this brief campaign could not be disputed; and the modest language of the young general's despatches to the Directory, lent additional grace to his fame. At this time the name of Buonaparte was spotless: and the eyes of all Europe were fixed in admiration on his career.

[Footnote 8: Berthier used to keep, as a curiosity, a general order, by which three louis-d'or were granted as a great supply to each general of division, dated on the very day of the victory at Albegna.]

CHAPTER V

The French cross the Po at Placenza--The Battle of Fombio--The Bridge of Lodi--Napoleon occupies Milan--Resigns, and resumes his command--Insurrection of Pavia--Military Executions--The French pass the Mincio at Borghetto--Beaulieu retreats behind the Adige--Mantua besieged--Peace with the King of the Two Sicilies--The Pope buys a Respite.

Piedmont being now in the hands of Buonaparte, the Austrian general concentrated his army behind the Po, with the purpose of preventing the invader from passing that great river and making his way to the capital of Lombardy.

Napoleon employed every device to make Beaulieu believe that he designed to attempt the passage of the Po at Valenza; and the Austrian, a man of routine, who had himself crossed the river at that point, was easily persuaded that these demonstrations were sincere. Meanwhile his crafty antagonist executed a march of incredible celerity upon Placenza, fifty miles lower down the river; and appeared there on the 7th of May, to the utter consternation of a couple of Austrian squadrons, who happened to be reconnoitring in that quarter. He had to convey his men across that great stream in the common ferry boats, and could never have succeeded had there been anything like an army to oppose him. Andreossi (afterwards so celebrated) was commander of the advanced guard; Lannes (who became in the sequel Marshal Duke of Montebello) was the first to throw himself ashore at the head of some grenadiers. The German hussars were driven rapidly from their position. Buonaparte himself has said that no operation in war is more critical than the passage of a great river, on this occasion the skill of his arrangements enabled him to pass one of the greatest in the world without the loss of a single man.

Beaulieu, as soon as he ascertained how he had been outwitted, advanced upon Placenza, in the hope of making the invader accept battle with the Po in his rear, and therefore under circumstances which must render any check in the highest degree disastrous. Buonaparte, in the meantime, had no intention to await the Austrian on ground so dangerous, and was marching rapidly towards Fomboi, where he knew he should have room to manoeuvre. The advanced divisions of the hostile armies met at that village on the 8th of

May. The Imperialists occupied the steeples and houses, and hoped to hold out until Beaulieu could bring up his main body. But the French charged so impetuously with the bayonet, that the Austrian, after seeing one-third of his men fall, was obliged to retreat, in great confusion, leaving all his cannon behind him, across the Adda; a large river which, descending from the Tyrolese mountains, joins the Po at Pizzighitone--and thus forms the immediate defence of the better part of the Milanese against any enemy advancing from Piedmont. Behind this river Beaulieu now concentrated his army, establishing strong guards at every ford and bridge, and especially at Lodi, where as he guessed (for once rightly) the French general designed to force his passage.

The wooden bridge of Lodi formed the scene of one of the most celebrated actions of the war; and will ever be peculiarly mixed up with the name of Buonaparte himself. It was a great neglect in Beaulieu to leave it standing when he removed his headquarters to the east bank of the Adda: his outposts were driven rapidly through the old struggling town of Lodi on the 10th; and the French sheltering themselves behind the walls and houses, lay ready to attempt the passage of the bridge. Beaulieu had placed a battery of thirty cannon so as to sweep it completely; and the enterprise of storming it in the face of this artillery, and the whole army drawn up behind, is one of the most daring on record.

Buonaparte's first care was to place as many guns as he could get in order in direct opposition to this Austrian battery. A furious cannonade on his side of the river also now commenced. The General himself appeared in the midst of the fire, pointing with his own hand two guns in such a manner as to cut off the Austrians from the only path by which they could have advanced to undermine the bridge; and it was on this occasion that the soldiery, delighted with his dauntless exposure of his person, conferred on him his honorary nickname of The Little Corporal. In the meantime he had sent General Beaumont and the cavalry to attempt the passage of the river by a distant ford (which they had much difficulty in effecting), and awaited with anxiety the moment when they should appear on the enemy's flank. When that took place, Beaulieu's line, of course, showed some confusion, and Napoleon instantly gave the word. A column of grenadiers, whom he had kept ready drawn up close to the bridge, but under shelter of the houses, were in a moment wheeled to the left, and their leading files placed upon the bridge.

They rushed on, shouting Vive la Republique! but the storm of grape-shot for a moment checked them. Buonaparte, Lannes, Berthier, and Lallemagne, hurried to the front, and rallied and cheered the men. The column dashed across the bridge in despite of the tempest of fire that thinned them. The brave Lannes was the first who reached the other side, Napoleon himself the second. The Austrian artillerymen were bayoneted at their guns, before the other troops, whom Beaulieu had removed too far back, in his anxiety to avoid the French battery, could come to their assistance. Beaumont pressing gallantly with his horse upon the flank, and Napoleon's infantry forming rapidly as they passed the bridge, and charging on the instant, the Austrian line became involved in inextricable confusion, broke up, and fled. The slaughter on their side was great; on the French there fell only 200 men. With such rapidity, and consequently with so little loss, did Buonaparte execute this dazzling adventure--"the terrible passage," as he himself called it, "of the bridge of Lodi."

It was indeed, terrible to the enemy. It deprived them of another excellent line of defence, and blew up the enthusiasm of the French soldiery to a pitch of irresistible daring. Beaulieu, nevertheless, contrived to withdraw his troops in much better style than Buonaparte had anticipated. He gathered the scattered fragments of his force together, and soon threw the line of the Mincio, another tributary of the Po, between himself and his enemy. The great object, however, had been attained: the Austrian general escaped, and might yet defend Mantua, but no obstacle remained between the victorious invader and the rich and noble capital of Lombardy. The garrison of Pizzighitone, seeing themselves effectually cut off from the Austrian army, capitulated. The French cavalry pursued Beaulieu as far as Cremona, which town they seized; and Napoleon himself prepared to march at once upon Milan.

It was after one of these affairs that an old Hungarian officer was brought prisoner to Buonaparte, who entered into conversation with him, and among other matters questioned him "what he thought of the state of the war?" "Nothing," replied the old gentleman, who did not know he was addressing the general-in-chief,--"nothing can be worse. Here is a young man who knows absolutely nothing of the rules of war; to-day he is in our rear, to-morrow on our flank, next day again in our front. Such violations of the principles of the art of war are intolerable!"

The Archduke, who governed in Lombardy for the Emperor, had made many a long prayer and procession; but the saints appeared to take no compassion on him, and he now withdrew from the capital. A revolutionary party had always existed there, as indeed in every part of the Austrian dominions beyond the Alps; and the tricolor cockade, the emblem of France, was now mounted by multitudes of the inhabitants. The municipality hastened to invite the conqueror to appear among them as their friend and protector; and on the 14th of May, four days after Lodi, Napoleon accordingly entered, in all the splendour of a military triumph, the venerable and opulent city of the old Lombard kings.

He was not, however, to be flattered into the conduct, as to serious matters, of a friendly general. He levied immediately a heavy contribution (eight hundred thousand pounds sterling) at Milan,--taking possession, besides, of twenty of the finest pictures in the Ambrosian gallery.

The conqueror now paused to look about and behind him; and proceeded still farther to replenish his chest by exactions, for which no justification can be adduced from the ordinary rules of international law. With Sardinia he had already reckoned; of the Austrian capital in Italy he had possession; there was only one more of the Italian governments (Naples) with which the French Republic was actually at war; although, indeed, he had never concealed his intention of revenging the fate of Basseville on the court of Rome. The other powers of Italy were, at worst, neutrals; with Tuscany and Venice, France had friendly relations. But Napoleon knew or believed, that all the Italian governments, without exception, considered the French invasion of Italy as a common calamity; the personal wishes of most of the minor princes (nearly connected as these were, by blood or alliance, with the imperial house of Austria) he, not unreasonably, concluded were strongly against his own success in this great enterprise. Such were his pretences--more or less feasible; the temptation was, in fact, great; and he resolved to consider and treat whatever had not been with him as if it had been against him. The weak but wealthy princes of Parma and Modena, and others of the same order, were forthwith compelled to purchase his clemency not less dearly than if they had been in arms. Besides money, of which he made them disburse large sums, he demanded from each a tribute of pictures and statues, to be selected at the discretion of Citizen Monge and other French connoisseurs, who now attended his march for such purposes.

In modern warfare the works of art had hitherto been considered as a species of property entitled in all cases to be held sacred; and Buonaparte's violent and rapacious infraction of this rule now excited a mighty clamour throughout Europe. Whether the new system originated with himself, or in the commands of the Directory, is doubtful. But from this time the formation of a great national gallery of pictures and statues at Paris was considered as an object of the first importance; and every victorious general was expected to bring trophies of this kind in his train. Whether the fine arts themselves are likely to be improved in consequence of the accumulation in any one place of such vast treasures as the Louvre were long exhibited, there has been, and will no doubt continue to be, much controversy. It is certain that the arts of France derived no solid advantage from Napoleon's museum. The collection was a mighty heap of incense for the benefit of the national vanity; and the hand which brought it together was preparing the means of inflicting on that vanity one of the most intolerable of wounds, in its ultimate dispersion.

The Duke of Modena would fain have redeemed the famous St. Jerome, of Correggio, at the price of ?0,000; and Buonaparte's lieutenants urged him to accept the money. "No," said he, "the duke's two millions of francs would soon be spent; but his Correggio will remain for ages to adorn Paris, and inspire the arts of France." The prophecy was not inspired. Of one thing there can be no doubt; namely, that the abstraction of these precious monuments of art from the Italian collections was deeply and permanently resented by the Italian people. This sacrilege, as those enthusiastic and intelligent lovers of all the elegant arts considered it, turned back many a half-made convert from the principles of the French Revolution.

Buonaparte remained but five days in Milan; the citadel of that place still held out against him; but he left a detachment to blockade it, and proceeded himself in pursuit of Beaulieu. The Austrian had now planted the remains of his army behind the Mincio, having his left on the great and strong city of Mantua, which has been termed "the citadel of Italy," and his right at Peschiera a Venetian fortress, of which he took possession in spite of the remonstrances of the Doge. Peschiera stands where the Mincio flows out of "its parent lake," the Lago di Guarda. That great body of waters, stretching many miles backwards towards the Tyrolese Alps, at once extended the line of defence, and kept the communication open with Vienna. The Austrian veteran occupied one of the strongest positions that it is possible to imagine. The invader hastened once more to dislodge him.

The French Directory, meanwhile, had begun to entertain certain not unnatural suspicions as to the ultimate designs of their young general, whose success and fame had already reached so astonishing a height. They determined to check, if they could, the career of an ambition which they apprehended might outgrow their control. Buonaparte was ordered to take half his army, and lead it against the Pope and the King of Naples, and leave the other half to terminate the contest with Beaulieu, under the orders of Kellerman. But he acted on this occasion with the decision which these Directors in vain desired to emulate. He answered by resigning his command. "One half of the army of Italy," said he, "cannot suffice to finish the matter with the Austrian. It is only by keeping my force entire that I have been able to gain so many battles and to be now in Milan. You had better have one bad general than two good ones." The Directory durst not persist in displacing the chief whose name was considered as the pledge of victory. Napoleon resumed the undivided command, to which now, for the last time, his right had been questioned.

Another unlooked-for occurrence delayed, for a few days longer, the march upon Mantua. The heavy exactions of the French, and even more perhaps the wanton contempt with which they treated the churches and the clergy, had produced or fostered the indignation of a large part of the population throughout Lombardy. Reports of new Austrian levies being poured down the passes of the Tyrol were spread and believed. Popular insurrections against the conqueror took place in various districts: at least 30,000 were in arms. At Pavia the insurgents were entirely triumphant; they had seized the town, and compelled the French garrison to surrender.

This flame, had it been suffered to spread, threatened immeasurable evil to the French cause. Lannes instantly marched to Benasco, stormed the place, plundered and burnt it, and put the inhabitants to the sword without mercy. The general in person appeared before Pavia; blew the gates open; easily scattered the townspeople; and caused the leaders to be executed, as if they had committed a crime in endeavouring to rescue their country from the arm of a foreign invader. Everywhere the same ferocious system was acted on.

The insurgent commanders were tried by courts-martial, and shot without ceremony. At Lugo, where a French squadron of horse had been gallantly and disastrously defeated, the whole of the male inhabitants were massacred. These bloody examples quelled the insurrections; but they fixed the first dark and indelible stain on the name of Napoleon Buonaparte.

The spirit of the Austrian and Catholic parties in Lombardy thus crushed, the French advanced on the Mincio. The general made such disposition of his troops, that Beaulieu doubted not he meant to pass that river, if he could, at Peschiera. Meantime he had been preparing to repeat the scene of Placenza;--and actually, on the 30th of May, forced the passage of the Mincio, not at Peschiera, but further down at Borghetto. The Austrian garrison at Borghetto in vain destroyed one arch of the bridge. Buonaparte supplied the breach with planks; and his men, flushed with so many victories, charged with a fury not to be resisted. Beaulieu was obliged to abandon the Mincio, as he had before the Adda and the Po, and to take up the new line of the Adige.

Meanwhile an occurrence, which may be called accidental, had nearly done more than repay the Austrians for all their reverses. The left of their line, stationed still further down the Mincio,--at Puzzuolo, no sooner learned from the cannonade that the French were at Borghetto, than they hastened to ascend the stream, with the view of assisting the defence of their friends. They came too late for this; the commander at Borghetto had retreated before they arrived. They, however, came unexpectedly; and, such was the chance, reached Valleggio after the French army had pursued the Austrians through it and onwards--and, at the moment when Buonaparte and a few friends, considering the work of the day to be over, and this village as altogether in the rear of both armies, were about to sit down to dinner in security. Sebetendorff, who commanded the Puzzuolo division, came rapidly, little guessing what a prize was near him, into the village. The French general's attendants had barely time to shut the gates of the inn, and alarm their chief by the cry "To arms." Buonaparte threw himself on horseback, and galloping out by a back passage, effected the narrowest of escapes from the most urgent of dangers. Sebetendorff was soon assaulted by a French column, and retreated, after Beaulieu's example, on the line of the Adige. Buonaparte, profiting by the perilous adventure of Valleggio, instituted a small corps of picked men, called Guides, to watch continually over his personal safety. Such was the germ from which sprung the famous Imperial Guard of Napoleon.

The Austrian had, in effect, abandoned for the time the open country of Italy. He now lay on the frontier, between the vast tract of rich provinces which Napoleon had conquered, and the Tyrol. The citadel of Milan, indeed, still held out; but the force there was not great, and, cooped up on every side, could not be expected to resist much longer. Mantua, which possessed prodigious natural advantages, and into which the retreating general had flung a garrison of full 15,000 men, was, in truth, the last and only Italian possession of the imperial crown, which, as it seemed, there might still be a possibility of saving. Beaulieu anxiously waited the approach of new troops from Germany, to attempt the relief of this great city; and his antagonist, eager to anticipate the efforts of the imperial government, sat down immediately before it.

Mantua lies on an island, being cut off on all sides from the main land by the branches of the Mincio, and approachable only by five narrow causeways, of which three were defended by strong and regular fortresses or entrenched camps, the other two by gates, drawbridges, and batteries. Situated amidst stagnant waters and morasses, its air is pestilential, especially to strangers. The garrison were prepared to maintain the position with their usual bravery; and it remained to be seen whether the French general possessed any new system of attack, capable of abridging the usual operations of the siege, as effectually as he had already done by those of the march and the battle. His commencement was alarming: of the five causeways, by sudden and overwhelming assaults, he obtained four; and the garrison were cut off from the main land, except only at the fifth causeway, the strongest of them all, named, from a palace near it, La Favorita. It seemed necessary, however, in order that this blockade might be complete, that the Venetian territory, lying immediately beyond Mantua, should be occupied by the French. The power of this ancient government was no longer such as to inspire much respect, and Buonaparte resolved that the claim of neutrality should form no obstacle to his measures. The French Directory had already most ungenerously trampled on the dignity of Venice, by demanding that she should no longer afford a retreat to the illustrious exile, the Count of Provence, eldest surviving brother of Louis XVI.[9] That unfortunate prince had, accordingly, though most reluctantly, been desired to quit the Venetian states, and had already passed to the Rhine, where his gallant cousin, the Prince of Cond? had long been at the head of a small and devoted army composed of the expatriated gentry of France. Buonaparte, however, chose to treat the reluctance with which Venice had been driven to this violation of her hospitality, as a new injury to his government: he argued that a power who had harboured in friendship, and unwillingly expelled, the Pretender to the French monarchy, had lost all title to forbearance on the part of the Revolutionary forces. This was a gross and ungenerous insult, and it was a gratuitous one; for he had a far better argument behind. The imperial general had, as we have seen, neglected the reclamations of the Doge, when it suited his purpose to occupy Peschiera. "You are too weak," said Buonaparte, when the Venetian envoy reached his headquarters, "to enforce neutrality on hostile nations such as France and Austria. Beaulieu did not respect your territory when his interest bade him violate it; nor shall I hesitate to occupy whatever falls within the line of the Adige." In effect, garrisons were placed forthwith in Verona, and all the strong places of that domain. The tricolor flag now waved at the mouth of the Tyrolese passes; and Napoleon, leaving Serrurier to blockade Mantua, returned to Milan, where he had important business to arrange.

The King of Naples, utterly confounded by the successes of the French, was now anxious to procure peace, almost on whatever terms, with the apparently irresistible Republic. Nor did it, for the moment, suit Buonaparte's views to contemn his advances. A peace with this prince would withdraw some valuable divisions from the army of Beaulieu; and the distance of the Neapolitan territory was such, that the French had no means of carrying the war thither with advantage, so long as Austria retained the power of sending new forces into Italy by the way of the Tyrol. He concluded an armistice accordingly, which was soon followed by a formal peace, with the King of the Two Sicilies; and the Neapolitan troops, who had recently behaved with eminent gallantry, abandoning the Austrian general, began their march to the south of Italy.

This transaction placed another of Napoleon's destined victims entirely within his grasp. With no friend behind him, the Pope saw himself at the mercy of the invader; and in terror prepared to submit. Buonaparte occupied immediately his legations of Bologna and Ferrara, making prisoners in the latter of these towns four hundred of the papal troops, and a cardinal, under whose orders they were. The churchman militant was dismissed on parole; but, being recalled to headquarters, answered that his master, the Pope, had given him a dispensation to break his promise. This exercise of the old dispensing power excited the merriment of the conquerors. The Vatican, meanwhile, perceived that no time was to be lost. The Spanish resident at the Roman court was despatched to Milan; and the terms on which the holy father was to obtain a brief respite were at length arranged. Buonaparte demanded and obtained a million sterling, a hundred of the finest pictures and statues in the papal gallery, a large supply of military stores, and the cession of Ancona, Ferrara, and Bologna, with their respective domains.

He next turned his attention to the grand duke of Tuscany,--a prince who had not only not taken any part in the war against the Republic, but had been the very first of the European rulers to recognise its establishment, and had kept on terms of friendship with all its successive authorities. Buonaparte, however, in pursuance of his system, resolved that the brother of the emperor should pay for his presumed inclinations. For the present, the Florentine museum and the grand duke's treasury were spared; but Leghorn, the seaport of Tuscany and great feeder of its wealth, was seized without ceremony; the English goods in that town were confiscated to the ruin of the merchants; and a great number of English vessels in the harbour made a narrow escape. The grand duke, in place of resenting these injuries, was obliged to receive Buonaparte with all the appearances of cordiality at Florence; and the spoiler repaid his courtesy by telling him, rubbing his hands with glee, during the princely entertainment provided for him, "I have just received letters from Milan; the citadel has fallen;--your brother has no longer a foot of land in Lombardy." "It is a sad case," said Napoleon himself long afterwards--speaking of these scenes of exaction and insolence,--"it is a sad case when the dwarf comes into the embrace of the giant; he is like enough to be suffocated--but 'tis the giant's nature to squeeze hard."

In the meantime the general did not neglect the great and darling plan of the French government, of thoroughly revolutionising the North of Italy, and establishing there a group of Republics modelled after their own likeness, and prepared to act as subservient allies in their mighty contest with the European monarchies. The peculiar circumstances of Northern Italy, as a land of ancient fame and high spirit, long split into fragments, and ruled, for the most part, by governors of German origin, presented many facilities for the realisation of this design; and Buonaparte was urged constantly by his government at Paris, and by a powerful party in Lombardy, to hasten its execution. He, however, had by this time learned to think of many idols of the

Directory with about as little reverence as they bestowed on the shrines of Catholicism; in his opinion more was to be gained by temporising with both the governments and the people of Italy, than by any hasty measures of the kind recommended. He saw well the deep disgust which his exactions had excited. "You cannot," said he, "at one and the same moment rob people and persuade them you are their friends." He fancied, moreover, that the Pope and other nerveless rulers of the land might be converted into at least as convenient ministers of French exaction, as any new establishments he could raise in their room. Finally he perceived that whenever the Directory were to arrange seriously the terms of a settlement with the great monarchy of Austria, their best method would be to restore Lombardy, and thereby purchase the continued possession of the more conveniently situated territories of Belgium and the Luxembourg. The general, therefore, temporised; content, in the meantime, with draining the exchequers of the governments, and cajoling from day to day the population. The Directory were with difficulty persuaded to let him follow his own course; but he now despised their remonstrances, and they had been taught effectually to dread his strength.

Napoleon, it is clear enough, had no intention to grant these Italian governments anything but a respite; nor is it to be doubted that their disposition to take part with Austria remained as it had been before they entered into these treaties with France. That the purpose of deceit was mutual, affords, however, no plea of justification--least of all to the stronger party. "It will be well," says Sir Walter Scott, "with the world, when falsehood and finesse are as thoroughly exploded in international communication as they are among individuals in civilised countries."

[Footnote 9: The same who became afterwards Louis XVIII. of France.]

CHAPTER VI

Wurmser supersedes Beaulieu--Jourdan and Moreau march into Germany, and are forced to retreat again--The Austrians advance from the Tyrol--Battle of Lonato--Escape of Napoleon--Battle near Castiglione--Wurmser retreats on Trent, and is recruited--Battle of Roveredo--Battle of Primolano--Battle of Bassano--Battle of St. George--Wurmser shut up in Mantua.

The general was now recalled to the war. The cabinet of Vienna, apt to be slow, but sure to be persevering, had at last resolved upon sending efficient aid to the Italian frontier. Beulieu had been too often unfortunate to be trusted longer: Wurmser, who enjoyed a reputation of the highest class, was sent to replace him: 300,000 men were drafted from the armies on the Rhine to accompany the new general; and he carried orders to strengthen himself further, on his march, by whatever recruits he could raise among the warlike and loyal population of the Tyrol.

The consequences of thus weakening the Austrian force on the Rhine were, for the moment, on that scene of the contest, inauspicious. The French, in two separate bodies, forced the passage of the Rhine--under Jourdan and Moreau; before whom the imperial generals, Wartensleben and the Archduke Charles, were compelled to retire. But the skill of the Archduke ere long enabled him to effect a junction with the columns of Wartensleben; and thus to fall upon Jourdan with a great superiority of numbers, and give him a signal defeat. The loss of the French in the field was great, and the bitter hostility of the German peasantry made their retreat a bloody one. Moreau, on the other hand, learning how Jourdan was discomfited, found himself compelled to give up the plan of pursuing his march further into Germany, and executed that famous retreat through the Black Forest which has made his name as splendid as any victory in the field could have done. But this reverse, however alleviated by the honours of Moreau's achievement, was attended with appearances of the most perilous kind. The genius of Carnot had devised a great scheme of operations, of which one half was thus at once cut short. He had meant Moreau and Jourdan, coalescing beyond the Rhine, to march upon the Tyrol; while Buonaparte should advance from the scene of his Italian conquests, join his brother generals on that frontier, and then march in union with them to dictate a peace before the gates of Vienna. All hope of this junction of forces was now at an end for this campaign. The French saw themselves compelled to resume the defensive on the western frontier of Germany; and the army of Italy had to await the overwhelming war which seemed ready to pour down upon Lombardy from the passes of the Tyrol.

Wurmser, when he fixed his headquarters at Trent, mustered in all 80,000; while Buonaparte had but 30,000, to hold a wide country, in which abhorrence of the French cause was now prevalent, to keep up the blockade of Mantua, and to oppose this fearful odds of numbers in the field. He was now, moreover, to act on the defensive, while his adversary assumed the more inspiriting character of invader. He awaited the result with calmness.

Wurmser might have learned from the successes of Buonaparte the advantages of compact movement; yet he was unwise enough to divide his great force into three separate columns, and to place one of these upon a line of march which entirely separated it from the support of the others. He himself, with his centre, came down on the left bank of the Lago di Guarda, with Mantua before him as his mark: his left wing, under Melas, was to descend the Adige, and drive the French from Verona; while the right wing, under Quasdonowich, were ordered to keep down the valley of the Chiese, in the direction of Brescia, and so to cut off the retreat of Buonaparte upon the Milanese;--in other words, to interpose the waters of the Lago di Guarda between themselves and the march of their friends--a blunder not likely to escape the eagle eye of Napoleon.

He immediately determined to march against Quasdonowich, and fight him where he could not be supported by the other two columns. This could not be done without abandoning for the time the blockade of Mantua; but it was not for Buonaparte to hesitate about purchasing a great ultimate advantage by a present sacrifice, however disagreeable. The guns were buried in the trenches during the night of the 31st July, and the French quitted the place with a precipitation which the advancing Austrians considered as the result of terror.

Napoleon meanwhile rushed against Quasdonowich, who had already come near the bottom of the Lake of Guarda. At Salo, close by the lake, and, further from it, at Lonato, two divisions of the Austrian column were attacked and overwhelmed. Augereau and Massena, leaving merely rear-guards at Borghetto and Peschiera, now marched also upon Brescia. The whole force of Quasdonowich must inevitably have been ruined by these combinations, had he stood his ground; but by this time the celerity of Napoleon had overawed him, and he was already in full retreat upon his old quarters in the Tyrol. Augereau and Massena, therefore, countermarched their columns, and returned towards the Mincio. They found that Wurmser had forced their rear-guards from their posts: that of Massena, under Pigeon, had retired in good order to Lonato; that of Augereau, under Vallette, had retreated in confusion, abandoning Castiglione to the Austrians.

Flushed with these successes, old Wurmser now resolved to throw his whole force upon the French, and resume at the point of the bayonet his communication with the scattered column of Quasdonowich. He was so fortunate as to defeat the gallant Pigeon at Lonato, and to occupy that town. But this great new success was fatal to him. In the exultation of victory he extended his line too much towards the right; and this over-anxiety to open the communication with Quasdonowich had the effect of so weakening his centre, that Massena, boldly and skilfully seizing the opportunity, poured two strong columns on Lonato, and regained the position; whereon the Austrian, perceiving that his army was cut in two, was thrown into utter confusion. Some of his troops, marching to the right, were met by those of the French, who had already defeated Quasdonowich in that quarter, and obliged to surrender: the most retreated in great disorder. At Castiglione alone a brave stand was made. But Augereau, burning to wipe out the disgrace of Vallette,[10] forced the position, though at a severe loss. Such was the battle of Lonato. Thenceforth nothing could surpass the discomfiture and disarray of the Austrians. They fled in all directions upon the Mincio, where Wurmser himself, meanwhile, had been employed in revictualling Mantua.

A mere accident had once more almost saved the Imperialist. One of the many defeated divisions of the army, wandering about in anxiety to find some means of reaching the Mincio, came suddenly on Lonato, the scene of the late battle, at a moment when Napoleon was there with only his staff and guards about him. He knew not that any considerable body of the enemy remained together in the neighbourhood; and, but for his presence of mind, must have been their prisoner. The Austrian had not the skill to profit by what fortune threw in his way; the other was able to turn even a blunder into an advantage. The officer sent to demand the surrender of the town was brought blindfolded, as is the custom, to his headquarters; Buonaparte, by a secret sign, caused his whole staff to draw up around him, and when the bandage was removed from the messenger's eyes, saluted him thus: "What means this insolence? Do you beard the French general in the middle of his army?" The German recognised the person of Napoleon, and retreated stammering and blushing. He assured his commander that Lonato was occupied by the French in numbers that made resistance impossible. Four thousand men laid down their arms; and then discovered that, if they had used them, nothing could have prevented Napoleon from being their prize.

Wurmser collected together the whole of his remaining force, and advanced to meet the conqueror. He, meanwhile, had himself determined on the assault, and was hastening to the encounter. They met between Lonato and Castiglione. Wurmser was totally defeated, and narrowly escaped being a prisoner; nor did he without great difficulty regain Trent and Roveredo, those frontier positions from which his noble army had so recently descended with all the confidence of conquerors. In this disastrous campaign the Austrians lost 40,000: Buonaparte probably understated his own loss at 7000. During the seven days which the campaign occupied he never took off his boots, nor slept except by starts. The exertions which so rapidly achieved this signal triumph were such as to demand some repose; yet Napoleon did not pause until he saw Mantua once more completely invested. The reinforcement and revictualling of that garrison were all that Wurmser could show, in requital of his lost artillery, stores, and 40,000 men.

During this brief campaign the aversion with which the ecclesiastics of Italy regarded the French manifested itself in various quarters. At Pavia, Ferrara, and elsewhere, insurrections had broken out, and the spirit was spreading rapidly at the moment when the report of Napoleon's new victory came to re-awaken terror and paralyse revolt. The conqueror judged it best to accept for the present the resubmission, however forced, of a party too powerful to be put down by examples. The Cardinal Mattei, Archbishop of Ferrara, being brought into his presence, uttered the single word peccavi: the victor was contented with ordering him a penance of seven days' fasting and prayer in a monastery: but he had no intention to forget these occurrences whenever another day of reckoning with the Pope should come.

While he was occupied with restoring quiet in the country, Austria, ever constant in adversity, hastened to place 20,000 fresh troops under the orders of Wurmser; and the brave veteran, whose heart nothing could chill, prepared himself to make one effort more to relieve Mantua, and drive the French out of Lombardy. His army was now, as before, greatly the superior in numbers; and though the bearing of his troops was more modest, their gallantry remained unimpaired. Once more the old general divided his army; and once more he was destined to see it shattered in detail.

He marched from Trent towards Mantua, through the defiles of the Brenta, at the head of 30,000; leaving 20,000 under Davidowich at Roveredo, to cover the Tyrol. Buonaparte instantly detected the error of his opponent. He suffered him to advance unmolested as far as Bassano, and the moment he was there, and consequently completely separated from Davidowich and his rear, drew together a strong force, and darted on Roveredo, by marches such as seemed credible only after they had been accomplished.

The battle of Roveredo (Sept. 4) is one of Napoleon's most illustrious days. The enemy had a strongly entrenched camp in front of the town; and behind it, in case of misfortune, Calliano, with its castle seated on a precipice over the Adige, where that river flows between enormous rocks and mountains, appeared to offer an impregnable retreat. Nothing could withstand the ardour of the French. The Austrians, though they defended the entrenched camp with their usual obstinacy, were forced to give way by the impetuosity of Dubois and his hussars. Dubois fell, mortally wounded, in the moment of his glory: he waved his sabre, cheering his men onwards with his last breath. "I die," said he, "for the Republic;--only let me hear, ere life leaves me, that the victory is ours." The French horse, thus animated, pursued the Germans, who were driven, unable to rally, through and beyond the town. Even the gigantic defences of Calliano proved of no avail. Height after height was carried at the point of the bayonet; 7000 prisoners and fifteen cannon remained with the conquerors. The Austrians fled to Levisa, which guards one of the chief defiles of the Tyrolese Alps, and were there beaten again. Vaubois occupied this important position with the gallant division who had forced it. Massena fixed himself in Wurmser's late headquarters at Trent; and Napoleon, having thus totally cut off the field-marshal's communication with Germany, proceeded to issue proclamations calling on the inhabitants of the Tyrol to receive the French as friends, and seize the opportunity of freeing themselves for ever from the dominion of Austria. He put forth an edict declaring that the sovereignty of the district was henceforth in the French Republic, and inviting the people themselves to arrange, according to their pleasure, its interior government.

The French general made a grievous mistake when he supposed that the Tyrolese were divided in their attachment to the Imperial government, because he had found the Italian subjects of that crown to be so. The Tyrol, one of the most ancient of the Austrian possessions, had also been one of the best governed; the people enjoyed all the liberty they wished under a paternal administration. They received with scornful coldness the flattering exhortations of one in whom they saw only a cunning and rapacious enemy; and Buonaparte was soon satisfied that it would cost more time than was then at his disposal to republicanise those gallant mountaineers. They, in truth, began to arm themselves, and waited but the signal to rise everywhere upon the invaders.

Wurmser heard with dismay the utter ruin of Davidowich; and doubted not that Napoleon would now march onwards into Germany, and joining Jourdan and Moreau, whose advance he had heard of, and misguessed to have been successful, endeavour to realise the great scheme of Carnot--that of attacking Vienna itself. The old general saw no chance of converting what remained to him of his army to good purpose, but by abiding in Lombardy, where he thought he might easily excite the people in his emperor's favour, overwhelm the slender garrisons left by Buonaparte, and so cut off, at all events, the French retreat through Italy, in case they should meet with any disaster in the Tyrol or in Germany. Napoleon had intelligence which Wurmser wanted. Wurmser himself was his mark; and he returned from Trent to Primolano where the Imperialist's vanguard lay, by a forced march of not less than sixty miles performed in two days. The surprise with which this descent was received may be imagined. The Austrian van was destroyed in a twinkling. The French, pushing everything before them, halted that night at Cismone-- where Napoleon was glad to have half a private soldier's ration of bread for his supper. Next day he reached Bassano where the aged Marshal once more expected the fatal rencounter. The battle of Bassano (Sept. 8) was a fatal repetition of those that had gone before it. Six thousand men laid down their arms. Quasdonowich, with one division of 4000, escaped to Friuli; while Wurmser himself, retreating to Vicenza, there collected with difficulty a remnant of 16,000 beaten and discomfited soldiers. His situation was most unhappy; his communication with Austria wholly cut off--his artillery and baggage all lost--the flower of his army no more. Nothing seemed to remain but to throw himself into Mantua, and there hold out to the last extremity, in the hope, however remote, of some succours from Vienna; and such was the resolution of this often outwitted but never dispirited veteran.

In order to execute his purpose, it was necessary to force a passage somewhere on the Adige; and the Austrian, especially as he had lost all his pontoons, would have had great difficulty in doing so, but for a mistake on the part of the French commander at Legnago, who, conceiving the attempt was to be made at Verona, marched to reinforce the corps stationed there, and thus left his proper position unguarded. Wurmser, taking advantage of this, passed with his army at Legnago, and after a series of bloody skirmishes, in which fortune divided her favours pretty equally, was at length enabled to throw himself into Mantua. Napoleon made another narrow escape, in one of these skirmishes, at Arcola. He was surrounded for a moment, and had just galloped off, when Wurmser coming up and learning that the prize was so near, gave particular directions to bring him in alive!

Buonaparte, after making himself master of some scattered corps which had not been successful in keeping up with Wurmser, re-appeared once more before Mantua. The battle of St. George--so called from one of the suburbs of the city--was fought on the 13th of September, and after prodigious slaughter, the French remained in possession of all the causeways; so that the blockade of the city and fortress was henceforth complete. The garrison, when Wurmser shut himself up, amounted to 26,000. Before October was far advanced the pestilential air of the place, and the scarcity and badness of provisions, had filled his hospitals, and left him hardly half the number in fighting condition. The misery of the besieged town was extreme; and if Austria meant to rescue Wurmser, there was no time to be lost.

[Footnote 10: Vallette was cashiered. Augereau was afterwards created Duke of Castiglione, in memory of this exploit.]

CHAPTER VII

Affairs of Corsica--Alvinzi assumes the Command of the Austrians on the Italian frontier--The three Battles of Arcola--Retreat of Alvinzi--Battle of Rivoli--Battle of La Favorita--Surrender of Mantua--Victor marches on Ancona--Despair of the Pope--Treaty of Tollentino.

The French party in Corsica had not contemplated without pride and exultation the triumphs of their countryman. His seizure of Leghorn, by cutting off the supplies from England, greatly distressed the opposite party in the island, and an expedition of Corsican exiles, which he now despatched from Tuscany, was successful in finally reconquering the country. To

Napoleon this acquisition was due; nor were the Directory insensible to its value. He, meanwhile, had heavier business on his hands.

The Austrian council well knew that Mantua was in excellent keeping; and being now relieved on the Rhenish frontier, by the failure of Jourdan and Moreau's attempts, were able to form once more a powerful armament on that of Italy. The supreme command was given to Marshal Alvinzi, a veteran of high reputation. He, having made extensive levies in Illyria, appeared at Friuli; while Davidowich, with the remnant of Quasdonowich's army, amply recruited among the bold peasantry of the Tyrol, and with fresh drafts from the Rhine, took ground above Trent. The marshal had in all 60,000 men under his orders. Buonaparte had received only twelve new battalions, to replace all the losses of those terrible campaigns, in which three imperial armies had already been annihilated. The enemy's superiority of numbers was once more such, that nothing but the most masterly combinations on the part of the French general could have prevented them from sweeping everything before them in the plains of Lombardy.

Buonaparte heard in the beginning of October that Alvinzi's columns were in motion: he had placed Vaubois to guard Trent, and Massena at Bassano to check the march of the field-marshal: but neither of these generals was able to hold his ground. The troops of Vaubois were driven from that position of Calliano, the strength of which has been already mentioned, under circumstances which Napoleon considered disgraceful to the character of the French soldiery. Massena avoided battle; but such was the overwhelming superiority of Alvinzi, that he was forced to abandon the position of Bassano. Napoleon himself hurried forward to sustain Massena; and a severe rencontre, in which either side claimed the victory, took place at Vicenza. The French, however, retreated, and Buonaparte fixed his headquarters at Verona. The whole country between the Brenta and the Adige was in the enemy's hands; while the still strong and determined garrison of Mantua in Napoleon's rear, rendering it indispensable for him to divide his forces, made his position eminently critical.

His first care was to visit the discomfited troops of Vaubois. "You have displeased me," said he, "you have suffered yourselves to be driven from positions where a handful of determined men might have bid an army defiance. You are no longer French soldiers! You belong not to the army of

Italy." At these words, tears streamed down the rugged cheeks of the grenadiers. "Place us but once more in the van," cried they, "and you shall judge whether we do not belong to the army of Italy." The general dropped his angry tone; and in the rest of the campaign no troops more distinguished themselves than these.

Having thus revived the ardour of his soldiery, Buonaparte concentrated his columns on the right of the Adige, while Alvinzi took up a very strong position on the heights of Caldiero, on the left bank, nearly opposite to Verona. In pursuance of the same system which had already so often proved fatal to his opponents, it was the object of Buonaparte to assault Alvinzi, and scatter his forces, ere they could be joined by Davidowich. He lost no time, therefore, in attacking the heights of Caldiero; but in spite of all that Massena, who headed the charge, could do, the Austrians, strong in numbers and in position, repelled the assailants with great carnage. A terrible tempest prevailed during the action, and Napoleon, in his despatches, endeavoured to shift the blame to the elements.

The country behind Caldiero lying open to Davidowich, it became necessary to resort to other means of assault, or permit the dreaded junction to occur. The genius of Buonaparte suggested to him on this occasion a movement altogether unexpected. During the night, leaving 1,500 men under Kilmaine to guard Verona, he marched for some space rearwards, as if he had meant to retreat on Mantua, which the failure of his recent assault rendered not unlikely. But his columns were ere long wheeled again towards the Adige: and finding a bridge ready prepared, were at once placed on the same side of the river with the enemy,--but in the rear altogether of his position, amidst those wide-spreading morasses which cover the country about Arcola. This daring movement was devised to place Napoleon between Alvinzi and Davidowich; but the unsafe nature of the ground, and the narrowness of the dykes, by which alone he could advance on Arcola, rendered victory difficult, and reverse most hazardous. He divided his men into three columns, and charged at daybreak (Nov. 15) by the three dykes which conduct to Arcola. The Austrian, not suspecting that the main body of the French had evacuated Verona, treated this at first as an affair of light troops; but as day advanced the truth became apparent, and these narrow passages were defended with the most determined gallantry. Augereau headed the first column that reached the bridge of Arcola, and was there, after a desperate effort, driven back with great loss. Buonaparte, perceiving the necessity of carrying the point ere Alvinzi could arrive, now threw himself on the bridge, and seizing a standard, urged his grenadiers once more to the charge.

The fire was tremendous: once more the French gave way. Napoleon himself, lost in the tumult, was borne backwards, forced over the dyke, and had nearly been smothered in the morass, while some of the advancing Austrians were already between him and his baffled column. His imminent danger was observed: the soldiers caught the alarm, and rushing forwards, with the cry, "Save the general," overthrew the Germans with irresistible violence, plucked Napoleon from the bog, and carried the bridge. This was the first battle of Arcola.

This movement revived in the Austrian lines their terror for the name of Buonaparte; and Alvinzi saw that no time was to be lost if he meant to preserve his communication with Davidowich. He abandoned Caldiero, and gaining the open country behind Arcola, robbed his enemy for the moment of the advantage which his skill had gained. Napoleon, perceiving that Arcola was no longer in the rear of his enemy but in his front, and fearful lest Vaubois might be overwhelmed by Davidowich, while Alvinzi remained thus between him and the Brenta, evacuated Arcola, and retreated to Ronco.

Next morning, having ascertained that Davidowich had not been engaged with Vaubois, Napoleon once more advanced upon Arcola. The place was once more defended bravely, and once more it was carried. But this second battle of Arcola proved no more decisive than the first; for Alvinzi still contrived to maintain his main force unbroken in the difficult country behind; and Buonaparte again retreated to Ronco.

The third day was decisive. On this occasion also he carried Arcola; and, by two stratagems, was enabled to make his victory effectual. An ambuscade, planted among some willows, suddenly opened fire on a column of Croats, threw them into confusion, and, rushing from the concealment, crushed them down into the opposite bog, where most of them died. Napoleon was anxious to follow up this success by charging the Austrian main body on the firm ground behind the marshes. But it was no easy matter to reach them there. He had, in various quarters, portable bridges ready for crossing the ditches and canals; but the enemy stood in good order, and three days' hard fighting had nearly exhausted his own men. In one of his conversations at St. Helena, he thus told the sequel. "At Arcola I gained the battle with twenty-five horsemen. I perceived the critical moment of lassitude in either army--when the oldest and bravest would have been glad to be in their tents. All my men had been engaged. Three times I had been obliged to re-establish the battle. There remained to me but some twenty-five Guides. I sent them round on the flank of the enemy with three trumpets, bidding them blow loud and charge furiously. Here is the French cavalry, was the cry; and they took to flight."... The Austrians doubted not that Murat and all the horse had forced a way through the bogs; and at that moment Buonaparte commanding a general assault in front, the confusion became hopeless. Alvinzi retreated finally, though in decent order, upon Montebello.

It was at Arcola that Muiron, who ever since the storming of Little Gibraltar had lived on terms of brotherlike intimacy with Napoleon, seeing a bomb about to explode threw himself between it and his general, and thus saved his life at the cost of his own. Napoleon, to the end of his life, remembered and regretted this heroic friend.

In these three days Buonaparte lost 8000 men: the slaughter among his opponents must have been terrible. Davidowich, in never coming up to join Alvinzi after his success over Vaubois, and Wurmser, in remaining quiet at Mantua, when by advancing with his garrison he might have incommoded the French rear, were guilty of grievous misjudgment or indecision. Once more the rapid combinations of Napoleon had rendered all the efforts of the Austrian cabinet abortive. For two months after the last day of Arcola, he remained the undisturbed master of Lombardy. All that his enemy could show, in set-off for the slaughter and discomfiture of Alvinzi's campaign, was that they retained possession of Bassano and Trent, thus interrupting Buonaparte's access to the Tyrol and Germany. This advantage was not trivial; but it had been dearly bought.

A fourth army had been baffled; but the resolution of the Imperial Court was indomitable, and new levies were diligently forwarded to reinforce Alvinzi. Once more (January 7, 1797) the Marshal found himself at the head of 60,000: once more his superiority over Napoleon's muster-roll was enormous; and once more he descended from the mountains with the hope of relieving Wurmser and reconquering Lombardy. The fifth act of the tragedy was yet to be performed.

We may here pause to notice some civil events of importance which occurred ere Alvinzi made his final descent. The success of the French naturally gave new vigour to the Italian party, who, chiefly in the large towns, were hostile to Austria, and desirous to settle their own government on the republican model. Napoleon had by this time come to be anything but a Jacobin in his political sentiments: his habits of command; his experience of the narrow and ignorant management of the Directory; his personal intercourse with the ministers of sovereign powers; his sense daily strengthened by events, that whatever good was done in Italy proceeded from his own skill and the devotion of his army,--all these circumstances conspired to make him respect himself and contemn the government, almost in despite of which he had conquered kingdoms for France. He therefore regarded now with little sympathy the aspirations after republican organisation which he had himself originally stimulated among the northern Italians. He knew, however, that the Directory had, by absurd and extravagant demands, provoked the Pope to break off the treaty of Bologna, and to raise his army to the number of 40,000,--that Naples had every disposition to back his Holiness with 30,000 soldiers, provided any reverse should befall the French in Lombardy,--and, finally, that Alvinzi was rapidly preparing for another march, with numbers infinitely superior to what he could himself extort from the government of Paris;[11] and considering these circumstances, he felt himself compelled to seek strength by gratifying his Italian friends. Two Republics accordingly were organised; the Cispadane and the Transpadane--handmaids rather than sisters of the great French democracy. These events took place during the period of military inaction which followed the victories of Arcola. The new Republics hastened to repay Napoleon's favour by raising troops, and placed at his disposal a force which he considered as sufficient to keep the Papal army in check during the expected renewal of Alvinzi's efforts.

Buonaparte at this period practised every art to make himself popular with the Italians; nor was it of little moment that they in fact regarded him more as their own countryman than a Frenchman; that their beautiful language was his mother tongue; that he knew their manners and their literature, and even in his conquering rapacity displayed his esteem for their arts. He was wise enough too, on farther familiarity with the state of the country, to drop that tone of hostility which he had at first adopted towards the priesthood; and to cultivate the most influential members of that powerful order by attentions which the Directory heard of with wonder, and would have heard of, had he been any other than Napoleon, with scorn and contempt.[12] Wherever he could have personal intercourse with the priesthood, he seems to have considerably softened their spleen. Meanwhile the clergy beyond the Apennines, and the nobility of Romagna, were combining all their efforts to rouse the population against him; and the Pope, pushed, as we have seen, to despair by the French Directory, had no reason to complain that his secular vassals heard such appeals with indifference.

Alvinzi's preparations were in the meantime rapidly advancing. The enthusiasm of the Austrian gentry was effectually stirred by the apprehension of seeing the conqueror of Italy under the walls of Vienna, and volunteer corps were formed everywhere and marched upon the frontier. The gallant peasantry of the Tyrol had already displayed their zeal; nor did the previous reverses of Alvinzi prevent them from once more crowding to his standard. Napoleon proclaimed that every Tyrolese caught in arms should be shot as a brigand. Alvinzi replied, that for every murdered peasant he would hang a French prisoner of war: Buonaparte rejoined, that the first execution of this threat would be instantly followed by the gibbeting of Alvinzi's own nephew, who was in his hands. These ferocious threats were laid aside, when time had been given for reflection; and either general prepared to carry on the war according to the old rules, which are at least sufficiently severe.

Alvinzi sent a peasant across the country to find his way if possible into the beleaguered city of Mantua, and give Wurmser notice that he was once more ready to attempt his relief. The veteran was commanded to make what diversion he could in favour of the approaching army; and if things came to the worst, to fight his way out of Mantua, retire on Romagna, and put himself at the head of the Papal forces. The spy who carried these tidings was intercepted, and dragged into the presence of Napoleon. The terrified man confessed that he had swallowed the ball of wax in which the despatch was wrapped. His stomach was compelled to surrender its contents; and Buonaparte prepared to meet his enemy. Leaving Serrurier to keep up the blockade of Mantua, he hastened to resume his central position at Verona, from which he could, according to circumstances, march with convenience on whatever line the Austrian main body might choose for their advance.

The Imperialists, as if determined to profit by no lesson, once more descended from the Tyrol upon two different lines of march; Alvinzi himself choosing that of the Upper Adige; while Provera headed a second army, with orders to follow the Brenta, and then, striking across to the Lower Adige, join the marshal before the walls of Mantua. Could they have combined their forces there, and delivered Wurmser, there was hardly a doubt that the French must retreat before so vast an army as would then have faced them. But Napoleon was destined once more to dissipate all these victorious dreams. He had posted Joubert at Rivoli, to dispute that important position, should the campaign open with an attempt to force it by Alvinzi; while Augereau's division was to watch the march of Provera. He remained himself at Verona until he could learn with certainty by which of these generals the first grand assault was to be made. On the evening of the 13th of January, tidings were brought him that Joubert had all that day been maintaining his ground with difficulty; and he instantly hastened to what now appeared to be the proper scene of action for himself.

Arriving about two in the morning (by another of his almost incredible forced marches) on the heights of Rivoli, he, the moonlight being clear, could distinguish five separate encampments, with innumerable watch-fires, in the valley below. His lieutenant, confounded by the display of this gigantic force, was in the very act of abandoning the position. Napoleon instantly checked this movement; and bringing up more battalions, forced the Croats from an eminence which they had already seized on the first symptoms of the French retreat. Napoleon's keen eye, surveying the position of the five encampments below, penetrated the secret of Alvinzi; namely, that his artillery had not yet arrived, otherwise he would not have occupied ground so distant from the object of attack. He concluded that the Austrian did not mean to make his grand assault very early in the morning, and resolved to force him to anticipate that movement. For this purpose, he took all possible pains to conceal his own arrival; and prolonged, by a series of petty manoeuvres, the enemy's belief that he had to do with a mere outpost of the French. Alvinzi swallowed the deceit; and, instead of advancing on some great and well-arranged system, suffered his several columns to endeavour to force the heights by insulated movements, which the real strength of Napoleon easily enabled him to baffle. It is true that at one moment the bravery of the Germans had nearly overthrown the French on a point of pre-eminent importance; but Napoleon himself galloping to the spot, roused by his voice and action the division of Massena, who, having marched all night, had lain down to rest in the extreme of weariness, and seconded by them and their gallant general,[13] swept everything before him. The French artillery was in position: the Austrian (according to Napoleon's shrewd guess) had not yet come up, and this circumstance decided the fortune of the day. The cannonade from the heights, backed by successive charges of horse and foot, rendered every attempt to storm the summit abortive; and the main body of the Imperialists was already in confusion, and, indeed, in flight, before one of their divisions, which had been sent round to outflank Buonaparte, and take higher ground in his rear, was able to execute its errand. When, accordingly, this division (that of Lusignan) at length achieved its destined object--it did so, not to complete the misery of a routed, but to swell the prey of a victorious enemy. Instead of cutting off the retreat of Joubert, Lusignan found himself insulated from Alvinzi, and forced to lay down his arms to Buonaparte. "Here was a good plan," said Napoleon, "but these Austrians are not apt to calculate the value of minutes." Had Lusignan gained the rear of the French an hour earlier, while the contest was still hot in front of the heights of Rivoli, he might have made the 14th of January one of the darkest, instead of one of the brightest days, in the military chronicles of Napoleon.

He, who in the course of this trying day had three horses shot under him, hardly waited to see Lusignan surrender, and to entrust his friends, Massena, Murat, and Joubert, with the task of pursuing the flying columns of Alvinzi. He had heard during the battle, that Provera had forced his way to the Lago di Guarda, and was already, by means of boats, in communication with Mantua. The force of Augereau having proved insufficient to oppose the march of the Imperialists' second column, it was high time that Napoleon himself should hurry with reinforcements to the Lower Adige, and prevent Wurmser from either housing Provera, or joining him in the open field, and so effecting the escape of his own still formidable garrison whether to the Tyrol or the Romagna.

Having marched all night and all next day, Napoleon reached the vicinity of Mantua late on the 15th. He found the enemy strongly posted, and Serrurier's situation highly critical. A regiment of Provera's hussars had but a few hours before nearly established themselves in the suburb of St. George. This Austrian corps had been clothed in white cloaks, resembling those of a well-known French regiment; and advancing towards the gate, would certainly have been admitted as friends--but for the sagacity of one sergeant, who could not help fancying that the white cloaks had too much of the gloss of novelty about them, to have stood the tear and wear of three Buonapartean campaigns. This danger had been avoided, but the utmost vigilance was necessary. The French general himself passed the night in walking about the outposts, so great was his anxiety.

At one of these he found a grenadier asleep by the root of a tree; and taking his gun, without wakening him, performed a sentinel's duty in his place for about half an hour; when the man, starting from his slumbers, perceived with terror and despair the countenance and occupation of his general. He fell on his knees before him. "My friend," said Napoleon, "here is your musket. You had fought hard, and marched long, and your sleep is excusable; but a moment's inattention might at present ruin the army. I happened to be awake, and have held your post for you. You will be more careful another time."

It is needless to say how the devotion of his men was nourished by such anecdotes as these flying ever and anon from column to column. Next morning there ensued a hot skirmish, recorded as the battle of St. George. Provera was compelled to retreat, and Wurmser, who had sallied out and seized the causeway and citadel of La Favorita, was fain to retreat within its old walls, in consequence of a desperate assault headed by Napoleon in person.

Provera now found himself entirely cut off from Alvinzi, and surrounded with the French. He and 5000 men laid down their arms on the 16th of January. Various bodies of the Austrian force, scattered over the country between the Adige and the Brenta, followed the example;[14] and the brave Wurmser, whose provisions were by this time exhausted, found himself at length under the necessity of sending an offer of capitulation.

General Serrurier, as commander of the blockade, received Klenau, the bearer of Wurmser's message, and heard him state, with the pardonable artifice usual on such occasions, that his master was still in a condition to hold out considerably longer, unless honourable terms were granted. Napoleon had hitherto been seated in a corner of the tent wrapped in his cloak; he now advanced to the Austrian, who had no suspicion in whose presence he had been speaking, and taking his pen, wrote down the conditions which he was willing to grant. "These," said he, "are the terms to which your general's bravery entitles him. He may have them to-day; a week, a month hence, he shall have no worse. Meantime, tell him that General Buonaparte is about to set out for Rome." The envoy now recognised Napoleon; and on reading the paper perceived that the proposed terms were more liberal than he had dared to hope for. The capitulation was forthwith signed.

On the 2nd of February, Wurmser and his garrison marched out of Mantua; but when the aged chief was to surrender his sword, he found only Serrurier ready to receive it. Napoleon's generosity, in avoiding being present personally to witness the humiliation of this distinguished veteran, forms one of the most pleasing traits in his story. The Directory had urged him to far different conduct. He treated their suggestions with scorn: "I have granted the Austrian," he wrote to them, "such terms as were, in my judgment, due to a brave and honourable enemy, and to the dignity of the French Republic."

The loss of the Austrians at Mantua amounted, first and last, to not less than 27,000 men. Besides innumerable military stores, upwards of 500 brass cannon fell into the hands of the conqueror; and Augereau was sent to Paris, to present the Directory with sixty stands of colours. He was received with tumults of exultation, such as might have been expected, on an occasion so glorious, from a people less vivacious than the French.

The surrender of Provera and Wurmser, following the total rout of Alvinzi, placed Lombardy wholly in the hands of Napoleon; and he now found leisure to avenge himself on the Pope for those hostile demonstrations which, as yet, he had been contented to hold in check. The terror with which the priestly court of the Vatican received the tidings of the utter destruction of the Austrian army, and of the irresistible conqueror's march southwards, did not prevent the Papal troops from making some efforts to defend the territories of the Holy See. General Victor, with 4000 French and as many Lombards, advanced upon the route of Imola. A Papal force, in numbers about equal, lay encamped on the river Senio in front of that town. Monks with crucifixes in their hands, ran through the lines, exciting them to fight bravely for their country and their Faith. The French general, by a rapid movement, threw his horse across the stream a league or two higher up, and then charged with his infantry through the Senio in their front. The resistance was brief. The Pope's army, composed mostly of new recruits, retreated in confusion. Faenza was carried by the bayonet. Colli and 3000 more laid down their arms; and the strong town of Ancona was occupied.[15] On the 10th of February the French entered Loretto, and rifled that celebrated seat of superstition of whatever treasures it still retained; the most valuable articles had already been packed up and sent to Rome for safety.[16]--Victor then turned westwards from Ancona, with the design to unite with another French column which had advanced into the papal dominion by Perugia.

The panic which the French advance had by this time spread was such, that the Pope had no hope but in submission. The peasants lately transformed into soldiers abandoned everywhere their arms, and fled in straggling groups to their native villages. The alarm in Rome itself recalled the days of Alaric.

The conduct of Buonaparte at this critical moment was worthy of that good sense which formed the original foundation of his successes, and of which the madness of pampered ambition could alone deprive him afterwards. He well knew that, of all the inhabitants of the Roman territories, the class who contemplated his approach with the deepest terror were the unfortunate French priests, whom the Revolution had made exiles from their native soil. One of these unhappy gentlemen came forth in his despair, and surrendering himself at the French headquarters, said he knew his fate was sealed, and that they might as well lead him at once to the gallows. Buonaparte dismissed this person with courtesy, and issued a proclamation that none of the class should be molested; on the contrary, allotting to each of them the means of existence in monasteries, wherever his arms were or should be predominant.

This conduct, taken together with other circumstances of recent occurrence, was well calculated to nourish in the breast of the Pope the hope that the victorious general of France had, by this time, discarded the ferocious hostility of the revolutionary government against the church of which he was head. He hastened, however, to open a negotiation, and Napoleon received his envoy not merely with civility, but with professions of the profoundest personal reverence for the holy father. The Treaty of Tollentino (Feb. 12, 1797) followed. By this the Pope conceded formally (for the first time), his ancient territory of Avignon. He resigned the legations of Ferrara, Bologna, and Romagna, and the port of Ancona; agreed to pay about a million and a half sterling, and to execute to the utmost the provisions of Bologna with respect to works of art. On these terms Pius was to remain nominal master of some shreds of the patrimony of St. Peter.

The French Directory heard with indignation that any semblance of sovereignty was still left to an enemy whose weakness had been made so manifest. But Buonaparte had now learned to act for himself. He knew that any formal dethronement of the Pope would invest his cause with tenfold strength wherever the Romish religion prevailed; that a new spirit of aversion would arise against France; and that Naples would infallibly profit by the first disturbances in the north of Italy, to declare war, and march her large army from the south. He believed also--and he ere long knew--that even yet Austria would make other efforts to recover Lombardy; and was satisfied, on the whole, that he should best secure his ultimate purposes by suffering the Vatican to prolong, for some time further, the shadow of that sovereignty which had in former ages trampled on kings and emperors.

[Footnote 11: Buonaparte, to replace all his losses in the two last campaigns, had received only 7000 recruits.]

[Footnote 12: He found among them a wealthy old canon of his own name, who was proud to hail the Corsican as a true descendant of the Tuscan Buonapartes; who entertained him and his whole staff with much splendour; amused the general with his anxiety that some interest should be applied to the Pope, in order to procure the canonisation of a certain long defunct worthy of the common lineage, by name Buonventara Buonaparte; and dying shortly afterwards, bequeathed his whole fortune to his new-found kinsman.]

[Footnote 13: Hence, in the sequel, Massena's title, "Duke of Rivoli."]

[Footnote 14: Such was the prevailing terror, that one body of 6000 under Ren?surrendered to a French officer who had hardly 500 men with him.]

[Footnote 15: The priests had an image of the Virgin Mary at this place, which they exhibited to the people in the act of shedding tears, the more to stimulate them against the impious Republicans. On entering the place, the French were amused with discovering the machinery by which this trick had been performed; the Madonna's tears were a string of glass beads, flowing by clockwork within a shrine which the worshippers were too respectful to approach very nearly. Little ormolu fountains, which stream on the same principle, are now common ornaments for the chimney-piece in Paris.]

[Footnote 16: The Santa Casa, or holy house of Loretto, is a little brick building, round which a magnificent church has been reared, and which the Romish calendar states to have been the original dwelling-house of the Virgin Mary in Nazareth, transported through the air to Italy by miracle. This was for ages the chief resort of Romish pilgrims, and the riches of the place were once enormous.]

CHAPTER VIII

Neutrality of Venice--The Archduke Charles--Battle of Tagliamento--Retreat of the Archduke--Treaty of Leoben--War with Venice--Venice conquered.

Napoleon was now master of all northern Italy, with the exception of the territories of Venice, which antique government, though no longer qualified to keep equal rank with the first princes of Europe, was still proud and haughty, and not likely to omit any favourable opportunity of aiding Austria in the great and common object of ridding Italy of the French. Buonaparte heard without surprise that the Doge had been raising new levies, and that the senate could command an army of 50,000, composed chiefly of fierce and semi-barbarous Sclavonian mercenaries. He demanded what these demonstrations meant, and was answered that Venice had no desire but to maintain a perfect neutrality. Meantime there was not wanting a strong party, throughout the Venetian territories of the mainland, who were anxious to emulate the revolutionary movements of the great cities of Lombardy, and to emancipate themselves from the yoke of the Venetian oligarchy, as their neighbours had done by that of the Austrian crown. Insurrections occurred at Bergamo, Brescia, and elsewhere; and Buonaparte, though little disposed to give the inhabitants of these places the boon they were in quest of, saw and profited by the opportunity of dividing, by their means, the resources, and shaking the confidence, of the senate. After some negotiation, he told the Venetian envoy that he granted the prayer of his masters. "Be neuter," said he, "but see that your neutrality be indeed sincere and perfect. If any insurrection occur in my rear, to cut off my communications in the event of my marching on Germany--if any movement whatever betray the disposition of your senate to aid the enemies of France, be sure that vengeance will follow--from that hour the independence of Venice has ceased to be."

More than a month had now elapsed since Alvinzi's defeat at Rivoli; in nine days the war with the Pope had reached its close; and, having left some garrisons in the towns on the Adige, to watch the neutrality of Venice, Napoleon hastened to carry the war into the hereditary dominions of the Emperor. Twenty thousand fresh troops had recently joined his victorious standard from France; and, at the head of perhaps a larger force than he had ever before mustered, he proceeded to the frontier of the Frioul, where, according to his information, the main army of Austria, recruited once more to its original strength, was preparing to open a sixth campaign--under the orders, not of Alvinzi, but of a general young like himself, and hitherto eminently successful--the same who had already by his combinations baffled two such masters in the art of war as Jourdan and Moreau--the Archduke Charles; a prince on whose high talents the last hopes of the empire seemed to repose.

To give the details of the sixth campaign, which now commenced, would be to repeat the story which has been already five times told. The Archduke, fettered by the Aulic Council of Vienna, saw himself compelled to execute a plan which he had discrimination enough to condemn. The Austrian army once more commenced operations on a double basis--one great division on the Tyrolese frontier, and a greater under the Archduke himself on the Friulese; and Napoleon--who had, even when acting on the defensive, been able, by the vivacity of his movements, to assume the superiority on whatever point he chose to select--was not likely to strike his blows with less skill and vigour, now that his numbers, and the acquiescence of Italy behind him, permitted him to assume the offensive.

Buonaparte found the Archduke posted behind the river Tagliamento, in front of the rugged Carinthian mountains, which guard the passage in that quarter from Italy to Germany. Detaching Massena to the Piave, where the Austrian division of Lusignan were in observation, he himself determined to charge the Archduke in front. Massena was successful in driving Lusignan before him as far as Belluno, (where a rear guard of 500 surrendered,) and thus turned the Austrian flank. Buonaparte then attempted and effected the passage of the Tagliamento. After a great and formal display of his forces, which was met by similar demonstrations on the Austrian side of the river, he suddenly broke up his line and retreated. The Archduke, knowing that the French had been marching all the night before, concluded that the general wished to defer the battle till another day; and in like manner withdrew to his camp. About two hours after Napoleon rushed with his whole army, who had merely lain down in ranks, upon the margin of the Tagliamento, no longer adequately guarded--and had forded the stream ere the Austrian line of battle could be formed. In the action which followed (March 12) the troops of the Archduke displayed much gallantry, but every effort to dislodge Napoleon failed; at length retreat was judged necessary. The French followed hard behind. They stormed Gradisca, where they made 5000 prisoners; and--the Archduke pursuing his retreat--occupied in the course of a few days Trieste, Fiume, and every stronghold in Carinthia. In the course of a campaign of twenty days, the Austrians fought Buonaparte ten times, but the overthrow on the Tagliamento was never recovered; and the Archduke, after defending Styria inch by inch as he had Carinthia, at length adopted the resolution of reaching Vienna by forced marches, there to gather round him whatever force the loyalty of his nation could muster, and make a last stand beneath the walls of the capital.

This plan, at first sight the mere dictate of despair, was in truth that of a wise and prudent general. The Archduke had received intelligence from two quarters of events highly unfavourable to the French. General Laudon, the Austrian commander on the Tyrol frontier, had descended thence with forces sufficient to overwhelm Buonaparte's lieutenants on the upper Adige, and was already in possession of the whole Tyrol, and of several of the Lombard towns. Meanwhile the Venetian Senate, on hearing of these Austrian successes, had plucked up courage to throw aside their flimsy neutrality, and not only declared war against France, but encouraged their partizans in Verona to open the contest with an inhuman massacre of the French wounded in the hospitals of that city. The vindictive Italians, wherever the French party was inferior in numbers, resorted to similar atrocities. The few troops left in Lombardy by Napoleon were obliged to shut themselves up in garrisons, which the insurgent inhabitants of the neighbouring districts invested. The Venetian army passed the frontier; and, in effect, Buonaparte's means of deriving supplies of any kind from his rear were for the time wholly cut off. It was not wonderful that the Archduke should, under such circumstances, anticipate great advantage from enticing the French army into the heart of Austria; where, divided by many wide provinces and mighty mountains and rivers from France, and with Italy once more in arms behind them, they should have to abide the encounter of an imperial army, animated by all the best motives that can lend vigour to the arm of man; fighting for their own hearths under the eyes of their own sovereign; seconded everywhere by the loyalty of the peasants; and well convinced that, if they could compel their enemy to a retreat, his total ruin must be the consequence.

The terror of the Aulic Council stepped in to prevent the Archduke from reaping either the credit or the disgrace of this movement. Vienna was panic-struck on hearing that Buonaparte had stormed the passes of the Julian Alps; the imperial family sent their treasure into Hungary; the middle ranks, whose interest is always peace, became clamorous for some termination to a war, which during six years had been so unfortunate; and the Archduke was ordered to avail himself of the first pretence which circumstances might afford for the opening of a negotiation.

That prince had already, acting on his own judgment and feelings, dismissed such an occasion with civility and with coldness. Napoleon had addressed a letter to his Imperial Highness from Clagenfurt, in which he called on him, as a brother soldier, to consider the certain miseries and the doubtful successes of war, and put an end to the campaign by a fair and equitable treaty. The Archduke replied, that he regarded with the highest esteem the personal character of his correspondent, but that the Austrian government had committed to his trust the guidance of a particular army, not the diplomatic business of the empire. The prince, on receiving these new instructions from Vienna, perceived, however reluctantly, that the line of his duty was altered; and the result was a series of negotiations--which ended in the provisional treaty of Leoben, signed April 18, 1797.

It was here, at Leoben, that Buonaparte's schoolfellow, De Bourienne, who had been summoned to act as secretary to the general, reached headquarters. He found his old comrade (whom he had not met with since the days of his envying small houses and cabriolets in Paris) in the midst of a splendid staff. "So thou art come at last," cried Napoleon, in the ancient tone of familiarity; but De Bourienne knew the world, and greeted the general of the army of Italy with profound and distant respect. When the company were gone, Buonaparte signified that he understood and approved this change of demeanour.

But to resume--no sooner was the negotiation in a fair train, than Napoleon, abandoning for the moment the details of its management to inferior diplomatists, hastened to retrace his steps, and pour the full storm of his wrath on the Venetians. The Doge and the Senate, whose only hopes had rested on the successes of Austria on the Adige, heard with utter despair that the Archduke had shared the fate of Beaulieu, of Wurmser, and of Alvinzi, and that the preliminaries of peace were actually signed. The rapidity of Buonaparte's return gave them no breathing-time. They hastened to send offers of submission, and their messengers were received with anger and contempt. "French blood has been treacherously shed," said Napoleon; "if you could offer me the treasures of Peru, if you could cover your whole dominion with gold--the atonement would be insufficient--the lion of St. Mark[17] must lick the dust." These tidings came like a sentence of death upon the devoted Senate. Their deliberations were unceasing; their schemes innumerable; their hearts divided and unnerved. Those secret chambers, from which that haughty oligarchy had for so many ages excluded every eye and every voice but their own, were invaded with impunity by strange-faced men, who boldly criticised their measures, and heaped new terrors on their heads, by announcing that the mass of the people had ceased to consider the endurance of their sway as synonymous with the prosperity of Venice. Popular tumults filled the streets and canals; universal confusion prevailed. The commanders of their troops and fleets received contradictory orders, and the city which

"--had held the gorgeous East in fee,"

seemed ready to yield everything to a ruthless and implacable enemy, without even striking a blow in defence.

Buonaparte appeared, while the confusion was at its height, on the opposite coast of the Lagoon. Some of his troops were already in the heart of the city, when (31st May) a hasty message reached him, announcing that the Senate submitted wholly. He exacted severe revenge. The leaders who had aided the Lombard insurgents were delivered to him. The oligarchy ceased to rule, and a democratical government was formed, provisionally, on the model of

France. Venice consented to surrender to the victor large territories on the mainland of Italy; five ships of war; 3,000,000 francs in gold, and as many more in naval stores; twenty of the best pictures, and 500 manuscripts. Lastly, the troops of the conqueror were to occupy the capital until tranquillity was established. It will be seen in what that tranquillity was destined to consist.

Such was the humiliation of this once proud and energetic, but now worn-out and enfeebled, oligarchy: so incapable was that hoary polity of contending with the youthful vigour of Napoleon.

[Footnote 17: The armorial bearing of Venice.]

CHAPTER IX

Pichegru--The Directory appeal to Buonaparte--The 18th Fructidor--The Court of Montebello--Josephine--The Treaty of Campo-Formio--Buonaparte leaves Italy.

In their last agony the Venetian Senate made a vain effort to secure the personal protection of the general, by offering him a purse of seven millions of francs. He rejected this with scorn. He had already treated in the same style a bribe of four millions, tendered on the part of the Duke of Modena. The friend employed to conduct the business reminded him of the proverbial ingratitude of all popular governments, and of the little attention which the Directory had hitherto paid to his personal interests. "That is all true enough," said Napoleon, "but for four millions I will not place myself in the power of this duke." Austria herself, it is said, did not hesitate to tamper in the same manner, though far more magnificently, as became her resources, with his republican virtue. He was offered, if the story be true, an independent German principality for himself and his heirs. "I thank the emperor," he answered, "but if greatness is to be mine, it shall come from France."

The Venetian Senate were guilty, in their mortal struggle, of another and a more inexcusable piece of meanness. They seized the person of Count D'Entraigues, a French emigrant, who had been living in their city as agent for the exiled house of Bourbon; and surrendered him and all his papers to the victorious general. Buonaparte discovered among these documents ample evidence that Pichegru, the French general on the Rhine, and universally honoured as the conqueror of Holland, had some time before this hearkened to the proposals of the Bourbon princes, and, among other efforts in favour of the royal cause, not hesitated even to misconduct his military movements with a view to the downfall of the government which had entrusted him with his command.

This was a secret, the importance of which Napoleon could well appreciate;[18] and he forthwith communicated it to the Directory at Paris.

The events of the last twelve months in France had made Pichegru a person of still higher importance than when he commenced his intrigues with the Bourbons as general on the Rhine. Some obscure doubts of his fidelity, or the usual policy of the Directory, which rendered them averse (wherever they could help it) to continue any one general very long at the head of one army, had induced them to displace Pichegru, and appoint Hoche, a tried republican, in his room. Pichegru, on returning to France, became a member of the Council of Five Hundred, and (the royalist party having at this season recovered all but a preponderance) was, on the meeting of the chambers, called to the chair of that in which he had his place.

The Five Directors had in truth done everything to undermine their own authority. They were known to be divided in opinion among themselves; three only of their number adhered heartily to the existing constitution: one was a royalist: another was a democrat of the Robespierre school. One of these new and uncourtly men excited laughter by affecting a princely state and splendour of demeanour and equipage. Another disgusted one set of minds, and annoyed all the rest, by procuring a law for the observation of the tenth day as the day of repose, and declaring it a crime to shut up shops on the Sabbath. A ridiculous ritual of an avowedly heathen worship followed, and was received with partial horror, universal contempt. A tyrannical law about the equalisation of weights and measures spread confusion through all mercantile transactions, and was especially unpopular in the provinces. A contemptible riot, set on foot by one who called himself Gracchus Barboeuf, for the purpose of bringing back the reign of terrorism was indeed suppressed; but the mere occurrence of such an attempt recalled too vividly the days of Robespierre, and by so doing tended to strengthen the cause of the royalists in public opinion. The truth is, that a vast number of the emigrants had found their way back again to Paris after the downfall of

Robespierre, and that the old sway of elegant manners and enlightened saloons was once more re-establishing itself where it had so long been supreme. The royalist club of Clichy corresponded with the exiled princes, and with the imperial government, and was gaining such influence as to fill Buonaparte himself with alarm. Everything indicated that the Directory (the five majesties of the Luxembourg, as they were called in derision) held their thrones by a very uncertain tenure; and those gentlemen, nothing being left them but a choice among evils, were fain to throw themselves on the protection of the armies which they dreaded, and of Hoche and Buonaparte-- which last name in particular had long filled them with jealousy proportioned to its splendour and popularity.

Napoleon's recent conduct, in more important points than one, had excited powerfully the resentment of the Directory, which now appealed to him for aid. He had taken upon himself the whole responsibility of the preliminary treaty of Leoben, although the French government had sent General Clarke into Italy for the express purpose of controlling him, and acting as his equal at least in the negotiation. A clause in that treaty, by which Mantua, the strongest fortress in Italy, was to be surrendered back to Austria, had been judged necessary at the time by the general, in order to obtain from the emperor the boundary of the Rhine and the cession of Belgium. But the Directory thought the conqueror underrated the advantages of his own position and theirs in consenting to it, and but for Carnot would never have ratified it.[19] At the other side of the Italian Peninsula, again, the victorious general, immediately after the fall of Venice, had to superintend the revolution of Genoa; in which great city also the democratic party availed themselves of the temper and events of the time, to emancipate themselves from their hereditary oligarchy. They would fain have excluded the nobility from all share in the remodelled government; and Napoleon rebuked and discountenanced this attempt in terms little likely to be heard with approbation by the "Sires of the Luxembourg." He told the Genoese, that to exclude the nobles was in itself as unjust as unwise, and that they ought to be grateful for the means of re-organising their constitution, without passing like France through the terrible ordeal of a revolution. The rulers of France might be excused for asking at this moment--Does the lecturer of the Ligurian Republic mean to be our Washington, our Monk, or our Cromwell?

He, however, received with alacrity the call of the trembling Directory. He harangued his soldiery, and made himself secure of their readiness to act as he might choose for them. He not only offered large pecuniary supplies, and sent his lieutenant Augereau to Paris to command the National Guard for the government, should they find it necessary to appeal immediately to force, but announced that he was himself prepared to "pass the Rubicon," (an ominous phrase) and march to their assistance, with 15,000 of his best troops.

The Directory, meanwhile, had in their extremity ventured to disregard the law against drawing regular troops within a certain distance of the capital, and summoned Hoche to bring a corps of his Rhenish army for their instant protection.

It was by this means that the new revolution, as it may be called, of the 18th Fructidor was effected. On that day, (Sept. 4, 1797,) the majority of the Directory, marching their army into Paris, dethroned their two opposition colleagues. Pichegru and the other royalists of note in the assemblies, to the number of more than 150, were arrested and sent into exile. The government, for the moment, recovered the semblance of security; and Buonaparte heard, with little satisfaction, that they had been able to accomplish their immediate object without the intervention of his personal appearance on the scene. He remonstrated, moreover, against the manner in which they had followed up their success. According to him, they ought to have executed Pichegru and a few ring-leaders, and set an example of moderation, by sparing all those whose royalism admitted of any doubt, or, if it was manifest, was of secondary importance. It would have been hard for the Directory at this time to have pleased Buonaparte, or for Buonaparte to have entirely satisfied them; but neither party made the effort.

The fall of Venice, however, gave Napoleon the means, which he was not disposed to neglect, of bringing his treaty with Austria to a more satisfactory conclusion than had been indicated in the preliminaries of Leoben.

After settling the affairs of Venice, and establishing the new Ligurian Republic, the general took up his residence at the noble castle of Montebello, near Milan. Here his wife, who, though they had been married in March, 1796, was still a bride, and with whom, during the intervening eventful months, he had kept up a correspondence full of the fervour, if not of the delicacy of love,[20] had at length rejoined him. Josephine's manners were worthy, by universal admission, of the highest rank; and the elegance with which she did the honours of the castle, filled the ministers and princes, who were continually to be seen in its precincts, with admiration. While Napoleon conducted his negotiations with as much firmness and decision as had marked him in the field, it was her care that nature and art should lend all their graces to what the Italians soon learnt to call the Court of Montebello. Whatever talent Milan contained, was pressed into her service. Music and dance, and festival upon festival, seemed to occupy every hour. The beautiful lakes of Lombardy were covered with gay flotillas; and the voluptuous retreats around their shores received in succession new life and splendour from the presence of Napoleon, Josephine, and the brilliant circle amidst whom they were rehearsing the imperial parts that destiny had in reserve for them. Montebello was the centre from which Buonaparte, during the greater part of this autumn, negotiated with the emperor, controlled all Italy, and overawed the Luxembourg.

The final settlement with the emperor's commissioners would have taken place shortly after the fall of Venice, but for the successful intrigues of the royalist Clichyens, the universal belief that the government of France approached some new crisis, and the Austrians' hope that from such an event their negotiation might derive considerable advantages. Buonaparte well knew the secret motive which induced Cobentzel, the emperor's chief envoy, to protract and multiply discussions of which he by this time was weary. One day, in this ambassador's own chamber, Napoleon suddenly changed his demeanour; "you refuse to accept our ultimatum," said he, taking in his hands a beautiful vase of porcelain, which stood on the mantelpiece near him. The Austrian bowed. "It is well," said Napoleon, "but mark me--within two months I will shatter Austria like this potsherd." So saying, he dashed the vase on the ground in a thousand pieces, and moved towards the door. Cobentzel followed him, and made submissions which induced him once more to resume his negotiations.

The result was the treaty of Campo-Formio, so-called from the village at which it was signed, on the 3d of October, 1797. By this act the emperor yielded to France, Flanders and the boundary of the Rhine, including the great fortress of Mentz. The various new republics of Lombardy were united and recognised under the general name of the Cisalpine Republic. To indemnify Austria for the loss of those territories, the fall of Venice afforded new means--of which Napoleon did not hesitate to propose, nor Austria to accept the use. The French general had indeed conquered Venice, but he had entered into a treaty subsequently, and recognised a wholly new government in place of the oligarchy. The emperor, on the other hand, well knew that the Doge and Senate had incurred ruin by rising to his own aid. Such considerations weighed little on either side. France and Austria agreed to effect a division of the whole territories of the ancient republic. Venice herself, and her Italian provinces, were handed over to the emperor in lieu of his lost Lombardy; and the French assumed the sovereignty of the Ionian islands and Dalmatia. This unprincipled proceeding excited universal disgust throughout Europe. It showed the sincerity of Buonaparte's love for the cause of freedom; and it satisfied all the world of the excellent title of the imperial court to complain of the selfishness and rapacity of the French democracy.

The emperor set his seal at Campo-Formio to another of Buonaparte's acts of dictatorship, which, though in one point of view even more unjustifiable than this, was not regarded by the world with feelings of the same order. The Italian territory of the Valteline had for ages been subject to the Grison League. The inhabitants, roused by the prevailing spirit all around them, demanded Napoleon's intercession with their Swiss masters, to procure their admission to all the political privileges of the other cantons. They refused; and Napoleon, in the plenitude of his authority, immediately supported the Valteline in throwing off the Grison yoke, and asserting its utter independence. This territory was now annexed to the Cisalpine Republic. A government, with which France was on terms of alliance and amity, was thus robbed of its richest possession; but the Valteline belonged by natural position, religion, and language, to Italy, and its annexation to the new Italian republic was regarded as in itself just and proper, however questionable Buonaparte's title to effect that event. He himself said at the time, "it is contrary to the rights of man that any one people should be subject to another;" a canon on which his after history formed a lucid commentary.

In concluding, and in celebrating the conclusion of his treaty, Napoleon's proud and fiery temperament twice shone out. Cobentzel had set down as the first article, "The Emperor recognises the French Republic." "Efface that," said Napoleon, sternly, "it is as clear as that the sun is in heaven. Woe to them that cannot distinguish the light of either!" At the TE DEUM after the proclamation of the peace, the imperial envoy would have taken the place prepared for Buonaparte, which was the most eminent in the church. The haughty soldier seized his arm and drew him back. "Had your master himself been here," said he, "I should not have forgotten that in my person the dignity of France is represented."

Various minor arrangements remained to be considered; and a congress of all the German powers being summoned to meet for that purpose at Rastadt, Napoleon received the orders of the Directory to appear there, and perfect his work in the character of ambassador of France. He took an affecting leave of his soldiery, published a temperate and manly address to the Cisalpine Republic, and proceeded, by way of Switzerland, (where, in spite of the affair of the Valteline, he was received with enthusiasm,) to the execution of his duty. He carried with him the unbounded love and devotion of one of the finest armies that ever the world had seen; and the attachment, hardly less energetic, of all those classes of society throughout Italy, who flattered themselves with the hope that the Cisalpine Republic, the creature of his hands, would in time prepare the way for, and ultimately merge in a republican constitution common to the whole Italian people. With what hopes or fears as to his future fortunes he abandoned the scene and the companions of his glory, the reader must form his own opinion.

[Footnote 18: Moreau knew it some months sooner, and said so after Napoleon had communicated it to the Directory. This is a suspicious circumstance when considered along with the sequel of Moreau's history.]

[Footnote 19: Mantua, as will appear hereafter, was saved to France under Napoleon's final treaty with Austria; but the events which rendered this possible were as yet unknown and unexpected.]

[Footnote 20: It would be painful to show, as might easily be done, from this correspondence, the original want of delicacy in Napoleon's mind. Many of his letters are such as no English gentleman would address to a mistress. In others, the language is worthy of a hero's passion. "Wurmser," says he, "shall pay dearly for the tears he causes you to shed."]

CHAPTER X

Napoleon at Rastadt--He arrives in Paris--His reception by the Directory--His

Conduct and Manners--He is appointed to command the Army for the Invasion of England--He recommends an Expedition to Egypt--Reaches Toulon--Embarks.

Napoleon was received by the ministers assembled at Rastadt with the respect due to the extraordinary talents which he had already displayed in negotiation as well as in war. But he stayed among them only two or three days, for he perceived that the multiplicity of minor arrangements to be discussed and settled, must, if he seriously entered upon them, involve the necessity of a long-protracted residence at Rastadt; and he had many reasons for desiring to be quickly in Paris. His personal relations with the Directory were of a very doubtful kind, and he earnestly wished to study with his own eyes the position in which the government stood towards the various orders of society in the all-influential capital. He abandoned the conduct of the diplomatic business to his colleagues, and reached Paris at the beginning of December. Nor was he without a feasible pretext for this rapidity. On the 2nd of October, the Directory had announced to the French people their purpose to carry the war with the English into England itself; the immediate organisation of a great invading army; and their design to place it under the command of "Citizen General Buonaparte."

During his brief stay at Rastadt the dictator of Campo-Formio once more broke out. The Swedish envoy was Count Fersen, the same nobleman who had distinguished himself in Paris, during the early period of the Revolution, by his devotion to King Louis and Marie-Antoinette. Buonaparte refused peremptorily to enter into any negotiation in which a man, so well known for his hostility to the cause of the Republic, should have any part; and Fersen instantly withdrew.

On quitting this congress Napoleon was careful to resume, in every particular, the appearance of a private citizen. Reaching Paris, he took up his residence in the same small modest house that he had occupied before he set out for Italy, in the Rue Chantereine, which, about this time, in compliment to its illustrious inhabitant, received from the municipality the new name of Rue de la Victoire. Here he resumed with his plain clothes his favourite studies and pursuits, and, apparently contented with the society of his private friends, seemed to avoid, as carefully as others in his situation might have courted, the honours of popular distinction and applause. It was not immediately known that he was in Paris, and when he walked the streets his person was rarely recognised by the multitude. His mode of life was necessarily somewhat different from what it had been when he was both poor and obscure; his society was courted in the highest circles, and he from time to time appeared in them, and received company at home with the elegance of hospitality over which Josephine was so well qualified to preside. But policy as well as pride moved him to shun notoriety. Before he could act again, he had much to observe; and he knew himself too well to be flattered by the stare either of mobs or of saloons. "They have memories for nothing here"-- he said at this time to his secretary--"if I remain long without doing anything, I am done. Fame chases fame in this great Babylon. If they had seen me three times at the spectacle, they would no longer look at me." Another day Bourienne could not help congratulating him on some noisy demonstration of popular favour. "Bah!" he answered, "they would rush as eagerly about me if I were on my way to the scaffold."

In his intercourse with society at this period, he was, for the most part, remarkable for the cold reserve of his manners. He had the appearance of one too much occupied with serious designs, to be able to relax at will into the easy play of ordinary conversation. If his eye was on every man, he well knew that every man's eye was upon him; nor, perhaps, could he have chosen a better method (had that been his sole object) for prolonging and strengthening the impression his greatness was calculated to create, than this very exhibition of indifference. He did not suffer his person to be familiarised out of reverence. When he did appear, it was not the ball or bon mot of the evening before, that he recalled:--he was still, wherever he went, the Buonaparte of Lodi, and Arcola, and Rivoli. His military bluntness disdained to disguise itself amidst those circles where a meaner parvenu would have been most ambitious to shine. The celebrated daughter of Necker made many efforts to catch his fancy and enlist him among the votaries of her wit, which then gave law in Paris. "Whom," said she, half wearied with his chillness, "do you consider as the greatest of women?" "Her, madam," he answered, "who has borne the greatest number of children." From this hour he had Madame de Sta 雠 for his enemy; and yet, such are the inconsistencies of human nature, no man was more sensitive than he to the assaults of a species of enemy whom he thus scorned to conciliate. Throughout his Italian campaigns--as consul--as emperor--and down to the last hour of the exile which terminated his life--Buonaparte suffered himself to be annoyed by sarcasms and pamphlets as keenly and constantly as if he had been a poetaster.

The haughtiness, for such it was considered, of his behaviour in the society of the capital, was of a piece with what he had already manifested in the camp. In the course of his first campaigns, his officers, even of the highest rank, became sensible, by degrees, to a total change of demeanour. An old acquaintance of the Toulon period, joining the army, was about to throw himself into the general's arms with the warmth of the former familiarity. Napoleon's cold eye checked him; and he perceived in a moment how he had altered with his elevation. He had always, on the other hand, affected much familiarity with the common soldiery. He disdained not on occasion to share the ration or to taste the flask of a sentinel; and the French private, often as intelligent as those whom fortune has placed above him, used to address the great general with even more frankness than his own captain. Napoleon, in one of his Italian despatches, mentions to the Directory the pleasure which he often derived from the conversation of the men: "But yesterday," says he, "a common trooper addressed me as I was riding, and told me he thought he could suggest the movement which ought to be adopted. I listened to him, and heard him detail some operations on which I had actually resolved but a little before." It has been noticed (perhaps by over-nice speculators) as a part of the same system, that Napoleon, on his return to Paris, continued to employ the same tradespeople, however inferior in their several crafts, who had served him in the days of his obscurity.[21]

If we may follow M. de Bourienne, Napoleon at this time laboured under intense anxiety of mind. Conscious of the daring heights to which he had ere now accustomed his ambitious imagination, he was fearful that others had divined his secret, and was haunted with the perpetual dread that some accident might unite Royalists and Republicans in the work of his personal ruin.

The first public appearance of Buonaparte occurred (January 2, 1798) when the treaty of Campo-Formio was to be formally presented to the Directory. The great court of the Luxembourg was roofed over with flags; an immense concourse, including all the members of the government and of the two legislative bodies, expected the victorious negotiator; and when he appeared, followed by his staff, and surrounded on all hands with the trophies of his glorious campaign, the enthusiasm of the mighty multitude, to the far greater part of which his person was, up to the moment, entirely unknown, outleaped all bounds, and filled the already jealous hearts of the directors with dark presentiments. They well knew that the soldiery, returning from Italy, had sung and said through every village that it was high time to get rid of the lawyers, and make the "little corporal" king. With uneasy hearts did they hear what seemed too like an echo of this cry, from the assembled leaders of opinion in Paris and in France. Anxious curiosity and mutual distrust were written in every face. The voice of Napoleon was for the first time heard in an energetic speech, ascribing all the glories that had been achieved to the zeal of the French soldiery--for "the glorious constitution of the year THREE"--the same glorious constitution which, in the year eight, was to receive the coup de grace from his own hand; and Barras, as presiding director, answering, that "Nature had exhausted all her powers in the creation of a Buonaparte," awoke a new thunder of unwelcome applauses.

Carnot had been exiled after the 18th Fructidor, and was at this time actually believed to be dead. The institute nominated Buonaparte to fill his place; and he was received by this learned body with enthusiasm not inferior to that of the Luxembourg. He thenceforth adopted, on all public occasions, the costume of this academy; and, laying aside as far as was possible, the insignia of his military rank, seemed to desire only the distinction of being classed with those whose scientific attainments had done honour to their country. In all this he acted on calculation. "I well knew," said he at St. Helena, "that there was not a drummer in the army, but would respect me the more for believing me to be not a mere soldier."

Some time before he left Italy, a motion had been made in one of the chambers for rewarding him with a grant of the estate of Chambord, and lost owing solely to the jealousy of the Directory. This opposition was on their part unjust and unwise, and extremely unpopular also; for it was known to all men that the general might easily have enriched himself during his wonderful campaigns, and it was almost as generally believed that he had brought with him to the Rue de la Victoire only 100,000 crowns, saved from the fair allowances of his rank. No one who considers the long series of intrigues which had passed between Buonaparte and the party that triumphed in Fructidor, can doubt how he regarded this part of their conduct. Every day confirmed them in their jealousy; nor did he take much pains on the other hand to conceal his feelings towards them. On many occasions they were willing to make use of him, although they dreaded in so doing to furnish him with new proofs of the vast superiority which he had reached in public opinion above themselves; and he was, on his part, chary of acceding to any of their proposals.

On the 21st of January, the anniversary of the death of Louis XVI. was to be celebrated, according to custom, as a great festival of the Republican calendar; and, conscious how distasteful the observance had by this time become to all persons capable of reflection, the government would fain have diverted attention from themselves, by assigning a prominent part in the ceremonial to him, on whom, as they knew, all eyes were sure to be fixed whenever he made his appearance. Napoleon penetrated their motives. He remonstrated against the ceremony altogether, as perpetuating the memory of a deed, perhaps unavoidable, but not the less to be regretted. He told them that it was unworthy of a great Republic to triumph, year after year, in the shedding of an individual enemy's blood. They answered by reminding him that the Athenians and Romans of old recorded, in similar festivals, the downfall of the Pisistratid?and the exile of the Tarquins. He might have replied, that it is easier for a nation to renounce Christianity in name, than to obliterate altogether the traces of its humanising influence. But this view did not as yet occur to Napoleon--or if it had, could not have been promulgated to their conviction. He stood on the impolicy of the barbarous ceremony; and was at length, with difficulty, persuaded to appear in it as a private member of the institute, along with the rest of that association. His refusal to be there as the great general of the Republic annoyed the timid Directory; and yet, on his being recognised in his civic dress, and pointed out to new myriads of observers, the effect which the government had desired to produce was brought about in spite of all Buonaparte's reluctance. The purpose of the assemblage was almost forgotten: the clamours of the people converted it into another f 陛 e for Napoleon.

It has already been said that as early as October, 1797, the Directory announced their intention of committing an army, destined for the invasion of England, to the conqueror of Italy. He wholly disapproved of their rashness in breaking off the negotiations of the preceding summer with the English envoy, Lord Malmesbury, and, above all, of the insolent abruptness of that procedure.[22] But the die was cast; and he willingly accepted the appointment now pressed upon him by the government, who, in truth, were anxious about nothing so much as to occupy his mind with the matters of his profession, and so prevent him from taking a prominent part in the civil business of the state. Solely owing to his celebrity two of his brothers were already distinguished members of the legislative bodies; and there could be no doubt that the gates of either would fly open for his own admission, if he chose it, on the next election.

Whatever views of ulterior ambition might have opened themselves to Napoleon at this period, he well knew that the hour was not yet come, in which he could serve his purpose better than by the pursuit of his military career. According to De Bourienne, he had for some time flattered himself that the law, which prevented a person so young as he from being a director, might be waived in his favour; not doubting, we may conclude, that such colleagues as Barras and Rewbell would soon sink into the mere ministers of his will: but the opposition to this scheme was so determined that it was never permitted to be proposed openly. The Directory were popular with no party; but there were many parties; and, numerically, probably the royalists were the strongest. The pure republicans were still powerful: the army of Italy was distant and scattered; that of the Rhine, far more numerous, and equally well disciplined, had its own generals--men not yet in reputation immeasurably inferior to himself; and, having been less fortunate than their brethren in Italy, and consequently acquired less wealth, it was no wonder that the soldiery of the Rhine regarded the others, if not their leader, with some little jealousy. In Napoleon's own language, "the pear was not yet ripe."

He proceeded, therefore, to make a regular survey of the French coast opposite to England, with the view of improving its fortifications, and (ostensibly at least) of selecting the best points for embarking an invading force. For this service he was eminently qualified; and many local improvements of great importance, long afterwards effected, were first suggested by him at this period. But, if he had really thought otherwise beforehand (which M. de Bourienne denies), the result of his examination was a perfect conviction that the time was not yet come for invading England. He perceived that extensive and tedious preparations were indispensable ere the French shipping on that coast could be put into a condition for such an attempt; and the burst of loyalty which the threat of invasion called forth in every part of Britain--the devotion with which all classes of the people answered the appeal of the government--the immense extent to which the regular and volunteer forces were increased everywhere--these circumstances produced a strong impression on his not less calculating than enterprising mind. He had himself, in the course of the preceding autumn, suggested to the minister for foreign affairs, the celebrated Talleyrand, the propriety of making an effort against England in another quarter of the world:--of seizing Malta, proceeding to occupy Egypt, and therein gaining at once a territory capable of supplying to France the loss of her West Indian colonies, and the means of annoying Great Britain in her Indian trade and empire. To this scheme he now recurred: the East presented a field of conquest and glory on which his imagination delighted to brood: "Europe," said he, "is but a molehill, all the great glories have come from Asia." The injustice of attacking the dominions of the Grand Seignior, an old ally of France, formed but a trivial obstacle in the eyes of the Directory: the professional opinion of Buonaparte that the invasion of England, if attempted then, must fail, could not but carry its due weight: the temptation of plundering Egypt and India was great; and great, perhaps above all the rest, was the temptation of finding employment for Napoleon at a distance from France. The Egyptian expedition was determined on: but kept strictly secret. The attention of England was still riveted on the coasts of Normandy and Picardy, between which and Paris Buonaparte studiously divided his presence--while it was on the borders of the Mediterranean that the ships and the troops really destined for action were assembling.

Buonaparte, having rifled to such purpose the cabinets and galleries of the Italian princes, was resolved not to lose the opportunity of appropriating some of the rich antiquarian treasures of Egypt; nor was it likely that he should undervalue the opportunities which his expedition might afford, of extending the boundaries of science, by careful observation of natural phenomena. He drew together therefore a body of eminent artists and connoisseurs, under the direction of Monge, who had managed his Italian collections: it was perhaps the first time that a troop of Savans (there were 100 of them) formed part of the staff of an invading army.[23]

The various squadrons of the French fleet were now assembled at Toulon; and everything seemed to be in readiness. Yet some time elapsed before Napoleon joined the armament: and it is said by Miot that he did all he could to defer joining it as long as possible, in consequence of certain obscure hopes which he had entertained of striking a blow at the existing government, and remodelling it, to his own advantage, with the assent, if not assistance, of Austria. This author adds that Barras, having intercepted a letter of Buonaparte to Cobentzel, went to him late one evening, and commanded him to join the fleet instantly, on pain of being denounced as the enemy of the government; that the general ordered his horses the same hour, and was on his way to Toulon ere midnight. These circumstances may or may not be truly given. It is not doubtful that the command of the Egyptian expedition was ultimately regarded, both by Napoleon and the Directory, as a species of honourable banishment. On reaching Toulon, Buonaparte called his army together, and harangued them. "Rome," he said, "combated Carthage by sea as well as land; and England was the Carthage of France.--He was come to lead them, in the name of the Goddess of Liberty, across mighty seas, and into remote regions, where their valour might achieve such glory and such wealth as could never be looked for beneath the cold heavens of the west. The meanest of his soldiers should receive seven acres of land;"--where he mentioned not. His promises had not hitherto been vain. The soldiery heard him with joy, and prepared to obey with alacrity.

The English government, meanwhile, although they had no suspicion of the real destination of the armament, had not failed to observe what was passing in Toulon. They probably believed that the ships there assembled were meant to take part in the great scheme of the invasion of England. However this might have been, they had sent a considerable reinforcement to Nelson, who then commanded on the Mediterranean station; and he, at the moment when Buonaparte reached Toulon, was cruising within sight of the port. Napoleon well knew that to embark in the presence of Nelson would be to rush into the jaws of ruin; and waited until some accident should relieve him from his terrible watcher. On the evening of the 19th of May fortune favoured him. A violent gale drove the English off the coast, and disabled some ships so much that Nelson was obliged to go into the harbours of Sardinia to have them repaired. The French general instantly commanded the embarkation of all his troops; and as the last of them got on board, the sun rose on the mighty armament: it was one of those dazzling suns which the soldiery delighted afterwards to call "the suns of Napoleon."

Seldom have the shores of the Mediterranean witnessed a nobler spectacle. That unclouded sun rose on a semicircle of vessels, extending in all to not less than six leagues: thirteen ships of the line and fourteen frigates (under the command of Admiral Brueyes); and 400 transports. They carried 40,000 picked soldiers, and officers whose names were only inferior to that of the general-in-chief;--of the men, as well as of their leaders, the far greater part already accustomed to follow Napoleon, and to consider his presence as the pledge of victory.

[Footnote 21: A silversmith, who had given him credit when he set out to Italy for a dressing-case worth ?0, was rewarded with all the business which the recommendation of his now illustrious debtor could bring to him; and, being clever in his trade, became ultimately, under the patronage of the imperial household, one of the wealthiest citizens of Paris. A little hatter, and a cobbler, who had served Buonaparte when a subaltern, might have risen in the same manner, had their skill equalled the silversmith's. Not even Napoleon's example could persuade the Parisians to wear ill-shaped hats and clumsy boots; but he, in his own person, adhered, to the last, to his original connection with these poor artisans.]

[Footnote 22: The Directory broke off the negotiation in a most insolent manner, by ordering Lord Malmesbury to quit France within twenty-four hours: this they did in their exultation after the 18th Fructidor.]

[Footnote 23: Before leaving Paris, Buonaparte ordered his secretary to prepare a camp library, of small volumes, arranged under the different heads of Science, Geography and Travels, History, Poetry, Romance, Politics. The "works on Politics" are six in number: viz. Montesquieu's Spirit of Laws, a compendium of Mythology, the Vedam, the Koran, and the Old and New Testaments--all in French.]

CHAPTER XI

The Voyage to Egypt--Malta surrendered--The French escape Nelson, and take Alexandria--The March up the Nile--The Battle of the Pyramids--Cairo surrenders--The Battle of Aboukir.

The French fleet was reinforced, ere it had proceeded far on its way, by General Dessaix, and his division from Italy; and, having prosperous winds, appeared on the 10th of June off Malta. The Knights of St. John were no longer those hardy and devout soldiers of the cross, who for ages inspired terror among the Mussulmans, and were considered as the heroic outguards of Christendom. Sunk in indolence and pleasure, these inheritors of a glorious name hardly attempted for a moment to defend their all but impregnable island, against the fleet which covered the seas around them. The Parisian authorities had tampered successfully beforehand with some of the French knights. Division of counsels prevailed: and in confusion and panic the gates were thrown open. As Napoleon was entering between the huge rocky barriers of La Valette, Caffarelli said to him: "It is well there was some one within to open the door for us; had there been no garrison at all, the business might have been less easy."

From Malta--where he left a detachment of troops to guard an acquisition which he expected to find eminently useful in his future communications with France--Buonaparte steered eastwards; but, after some days, ran upon the coast of Candia to take in water and fresh provisions, and, by thus casually diverging from his course, escaped imminent danger. For Nelson, soon returning to Toulon, missed the shipping which had so lately crowded the harbour, and ascertaining that they had not sailed towards the Atlantic, divined on the instant that their mark must be Egypt. His fleet was inferior in numbers, but he pursued without hesitation; and taking the straight line, arrived off the Nile before any of the French ships had appeared there. Buonaparte, on hearing off Candia that the English fleet was already in the Levant, directed Admiral Brueyes to steer not for Alexandria, but for a more northerly point of the coast of Africa. Nelson, on the other hand, not finding the enemy where he had expected, turned back and traversed the sea in quest of him, to Rhodes--and thence to Syracuse. It is supposed that on the 20th of June the fleets almost touched each other; but that the thickness of the haze, and Nelson's want of frigates, prevented an encounter. Napoleon, reconnoitring the coast, ascertained that there was no longer any fleet off Alexandria, and in effect reached his destination undisturbed on the 1st of July. At that moment a strange sail appeared on the verge of the horizon. "Fortune," exclaimed he, "I ask but six hours more--wilt thou refuse them?" The vessel proved not to be English; and the disembarkation immediately took place, in spite of a violent gale and a tremendous surf. The Admiral Brueyes in vain endeavoured to persuade Buonaparte to remain on board until the weather should be more calm. He sternly refused, and landed at Marabout, three leagues to the eastward of Alexandria, about one in the morning of the 2nd July--having lost many by drowning.

Egypt, a province of the Ottoman empire, then at peace with France, was of course wholly unprepared for this invasion. The Turks, however, mustered what force they could, and, shutting the gates of the city, held out--until a division, headed by Napoleon in person, forced their way, at three in the morning, through the old crumbling walls, and it was no longer possible to resist at once superior numbers and European discipline. Two hundred French died in the assault; the Turkish loss was much greater: and, if we are to believe almost all who have written concerning this part of his history, Buonaparte, after taking possession, abandoned the place for three hours to the unbridled licence of military execution and rapine--an atrocity for which, if it really occurred, there could have been only one pretext; namely, the urgent necessity of striking awe and terror into the hearts of the population, and so preventing them from obeying the call of their military chieftains, to take arms in defence of the soil. De Bourienne and Berthier, however, wholly deny this story.

If Napoleon's conduct on this occasion was as it has been commonly represented, it was strangely contrasted with the tenor of his _General Order_ to the army, issued immediately before their disembarkation. "The people," he then said, "with whom we are about to live, are Mahometans; the first article of their faith is, _There is no God but God, and Mahomet is his Prophet._ Do not contradict them: deal with them as you have done with the Jews and the Italians. Respect their muphtis and imans, as you have done by the rabbis and the bishops elsewhere.... The Roman legions protected all religions. You will find here usages different from those of Europe: you must accustom yourselves to them. These people treat their women differently from us; but _in all countries he who violates is a monster; pillage enriches only a few; it dishonours us, destroys our resources, and makes those enemies whom it is our interest to have for friends_."

To the people of Egypt, meanwhile, Napoleon addressed a proclamation in these words:--"They will tell you that I come to destroy your religion; believe them not: answer that I come to restore your rights, to punish the usurpers, and that I respect, more than the Mamelukes ever did, God, his Prophet, and the Koran. Sheiks and Imans, assure the people that we also are true Mussulmans. Is it not we that have ruined the Pope and the Knights of Malta?

Thrice happy they who shall be with us! Woe to them that take up arms for the Mamelukes! they shall perish!"[24]

Buonaparte was a fatalist--so that one main article of the Mussulman creed pleased him well. He admired Mahomet as one of those rare beings, who, by individual genius and daring, have produced mighty and permanent alterations in the world. The General's assertion of his own belief in the inspiration of the Arab impostor, was often repeated in the sequel; and will ever be appreciated, as it was at the time by his own soldiery--whom indeed he had addressed but the day before in language sufficiently expressive of his real sentiments as to all forms of religion. Rabbi, muphti, and bishop, the Talmud, the Koran, and the Bible, were much on a level in his estimation. He was willing to make use of them all as it might serve his purpose; and, though not by nature cruel, he did not hesitate, when his interest seemed to demand it, to invest his name with every circumstance of terror, that could result from the most merciless violation of those laws of humanity which even his Koran enforces, and which his own address to his army had so recently inculcated.

Napoleon left Alexandria on the 7th July, being anxious to force the Mamelukes to an encounter with the least possible delay. He had a small flotilla on the Nile, which served to guard his right flank: the infantry marched over burning sand at some distance from the river. The miseries of this progress were extreme. The air is crowded with pestiferous insects, the glare of the sand weakens most men's eyes, and blinds many; water is scarce and bad: and the country had been swept clear of man, beast, and vegetable. Under this torture even the gallant spirits of such men as Murat and Lannes could not sustain themselves:--they trod their cockades in the sand. The common soldiers asked, with angry murmurs, if it was here the General designed to give them their seven acres? He alone was superior to all these evils. Such was the happy temperament of his frame, that--while others, after having rid them of their usual dress, were still suffused in perpetual floods of perspiration, and the hardiest found it necessary to give two or three hours in the middle of the day to sleep--Napoleon altered nothing; wore his uniform buttoned up as at Paris; never showed one bead of sweat on his brow; nor thought of repose except to lie down in his cloak the last at night, and start up the first in the morning. It required, however, more than all his example of endurance and the general influence of Napoleon's character, could do to prevent the army from breaking into open mutiny. "Once," said he at St.

Helena, "I threw myself suddenly amidst a group of generals, and, addressing myself to the tallest of their number with vehemence, said, _You have been talking sedition: take care lest I fulfil my duty: your five feet ten inches would not hinder you from being shot within two hours._"

For some days no enemy appeared; but at length scattered groups of horsemen began to hover on their flanks; and the soldier, who quitted the line but for a moment, was surrounded and put to death ere his comrades could rescue him. The rapidity with which the Mamelukes rode, and their skill as marksmen, were seconded by the character of the soil and the atmosphere; the least motion or breath of wind being sufficient to raise a cloud of sand, through which nothing could be discerned accurately, while the constant glare of the sun dazzled almost to blindness. It was at Chebreis that the Mamelukes first attacked in a considerable body; and at the same moment the French flotilla was assaulted. In either case the superiority of European discipline was made manifest; but in either case also the assailants were able to retreat without much loss. Meantime the hardships of the march continued; the irregular attacks of the enemy were becoming more and more numerous; so that the troops, continually halting and forming into squares to receive the charge of the cavalry by day, and forced to keep up great watches at night, experienced the extremes of fatigue as well as of privation. In the midst of this misery the common men beheld with no friendly eyes the troop of savans mounted on asses (the common conveyance of the country), with all their instruments, books and baggage. They began to suspect that the expedition had been undertaken for some merely scientific purposes; and when, on any alarm, they were ordered to open the square and give the learned party safe footing within, they used to receive them with military jeerings. "Room for the asses:--stand back, here come the savans and the demi cavans."

On the 21st of July the army came within sight of the Pyramids, which, but for the regularity of the outline, might have been taken for a distant ridge of rocky mountains. While every eye was fixed on these hoary monuments of the past, they gained the brow of a gentle eminence, and saw at length spread out before them the vast army of the beys, its right posted on an entrenched camp by the Nile, its centre and left composed of that brilliant cavalry with which they were by this time acquainted. Napoleon, riding forwards to reconnoitre, perceived (what escaped the observation of all his staff) that the guns on the entrenched camp were not provided with carriages; and instantly decided on his plan of attack. He prepared to throw his force on the left, where the guns could not be available. Mourad Bey, who commanded in chief, speedily penetrated his design; and the Mamelukes advanced gallantly to the encounter. "Soldiers," said Napoleon, "from the summit of yonder pyramids forty ages behold you;" and the battle began.

The French formed into separate squares, and awaited the assault of the Mamelukes. These came on with impetuous speed and wild cries, and practised every means to force their passage into the serried ranks of their new opponents. They rushed on the line of bayonets, backed their horses upon them, and at last, maddened by the firmness which they could not shake, dashed their pistols and carbines into the faces of the men. They who had fallen wounded from their seats, would crawl along the sand, and hew at the legs of their enemies with their scimitars. Nothing could move the French: the bayonet and the continued roll of musketry by degrees thinned the host around them; and Buonaparte at last advanced. Such were the confusion and terror of the enemy when he came near the camp, that they abandoned their works, and flung themselves by hundreds into the Nile. The carnage was prodigious. Multitudes more were drowned. Mourad and a remnant of his Mamelukes retreated on Upper Egypt. Cairo surrendered: Lower Egypt was entirely conquered.

Such were the immediate consequences of the Battle of the Pyramids. The name of Buonaparte now spread panic through the East; and the "Sultan Kebir" (or King of Fire--as he was called from the deadly effects of the musketry in this engagement) was considered as the destined scourge of God, whom it was hopeless to resist.

The French now had recompense for the toils they had undergone. The bodies of the slain and drowned Mamelukes were rifled, and, it being the custom for those warriors to carry their wealth about them, a single corpse often made a soldier's fortune. In the deserted harems of the chiefs at Cairo, and in the neighbouring villages, men at length found proofs that "eastern luxury" is no empty name. The savans ransacked the monuments of antiquity, and formed collections which will ever reflect honour on their zeal and skill. Napoleon himself visited the interior of the Great Pyramid, and on entering the secret chamber, in which, 3000 years before, some Pharaoh had been inurned, repeated once more his confession of faith--"There is no God but God, and Mahomet is his prophet." The bearded orientals who accompanied him, concealed their doubts of his orthodoxy, and responded very solemnly, "God is merciful. Thou hast spoken like the most learned of the prophets."

While Napoleon was thus pursuing his career of victory in the interior, Nelson, having scoured the Mediterranean in quest of him, once more returned to the coast of Egypt. He arrived within sight of the towers of Alexandria on the 1st of August--ten days after the battle of the Pyramids had been fought and won--and found Brueyes still at his moorings in the bay of Aboukir. Nothing seems to be more clear than that the French admiral ought to have made the best of his way to France, or at least to Malta, the moment the army had taken possession of Alexandria. Napoleon constantly asserted that he had urged Brueyes to do so. Brueyes himself lived not to give his testimony; but Gantheaume, the vice-admiral, always persisted in stating, in direct contradiction to Buonaparte, that the fleet remained by the General's express desire. The testimonies being thus balanced, it is necessary to consult other materials of judgment; and it appears extremely difficult to doubt that the French admiral,--who, it is acknowledged on all hands, dreaded the encounter of Nelson--remained off Alexandria for the sole purpose of aiding the motions of the army, and in consequence of what he at least conceived to be the wish of its general. However this might have been, the results of his delay were terrible.

The French fleet were moored in a semicircle in the bay of Aboukir, so near the shore, that, as their admiral believed, it was impossible for the enemy to come between him and the land. He expected, therefore, to be attacked on one side only, and thought himself sure that the English could not renew their favourite manoeuvre of breaking the line,[25] and so at once dividing the opposed fleet, and placing the ships individually between two fires. But Nelson daringly judged that his ships might force a passage between the French and the land, and succeeding in this attempt, instantly brought on the conflict, in the same dreaded form which Brueyes had believed impossible. The details of this great sea fight belong to the history of the English hero.[26] The battle was obstinate--it lasted more than twenty hours, including the whole night. A solitary pause occurred at midnight, when the French admiral's ship L'Orient, a superb vessel of 120 guns, took fire, and blew up in the heart of the conflicting squadrons, with an explosion that for a moment silenced rage in awe. The admiral himself perished. Next morning two shattered ships, out of all the French fleet, with difficulty made their escape to the open sea. The rest of all that magnificent array had been utterly destroyed, or remained in the hands of the English.

Such was the battle of Aboukir, in which Nelson achieved, with a force much inferior to the French, what he himself called, "not a victory, but a conquest." Three thousand French seamen reached the shore: a greater number died. Had the English admiral possessed frigates, he must have forced his way into the harbour of Alexandria, and seized the whole stores and transports of the army. As things were, the best fleet of the Republic had ceased to be; the blockade of the coast was established: and the invader, completely isolated from France, must be content to rely on his own arms and the resources of Egypt.

[Footnote 24: At this period Egypt, though nominally governed by a pacha appointed by the Grand Seignior, was in reality in the hands of the Mamelukes; a singular body of men, who paid but little respect to any authority but that of their own chiefs. Of these chiefs or beys there were twenty-four; each one of whom ruled over a separate district; who often warred with each other; and were as often in rebellion against their nominal sovereign. According to the institutions of the Mamelukes their body was recruited solely by boys, chiefly of European birth, taken captive, and brought up from their earliest days in all military exercises. These were promoted according to their merits; it being the custom that when a bey died, the bravest of his band succeeded him. The Mamelukes thus formed a separate caste; and they oppressed most cruelly the population of the country which had fallen into their keeping. The fellahs, or poor Arabs, who cultivate the soil, being compelled to pay exorbitantly for permission to do so, suffered the extreme of misery in the midst of great natural wealth. The Cophts, supposed to be descended from the ancient Egyptian nation, discharged most civil functions under the Mamelukes, and had the trades and professions in their hands, but they also were oppressed intolerably by those haughty and ferocious soldiers.

The Mamelukes were considered by Napoleon to be, individually, the finest cavalry in the world. They rode the noblest horses of Arabia, and were armed with the best weapons which the world could produce: carbines, pistols, etc., from England, and sabres of the steel of Damascus. Their skill in horsemanship was equal to their fiery valour. With that cavalry and the French infantry, Buonaparte said, it would be easy to conquer the world.]

[Footnote 25: This manoeuvre was first practised on the 12th of August, 1782, by Lord Rodney's fleet; and, as appears to be now settled, at the suggestion of that admiral's captain of the fleet, the late Sir Charles Douglas, Bart.]

[Footnote 26: See the admirable Life of Nelson, by Southey; which will form one of the volumes of this Library.]

CHAPTER XII

Buonaparte's Administration in Egypt--Armaments of the Porte--Buonaparte at Suez--At El-Arish--Gaza, Jaffa, Acre--Retreat to Egypt--Defeat of the Turks at Aboukir--Napoleon embarks for France.

Before Nelson's arrival, Buonaparte is said to have meditated returning to France, for the purpose of extorting from the government those supplies of various kinds which, on actual examination, he had perceived to be indispensable to the permanent occupation of Egypt, and which he well knew the Directors would refuse to any voice but his own. He intended, it is also said, to urge on the Directory the propriety of resuming the project of a descent on England itself, at the moment when the mind of that government might be supposed to be engrossed with the news of his dazzling successes in Egypt. All these proud visions died with Brueyes. On hearing of the battle of Aboukir a solitary sigh escaped from Napoleon. "To France," said he, "the fates have decreed the empire of the land--to England that of the sea."

He endured this great calamity with the equanimity of a masculine spirit. He gave orders that the seamen landed at Alexandria should be formed into a marine brigade, and thus gained a valuable addition to his army; and proceeded himself to organise a system of government, under which the great natural resources of the country might be turned to the best advantage. We need not dwell on that vain repetition of his faith in Mahomet, to which he would not and could not give effect by openly adopting the rules and ceremonies of the Koran; which accordingly but amused his own followers;

and which deceived none of the Mussulman people. This was the trick of an audacious infidel, who wanted wholly that enthusiasm without which no religious impostor can hope to partake the successes of the Prophet of Mecca. Passing over this worthless preliminary, the arrangements of the new administration reflect honour on the consummate understanding, the clear skill, and the unwearied industry of this extraordinary man.

He was careful to advance no claim to the sovereignty of Egypt, but asserted, that having rescued it from the Mameluke usurpation, it remained for him to administer law and justice, until the time should come for restoring the province to the dominion of the Grand Seignior. He then established two councils, consisting of natives, principally of Arab chiefs and Moslem of the church and the law, by whose advice all measures were, nominally, to be regulated. They formed of course a very subservient senate. He had no occasion to demand more from the people than they had been used to pay to the beys; and he lightened the impost by introducing as far as he could the fairness and exactness of a civilised power in the method of levying it. He laboured to make the laws respected, and this so earnestly and rigidly, that no small wonder was excited among all classes of a population so long accustomed to the licence of a barbarian horde of spoilers. On one occasion one of the Ulemahs could not help smiling at the zeal which he manifested for tracing home the murder of an obscure peasant to the perpetrator. The Mussulman asked if the dead man were anywise related to the blood of the Sultan Kebir? "No," answered Napoleon, sternly--"but he was more than that--he was one of a people whose government it has pleased Providence to place in my hands." The measures which he took for the protection of travellers to Mecca were especially acceptable to the heads of the Moslem establishment, and produced from them a proclamation, (in direct contradiction to the Koran,) signifying that it was right and lawful to pay tribute to the French. The virtuosi and artists in his train, meanwhile, pursued with indefatigable energy their scientific researches; they ransacked the monuments of Egypt, and laid the foundation, at least, of all the wonderful discoveries, which have since been made concerning the knowledge, arts, polity (and even language) of the ancient nation. Nor were their objects merely those of curiosity. They, under the General's direction, examined into the long-smothered traces of many an ancient device for improving the agriculture of the country. Canals that had been shut up for centuries were re-opened: the waters of the Nile flowed once more where they had been guided by the skill of the Pharaohs or the Ptolemies. Cultivation was extended; property secured; and it cannot be doubted that the signal improvements since introduced in Egypt, are attributable mainly to the wise example of the French administration. At Cairo itself there occurred one stormy insurrection, provoked, as may be supposed, by some wantonness on the part of the garrison; but, after this was quelled by the same merciless vigour which Napoleon had displayed on similar occasions in Italy, the country appears to have remained in more quiet, and probably enjoyed, in spite of the presence of an invading army, more prosperity, than it had ever done during any period of the same length, since the Saracen government was overthrown by the Ottomans.

In such labours Napoleon passed the autumn of 1798. "At this period," writes his secretary, "it was his custom to retire early to bed, and it was my business to read to him as long as he remained awake. If I read poetry, he soon fell asleep, but if, as sometimes happened, he called for The Life of Cromwell, I made up mind to want repose for that night."

General Dessaix, meanwhile, had pursued Mourad Bey into Upper Egypt, where the Mamelukes hardly made a single stand against him, but contrived, by the excellence of their horses, and their familiarity with the deserts, to avoid any total disruption of their forces. Mourad returned to the neighbourhood of Cairo on hearing of the insurrection already mentioned; but departed when he learned its suppression. Those gallant horsemen were gradually losing numbers in their constant desert marches--they were losing heart rapidly: and everything seemed to promise, that the Upper Egypt, like the Lower, would soon settle into a peaceful province of the new French colony.

The General, during this interval of repose, received no communication from the French government; but rumours now began to reach his quarters which might well give him new anxieties. The report of another rupture with Austria gradually met with more credence; and it was before long placed beyond a doubt, that the Ottoman Porte, instead of being tempted into any recognition of the French establishment in Egypt, had declared war against the Republic, and summoned all the strength of her empire to pour in overwhelming numbers on the isolated army of Buonaparte.

As yet, however, there was no appearance of an enemy; and Napoleon seized the opportunity to explore the Isthmus of Suez, where a narrow neck of land divides the Red Sea from the Mediterranean, partly with the view of restoring the communication which in remote times existed between them, and partly of providing for the defence of Egypt, should the Ottomans attempt their invasion by the way of Syria.

He visited the Maronite monks of Mount Sinai, and, as Mahomet had done before him, affixed his name to their charter of privileges; he examined also the fountain of Moses: and nearly lost his life in exploring, during low water, the sands of the Red Sea, where Pharaoh is supposed to have perished in the pursuit of the Hebrews. "The night overtook us," says Savary in his Memoirs, "the waters began to rise around us, the guard in advance exclaimed that their horses were swimming. Buonaparte saved us all by one of those simple expedients which occur to an imperturbable mind. Placing himself in the centre, he bade all the rest form a circle round him, and then ride out each man in a separate direction, and each to halt as soon as he found his horse swimming. The man whose horse continued to march the last, was sure, he said, to be in the right direction; him accordingly we all followed, and reached Suez at two in the morning in safety, though so rapidly had the tide advanced, that the water was at the poitrels of our horses ere we made the land."

On his return to Cairo, the General despatched a trusty messenger into India, inviting Tippoo Saib to inform him exactly of the condition of the English army in that region, and signifying that Egypt was only the first post in a march destined to surpass that of Alexander! "He spent whole days," writes his secretary, "in lying flat on the ground stretched upon maps of Asia."

At length the time for action came. Leaving 15,000 in and about Cairo, the division of Dessaix in Upper Egypt, and garrisons in the chief towns,-- Buonaparte on the 11th of February 1799 marched for Syria at the head of 10,000 picked men, with the intention of crushing the Turkish armament in that quarter, before their chief force (which he now knew was assembling at Rhodes) should have time to reach Egypt by sea. Traversing the desert which divides Africa from Asia, he took possession of the fortress El-Arish, (15 Feb.) whose garrison, after a vigorous assault, capitulated on condition that they should be permitted to retreat into Syria, pledging their parole not to serve again during the war. Pursuing his march, he took Gazah (that ancient city of the Philistines) without opposition; but at Jaffa (the Joppa of holy writ) the Moslem made a resolute defence. The walls were carried by storm, 3000 Turks died with arms in their hands, and the town was given up during three hours to the fury of the French soldiery--who never, as Napoleon confessed, availed themselves of the licence of war more savagely than on this occasion.

A part of the garrison--amounting, according to Buonaparte, to 1200 men, but stated by others as nearly 3000 in number--held out for some hours longer in the mosques and citadel; but at length, seeing no chance of rescue, grounded their arms on the 7th of March. Eugene Beauharnois, who in person accepted their submission, was violently rebuked by Napoleon for having done so: the soldiery murmured, asking how these barbarians were to be fed, when they themselves were already suffering severe privations. The General summoned his chief officers to council and, after long discussion, it was resolved that, in this case, necessity left no room for mercy. On the 10th--three days after their surrender--the prisoners were marched out of Jaffa, in the centre of a battalion under General Bon. When they had reached the sand-hills, at some distance from the town, they were divided into small parties, and shot or bayoneted to a man. They, like true fatalists, submitted in silence; and their bodies were gathered together into a pyramid, where, after the lapse of thirty years, their bones are still visible whitening the sand.

Such was the massacre of Jaffa, which will ever form one of the darkest stains on the name of Napoleon. He admitted the fact himself;--and justified it on the double plea, that he could not afford soldiers to guard so many prisoners, and that he could not grant them the benefit of their parole, because they were the very men who had already been set free on such terms at El-Arish. To this last defence the answer is, unfortunately for him, very obvious. He could not possibly have recognised in every one of these victims, an individual who had already given and broken his parole. If he did-- still that would not avail him:--the men surrendered with arms in their hands. No general has a right to see men abandon the means of defence, and then-- after the lapse of three days too!--inflict on them the worst fate that could have befallen them had they held out. The only remaining plea is that of expediency; and it is one upon which many a retail as well as wholesale murderer might justify his crime.

Buonaparte had now ascertained that the Pacha of Syria, Achmet-

Djezzar,[27] was at St. Jean d'Acre, (so renowned in the history of the crusades,) and determined to defend that place to extremity, with the forces which had already been assembled for the invasion of Egypt. He in vain endeavoured to seduce this ferocious chief from his allegiance to the Porte, by holding out the hope of a separate independent government, under the protection of France. The first of Napoleon's messengers returned without an answer; the second was put to death; and the army moved on Acre in all the zeal of revenge, while the necessary apparatus of a siege was ordered to be sent round by sea from Alexandria.

Sir Sydney Smith was then cruising in the Levant with two British ships of the line, the Tigre and the Theseus; and, being informed by the Pacha of the approaching storm, hastened to support him in the defence of Acre. Napoleon's vessels, conveying guns and stores from Egypt, fell into his hands, and he appeared off the town two days before the French army came in view of it. He had on board his ship Colonel Philippeaux, a French royalist of great talents (formerly Buonaparte's school-fellow at Brienne);[28] and the Pacha willingly permitted the English commodore and this skilful ally, to regulate for him, as far as was possible, the plan of his defence.

The loss of his own heavy artillery and the presence of two English ships, were inauspicious omens; yet Buonaparte doubted not that the Turkish garrison would shrink before his onset, and he instantly commenced the siege. He opened his trenches on the 18th of March. "On that little town," said he to one of his generals, as they were standing together on an eminence, which still bears the name of Richard Coeur-de-lion--"on yonder little town depends the fate of the East. Behold the key of Constantinople, or of India."--"The moment Acre falls," said he about the same time to De Bourienne, "all the Druses will join me; the Syrians, weary of Djezzar's oppressions, will crowd to my standard. I shall march upon Constantinople with an army to which the Turk can offer no effectual resistance--and it seems not unlikely that I may return to France by the route of Adrianople and Vienna--destroying the house of Austria on my way!"

From the 18th to the 28th of March, the French laboured hard in their trenches, being exposed to the fire of extensive batteries, arranged by Philippeaux so as to command their approach, and formed chiefly of Buonaparte's own artillery, captured on the voyage from Alexandria. The

Turks also were constantly sallying out, and their Pacha personally set the example of the most heroic resolution. Nevertheless, on the 28th, a breach was at last effected, and the French mounted with such fiery zeal that the garrison gave way, until Djezzar appeared on the battlements, and flinging his own pistols at the heads of the flying men, urged and compelled them to renew the defence. In the end the French retreated with great loss, and--the Turks, headed by the English seamen, pursuing them to their lines--a great mine, designed to blow up the chief tower of Acre, was explored, and means taken for countermining it.

Meanwhile a vast Mussulman army had been gathered among the mountains of Samaria, and was preparing to descend upon Acre, and attack the besiegers in concert with the garrison of Djezzar. Junot, with his division, marched to encounter them, and would have been overwhelmed by their numbers, had not Napoleon himself followed and rescued him (April 8) at Nazareth, where the splendid cavalry of the orientals were, as usual, unable to resist the solid squares and well-directed musketry of the French. Kleber, with another division, was in like manner endangered, and in like manner rescued by the general-in-chief at Mount Tabor (April 15). The Mussulmans dispersed on all hands; and Napoleon, returning to his siege, pressed it on with desperate assaults, day after day, in which his best soldiers were thinned, before the united efforts of Djezzar's gallantry, and the skill of his allies. At length, however, a party of French succeeded in forcing their way into the great tower, and in establishing themselves in one part of it, in despite of all the resolution that could be opposed to them. At the same critical moment, there appeared in the offing a Turkish fleet, which was known to carry great reinforcements for the Pacha. Everything conspired to prompt Napoleon to finish his enterprise at whatever cost, and he was bravely seconded.

Sir Sydney Smith, however, was as resolute to hold out until the fleet should arrive, as Napoleon was eager to anticipate its coming. The English commander repaired with his handful of seaman to the tower, and after a furious assault dislodged the occupants. Buonaparte did not renew the attack in that quarter, but succeeded in breaking the wall in another part of the town; and the heroic Lannes headed a French party who actually entered Acre at that opening. But Djezzar was willing they should enter. He suffered them to come in unmolested; and then, before they could form, threw such a crowd of Turks upon them, that discipline was of no avail: it was a mere multitude of duels, and the brave orientals with their scimitars and pistols, overpowered their enemies, and put them to death--almost to a man. Lannes himself was with difficulty carried back desperately wounded.

The rage of Buonaparte at these repeated discomfitures may be imagined. The whole evil was ascribed, and justly, to the presence of Sir Sydney Smith; and he spoke of that chivalrous person ever after with the venom of a personal hatred. Sir Sydney, in requital of Buonaparte's proclamation-- inviting (as was his usual fashion) the subjects of the Pacha to avoid his yoke, and ally themselves with the invaders--put forth a counter address to the Druses and other Christian inhabitants of Syria, invoking their assistance in the name of their religion, against the blasphemous general of a nation which had renounced Christianity. Napoleon upon this said that Sir Sydney was a madman; and if his story be true, Sir Sydney challenged him to single combat; to which he made answer, that he would not come forth to a duel unless the English could fetch Marlborough from his grave, but that, in the meantime, any one of his grenadiers would willingly give the challenger such satisfaction as he was entitled to demand. Whatever inaccuracy there may be in some of these circumstances, there is no doubt of the fact that Buonaparte and the brave commodore strove together at Acre, under the highest influence of personal resentment, as well as martial skill and determination.

[21st May.] The siege had now lasted sixty days. Once more Napoleon commanded an assault, and his officers and soldiery once more obeyed him with devoted and fruitless gallantry. The loss his army had by this time undergone was very great. Caffarelli and many other officers of the highest importance were no more. The plague had some time before this appeared in the camp; every day the ranks of his legions were thinned by this pestilence, as well as by the weapons of the defenders of Acre. The hearts of all men were quickly sinking. The Turkish fleet was at hand to reinforce Djezzar; and upon the utter failure of the attack of the 21st of May, Napoleon yielded to stern necessity, and began his retreat upon Jaffa.

The plague now raged in the army. The very name of this horrible scourge shook the nerves of the Europeans; its symptoms filled them with indescribable horror. The sick despaired utterly; the healthy trembled to minister to them in their misery. Napoleon went through the hospitals, and at once breathed hope into the sufferers, and rebuked the cowardice of their attendants, by squeezing and relieving with his own hand the foul ulcers which no one had dared to touch. Pity that this act of true heroism must ever be recorded on the same page that tells the story of the sand-hills!

The name of Jaffa was already sufficiently stained; but fame speedily represented Napoleon as having now made it the scene of another atrocity, not less shocking than that of the massacre of the Turkish prisoners.

The accusation, which for many years made so much noise throughout Europe, amounts to this: that on the 27th of May, when it was necessary for Napoleon to pursue his march from Jaffa for Egypt, a certain number of the plague-patients in the hospital were found to be in a state that held out no hope whatever of their recovery; that the general, being unwilling to leave them to the tender mercies of the Turks, conceived the notion of administering opium, and so procuring for them at least a speedy and an easy death; and that a number of men were accordingly taken off in this method by his command. The story, the circumstances of which were much varied in different accounts, especially as regards the numbers of the poisoned (raised sometimes as high as 500), was first disseminated by Sir Robert Wilson, and was in substance generally believed in England. In each and all of its parts, on the contrary, it was wholly denied by the admirers of Buonaparte, who treated it as one of the many gross falsehoods, which certainly were circulated touching the personal character and conduct of their idol, during the continuance of his power.

Buonaparte himself, while at St. Helena, referred to the story frequently; and never hesitated to admit that it originated in the following occurrence. He sent, he said, the night before the march was to commerce, for Desgenettes, the chief of the medical staff, and proposed to him, under such circumstances as have been described, the propriety of giving opium, in mortal doses, to seven men, adding that, had his son been in their situation, he would have thought it his duty, as a father, to treat him in the same method; and that, most certainly, had he himself been in that situation, and capable of understanding it, he would have considered the deadly cup as the best boon that friendship could offer him. M. Desgenettes, however, (said the ex-Emperor) did not consider himself as entitled to interfere in any such method with the lives of his fellow men: the patients were abandoned; and, at least, one of the number fell alive into the hands of Sir Sidney Smith, and recovered.

Such is Napoleon's narrative; and it is confirmed in all particulars of importance, save two, by De Bourienne. That writer states distinctly that he was present when Napoleon, Berthier and the usual suite, examined the hospital--heard the discussion which followed, and _the order given_ for administering mortal potions to the hopeless patients--in number sixty. He does not assert that he saw the poison administered, but says he has no doubt the order was executed; and concludes with defending the measure by arguments similar to those already quoted from the lips of his master.

Whether the opium was really administered or not--that the audacious proposal to that effect was made by Napoleon, we have his own admission; and every reader must form his opinion--as to the degree of guilt which attaches to the fact of having meditated and designed the deed in question, under the circumstances above detailed. That Buonaparte, accustomed to witness slaughter in every form, was in general but a callous calculator when the loss of human life was to be considered, no one can doubt. That his motives, on this occasion, were cruel, no human being, who considers either the temper or the situation of the man, will ever believe. He doubtless designed, by shortening those men's lives, to do them the best service in his power. The presumption of thus daring to sport with the laws of God and man, when expedience seemed to recommend such interference, was quite in the character of the young General: cruelty was not; least of all, cruelty to his own soldiery--the very beings on whose affection all his greatness depended.

The march onwards was a continued scene of misery; for the wounded and the sick were many, the heat oppressive, the thirst intolerable; and the ferocious Djezzar was hard behind, and the wild Arabs of the desert hovered round them on every side, so that he who fell behind his company was sure to be slain. How hard and callous the hearts of brave men can become when every thought is occupied with self, the story of that march presents a fearful picture. When a comrade, after quitting his ranks, being stimulated by the despair of falling into the hands of the Turks or Arabs, yet once again reared himself from the burning sand, and made a last attempt to stagger after the column, his painful and ineffectual efforts furnished matter for military merriment. "He is drunk," said one; "his march will not be a long one," answered another; and when he once more sank helpless and hopeless, a third remarked, "our friend has at length taken up his quarters." It is not to be omitted, that Napoleon did, on this occasion, all that became his situation. He issued an order that every horse should be given up to the service of the sick. A moment afterwards one of his attendants came to ask which horse the General wished to reserve for himself: "Scoundrel!" cried he, "do you not know the order? Let everyone march on foot--I the first.--Begone." He accordingly, during the rest of the march, walked by the side of the sick, cheering them by his eye and his voice, and exhibiting to all the soldiery the example at once of endurance and of compassion.

[June 14.] Having at length accomplished this perilous journey, Buonaparte repaired to his old headquarters at Cairo, and re-entered on his great functions as the establisher of a new government in the state of Egypt. But he had not long occupied himself thus, ere new rumours concerning the beys on the Upper Nile, who seemed to have some strong and urgent motive for endeavouring to force a passage downwards, began to be mingled with, and by degrees explained by, tidings daily repeated of some grand disembarkation of the Ottomans, designed to have place in the neighbourhood of Alexandria. Leaving Dessaix, therefore, once more in command at Cairo, he himself descended the Nile, and travelled with all speed to Alexandria, where he found his presence most necessary. For, in effect, the great Turkish fleet had already run into the bay of Aboukir; and an army of 18,000, having gained the fortress, were there strengthening themselves, with the view of awaiting the promised descent and junction of the Mamelukes, and then, with overwhelming superiority of numbers, advancing to Alexandria, and completing the ruin of the French invaders.

Buonaparte, reaching Alexandria on the evening of the 24th of July, found his army already posted in the neighbourhood of Aboukir, and prepared to anticipate the attack of the Turks on the morrow. Surveying their entrenched camp from the heights above with Murat, he said, "Go how it may, the battle of to-morrow will decide the fate of the world." "Of this army at least," answered Murat; "but the Turks have no cavalry, and, if ever infantry were charged to the teeth by horse, they shall be so by mine." Murat did not penetrate the hidden meaning of Napoleon's words, but he made good his own.

The Turkish outposts were assaulted early next morning, and driven in with great slaughter; but the French, when they advanced, came within the range of the batteries, and also of the shipping that lay close by the shore, and were checked. Their retreat might have ended in a rout, but for the undisciplined eagerness with which the Turks engaged in the task of spoiling and maiming those that fell before them--thus giving to Murat the opportunity of charging their main body in flank with his cavalry, at the moment when the French infantry, profiting by their disordered and scattered condition, and rallying under the eye of Napoleon, forced a passage to the entrenchments. From that moment the battle was a massacre. The Turks, attacked on all sides, were panic-struck; and the sea was covered with the turbans of men who flung themselves headlong into the waves rather than await the fury of _Le Beau Sabreur,[29] or the steady rolling fire of the Sultan Kebir_. Six thousand surrendered at discretion: twelve thousand perished on the field or in the sea. Mustapha Pacha, the general, being brought into the presence of his victor, was saluted with these words:--"It has been your fate to lose this day; but I will take care to inform the sultan of the courage with which you have contested it." "Spare thyself that trouble," answered the proud pacha, "my master knows me better than thou."

Napoleon once more returned to Cairo on the 9th of August; but it was only to make some parting arrangements as to the administration, civil and military; for, from the moment of his victory at Aboukir, he had resolved to entrust Egypt to other hands, and Admiral Gantheaume was already preparing in secret the means of his removal to France.

Buonaparte always asserted, and the Buonapartist writers of his history still maintain, that this resolution was adopted in consequence of a mere accident;[30] namely, that Sir Sydney Smith, in the course of some negotiations about prisoners which followed after the battle of Aboukir, sent a file of English newspapers for the amusement of the General. Some say the English Commodore did so out of mere civility: others, that he designed to distract the movements of Napoleon, by showing him the dangerous condition to which, during his absence, the affairs of France, both at home and abroad, had been reduced. It seems, however, to be generally believed (as without doubt it is the more probable case) that Buonaparte had long ere now received intelligence of the great events in which he was so deeply concerned. He had, assuredly, many friends in Paris, who were watching keenly over his interests, and who must have been singularly ill served if they never were able to communicate with him during so many months.

However this might have been, the General succeeded in preventing any suspicion of his projected evasion from arising among the soldiery; and when he finally turned his back on Cairo, it was universally believed that it was but to make a tour in the Delta.

Napoleon reached the coast on the 22nd August, and was there met by Berthier, Andreossi, Murat, Lannes, Marmont, and the savans Monge and Berthollet; none of whom had suspected for what purpose they were summoned. Admiral Gantheaume had by this time two frigates and two smaller vessels (which had been saved in the harbour of Alexandria) ready for sea; and on the morning of the 23rd, the wind having fortunately driven the English squadron of blockade off the coast, Buonaparte and his followers embarked at Rosetta.

The same day the event was announced to the army by a proclamation which the General left behind him, naming Kleber as his successor in the command. The indignation of the soldiery, who thought themselves deserted by their chief, was for a time violent; but, by degrees, the great qualities displayed by Kleber softened this feeling, and Buonaparte had left agents well qualified to explain what had happened, in the manner most favourable for himself.

Kleber received at the same time a parting letter of instructions--one of the most singular pieces that ever proceeded from Napoleon's pen. "I send you," said he, "English gazettes to the 10th of June. You will there see that we have lost Italy; that Mantua, Turin, and Tortona are blockaded. I hope, if fortune smiles on me, to reach Europe before the beginning of October.... It is the intention of government that General Dessaix should follow me, unless great events interpose themselves, in the course of November.... There is no doubt that, on the arrival of our squadron at Toulon, means will be found of sending you the recruits and munitions necessary for the army of Egypt. The government will then correspond with you directly; while I, both in my public and in my private capacity, will take measures to secure for you frequent intelligence."

Buonaparte proceeds, after thus boldly assuming to himself the right of speaking for the government--and in terms, it will be observed, calculated to leave no doubt that his own departure was the result of orders from Paris--to impress upon Kleber the necessity of always considering the possession of Egypt as a point of the highest importance to France; and, nevertheless, of negotiating, as long as possible, with the Porte, on the basis that the French Republic neither had now, nor ever had had, the smallest wish to be permanently mistress of that country. He finally authorised Kleber, if not released or recruited by May following, to make a peace with the Porte, even if the first of its conditions should be the total evacuation of Egypt.

Then follow directions for the internal administration of Egypt, in which, among other sufficiently characteristic hints, Kleber is desired to cultivate the good will of the Christians, but, nevertheless, to avoid carefully giving the Mussulmans any reason to confound _the Christians with the French_. "Above all," says Napoleon, "gain the Sheiks, who are timid, who cannot fight, and who, like all priests, inspire fanaticism without being fanatics."

The conclusion is in these words. "The army which I confide to you is composed of my children; in all times, even in the midst of the greatest sufferings, I have received the marks of their attachment: keep alive in them these sentiments. You owe this to the particular esteem and true attachment which I bear towards yourself."

[Footnote 27: Djezzar means butcher: he had well earned this title by the mercilessness of his administration.]

[Footnote 28: Sir Sydney Smith, having been taken prisoner and most unjustifiably confined by the French government in the dungeons of the Temple, had made his escape through the zeal of certain of the royalist party, and chiefly of Philippeaux.]

[Footnote 29: The handsome swordsman--i.e. Murat.]

[Footnote 30: De Bourienne, whose curious work has appeared since the first edition of this narrative was published, confirms this statement of Napoleon: but Napoleon, it is obvious, might have received letters which he did not choose to communicate to his secretary.]

CHAPTER XIII

Retrospect--Buonaparte arrives in France--The Revolution of the 18th Brumaire--The Provisional Consulate.

We must now pause for a moment to indicate, however briefly and imperfectly, the course of events which had determined Napoleon to abandon the army of Egypt.

While the negotiations at Rastadt were still in progress, the Directory, on the most flimsy of pretences, marched an army into Switzerland; and, by vast superiority of numbers, overwhelmed the defence of the unprepared mountaineers. The conquered cantons were formed into another republic of the new kind--to wit, "the Helvetian:" nominally a sister and ally, but really a slave of the French. Another force, acting under orders equally unjustifiable, seized Turin, and dethroned the King of Sardinia. Lastly, the Pope, in spite of all his humiliating concessions at Tollentino, saw a republican insurrection, roused by French instigation, within his capital. Tumults and bloodshed ensued; and Joseph Buonaparte, the French ambassador, narrowly escaped with his life. A French army forthwith advanced on Rome; the Pope's functions as a temporal prince were terminated; he retired to the exile of Siena; and another of those feeble phantoms, which the Directory delighted to invest with glorious names, appeared under the title of "the Roman Republic."

These outrages roused anew the indignation, the first, of all true lovers of freedom, the second, of the monarchs whose representatives were assembled at Rastadt, and the third, of the Catholic population throughout Europe. England was not slow to take advantage of the unprincipled rashness of the Directory, and of the sentiments which it was fitted to inspire; and the result was a new coalition against France, in which the great power of Russia now, for the first time, took a part. The French plenipotentiaries were suddenly ordered to quit Rastadt; and, within a few hours afterwards, they were murdered on their journey by banditti clad in the Austrian uniform, most assuredly not acting under orders from the Austrian government--and now commonly believed to have been set on by certain angry intriguers of the Luxembourg.

The King of Naples had, unfortunately for himself, a greater taste for arms than the nation he governed; and, justly concluding that the conquerors of Rome would make himself their next object, he rashly proclaimed war, ere the general measures of the coalition were arranged. The arrival of Nelson in his harbour, bringing the news of the destruction of the French fleet at Aboukir, and the consequent isolation of Napoleon, gave him courage to strike a blow which the officers of his army were little likely to second. The result of his hasty advance to the northwards was not a battle, but a flight: and though the Lazzaroni of Naples, rising in fury, held the capital for some days against the French, their defences were at length overcome; the king passed over to his Sicilian dominions; and another tributary of France was announced by the name of the Parthenopean Republic.

Far different success attended the better-considered movements by which the great powers of the new coalition re-opened the war. The details of those bloody campaigns by which Holland and Belgium were for a moment rescued from the grasp of the Republic; Jourdan beaten beyond the Rhine by the Archduke Charles; and the north of Italy, the whole of Buonaparte's mighty conquests, recovered by the Austro-Russians under Suwarrow; as also of the ultimate reverses of the allies in the direction of Holland,--of the concentration of their forces in two great armies, one on the frontier of Switzerland, and another lower down on the Rhine, for the purpose of carrying the war by two inlets into the heart of France--and finally, of the masterly retreat of Macdonald, by which he succeeded in leading the army which had occupied Naples quite through Italy into Provence;--all these details belong rather to the general history of the period, than to the biography of Buonaparte. Neither is it possible that we should here enter upon any minute account of the internal affairs of France during the period of his Egyptian and Syrian campaigns. It must suffice to say that the generally unfortunate course of the war had been accompanied by the growth of popular discontent at home; that the tottering Directory for a moment gathered strength to themselves by associating Sieyes to their number; that the mean and selfish conduct of the rulers soon nullified the results of that partial change; that the Directory at length found it impossible to maintain the favourite system of balancing faction against faction, and so neutralising their efforts; in a word, that the moderates (under which name the royalists are included) had obtained a decided command in the Council of Ancients, and the republicans, or democratical party, an equally overpowering majority in the Assembly of the Five Hundred; while the Directors, as a body, had no longer the slightest power to control either. Finally, the Chouans (as the royalists of Bretagne were called) had been stimulated by the disordered appearance of things at home and abroad, and 40,000 insurgents appeared in arms, withstanding, with varied success, the troops of the Republic, and threatening, by their example, to rekindle a general civil war in France. Such was, or had recently been, the state of affairs when Buonaparte landed at Frejus, and sent before him to Paris, to the inexpressible delight of a nation of late accustomed to hear of nothing but military disasters, the intelligence of that splendid victory which had just destroyed the great Turkish armament at Aboukir. He arrived at a moment when all men, of all parties, were satisfied that a new revolution was at hand; and when the leaders of all the contending factions were equally desirous of invoking arms to their support in the inevitable struggle. Napoleon's voyage had been one of constant peril; for the Mediterranean was traversed in all directions by English ships of war, in whose presence resistance would have been hopeless. He occupied his time, during this period of general anxiety, in very peaceful studies: he read the Bible, the Koran, Homer; conversed with his savans on the old times and manners of the East; and solved problems in geometry. He also spent many hours in playing at the game of vingt-un; and M. de Bourienne says, that he never hesitated to play unfairly when it suited his purpose, though he always returned whatever he had gained on rising from the table. On the 30th of September they reached Ajaccio, and he was received with enthusiasm at the place of his birth. But, according to his own phrase, "it rained cousins:" he was wearied with solicitations, and as soon as the wind proved favourable, on the 7th of October, the voyage was resumed. Gantheaume, descrying an English squadron off the French coast, would have persuaded him to take to the long boat; but he refused, saying, "that experiment may be reserved for the last extremity." His confidence in fortune was not belied. They passed at midnight, unseen, through the English ships, and on the morning of the 9th were moored in safety in the bay of Frejus; and no sooner was it known that Buonaparte was at hand, than, in spite of all the laws of quarantine, persons of every description, including the chief functionaries, both civil and military, repaired on board to welcome him. He had looked forward with the utmost disgust to a long quarantine: this dread was dissipated in a moment; the deck was crowded with persons, crying aloud, "We prefer the plague to the Austrians!" His presence alone was considered as the pledge of victory. The story of Aboukir gave new fuel to the flame of universal enthusiasm; and he landed, not so much like a general who had quitted his post without orders, as a victorious prince, who had returned to restore the lost hearts and fortunes of a people that confided only in him. His progress towards the capital, wherever his person was recognised, bore all the appearance of a triumphal procession. He reached his own house, in the Rue de la Victoire, on the 16th October.

The trembling Directory received him, when he presented himself at the Luxembourg, with every demonstration of joy and respect. Not a question was asked as to his abandonment of his army; for all dreaded the answer which they had the best reason for anticipating. He was invited to accept of a public dinner, and agreed to do so. The assemblage was magnificent, and his reception enthusiastic; but his demeanour was cold and reserved. After proposing as a toast, "the union of all parties"--ominous words from those lips--he withdrew at an early hour of the evening.

He continued for some little time to avoid public notice, resuming apparently the same studious and sequestered life which he had led when last in Paris. It was, however, remarked that, when recognised by the populace, he received their salutations with uncommon affability; and that if he met any old soldier of the army of Italy, he rarely failed to recollect the man, and take him by the hand.

Buonaparte had been tormented when in Egypt by certain rumours concerning the conduct of Josephine in his absence from Paris. She had quitted the capital with the purpose of meeting him on his journey thither, the moment his arrival at Frejus was known; but taking the road of Burgundy, while he was travelling by that of Lyons, missed him. When she at length joined him in Paris, he received her with marked coldness; but, after a few days, the intercessions and explanations of friends restored harmony between them. He felt acutely, says De Bourienne, the ill effects which a domestic fracas must produce at the moment when all France was expecting him to take the chief part in some great political revolution.

The universal enthusiasm which waited on his person at this crisis appears to have at length given definite shape to his ambition. All parties equally seemed to be weary of the Directory, and to demand the decisive interference of the unrivalled soldier. The members of the tottering government were divided bitterly among themselves; and the moderates, with the Director Sieyes at their head, on the one side, the democrats, under the Director Barras, on the other, were equally disposed to invoke his assistance. He received the proposals of both parties; and at length decided on closing with those of the former, as consisting of a class of men less likely than the others to interfere with his measures--when the new government, which he had determined should be his, had been arranged. His brother Lucien, recently elected President of the Council of Five Hundred--the acute and spirited Abb?Sieyes, for whom, as "a man of systems," Buonaparte had formerly manifested great repugnance, but who was now recommended effectually by his supposed want of high ambition--and Fouche minister of police--these were his chief confidants; nor could any age or country have furnished instruments more admirably qualified for his purpose. Josephine, too, exerted indefatigably in his cause all the arts of address, and contrived to neutralise by flattery many whom promises had failed to gain. Meanwhile his house was frequented by the principal officers who had accompanied him from Egypt, and by others who had served in his Italian campaigns; and though no one pretended to say what was about to happen, the impression became universal throughout Paris, that some great and decisive event was at hand, and that it was to be brought about by means of Buonaparte.

His friends at first busied themselves with schemes for making him one of the directorial body; but the law, requiring that every candidate for that office should be forty years of age, still subsisted; and this presented an obstacle which Napoleon chose rather to avoid than to overcome. The conspirators in his confidence were from day to day more numerous, and, before he had been three weeks in Paris, audacity reached its height. "During this crisis" (writes Bourienne) "there occurred nothing a whit more elevated, more grand, more noble, than had been observed in our preceding revolutionary commotions. In these political intrigues, all is so despicable--so made up of trickery, lying, spying, treachery, and impudence--that for the honour of human nature the details ought to be buried under an eternal veil."

Sieyes governed absolutely one of his colleagues in the Directory, Ducos; and the party of which he was the chief predominated strongly, as has been mentioned, in the Council of Ancients. It was through the instrumentality of that council, accordingly, that the conspirators resolved to strike their first blow. And how well their measures had been preconcerted, will sufficiently appear from the most naked statement of the events of the 18th and 19th Brumaire (Nov. 10 and 11, 1799), in the order of their occurrence.

As soon as Buonaparte's arrival was known, three regiments of dragoons, forming part of the garrison of Paris, petitioned for the honour of being reviewed by him. He had promised to do this, but delayed naming the day. In like manner the forty adjutants of the National Guard of Paris (which, as we have seen, was remodelled by himself while General of the Interior) had requested leave to wait upon him, and congratulate him on his arrival: these also had been told that he would soon appoint the time for receiving them. Lastly, the officers of the garrison, and many besides, had sent to beg admittance to Napoleon's presence, that they might tender him the expression of their admiration and attachment; and to them also an answer of the same kind had been given.

On the evening of the 17th Brumaire all the officers above-mentioned received, separately, the General's invitation to come to his house in the Rue de la Victoire, at six o'clock the next morning; and the three regiments of dragoons were desired to be mounted for their review, at the same early hour, in the Champs Elyseess. How many of these persons knew the real purpose of the assemblage it is impossible to tell; but Moreau, Macdonald, and other generals of the first reputation, avowedly attached to the moder 閿, were in the number of those who attended,--having, it is not to be doubted, received sufficient intimation that the crisis was at hand, though not of the manner in which Buonaparte designed it to terminate. However, at the appointed hour, the dragoons were at their post in the Champs Elyseess; and the concourse of officers at Napoleon's residence was so great that, the house being small, he received them in the courtyard before it, which they entirely filled.

Among those who came thither was Bernadotte; but he certainly came without any precise notion of the purposes of his friend Joseph Buonaparte, who invited him. He was, next to Napoleon, the general who possessed the greatest influence at the period in Paris; in fact, the fate of the government depended on whether the one party in the Directory should be the first to summon him to interfere, or the others to throw themselves on Buonaparte.

He came; but, unlike the rest, he came not in uniform, nor on horseback. Being introduced into Napoleon's private chamber, he was informed, with little preface, that a change in the government was necessary, and about to be effected that very day. Bernadette had already been tampered with by Sieyes and Ducos, and he rejected Napoleon's flatteries as he had theirs. It was well known to Buonaparte that, had this great officer's advice been taken, he would, immediately on his arrival from Egypt, have been arrested as a deserter of his post: he in vain endeavoured now to procure his co-operation; and at last suffered him to depart, having with difficulty extorted a promise, that he would not, at least, do anything against him as a citizen. It will soon be seen that he could have little reason to apprehend Bernadotte' s interference in his military capacity.

In effect the Council of the Ancients assembled the same morning, in the Tuileries, at the early hour of seven; one of the conspirators forthwith declared that the salvation of the state demanded vigorous measures, and proposed two decrees for their acceptance; one by which the meetings of the legislative bodies should be instantly transferred to the Chateau of St. Cloud, some miles from Paris: and another investing Napoleon with the supreme command of all the troops in and about the capital, including the National Guard. These motions were instantly carried; and, in the course of a few minutes, Buonaparte received, in the midst of his martial company, the announcement of his new authority. He instantly mounted and rode to the Tuileries, where, being introduced into the council, together with all his staff, he pronounced those memorable words--"You are the wisdom of the nation: I come, surrounded by the generals of the Republic, to promise you their support. Let us not lose time in looking for precedents. Nothing in history resembled the close of the eighteenth century--nothing in the eighteenth century resembled this moment. Your wisdom has devised the necessary measure; our arms shall put it in execution." Care had been taken to send no summons to the members of the council whom the conspirators considered as decidedly hostile to their schemes; yet several began to murmur loudly at this tone. "I come," resumed Napoleon, sternly, "I come accompanied by the God of War and the God of Fortune." His friends were alarmed lest this violence should produce some violent re-action in the assembly, and prevailed on him to withdraw. "Let those that love me follow me" said he, and was immediately on horseback again. "In truth," says De Bourienne, "I know not what would have happened, had the President, when he saw the

General retiring, exclaimed, Grenadiers, let no one go out: it is my conviction that, instead of sleeping the day after at the Luxembourg, he would have ended his career on the _Place de la Revolution_."

The command entrusted to Napoleon was forthwith announced to the soldiery; and they received the intelligence with enthusiasm--the mass of course little comprehending to what, at such a moment, such authority amounted.

The three Directors, meanwhile, who were not in the secret, and who had been much amused with seeing their colleague Sieyes set off on horseback an hour or two earlier from the Luxembourg, had begun to understand what that timely exhibition of the Abb?s awkward horsemanship portended. One of them, Moulins, proposed to send a battalion to surround Buonaparte's house and arrest him. Their own guard laughed at them. Buonaparte was already in the Tuileries, with many troops around him; and the Directorial Guard, being summoned by one of his aides-de-camp, instantly marched thither also, leaving the Luxembourg at his mercy. Barras sent his secretary to expostulate. Napoleon received him with haughtiness. "What have you done," cried he, "for that fair France which I left you so prosperous? For peace I find war; for the wealth of Italy, taxation and misery. Where are the 100,000 brave French whom I knew--where are the companions of my glory?--They are dead." Barras, who well knew that Buonaparte would never forgive him for having boasted that the conqueror of Italy and Egypt owed everything to his early favour, and whose infamous personal conduct in the articles of bribery and exaction made him tremble at the thought of impeachment, resigned his office: so did his colleagues, Gohier and Moulins. Sieyes and Ducos had done so already. Bernadotte, indeed, repaired to the Luxembourg ere Moulins and Gohier had resigned, and offered his sword and influence, provided they would nominate him to the command of the forces jointly with Napoleon. They hesitated: his word of honour given to Buonaparte, that he would do nothing as a citizen, rendered it indispensable that they should take that decisive step; by doing so they would at least have given the soldiery a fair choice--they hesitated--and their power was at an end. The Luxembourg was immediately guarded by troops in whom Napoleon could place implicit confidence. The Directory was no more.

Barras, in his letter, said that "he had undertaken his office solely for the purpose of serving the cause of liberty, and that now, seeing the destinies of the Republic in the hands of her young and invincible general, he gladly resigned it." By this courtly acquiescence he purchased indemnity for the past, and the liberty of retiring to his country-seat, there to enjoy the vast fortune he had so scandalously accumulated. The other two remained for the present under surveillance.

At ten o'clock on the same morning, the adverse Council of Five Hundred assembled also, and heard, with astonishment and indignation, of the decree by which their sittings were transferred from Paris (the scene of their popular influence) to St. Cloud. They had, however, no means of disputing that point: they parted with cries of "_Vive la Republique! Vive la Constitution!_" and incited the mob, their allies, to muster next morning on the new scene of action--where, it was evident, this military revolution must either be turned back, or pushed to consummation. During the rest of the day, Napoleon remained at the Tuileries: the troops were in arms; the population expected with breathless anxiety the coming of the decisive day. A strong body of soldiery marched to St. Cloud under the orders of Murat.

The members of both assemblies repaired thither early in the morning of the 19th; and those of the opposite party beheld with dismay the military investment of the Chateau. Scattered in groups about the courts and gardens, surrounded with the mob from the city, and watched by Murat and his stern veterans, they awaited with impatience the opening of the doors; which, in consequence of some necessary preparations, did not occur until two o'clock in the afternoon.

The Council of Ancients were ushered into the Gallery of Mars, and, the minority having by this time recovered from their surprise, a stormy debate forthwith commenced touching the events of the preceding day. Buonaparte entered the room, and, by permission of the subservient president, addressed the assembly. "Citizens," said he, "you stand over a volcano. Let a soldier tell the truth frankly. I was quiet in my home when this council summoned me to action. I obeyed: I collected my brave comrades, and placed the arms of my country at the service of you who are its head. We are repaid with calumnies--they talk of Cromwell--of Caesar. Had I aspired at power the opportunity was mine ere now. I swear that France holds no more devoted patriot. Dangers surround us. Let us not hazard the advantages for which we have paid so dearly--Liberty and Equality!--"

A democratic member, Linglet, added aloud--"and the Constitution--"

"The Constitution!" continued Napoleon, "it has been thrice violated already--all parties have invoked it--each in turn has trampled on it: since that can be preserved no longer, let us, at least, save its foundations--Liberty and Equality. It is on you only that I rely. The Council of Five Hundred would restore the Convention, the popular tumults, the scaffolds, the reign of terror. I will save you from such horrors--I and my brave comrades, whose swords and caps I see at the door of this hall; and if any hireling prater talks of outlawry, to those swords shall I appeal." The great majority were with him, and he left them amidst loud cries of "Vive Buonaparte!"

A far different scene was passing in the hostile assembly of the Five Hundred. When its members at length found their way into the Orangery, the apartment allotted for them, a tumultuous clamour arose on every side. _Live the Constitution! The Constitution or death! Down with the Dictator!_--such were the ominous cries. Lucien Buonaparte, the president, in vain attempted to restore order: the moderate orators of the council, with equal ill success, endeavoured to gain a hearing. A democrat member at length obtained a moment's silence, and proposed that the council should renew, man by man, the oath of fidelity to the Constitution of the year three. This was assented to, and a vain ceremony, for it was no more, occupied time which might have been turned to far different account. Overpowered, however, by the clamour, the best friends of Napoleon, even his brother Lucien, took the oath. The resignatory letter of Barras was then handed in, and received with a shout of scorn. The moment was come; Napoleon, himself, accompanied by four grenadiers, walked into the chamber--the doors remained open, and plumes and swords were visible in dense array behind him. His grenadiers halted near the door, and he advanced alone towards the centre of the gallery. Then arose a fierce outcry--_Drawn swords in the sanctuary of the laws! Outlawry! Outlawry! Let him be proclaimed a traitor! Was it for this you gained so many victories?_ Many members rushed upon the intruder, and, if we may place confidence in his own tale, a Corsican deputy, by name, Arena, aimed a dagger at his throat. At all events there was such an appearance of personal danger as fired the grenadiers behind him. They rushed forwards, and extricated him almost breathless; and one of their number (Thom? was at least rewarded on the score of his having received a wound meant for the General.

It seems to be admitted that at this moment the iron nerves of Buonaparte were, for once, shaken. With the dangers of the field he was familiar--in order to depict the perfect coolness of his demeanour during the greater part of this very day, his secretary says--"_he was as calm as at the opening of a great battle_;" but he had not been prepared for the manifestations of this civil rage. He came out, staggering and stammering, among the soldiery, and said, "I offered them victory and fame, and they have answered me with daggers."

Sieyes, an experienced observer of such scenes, was still on horseback in the court, and quickly re-assured him. General Augereau came up but a moment afterwards, and said, "You have brought yourself into a pretty situation." "Augereau," answered Napoleon (once more himself again), "things were worse at Arcola. Be quiet: all this will soon right itself." He then harangued the soldiery. "I have led you to victory, to fame, to glory. Can I count upon you?" "Yes, yes, we swear it" (was the answer that burst from every line), "Vive Buonaparte!"

In the council, meantime, the commotion had increased on the retreat of Napoleon. A general cry arose for a sentence of outlawry against him; and Lucien, the President, in vain appealed to the feelings of nature, demanding that, instead of being obliged to put that question to the vote, he might be heard as the advocate of his brother. He was clamorously refused, and in indignation flung off the insignia of his office. Some grenadiers once more entered, and carried him also out of the place.

Lucien found the soldiery without in a high state of excitement. He immediately got upon horseback, that he might be seen and heard the better, and exclaimed: "General Buonaparte, and you, soldiers of France, the President of the Council of Five Hundred announces to you that factious men with daggers interrupt the deliberations of the senate. He authorises you to employ force. The Assembly of Five Hundred is dissolved."

Napoleon desired Le Clerc to execute the orders of the President, and he, with a detachment of grenadiers, forthwith marched into the hall. Amidst the reiterated screams of "Vive la Republique" which saluted their entrance, an aide-de-camp mounted the tribune, and bade the assembly disperse. "Such," said he, "are the orders of the General." Some obeyed; others renewed their shouting. The drums drowned their voices. "Forward, grenadiers," said Le Clerc; and the men, levelling their pieces as if for the charge, advanced. When the bristling line of bayonets at length drew near, the deputies lost heart, and the greater part of them, tearing off their scarfs, made their escape, with very undignified rapidity, by way of the windows. The apartment was cleared. It was thus that Buonaparte, like Cromwell before him,

"Turn'd out the members, and made fast the door."[31]

Some of his military associates proposed to him that the unfriendly legislators should be shot, man by man, as they retreated through the gardens; but to this he would not for a moment listen.

Lucien Buonaparte now collected the moderate members of the Council of Five Hundred; and that small minority, assuming the character of the assembly, communicated with the Ancients on such terms of mutual understanding, that there was no longer any difficulty about giving the desired colouring to the events of the day. It was announced by proclamation, that a scene of violence and uproar, and the daggers and pistols of a band of conspirators, in the Council of Five Hundred, had suggested the measures ultimately resorted to. These were--the adjournment of the two councils until the middle of February next ensuing; and the deposition, meantime, of the whole authority of the state in a provisional consulate--the consuls being Napoleon Buonaparte, Sieyes, and Ducos.

Thus terminated the 19th of Brumaire. One of the greatest revolutions on record in the history of the world was accomplished, by means of swords and bayonets unquestionably, but still without any effusion of blood. From that hour the fate of France was determined. The Abb?Sieyes, Talleyrand, and other eminent civilians, who had a hand in this great day's proceedings, had never doubted that, under the new state of things to which it should lead, they were to have the chief management of the civil concerns of France. The ambition of Buonaparte, they questioned not, would be satisfied with the control of the armies and military establishments of the Republic. But they reckoned without their host. Next day the three consuls met in Paris; and a lengthened discussion arose touching the internal condition and foreign relations of France, and the measures not only of war, but of finance and diplomacy, to be resorted to. To the astonishment of Sieyes, Napoleon entered readily and largely upon such topics, showed perfect familiarity with them in their minutest details, and suggested resolutions which it was impossible not to approve. "Gentlemen," said the Abb? on reaching his own house, where Talleyrand and the others expected him--and it is easy so imagine the sensations with which Sieyes spoke the words, and Talleyrand heard them--"Gentlemen, I perceive that you have got a master. Buonaparte can do, and will do, everything himself. But" (he added, after a pause) "it is better to submit than to protract dissension for ever."

Buonaparte sent word next morning to Gohier and Moulins that they were at liberty. These ex-Directors were in haste to seclude themselves from public view; and the new ruler took possession the same evening of the Palace of the Luxembourg.

[Footnote 31: Crabbe.]

CHAPTER XIV

The Provisional Consulate--Reforms in France--Pacification of the Chouans--Constitution of the year VIII.--Buonaparte Chief Consul.

The upper population of Paris had watched the stormy days of the 18th and 19th Brumaire with the most anxious fears, lest the end should be anarchy and the re-establishment of the reign of terror. Such, in all likelihood, must have been the result, had Buonaparte failed, after once attempting to strike his blow. His success held out the prospect of victory abroad, and of a firm and stable government at home, under which life and property might exist in safety; and wearied utterly with so many revolutions and constitutions, each in turn pretending everything, and ending in nothing but confusion, the immense majority of the nation were well prepared to consider any government as a blessing which seemed to rest on a solid basis, and to bid fair for endurance. The revolutionary fever had in most bosoms spent its strength ere now; and Buonaparte found henceforth little opposition to any of his measures, unless in cases where the substantial personal comforts of men--not abstract theories or dogmas--nor even political rights of unquestionable value and importance--were invaded by his administration.

The two chambers, on breaking up, appointed small committees to take counsel during the recess with the new heads of the executive; and, in concert with these, Buonaparte and Sieyes entered vigorously on the great task of restoring confidence and peace at home. The confusion of the finances was the most pressing of many intolerable evils; and the first day was devoted to them. In lieu of forced loans, by which the Directory had systematically scourged the people, all the regular taxes were at once raised 25 per cent.; and the receipt and expenditure of the revenue arranged on a business-like footing. The repeal of the "Law of Hostages"--a tyrannical act, by which the relations of emigrants were made responsible for the behaviour of their exiled kinsmen,--followed immediately, and was received with universal approbation. A third and a bolder measure was the discarding of the heathen ritual, and re-opening of the churches for Christian worship; and of this the credit was wholly Napoleon's, who had to oppose the philosophic prejudices of almost all his colleagues. He, in his conversations with them, made no attempt to represent himself as a believer in Christianity; but stood on the necessity of providing the people with the regular means of worship, wherever it is meant to have a state of tranquillity. The priests who chose to take the oath of fidelity to government were re-admitted to their functions; and this wise measure was followed by the adherence of not less than 20,000 of these ministers of religion, who had hitherto languished in the prisons of France. Cambaceres, an excellent lawyer and judge, was of great service to Napoleon in these salutary reforms.

Many other judicious measures might be mentioned in this place. Some emigrants, cast on the shores by shipwreck, had been imprisoned and destined for trial by the Directory. They were at once set free: and, in like manner, La Fayette and other distinguished revolutionists, who had been exiled for not adhering to all the wild notions of the preceding administrations, were at once recalled. Carnot was one of these: Buonaparte forthwith placed him at the head of the war department; and the reform of the army was prosecuted with the vigour which might have been expected from the joint skill and talent of the provisional head of the government and this practised minister. The confusion which had of late prevailed in that department was extreme. The government did not even know the existence of regiments raised in the provinces: arms, clothing, discipline in every article, had been neglected. The organisation of the army was very speedily mended.

The insurgent Chouans next claimed attention: and here the personal character of Napoleon gave him advantages of the first importance. The leaders of those brave bands were disposed to consider such a soldier as a very different sort of ruler from the Pentarchy of the Luxembourg; and their admiration for his person prepared them to listen to his terms. The first measures of the new government were obviously calculated to soothe their prejudices, and the general display of vigour in every branch of the administration to overawe them. Chatillon, D'Antichamp, Suzannet, and other royalist chiefs, submitted in form. Bernier, a leading clergyman in La Vend 閑, followed the same course, and was an acquisition of even more value. Others held out; but were soon routed in detail, tried and executed. The appearances of returning tranquillity were general and most welcome.

Some of the party vanquished on the 18th Brumaire, however, still lingered in Paris, and were busy in plotting new convulsions. It was therefore the advice of all the ministers to condemn them to exile; and lists of proscription were drawn up and published. But Buonaparte only meant to overawe these persons: no one was apprehended: they kept quiet for a season; and the edict of exile sank by degrees into oblivion.

Meanwhile it was necessary that the government itself should assume some permanent form, ere the time arrived for the re-assembly of the legislative bodies. Their two committees met in one chamber with the consuls, and the outline of a new constitution was laid before them by Sieyes; who enjoyed the reputation of being the greatest of scientific politicians. The Abb? however, had soon perceived that Napoleon was to be the real creator of whatever should be adopted; and, in the progress of the ensuing consultations, submitted, step by step, to the laconic Dictator, who accepted or discarded propositions, exactly as they happened to coincide, or be at variance with, his own notions of his own personal interest. He cared little in what manner the structure of the future representative assemblies might be arranged; but there must be no weakening of the executive power, which he was determined to vest virtually in himself alone, and by means of which, he doubted not, it would be easy to neutralise all other influences.

The metaphysical Abb?proposed a scheme by far too delicately complicated for the tear and wear of human business and human passions. The absurdity, even of the parts which Napoleon consented to adopt, became apparent to all when the machine was set in motion. The two most prominent and peculiar devices--namely, that of placing at the head of the state a sort of mock sovereign, destitute of any effective power, and capable at any time of being degraded by the vote of a single legislative body, under the title of GRAND ELECTOR; and secondly, that of committing the real executive power to two separate consuls, one for war and one for peace, nominally the inferiors of the Elector, but in influence necessarily quite above him, and almost as necessarily the rivals and enemies of each other; these ingenious twins were strangled in the birth by Napoleon's shrewd practical sense. "Who," said he, "would accept an office, the only duties of which were to fatten like a pig, on so many millions a year? And your two consuls--the one surrounded with churchmen, lawyers, and civilians--the other with soldiers and diplomatists--on what footing would be their intercourse? the one demanding money and recruits, the other refusing the supplies? A government, made up of such heterogeneous and discordant materials, would be the shadow of a state." He added two words, which at once decided the main question; "I, for one, would never be your Grand Elector."

The constitution actually announced by proclamation on the 14th of December, 1799, presents the following principal features. I. The male citizens who are of age, and who pay taxes, in every commune shall choose a tenth of their number to be the notables of the commune; and out of those notables the officers of the commune shall be appointed. II. The notables of the communes constituting a department, shall choose, in like manner, the tenth of their number to be the notables of the department; and out of these the officers of the department shall be appointed. III. The notables of all the departments shall, in the same way, choose the tenth of their number to be notables of France; and out of these the public functionaries of The State shall be chosen. IV. Three assemblies shall be composed of persons chosen from the notables of France, viz.--1. The Conservative Senate, consisting (at first) of twenty-four men, of forty years of age, to hold their places for life, and to receive, each, a salary equal to 1-20th of that of the chief consul: 2. The Tribunate, to be composed of 100 men, of twenty-five years of age and upwards, of whom 1-5th go out every year, but re-eligible indefinitely; the salary of each 15,000 francs (?25); and thirdly, The Legislative Senate, composed of 300 members, of thirty years of age, renewable by fifths every year, and having salaries of 10,000 francs (?16). V. The executive power shall be vested in three consuls, chosen individually, as chief consul, second and third; the two former for ten years, the last for five. VI. In order that the administration of affairs may have time to settle itself, the tribunate and legislative senate shall remain as first constituted for ten years, without any re-elections. VII. With the same view, of avoiding discussions during the unsettled state of opinion, a majority of the members of the conservative senate are for the present appointed by the consuls, Sieyes and Ducos, going out of office, and the consuls, Cambaceres and Lebrun, about to come into office; they shall be held to be duly elected, if the public acquiesce; and proceed to fill up their own number, and to nominate the members of the tribunate and legislative senate. VIII. The acts of legislation shall be proposed by the consuls: the tribunate shall discuss and propound them to the legislative senate, but not vote: the legislative senate shall hear the tribunate, and vote, but not debate themselves; and the act thus discussed and voted, shall become law on being promulgated by the chief consul. IX. Buonaparte is nominated chief consul, Cambaceres (minister of justice) second, and Lebrun third consul.

It would be rash to say that this could never have turned out in practice a free constitution. Circumstances might have modified its arrangements, and given the spirit of freedom to institutions not ex-facie favourable to it. But for the present it was universally admitted that, under these new forms, the power of the state must be virtually lodged in Buonaparte. He, in fact, named himself chief consul. His creatures chose the conservative senate, and the conservative senate were to choose the members of the other two assemblies. The machinery, thus set in motion, could hardly fail to remain under his control; and, looking at things more largely, the contrivances of making the electoral bodies in the departments choose, not their actual representatives, but only the persons from among whom these were to be chosen by the conservative senate, and of preventing the legislative senate from debating for themselves on the measures destined to pass into law, appear to have been devised for the purpose of reducing to a mere nullity the forms of a representative government.[32] However, the consuls announced their manufacture to the people in these terms:--"Citizens, the Constitution is grounded on the true principles of a representative government, on the sacred rights of property, of equality, and of liberty. The powers which it institutes will be vigorous and permanent: such they should be to secure the rights of the citizens and the interests of the state. Citizens! the Revolution is fixed on the principles from which it originated: IT IS ENDED." And in effect, books being opened throughout France, the names of the citizens who inscribed their acceptance of this new constitution amounted to four millions, while but a few votes to the contrary were registered--an irrefragable proof that the national mind was disposed to think no sacrifice too dear, so tranquillity could be obtained.

The circumstance, perhaps, which occasioned most surprise on the promulgation of the new constitution, was the non-appearance of the name of Sieyes in the list of permanent consuls. It is probable that the Abb?made up his mind to retire, so soon as he found that Buonaparte was capable not only of mutilating his ideal republican scheme, but of fulfiling in his own person all the functions of a civil ruler of France. Howbeit the ingenious metaphysician did not disdain to accept of a large estate (part of the royal domain of Versailles!) and a large pension besides, by way of "public recompense"--when he withdrew to a situation of comparative obscurity, as President of the Conservative Senate.

One of Buonaparte's first acts was to remove the seat of government from the Luxembourg to the old Palace of the Tuileries, "which," he significantly said to his colleagues, "is a good military position." It was on the 19th of February, 1800, that the Chief Consul took possession of the usual residence of the French kings. Those splendid halls were re-opened with much ceremony, and immediately afterwards Napoleon held a great review in the Place du Carousel. This was the first public act of the Chief Consul. Shortly after, he appeared in his new official costume, a dress of red silk and a black stock. Someone observed to him that this last article was out of keeping with the rest: "No matter," answered he, smiling, "a small remnant of the military character will do us no harm." It was about the same time that Buonaparte heard of the death of Washington. He forthwith issued a general order, commanding the French army to wrap their banners in crape during ten days in honour of "a great man who fought against tyranny and consolidated the liberties of his country."

Talleyrand, appointed minister of foreign affairs by Buonaparte, was now the chief partner of his counsels. The second Consul, Cambaceres, soon learned to confine himself to the department of justice, and Lebrun to that of finance. The effective branches of government were, almost from the first, engrossed by Napoleon. Yet, while with equal audacity and craft he was rapidly consolidating the elements of a new monarchy in his own person--the Bourbonists, at home and abroad, had still nourished the hope that this ultimate purpose was the restoration of the rightful king of France. Very shortly after the 18th Brumaire, one of the foreign ambassadors resident at Paris had even succeeded in obtaining a private audience for Messieurs Hyde de Neuville and Dandign? two agents of the exiled princes. Buonaparte received them at night in a small closet of the Tuileries, and requested them to speak with frankness. "You, sir," they said, "have now in your hands the power of re-establishing the throne, and restoring to it its legitimate master. Tell us what are your intentions; and, if they accord with ours, we, and all the Vendeans, are ready to take your commands." He replied that the return of the Bourbons could not be accomplished without enormous slaughter; that his wish was to forget the past, and to accept the services of all who were willing henceforth to follow the general will of the nation; but that he would treat with none who were not disposed to renounce all correspondence with the Bourbons and the foreign enemies of the country. The conference lasted half-an-hour; and the agents withdrew with a fixed sense that Buonaparte would never come over to their side. Nevertheless, as it will appear hereafter, the Bourbons themselves did not as yet altogether despair; and it must be admitted, that various measures of the provisional government were not unlikely to keep up their delusive hopse. We may notice in particular a change in the national oath of allegiance, by which one most important clause was entirely erased: namely, that expressive of hatred to royalty: and an edict, by which the celebration of the day on which Louis XVI. died, was formally abolished. Sieyes, in opposing this last measure, happened to speak of Louis as "the tyrant":--"Nay, nay," said Napoleon, "he was no tyrant: had he been one, I should this day have been a captain of engineers--and you saying maco." The Bourbons were very right in considering these as monarchical symptoms; but shrewd observers perceived clearly in whose favour such changes were designed to operate. It appears that some of Napoleon's colleagues made a last effort to circumscribe his power, by urging on him the necessity of his immediately placing himself at the head of the armies in the field; expecting, no doubt, great advantages, could they remove him from the seat of government, at the time when the new machinery was getting into a regular course of motion. He sternly resisted all such suggestions. "I am Chief Consul," said he, biting his nails to the quick, "I will remain in Paris."

And it was, indeed, most necessary for his success that he should remain there at this critical epoch; for, in the arrangement of every branch of the new government, he had systematically sought for his own security in balancing against each other the lovers of opposite sets of principles -men, who, by cordially coalescing together, might still have undone him; or by carrying their animosities to extremity, overturned the whole fabric of his manufacture. It was thus that he had chosen one consul from the Republican party, and another from the Royalist; either of whom might, in his absence, have been tempted to undermine his sway; whereas both Cambaceres and Lebrun, overawed by his presence, proved eminently serviceable in drawing over to the interests of the Chief Consul innumerable persons, of their own ways of thinking originally, but no longer such zealous theorists as to resist the arguments of self-interest--those strong springs of hope and fear, of both of which Napoleon, while at the Tuileries, held the master-key. It was thus, also, that, in forming his ministry, he grouped together men, each of whom detested or despised the others; but each unquestionably fitted, in the highest degree, for the particular office assigned to him; and each, therefore, likely to labour in his own department, communicating little with his colleagues, and looking continually to the one hand that had invested him with his share of power. It was in vain that one party objected to the weathercock politics of Talleyrand. "Be it so," answered the Chief Consul: "but he is the ablest minister for foreign affairs in our choice, and it shall be my care that he exerts his abilities." Carnot, in like manner, was objected to as a firm republican. "Republican or not," answered Napoleon, "he is one of the last Frenchmen that would wish to see France dismembered. Let us avail ourselves of his unrivalled talents in the war department, while he is willing to place them at our command." All parties equally cried out against the falsehood, duplicity, and, in fact, avowed profligacy of Fouche "Fouche" said Buonaparte, "and Fouchealone, is able to conduct the ministry of the police: he alone has a perfect knowledge of all the factions and intrigues which have been spreading misery through France. We cannot create men: we must take such as we find; and it is easier to modify by circumstances the feelings and conduct of an able servant, than to supply his place." Thus did he systematically make use of whatever was willing to be useful--counting on the ambition of one man, the integrity of a second, and the avarice of a third, with equal confidence; and justified, for the present time (which was all he was anxious about) by the results of each of the experiments in question.

It is impossible to refuse the praise of consummate prudence and skill to these, and indeed, to all the arrangements of Buonaparte, at this great crisis of his history. The secret of his whole scheme is unfolded in his own memorable words to Sieyes: "We are creating a new era,--of the past we must forget the bad, and remember only the good." From the day when the consular government was formed, a new epoch was to date. Submit to that government, and no man need fear that his former acts, far less opinions, should prove any obstacle to his security--nay, to his advancement. Henceforth the regicide might dismiss all dread of Bourbon revenge; the purchaser of forfeited property of being sacrificed to the returning nobles; provided only they chose to sink their theories and submit. To the royalist, on the other hand, Buonaparte held out the prospect, not indeed of Bourbon restoration, but of the re-establishment of a monarchical form of government, and all the concomitants of a court; for the churchman the temples were at once opened; and the rebuilding of the hierarchical fabric, in all its wealth, splendour and power, was offered in prospective. Meanwhile, the great and crying evil, from which the revolution had really sprung, was for ever abolished. The odious distinction of castes was at an end. Political liberty existed, perhaps, no longer; but civil liberty--the equality of all Frenchmen in the eye of the law--was, or seemed to be, established. All men henceforth must contribute to the state in the proportion of their means: all men appeal to the same tribunals; and no man, however meanly born, had it to say, that there was one post of power or dignity in France to which talent and labour never could elevate him. Shortly after Napoleon took possession of the Tuileries, Murat, who had long been the lover of his sister Caroline, demanded her hand in marriage. The gallantry and military talents of this handsome officer had already raised him to a distinguished rank in the army, and Josephine warmly espoused his interests, but Buonaparte was with difficulty persuaded to give his consent to the match. "Murat is the son of an innkeeper," said he,--"in the station to which events have elevated me, I must not mix my blood with his." These objections, however, were overcome by the address of Josephine, who considered Napoleon's own brothers as her enemies, and was anxious, not without reason, to have some additional support in the family. Her influence, from this time, appears to have remained unshaken; though her extravagance and incurable habit of contracting debts gave rise to many unpleasing scenes between her and the most methodical of mankind.

[Footnote 32: The morning after the constitution was announced, the streets of Paris were placarded with a pasquil.

CHAPTER XV

The Chief Consul writes to the King of England--Lord Grenville's Answer--Napoleon passes the Great St. Bernard--The taking of St. Bard--The Siege of Genoa--The Battle of Montebello--The Battle of Marengo--Napoleon returns to Paris--The Infernal Machine--The Battle of Hohenlinden--The Treaty of Luneville.

Much had been already done towards the internal tranquillisation of France: but it was obvious that the result could not be perfect until the war, which had so long raged on two frontiers of the country, should have found a termination. The fortune of the last two years had been far different from that of the glorious campaigns which ended in the treaty--or armistice, as it might more truly be named--of Campo-Formio. The Austrians had recovered the north of Italy, and already menaced the Savoy frontier, designing to march into Provence, and there support a new insurrection of the royalists. The force opposed to them in that quarter was much inferior in numbers, and composed of the relics of armies beaten over and over again by Suwarrow. The Austrians and French were more nearly balanced on the Rhine frontier; but even there, there was ample room for anxiety. On the whole, the grand attitude in which Buonaparte had left the Republic when he embarked for Egypt, was exchanged for one of a far humbler description; and, in fact, as has been intimated, the general disheartening of the nation, by reason of those reverses, had been of signal service to Napoleon's ambition. If a strong hand was wanted at home, the necessity of having a general who could bring back victory to the tricolor banners in the field had been not less deeply felt. And hence the decisive revolution of Brumaire.

Of the allies of Austria, meanwhile, one had virtually abandoned her. The Emperor Paul, of Russia, resenting the style in which his army under Suwarrow had been supported, withdrew it altogether from the field of its victories; and that hare-brained autocrat, happening to take up an enthusiastic personal admiration for Buonaparte, was not likely for the present to be brought back into the Antigallican league. England appeared steadfast to the cause; but it remained to be proved whether the failure of her expedition to Holland under the Duke of York, or the signal success of her naval arms in the Mediterranean under Lord Nelson, had had the greater influence on the feelings of the government of St. James's. In the former case Napoleon might expect to find his advances towards a negotiation, in his new character of Chief Consul, received with better disposition than his predecessors of the Directory had extended to the last overtures of the English cabinet tendered by Lord Malmesbury. He resolved to have the credit of making the experiment at least, ere the campaign with the Austrians should open; and, discarding, as he had on a former occasion,[33] the usual etiquettes of diplomatic intercourse, addressed a letter to King George III., in person, almost immediately after the new consulate was established in the Tuileries, in these terms (Dec. 25, 1799).

"_French Republic--Sovereignty of the People-- Liberty and Equality._ "_Buonaparte, First Consul of the Republic, to his Majesty the King of Great Britain and Ireland._

"Called by the wishes of the French nation to occupy the first magistracy of the Republic, I have thought proper, in commencing the discharge of its duties, to communicate the event directly to your Majesty.

"Must the war, which for eight years has ravaged the four quarters of the world, be eternal? Is there no room for accommodation? How can the two most enlightened nations of Europe, stronger and more powerful than is necessary for their safety and independence, sacrifice commercial advantages, internal prosperity, and domestic happiness, to vain ideas of grandeur? Whence comes it that they do not feel peace to be the first of wants as well as of glories? These sentiments cannot be new to the heart of your Majesty, who rule over a free nation with no other view than to render it happy. Your Majesty will see in this overture only my sincere desire to contribute effectually, for the second time, to a general pacification--by a prompt step taken in confidence, and freed from those forms, which, however necessary to disguise the apprehensions of feeble states, only serve to discover in the powerful a mutual wish to deceive.

"France and England, abusing their strength, may long defer the period of its utter exhaustion; but I will venture to say, that the fate of all civilised nations is concerned in the termination of a war, the flames of which are raging throughout the whole world. I have the honour to be, &c. &c.

"BUONAPARTE."

It is manifest that the Chief Consul was wonderfully ignorant of the English constitution, if he really believed that the King (whose public acts must all be done by the hands of responsible ministers) could answer his letter personally. The reply was an official note from Lord Grenville, then secretary of state for the department of foreign affairs, to Talleyrand. It stated "that the King of England had no object in the war but the security of his own dominions, his allies, and Europe in general; he would seize the first favourable opportunity to make peace--at present he could see none. The same general assertions of pacific intentions had proceeded, successively, from all the revolutionary governments of France; and they had all persisted in conduct directly and notoriously the opposite of their language. Switzerland, Italy, Holland, Germany, Egypt,--what country had been safe from French aggression? The war must continue until the causes which gave it birth ceased to exist. The restoration of the exiled royal family would be the easiest means of giving confidence to the other powers of Europe. The King of England by no means pretended to dictate anything as to the internal polity of France; but he was compelled to say, that he saw nothing in the circumstances under which the new government had been set up, or the principles it professed to act upon, which could tend to make foreign powers regard it as either more stable or more trustworthy than the transitory forms it had supplanted."

Such was the tenor of Lord Grenville's famous note. It gave rise to an animated discussion in both Houses immediately on the meeting of the British Parliament; and, in both, the conduct of the ministry was approved by very great majorities. When, however, the financial preparations were brought forward, and it turned out that Russia was no longer to be subsidised--or, in other words, had abandoned the league against France--the prospects of the war were generally considered as much less favourable than they had been during this discussion. In the meantime the French government put forth, by way of commentary on Lord Grenville's state paper, a pretended letter from the unfortunate heir of the House of Stuart to George III., demanding from him the throne of England, which, now that the principle of legitimacy seemed to be recognised at St. James's, there could (said the pasquinade) be no fair pretext for refusing. Some other trifles of the same character might be noticed; but the true answer to Mr. Pitt was the campaign of Marengo.

Buonaparte rejoiced cordially in the result of his informal negotiation. It was his policy, even more clearly than it had been that of his predecessors, to buy security at home by battle and victory abroad. The national pride had been deeply wounded during his absence; and something must be done in Europe, worthy of the days of Lodi, and Rivoli, and Tagliamento, ere he could hope to be seated firmly on his throne. On receiving the answer of the British minister, he said to Talleyrand (rubbing his hands, as was his custom when much pleased), "it could not have been more favourable." On the same day, the 7th of January (just three days after the date of Lord Grenville's note), the First Consul issued his edict for the formation of an army of reserve, consisting of all the veterans who had ever served, and a new levy of 30,000 conscripts.

At this time France had four armies on her frontiers: that of the North, under Brune, watched the partisans of the House of Orange in Holland, and guarded those coasts against any new invasion from England; the defeat of the Duke of York had enabled the government to reduce its strength considerably. The second was the army of the Danube, under Jourdan, which, after the defeat at Stockach, had been obliged to repass the Rhine. The third, under Massena, styled the army of Helvetia, had been compelled in the preceding campaign to evacuate great part of Switzerland; but, gaining the battle of Zurich against the Russians, now re-occupied the whole of that republic. The fourth was that broken remnant which still called itself the "army of Italy." After the disastrous conflict of Genola it had rallied in disorder on the Apennine and the heights of Genoa, where the spirit of the troops was already so much injured, that whole battalions deserted en masse, and retired behind the Var. Their distress, in truth, was extreme; for they had lost all means of communication with the valley of the Po, and the English fleet effectually blockaded the whole coasts both of Provence and Liguria; so that, pent up among barren rocks, they suffered the hardships and privations of a beleaguered garrison.

The Chief Consul sent Massena to assume the command of the "army of Italy"; and issued, on that occasion, a general order, which had a magical effect on the minds of the soldiery, Massena was highly esteemed among them; and after his arrival at Genoa, the deserters flocked back rapidly to their standards. At the same time Buonaparte ordered Moreau to assume the command of the two corps of the Danube and Helvetia, and consolidate them into one great "army of the Rhine." Lastly, the rendezvous of the "army of reserve" was appointed for Dijon: a central position from which either Messena or Moreau might, as circumstances demanded, be supported and reinforced; but which Napoleon really designed to serve for a cloak to his main purpose. For he had already, in concert with Carnot, sketched the plan of that which is generally considered as at once the most daring and the most masterly of all the campaigns of the war; and which, in so far as the execution depended on himself, turned out also the most dazzlingly successful.

In placing Moreau at the head of the army of the Rhine, full 150,000 strong, and out of all comparison the best disciplined as well as largest force of the Republic, Buonaparte exhibited a noble superiority to all feelings of personal jealousy. That general's reputation approached the most nearly to his own, but his talents justified this reputation, and the Chief Consul thought of nothing but the best means of accomplishing the purposes of the joint campaign. Moreau, in the sequel, was severely censured by his master for the manner in which he executed the charge entrusted to him. His orders were to march at once upon Ulm, at the risk of placing the great Austrian army under Kray between him and France; but he was also commanded to detach 15,000 of his troops for the separate service of passing into Italy by the defiles of St. Gothard; and given to understand that it must be his business to prevent Kray, at all hazards, from opening a communication with Italy by way of the Tyrol. Under such circumstances, it is not wonderful that a general, who had a master, should have proceeded more cautiously than suited the gigantic aspirations of the unfettered Napoleon. Moreau, however, it must be admitted, had always the reputation of a prudent rather than a daring commander. The details of his campaign against Kray must be sought elsewhere. A variety of engagements took place with a variety of fortune. Moreau, his enemies allow, commenced his operations by crossing the Rhine in the end of April; and, on the 15th of July, had his headquarters at Augsburg, and was in condition either to reinforce the French in Italy, or to march into the heart of the Austrian states, when the success of Buonaparte's own expedition rendered either movement unnecessary.

The Chief Consul had resolved upon conducting, in person, one of the most adventurous enterprises recorded in the history of war. The formation of the army of reserve at Dijon was a mere deceit. A numerous staff, indeed, assembled in that town; and the preparation of the munitions of war proceeded there as elsewhere with the utmost energy: but the troops collected at Dijon were few; and--it being universally circulated and believed, that they were the force meant to re-establish the once glorious army of Italy, by marching to the headquarters of Massena at Genoa,--the Austrians received the accounts of their numbers and appearance, not only with indifference but with derision. Buonaparte, meanwhile, had spent three months in recruiting his armies throughout the interior of France; and the troops, by means of which it was his purpose to change the face of affairs beyond the Alps, were already marching by different routes, each detachment in total ignorance of the other's destination, upon the territory of Switzerland. To that quarter Buonaparte had already sent forward Berthier, the most confidential of his military friends, and other officers of the highest skill, with orders to reconnoitre the various passes in the great Alpine chain, and make every other preparation for the movement, of which they alone were, as yet, in the secret.

The statesmen who ventured, even after Brumaire, to oppose the investiture of Buonaparte with the whole power of the state, had, at first (as we have seen) attempted to confine him to the military department; or so arrange it that his orders, as to civil affairs, should, at least, not be absolute. Failing in this, they then proposed that the Chief Consul should be incapable of heading an army in the field, without abdicating previously his magistracy; and to their surprise, Napoleon at once acceded to a proposition which, it had been expected, would rouse his indignation. It now turned out how much the saving clause in question was worth. The Chief Consul could not, indeed, be general-in-chief of an army; but he could appoint whom he pleased to that post; and there was no law against his being present, in his own person, as a spectator of the campaign. It signified little that a Berthier should write himself commander, when a Napoleon was known to be in the camp.

It was now time that the great project should be realised. The situation of the "army of Italy" was become most critical. After a variety of petty engagements, its general saw his left wing (under Suchet) wholly cut off from his main body; and, while Suchet was forced to retire behind the Var, where his troops had the utmost difficulty in presenting any serious opposition to the Austrians, Massena had been compelled to throw himself with the remainder into Genoa. In that city he was speedily blockaded by the Austrian general Ott; while the imperial commander-in-chief, Melas, advanced with 30,000 upon Nice--of which place he took possession on the 11th of May. The Austrians, having shut up Massena, and well knowing the feebleness of Suchet's division, were in a delirium of joy. The gates of France appeared, at length, to be open before them; and it was not such an army of reserve as had excited the merriment of their spies at Dijon that could hope to withstand them in their long-meditated march on Provence--where Pichegru, as they supposed, was prepared to assume the command of a numerous body of royalist insurgents, as soon as he should receive intelligence of their entrance into France. But they were soon to hear news of another complexion from whence they least expected it--from behind them.

The Chief Consul remained in Paris until he received Berthier's decisive despatch from Geneva--it was in these words: "I wish to see you here. There are orders to be given by which three armies may act in concert, and you alone can give them in the lines. Measures decided on in Paris are too late." He instantly quitted the capital; and, on the 7th of May appeared at Dijon, where he reviewed, in great form, some 7000 or 8000 raw and half-clad troops, and committed them to the care of Brune. The spies of Austria reaped new satisfaction from this consular review: meanwhile Napoleon had halted but two hours at Dijon; and, travelling all night, arrived the next day, at Geneva. Here he was met by Marescot, who had been employed in exploring the wild passes of the Great St. Bernard, and received from him an appalling picture of the difficulties of marching an army by that route into Italy. "Is it possible to pass?" said Napoleon, cutting the engineer's narrative short. "The thing is barely possible," answered Marescot. "Very well," said the Chief Consul, "en avant--let us proceed."

While the Austrians were thinking only of the frontier where Suchet commanded an enfeebled and dispirited division,--destined, as they doubted not, to be reinforced by the army, such as it was, of Dijon,--the Chief Consul had resolved to penetrate into Italy, as Hannibal had done of old, through all the dangers and difficulties of the great Alps themselves. The march on the Var and Genoa might have been executed with comparative ease, and might, in all likelihood, have led to victory; but mere victory would not suffice. It was urgently necessary that the name of Buonaparte should be surrounded with some blaze of almost supernatural renown; and his plan for purchasing this splendour was to rush down from the Alps, at whatever hazard, upon the rear of Melas, cut off all his communications with Austria, and then force him to a conflict, in which, Massena and Suchet being on the other side of him, reverse must needs be ruin.

For the treble purpose of more easily collecting a sufficient stock of provisions for the march, of making its accomplishment more rapid, and of perplexing the enemy on its termination, Napoleon determined that his army should pass in four divisions, by as many separate routes. The left wing, under Moncey, consisting of 15,000 detached from the army of Moreau, was ordered to debouch by the way of St. Gothard. The corps of Thureau, 5000 strong, took the direction of Mount Cenis: that of Chabran, of similar strength, moved by the Little St. Bernard. Of the main body, consisting of 35,000, the Chief Consul himself took care; and he reserved for them the gigantic task of surmounting, with the artillery, the huge barriers of the Great St. Bernard. Thus along the Alpine Chain--from the sources of the Rhine and the Rhone to Isere and Durance--about 60,000 men, in all, prepared for the adventure. It must be added, if we would form a fair conception of the enterprise, that Napoleon well knew not one-third of these men had ever seen a shot fired in earnest.

The difficulties encountered by Moncey, Thureau, and Chabran will be sufficiently understood from the narrative of Buonaparte's own march. From the 15th to the 18th of May all his columns were put in motion; Lannes, with the advanced guard, clearing the way before them; the general, Berthier, and the Chief Consul himself superintending the rear guard, which, as having with it the artillery, was the object of highest importance. At St. Pierre all semblance of a road disappeared. Thenceforth an army, horse and foot, laden with all the munitions of a campaign, a park of forty field-pieces included, were to be urged up and along airy ridges of rock and eternal snow, where the goatherd, the hunter of the chamois, and the outlaw-smuggler are alone accustomed to venture; amidst precipices where to slip a foot is death; beneath glaciers from which the percussion of a musket-shot is often sufficient to hurl an avalanche; across bottomless chasms caked over with frost or snow-drift; and breathing

"The difficult air of the iced mountain top, Where the birds dare not build, nor insect's wing Flit o'er the herbless granite."[34]

The transport of the artillery and ammunition was the most difficult point; and to this, accordingly, the Chief Consul gave his personal superintendence. The guns were dismounted, grooved into the trunks of trees hollowed out so as to suit each calibre, and then dragged on by sheer strength of muscle--not less than an hundred soldiers being sometimes harnessed to a single cannon. The carriages and wheels, being taken to pieces, were slung on poles, and borne on men's shoulders. The powder and shot, packed into boxes of fir-wood, formed the lading of all the mules that could be collected over a wide range of the Alpine country. These preparations had been made during the week that elapsed between Buonaparte's arrival at Geneva and the commencement of Lannes's march. He himself travelled sometimes on a mule, but mostly on foot, cheering on the soldiers who had the burden of the great guns. The fatigue undergone is not to be described. The men in front durst not halt to breathe, because the least stoppage there might have thrown the column behind into confusion, on the brink of deadly precipices; and those in the rear had to flounder knee deep, through snow and ice trampled into sludge by the feet and hoofs of the preceding divisions. Happily the march of Napoleon was not harassed, like that of Hannibal, by the assaults of living enemies. The mountaineers, on the contrary, flocked in to reap the liberal rewards which he offered to all who were willing to lighten the drudgery of his troops.

On the 16th of May Napoleon slept at the convent of St. Maurice; and, in the course of the four following days, the whole army passed the Great St. Bernard. It was on the 20th that Buonaparte himself halted an hour at the convent of the Hospitallers, which stands on the summit of this mighty mountain. The good fathers of the monastery had been warned beforehand of the march, and they had furnished every soldier as he passed with a luncheon of bread and cheese and a glass of wine; for which seasonable kindness, they now received the warm acknowledgments of the chief.[35] It was here that he took his leave of a peasant youth, who had walked by him, as his guide, all the way from the convent of St. Maurice. Napoleon conversed freely with the young man, and was much interested with his simplicity. At parting, he asked the guide some particulars about his personal situation; and, having heard his reply, gave him money and a billet to the head of the monastery of St. Maurice. The peasant delivered it accordingly, and was surprised to find that, in consequence of a scrap of writing which he could not read, his worldly comforts were to be permanently increased. The object of his generosity remembered, nevertheless, but little of his conversation with the Consul. He described Napoleon as being "a very dark man" (this was the effect of the Syrian sun), and having an eye that, notwithstanding his affability, he could not encounter without a sense of fear. The only saying of the hero which he treasured in his memory was, "I have spoiled a hat among your mountains: well, I shall find a new one on the other side."--Thus spoke Napoleon, wringing the rain from his covering as he approached the hospice of St. Bernard.--The guide described, however, very strikingly, the effects of Buonaparte's appearance and voice, when any obstacle checked the advance of his soldiery along that fearful wilderness which is called emphatically, "The Valley of Desolation." A single look or word was commonly sufficient to set all in motion again. But if the way presented some new and apparently insuperable difficulty, the Consul bade the drums beat and the trumpets sound, as if for the charge; and this never failed. Of such gallant temper were the spirits which Napoleon had at command, and with such admirable skill did he wield them!

On the 16th the vanguard, under Lannes, reached the beautiful vale of Aosta, and the other divisions descended rapidly on their footsteps. This part of the progress was not less difficult than the ascent before. The horses, mules, and guns, were to be led down one slippery steep after another--and we may judge with what anxious care, since Napoleon himself was once contented to slide nearly a hundred yards together, seated.

On the 17th Lannes arrived at Chatillon, where he attacked and defeated a corps of 5000 Austrians who received the onset of a French division in that quarter, with about as much surprise as if an enemy had dropped on them from the clouds. Every difficulty now seemed to be surmounted, and corps after corps came down into the plentiful and verdant valley, full of joy. But suddenly the march of the vanguard was arrested by an obstacle unforeseen, or, at least, grievously under-estimated. Midway between Aosta and Ivrea the Dora flows through a defile, not more than fifty yards in width: the heights on either hand rise precipitous; and in the midst an abrupt conical rock, crowned with the fortress of St. Bard, entirely commands the river, and a small walled town, through the heart of which lies the only passage. Lannes having vainly attempted to force the place by a coup de main, a panic arose, and this spreading to the rear, orders were given for stopping the descent of the artillery. The Consul had come as far as the town of Aosta when this intelligence reached him. He immediately hastened to St. Bard, where he found the troops in much confusion.

On occasions like this Napoleon rarely failed to vindicate the prestige of his reputation. After hastily surveying the localities, he climbed the height of the Albaredo, which rises on the one side above the fort, and satisfied himself that, though the path had hitherto been trodden only by solitary huntsmen, the army who had crossed the St. Bernard might, by similar efforts, find or make their way here also. A single cannon being, with the last difficulty, hoisted to the summit, he planted it so as to play full on the chief bastion of St. Bard. The moment this was arranged the troops began their painful march; and they accomplished it without considerable loss; for the Consul's gun was so excellently placed that the main battery of the subjacent castle, was, ere long, silenced. The men crept along the brow of the Albaredo in single file, each pausing (says an eye-witness) to gaze for a moment on Napoleon, who, overcome with his exertions, had lain down and fallen fast asleep upon the summit of the rock. Thus passed the main body, slowly, but surely. Meantime Colonel Dufour had been ordered to scale the wall of the town at nightfall; and his regiment (the 58th) performed this service so impetuously, that the Austrian troops took refuge in the castle, and the French made good their lodgment in the houses below. For some hours the garrison poured down grape-shot at half-musket distance upon the French, but at last out of compassion for the inhabitants, the fire slackened, and ere day broke Buonaparte had effected his main purpose. The streets of the town having been strewn with litter to deafen sound, the guns, covered with straw and branches of trees, were dragged through it under the very guns of St. Bard, and without exciting the least suspicion in its garrison. Next morning the Austrian sent on a messenger to Melas, with tidings that a large division of the French had indeed passed by the goat-tracks of Albaredo, but that most certainly not one great gun was with them. Buonaparte, meantime, was hurrying forwards with horse, foot, and artillery too, upon Ivrea.

The march of the Consul received no new check until he reached the town of Ivrea, where, after two days' hard fighting, Lannes at length forced an entrance, and the garrison, with severe loss, withdrew. Buonaparte then took the road to Turin, and the vanguard had another severe piece of service at the bridge of Chiusilla, where 10,000 Austrians had been very strongly posted. Lannes broke them, and pursuing as far as Orca, cut them off from their magazines at Chevagno, and seized a vast quantity of stores which had been embarked on the Po. The advance was now within one march of Turin, while Murat occupied Vercelli, and the other divisions (those of Moncey, Chabran, and Thureau), having accomplished their several Alpine journeys, were pouring down upon the low country, and gradually converging towards the appointed rendezvous on the Ticino. Buonaparte had thus overcome the great difficulties of his preparation, and was ready with his whole army to open the campaign in good earnest against Melas.

The blockade of Genoa had been kept up all this time; while Suchet resolutely maintained the last line of defence on the old frontier of France. On the 22nd of May Melas made a desperate effort to force the passage of the Var, but failed; and immediately afterwards received his first intelligence of the movements of Buonaparte, and the defeat of his own detachment at the bridge of Chiusilla. He perceived that it was high time to leave Suchet to inferior hands, and set off to oppose in person "the army of reserve." Suchet, on his part, was not slow to profit by the departure of the Austrian Commander-in-chief: he, being informed of Buonaparte's descent, forthwith resumed the offensive, re-crossed the Var, and carried Vintimiglia at the point of the bayonet. Pursuing his advantage, Suchet obtained the mastery, first of the defile of Braus, and then of that of Tende, and at length re-occupied his old position at Melagno, whence his advanced guard pushed on as far as Savona.

The garrison of Genoa, meantime, had been holding out gallantly. Massena for some time kept possession of the semicircular chain of heights on the land side, and was thus enabled to obtain provisions, despite the 40,000 Austrians under General Ott who lay watching him, and the English fleet under Lord Keith which completely blockaded the shore. A great effort made to dislodge him from the heights on the 3rd of April had failed. But by degrees the superiority of numbers proved too much for him, and being shut at last within the walls--where, to increase all his difficulties, a great part of the population was violently hostile to the French cause--his sufferings from want of provisions, and the necessity of constant watchfulness and daily skirmishes, began to be severe. In his sorties, Massena had for the most part the advantage; and never in the whole war was the heroism of the French soldiery more brilliantly displayed than during this siege.[36] The news of the expedition of Napoleon at length penetrated to the beleaguered garrison, and the expectation of relief gave them from day to day new courage to hold out. But day passed after day without any deliverer making his appearance, and the scarcity of food rendered it almost impossible to keep the inhabitants from rising en masse to throw open the gates. The English, meanwhile, anchored closer to the city, and having cut out the vessels which guarded the entrance of the harbour, were bombarding the French quarters at their pleasure. Everything eatable, not excepting the shoes and knapsacks of the soldiers, had been devoured, ere Massena at length listened to the proposal of a conference with General Ott and Lord Keith. If the French general's necessities were urgent, the English admiral's desire to get possession of Genoa, ere Buonaparte could make further progress, was not less vehement. Lord Keith frankly told Massena, that his gallantry had been such that no terms could be too good for him. The word capitulation Was omitted: the French marched out of the town with arms and baggage, and were allowed to proceed to Suchet's headquarters; and, on the 5th of June, Ott occupied Genoa.

General Ott, notwithstanding this success, had been very ill-employed in lingering before Genoa while Napoleon was so rapidly advancing; and Melas, utterly perplexed between Suchet on the one side and the Consul on the other, had in fact lain still, and done nothing. Buonaparte, between the 1st and 4th of June, crossed the Ticino with his whole army. Murat carried Turbigo on the 5th, the very day that Genoa fell; and on the 2nd, the Chief Consul himself once more entered Milan, where he was received with enthusiasm. Lannes, after various conflicts, occupied Pavia. Chapon and Thureau threatened Turin by two different routes; and Melas, at last roused to a sense of his imminent danger, abandoned the open country of Piedmont, took up his headquarters at Alessandria, and began to draw together his widely separated columns, and concentrate them for the inevitable battle which must decide the fate of Italy.

Buonaparte, meanwhile, was ignorant of the fall of Genoa. He supposed, therefore, that the army of Ott was still at a wide distance from that of the Austrian commander-in-chief, and meditated to pass the Po suddenly, and either attack Ott and relieve Genoa, ere Melas knew that he was in that neighbourhood, or, if he should find this more practicable, force Melas himself to accept battle unsupported by Ott. Lannes and the van, accordingly, pushed on as far as Montebello, where, to their surprise, they found the Austrians in strength. Early in the morning of the 9th of June, Lannes was attacked by a force which he had much difficulty in resisting. The Austrians were greatly superior in cavalry, and the ground was favourable for that arm. But at length Victor's division came up, and, after a severe struggle, turned the tide. The battle was a most obstinate one. The fields being covered with very tall crops of rye, the hostile battalions were often almost within bayonet's length ere they were aware of each other's presence; and the same circumstances prevented the generals, on either side, from displaying much science in their manoeuvres. It was a conflict of man against man, and determined at a dear cost of blood. The field was strewn with dead, and the retiring Austrians left 5000 prisoners in the hands of Lannes--who, in memory of this day of slaughter, was created afterwards Duke of Montebello. It was from the prisoners taken here that the Consul learned the fate of Genoa. He immediately concluded that Melas had concentrated his army; and, having sent messengers to Suchet, urging him to cross the mountains by the Col di Cadibona, and march on the Scrivia (which would place him in the rear of the enemy), halted his whole line upon the strong position of Stradella.

It was on the evening after Montebello, that General Dessaix, whom Napoleon considered as second only to himself in military genius, arrived at headquarters. Buonaparte had, as we have seen, on leaving Egypt, ordered Kleber to send Dessaix to France in the course of November. He had accordingly landed at Frejus shortly after the establishment of the new government, where he found letters from the Chief Consul, urging him to join him without delay. In these letters there were some melancholy phrases, and Dessaix, who really loved Napoleon, was heard to say, "He has gained all, and yet he is not satisfied." A hundred obstacles rose up to keep Dessaix from joining his friend so speedily as both wished. He was yet in France when the news of St. Bernard came thither, and exclaiming, "He will leave us nothing to do," travelled night and day until he was able to throw himself into his arms. Napoleon immediately gave him the command of a division; and they spent the night together in conversing about the affairs of Egypt.

The First Consul was anxious to tempt Melas to attack him at Stradella, where the ground was unfavourable to cavalry movements; but, after lying there unmolested for three days, he began to fear that the Austrian had resolved, either on moving to the left flank, crossing the Ticino, occupying Milan, and so re-opening his communications with Vienna;--or, on falling back to Genoa, overwhelming Suchet, and taking up a position where the British fleet could supply him with provisions--or even, in case of necessity, embark his army, carry it round to the other side of Italy, and by that means place him once more between his enemy and the German states. Buonaparte, being perplexed with these apprehensions, at last descended into the great plain of Marengo, on which he had, not without reason, feared to abide the onset of Melas and the Austrian horse. He was at Volghera on the 11th, and the next day at St. Juliano, in the very centre of the plain; but still no enemy appeared. On the 13th, he advanced to the village of Marengo itself, and finding nothing even there but a scanty outpost, which retreated before him, concluded certainly that Melas had given him the slip, and marched either to the left on the Ticino, or to the right on Genoa. In great anxiety he detached one division under Dessaix to watch the road to Genoa, and another under Murat towards the Scrivia. Dessaix was already half-a-day's journey from headquarters, when Napoleon received intelligence which made him hastily recall all his detachments. The Austrian general, after a long hesitation, had at length resolved to let a fair field decide once more the fate of Italy. On the evening of the 13th, his whole army mustered in front of Alessandria having only the river Bormida between them and the plain of Marengo; and early in the following morning, they passed the stream at three several points, and advanced towards the French position in as many columns.

The Austrians were full 40,000 strong; while, in the absence of Dessaix and the reserve, Napoleon could, at most, oppose to them 20,000, of whom only 2500 were cavalry. He had, however, no hesitation about accepting the battle. His advance, under Gardanne, occupied the small hamlet of Padre Bona, a little in front of Marengo. At that village, which overlooks a narrow ravine, the channel of a rivulet, Napoleon stationed Victor with the main body of his first line--the extreme right of it resting on Castel Ceriolo, another hamlet almost parallel with Marengo; Kellerman, with a brigade of cavalry, was posted immediately behind Victor for the protection of his flanks. A thousand yards in the rear of Victor was the second line, under Lannes, protected in like fashion by the cavalry of Champeaux. At about an equal distance, again, behind Lannes, was the third line, consisting of the division of St. Cyr, and the consular guard, under Napoleon in person. The Austrian heavy infantry, on reaching the open field, formed into two lines, the first, under General Haddick, considerably in advance before the other, which Melas himself commanded, with General Zach for his second. These moved steadily towards Marengo; while the light infantry and cavalry, under General Elsnitz, made a detour round Castel Ceriolo with the purpose of outflanking the French right.

Such was the posture of the two armies when this great battle began. Gardanne was unable to withstand the shock, and abandoning Padre Bona, fell back to strengthen Victor. A furious cannonade along the whole front of that position ensued; the tirailleurs of either army posted themselves along the margins of the ravine, and fired incessantly at each other, their pieces almost touching. Cannon and musketry spread devastation everywhere--for the armies were but a few toises apart. For more than two hours Victor withstood singly the vigorous assaults of a far superior force; Marengo had been taken and retaken several times, ere Lannes received orders to reinforce him. The second line at length advanced, but they found the first in retreat, and the two corps took up a second line of defence considerably to the rear of Marengo. Here they were, again, charged furiously--and again, after obstinate resistance, gave way. General Elsnitz, meantime, having effected his purpose, and fairly marched round Castel Ceriolo, appeared on the right flank, with his splendid cavalry, and began to pour his squadrons upon the retreating columns of Lannes. That gallant chief formed his troops _en echelon_; and retired in admirable order--but the retreat was now general; and, had Melas pursued the advantage with all his reserve, the battle was won. But that aged general (he was eighty-four years old) doubted not that he had won it already; and at this critical moment, being quite worn out with fatigue, withdrew to the rear, leaving Zach to continue what he considered as now a mere pursuit.

At the moment when the Austrian horse were about to rush on Lannes's retreating corps, the reserve under Dessaix appeared on the outskirts of the field. Dessaix himself, riding up to the First Consul, said, "I think this is a battle lost." "I think it is a battle won," answered Napoleon. "Do you push on, and I will speedily rally the line behind you."--And in effect the timely arrival of this reserve turned the fortune of the day.

Napoleon in person drew up the whole of his army on a third line of battle, and rode along the front, saying, "Soldiers, we have retired far enough. Let us now advance. You know it is my custom to sleep on the field of battle." The enthusiasm of the troops appeared to be revived, and Dessaix prepared to act on the offensive; he led a fresh column of 5000 grenadiers to meet and check the advance of Zach. The brave Dessaix fell dead at the first fire, shot through the head. "Alas! it is not permitted to me to weep," said Napoleon; and the fall of that beloved chief redoubled the fury of his followers. The first line of the Austrian infantry charged, however, with equal resolution. At that moment Kellerman's horse came on them in flank; and being, by that unexpected assault, broken, they were, after a vain struggle, compelled to surrender:--General Zach himself was here made prisoner. The Austrian columns behind, being flushed with victory, were advancing too carelessly, and proved unable to resist the general assault of the whole French line, which now pressed onwards under the immediate command of Napoleon. Post after post was carried. The noble cavalry of Elsnitz, perceiving the infantry broken and retiring, lost heart; and, instead of forming to protect their retreat, turned their horses' heads and galloped over the plain, trampling down every thing in their way. When the routed army reached at length the Bormida, the confusion was indescribable. Hundreds were drowned--the river rolled red amidst the corpses of horse and men. Whole corps, being unable to effect the passage, surrendered: and at ten at night the Austrian commander with difficulty rallied the remnant of that magnificent array on the very ground which they had left the same morning in all the confidence of victory.

It is not to be denied that Napoleon was saved on this occasion by the arrival of the reserve under Dessaix, and the timely charge of Kellerman. On the other hand it is impossible not to condemn the rashness with which the Austrian generals advanced after their first successes.

The discomfiture of the imperialists was so great, that rather than stand the consequences of another battle, while Suchet was coming on their rear, they next day entered into a negotiation. Melas offered to abandon Genoa and all the strong places in Piedmont, Lombardy, and the Legations--provided Buonaparte would allow him to march the remains of his army unmolested to the rear of Mantua. Napoleon accepted this offer. By one battle he had regained nearly all that the French had lost in the unhappy Italian campaign of 1799: at all events he had done enough to crown his own name with unrivalled splendour, and to show that the French troops were once more what they had used to be--when he was in the field to command them. He had another motive for closing with the propositions of General Melas. It was of urgent importance to regain Genoa, ere an English army, which he knew was on its voyage to that port, could reach its destination.

On the 17th of June Napoleon returned in triumph to Milan, where he formally re-established the Cisalpine Republic, and was present at a festival of high state and magnificence. He then gave the command of the army of Italy to Massena; and appointed Jourdan French minister in Piedmont--in other words, governor of that dominion; and set out on his journey to Paris. He halted at Lyons to lay the first stone of the new Place de Bellecour, erected on the ruins of a great square destroyed by the Jacobins during the revolutionary madness; and reached the Tuileries on the 2nd of July. He had set out for Switzerland on the 6th of May. Two months had not elapsed, and in that brief space what wonders had been accomplished! The enthusiasm of the Parisians exceeded all that has been recorded of any triumphal entry. Night after night every house was illuminated; and day following day the people stood in crowds around the palace, contented if they could but catch one glimpse of the preserver of France.

The effusion of joy was the greater--because the tale of victory came on a people prepared for other tidings. About noontide on the 14th of June, when the French had been driven out of Marengo, and were apparently in full and disastrous retreat, a commercial traveller left the field, and arriving, after a rapid journey, in Paris, announced that Buonaparte had been utterly defeated by Melas. It is said that the ill-wishers of the First Consul immediately set on foot an intrigue for removing him from the government, and investing Carnot with the chief authority. It is not doubtful that many schemes of hostility had been agitated during Napoleon's absence, or that, amidst all the clamour and splendour of his triumphant reception in Paris, he wore a gloomy brow; nor has any one disputed that, from this time, he regarded the person of Carnot with jealousy and aversion.

The tidings of the great battle, meanwhile, kindled the emulation of the Rhenish army; and they burned with the earnest desire to do something worthy of being recorded in the same page with Marengo. But the Chief Consul, when he granted the armistice to Melas, had extended it to the armies on the German frontier likewise; and Moreau, consequently, could not at once avail himself of the eagerness of his troops. The negotiations which ensued, however, were unsuccessful. The emperor, subsidised as he had been, must have found it very difficult to resist the remonstrances of England against the ratification of any peace in which she should not be included; and it is natural to suppose, that the proud spirit of the Austrian cabinet revolted from setting the seal to an act of humiliation, not yet, as the English government insisted, absolutely necessary. News, meantime, were received, of the surrender of Malta to an English expedition under Lord Keith and Sir Ralph Abercrombie;[37] and this timely piece of good fortune breathed fresh spirit into the Antigallican league. In fine, insincerity and suspicion protracted, from day to day, a negotiation not destined to be concluded until more blood had been shed.

During this armistice, which lasted from the 15th of June to the 10th of November, the exiled princes of the House of Bourbon made some more ineffectual endeavours to induce the Chief Consul to be the Monk of France. The Abb?de Montesquiou, secret agent for the Count de Lille (afterwards Louis XVIII.), prevailed on the Third Consul, Le Brun, to lay before Buonaparte a letter addressed to him by that prince--in these terms: "You are very tardy about restoring my throne to me: it is to be feared that you may let the favourable moment slip. You cannot establish the happiness of France without me; and I, on the other hand, can do nothing for France without you. Make haste, then, and point out, yourself, the posts and dignities which will satisfy you and your friends." The First Consul answered thus: "I have received your Royal Highness's letter. I have always taken a lively interest in your misfortunes and those of your family. You must not think of appearing in France--you could not do so without marching over five hundred thousand corpses. For the rest, I shall always be zealous to do whatever lies within my power towards softening your Royal Highness's destinies, and making you forget, if possible, your misfortunes." The Comte D'Artois (Charles X. of France) took a more delicate method of negotiating. He sent a very beautiful and charming lady, the Duchesse de Guiche, to Paris; she without difficulty gained access to Josephine, and shone, for a time, the most brilliant ornament of the consular court. But the moment Napoleon discovered the fair lady's errand, she was ordered to quit the capital within a few hours. These intrigues, however, could not fail to transpire; and there is no doubt that, at this epoch, the hopes of the royalists were in a high state of excitement.

Meantime, among the meaner orders of both the great parties, who regarded with aversion the sovereign authority of the Chief Consul, there wanted not hearts wicked enough, nor hands sufficiently desperate, for attempts far different from these. The lawfulness, nay, the merit and the glory of tyrranicide, were ideas familiar to the Jacobins of every degree; and, during the years of miserable convulsion which followed the imprisonment and murder of Louis XVI., the royalist bands had often been joined, and sometimes guided, by persons in whom a naturally fanatical spirit, goaded by the sense of intolerable wrongs, dared to think of revenge--no matter how accomplished--as the last and noblest of duties: nor is it wonderful that amidst a long protracted civil war, when scenes of battle and slaughter were relieved only by the hardships of skulking in woods and the fears of famine, the character of others, originally both pure and gentle, had come to be degraded into a callous indifference of dark sullenness of temper, fit preparatives for deeds, the thought of which, in earlier and better days, would have been horror and loathing.

It was among the Jacobins, who had formerly worshipped Buonaparte as the "child and champion" of their creed, that the first schemes of assassination were agitated. An Italian sculptor, by name Ceracchi, who had modelled the bust of Napoleon while he held his court at Montebello, arrived in Paris, and, under pretence of retouching his work, solicited admission to the presence of the new Caesar, whose Brutus he had resolved to be. The occupations of the Consul did not permit of this, and the Italian, having opened his purpose to Topineau, Lebrun, a painter, the adjutant-general Arena, Damerville, and others of kindred sentiments, arranged a plan by which Buonaparte was to have been surrounded and stabbed in the lobby of the opera house. But one of the accomplices betrayed the conspiracy, and Ceracchi and his associates were arrested in the theatre, at the moment when they were expecting their victim.

This occurred towards the middle of August; and it has been said that the Jacobin conspirators, being thrown into the same prison with some desperadoes of the Chouan faction, gave to these last the outline of another scheme of assassination, which had more nearly proved successful. This was the plot of the infernal machine. A cart was prepared to contain a barrel of gunpowder, strongly fastened in the midst of a quantity of grape-shot, which, being set on fire by a slow match, was to explode at the moment when Buonaparte was passing through some narrow street, and scatter destruction in every direction around it. The night selected was that of the 10th of October, when the Chief Consul was expected to visit the opera, and the machine was planted in the Rue St. Nicaise, through which he must pass in his way thither from the Tuileries. Napoleon told his friends at St. Helena, that having laboured hard all day, he felt himself overpowered with sleep after dinner, and that Josephine, who was anxious to be at the opera, had much difficulty in at last rousing and persuading him to go. "I fell fast asleep again" (he said), "after I was in my carriage; and at the moment when the explosion took place, I was dreaming of the danger I had undergone some years before in crossing the Tagliamento at midnight, by the light of torches, during a flood." He awoke, and exclaimed to Lannes and Bessieres, who were with him in the coach, "We are blown up." The attendants would have stopped the carriage, but, with great presence of mind, he bade them drive as fast as they could to the theatre, which he alone of all the party entered with an unruffled countenance. He had escaped most narrowly. The coachman, happening to be intoxicated, drove more rapidly than was his custom.[38] The engine exploded half a minute after the carriage had passed it--killing twenty persons, wounding fifty-three (among whom was St. Regent, the assassin who fired the train), and shattering the windows of several houses on both sides of the street.

The audience in the opera-house, when the news was divulged, testified their feelings with enthusiasm. The atrocity of the conspiracy roused universal horror and indignation, and invested the person of the Chief Consul with a new species of interest. The assassins were tried fairly, and executed, glorying in their crime: and, in the momentary exaltation of all men's minds, an edict of the senate, condemning to perpetual exile 130 of the most notorious leaders of the Terrorists, was received with applause. But Napoleon himself despised utterly the relics of that odious party; and the arbitrary decree in question was never put into execution.

The Chief Consul, nevertheless, was not slow to avail himself of the state of the public mind, in a manner more consistent with his prudence and farsightedness. It was at this moment that the erection of a new tribunal, called the Special Commission, consisting of eight judges, without jury, and without revision or appeal, was proposed to the legislative bodies. To their honour the proposal was carried by very narrow majorities; for after that judicature was established, the Chief Consul had, in effect, the means of disposing of all who were suspected of political offences, according to his own pleasure. Another law which soon succeeded, and which authorised the chief magistrate to banish disaffected persons, as "enemies of the state," from Paris or from France, whenever such steps should seem proper, without the intervention of any tribunal whatever, completed (if it was yet incomplete) the despotic range of his power: and the police, managed as that fearful engine was by Fouche presented him with the most perfect means of carrying his purposes into execution.

A singular anecdote belongs to this time--(December, 1800). During the effervescence of public opinion consequent on the affair of the infernal machine, there appeared a pamphlet, entitled, "Parallel between Caesar, Cromwell, Monk, and Bonaparte"[39]--a production evidently designed to favour the assumption of regal dignity by the Consul. Appearing at such a moment, it could not fail to excite a vivid sensation; the confidential friends of Napoleon assured him, in one voice, that the publication was likely to injure him. He sent for Fouche and reproached him violently for suffering such a pamphlet to appear. The minister of police heard him with perfect coolness, and replied that he had not chosen to interfere, because he had traced the manuscript to the hotel of his brother Lucien. "And why not denounce Lucien?" cried Napoleon; "he ought to have been arrested instantly, and confined in the Temple." The Consul having spoken thus, quitted the apartment, shutting the door with violence. Fouchesmiled, and whispered to De Bourienne--"Confine the author in the Temple! Lucien showed me the manuscript; I found it full of corrections in the handwriting of--the First Consul!" Lucien, informed of his brother's wrath, came forthwith to the Tuileries, and complained that "he had been made a puppet and abandoned." "The fault is your own," answered Napoleon; "it was your business not to be detected. Fouchehas shown himself more dexterous--so much the worse for you." Lucien resigned forthwith the office which he held in the ministry, and proceeded as ambassador to Spain.

How far these disturbances in the French capital might have contributed to the indecision of the Austrian cabinet during this autumn, we know not. Five months had now elapsed since the armistice after Marengo; and the First Consul, utterly disgusted with the delay, determined to resume arms, and to be first in the field. Between the 17th and the 27th of November his generals received orders to set all their troops once more in motion. Everywhere the French arms had splendid success. Brune defeated the Austrians on the Mincio, and advanced within a few miles of Venice. Macdonald occupied the mountains of the Tyrol, and was prepared to reinforce either the army of Italy or that of the Rhine, as might be desired. Moreau, finally, advanced into the heart of Germany, and was met by the Archduke John of Austria, who obtained considerable advantages in an affair at Haag. The Archduke, elated by this success, determined on a general engagement, and appeared in front of the French on the evening of the 2nd December, at Hohenlinden, between the Inn and the Iser.[40] At seven, on the morning of the 3rd, the conflict began. The deep snow had obliterated the tracks of roads; several Austrian columns were bewildered; and either came not at all into their positions, or came too late. Yet the battle was obstinate and severe: 10,000 Imperialists were left dead on the field: and Moreau, improving his success, marched on immediately, and occupied Salzburg.

The Austrian capital now lay exposed to the march of three victorious armies; and the Emperor was at last compelled to release himself from his English obligations, and negotiate in sincerity for a separate peace. Mr. Pitt himself considered the prosecution of the continental war as for the time hopeless. On reading the bulletin of Marengo, he said, "Fold up that map" (the map of Europe); "it will not be wanted for these twenty years."

A definitive treaty was signed at Luneville on the 9th February, 1801; by which the Emperor, not only as the head of the Austrian monarchy, but also in his quality of Chief of the German empire, guaranteed to France the boundary to the Rhine; thereby sacrificing certain possessions of Prussia and other subordinate princes of the empire, as well as his own. Another article, extremely distasteful to Austria, yielded Tuscany; which Napoleon resolved to transfer to a prince of the House of Parma, in requital of the good offices of Spain during the war. The Emperor recognised the union of the Batavian Republic with the French;--and acknowledged the Cisalpine and Ligurian Commonwealths; both virtually provinces of the great empire, over which the authority of the First Consul seemed now to be permanently established.

[Footnote 33: When he wrote from Clagenfurt to the Archduke Charles.]

[Footnote 34: Byron's "Manfred."]

[Footnote 35: The worthy Hospitallers of St. Bernard have stationed themselves on that wild eminence, for the purpose of alleviating the misery of travellers lost or bewildered amidst the neighbouring defiles. They entertain a pack of dogs, of extraordinary sagacity, who roam over the hills night and day, and frequently drag to light and safety pilgrims who have been buried in the snow.]

[Footnote 36: The following anecdote is given by Dumas:--"On one of these occasions, when a desperate attack was led on by Soult, there occurred a circumstance as honourable as it was characteristic of the spirit which animated the French. The soldiers of two regiments or demi-brigades, of the army of Italy, namely, the 25th Light, and the 24th of the Line, had sworn eternal enmity against one another, because that, previous to the opening of the campaign, when desertion and all the evils of insubordination prevailed in that army, disorganised by suffering, the former, in which discipline had been maintained, was employed to disarm the latter. The utmost care had been taken to keep them separate; but it so happened that these two corps found themselves one day made rivals as it were in valour, the one before the eyes of the other. The same dangers, the same thirst of glory, the same eagerness to maintain themselves, at once renewed in all hearts generous sentiments; the soldiers became instantly intermingled; they embraced in the midst of the fire, and one half of the one corps passing into the ranks of the other, they renewed the combat, after the exchange, with double ardour."]

[Footnote 37: Sept. 5, 1800.]

[Footnote 38: The man took the noise for that of a salute.]

[Footnote 39: "Napoleon dropped the u in his surname after his first campaign in Italy."--Bourienne.]

[Footnote 40: The poet Campbell has vividly painted the opening of the great battle which followed.

"On Linden, when the sun was low, All bloodless lay the untrodden snow, And dark as winter was the flow Of Iser rolling rapidly:

But Linden saw another sight When the drums beat at dead of night, Commanding fires of death to light The darkness of her scenery," &c.]

CHAPTER XVI

Affairs of Naples and of the Pope--The Emperor Paul of Russia--Northern confederacy against England--Battle of Copenhagen--Nelson's Victory--Death of Paul--Expedition to Egypt under Sir Ralph Abercrombie--Battle of Alexandria--Conquest of Egypt--The Flotilla of Boulogne--Negotiations with England--Peace of Amiens.

England alone remained steadfast in her hostility; and, as we shall presently see, the Chief Consul was even able to secure for himself the alliance against her of some of the principal powers in Europe; but before we proceed to the eventful year of 1801, there are some incidents of a minor order which must be briefly mentioned.

It has been already said that the half-crazy Emperor of Russia had taken up a violent personal admiration for Buonaparte, and, under the influence of that feeling, virtually abandoned Austria before the campaign of Marengo. Napoleon took every means to flatter the Autocrat and secure him in his interests. Paul had been pleased to appoint himself Grand Master of the ruined Order of the Knights of St. John. It was his not idle ambition to obtain, in this character, possession of the Island of Malta; and Buonaparte represented the refusal of the English government to give up that stronghold as a personal insult to Paul. Some 10,000 Russian prisoners of war were not only sent back in safety, but new clothed and equipped at the expense of France; and the Autocrat was led to contrast this favourably with some alleged neglect of these troops on the part of Austria, when arranging the treaty of Luneville. Lastly, the Queen of Naples, sister to the German Emperor, being satisfied that, after the battle of Marengo, nothing could save her husband's Italian dominions from falling back into the hands of France (out of which they had been rescued, during Napoleon's Egyptian campaign, by the English, under Lord Nelson), took up the resolution of travelling in person to St. Petersburg in the heart of the winter, and soliciting the intercession of Paul. The Czar, egregiously flattered with being invoked in this fashion, did not hesitate to apply in the Queen's behalf to Buonaparte; and the Chief

Consul, well calculating the gain and the loss, consented to spare Naples for the present, thereby completing the blind attachment of that weak-minded despot.

At the same time when Nelson delivered Naples from the French, a party of English seamen, under Commodore Trowbridge, had landed at the mouth of the Tiber, marched to Rome, and restored the Pope. The French army, after the great victory which gave them back Lombardy and Piedmont, doubted not that the re-establishment of "the Roman Republic" would be one of its next consequences. But Buonaparte, who had in the interim re-opened the churches of France, was now disposed to consider the affairs of the Pope with very different eyes. In a word, he had already resolved to make use of the Holy Father in the consolidation of his own power as a monarch; and, as the first step to this object, the government of the Pope was now suffered to continue--not a little to the astonishment of the French soldiery, and to the confusion, it may be added, and regret, of various powers of Europe.

The First Consul, meanwhile, proceeded to turn the friendship of the Russian Emperor to solid account. It has never, in truth, been difficult to excite angry and jealous feelings, among the minor maritime powers, with regard to the naval sovereignty of England. The claim of the right of searching neutral ships, and her doctrine on the subject of blockades, had indeed been recognised in many treaties by Russia, and by every maritime government in Europe. Nevertheless, the old grudge remained; and Buonaparte now artfully employed every engine of diplomacy to awaken a spirit of hostility against England, first, in the well-prepared mind of the Czar, and then in the cabinets of Prussia, Denmark, and Sweden. The result was, in effect, a coalition of these powers against the mistress of the seas; and, at the opening of the nineteenth century, England had to contemplate the necessity of encountering single-handed the colossal military force of France, and the combined fleets of Europe. To deepen the shadows of her prospects at that great crisis of her history, the people suffered severely under a scarcity of food, in consequence of bad harvests; and the efforts which England made, under such an accumulation of adverse circumstances, must ever be treasured among the proudest of her national recollections.

In January, 1801, the first imperial parliament of Great Britain and Ireland assembled; and, shortly afterwards, in consequence of a difference of opinion, touching the Roman Catholic Question, between George III. and Mr. Pitt, that great minister resigned his office, and a new cabinet was formed, with Mr. Addington (afterwards Viscount Sidmouth) at its head. These changes were a new source of embarrassment; yet the prosecution of the war was urged with undiminished vigour.

Early in March, Admiral Sir Hyde Parker and Vice-Admiral Lord Nelson conducted a fleet into the Baltic, with the view of attacking the northern powers in their own harbours, ere they could effect their meditated junction with the fleets of France and Holland. The English passed the Sound on the 13th of March, and reconnoitred the road of Copenhagen, where the Crown-Prince, Regent of Denmark, had made formidable preparations to receive them. It was on the 2nd of April that Nelson, who had volunteered to lead the assault, having at length obtained a favourable wind, advanced with twelve ships of the line, besides frigates and fire-ships, upon the Danish armament, which consisted of six sail of the line, eleven floating batteries, and an enormous array of small craft, all chained to each other and to the ground, and protected by the Crown-batteries, mounting eighty-eight guns, and the fortifications of the isle of Amack. The battle lasted for four hours, and ended in a signal victory. Some few schooners and bomb-vessels fled early, and escaped: the whole Danish fleet besides were sunk, burnt, or taken. The Prince Regent, to save the capital from destruction, was compelled to enter into a negotiation, which ended in the abandonment of the French alliance by Denmark. Lord Nelson then reconnoitred Stockholm; but, being unwilling to inflict unnecessary suffering, did not injure the city, on discovering that the Swedish fleet had already put to sea. Meantime, news arrived that Paul had been assassinated in his palace at St. Petersburg; and that the policy which he had adopted, to the displeasure of the Russian nobility, was likely to find no favour with his successor. The moving spirit of the northern confederacy was, in effect, no more, and a brief negotiation ended in its total disrupture.[41]

In the same month of March the British arms were crowned with a more pleasing triumph in a more distant region. From the time when Buonaparte landed in Egypt, the occupation of that country by a French army, and its possible consequences to our empire in the East, had formed a subject of anxious solicitude in the cabinet of St. James's; and the means for attacking the army which Napoleon had entrusted to Kleber, had, at length, been combined and set in motion, in opposition to the sentiments both of the King and Mr. Pitt, by the bold spirit of Lord Melville, then at the head of the Indian Board of Control. The fleet of Lord Keith, carrying Sir Ralph Abercrombie and his army, were already in possession of Malta; another army of 7000, composed partly of English troops and partly of sepoys, had been dispatched from India, and approached Egypt by the way of the Red Sea; and, lastly, the Ottoman Porte was prepared to co-operate with General Abercrombie, whenever he should effect a landing in the neighbourhood of Alexandria. That event occurred on the 13th of March, the British troops disembarking in the face of the French, who were very strongly posted; and, at length, driving them from the shore. On the 21st a general engagement took place in front of Alexandria; and Sir Ralph Abercrombie fell, mortally wounded, in the moment of victory. General Hutchinson (afterwards Earl of Donoughmore), on whom the command devolved, pursued the advantage. Kleber, who by his excellent administration had earned the title of the Just Sultan, had been assassinated by an obscure fanatic on the same day when Dessaix died gloriously at Marengo; and Menou, who succeeded to the command of the French army in Egypt, was found wholly incapable of conducting either the civil or the military business of the colony to advantage. He shut himself up in Alexandria with the relics of the army defeated on the 21st. The English, forthwith, let the sea into the lake Martis: the capital was thus made an island, and all communication with the country cut off. Hutchinson was now joined by the Turkish Capitan-pasha and 6000 men; and intelligence reached him that the Indian reinforcement, under General Baird, had landed at Cossire. Rosetta was soon captured; and, after various skirmishes, Cairo was invested. On the 28th of June General Belliard and a garrison of 13,000 surrendered, on condition that they should be transported in safety to France: and Menou, perceiving that defence was hopeless and famine at hand, followed, ere long, the same example. Thus, in one brief campaign, was Egypt entirely rescued from the arms of France. But even that great advantage was a trifle, when compared with the stimulus afforded to national confidence at home, by this timely re-assertion of the character of the English army. At sea we had never feared an enemy; but the victories of Abercrombie destroyed a fatal prejudice which had, of recent days, gained ground,--that the military of Great Britain were unfit to cope with those of revolutionary France. Nor should it be forgotten, that if Abercrombie had the glory of first leading English soldiers to victory over the self-styled Invincibles of Buonaparte, he owed the means of his success to the admirable exertions of the Duke of York, in reforming the discipline of the service as commander-in-chief.

On learning the fate of Egypt, Buonaparte exclaimed, "Well, there remains only the descent on Britain;" and, in the course of a few weeks, not less than 100,000 troops were assembled on the coasts of France. An immense flotilla of flat-bottomed boats was prepared to carry them across the Channel, whenever, by any favourable accident, it should be clear of the English fleets; and both the soldiery and the seamen of the invading armament were trained and practised incessantly, in every exercise and manoeuvre likely to be of avail when that long-looked-for day should arrive. These preparations were met, as might have been expected, on the part of the English government and nation. Nelson was placed in command of the Channel fleet; and the regular army was reinforced on shore by a multitude of new and enthusiastic volunteers; men of all parties and ranks joining heart and hand in the great and sacred cause. Lord Nelson, more than once, reconnoitred the flotilla assembled at Boulogne, and, at length, attempted the daring movement of cutting out the vessels, in the teeth of all the batteries. The boats being chained to the shore, crowded with soldiery, and placed immediately under the fortifications, the attempt was unsuccessful; but the gallantry with which it was conducted struck new terror into the hearts of the French marine, and, Nelson continuing to watch the Channel with unsleeping vigilance, the hopes of the First Consul, ere long, sunk.

The successes of the English in the Baltic and in Egypt were well calculated to dispose Napoleon for negotiation: and the retirement of Mr. Pitt, who was considered throughout Europe as the author and very soul of the anti-revolutionary war, was not without its influence. On the other hand, Napoleon's mighty successes against the German emperor had been followed up this same year by the march of a French and Spanish army into Portugal, in consequence of which that last ally of England had been compelled to submit to the general fate of the continent. On both sides there existed the strongest motives for accommodation; and, in effect, after a tedious negotiation, the preliminaries of peace were signed, on the 10th of October, at Amiens. By this treaty England surrendered all the conquests which she had made during the war, except Ceylon and Trinidad. France, on the other hand, restored what she had taken from Portugal, and guaranteed the independence of the Ionian Islands. Malta was to be restored to the Knights of St. John, and declared a free port: neither England nor France was to have any representatives in the order; and the garrison was to consist of the troops of a neutral power. This article was that which cost the greatest difficulty--and Malta was destined to form the pretext, at least, for the re-opening of the war at no distant date.

Meantime, except by a small party, who thought that England should never make peace unless the Bourbon family were restored to the throne of France, this news was received with universal satisfaction throughout Great Britain. "It was," as Mr. Sheridan summed up the matter, "a peace which all men were glad of, and of which no man could be proud." The definitive treaty was signed on the 25th of March, 1802: and nothing could surpass the demonstrations of joy on this occasion, both in London and in Paris--or the enthusiastic display of good-will with which the populace of either capital welcomed the plenipotentiaries.

[Footnote 41: For the details of the battle of Copenhagen see Southey's Life of Nelson. That conflict has been celebrated, in a noble lyric, by Campbell--

"Of Nelson and the North Sing the glorious day's renown, When to the battle fierce came forth All the might of Denmark's crown," &c.]

CHAPTER XVII

Peace of Amiens--The Concordat--The Legion of Honour--Buonaparte President of the Cisalpine Republic--First Consul for Life--Grand Mediator of the Helvetic Confederacy--St. Domingo--Toussaint L'Ouverture--Dissatisfaction of England--Trial of Peltier--Lord Whitworth--Rupture of the Peace of Amiens--Detention of English Travellers in France.

The peace of Amiens, like that of Campo-Formio, turned out a mere armistice. It was signed in the midst of mutual suspicion; and the audacious ambition of the French government, from the very day of its ratification, accumulated the elements of an inevitable rupture. The continent, however, had been virtually shut against the English for ten years; and now, in the first eagerness of curiosity, travellers of all ranks, ages, and sexes poured across the Channel, to contemplate, with their own eyes, the scenes and effects of the many wonderful deeds and changes which had been wrought since the outbreaking of the French Revolution. The chief object of curiosity was Napoleon himself; and English statesmen, of the highest class, were among those who now thronged the levees of the Tuileries. Mr. Fox, in particular, seems to have been courted and caressed by the Chief Consul; and these two great men parted with feelings of mutual admiration. Our countrymen, in general, were received in Paris with extraordinary attentions and civilities; and for a brief space, the establishment of friendly feelings between the two nations was confidently expected.

The English were agreeably disappointed with the condition of Paris. To their great surprise they found the consular court already arranged, in many particulars, upon the old model of the monarchy, and daily approximating to that example, step by step. Josephine had restored, titles alone excepted, the old language of polite intercourse: Citoyenne had been replaced by Madame; and Citoyen was preparing to make way for Monsieur. The emigrant nobility had flocked back in great numbers; and Buonaparte, dispensing with the awkward services of his aides-de-camp in the interior of the palace, was now attended by chamberlains and other officers of state--chosen for the most part, from the highest families of the monarchy; and who studiously conducted themselves towards the Chief Consul exactly as if the crown of Louis XVI. had descended to him by the ordinary laws of inheritance. Napoleon himself, if we may believe Madame had the weakness to affect, in many trivial matters, a close imitation of what his new attendants reported to have been the personal demeanour of the Bourbon princes. His behaviour as the holder of a court was never graceful. He could not, or would not, control the natural vehemence of his temper, and ever and anon confounded the old race of courtiers, by ebullitions which were better suited to the camp than the saloons of the Tuileries. But whenever he thought fit to converse with a man capable of understanding him, the Consul failed not to create a very lively feeling in his own favour; and, meantime, Josephine was admirably adapted to supply his deficiencies in the management of circles and festivals.

The labour which Napoleon underwent at this period, when he was consolidating the administration throughout France (in every department of which intolerable confusion had arisen during the wars and tumults of the preceding years), excited the astonishment of all who had access to his privacy. He exhausted the energies of secretary after secretary; seemed hardly to feel the want of sleep; and yet sustained the unparalleled fatigue without having recourse to any stimulus stronger than lemonade. Of the many great measures adopted and perfected during this short-lived peace we may notice in particular the following:--

A decree of the senate, dated 26th April, 1802, allowed all emigrants to return to France, provided they chose to do so within a certain space of time, and to pledge allegiance to the consular government; and offered to restore to such persons whatever property of theirs, having been confiscated during the Revolution, still remained at the disposal of the state. From this amnesty about 5000 persons, however, were excepted; these were arranged under five heads, viz.: those who had headed bodies of royalist insurgents; who had served in the armies of the allies; who had belonged to the household of the Bourbons during their exile; who had been agents in stirring up foreign or domestic war; and lastly, generals, admirals, Representatives of the People, who had been banished for treason to the Republic; together with bishops who were obstinate in refusing to accept of the conditions on which the exercise of ecclesiastical functions had been sanctioned by the consuls. The event, in a great measure, justified the prudence of this merciful edict. The far greater part of the emigrants returned, and became peaceful subjects of Napoleon--even although the restoration of forfeited property never took place to anything like the promised extent. He, having yielded back a few princely estates to their rightful lords, was, it is said, made aware, by sufficiently significant behaviour on their parts, that they had now obtained all they wished, and would not in future trouble themselves to merit his favour. Some instances of haughty ingratitude may, very probably, have occurred; but the Consul, in breaking his word with the despoiled emigrants as a body, was preparing for himself dangers greater than those he removed by permitting their return to France.

A still more important measure was that by which the Romish religion was finally re-established as the national faith. The sparing of the Papal dominion after Marengo, and the re-opening of the churches in France, were the preliminaries of the peace, which was, at length, signed on the 18th of September, 1802, between the Pope and the revolutionary government. This famous concordat was the work of Napoleon himself, who seems to have met with more opposition, whenever he touched the matter of religion, than the men of the Revolution, with whom he consulted, thought fit to exhibit on any other occasions whatever. The question was argued one evening, at great length, on the terrace of the garden, at Buonaparte's favourite villa of Malmaison. The Chief Consul avowed himself to be no believer in Christianity;

"But religion," said he, "is a principle which cannot be eradicated from the heart of man." "Who made all that?" he continued, looking up to the heaven, which was clear and starry. "But last Sunday evening I was walking here alone when the church bells of the village of Ruel rung at sunset. I was strongly moved, so vividly did the image of early days come back with that sound. If it be thus with me, what must it be with others? In re-establishing the church, I consult the wishes of the great majority of my people."

Volney, the celebrated traveller, was present. "You speak of the majority of the people," said he: "if that is to be the rule, recall the Bourbons to-morrow." Napoleon never conversed with this bold infidel afterwards.

The concordat gave no satisfaction to the high Catholic party, who considered it as comprehending arrangements wholly unworthy of the dignity of the Pope, and destructive of the authority of the church. The great majority of the nation, however, were wise enough to be contented with conditions which the Vatican had found it necessary to admit. The chief articles were these: I. The Roman Catholic religion is recognised as the national faith. II. The Pope, in concert with the French government, shall make a new division of dioceses, requiring, if necessary, the resignation of any existing prelate. III. Vacant sees now and henceforth shall be filled by the Pope _on nominations by the government_. IV. No bishops shall hold their sees unless they swear allegiance to the government, and adopt a ritual in which prayers are offered up for the Consuls. V. The church livings shall be, like the dioceses, rearranged; and the cur 閣 be appointed by the bishop, but not without the approbation of the government. VI. The French government shall make provision for the prelates and clergy, and the Pope renounces for ever all right to challenge the distribution of church property consequent on the events of the revolutionary period.

The Pope, in acceding to these terms, submitted to "the exigence of the time--which," said his Holiness in the deed itself, "lays its violence even upon us." The most bitter point of execution was that which regarded the bishops-- the great majority of whom were yet in exile. These prelates were summoned to send in, each separately, and within fifteen days, his acceptance of the terms of the concordat, or his resignation of his see. Thus taken by surprise, having no means of consultation, and considering the concordat as fatal to the rights of the church, and the Pope's assent as extorted by mere necessity, almost all of them, to their honour be it said, declined complying with either of these demands. That these bishops should prefer poverty and exile to submission, was not likely to increase the popularity of the concordat with the more devout part of the nation. Meantime, the self-called philosophers looked on with scorn; and the republicans, of every sect, regarded with anger and indignation a course of policy which, as they justly apprehended, provided for the re-establishment of the church, solely because that was considered as the likeliest means of re-establishing the monarchy--in a new dynasty indeed, but with all, or more than all, the old powers.

In moments of spleen Napoleon is known to have sometimes expressed his regret that he should ever have had recourse to this concordat: but at St. Helena, when looking back calmly, he said that it was so needful a measure that had there been no Pope, one ought to have been created for the occasion.

The name of the First Consul was now introduced into the church service at least as often as that of the king had used to be. The cathedral of Notre Dame was prepared for the solemn reception of the concordat. Napoleon appeared there with the state and retinue of a monarch; and in every part of the ceremonial the ancient rules were studiously attended to. The prelate who presided was the same Archbishop of Aix who had preached the coronation sermon of Louis XVI.

It was not easy, however, to procure the attendance of some of the revolutionary generals of the true republican race. Berthier had invited a large party of them long beforehand to breakfast: he carried them from thence to the levee of the Chief Consul, and they found it impossible not to join in the procession. Buonaparte asked one of these persons, after the ceremony was over, what he thought of it? "It was a true Capucinade" was the answer. To another of these, whom he thought less sincere, he said with a smile, "Things, you see, are returning to the old order." "Yes," the veteran replied, "all returns--all but the two millions of Frenchmen who have died for the sake of destroying the very system which you are now rebuilding." These officers are said to have paid dearly for their uncourtly language. Moreau was not to be tampered with by Berthier. The Chief Consul personally invited him to be present at the Te Deum in Notre Dame, to attend afterwards at the consecration of some colours, and, lastly, to dine at the Tuileries. Moreau answered, "I accept the last part of your invitation."

A third great measure, adopted about the same period, was received with unqualified applause. This was the establishment of a national system of education, the necessity of which had been much felt, since the old universities and schools under the management of the clergy had been broken up amidst the first violence of the Revolution. The Polytechnic School, established under the direction of Monge, dates from this epoch; and furnished France, in the sequel, with a long train of eminent men for every department of the public service.

It was now also that the Chief Consul commenced the great task of providing France with an uniform code of laws. He himself took constantly an earnest share in the deliberations of the jurists, who were employed in this gigantic undertaking; and astonished them by the admirable observations which his native sagacity suggested, in relation to matters commonly considered as wholly out of the reach of unprofessional persons. But of the new code we shall have occasion to speak hereafter.

Buonaparte at this period devised, and began to put into execution, innumerable public works of the highest utility. The inland navigation of Languedoc was to be made complete: a great canal between the Yonne and the Saonne was begun, for the purpose of creating a perfect water communication quite across the republican dominion--from Marseilles to Amsterdam. Numberless bridges, roads, museums, were planned; and the vain were flattered with rising monuments of magnificence, while the wise recognised in every such display the depths and forecast of a genius made for empire.

Thus far the measures of the Consulate may be said to have carried with them the approbation of all but a few individuals. They were accompanied or followed by proceedings, some of which roused, or strengthened and confirmed, sentiments of a very different description among various important classes of the French community; while others were well calculated to revive the suspicion of all the neighbouring nations.

It is said that the first idea of the Legion of Honour arose in the breast of Napoleon on witnessing one day, from a window at the Tuileries, the admiration with which the crowd before the palace regarded the stars and crosses worn by the Marquis Lucchesini, ambassador of Prussia, as he descended from his carriage. The republican members of the senate could not be persuaded that the institution of an order, with insignia, was anything but the first step to the creation of a new body of nobility; and they resisted the proposed measure with considerable pertinacity. On this head, as on that of the concordat with the Pope, the Consul condescended to enter personally into discussion with the chief persons who differed from his opinion, or suspected his intentions; and if any, who heard his language on this occasion, doubted that both nobility and monarchy were designed to follow hard behind the Legion of Honour, they must have been singularly slow of understanding. Berthier had called ribbons and crosses "the playthings of monarchy," and cited the Romans of old as "having no system of honorary rewards." "They are always talking to us of the Romans," said Buonaparte. "The Romans had patricians, knights, citizens, and slaves:--for each class different dresses and different manners--honorary recompenses for every species of merit--mural crowns--civic crowns--ovations--triumphs--titles. When the noble band of patricians lost its influence, Rome fell to pieces--the people were vile rabble. It was then that you saw the fury of Marius, the proscriptions of Sylla, and afterwards of the emperors. In like manner Brutus is talked of as the enemy of tyrants: he was an aristocrat, who stabbed Caesar, because Caesar wished to lower the authority of the noble senate. You talk of child's rattles--be it so: it is with such rattles that men are led. I would not say that to the multitude; but in a council of statesmen one may speak the truth. I do not believe that the French people love liberty and equality. Their character has not been changed in ten years: they are still what their ancestors, the Gauls, were--vain and light. They are susceptible but of one sentiment--honour. It is right to afford nourishment to this sentiment: and to allow of distinctions. Observe how the people bow before the decorations of foreigners. Voltaire calls the common soldiers Alexanders at five sous a day. He was right: it is just so. Do you imagine that you can make men fight by reasoning? Never. You must bribe them with glory, distinctions, rewards. To come to the point: during ten years there has been a talk of institutions. Where are they? All has been overturned: our business is to build up. There is a government with certain powers: as to all the rest of the nation what is it but grains of sand? Before the Republic can be definitely established, we must, as a foundation, cast some blocks of granite on the soil of France. In fine, it is agreed that we have need of some kind of institutions. If this Legion of Honour is not approved, let some other be suggested. I do not pretend that it alone will save the state; but it will do its part." Such were the words of Napoleon when the scheme was in preparation. Many years afterwards, in his exile at St. Helena, he thus spoke of his Order. "It was the reversion of every one who was an honour to his country, stood at the head of his profession, and contributed to the national prosperity and glory. Some were dissatisfied because the decoration was alike for officers and soldiers; others because it was given to civil and military merit indiscriminately. But if ever it cease to be the recompense of the brave private, or be confined to soldiers alone, it will cease to be the Legion of Honour."

On the 15th of May, 1802, the Legion of Honour was formally instituted; large national domains were set apart for its maintenance; and crosses (each of which entitled the bearer to certain precedence and a pension) widely distributed among the soldiery, and among citizens of almost all professions.

The personal authority of the future emperor, meantime, was daily widening and strengthening. After the Consulate was established in France, some corresponding change in the government of the Cisalpine Republic was judged necessary, and Napoleon took care that it should be so conducted as to give himself not only permanent, but wholly independent, power beyond the Alps. A convention of 450 Italian deputies was summoned to meet at Lyons; and there Talleyrand was ready to dictate the terms of a new constitution, by which the executive functions were to be lodged in a president and vice-president, the legislative in a council chosen from three electoral colleges. It was next proposed that Buonaparte should be invited to take on him the office of president--Buonaparte, it was studiously explained, not as Chief Consul of France, but in his own individual capacity. He repaired to Lyons in person, and having harangued the convention in the Italian tongue, assumed the dignity thus conferred on him on the 2nd of January, 1802.

The next step was to prolong the period of his French Consulate. Chabot de L'Allier, his creature, moved in the Tribunate that the Conservative Senate should be requested to mark the national feelings of gratitude by conferring some new honour on Napoleon. The Senate proposed accordingly that he should be declared Consul for a second period of ten years, to commence on the expiration of his present magistracy. He thanked them; but said he could not accept of any such prolongation of his power except from the suffrages of the people. To the people the matter was to be referred; but the Second and Third Consuls, in preparing the edict of the Senate for public inspection and ratification, were instructed by their master-colleague to introduce an important change in its terms. The question which they sent down was, "Shall Buonaparte be Chief Consul for life?" No mention was made of ten years. Books were opened as on a former occasion: the officers of government in the departments well knew in what method to conduct the business, and the voice of the nation was declared to be in favour of the decree. Some few hundreds of sturdy republicans alone recorded their opposition; and Carnot, who headed them, said he well knew he was signing his own sentence of exile. But Napoleon was strong enough to dispense with any such severities; Carnot remained in safety, but out of office, until, many years afterwards, his services were tendered and accepted on the entrance of foreign invaders into France. Buonaparte was proclaimed Consul for life on the 2nd of August.

Shortly afterwards, in the committee occupied with the Code, Napoleon entered upon a long disquisition in favour of the Roman law of adoption; urging with intrepid logic, that an heir so chosen ought to be even dearer than a son. The object of this harangue was not difficult of detection. Napoleon had no longer any hope of having children by Josephine; and meditated the adoption of one of his brother's sons as his heir. In the course of the autumn a simple edict of the Conservative Senate authorised him to appoint his successor in the consulate by a testamentary deed. By this act (Aug. 4, 1802) a new dynasty was called to the throne of France. The farce of opening books in the departments was dispensed with. Henceforth the words "_Liberty, Equality, Sovereignty of the People_," disappeared from the state papers and official documents of the government--nor did the change attract much notice. The nation had a master, and sate by, indifferent speculators, while he, under whose sway life and property were considered safe, disposed of political rights and privileges according to his pleasure.[42]

This year was distinguished by events of another order, and not likely to be contemplated with indifference by the powers of Europe. After the peace of Amiens was ratified, certain treaties which the Chief Consul had concluded with Turkey, Spain, and Portugal, and hitherto kept profoundly secret, were made known. The Porte, it now appeared, had yielded to France all the privileges of commerce which that government had ever conceded to the most favoured nations. Spain had agreed that Parma, after the death of the reigning prince, should be added to the dominions of France: and Portugal had actually ceded her province in Guyana. In every quarter of the world the grasping ambition of Buonaparte seemed to have found some prey.

Nearer him, in the meantime, he had been preparing to strike a blow at the independence of Switzerland, and virtually unite that country also to his empire. The contracting parties in the treaty of Luneville had guaranteed the independence of the Helvetic Republic, and the unquestionable right of the Swiss to settle their government in what form they pleased. There were two parties there as elsewhere--one who desired the full re-establishment of the old federative constitution--another who preferred the model of the French Republic "one and indivisible." To the former party the small mountain cantons adhered--the wealthier and aristocratic cantons to the latter. Their disputes at last swelled into civil war--and the party who preferred the old constitution, being headed by the gallant Aloys Reding, were generally successful. Napoleon, who had fomented their quarrel, now, unasked and unexpected, assumed to himself the character of arbiter between the contending parties. He addressed a letter to the eighteen cantons, in which these words occur:--"Your history shows that your intestine wars cannot be terminated, except through the intervention of France. I had, it is true, resolved not to intermeddle in your affairs--but I cannot remain insensible to the distress of which I see you the prey--I recall my resolution of neutrality--I consent to be the mediator in your differences." Rapp, adjutant-general, was the bearer of this insolent manifesto. To cut short all discussion, Ney entered Switzerland at the head of 40,000 troops. Resistance was hopeless. Aloys Reding dismissed his brave followers, was arrested, and imprisoned in the castle of Aarburg. The government was arranged according to the good pleasure of Napoleon, who henceforth added to his other titles that of "Grand Mediator of the Helvetic Republic." Switzerland was, in effect, degraded into a province of France; and became bound to maintain an army of 16,000 men, who were to be at the disposal, whenever it should please him to require their aid, of the Grand Mediator. England sent an envoy to remonstrate against this signal and unprovoked rapacity: but the other powers suffered it to pass without any formal opposition. The sufferings, however, of Aloys Reding and his brave associates, and this audacious crushing-down of the old spirit of Swiss freedom and independence, were heard of throughout all Europe with deep indignation.

Feelings of the same kind were nourished everywhere by the results of an expedition which Buonaparte sent, before the close of 1801, to St. Domingo, for the purpose of reconquering that island to France. The black and coloured population had risen, at the revolutionary period, upon their white masters, and, after scenes of terrible slaughter and devastation, emancipated themselves. The chief authority was, by degrees, vested in Toussaint L'Ouverture, a negro, who, during the war, displayed the ferocity of a barbarian, but after its conclusion, won the applause and admiration of all men by the wisdom and humanity of his administration. Conscious that, whenever peace should be restored in Europe, France would make efforts to recover her richest colony, Toussaint adopted measures likely to conciliate the exiled planters and the government of the mother country. A constitution on the consular model was established, Toussaint being its Buonaparte: the supremacy of France was to be acknowledged to a certain extent; and the white proprietors were to receive half the produce of the lands of which the insurgents had taken possession. But Napoleon heard of all these arrangements with displeasure and contempt. He fitted out a numerous fleet, carrying an army full 20,000 strong, under the orders of General Leclerc, the husband of his own favourite sister Pauline. It has often been said, and without contradiction, that the soldiers sent on this errand were chiefly from the army of the Rhine, whose good-will to the Consul was to be doubted. Leclerc summoned Toussaint (Jan. 2, 1802) to surrender, in a letter which conveyed expressions of much personal respect from Buonaparte. The negro chief, justly apprehending insincerity, stood out and defended himself gallantly for a brief space; but stronghold after stronghold yielded to numbers and discipline; and at length he too submitted, on condition that he should be permitted to retire in safety to his plantation. Some obscure rumours of incurroction were soon made the pretext for arresting him, and he, being put on board ship, and sent to France, was shut up in a dungeon, where either the midnight cord or dagger, or the wasting influence of confinement and hopeless misery, ere long put an end to his life. His mysterious fate, both before and after its consummation, excited great interest.[43] The atrocious cruelty of the French soldiery, in their subjugation of St. Domingo, equalled (it could not have surpassed) that of the barbarous negroes whom they opposed; but was heard of with disgust and horror, such as no excesses of mere savages could have excited. As if Heaven had been moved by these bloody deeds of vengeance, disease broke out in the camp; thousands, and among them Leclerc himself, died. For the time, however, the French armament triumphed--and, in the exultation of victory, the government at home had the extreme and seemingly purposeless ungenerosity, to publish an edict banishing all of the negro race from their European dominions.[44] But the yellow fever was already rapidly consuming the French army in St. Domingo; and its feeble remnant, under Rochambeau, having been at length expelled, in November, 1803, the independence of Hayti was formally proclaimed on the 1st of January, 1804.

The course of Napoleon's conduct, in and out of Europe, was calculated to fill all independent neighbours with new or aggravated suspicion; and in England, where public opinion possesses the largest means of making itself heard, and consequently the greatest power, the prevalence of such feelings became, from day to day, more marked. The British envoy's reclamation against the oppression of Switzerland, was but one of many drops, which were soon to cause the cup of bitterness to overflow. As in most quarrels, there was something both of right and of wrong on either side. When the English government remonstrated against any of those daring invasions of the rights of independent nations, or crafty enlargements, through diplomatic means, of the power of France, by which this period of peace was distinguished, the Chief Consul could always reply that the cabinet of St. James's, on their part, had not yet fulfilled one article of the treaty of Amiens, by placing Malta in the keeping of some power which had been neutral in the preceding war. The rejoinder was obvious: to wit, that Napoleon was every day taking measures wholly inconsistent with that balance of power which the treaty of Amiens contemplated. It is not to be denied that he, in his audaciously ambitious movements, had contrived to keep within the strict terms of the treaty: and it can as little be disputed that the English cabinet had equity with them, although they violated the letter of the law, in their retention of the inheritance of the worthless and self-betrayed Knights of St. John.

The feelings of the rival nations, however, were soon kindled into rage; and, on either side of the Channel the language of the public prints assumed a complexion of even more bitter violence than had been observable during the war. The English journalists resorted to foul, and often false and even absurd, personal criminations of the Chief Consul: and the Parisian newspapers replied in language equally indefensible on the score of truth and decency, but with this most essential difference, that whereas the press of England was free, that of France, being entirely under the control of Foucheand the police, could not, as all men knew, put forth any such calumnies otherwise than with the consent of the consular government. When Napoleon complained to the English ministers, their answer was obvious: "Our courts of law are open--we are ourselves accustomed to be abused as you are, and in them we, like you, have our only resource." The paragraphs in the Moniteur, on the other hand, were, it was impossible to deny, virtually so many manifestoes of the Tuileries.

Of all the popular engines which moved the spleen of Napoleon, the most offensive was a newspaper (L'Ambigu) published in the French language, in London, by one Peltier, a royalist emigrant; and, in spite of all the advice which could be offered, he at length condescended to prosecute the author in the English courts of law. M. Peltier had the good fortune to retain, as his counsel, Mr. Mackintosh,[45] an advocate of most brilliant talents, and, moreover, especially distinguished for his support of the original principles of the French Revolution. On the trial which ensued, this orator, in defence of his client, delivered a philippic against the personal character and ambitious measures of Napoleon, immeasurably more calculated to injure the Chief Consul in public opinion throughout Europe, than all the efforts of a thousand newspapers; and, though the jury found Peltier guilty of libel, the result was, on the whole, a signal triumph to the party of whom he had been the organ.

This was a most imprudent, as well as undignified proceeding; but ere the defendant, Peltier, could be called up for judgment, the doubtful relations of the Chief Consul and the cabinet of St. James's were to assume a different appearance. The truce of St. Amiens already approached its close. Buonaparte had, perhaps, some right to complain of the unbridled abuse of the British press: but the British government had a far more serious cause of reclamation against him. Under pretence of establishing French consuls for the protection of commerce, he sent persons, chiefly of the military profession, who carried orders to make exact plans of all the harbours and coasts of the United Kingdom. These gentlemen endeavoured to execute their commission with all possible privacy; but the discovery of their occupation was soon made; they were sent back to France without ceremony; and this treacherous measure of their government was openly denounced as a violation of every rule of international law, and a plain symptom of warlike preparation.

Ere hostilities were renewed, Buonaparte employed M. Meyer, president of the regency of Warsaw, to open a negotiation with the head of the House of Bourbon, then resident in Poland. He proposed that Louis should execute a formal deed resigning for himself and his family all pretensions to the throne of France, and offered in return to put the Bourbon princes in possession of independent dominions in Italy. The heir of the French kings answered in language worthy of his birth: "I do not confound Monsieur Buonaparte," said he, "with those who have preceded him. I esteem his bravery and military genius, and I owe him goodwill for many of the acts of his government--for benefits done to my people I will always consider as done to me. But he is mistaken if he supposes that my rights can ever be made the subject of bargain and compromise. Could they have been called in question, this very application would have established them. What the designs of God may be for me and my house I know not; but of the duties imposed on me by the rank in which it was His pleasure I should be born, I am not wholly ignorant. As a Christian, I will perform those duties while life remains. As a descendant of St. Louis, I will know how to respect myself, were I in fetters. As the successor of Francis the First, I will, at least, say with him--'all is lost except honour.'"

Such is the account of the Bourbon princes. Buonaparte utterly denied having given any authority for such a negotiation; and added, that in doing so he should have played the part of a madman, since any application to Louis must have been an admission that his own authority in France was imperfect in title. It is obvious that the Consul would have acted most imprudently in avowing such an attempt--after it had proved unsuccessful; but the veracity of the exiled king lies under no suspicion; nor is it easy to believe that Meyer would have dared to open such a negotiation without sufficient authority from Napoleon. Hitherto he had betrayed no symptom of personal malevolence towards the House of Bourbon--but henceforth the autocrat, insulted as he thought in the style of "Monsieur Buonaparte," appears to have meditated some signal act of revenge.

He resented the refusal of Louis the more because he doubted not that that prince well understood how little the great powers of Europe were disposed to regard, with favourable eyes, the establishment of the Buonapartes as a new dynasty in France. He suspected, in a word, that his recent disputes with the cabinet of St. James's, had inspired new hopes into the breasts of the exile family.

It was at this period that Napoleon published, in the Moniteur, a long memorial, drawn up by General Sebastiani, who had just returned from a mission to the Levant, abounding in statements, and clothed in language, such as could have had no other object but to inflame the government of England to extremity. Sebastiani detailed the incidents of his journey at great length, representing himself as having been everywhere received with honour, and even with enthusiasm, as the envoy of Napoleon. Such, he said, were the dispositions of the Mussulmans, that 6000 French would now suffice to restore Egypt to the republic; and it was in vain that General Stuart, who represented the English king in that country, had endeavoured to excite the Turkish government to assassinate him, Sebastiani. Lastly, the report asserted, that the Ionian Islands would, on the first favourable occasion, declare themselves French.

The English government reclaimed against this publication, as at once a confession of the dangerous ambition of Buonaparte, and a studied insult to them, whose representative's character and honour one of its chief statements must have been designed to destroy, at a wilful sacrifice of truth. The French minister replied, that the Chief Consul had as much right to complain of the recent publication of Sir Robert Wilson's Narrative of the English Expedition to Egypt, which contained statements in the highest degree injurious to his character and honour;[46] and had, nevertheless, been dedicated by permission to the Duke of York. The obvious answer, namely, that Sir Robert Wilson's book was the work of a private individual, and published solely on his own responsibility, whereas Sebastiani's was a public document set forth by an official organ, was treated as a wanton and insolent evasion. Meanwhile the language of the press on either side became from day to day more virulently offensive; and various members of the British Parliament, of opposite parties, and of the highest eminence, did not hesitate to rival the newspapers in their broad denunciations of the restless and insatiable ambition of the Chief Consul.--"Buonaparte," said Mr. Wyndham, "is the Hannibal who has sworn to devote his life to the destruction of England. War cannot be far off, and I believe it would be much safer to anticipate the blow than to expect it. I would advise ministers to appeal to the high-minded and proud of heart--whether they succeed or not, we shall not then go down like the Augustuli." "The destruction of this country," said Mr. Sheridan, "is the first vision that breaks on the French Consul through the gleam of the morning: this is his last prayer at night, to whatever deity he may address it, whether to Jupiter or to Mahomet, to the Goddess of Battles or the Goddess of Reason. Look at the map of Europe, from which France was said to be expunged, and now see nothing but France. If the ambition of Buonaparte be immeasurable, there are abundant reasons why it should be progressive."

Stung to the quick by these continual invectives, Napoleon so far descended from his dignity as to make them the subject of personal complaint and reproach to the English Ambassador. He obtruded himself on the department of Talleyrand, and attempted to shake the resolution of the ambassador, Lord Whitworth, by a display of rude violence, such as had, indeed, succeeded with the Austrian envoy at Campo-Formio, but which produced no effect whatever in the case of this calm and high-spirited nobleman. The first of their conferences took place in February, when the Consul harangued Lord Whitworth for nearly two hours, hardly permitting him to interpose a word on the other side of the question. "Every gale that blows from England is burdened with enmity," said he; "your government countenances Georges, Pichegru, and other infamous men, who have sworn to assassinate me. Your journals slander me, and the redress I am offered is but adding mockery to insult. I could make myself master of Egypt to-morrow, if I pleased. _Egypt, indeed, must sooner or later belong to France_; but I have no wish to go to war for such a trivial object. What could I gain by war? Invasion would be my only means of annoying you; and invasion you shall have, if war be forced on me--but I confess the chances would be an hundred to one against me in such an attempt. In ten years I could not hope to have a fleet able to dispute the seas with you: but, on the other hand, the army of France could be recruited in a few weeks to 480,000 men. United, we might govern the world:--Why can we not understand each other?" Lord Whitworth could not but observe the meaning of these hints, and answered, as became him, that the King of England had no wish but to preserve his own rights, and scorned the thought of becoming a partner with France in a general scheme of spoliation and oppression. They parted with cold civility, and negotiations were resumed in the usual manner: but England stood firm in the refusal to give up Malta--at least for ten years to come. The aggressions of Napoleon had wholly changed the arrangement of territory and power contemplated when the treaty of Amiens was drawn up; what security could there be for the retention of Malta by Naples, or any such minor power, if Buonaparte wished to have it? To surrender it would in fact be to yield an impregnable harbour and citadel in the heart of the Levant, to a government which had gone on trampling down the independence of state after state in the west. Meanwhile the English government openly announced, in Parliament, that the position of affairs seemed to be full of alarm--that the French were manning fleets and recruiting their armies, and that it was necessary to have recourse to similar measures; and, accordingly, a considerable addition to the military establishment was agreed to.

Thus stood matters on the 13th of March, when Lord Whitworth made his appearance at the levee of the Chief Consul, in company with all the rest of the diplomatic body. Napoleon no sooner entered, than, fixing his eye on the English Ambassador, he exclaimed aloud and fiercely, in presence of the circle, "You are then determined on war!" Lord Whitworth denied the charge, but the Consul drowned his voice, and pursued thus:--"We have been at war for fifteen years--you are resolved to have fifteen years more of it--you force me to it." He then turned to the other ministers, and said, in the same violent tone: "The English wish for war; but if they draw the sword first, I will be the last to sheath it again. They do not respect treaties--henceforth we must cover them with black crape." Then, turning again to Whitworth, "To what purpose," he cried, "are these armaments? If you arm, I will arm too; if you fight, I can fight also. You may destroy France, but you cannot intimidate her." "We desire neither to injure nor to alarm her, but to live on terms of good intelligence," said Lord Whitworth. "Respect treaties, then," said Napoleon; "woe to those by whom they are not respected!--they shall be responsible to Europe for the result." He repeated these last words sternly, and immediately quitted the apartment, leaving the assembled ministers utterly confounded by this indecent display of violence.

Some persons, who knew Buonaparte well, have always asserted that this undignified scene was got up with calm premeditation, and that the ferocity of passion on the occasion was a mere piece of acting. Lord Whitworth, however, was an excellent judge of men and manners, and he never doubted that the haughty soldier yielded to the uncontrollable vehemence of wrath. The cautious Talleyrand made various efforts to explain away the intemperate words of his master; but they, and the tone in which they had been uttered, went far to increase the jealousy and animosity of the English government and nation, and to revive or confirm the suspicion with which the other powers of Europe had had but too much reason to regard the career of revolutionary France.

On the 18th of May Great Britain declared war. Orders had previously been given for seizing French shipping wherever it could be found, and it is said that 200 vessels, containing property to the amount of three millions sterling, had been laid hold of accordingly, ere the proclamation of hostilities reached Paris. Whether the practice of thus unceremoniously seizing private property, under such circumstances, be right on abstract principle, or wrong, there can be no doubt that the custom had been long established, acted upon by England on all similar occasions, and of course considered, after the lapse of ages, and the acquiescence of innumerable treaties, as part and parcel of the European system of warfare. This was not denied by Napoleon; but he saw the opportunity, and determined to profit by it, of exciting the jealousy of other governments, by reclaiming against the exercise, on the part of England, of a species of assault which England, from her maritime predominance, has more temptations and better means to adopt than any other power. He resolved, therefore, to retaliate by a wholly unprecedented outrage. The very night that the resolution of the cabinet of St. James's reached Paris, orders were given for arresting the persons of all English subjects residing or travelling within the dominion of France.

Not less than 10,000 persons, chiefly of course of the higher classes of society, thus found themselves condemned to captivity in a hostile land. Had Napoleon adopted less violent measures, his reclamations against the English government might have been favourably attended to throughout Europe. But this despotic and unparalleled infliction of exile and misery on a host of innocent private individuals, was productive of far different effects. It moved universal sympathy, indignation, and disgust.

[Footnote 42: See Wordsworth's verses, "written at Calais the 15th Aug. 1802," in which the indifference of the people is contrasted with their enthusiasm in the early days of the Revolution.

"Festivals have I seen that were not names:-- This is young Buonaparte's natal day; And his is henceforth an established sway, Consul for life. With worship France proclaims Her approbation, and with pomps and games Heaven grant that other cities may be gay! Calais is not: and I have bent my way To the sea coast, noting that each man frames His business as he likes. Another time That was, when I was here long years ago, The senselessness of joy was then sublime!" &c.]

[Footnote 43: Witness, among other evidences, the noble sonnet of Wordsworth:--

"TOUSSAINT, the most unhappy Man of Men! Whether the all-cheering sun be free to shed His beams around thee, or thou rest thy head Pillowed in some dark dungeon's noisome den O, miserable chieftain! where and when Wilt thou find patience! Yet die not; do thou Wear rather in thy bonds a cheerful brow: Though fallen Thyself, never to rise again, Live and take comfort. Thou hast left behind Powers that will work for thee--Air, Earth, and Skies; There's not a breathing of the common Wind That will forget thee; thou hast great Allies; Thy friends are Exultations, Agonies, And Love, and Man's unconquerable Mind."]

[Footnote 44: See Wordsworth's sonnet, "22nd Sept. 1802."

"We had a fellow-passenger who came From Calais with us, gaudy in array,-- A Negro Woman like a Lady gay, Yet silent as a woman fearing blame; Dejected, meek, yet pitiably tame, She sate, from notice turning not away, But on our proffered kindness still did lay A weight of languid speech, or at the same Was silent, motionless in eyes and face, She was a Negro Woman, driven from France-- Rejected, like all others of that race, Not one of whom may now find footing there; Thus the poor outcast did to us declare, Nor murmured at the unfeeling Ordinance."]

[Footnote 45: Afterwards Sir James.]

[Footnote 46: It was by this book that the two dark stories of Jaffa were first promulgated through Europe: and it is proper to add, that Sir R. Wilson publicly presented a copy to George III. at his levee.]

CHAPTER XVIII

Recommencement of the War--French seize Hanover and Naples--the English seize various French colonies--Scheme of invading England resumed--Moreau--Pichegru--Georges Cadoudal--Captain Wright--Murder of the Duke d'Enghien--Napoleon Emperor of France--King of Italy--Genoa united to the Empire.

The war was re-opened vigorously on both sides. The English fleets rapidly reconquered various colonies surrendered back to France by the treaty of Amiens, and assisted in compelling the dwindled army which Leclerc had commanded to evacuate St. Domingo. Buonaparte, on the other hand, despised utterly the distinction between the British Empire and Hanover--a possession indeed of the same prince, but totally unconnected with the English Constitution, and, as belonging to the Germanic Empire, entitled, if it chose, to remain neutral--and having first marched an army into Holland, ordered Mortier, its chief, to advance without ceremony and seize the Electorate. At the same time, and with the same pretext, French troops poured into the South of Italy, and occupied Naples.

General Mortier's appearance on the Hanoverian frontier was such as to satisfy the Duke of Cambridge, governor for the Elector, that resistance was hopeless. He entered into a negotiation (May, 1803), by which the territory was to be surrendered, provided his army were permitted to retire unbroken behind the Elbe, pledging themselves not to take the field again against France during this war. But the ministers of George III. advised him not to ratify this treaty. Mortier demanded of General Walmsloden, commander-in-chief of the Hanoverian army, to surrender his arms--or abide the consequences of being attacked beyond the Elbe--and that fine body of men was accordingly disarmed and disbanded. The cavalry, being ordered to dismount and yield their horses to the French, there ensued a scene which moved the sympathy of the invading soldiery themselves. The strong attachment between the German dragoon and his horse is well known; and this parting was more like that of dear kindred than of man and beast.

The emperor, whose duty it was, as head of the German body, to reclaim against this invasion of its territory, was obliged to put up with the Consul's explanation, viz. that he had no wish to make the conquest of Hanover, but merely to hold it until England should see the necessity of fulfilling the

Maltese article in the treaty of Amiens. Prussia, alarmed by the near neigbourhood of Mortier, hardly dared to remonstrate. Denmark alone showed any symptom of active resentment. She marched 30,000 men into her German provinces; but finding that Austria and Prussia were resolved to be quiescent, was fain to offer explanations, and recall her troops. The French General, meantime, scourged Hanover by his exactions, and even, without the shadow of a pretext, levied heavy contributions in Bremen, Hamburg, and the other Hansetowns in the vicinity of the Electorate.

These successes enabled Napoleon to feed great bodies of his army at the expense of others, and to cripple the commerce of England, by shutting up her communication with many of the best markets on the continent. But he now recurred to his favourite scheme, that of invading the island itself, and so striking the fatal blow at the heart of his last and greatest enemy. Troops to the amount of 160,000, were mustered in camps along the French and Dutch coasts, and vast flotillas, meant to convey them across the Channel, were formed, and constantly manoeuvred in various ports, that of Boulogne being the chief station.

The spirit of England, on the other hand, was effectually stirred. Her fleets, to the amount of not less than 500 ships of war, traversed the seas in all directions, blockaded the harbours of the countries in which the power of the Consul was predominant, and from time to time made inroads into the French ports, cutting out and destroying the shipping, and crippling the flotillas. At home the army, both regular and irregular, was recruited and strengthened to an unexampled extent. Camps were formed along the English coasts opposite to France, and the King in person was continually to be seen in the middle of them. By night beacons blazed on every hill-top throughout the island, and the high resolution of the citizen-soldiery was attested, on numberless occasions of false alarm, by the alacrity with which they marched on the points of supposed danger.[47] There never was a time in which the national enthusiasm was more ardent and concentrated; and the return of Pitt to the prime-ministry (March, 1804) was considered as the last and best pledge that the councils of the sovereign were to exhibit vigour commensurate with the nature of the crisis. The regular army in Britain amounted, ere long, to 100,000; the militia to 80,000; and of volunteer troops there were not less than 350,000 in arms.

Soult, Ney, Davoust, and Victor were in command of the army designed to invade England, and the Chief Consul personally repaired to Boulogne, and inspected both the troops and the flotilla. He constantly gave out that it was his fixed purpose to make his attempt by means of the flotilla alone; but while he thus endeavoured to inspire his enemy with false security (for Nelson had declared this scheme of a boat invasion to be mad, and staked his whole reputation on its miserable and immediate failure, if attempted), the Consul was in fact providing indefatigably a fleet of men-of-war, designed to protect and cover the voyage. These ships were preparing in different ports of France and Spain, to the number of fifty; Buonaparte intended them to steal out to sea individually or in small squadrons, rendezvous at Martinico, and, returning thence in a body, sweep the Channel free of the English for such a space of time at least as might suffice for the execution of his great purpose. These designs, however, were from day to day thwarted by the watchful zeal of Nelson and the other English admirals; who observed Brest, Toulon, Genoa, and the harbours of Spain so closely, that no squadron, nor hardly a single vessel, could force a passage to the Atlantic.

Napoleon persisted to the end of his life in asserting his belief that the invasion of England was prevented merely by a few unforeseen accidents, and that, had his generals passed the sea, they must have been successful. The accidents to which he attributed so much influence, were, it is to be supposed, the presence and zeal of Nelson, Pellew, Cornwallis, and their respective fleets of observation. As for the results of the expedition, if the Channel had once been crossed--Napoleon never seemed to doubt that a single great battle would have sufficed to place London in his hands. Once arrived in the capital, he would, he said, have summoned a convention, restored the mass of the English people to their proper share of political power,--in a word, banished the King, and revolutionised England on the model of France: the meaning of all which is--reduced this island to be a province of the French empire, and yet bestowed upon its people all those rights and liberties of which he had already removed the last shadow, wherever his own power was established on the continent.

There can be little doubt that Napoleon egregiously underrated the resistance which would have been opposed to his army, had it effected the voyage in safety, by the spirit of the British people, and the great natural difficulties of the country through which the invaders must have marched.

Nevertheless, it is not to be denied that, had the attempt been made instantly on the rupture of the peace, the chances of success might have been considerable--of success, temporary and short-lived indeed, but still sufficient to inflict a terrible injury upon this country--to bathe her soil in blood--to give her capital to the flames--and not impossibly to shake some of her institutions. The enemy himself was, in all likelihood, unprepared to make the attempt, until England had had time to make adequate preparation for its encounter. It was otherwise ordered of God's providence, than that the last bulwark of liberty should have to sustain the shock of battle at its own gates.

The invasion of England was the great object of attention throughout Europe during the autumn and winter of 1803. Early in the succeeding year Paris itself became the theatre of a series of transactions which for a time engrossed the public mind.

Even before Buonaparte proclaimed himself Consul for life, it appears that, throughout a considerable part of the French army, strong symptoms of jealousy had been excited by the rapidity of his advance to sovereign power. After the monarchy of France was in effect re-established in him and his dynasty, by the decrees of the 2nd and 4th of August, 1802, this spirit of dissatisfaction showed itself much more openly; and ere long it was generally believed that the republican party in the army looked up to Moreau as their head, and awaited only some favourable opportunity for rising in arms against Napoleon's tyranny. Moreau was known to have treated both the Concordat and the Legion of Honour with undisguised contempt; and Buonaparte's strictures on his conduct of the campaign of 1801 were not likely to have nourished feelings of personal goodwill in the bosom of him whom all considered as second only to the Chief Consul himself in military genius. It has already been intimated that the army of the Rhine had been all along suspected of regarding Napoleon with little favour. He had never been their general; neither they nor their chiefs had partaken in the plunder of Italy, or in the glory of the battles by which it was won. It was from their ranks that the unhappy expedition under Leclerc had been chiefly furnished, and they considered their employment in that unwholesome climate as dictated, more by the Consul's doubts of their fidelity to himself, than his high appreciation of their discipline and gallantry. How far Pichegru, while corresponding with the Bourbons as head of the army of the Rhine, had intrigued among his own soldiery, no evidence has as yet appeared. But after

Pichegru's banishment, Moreau possessed the chief sway over the minds of one great division of the armed force of the Republic.

Carnot, meantime, and other genuine republicans in the legislative bodies, had been occupied with the endeavour, since they could not prevent Napoleon from sitting on the throne of France, to organise at least something like a constitutional opposition (such as exists in the Parliament of England) whereby the measures of his government might be, to a certain extent, controlled and modified. The creation of the Legion of Honour, the decree enabling Buonaparte to appoint his successor, and other leading measures, had accordingly been carried through far less triumphantly than could be agreeable to the self-love of the autocrat.

On the other hand, the return of so many emigrants--(a great part of whom, not receiving back the property promised to them, were disappointed and aggrieved anew)--could not fail to strengthen the influence of the royalists in the private society of Paris; and by degrees, as has often happened in the history of parties, the leaders of the republicans and those of the Bourbonists came together, sinking for the time the peculiar principles of either side, in the common feeling of hatred to Napoleon.

Pichegru returned from his exile at Cayenne, and after spending some time in England, where he, no doubt, communicated with the Bourbon princes, and with some members of Mr. Addington's government, passed over secretly into France. Georges Cadoudal and other Chouan chiefs were busy in stirring up their old adherents, and communicated with Pichegru on his arrival in Paris.

Suddenly, on the 12th of February, Paris was surprised with the announcement, that a new conspiracy against the life of the Chief Consul had been discovered by the confession of an accomplice; that 150 men had meant to assemble at Malmaison in the uniform of the consular guard, and seize Buonaparte while hunting; that Georges, the Chouan, had escaped by a quarter of an hour--but that Mairn, La Jollais, and other leaders of the conspiracy had been taken; finally, that Moreau had held various conferences with Georges, La Jollais and Pichegru, and that he also was under arrest.

It is said that Georges Cadoudal had once actually penetrated into the chamber of Napoleon at the Tuileries, and been prevented by the merest accident from assassinating him: others of the conspirators had approached his person very nearly on pretext of presenting petitions. Buonaparte attributed his escape chiefly to the irregular mode of living which his multifarious occupations involved; he seldom dined two days following at the same hour, hardly ever stirred out of the palace except with his attendants about him for some review or public ceremony, and perhaps never appeared unguarded except where his appearance must have been totally unexpected. The officer who betrayed Cadoudal and his associates, was, it seems, a violent republican, and as such desired the downfall of the Consul; but he had also served under Napoleon, and learning at a late hour that the life of his old leader was to be sacrificed, remonstrated vehemently, and rather than be accessary to such extremities, gave the necessary information at the Tuileries. Moreau was forthwith arrested; but Pichegru lurked undiscovered in the heart of Paris until the 28th; six gens-d'armes then came upon his privacy so abruptly that he could not use either his dagger or pistols, though both were on his table. He wrestled for a moment, and then attempted to move compassion--but was immediately fettered. Shortly after Cadoudal himself, who had for days traversed Paris in cabriolets, not knowing where to lay his head, was detected while attempting to pass one of the barriers. Captain Wright, an English naval officer, who had distinguished himself under Sir Sydney Smith at Acre, and from whose vessel Pichegru was known to have disembarked on the coast of France, happened about the same time to encounter a French ship of much superior strength, and become a prisoner of war. On pretext that this gentleman had acted as an accomplice in a scheme of assassination, he also was immediately placed in solitary confinement in a dungeon of the Temple.

It was now openly circulated that England and the exiled Bourbons had been detected in a base plot for murdering the Chief Consul; that the proof of their guilt was in the hands of the government, and would soon be made public. The Duke de Berri himself, it was added, had been prepared to land on the west coast of France, whenever Pichegru or Cadoudal should inform him that the time was come; while another of the royal exiles lay watching the event, and in readiness to profit by it, on the other side, immediately behind the Rhine.

The name of this last prince, the heir of Cond? well known for the brilliant gallantry of his conduct while commanding the van of his grandfather's little army of exiles, and beloved for many traits of amiable and generous character, had hardly been mentioned in connection with these rumours, ere the inhabitants of Paris heard, in one breath, with surprise and horror, that the Duke d'Enghien had been arrested at Ettenheim, and tried and executed within sight of their own houses at Vincennes. This story will ever form the darkest chapter in the history of Napoleon.

The duke had his residence at a castle in the Duchy of Baden, where, attended by a few noble friends, the partakers of his exile, he was chiefly occupied with the diversions of the chase. On the evening of the 14th of March, a troop of French soldiers and gens-d'armes, under Colonel Ordonner (who derived his orders from Caulaincourt) suddenly passed the frontier into the independent territory of Baden, surrounded the Castle of Ettenheim, rushed into the apartment of the prince, and seized him and all his company. He would have used his arms, but his attendants, representing the overpowering number of the assailants, persuaded him to yield without resistance. He was forthwith conveyed to the citadel of Strasburg, and separated from all his friends except one aide-de-camp, the Baron de St. Jaques, and allowed no communication with any one else. After being here confined three days, he was called up at midnight on the 18th and informed that he must prepare for a journey. He desired to have the assistance of his valet-de-chambre, and was refused: they permitted him to pack up two shirts, and the journey immediately begun.

The duke reached Paris early on the 20th; and after lying a few hours in the Temple, was removed to the neighbouring Castle of Vincennes, used for ages as a state prison. Being much fatigued he fell asleep, but was presently roused, and his examination forthwith commenced. Weary and wholly unprepared as he must have been, the unfortunate prince conducted himself throughout in such a manner as to command the respect of his inquisitors. He at once avowed his name and his services in the army of Cond? but utterly denied all knowledge of Pichegru and his designs. To this the whole of his evidence (and there was no evidence but his own) amounted; and having given it; he earnestly demanded an audience of the Consul. "My name," said he, "my rank, my sentiments, and the peculiar distress of my situation, lead me to hope that this request will not be refused."

At midnight the duke was again called from his bed, to attend the court which had been constituted for his trial. It consisted of eight military officers, appointed by Murat, Napoleon's brother-in-law, then governor of Paris. General Hullin, president of the military commission, commanded him to listen to the charges on which he was to be tried: of having fought against France; of being in the pay of England; and of plotting with England against the internal and external safety of the Republic. The Duke was again examined, and the second interrogatory was a mere repetition of the first, with this addition, that the prisoner avowed his readiness to take part again in the hostilities against France, if the opportunity should present itself. No other evidence whatever was adduced, except the written report of a spy of the police, who testified that the duke received many emigrants at his table at Ettenheim, and occasionally left the castle for several days together, without the spy's being able to trace where he was: a circumstance sufficiently explained by the duke's custom of hunting in the Black Forest.

General Hullin, in his account of the proceedings,[48] says, "He uniformly maintained that 'he had only sustained the rights of his family, and that a Cond?could never enter France but with arms in his hands. My birth,' said he, 'and my opinions must ever render me inflexible on this point.'"--"The firmness of his answers," continues Hullin, "reduced the judges to despair. Ten times we gave him an opening to retract his declarations, but he persisted in them immovably. 'I see,' he said, 'the honourable intentions of the commissioners, but I cannot resort to the means of safety which they indicate.' Being informed that the military commission judged without appeal, 'I know it,' answered he, 'nor do I disguise to myself the danger which I incur. My only desire is to have an interview with the First Consul.'"

The irregularities of all this procedure were monstrous. In the first place, the duke owed no allegiance to the existing government of France. 2ndly, The seizure of his person was wholly illegal; it took place by means of a violation of an independent territory: an outrage for which it is impossible to offer the smallest excuse. 3rdly, Had the arrest been ever so regular, the trial of a prisoner accused of a political conspiracy was totally beyond the jurisdiction of a court-martial. 4thly, It was against the laws of France to hold any trial at midnight. 5thly, The interrogatory was not read over to the prisoner, which the law imperatively demanded; and, 6thly, No defender was assigned to him--an indulgence which the French code refuses not to the meanest or most atrocious criminal, by what tribunal soever he may be tried.

But to proceed--The judges were moved by the conduct of the prisoner, and inclined to listen to his request of an audience of the Chief Consul. But Savary, then minister of police, had by this time introduced himself into the chamber, and watched the course of procedure from behind the chair of the president. He now leaned forward, and whispered into Hullin's ear, "this would be inopportune."--These significant words were obeyed. The court pronounced the duke guilty of the capital crimes of having fought against the Republic; of having intrigued with England; of having maintained intelligence with Strasburg, with the view of seizing that place; and of having conspired against the life of the Chief Consul. The prisoner, being remanded to his confinement, the report was instantly forwarded to Buonaparte, with a request that his further pleasure might be made known.

The court remained sitting until their messenger returned: he brought back their own letter with these words inscribed on it, "Condemned to death." The prisoner being called in again, heard his sentence with perfect composure. He requested the attendance of a confessor, and was answered,--"Would you die like a monk?" Without noticing this brutality he knelt for a moment, as in prayer, and rising, said, "Let us go."

He was immediately led down a winding stair by torch-light; and, conceiving that he was descending into some subterraneous dungeon, said to one of the soldiers of the escort, "Am I to be immured in an oubliette?" "Monseigneur," the man replied, sobbing, "be tranquil on that point." They emerged from a postern into the ditch of the castle, where a party of gens-d'armes were drawn up, Savary, their master, standing on the parapet over them. It was now six o'clock in the morning, and the gray light of the dawn was mingled with the gleam of torches. The prince refused to have his eyes bandaged--the word was given, and he fell. The body, dressed as it was, was immediately thrown into a grave--which had been prepared beforehand; at least, so say all the witnesses, except M. Savary.

To resume our notice of the mere informalities of the procedure:--1. The sentence was altogether unsupported by the evidence, except as to the mere fact of D'Enghien's having borne arms against France; but this could be no crime in him: he owed no allegiance to the French government; on the contrary, he and all his family had been expressly excepted from every act of amnesty to emigrants, and thereby constituted aliens. 2. The execution took place immediately after the sentence was pronounced; this is contrary to the laws of all civilised nations, and in direct contradiction to an article in the French code then in force, which gave twenty-four hours to every prisoner convicted by a court-martial, that he might, if he chose, appeal from their sentence. But, 3rdly, the publications (long afterwards extorted) of Savary and Hullin, prove that the court, perplexed with the difficulty of making their sentence appear to have any conformity with the charge and the evidence, drew up in fact, two different sentences: one before the duke was executed, which bore the article, "immediate execution"; the other a more careful document, intended alone to meet the public eye, in which not a word about immediate execution occurs. The duke was not executed, therefore, at six in the morning of the 21st of March, upon that sentence which was made public at the time, as the authority for his death.

Every circumstance in the dismal tale, from the quantity of linen packed up at Strasburg, to the preparation of the grave in the ditch of Vincennes, attests the fact that the fate of the unfortunate young man (for he was but 32 years old when he fell) had been determined on, to the minutest particular, long before he was summoned to a mock trial, before an incompetent tribunal. If ever man was murdered, it was the Duke d'Enghien.

Such was the fate of the gallant and generous youth, who, by his fiery courage, won the battle of Bertsheim; and who, when his followers, to whom the republicans had so often refused quarter, seemed disposed to retaliate in the hour of victory, threw himself between them and their discomfited countrymen, exclaiming, "They are French--they are unfortunate; I place them under the guardianship of your honour."

The horror with which this remorseless tragedy was heard of in Paris, soon spread throughout all Europe; and from that day the name of Buonaparte was irremediably associated with the ideas of sullen revenge and tyrannic cruelty. The massacre of Jaffa had been perpetrated in a remote land, and many listened with incredulity to a tale told by the avowed enemies of the homicide. But this bloody deed was done at home, and almost in the sight of all Paris. Of the fact there could be no doubt; and of the pretexts set forth by the organs of the French government, there were few men of any party who affected not to perceive the futility. Hitherto Napoleon had been the fortunate heir of a revolution, in whose civil excesses he had scarcely participated--henceforth he was the legitimate representative and symbol of all its atrocities.

In so far as Buonaparte had the power to suppress all mention of this catastrophe, it was, at the time, suppressed. But in after days, at St. Helena, when dictating the apology of his life to the companions of his exile, he not only spoke openly of the death of the Duke d'Enghien, but appears to have dwelt upon it often and long. Well aware that this was generally regarded as the darkest trait in his history, he displayed a feverish anxiety to explain it away. But the Sultan Akber wore a signet, inscribed, "I never knew any one that lost his way in a straight road;" and he that is conscious of innocence can have no temptation to multiply the lines of his defence. Buonaparte, according to the mood of the moment, or the companion whom he addressed, adopted different methods of vindicating himself. They were inconsistent as well as diverse; and even Las Cases seems to have blushed for his hero when he recorded them.

At one time Napoleon represents himself as having been taken by surprise: his ministers come on him when he is alone, at midnight, and inform him that the Bourbons have conspired to assassinate him--that the proofs are in their hands--that the Duke d'Enghien has already been more than once in Paris, and is lying close to the frontier, expecting the signal to return and head the conspirators in person.--In the first flush of indignation he gives the order for arresting the duke--every artifice is adopted to prevent him from interfering afterwards--everything is arranged by Talleyrand--the duke addresses a letter to him from Strasburg--that letter Talleyrand suppresses until the tragedy is over--had it been delivered in time, the life of the unhappy prince had been saved.

Unfortunately for Buonaparte, eight days elapsed between the order for the arrest and the order for the execution, a much longer period than was ever necessary for restoring the composure of his strong understanding. Further, the Duke d'Enghien kept a diary during his imprisonment, in which the minutest incidents are carefully recorded; it contains no hint of the letter to Napoleon; and the Baron de St. Jaques, who never quitted his master's chamber while he remained at Strasburg, bears distinct testimony that no such letter was written there. Moreover, neither Talleyrand nor any other individual in the world, except Buonaparte, could have had the slightest motive for desiring the death of D'Enghien. On the contrary, every motive that has weight with mankind in general, must have swayed the other way with Talleyrand; a member of one of the noblest families in France; a man unstained by participation in any of the butcheries of the revolution; and, above all, a man whose consummate skill has through life steadily pursued one object, namely, his own personal interest, and who must have been mad to perpetrate a gratuitous murder. And, lastly, Talleyrand was minister for foreign affairs. A letter written at Strasburg could by no accident have been forwarded through his department in the government; and, in fact, there is perfect proof that the whole business was done by the police, whose chief, Savary, communicated directly with the Chief Consul, and the military, who acted under the orders either of Buonaparte's aide-de-camp, Caulaincourt (afterwards Duke of Vicenza), or of his brother-in-law, Murat, the governor of Paris. It is needless to observe, that Napoleon's accusation of Talleyrand dates after that politician had exerted all his talents and influence in the work of procuring his own downfall, and the restoration of the House of Bourbon. But in truth whether Talleyrand, or Savary, or Caulaincourt, had the chief hand in the death of the Duke d'Enghien, is a controversy about which posterity will feel little interest. It is obvious to all men, that not one of them durst have stirred a finger to bring about a catastrophe of such fearful importance, without the express orders of Napoleon.

At other times the exile of St. Helena told a shorter and a plainer tale. "I was assailed," said he, "on all hands by the enemies whom the Bourbons had raised up against me: threatened with air-guns, infernal machines, and stratagems of every kind. There was no tribunal to which I could appeal for protection; therefore I had a right to protect myself. By putting to death one of those whose followers threatened my life, I was entitled to strike a salutary terror into all the rest."

The princes of the House of Bourbon, so far from stimulating assassins to take off the usurper of their throne, never failed, when such schemes were suggested, to denounce them as atrocities hateful in the sight of God and man. As to this part of their conduct, the proofs are abundant, clear, and irrefragable. But it is very possible that Buonaparte entertained the foul suspicion on which he justifies his violence. And indeed it is only by supposing him to have sincerely believed that the Bourbons were plotting against his life, that we can at all account for the shedding of D'Enghien's blood.--Unless Josephine spake untruly, or her conversation has been wilfully misrepresented, she strenuously exerted her influence to procure mercy for the royal victim; and so, unquestionably, did his venerable mother. But it demanded neither affection for Napoleon's person, nor regard for his interest, nor compassion for the youth and innocence of the Duke d'Enghien, to perceive the imprudence, as well as wickedness, of the proceeding. The remark of the callous Fouchehad passed into a proverb, "It was worse than a crime--it was a blunder."

A few days after the execution of the Duke d'Enghien (on the morning of the 7th of April) General Pichegru was found dead in prison: a black handkerchief was tied round his neck, and tightened by the twisting of a short stick, like a tourniquet. It could not appear probable that he should have terminated his own life by such means; and, accordingly, the rumour spread that he had been taken off in the night by some of the satellites of Savary; or, according to others, by some Mamelukes whom Napoleon had brought with him from the East, and now retained near his person, as an interior body-guard of the palace. This is a mystery which has never been penetrated. The recent fate of D'Enghien had prepared men to receive any story of this dark nature; and it was argued that Buonaparte had feared to bring Pichegru, a bold and dauntless man, into an open court, where he might have said many things well calculated to injure the Consul in public opinion.[49]

The other prisoners were now brought to trial. There was not a shadow of evidence against General Moreau, except the fact, admitted by himself, that he had been twice in company with Pichegru since his return to Paris. He in vain protested that he had rejected the proposals of Pichegru, to take part in a royalist insurrection; and, as for the murderous designs of Georges Cadoudal, that he had never even heard of them. He was sentenced to two years' confinement: but, on the intercession of his wife with Josephine, or rather on finding that a great part of the soldiery considered so eminent a commander as hardly used, the Chief Consul ere long, commuted this punishment for two years of exile.

Moreau was innocent; by his side, on the day of trial, appeared men who would have scorned to be so. Georges Cadoudal appeared in court with the miniature of Louis XVI. suspended round his neck, and gloried in the avowal of his resolution to make war personally on the usurper of the throne. The presiding judge, Thuriot, had been one of those who condemned the king to death. Georges punned on his name, and addressed him as "Monsieur Tue-Roi."[50] When called up for sentence, the judge missed the miniature, and asked him what he had done with it? "And you," answered the prisoner, "what have you done with the original?"--a retort which nothing could prevent the audience from applauding. Georges and eighteen more were condemned to death; and he, and eleven besides, suffered the penalty with heroic firmness. Of the rest, among whom were two sons of the noble house of Polignac, some were permitted to escape on condition of perpetual banishment: others had their punishment commuted to imprisonment.

With what indignation the death of the Duke d'Enghien had been heard of throughout Europe, now began to appear. The Emperor of Russia and the Kings of Sweden and Denmark put their courts into mourning, and made severe remonstrances through their diplomatic agents; and the correspondence which ensued laid the train for another general burst of war. Austria was humbled for the time, and durst not speak out: Prussia could hardly be expected to break her long neutrality on such an occasion: but wherever the story went, it prepared the minds of princes as of subjects, to take advantage of the first favourable opportunity for rising against the tyranny of France.

A conspiracy suppressed never fails to strengthen the power it was meant to destroy: and Buonaparte, after the tragedies of D'Enghien and Pichegru, beheld the French royalists reduced everywhere to the silence and the inaction of terror. Well understanding the national temper, he gave orders that henceforth the name of the exiled family should be as much as possible kept out of view; and accordingly after this time it was hardly ever alluded to in the productions of the enslaved press of Paris. The adherents of the Bourbons were compelled to content themselves with muttering their resentment in private saloons, where, however, the Chief Consul commonly had spies--who reported to him, or to his Savarys and Fouche, the jests and the caricatures in which the depressed and hopeless party endeavoured to find some consolation.

In order to check the hostile feeling excited among the sovereigns of the continent by the murder of the Bourbon Prince, the French government were now indefatigable in their efforts to connect the conspiracy of Georges Cadoudal with the cabinet of England. The agents of the police transformed themselves into numberless disguises, with the view of drawing the British ministers resident at various courts of Germany into some correspondence capable of being misrepresented, so as to suit the purpose of their master. Mr. Drake, envoy at Munich, and Mr. Spencer Smith, at Stuttgard, were deceived in this fashion; and some letters of theirs, egregiously misinterpreted, furnished Buonaparte with a pretext for complaining, to the sovereigns to whom they were accredited, that they had stained the honour of the diplomatic body by leaguing themselves with the schemes of the Chouan conspirators. The subservient princes were forced to dismiss these gentlemen from their residences; but the English ministry made such explanations in open Parliament as effectually vindicated the name of their country. Lord Elgin, British ambassador at Constantinople, had been one of those travellers detained at the out-breaking of the war, and was now resident on his parole in the south of France. He was, on some frivolous pretext, confined in a solitary castle among the Pyrenees; and there every device was practised to induce him to, at least, receive letters calculated, if discovered in his possession, to compromise him. But this nobleman, sagaciously penetrating the design, baffled it by his reserve. Being liberated from confinement shortly after, he communicated what had happened to a friend, a member of the French Senate, who traced the matter home to some of Fouches creatures, and congratulated Lord Elgin on having avoided very narrowly the fate of Pichegru.

Sir George Rumbold, the British minister at Hamburg, escaped that consummation still more narrowly. During the night of the 23rd October a party of French soldiers passed the Elbe, as Ordonner and his gang had crossed the Rhine on the 14th of March, and boldly seized Rumbold within the territory of an independent and friendly state. He was hurried to Paris, and confined in the fated dungeons of the Temple: but none of his papers afforded any plausible pretext for resisting the powerful remonstrance which the King of Prussia thought fit to make against an outrage perpetrated almost within sight of his dominions; and, after a few days, Sir George was set at liberty.

Meantime, while all the princes of Europe regarded with indignation (though few of them, indeed, cared to express the feeling openly) the cruel tragedies which had been acted in France, the death of Pichegru had suppressed effectually the hopes of the royalists in that country, and the exile of Moreau deprived the republicans of the only leader under whom there was any likelihood of their taking arms against the Chief Consul. He resolved to profit by the favourable moment for completing a purpose which he had long meditated; and, on the 30th of April, little more than a month after the Duke d'Enghien died, one Curacao was employed to move, in the Tribunate, "that it was time to bid adieu to political illusions--that victory had brought back tranquillity--the finances of the country had been restored, and the laws renovated--and that it was a matter of duty to secure those blessings to the nation in future, by rendering the supreme power hereditary in the person and family of Napoleon."--"Such," he said, "was the universal desire of the army and of the people. The title of Emperor, in his opinion, was that by which Napoleon should be hailed, as best corresponding to the dignity of the nation."

This motion was carried in the Tribunate, with one dissenting voice, that of Carnot; who, in a speech of great eloquence, resisted the principle of hereditary monarchy altogether. He admitted the merits in war and in policy of the Chief Consul--he was at present the Dictator of the Republic, and, as such, had saved it.--"Fabius, Camillus, Cincinnatus were dictators also. Why should not Buonaparte, like them, lay down despotic power, after the holding of it had ceased to be necessary to the general good? Let the services of a citizen be what they might, was there to be no limit to the gratitude of the nation? But at all events, even granting that Buonaparte himself could not be too highly rewarded, or too largely trusted, why commit the fortunes of posterity to chance? Why forget that Vespasian was the father of Domitian, Germanicus of Caligula, Marcus Aurelius of Commodus?" In effect Carnot, colleague as he had been of Robespierre, and stained as he was with the blood of Louis XVI., was a sincere republican; and, after his own fashion, a sincere patriot. He was alone in the Tribunate--the rest of whose members prolonged, during three whole days, a series of fulsome harangues, every one of which terminated in the same implicit agreement to the proposal of Curacao.

The legislative body, without hesitation, adopted it; and a senatus-consultum forthwith appeared, by which Napoleon Buonaparte was declared

Emperor of the French: the empire to descend in the male line of his body: in case of having no son, Napoleon might adopt any son or grandson of his brothers as his heir: in default of such adoption, Joseph and Louis Buonaparte were named as the next heirs of the crown (Lucien and Jerome being passed over, as they had both given offence to Napoleon by their marriages). The members of Napoleon's family were declared princes of the blood of France.

This decree was sent down to the departments: and the people received it with indifference. The Prefects reported on the 1st of December, that between three and four millions of citizens had subscribed their assent to the proposed measure, while not many more than three thousand voted in opposition to it. This result indicated, as these functionaries chose to say, the unanimous approbation of the French people. That nation, however, consisted at the time of more than thirty millions!

But Napoleon did not wait for this authority, such as it proved to be. On the 18th of May (more than six months ere the report reached him) he openly assumed the imperial title and dignity. On the same day he nominated his late colleagues in the Consulate, Cambaceres and Le Brun, the former to be Arch-Chancellor, the latter Arch-Treasurer of the Empire. The offices of High-Constable, Grand Admiral, &c., were revived and bestowed on his brothers, and others of his immediate connections. Seventeen generals (viz. Berthier, Murat, Moncey, Jourdan, Massena, Augereau, Bernadotte, Soult, Brune, Lannes, Mortier, Ney, Davoust, Bessieres, Kellerman, Lefebre, Perignon, Serrurier) were named Marshals of the Empire; Duroc, Grand Marshal of the Palace; Caulaincourt, Master of the Horse; Berthier, Grand Huntsman; and Count Segur, a nobleman of the ancient regime, Master of the Ceremonies. It was in vain attempted to excite popular enthusiasm. "It appeared," says an eye-witness, "as if the shades of D'Enghien and Pichegru had hovered over the scene, and spread coldness on all that was meant for the manifestation of joy."

It was not so with the soldiery. Napoleon, with his empress, visited the camps at Boulogne, and was received with the excess of military applause and devotion. He made a progress to Aix-la-Chapelle, and along the Rhenish frontier, flattered and extolled at every station. Except Russia, Sweden, and England, every crown in Europe sent to congratulate him on his enrolment in the body of hereditary monarchs. Nay, not a few of the smaller German potentates came in person, to swell, on this great occasion, the state and magnificence of the new imperial court.

In assuming the title of Emperor, not of King, it escaped not observation, that Napoleon's object was to carry back the minds of the French to a period antecedent to the rule of the recently dethroned dynasty--to the days of Charlemagne, who, with the monarchy of France, combined both a wider dominion and a loftier style. As that great conqueror had caused himself to be crowned by Pope Leo, so Napoleon now determined that his own inauguration should take place under the auspices of Pius VII.; nay, that the more to illustrate his power, the head of the Catholic church should repair to Paris for this purpose. It may be doubted whether, in this measure, he regarded more the mere gratification of his pride or the chance of conferring a character of greater solemnity on the installation of the new dynasty, in the eyes of the Catholic population of France. On the 5th of November, however, the unresisting Pope left Rome, and, having been received throughout his progress with every mark of respect and veneration, arrived in Paris to bear his part in the great pageant. On the 2nd of December Buonaparte and Josephine appeared, amidst all that was splendid and illustrious in their capital, and were crowned in Notre-Dame. The Pope blessed them and consecrated the diadems; but these were not placed on their heads by his hand. That office, in either case, Napoleon himself performed. Throughout the ceremonial his aspect was thoughtful: it was on a stern and gloomy brow that he with his own hands planted the symbol of successful ambition and uneasy power, and the shouts of the deputies present, carefully selected for the purpose, sounded faint and hollow amidst the silence of the people.

As a necessary sequel to these proceedings in Paris, the senators of the Italian republic now sent in their humble petition, that their president might be pleased to do them also the favour to be crowned as their king at Milan. The Emperor proceeded to that city accordingly, and in like fashion, on the 26th of May, 1805, placed on his own head the old iron crown of the Lombard kings, uttering the words which, according to tradition, they were accustomed to use on such occasions, "_God hath given it me. Beware who touches it._"--Napoleon henceforth styled himself Emperor of the French and King of Italy, but announced that the two crowns should not be held by the same person after his death.

It was not, however, for mere purposes of ceremonial that he had once more passed the Alps. The Ligurian republic sent the Doge to Milan to congratulate the King of Italy, and also to offer their territories for the formation of another department of the French empire. But this was a step of his ambition which led to serious results.

Meanwhile Eugene Beauharnois, son to Josephine, was left Viceroy at Milan, and the imperial pair returned to Paris.

[Footnote 47: To this period belong Sir W. Scott's song to the Edinburgh Volunteers:--

"If ever breath of British gale Shall fan the tricolor, Or footstep of invader rude, With rapine foul and red with blood, Pollute our happy shore-- Then farewell home! and farewell friends! Adieu each tender tie! Resolved, we mingle in the tide Where charging squadron furious ride, To conquer or to die," &c.

And various sonnets of Mr. Wordsworth; such as--

"It is not to be thought of that the flood Of British freedom," &c.

"Vanguard of liberty! ye men of Kent, Ye children of a soil that doth advance Its haughty brow against the coast of France, Now is the time to prove your hardiment!" &c.]

[Footnote 48: This account was published _more than twenty years afterwards_, in consequence of a pamphlet by Savary (Duke of Rovigo).]

[Footnote 49: About a year afterwards Captain Wright was found dead in his dungeon in the Temple, with his throat cut from ear to ear. This mystery has hitherto remained in equal darkness; but Buonaparte was far from Paris at the period of Wright's death, and, under all the circumstances of the case, there seems to be no reason for supposing that he could have had any concern in that tragedy.]

[Footnote 50: i.e. Kill-king.]

CHAPTER XIX

New coalition against France--Sweden--Russia--Austria joins the Alliance--
Napoleon heads the Army in Germany--Ulm surrendered by Mack--Vienna
taken--Naval Operations--Battle of Trafalgar--Battle of Austerlitz--Treaty of
Presburg--Joseph Buonaparte King of Naples--Louis Buonaparte King of
Holland--Confederation of the Rhine--New Nobility in France.

On the 27th of January, 1805, Napoleon, in his new character of Emperor,
addressed a letter (as he had done before at the commencement of his
Consulate) to King George III. in person; and was answered, as before, by the
British Secretary of State for Foreign Affairs. The new Emperor's letter
contained many well-turned sentences about the blessings of peace, but no
distinct proposition of any kind--least of all any hint that he was willing to
concede Malta. The English minister, however, answered simply, that in the
present state of relations between the cabinet of St. James's and that of St.
Petersburg, it was impossible for the former to open any negotiation without
the consent of the latter.

This sufficiently indicated a fact of which Napoleon had just suspicion some
time before. The murder of the Duke d'Enghien had been regarded with
horror by the young Emperor of Russia; he had remonstrated vigorously, and
his reclamations had been treated with indifference. The King of Sweden,
immediately after he heard of the catastrophe of Vicennes, had made known
his sentiments to the Czar: a strict alliance had been signed between those
two courts about a fortnight before Napoleon wrote to the King of England;
and it was obvious that the northern powers had resolved to take part with
Great Britain in her struggle against France. The Consul now made the
Moniteur the vehicle of continual abuse against the sovereigns of Russia and
Sweden; and the latter caused a note to be handed to the French minister at
Stockholm, complaining of the "indecent and ridiculous insolence which
Monsieur Buonaparte had permitted to be inserted" in that official journal.

The cabinets of London, Petersburg, and Stockholm were parties in a league
which had avowedly the following objects: to restore the independence of
Holland and Switzerland: to free the north of Germany from the presence of
French troops: to procure the restoration of Piedmont to the King of Sardinia;
and, finally, the evacuation of Italy by Napoleon. Until, by the attainment of

these objects, the sway of France should be reduced to limits compatible with the independence of the other European states, no peace was to be signed by any of the contracting powers; and, during several months, every means was adopted to procure the association of Austria and Prussia. But the latter of these sovereigns had the misfortune at this time to have a strong French party in his council, and, though personally hostile to Napoleon, could not as yet count on being supported in a war against him by the hearty goodwill of an undivided people. Austria, on the other hand, had been grievously weakened by the campaign of Marengo, and hesitated, on prudential grounds, to commit herself once more to the hazard of arms.

Alexander repaired in person to Berlin, for the purpose of stimulating the King of Prussia. The two sovereigns met in the vault where the great Frederick lies buried, and swore solemnly, over his remains, to effect the liberation of Germany. But though thus pledged to the Czar, the King of Prussia did not hastily rush into hostilities. He did not even follow the example of the Austrian, whose forbearance was at length wholly exhausted by the news of the coronation at Milan, and the annexation of Genoa to the empire of France.

The government of Vienna no sooner heard of this new aggrandisement, than it commenced warlike preparations, rashly and precipitately, without making sure of the co-operation of Berlin, or even waiting until the troops of Russia could perform the march into Germany. But this great fault was not the greatest. The Emperor haughtily demanded that the Elector of Bavaria should take the field also; nay, that he should suffer his army to be entirely incorporated with the Austrian, and commanded by its chiefs. The Elector, who had a son travelling in France, resisted anxiously and strenuously. "On my knees," he wrote to the Emperor, "I beg of you that I may be permitted to remain neutral." This appeal was disregarded. The Austrian troops advanced into Bavaria, where they appear to have conducted themselves as in an enemy's country; and the indignant Elector withdrew his army into Franconia, where he expected the advance of the French as liberators.

This unjustifiable behaviour was destined to be severely punished. No sooner did Napoleon understand that war was inevitable, than he broke up his great army on the coast opposite to England, and directed its march upon the German frontier; while Massena received orders to assume, also, the offensive in Italy, and force his way, if possible, into the hereditary states of Austria. The favourite scheme of Carnot was thus revived, and two French armies, one crossing the Rhine, and the other pushing through the Tyrolese, looked forward to a junction before the walls of Vienna.

The rashness which had characterised the conduct of the Cabinet of Vienna, was fatally followed out in that of its general, Mack: instead of occupying the line of the river Inn, which, extending from the Tyrol to the Danube at Passau, affords a strong defence to the Austrian territory, and on which he might have expected, in comparative safety, the arrival of the Russians--this unworthy favourite of the Emperor left the Inn behind him, and established his headquarters on the western frontier of Bavaria, at Ulm.

Napoleon hastened to profit by this unpardonable error. Bernadotte advanced from Hanover, with the troops which had occupied that electorate, towards Wurtzburg, where the Bavarian army lay ready to join its strength to his; five divisions of the great force lately assembled on the coasts of Normandy, under the orders of Davoust, Ney, Soult, Marmont, and Vandamme, crossed the Rhine at different points, all to the northward of Mack's position; while a sixth, under Murat, passing at Kehl, manoeuvred in such a manner as to withdraw the Austrian's attention from these movements, and to strengthen him in his belief that Napoleon and all his army were coming against him through the Black Forest in his front.

The consequence of Buonaparte's combinations was, that while Mack lay expecting to be assaulted in front of Ulm, the great body of the French army advanced into the heart of Germany, by the left side of the Danube, and then, throwing themselves across that river, took ground in his rear, interrupting his communication with Vienna, and isolating him. In order that Bernadotte and the Bavarians might have a part in this great manoeuvre, it was necessary that they should disregard the neutrality of the Prussian territories of Anspach and Bareuth; and Napoleon, well aware of the real sentiments of the court of Berlin, did not hesitate to adopt this course. Prussia remonstrated indignantly, but still held back from proclaiming war; and Napoleon cared little for such impediments as mere diplomacy could throw in the way of his campaign. He did not, however, effect his purpose of taking up a position in the rear of Mack without resistance. On the contrary, at various places, at Wertenghen, Guntzburg, Memingen, and Elchingen, severe skirmishes occurred with different divisions of the Austrian army, in all of which the French had the advantage. General Spangenburg and 5000 men laid down their arms at Memingen; and, in all, not less than 20,000 prisoners fell into the hands of the French between the 26th of September, when they crossed the Rhine, and the 13th of October, when they were in full possession of Bavaria and Swabia, holding Mack cooped up behind them in Ulm--as Wurmser had been in Mantua, during the campaign of Alvinzi.

But Mack was no Wurmser. Napoleon's recent movements had perplexed utterly the counsels of the Austrians, whose generals, adopting different views of the state of the campaign, no longer acted in unison. Schwartzenberg, and the Archduke Ferdinand, considering further resistance in Bavaria as hopeless, cut their way, at the head of large bodies of cavalry, into Bohemia, and began to rouse the inhabitants of that kingdom to a levy en masse. The French Emperor, perceiving that they had for the present escaped him, drew back upon Ulm, invested that town on every side, and summoned Mack to surrender.

The garrison consisted of full 20,000 good troops; the place was amply victualled and stored; the advance of the great Russian army could not be distant; the declaration of war against Napoleon by Berlin was hourly to be expected: and the armies of Austria, though scattered for the present, would be sure to rally and make every effort for the relief of Ulm. Under circumstances comparatively hopeless the brave Wurmser held Mantua to extremity. But in spite of example or argument, in terror or in treachery, General Mack capitulated without hazarding a blow.

On the 16th he published a proclamation, urging his troops to prepare for the utmost pertinacity of defence, and forbidding, on pain of death, the very word surrender to be breathed within the walls of Ulm. On the 17th he signed articles by which hostilities were immediately to cease, and he and all his men to surrender themselves prisoners of war within ten days, unless some Austrian or Russian force should appear in the interval, and attempt to raise the blockade. After signing this document, Mack visited, in person, the headquarters of Napoleon; and, whatever the nature of their conversation may have been, the result was, a revision of the treaty on the 19th, and the formal evacuation of Ulm on the 20th. Twenty thousand soldiers filed off, and laid down their arms before Napoleon and his staff.--Eighteen generals were dismissed on parole; an immense quantity of ammunition of all sorts fell into the hands of the victor; and a waggon filled with Austrian standards was sent to gratify the vanity of the Parisians.

The catastrophe of Ulm, striking new terror into the Prussian counsels, prevented the violation of the territory of Anspach from being immediately followed by the declaration of war, for which Buonaparte must have made up his mind when he hazarded that measure. Meantime success had attended Massena in his advance from Lombardy towards the Venetian states, where the Archduke Charles commanded an army of 60,000 men for Austria. The Archduke, after sustaining various reverses, was forced to abandon Italy; and retreated, though slowly and leisurely, before Massena, through the strong passes of the Carinthian mountains.

Nor had Marshal Ney, whom Napoleon had detached from his own main army with orders to advance in the Tyrol, been less successful than Massena. The Archduke John, who commanded in that province, was beaten like his brother; and the outposts of the army of Massena from Italy and that of Ney from the Upper Rhine, at length met and saluted in triumph at Clagenfurt. The Archduke Charles, understanding how Ney was prospering in the Tyrol, had given up the design of retreating by that way into Germany, and proceeded through the Carinthian Mountains towards Hungary. Prince John now followed his brother's example; and, the remains of those two armies thus coalescing in a distant region, the divisions of Ney and Messena came to be at the immediate disposal of Napoleon, who was now concentrating his force for the purpose of attacking Vienna.

While the victorious corps of Ney thus secured his right--Murat, on his left, watched the Austrians who had made their way into Bohemia, and Augereau, who had now advanced at the head of a large reserve from France, remained behind him in Swabia, to guard the passes from the Voralberg, in case of any hostile movement from that mountainous province, and, at the same time, to be ready for action against the Prussians, should that army at length receive orders to take part in the war, and cross the Danube. Thus guarded, as he judged, against any chance of having his communications intercepted in the rear or flanks, Napoleon himself, with the main body, now moved on the capital of the German Emperor. Austrian and Russian troops, to the number of 45,000, had been thrown together with the view of relieving Ulm, and advanced considerably for that purpose ere they heard of the treacherous capitulation of Mack. They now retired again before the movement of Napoleon, halting, indeed, occasionally, and assuming the aspect of determination; but, whenever the outposts met, losing heart, and continuing their progress towards Moravia:--for there, at length, the Czar, with his principal army, had made his appearance; and there, around that standard, every disposable force was now to be rallied. The Emperor Francis himself, perceiving that Vienna was incapable of defence, quitted his capital on the 7th of November, and proceeded to Brunn, in Moravia, the headquarters of Alexander.

On the same evening Count Giulay reached Napoleon's headquarters at Lintz, with proposals for an immediate armistice and negotiation. Buonaparte refused to pause unless the Tyrol and Venice were instantly ceded to him. These were terms to which the Austrian envoy had no authority to submit. On the 13th of November, accordingly, the French entered Vienna, and Napoleon took up his residence in the castle of Schoenbrunn, the proud palace of the Austrian Caesars. General Clarke was appointed governor of the city; and the Elector of Bavaria was gratified with a large share of the military stores and equipments found in its arsenals.

But the intoxication of this success was to be sobered by a cup of bitterness--and from a hand which had already dashed more than one of Napoleon's proudest triumphs.

When Buonaparte took up arms again, and devoted every energy of his mind to the descent upon England, Spain, the next maritime power after France, professed, indeed, neutrality,--but by some of her proceedings raised the suspicion that her fleet was really destined to act along with that of the invader. The English government resolved to bring this matter to the test: and a squadron of four ships demanded a similar force of the Spaniards to yield themselves into their keeping as a pledge of neutrality. The British squadron sent on such an errand ought, on every principle of policy and humanity, to have been much stronger than that which Commodore Moore commanded on this occasion. The Castilian pride took fire at the idea of striking to an equal foe; and, unhappily, an action took place, in which three of the Spanish ships were captured, and one blown up. This catastrophe determined, as might have been expected, the wavering counsels of Madrid. Spain declared war against England, and placed her fleets at the command of the French Emperor.

Two of his own squadrons, meantime, had, in pursuance of the great scheme traced for the ruin of England, escaped early in this year out of Rochefort and Toulon. The former, passing into the West Indies, effected some trivial services, and returned in safety to their original port. The latter, under Villeneuve, had like fortune; and, venturing on a second sortie, joined the great Spanish fleet under Gravina at Cadiz. The combined fleets then crossed the Atlantic, where they captured an insignificant island, and once more returned towards Europe. Nelson had spent the summer in chasing these squadrons across the seas--and on this occasion they once more eluded his grasp: but on approaching Cape Finisterre (22nd July), another English squadron of fifteen sail of the line and two frigates, under Sir Robert Calder, came in view: and the allied admirals, having twenty sail of the line, three fifty-gun ships, and four frigates, did not avoid the encounter. They were worsted, notwithstanding their superiority of strength, and Calder captured two of their best ships. But that they escaped from an English fleet, howsoever inferior in numbers, without sustaining severer loss than this, was considered as a disgrace by the British public.--Calder, being tried by a court-martial, was actually censured for not having improved his success more signally; a striking example of the height to which confidence in the naval superiority of the English had been raised, at the very time when no arm appeared capable of thwarting the career of French victory by land.

Villeneuve and Gravina now made their way to Vigo, and thence finally to Cadiz: while Nelson, having at length received accurate intelligence of their motions, took the command in the Mediterranean, and lay watching for the moment in which they should be tempted to hazard another egress. The coasts of Spain being strictly blockaded, some difficulty began to be felt about providing necessaries for the numerous crews of the allied fleets; but the circumstance which had most influence in leading them to quit, once more, their place of safety, was, according to general admission, the impatience of Villeneuve under some unmerited reproaches with which Napoleon visited the results of the battle off Cape Finisterre. Villeneuve, a man of dauntless gallantry and the highest spirit, smarting under this injury, was anxious to take the noble revenge of victory. And, in truth, had numbers been to decide the adventure, he ran little risk: for Nelson commanded only twenty-seven sail of the line, and three frigates, manned in the ordinary manner; whereas the fleet in Cadiz mustered thirty-three ships of the line, and seven frigates; and, besides the usual crews, carried 4000 troops, chiefly rifle-men. The result was the most glorious day in the proud annals of the English Marine. The combined fleets sailed from Cadiz on the 19th of October, and on the morning of the 21st--the very day after Mack surrendered at Ulm--they came in sight of the English Admiral, off Cape Trafalgar.

The reader is referred to the historian of Lord Nelson for the particulars of this great action. The French and Spaniards awaited the attack in a double line. Nelson hoisted the famous signal--"England expects every man to do his duty"; charged in two columns, and broke their array at the first onset. The battle, nevertheless, was sternly contested. In the end nineteen ships of the line were taken; and of those Spanish vessels which escaped into Cadiz, seven had been rendered wholly unserviceable. Four French ships of the line, under Commodore Dumanoir, made way for the Straits, and were captured a few days after by Sir Richard Strachan, commander of the English squadron off Rochefort. The fleets of France and Spain were annihilated: yet, great as was the triumph, glorious and unrivalled, it was dearly purchased--for Nelson fell, mortally wounded, early in the action. The hero lived just long enough to hear the cheer of consummated victory; and then breathed out his noble spirit, in words worthy of his life, "Thank God! I have done my duty."[51]

The French and Spaniards had fought together against Nelson; but not in the same spirit. The former were determined and malignant enemies; the latter generous friends, hurried, by the excitement of temporary and pardonable passion, into hostilities against the only power which could afford their country any chance of avoiding that political slavery, under which it was now the settled purpose of Napoleon's ambition to crush every nation of Europe. But the unprincipled conduct of Dumanoir, who escaped from Nelson to be captured shortly after, as has been mentioned, by Strachan, at once brought out the different feelings under which the two allied fleets had been acting. This French officer, retreating with his four ships, which had had no part in the battle, discharged his broadsides, as he passed, into English vessels no longer capable of pursuit,--conduct which, as the victory was complete, could have no object but that of carnage. Nay, such was the ruffian nature of this man's soul, he fired into the Spanish ships which had yielded to the English, thus, for the sake of trivially injuring his enemy, sacrificing without scruple the blood of his own unfortunate friends. The Spanish prisoners, in their indignation at this brutality, asked their English captors to permit them to man their guns against the retreating French; and such was the earnestness of their entreaty, and the confidence of Englishmen in the honour of Spaniards, that these men actually were permitted to do as they had requested. A mutual interchange of good offices ensued. In the evening after the battle a gale sprung up, and some of the captured vessels drifting on shore, a number of British seamen fell into the hands of the garrison of Cadiz. They were received as friends: for the accommodation of their wounded the Spanish soldiers gave up their own beds. Collingwood, who succeeded to Nelson's command, sent all the wounded Spaniards on shore to be cured in their own country, merely taking their parole that they would not serve again during the war: and the governor of Cadiz, with still more romantic generosity, offered his hospitals for the use of Collingwood's wounded seamen, pledging the honour of the Spanish name that they should be cared for like his own men, and sent back to their admiral whenever they had recovered. It will appear, hereafter, what illustrious consequences the kindly feelings thus manifested were destined to produce.

Buonaparte, when he heard of this mighty discomfiture, which for ever put an end to all his visions of invading England, is said to have lost that possession of himself, which he certainly maintained when the catastrophe of Aboukir was announced to him at Cairo. Yet arrogance mingled strangely in his expressions of sorrow.--"I cannot be everywhere," said he to the messenger of the evil tidings--as if Napoleon could have had any more chance of producing victory by his presence at Trafalgar, than Nelson would have dreamed of having by appearing on horseback at Marengo. In his newspapers, and even in his formal messages to the senate at Paris, Buonaparte always persisted in denying that there had been a great defeat at Trafalgar, or even a great battle. But how well he appreciated the facts of the case was well known to the unfortunate Admiral Villeneuve. That brave officer, after spending a short time in England, was permitted to return to France on his parole. He died almost immediately afterwards at Rennes: whether by his own hand, in the agony of despair, as the French Gazette asserted, or assassinated, as was commonly believed at the time, by some of the blood-hardened minions of Fouches police, is a mystery not yet cleared up; and, perhaps, never destined to be so until the day comes in which nothing shall be hid.

The tidings of Trafalgar, after the first moment, served but as a new stimulus to the fire of Napoleon's energy. He quitted Vienna, and put himself at the head of his columns, which, passing the Danube into Moravia, soon found themselves within reach of the forces of Russia and Austria, at length combined, and prepared for action, under the eyes of their respective emperors. These princes, on the approach of the French, drew back as far as Olmutz, in order that a reserve of Russians, under Bexhowden, might join them before the decisive struggle took place. Napoleon fixed his headquarters at Brunn, and, riding over the plain between Brunn and Austerlitz (a village about two miles from that town), said to his generals, "study this field--we shall, ere long, have to contest it."

Buonaparte has been much criticised by strategists for the rashness of thus passing the Danube into Moravia, while the Archduke Ferdinand was organising the Bohemians on his left, the Archdukes Charles and John in Hungary, with still formidable and daily increasing forces on his right, the population of Vienna and the surrounding territories ready to rise, in case of any disaster, in his rear; and Prussia as decidedly hostile in heart as she was wavering in policy. The French leader did not disguise from himself the risk of his adventure; but he considered it better to run all that risk, than to linger in Vienna until the armies in Hungary and Bohemia should have had time to reinforce the two emperors.

Napoleon's preparations were as follows:--his left, under Larmes, lay at Santon, a strongly fortified position: Soult commanded the right wing: the centre, under Bernadotte, had with them Murat and all the cavalry. Behind the line lay the reserve, consisting of 20,000, 10,000 of whom were of the Imperial guard, under Oudinot: and here Napoleon himself took his station. But besides these open demonstrations, Davoust, with a division of horse and another of foot, lay behind the convent of Raygern, considerably in the rear of the French right--being there placed by the Emperor, in consequence of a false movement, into which he, with a seer-like sagacity, foresaw the enemy might, in all likelihood, he tempted; and to which he lured them on accordingly by every engine of his craft.

Buonaparte, on learning that the Emperor Alexander was personally in the hostile camp, sent Savary to present his compliments to that sovereign; but really, as we may suppose, to observe as much as he could of the numbers and condition of the troops. Savary, on his return, informed his master that the Russian prince was surrounded by a set of young coxcombs, whose every look and gesture expressed overweening confidence in themselves and contempt for their opponents. All the reverses of the previous campaign were, as they took care to signify, the result of unpardonable cowardice among the Austrians, whose spirit had been quite broken by the wars in Italy: but they were the countrymen of the same Suwarrow who had beaten the French out of all Buonaparte's Lombard conquests, and the first general battle would show what sort of enemies the Russians were. How much of this statement is true we know not: it was openly made at the time in one of Buonaparte's bulletins--and, what is of more moment, he appears to have acted on the belief that Savary told the truth. Having, ere he received it, advanced several leagues beyond the chosen field of battle, near Austerlitz, he forthwith retreated on that position, with a studied semblance of confusion. The Czar sent a young aide-de-camp to return the compliment carried by Savary; and this messenger found the French soldiery actively engaged in fortifying their position--the very position which their Emperor had all along determined to occupy. The account of what the young Russian saw in the French lines gave, as Napoleon wished, a new stimulus to the presumption of his enemy; and, having made the preparations above described, he calmly expected the consequences of their rashness and inexperience.

On the 1st of December he beheld the commencement of those false movements which he had desired and anticipated. On seeing the Russians begin to descend from the heights, on which they might have lain in safety until the Archdukes could come to swell their array with the forces in Bohemia and Hungary, Napoleon did not repress his rapturous joy. "In twenty-four hours," said he, "that army is mine."

Shortly afterwards there arrived Count Haugwitz, an envoy from the King of Prussia, who being introduced into the Emperor's presence, signified that he was the bearer of an important communication. "Count," said Napoleon, "you may see that the outposts of the armies are almost meeting--there will be a battle to-morrow--return to Vienna, and deliver your message when it is over." The envoy did not require two biddings. Napoleon had all this year been protracting the indecision of the Prussian counsels by holding out the delusive hope, that, were Austria effectually humbled, the imperial crown of Germany might be transferred to the house of Brandenburg. The old jealousies, thus artfully awakened, had been sufficient to prevent a declaration of war from immediately following on the violation of the territory of Anspach and Bareuth. The intervention of the Czar had, it is not to be doubted, at length determined the Court of Berlin to close their unworthy neutrality:--but Haugwitz had no Prussian army in his train; and, seeing what was before him, he certainly did prudently to defer that which had been so unwisely as well as ungenerously put off from month to month, for one day more.

At one o'clock in the morning of the 2nd of December, Napoleon, having slept for an hour by a watch-fire, got on horseback, and proceeded to reconnoitre the front of his position. He wished to do so without being recognised, but the soldiery penetrated the secret, and, lighting great fires of straw all along the line, received him from post to post with shouts of enthusiasm. They reminded him that this was the anniversary of his coronation, and assured him they would celebrate the day in a manner worthy of its glory. "Only promise us," cried an old grenadier, "that you will keep yourself out of the fire." "I will do so," answered Napoleon, "I shall be with the reserve until you need us." This pledge, which so completely ascertains the mutual confidence of the leader and his soldiers, he repeated in a proclamation issued at daybreak. The sun rose with uncommon brilliancy: on many an after-day the French soldiery hailed a similar dawn with exultation as the sure omen of victory, and "the Sun of Austerlitz" has passed into a proverb.

The Russian General-in-Chief, Kutusoff, fell into the snare laid for him, and sent a large division of his army to turn the right of the French. The troops detached for this purpose met with unexpected resistance from Davoust, and were held in check at Raygern. Napoleon immediately seized the opportunity. They had left a deep gap in the line, and upon that space Soult forthwith poured a force, which entirely destroyed the communication between the Russian centre and left. The Czar perceived the fatal consequences of this movement, and his guards rushed to beat back Soult. It was on an eminence, called the hill of Pratzen, that the encounter took place. The Russians drove the French infantry before them: Napoleon ordered Bessieres to hurry with the imperial guard to their rescue. The Russians were in some disorder from the impatience of victory. They resisted sternly, but were finally broken, and fled. The Grand Duke Constantine, who had led them gallantly, escaped by the fleetness of his horse.

The French centre now advanced, and the charges of its cavalry under Murat were decisive. The Emperors of Russia and Germany beheld from the heights of Austerlitz the total ruin of their centre, as they had already of their left. Their right wing had hitherto contested well against all the impetuosity of Lannes: but Napoleon could now gather round them on all sides, and, his artillery plunging incessant fire on them from the heights, they at length found it impossible to hold their ground. They were forced down into a hollow, where some small frozen lakes offered the only means of escape from the closing cannonade. The French broke the ice about them by a storm of shot, and nearly 20,000 men died on the spot, some swept away by the artillery, the greater part drowned. Buonaparte, in his bulletin, compares the horrid spectacle of this ruin to the catastrophe of the Turks at Aboukir, when "the sea was covered with turbans." It was with great difficulty that the two emperors rallied some fragments of their armies around them, and effected their retreat. Twenty thousand prisoners, forty pieces of artillery, and all the standards of the imperial guard of Russia, remained with the conqueror. Such was the battle of Austerlitz;--or, as the French soldiery delighted to call it, "the battle of the emperors."

The Prussian envoy now returned, and presented to Napoleon his master's congratulations on the victory thus achieved. The Emperor whispered to Haugwitz, "Here is a message, of which circumstances have altered the address." Frederick-William, however, had 150,000 men under arms, and it by no means suited Napoleon's views to provoke him to extremities at this moment. He entered into a treaty with Haugwitz; and Prussia was bribed to remain quiescent, by a temptation which she wanted virtue to resist. The French Emperor offered her Hanover, provided she would oppose no obstacle to any other arrangements which he might find it necessary to form: and the house of Brandenburg did not blush to accept at his hands the paternal inheritance of the royal family of England.

The Austrian, understanding how Prussia was disposed of, perceived too clearly that further resistance was hopeless; and negotiations immediately begun.

The haughty Emperor of Germany repaired to the French headquarters. He was received at the door of a miserable hut. "Such," said Buonaparte, "are the palaces you have compelled me to occupy for these two months." "You have made such use of them," answered Francis, "that you ought not to complain of their accommodation."

The humiliated sovereign, having ere this obtained an armistice for himself, demanded of Napoleon that the Czar might be permitted to withdraw in safety to his own states. To this the conqueror assented: and on the 6th of December the Russians commenced their retreat.

The definitive treaty with Francis was signed at Presburg on the 15th of December, another with Prussia on the 26th, at Vienna:--and the terms of both arranged, on Napoleon's side, by Talleyrand, corresponded with the signal and decisive events of the campaign.

Austria yielded the Venetian territories to the kingdom of Italy: her ancient possessions of the Tyrol and Voralberg were transferred to Bavaria, to remunerate that elector for the part he had taken in the war; Wirtemberg, having also adopted the French side, received recompense of the same kind at the expense of the same power, and both of these electors were advanced to the dignity of kings. Bavaria received Anspach and Bareuth from Prussia, and, in return, ceded Berg, which was erected into a grand duchy, and conferred, in sovereignty, on Napoleon's brother-in-law, Murat. Finally, Prussia added Hanover to her dominions, in return for the cession of Anspach and Bareuth, and acquiescence in the other arrangements above-mentioned.

Eugene Beauharnois, son of Josephine, and Viceroy of Italy, received in marriage the eldest daughter of the new king of Bavaria: this being the first occasion on which Napoleon manifested openly his desire to connect his family with the old sovereign houses of Europe. It was announced at the same time, that in case the Emperor should die without male issue, the crown of Italy would descend to Eugene.

Other events of the same character now crowded on the scene. The king, or rather the queen of Naples, had not failed, during the recent campaign, to manifest the old aversion to the French cause. St. Cyr's army, which on the first rupture of the peace of Amiens had occupied the seaports of that kingdom, being called into the north of Italy to reinforce Massena against the Archduke Charles, an Anglo-Russian expedition soon landed in Naples, and were welcomed cordially by the court. Napoleon, immediately after the battle of Austerlitz, issued a proclamation, declaring that "the royal house of Naples had ceased to reign for ever." On hearing of the decisive battle, and the retreat of the Czar, the English and Russians evacuated the Neapolitan territories on the mainland of Italy. Joseph Buonaparte conducted a French army towards the frontier; the court passed over into Sicily; and Joseph was proclaimed King of Naples.

The King of Sweden, rushing as hastily and inconsiderately as he of Naples into the war of 1805, landed with a small army in Germany, and besieged Hamelen, a fortress of Hanover, where Bernadotte had left a strong garrison. This movement, had Prussia broken her neutrality, might have been of high importance to the general cause; as events turned out, it was fruitless. The Swedes raised their siege in confusion, on receiving the news of Austerlitz; and Napoleon from that hour meditated the dethronement of the dynasty of Gustavus--but this object was not yet within reach.

The Principalities of Lucca, Massa-Carrara, and Garfagnana, were now conferred on Napoleon's sister, Eliza (Madame Bacciochi): on Pauline, the younger sister, who, after the death of General Leclerc, had married the Prince Borghese, the sovereignty of Guastalla was in like manner bestowed.

The Batavian republic had for years been in effect enslaved by France. On pretence that her leading men, however, still yearned after the alliance of England, and thwarted him in his designs on the commerce of that great enemy, Napoleon now resolved to take away even the shadow of Dutch independence. The Batavian Senate were commanded to ask Louis Buonaparte for their king; and these republicans submitted with the better grace, because the personal character of Louis was amiable, and since Holland must be an appendage to France, it seemed probable that the connection might be rendered the less galling in many circumstances, were a prince of Napoleon's own blood constituted her natural guardian. Louis had married the beautiful Hortense-Fanny de Beauharnois, daughter of Josephine--so that, by this act, two members of the imperial house were at once elevated to royalty.--They began their reign at the Hague in May, 1806.

Another great consequence of Austerlitz remains to be mentioned. The Kings of Wirtemberg and Bavaria, the Grand Duke of Berg, and other sovereigns of the West of Germany, were now associated together in a close alliance under the style of the Confederation of the Rhine: Napoleon added to his other titles that of Protector of this confederacy; and the princes of the league were bound to place 60,000 soldiers at his command.

Finally, it was on his return from the triumph of Austerlitz, that Napoleon trampled down the last traces of the revolutionary organisation in France, by creating a new order of nobility. Talleyrand became Prince of Benevento, Bernadotte, of Ponte Corvo, Berthier, of Neufchatel; the most distinguished of the Marshals received the title of Duke, and a long array of Counts of the Empire filled the lower steps of the throne.

These princedoms and dukedoms were accompanied with grants of extensive estates in the countries which the French arms had conquered; and the great feudatories of the new empire accordingly bore titles not domestic, but foreign. In everything it was the plan of Napoleon to sink the memory of the Bourbon Monarchy, and revive the image of Charlemagne, Emperor of the West.

[Footnote 51:

"Lamented hero! when to Britain's shore Exulting Fame those awful tidings bore, Joy's bursting shout in whelming grief was drowned And Victory's self unwilling audience found; On every brow the cloud of sadness hung; The sounds of triumph died on every tongue. Yet not the vows thy weeping country pays; Not that high meed, thy mourning sovereign's praise, Not that the great, the beauteous, and the brave Bend in mute reverence o'er thy closing grave; That with such grief as bathes a kindred bier Collective nations mourn a death so dear; Not these alone shall soothe thy sainted shade, And consecrate the spot where thou art laid-- Not these alone!--but bursting thro' the gloom, With radiant glory from thy trophied tomb, The sacred splendour of thy deathless name Shall grace and guard thy country's martial fame; Far seen shall blaze the unextinguished ray, A mighty beacon lighting glory's way-- With living lustre this proud land adorn, And shine, and save, thro' ages yet unborn."[52]]

CHAPTER XX

Discontent of Prussia--Death of Pitt--Negotiation of Lords Yarmouth and Lauderdale broken off--Murder of Palm, the bookseller--Prussia declares War--Buonaparte heads the Army--Naumburg taken--Battle of Jena--Napoleon enters Berlin--Fall of Magdeburg, &c.--Humiliation of Prussia--Buonaparte's cruelty to the Duke of Brunswick--his rapacity and oppression in Prussia.

The establishment of the Confederation of the Rhine rendered Napoleon, in effect, sovereign of a large part of Germany; and seemed to have so totally revolutionised Central Europe, that Francis of Austria declared the Imperial Constitution at an end. He retained the title of Emperor as sovereign of his own hereditary dominions; but "The Holy Roman Empire," having lasted full one thousand years, was declared to be no more; and of its ancient influence the representative was to be sought for not at Vienna, but at Paris.

The vacillating court of Berlin heard with much apprehension of the formation of the Rhenish confederacy;[53] and with deep resentment of its immediate consequence, the dissolution of the Germanic Empire. The house of Brandenburg had consented to the humiliation of Francis in the hope of succeeding, at the next election, to the imperial crown so long worn by the princes of Austria; and now, not only was that long-cherished hope for ever dispelled, but it appeared that Napoleon had laid the foundation of a new system, under which the influence of the house of Brandenburg must, in all probability, be overruled far more effectually than it ever had been, of recent times, by the imperial prerogative of Austria.

The only method of counteracting the consolidation of French power all over Germany, seemed to be that of creating another confederacy in the northern circles, capable of balancing the league of the Rhine. The Elector of Saxony, however, perceived that Napoleon was not likely to acquiesce in the realisation of this scheme; and his Minister at Berlin continued to decline acceding to the Northern alliance. The Prince of Hesse-Cassel took a similar view of the case; but acted with a degree of vacillation worthy of the late conduct of Prussia herself, refusing on the one hand to embrace the confederation proposed by the Cabinet of Berlin, and yet declining, on the other, to form part of the Rhenish league, to which effect Buonaparte had frequently and urgently invited this elector. In the reluctance, however, of these princes, Prussia saw nothing but the determination of Napoleon to suppress, in the beginning, any such confederation of the Northern German States as had been contemplated; and irritation and jealousy from day to day increased.

The relations of France and Prussia continued in this dubious state, until the Cabinet of Berlin learned some particulars of a negotiation between Napoleon and the English Government, which took place in the summer of 1806.

Mr. Pitt, who despaired of opposing Buonaparte on the continent after Marengo, did not long survive the disastrous intelligence of Austerlitz. Worn out and broken by the endless anxieties of his situation, not even the glorious tidings of Trafalgar could revive the sinking spirit of this great minister. He died on the 23rd of January, 1806, and was succeeded in the government by Mr. Fox, the same statesman who had, throughout every variety of fortune, arraigned his conduct of the war as imbecile and absurd, and who all along professed his belief that in the original quarrel between Great Britain and revolutionised France, the blame lay with his own country, and above all with Mr. Pitt.

The personal intercourse which took place between Fox and Napoleon, during the peace of Amiens, has already been alluded to. It was calculated to make all men regard the chances of a solid peace between France and England as increased by the event which transferred the reins of government, in the latter country, into the hands of the illustrious opponent of Mr. Pitt. But the peculiar feelings of English politicians have seldom been understood by foreigners--never more widely misunderstood than by Buonaparte. When Fox visited him, as First Consul, at the Tuileries, he complained that the English Government countenanced the assassins who were plotting against his life. Mr. Fox, forgetting all his party prejudice when the honour of his country was assailed, answered in terms such as Napoleon's own military bluntness could not have surpassed--"Clear your head of that nonsense." And now, in like manner, Mr. Fox, once placed in the responsible management of his country's interests, was found, not a little to the surprise and disappointment of Napoleon, about as close and watchful a negotiator as he could have had to deal with in Pitt himself. The English minister employed on this occasion, first, Lord Yarmouth,[54] one of the detenus of 1803, and afterwards Lord Lauderdale. For some time strong hopes of a satisfactory conclusion were entertained; but, in the end, the negotiation broke up, on the absolute refusal of Napoleon to concede Malta to England, unless England would permit him to conquer Sicily from the unfortunate sovereign whose Italian Kingdom had already been transferred to his brother Joseph. Mr. Fox was lost to his country in September, 1806; and Napoleon ever afterwards maintained that, had that great statesman lived, the negotiation would have been resumed, and pushed to a successful close. Meantime, however, the diplomatic intercourse of the Tuileries and St. James's was at an end, and the course which the negotiation had taken transpired necessarily in Parliament.

It then came out that the article of Hanover had not formed one of the chief difficulties;--in a word, Napoleon had signified that, although the Electorate had been ceded by him to Prussia under the treaty of Vienna, at the close of 1805, Prussia yielding to him in return the principalities of Anspach, Bareuth and Neufchatel, still, if the English Government would agree to abandon Sicily, he, on his part, would offer no opposition to the resumption of Hanover by its rightful sovereign, George III. This contemptuous treachery being ascertained at Berlin, the ill-smothered rage of the court and nation at length burst into a flame. The beautiful Queen of Prussia, and Prince Louis, brother to the king, two characters whose high and romantic qualities rendered them the delight and pride of the nation, were foremost to nourish and kindle the popular indignation. The young nobility and gentry rose in tumult, broke the windows of the ministers who were supposed to lean to the French interest, and openly whetted their sabres on the threshold-stone of Napoleon's ambassador. The lovely Queen appeared in the uniform of the regiment which bore her name, and rode at its head. The enthusiasm of the people thus roused might be directed, but could hardly be repressed.

Nor was it in Prussia alone that such sentiments prevailed. Split as Germany has for ages been into many independent states, there has always, nevertheless, been felt, and acknowledged, a certain national unity of heart as well as head among all that speak the German language: the dissolution of the empire was felt all over the land as a common wrong and injury: Napoleon's insulting treatment of Prussia was resented as indicative of his resolution to reduce that power also (the only German power now capable of opposing any resistance to French aggression) to a pitch of humiliation as low as that in which Austria was already sunk; and, lastly, another atrocious deed of the French Emperor--a deed as darkly unpardonable as the murder of D'Enghien--was perpetrated at this very crisis, and arrayed against him, throughout all Germany, every feeling, moral and political, which could be touched either by the crimes or the contumelies of a foreign tyrant.

Palm, a bookseller of the free city of Naumburg, having published a pamphlet in which the ambition of Napoleon was arraigned, a party of French gens-d'armes passed the frontier, and seized the unsuspecting citizen, exactly as the Duke d'Enghien had been arrested at Ettingen, and Sir George Rumbold at Hamburg, the year before. The bookseller was tried for a libel against Napoleon, at Braunau, before a French court-martial; found guilty, condemned to death, and shot immediately, in pursuance of his sentence. It is needless to dwell upon this outrage: the death of D'Enghien has found advocates or palliators--this mean murder of a humble tradesman, who neither was nor ever had been a subject either of France or Buonaparte, has been less fortunate.

The Emperor of Russia once more visited Berlin, when the feelings of Prussia, and indeed of all the neighbouring states, were in this fever of excitement. He again urged Frederick William to take up arms in the common cause, and offered to back him with all the forces of his own great empire. The English Government, taking advantage of the same crisis, sent Lord Morpeth[55] to Berlin, with offers of pecuniary supplies--about the acceptance of which, however, the anxiety of Prussia on the subject of Hanover created some difficulty. Lastly, Buonaparte, well informed of what was passing in Berlin, and desirous, since war must be, to hurry Frederick into the field ere the armies of the Czar could be joined with his, now poured out in the Moniteur such abuse on the persons and characters of the Queen, Prince Louis, and every illustrious patriot throughout Prussia, that the general wrath could no longer be held in check. Warlike preparations of every kind filled the kingdom during August and September. On the first of October the Prussian Minister at Paris presented a note to Talleyrand, demanding, among other things, that the formation of a Confederacy in the North of Germany should no longer be thwarted by French interference, and that the French troops within the territories of the Rhenish League should recross the Rhine into France, by the 8th of the same month of October.

But Napoleon was already in person on the German side of the Rhine; and his answer to the Prussian note was a general order to his own troops, in which he called on them to observe in what manner a German sovereign still dared to insult the soldiers of Austerlitz.

The conduct of Prussia, in thus rushing into hostilities, without waiting for the advance of the Russians, was as rash as her holding back from Austria, during the campaign of Austerlitz, had been cowardly. As if determined to profit by no lesson, the Prussian council also directed their army to advance towards the French, instead of lying on their own frontier--a repetition of the great leading blunder of the Austrians in the preceding year. The Prussian army accordingly invaded the Saxon provinces, and the Elector, seeing his country treated as rudely as that of Bavaria had been on a similar occasion by the Austrians, and wanting the means to withdraw his own troops as the Bavarian had succeeded in doing under like provocation, was compelled to accept the alliance which the Cabinet of Berlin urged on him, and to join his troops with those of the power by which he had been thus insulted and wronged.

No sooner did Napoleon know that the Prussians had advanced into the heart of Saxony, than he formed the plan of his campaign: and they, persisting in their advance, and taking up their position finally on the Saale, afforded him, as if studiously, the means of repeating, at their expense, the very manoeuvres which had ruined the Austrians in the preceding campaign. In a word, he perceived that the Prussian army was extended upon too wide a line, and the consequent possibility of destroying it in detail. He further discovered that the enemy had all his principal stores and magazines at Naumburg, to the rearward, not of his centre, but of his extreme right; and resolved to commence operations by an attempt to turn the flank, and seize those magazines, ere the main body of the Prussians, lying at Weimar, could be aware of his movement. The French came forward in three great divisions; the corps of Soult and Ney, in the direction of Hof; Murat, Bernadotte and Davoust, towards Saalburg and Schleitz; and Lannes and Augereau upon Coburg and Saalfield. These last generals were opposed sternly, at Saalfield, by the corps of Prince Louis of Prussia. This brave young officer imprudently abandoned the bridge over the Saale, which he might have defended with success, and came out into the open plain, where his troops were overpowered by the French impetuosity. He himself, fighting hand to hand with a subaltern, was desired to surrender, and replying by a sabre cut, was immediately struck down with a mortal thrust. The Prussians fled; the bridge, which ought to have defended, gave the French access to the country behind the Saale. The flank of the Prussian position was turned: the French army passed entirely round them; Napoleon seized Naumburg, and blew up the magazines there,--announcing, for the first time, by this explosion, to the King of Prussia and his Generalissimo, the Duke of Brunswick, that he was in their rear.

From this moment the Prussians were isolated, and cut off from all their resources, as completely as the army of Mack was at Ulm, when the French had passed the Danube and overrun Suabia. The Duke of Brunswick hastily endeavoured to concentrate his forces for the purpose of cutting his way back again to the frontier which he had so rashly abandoned. Napoleon, meantime, had posted his divisions so as to watch the chief passages of the Saale, and expected, in confidence, the assault of his outwitted opponent. It was now that he found leisure to answer the manifesto of Frederick William, which had reached Paris a day or two after he himself quitted that capital for the camp. His letter, dated at Gera, is written in the most elaborate style of insult. The King of Prussia (said he) had sent him a silly pamphlet of twenty pages, in very bad French--such a pamphlet as the English ministry were in the habit of commanding their hireling scribblers to put forth--but he acquitted the King of having read this performance. He was extremely anxious to live on the most friendly terms with his "good brother," and begged him, as the first token of equal goodwill, to dismiss the counsellors who had hurried him into the present unjust and unequal war. Such was the language of this famous note. Napoleon, now sure of his prey, desired his own generals to observe how accurately he had already complied with one of the requests of the Prussian Manifesto--"The French army," said he, "has done as it was bidden. This is the 8th of October, and we have evacuated the territories of the Confederation of the Rhine."

The Prussian King understood well, on learning the fall of Naumburg, the imminent danger of his position; and his army was forthwith set in motion, in two great masses; the former, where he was in person present, advancing towards Naumburg; the latter attempting, in like manner, to force their passage through the French line in the neighbourhood of Jena. The King's march was arrested at Auerstadt by Davoust, who, after a severely contested action, at length repelled the assailant. Napoleon himself, meanwhile, was engaged with the other great body of the Prussians. Arriving on the evening of the 13th October at Jena, he perceived that the enemy were ready to attempt the advance next morning, while his own heavy train were still six-and-thirty hours' march in his rear. Not discouraged with this adverse circumstance, the Emperor laboured all night in directing and encouraging his soldiery to cut a road through the rocks, and draw up by that means such light guns as he had at command to a position, on a lofty plateau in front of Jena, where no man could have expected beforehand that any artillery whatever should be planted, and where, accordingly, the effect even of a small park proved more decisive than that of a much larger one might have been under other circumstances. Buonaparte spent all the night among the men, offering large sums of gold for every piece that should be dragged to the position, and continually reminding his followers that the Prussians were about to fight not for honour, but for safety,--that they were already isolated as completely as Mack's army had been at Ulm, and on stern resistance must needs submit to the fate of the Austrians. Lannes commanded the centre; Augereau the right; Soult the left; and Murat the reserve and cavalry.

Soult had to sustain the first assault of the Prussians, which was violent--and sudden; for the mist lay so thick on the field that the armies were within half gunshot of each other ere the sun and wind rose and discovered them; and on that instant Mollendorf charged. The battle was contested well for some time on this point; but at length Ney appeared in the rear of the Emperor with a fresh division; and then the French centre advanced to a general charge, before which the Prussians were forced to retire. They moved for some space in good order; but Murat now poured his masses of cavalry on them, storm after storm, with such rapidity and vehemence that their rout became inevitable. It ended in the complete breaking up of the army--horse and foot all flying together, in the confusion of panic, upon the road to Weimar. At that point the fugitives met and mingled with their brethren flying, as confusedly as themselves, from Auerstadt. In the course of this disastrous day 20,000 Prussians were killed or taken; 300 guns, twenty generals, and sixty standards. The Commander-in-Chief, the Duke of

Brunswick, being wounded in the face with a grape-shot, was carried early off the field, never to recover. The loss of superior officers on the Prussian side was so great, that of an army which, on the evening of the 13th of October, mustered not less than 150,000, but a few regiments were ever able to act in concert for some time after the 14th. The various routed divisions roamed about the country, seeking separately the means of escape: they were in consequence destined to fall an easy prey. Mollendorf and the Prince of Orange-Fulda laid down their arms at Erfurt. General Kalkreuth's corps was overtaken and surrounded among the Hartz Mountains: Prince Eugene of Wirtemberg, and 16,000 men, surrendered to Bernadotte at Halle. The Prince of Hohenlohe at length drew together not less than 50,000 of these wandering soldiers, and threw himself, at their head, into Magdeburg. But it turned out that that great fortress had been stripped of all its stores for the service of the Duke of Brunswick's army before Jena. Hohenlohe, therefore, was compelled to retreat towards the Oder. He was defeated in a variety of skirmishes; and at length, finding himself devoid of ammunition or provisions, laid down his arms at Prenzlow; 20,000 surrendered with the Prince. His rear, consisting of about 10,000, under the command of the celebrated General Blucher, were so far behind as to render it possible for them to attempt escape. Their heroic leader traversed the country with them for some time unbroken, and sustained a variety of assaults, from far superior numbers, with the most obstinate resolution. By degrees, however, the French, under Soult, hemmed him in on one side, Murat on the other, and Bernadotte appeared close behind him. He was thus forced to throw himself into Lubeck, where a severe action was fought in the streets of the town, on the 6th of November. The Prussian, in this battle, lost 4000 prisoners, besides the slain and wounded: he retreated to Schwerta, and there, it being impossible for him to go farther without violating the neutrality of Denmark, on the morning of the 7th, Blucher at length laid down his arms--having exhibited a specimen of conduct and valour such as certainly had not been displayed by any of his superiors in the campaign.

The strong fortresses of the Prussian monarchy made as ineffectual resistance as the armies in the field. In how far the charge of actual treachery, brought then, and still continued, against the commanders of those places, be just, we know not; but the fact is certain that the Governors of Spandau, Stettin, Custrin, Hamelen, and Magdeburg itself, yielded successively to the French Generals, under circumstances which roused the indignant suspicion of the Prussian people, as well as the soldiery and their unfortunate King. Buonaparte, in person, entered Berlin on the 25th of October: and before the end of November, except Konigsberg--where the King himself had found refuge, and gathered round him a few thousand troops, the sad relics of an army which had been considered as not unable to withstand the whole power of France,--and a few less important fortresses, the whole of the German possessions of the house of Brandenburg were in the hands of the conqueror. Louis Buonaparte, King of Holland, meanwhile, had advanced into Westphalia, and occupied that territory also, with great part of Hanover, East Friesland, Embden, and the dominions of Hesse-Cassel.

Thus in the course of a few short weeks, was the proud fabric of the Prussian monarchy levelled with the ground. The government being of a strictly military character, when the army, the pride and strength of the nation, disappeared, every bond of union among the various provinces of the crown seemed to be at once dissolved. To account for the unexampled rapidity of such a downfall, it must be remembered, first, that the Prussian states, many of them the fruits of recent military conquest, were held together by little but the name of the great Frederick, and the terror of the highly disciplined force, which he had bequeathed to his successors; that, in a word, they had not yet had time to be blended and melted thoroughly into a national whole: secondly, that Prussia had rushed into this war not only with imprudent rashness, but with the stain of dishonour on her hands. The acceptance of Hanover, as a bribe, from the French despot, and the hard and brazen reluctance to part with that ill-gotten spoil, even when the preservation of peace with France seemed hopeless--these circumstances, together with the mean desertion of Austria during the preceding campaign of Austerlitz--had, in effect, injured the government deeply and degradingly in the opinion of its own subjects, as well as of other nations: but, thirdly, the imbecile conduct of the chief Prussian officers, in the campaign of Jena, was as little likely to have been foreseen or expected, as the pusillanimous, if not treacherous, baseness of those who, after the army was defeated, abandoned so easily a chain of the best fortresses in Europe.

The personal character of King Frederick William was never calumniated, even when the measures of his government were most generally and most justly exposed to suspicion and scorn. On the contrary, the misfortunes of this virtuous sovereign and his family were heard of with unmixed regret and compassion.

These sentiments, and all sentiments likely in their consequences to be injurious to the cause of Napoleon, the conduct of the Conqueror in Prussia, at this time of national humiliation and sorrow, was well calculated to strengthen and confirm. The Duke of Brunswick, retiring wounded from Jena to the capital of his own hereditary principality, addressed a letter from thence to Napoleon, requesting that the territory of Brunswick might not be confounded with that of Prussia, although he, as an individual, had appeared in Prussian uniform against him. Buonaparte answered with insolence as well as harshness. He styled the Duke "General Brunswick," and said he was determined to destroy his city, and displace his family for ever. The brave, though unfortunate Duke, retired on this to Altona, a Danish town, from which he meant to embark for England; but his wound being inflamed by these untimely movements, he died ere a vessel could be prepared for him. His son, considering him as murdered, vowed eternal revenge--and how he kept his vow, we shall see hereafter. The Prussian nobility and gentry were treated on almost every occasion with like brutality. The great Conqueror did not hesitate to come down from his dignity for the petty pleasure of personally insulting gentlemen, who had done him no injury except that of being loyal to their own prince. The exactions of the victorious military were beyond all former example of licence; and studied contempt was everywhere mingled with their rapacity. It was now that the French laid the foundation of that universal hatred with which the Prussian nation, in the sequel, regarded them, and which assumed everywhere the virulence of a private and personal passion.

In justice to Buonaparte, a solitary instance of generous conduct, which occurred ere he had been long in Berlin, must be noticed. The Prince of Hatzsfeld, continuing to reside in Berlin under his protection, corresponded, nevertheless, with Hohenlohe, then in the field, and sent information of the state and movements of the French army. One of his letters fell into the hands of the French--the Prince was arrested--his wife gained access to the Emperor, and, ignorant of her husband's conduct, spoke with the boldness of innocence in his favour. He handed to her the Prince's letter; and, confounded with the clearness of that evidence, she fell on her knees in silence. "Put the paper in the fire, madam," said Napoleon, "and there will then be no proof."

Perhaps no part of Buonaparte's conduct at this time gave more general disgust than his meanness in robbing the funeral monument of Frederick the Great of his sword and orders. These unworthy trophies he transmitted to Paris, along with the best statues and pictures of the galleries of Berlin and Potsdam, thus dealt with according to the example of Lombardy and Venice.

[Footnote 53: Published 27th July, 1806.]

[Footnote 54: Afterwards third Marquis of Hertford.]

[Footnote 55: Afterwards sixth Earl of Carlisle.]

CHAPTER XXI

The Decrees of Berlin--Napoleon renews the campaign--Warsaw taken--Enthusiasm of the Poles--Retreat of the Russians--Battle of Pultusk--The French go into winter quarters--Battle of Preuss-Eylau--Taking of Dantzick--Battle of Friedland--Armistice--Expeditions of the English to Calabria, Constantinople, Egypt, and Buenos Ayres--Peace of Tilsit.

Napoleon had achieved the total humiliation of the Prussian monarchy in a campaign of a week's duration: yet severe as the exertions of his army had been, and splendid his success, and late as the season was now advanced, there ensued no pause of inaction: the Emperor himself remained but a few days in Berlin.

This brief residence, however, was distinguished by the issue of the famous decrees of Berlin; those extraordinary edicts by which Buonaparte hoped to sap the foundations of the power of England--the one power which he had no means of assailing by his apparently irresistible arms.

Napoleon declared the British Islands to be in a state of blockade: any intercourse with that country was henceforth to be a crime; all her citizens found in any country in alliance with France to be prisoners; every article of English produce or manufacture, wherever discovered, to be confiscated. In a word, wherever France had power, the slightest communication with England was henceforth to be treason against the majesty of Napoleon; and every coast of Europe was to be lined with new armies of douaniers and gens-d'armes, for the purpose of carrying into effect what he called "the continental system."

He had long meditated the organisation of this system, and embraced, as a favourable opportunity for its promulgation, the moment which saw him at length predominant in the North of Germany, and thus, in effect, master of the whole coasts of Europe from the mouth of the Oder round to the Adriatic Gulf. The system, however, could not be carried into effect, because from long habit the manufactured goods and colonial produce of Britain had come to be necessaries of life among every civilised people of the world; and consequently every private citizen found his own domestic comforts invaded by the decree, which avowedly aimed only at the revenues of the English crown. Every man, therefore, was under continual temptation, each in his own sphere and method, to violate the decrees of Berlin. The custom-house officers were exposed to bribes which their virtue could not resist. Even the most attached of Napoleon's own functionaries connived at the universal spirit of evasion--his brothers themselves, in their respective dominions, could not help sympathising with their subjects, and winking at the methods of relief to which they were led by necessity, the mother of invention. The severe police, however, which was formed everywhere as a necessary part of the machinery for carrying these edicts into execution--the insolence of the innumerable spies and informers whom they set in motion--and the actual deprivation of usual comforts, in so far as it existed--all these circumstances conspired to render the name of the Berlin decrees odious throughout Europe and in France itself. It may be added that the original conception of Napoleon was grounded on a mistaken opinion, to which, however, he always clung--namely, that England derives all her strength from her foreign commerce. Great as that commerce was, and great as, in spite of him, it continued to be, it never was anything but a trifle when compared with the internal traffic and resources of Great Britain--a country not less distinguished above other nations for its agricultural industry, than for its commercial.

Napoleon received at Berlin a deputation of his Senate, sent from Paris to congratulate him on the successes of his campaign. To them he announced these celebrated decrees: he made them the bearers of the trophies of his recent victories, and, moreover, of a demand for the immediate levying of 80,000 men, being the first conscription for the year 1808--that for the year

1807 having been already anticipated. The subservient Senate recorded and granted whatever their master pleased to dictate; but the cost of human life which Napoleon's ambition demanded had begun, ere this time, to be seriously thought of in France. He, meanwhile, prepared, without further delay, to extinguish the feeble spark of resistance which still lingered in a few garrisons of the Prussian Monarchy, beyond the Oder: and to meet, before they could reach the soil of Germany, those Russian legions which were now advancing, too late, to the assistance of Frederick William. That unfortunate Prince sent Lucchesini to Berlin, to open, if possible, a negotiation with the victorious occupant of his capital and palace; but Buonaparte demanded Dantzick, and two other fortified towns, as the price of even the briefest armistice; and the Italian envoy returned to inform the King, that no hope remained for him except in the arrival of the Russians.

Napoleon held in his hands the means of opening his campaign with those allies of Prussia, under circumstances involving his enemy in a new, and probably endless train of difficulties. The Partition of Poland--that great political crime, for which every power that had a part in it has since been severely, though none of them adequately punished--had left the population of what had once been a great and powerful kingdom, in a state of discontent and irritation, of which, had Napoleon been willing to make full use of it, the fruits might have been more dangerous for the Czar than any campaign against any foreign enemy. The French Emperor had but to announce distinctly that his purpose was the restoration of Poland as an independent state, and the whole mass, of an eminently gallant and warlike population would have risen instantly at his call. But Buonaparte was withheld from resorting to this effectual means of annoyance by various considerations; of which the chief were these: first, he could not emancipate Poland without depriving Austria of a rich and important province, and consequently provoking her once more into the field: and secondly, he foresaw that the Russian Emperor, if threatened with the destruction of his Polish territory and authority, would urge the war in a very different manner from that which he was likely to adopt while acting only as the ally of Prussia. In a word, Napoleon was well aware of the extent of the Czar's resources, and had no wish at this time to give a character of irremediable bitterness to their quarrel.

Though, however, he for these and other reasons refrained from openly appealing in his own person to the Poles as a nation, Buonaparte had no scruple about permitting others to tamper, in his behalf, with the justly indignant feelings of the people. Some of the heroic leaders of the Poles, in the struggles for their expiring independence, had long been exiles in France-- not a few of them had taken service in her armies. These men were allowed, and encouraged, to address themselves to the body of their countrymen, in language which could hardly fail to draw eager and enthusiastic recruits to the French standard, and increase mightily the perplexities of the Russian counsels. Nor did Napoleon scruple to authorise the circulation of an appeal of like tendency, bearing falsely[56] the venerated signature of Kosciusko. "Dear countrymen and friends," said the forgery, "arise! the Great Nation is before you--Napoleon expects, and Kosciusko calls on you. We are under the 荄 is of the Monarch who vanquishes difficulties as if by miracles, and the re-animation of Poland is too glorious an achievement not to have been reserved for him by the Eternal." Dombrowski and Wibichi, two Polish officers in Buonaparte's own army, sent forward from Berlin, on the 8th of the same month, a proclamation, which commenced in these words:--"Poles! Napoleon, the Great, the Invincible, enters Poland with an army of 300,000 men. Without wishing to fathom the mystery of his views, let us strive to merit his magnanimity. I will see (he has said to us) whether you deserve to be a nation. Poles! it depends then on yourselves to exert a national spirit, and possess a country. Your avenger, your restorer is here. Crowd from all quarters to his presence, as children in tears hasten to behold a succouring father. Present to him your hearts, your arms. Rise to a man, and prove that you do not grudge your blood to your country!" Lastly, in one of Napoleon's own bulletins, the following ominous sentences were permitted to appear:--"Shall the Polish throne be re-established, and shall the Great Nation secure for it respect and independence? Shall she recall it to life from the grave? God only, who directs all human affairs, can resolve this great mystery!" These appeals produced various eager addresses from Poland--and Buonaparte prepared to visit that country, though not as her liberator.

Before re-opening the great campaign, Buonaparte received the submission and explanation of the Elector of Saxony, who truly stated that Prussia had forced him to take part in the war. The apology was accepted, and from this time the Elector adhered to the League of the Rhine, and was a faithful ally of Napoleon. The Landgrave of Hesse-Cassel had worse fortune. The answer to all his applications was, that he had ceased to reign. What use the Conqueror designed to make of the territories thus confiscated, we shall presently see.

The Saxon army, and that of Hesse-Cassel, were both, however, at his disposal, and they both accordingly were marched forwards, and blended with the forces occupying Prussia.

The French, having invested Glogau, Breslau, and Graudentz, and left detachments to urge these sieges, moved towards the Polish frontier. General Bennigsen, with a considerable Russian army, had advanced to overawe the dissatisfied population, and was now at Warsaw. But the march of the French van, under Murat, soon alarmed him in these quarters. After some skirmishes of little moment the Russians retired behind the Vistula, and Murat took possession of the Polish metropolis on the 28th of November. On the 25th Napoleon himself had reached Posen, and found himself surrounded by a population in a high state of excitement and enthusiasm. The ancient national dress reappeared: hope and exultation beamed in every countenance; the old nobles, quitting the solitary castles in which they had been lamenting over the downfall of Poland, crowded the levees of the Victor, and addressed him in language which recalled the half-oriental character and manners of their nation. "We adore you," said the Palatine of Gnesna, "and with confidence repose in you all our hopes, as upon him who raises empires and destroys them, and humbles the proud--the regenerator of our country, the legislator of the universe." "Already," said the President of the Council of Justice, "already our country is saved, for we adore in your person the most just and the most profound Solon. We commit our fate into your hands, and implore the protection of the most august Caesar."

Having largely recruited his armies with brave Poles, who fancied him both a Solon and Caesar, Napoleon now moved forwards. General Bennigsen found himself under the necessity of abandoning first the line of the Vistula, and then that of the Bug, and, the French still advancing in numbers not to be resisted by his division, at length threw himself behind the river Wkra, where Kaminskoy, the Russian commander-in-chief, and three other divisions of the army, had by this time taken their ground. On the 23rd of December Napoleon reached and crossed the Wkra, and Kaminskoy ordered his whole army to fall back upon the line of the Niemen. Bennigsen accordingly retired towards Pultusk, Galitzin upon Golymin, both followed by great bodies of the French, and both sustaining with imperturbable patience and gallantry the severity of a march through probably the very worst roads in Europe, and of frequent skirmishes with their pursuers. But the minor divisions of D'Anrep and Bexhouden retreated without keeping up the requisite communications with either Bennigsen or Galitzin, and consequently suffered considerably, though the matter was grossly exaggerated in the French bulletins.

Bennigsen, in spite of Kaminskoy's orders to retreat at all hazards, made a stand, and a most gallant one at Pultusk. Having his left in that town, and his right on a wood, the general conceived his position to be too favourable for speedy abandonment, and on the 26th of December expected the onset of Lannes, Davoust, and the imperial guard of France. They charged with their usual impetuosity, and drove the Russian right wing, under General Barclay de Tolly, out of the wood; but Bennigsen skilfully availed himself of this occurrence; by his orders Barclay de Tolly retired much further than was necessary for his own safety, and the French, advancing unguardedly, found themselves confronted on very unfavourable ground with the Russian main body, which had now been arranged on a new line of battle, and of a battery of 120 guns, placed so as to command their march with terrible efficacy. The result was that the Russians lost 5000 in killed and wounded, the French 8000--one of their wounded being Marshal Lannes himself; and the French drew back from the hardly contested field with such haste, that all next day the advancing Cossacks sought in vain for their rear-guard. On the same day, and with nearly as much success, Prince Galitzin halted also, and awaited and repelled his pursuers at Golymin; and had either Bennigsen or Galitzin been supported by the other divisions which were doing nothing within a few miles of their respective marches, these events might have been improved so as to involve the French army in great and immediate perplexity. But in truth, the total want of plan and combination on the part of Kaminskoy was by this time apparent to the veriest tyro in his camp. Symptoms of actual insanity appeared shortly afterwards, and the chief command was transferred, with universal approbation, to Bennigsen.

The affairs of Pultusk and Golymin, however, were productive of excellent effects. They raised to a high pitch the spirits of the Russian soldiery; and they afforded Napoleon such a specimen of the character of his new enemy, that instead of pursuing the campaign, as he had announced in his bulletins, he thought fit to retire, and place his troops in winter quarters. He himself took up his residence at Warsaw, and the army occupied cantonments in various towns to the eastward.

But General Bennigsen, having proved at Pultusk what Russian troops could do when under a determined commander, no sooner found himself at the head of an army of nearly 100,000 men, than he resolved to disturb the French in their quarters, and at all events give them such occupation as might enable the King of Prussia to revictual Konigsberg, where the few troops, gathered round that unfortunate sovereign, were already beginning to suffer many privations. With this view Bennigsen advanced as far as Mohrungen, where the French sustained considerable damage in a skirmish, and from whence his Cossacks spread themselves abroad over the country--creating such confusion, that the leaguer of Konigsberg being for the moment relaxed, the Prussian garrison received welcome supplies of all kinds, and Napoleon himself perceived the necessity of breaking up his cantonments, and once more concentrating the army for active war.

His design was to occupy Willensberg, to the rear of the great Russian camp at Mohrungen; thus cutting off the new enemy's communications with his own means of resource, in the same manner which had proved so fatal to the Austrians at Ulm, and the Prussians at Jena. But Bennigsen, having learned the plan from an intercepted despatch, immediately countermarched his army with masterly skill, and thus involved Napoleon in a long series of manoeuvres, not to be executed in such a country at that dismal season without the extremity of hardship. The Russians themselves, inured as they were to northern climates, and incapable of even dreaming that a soldier could seek safety in flight, were reduced to the border of frenzy by the privations of these long marches. Their commissariat was wretched: the soldiers had often no food, except such frozen roots as they could dig out of the ground; and, tortured with toil and famine, they at length demanded battle so vehemently, that, against his own judgment, General Bennigsen consented to grant the prayer. He selected the town of Preuss Eylau, and a strong position behind it, as his field of battle; and--after two skirmishes, one at Landsberg, the other nearer the chosen ground, in the former of which the French, in the latter the Russians, had the advantage,--the whole army reached Preuss-Eylau on the 7th of February.

In the confusion of so great a movement, a division designed by Bennigsen to occupy the town itself, misunderstood the order, and evacuated it at the approach of the enemy's van. The French took possession of the place accordingly, and--General Bennigsen commanding it to be regained, as soon as he learned the mistake that had occurred--the whole day was spent in severe fighting within the town, which was taken and retaken several times, and at the fall of night remained in the hands of the French. On either side the loss had been very great, and Napoleon coming up in person, perceived that the contest must needs be renewed at daybreak. The night was clear, and he could trace the enemy's line darkening the whole of an admirably selected position, between which and the dearly contested town, a level space covered with snow, and two or three small frozen lakes, glittered in the mingled light of an unclouded moon and innumerable watch-fires.

The great battle of PREUSS-EYLAU was fought on the 8th of February. At dawn of day the French charged at two different points in strong columns, and were unable to shake the iron steadiness of the infantry, while the Russian horse, and especially the Cossacks under their gallant Hetman Platoff, made fearful execution on each division, as successively they drew back from their vain attempt. A fierce storm arose at mid-day: the snow drifted right in the eyes of the Russians; the village of Serpallen, on their left, caught fire, and the smoke also rolled dense upon them. Davoust skilfully availed himself of the opportunity, and turned their flank so rapidly, that Serpallen was lost, and the left wing compelled to wheel backwards so as to form almost at right angles with the rest of the line. The Prussian corps of L'Estocq, a small but determined fragment of the campaign of Jena, appeared at this critical moment in the rear of the Russian left; and, charging with such gallantry as had in former times been expected from the soldiery of the Great Frederick, drove back Davoust and restored the Russian line. The action continued for many hours along the whole line--the French attacked boldly, the Russians driving them back with unfailing resolution. Ney, and a fresh division, at length came up, and succeeded in occupying the village of Schlodtten, on the road to Konigsberg. To regain this, and thereby recover the means of communicating with the King of Prussia, was deemed necessary; and it was carried accordingly at the point of the bayonet. This was at ten o'clock at night. So ended the longest and by far the severest battle in which Buonaparte had as yet been engaged. The French are supposed to have had 90,000 men under arms at its commencement; the Russians not more than 60,000. After fourteen hours of fighting, either army occupied the same position as in the morning. Twelve of Napoleon's eagles were in the hands of Bennigsen, and the field between was covered with 50,000 corpses, of whom at least half were French.

Either leader claimed the victory; Bennigsen exhibiting as proof of his success the twelve eagles which his army, admitted to be inferior in numbers, bore off the field: Buonaparte, that he kept possession of the field, while the enemy retired, the very night after the battle, from Eylau towards Konigsberg. It was, in truth, a drawn battle; and to have found an equal was sufficient bitterness to Napoleon. The Russian general-in-chief had retreated, in opposition to the opinion of most of his council, out of anxiety for the personal safety of the King of Prussia at Konigsberg, and desire to recruit his army ere another great action should be hazarded. The French, triumphant as was the language of their bulletins, made no effort to pursue. Bennigsen conducted his army in perfect order to Konigsberg, and the Cossacks issuing from that city continued for more than a week to waste the country according to their pleasure, without any show of opposition from the French. But the best proof how severely Napoleon had felt the struggle of Preuss-Eylau, is to be found in a communication which he made to Frederick William, on the 13th of February, five days after the battle, offering him, in effect, the complete, or nearly complete restoration of his dominions, provided he would accept of a separate peace: with the king's answer; namely, that it was impossible for him to enter on any treaty unless the Czar were a party in it. Finally, on the 19th of February, Napoleon left Eylau, and retreated with his whole army on the Vistula; satisfied that it would be fatal rashness to engage in another campaign in Poland, while several fortified towns, and, above all, Dantzick, held out in his rear; and determined to have possession of these places, and to summon new forces from France, ere he should again meet in the field such an enemy as the Russian had proved to be.

Dantzick was defended with the more desperate resolution, because it was expected that, as soon as the season permitted, an English fleet and army would certainly be sent to its relief. But the besiegers having a prodigious superiority of numbers, and conducting the siege with every advantage of skill, the place was at length compelled to surrender, on the 7th of May; after which event, Napoleon's extraordinary exertions in hurrying supplies from France, Switzerland and the Rhine country, and the addition of the division of 25,000, which had captured Dantzick, enabled him to take the field again at the head of not less than 280,000 men. The Russian general also had done what was in his power to recruit his army during this interval; but his utmost zeal could effect no more than bringing his muster up again to its original point--90,000; the chief blame lying, as it was alleged, with the coldness of the English cabinet, who, instead of lavishing gold on the Emperor of Russia, as had been done in other similar cases, were with difficulty persuaded to grant him at this critical time, so small a supply as ?0,000. Russia has men to any amount at her command; but the poverty of the national purse renders it at all times very difficult for her to maintain a large army in a distant contest.

Bennigsen, nevertheless, was the first to reappear in the field. In the beginning of June he attacked Ney's division stationed at Gustadt, and pursued them to Deppen, where, on the 8th, a smart action took place, and Napoleon arrived in person to support his troops. The Russians were then forced to retire towards Heilsberg, where they halted, and maintained their position, during a whole day, in the face of an enemy prodigiously superior in numbers. The carnage on both sides was fearful; and Bennigsen, continuing his retreat, placed the river Aller between him and Napoleon.

The French Emperor now exerted all his art to draw the Russian into a general action: the resistance he had met with had surprised and enraged him, and he was eager to overpower and extinguish Bennigsen before further supplies of these hardy Muscovities should come up to swell his ranks. The Russian general was on the eastern bank of the Aller, opposite to the town of Friedland, when Buonaparte once more came up with him on the 13th of June. There was a long and narrow wooden bridge over the river, close by, which might have been destroyed if not defended; and Napoleon's object was to induce Bennigsen, instead of abiding by his position, to abandon its advantages, pass over to the western bank, and accept battle with the town and river in his rear. His crafty management outwitted the Russian, who, being persuaded that the troops which appeared in front of him were only a small division of the French army, was tempted to send some regiments over the river for the purpose of chastising them. The French, sometimes retreating, and then again returning to the combat, the Russians were by degrees induced to cross in greater numbers; until at length Bennigsen found himself and his whole army on the western bank, with the town and bridge in their rear--thus completely entrapped in the snare laid for him by his enemy.

On the 14th of June, under circumstances thus disadvantageous, the Russian general was compelled to accept battle. His army occupied open ground; the intricate and narrow streets of the town of Friedland, and the bridge behind it, appeared to be his only means of retreat in case of misadventure; and in front, and on either flank, extended those woods which had covered Buonaparte's stratagems of the preceding day, and which now afforded complete shelter to the Imperial army--the means of attacking from whatever point they might select--and of retiring with safety as often as it might be found advisable.

The battle commenced at ten in the morning, and the Russians stood their ground with unbroken resolution until between four and five in the evening; sustaining numberless charges of foot and horse, and exposed all the while to a murderous cannonade. At length Napoleon put himself at the head of the French line, and commanded a general assault of all arms, which was executed with overpowering effect. Having lost full 12,000 men, General Bennigsen was at last compelled to attempt a retreat; the French poured after him into the town: the first Russian division which forced the passage of the river destroyed the bridge behind them in their terror; and the rest of the army escaped by means of deep and dangerous fords, which, desperate as the resource they afforded was, had been discovered only in the moment of necessity. Nevertheless such were the coolness and determination of the Russians, that they saved all their baggage, and lost only seventeen cannon; and such was the impression which their obstinate valour left on the enemy, that their retreat towards the Niemen was performed without any show of molestation.

The results of the battle of Friedland were, however, as great as could have been expected from any victory. On the retreat of Bennigsen towards the Niemen, the unfortunate King of Prussia, evacuating Konigsberg, where he now perceived it must be impossible to maintain himself, sought a last and precarious shelter in the seaport of Memel; and the Emperor Alexander, overawed by the genius of Napoleon, which had triumphed over troops more resolute than had ever before opposed him, and alarmed for the consequence of some decisive measure towards the re-organisation of the Poles as a nation, began to think seriously of peace. Buonaparte, on his part also, had many reasons for being anxious to bring hostilities to a close. The Swedish king was in Pomerania, besieging Stralsund, and hourly expecting reinforcements from England, which might have ended in a formidable diversion in the rear of the French army. Schill, an able partizan, was in arms in Prussia, where the general discontent was such, that nothing by opportunity seemed wanting for a national insurrection against the conquerors. The further advance of the French towards the north could hardly have failed to afford such an opportunity. Neither could this be executed, to all appearance, without involving the necessity of proclaiming the independence of Poland; thereby giving a character of mortal rancour to the war with Russia, and, in all likelihood, calling Austria once more into the field. Under such circumstances the minds of Napoleon and Alexander were equally disposed towards negotiation: General Bennigsen sent, on the 21st of June, to demand an armistice; and to this proposal the victor of Friedland yielded immediate assent.

In truth over and above the parsimony of the court of St. James in regard to subsidies, the recent conduct of the war on the part of England had been so ill-judged, and on the whole so unfortunate, that the Czar might be excused for desiring to escape from that alliance. Almost the only occasion on which the character of the British arms had been gloriously maintained, was the battle of Maida, in Calabria, fought July the 4th, 1806--when Sir John Stuart and 7000 English soldiers encountered a superior French force under General Regnier, and drove them from the field with great loss. This was one of those rare occasions on which French and English troops have actually crossed bayonets--the steadiness of the latter inspired the former with panic, and they fled in confusion. But this occurrence, except for its moral influence on the English soldiery, was of small importance. General Stuart had been sent to support the Calabrian peasantry in an insurrection against Joseph Buonaparte; the insurgents were on the whole unable to stand their ground against the regular army of the intrusive king; and the English, soon after their fruitless victory, altogether withdrew. The British had, indeed, taken possession of Curacao, and of the Cape of Good Hope (this last an acquisition of the highest moment to the Indian empire); but on the whole the ill success of our measures had been answerable to the narrow and shallow system of policy in which they originated--the system of frittering away blood and gold upon detached objects, instead of rallying the whole resources of the empire around some one great leader for some one great purpose. The British expeditions of this period to the Turkish dominions and to Spanish America were especially distinguished for narrowness of design, imbecility of execution, and consequent misadventure.

On the assumption of the Imperial dignity by Napoleon, the Ottoman Porte, dazzled by the apparently irresistible splendour of his fate, sent an embassy to congratulate him; and in effect the ancient alliance between France and Turkey was re-established. Napoleon consequently had little difficulty in procuring from Constantinople a declaration of war against Russia, the great hereditary enemy of the Turk, at the time when he was about to encounter the armies of the Czar in Poland. The Dardanelles were shut against Russian vessels; and the English government, considering this as sufficient evidence that the Grand Seignior was attaching himself to the Antibritannic Confederacy, despatched a squadron of ships under Admiral Duckworth, in February, 1807, with orders to force the passage of the Dardanelles, present themselves before Constantinople, and demand from the Porte the custody pro tempore of all her ships of war. The Turks negotiated for a week upon this proposal, but in the meantime increased and manned their fortifications, under the direction of French engineers, with such skill, that the English admiral began to be seriously alarmed for his own safety; and at length, on the 1st of March, effected his retreat through the Straits with considerable loss--this disgrace being the only result of his expedition. On the 20th of the same month (of March, 1807) another English expedition under General Fraser, having sailed from Sicily to Egypt, took possession of Alexandria. But every subsequent step they took proved unfortunate: after severe loss the English were compelled to enter into a convention with the Turks, and wholly evacuate Egypt on the 20th of September.

In January, 1807, an English expedition landed near Montevideo, and carried that city by assault. Sir Home Popham, the admiral, was recalled, and tried by a court-martial, on the ground that he had undertaken this warfare without due authority; but he escaped with a reprimand, and new reinforcements were sent out, first under General Crawford, and secondly under General Whitelocke. The last named officer invested Buenos Ayres, and commanded a general assault of that town on the 5th of July; on which occasion, notwithstanding the excellent behaviour of the soldiery, he was repulsed with a loss of 2000 killed, wounded, and prisoners; and reduced to such extremity, that he was soon afterwards glad to enter into a convention, and wholly withdraw the armament. The timid and incompetent Whitelocke was tried and cashiered. Some of these disasters were unknown at the time when Bennigsen demanded an armistice; but the general ill success of the British expeditions was notorious, and produced without doubt a very serious impression on the mind of Alexander.

The armistice was ratified on the 23rd of June, and on the 25th the Emperors of France and Russia met personally, each accompanied by a few attendants, on a raft moored on the river Niemen, near the town of Tilsit. The sovereigns embraced each other, and retiring under a canopy had a long conversation, to which no one was a witness. At its termination the appearances of mutual goodwill and confidence were marked: immediately afterwards the town of Tilsit was neutralised, and the two Emperors established their courts there, and lived together, in the midst of the lately hostile armies, more like old friends who had met on a party of pleasure, than enemies and rivals attempting by diplomatic means the arrangement of differences which had for years been deluging Europe with blood. Whatever flatteries could be suggested by the consummate genius and mature experience of Napoleon, were lavished, and produced their natural effects, on the mind of a young autocrat, of great ambition, and as great vanity. The intercourse of the Emperors assumed by degrees the appearance of a brotherlike intimacy. They spent their mornings in reviewing each other's troops, or in unattended rides; their evenings seemed to be devoted to the pleasures of the table, the spectacle, music, dancing and gallantry. Meanwhile the terms of a future alliance were in effect discussed, and settled much more rapidly than could have been expected from any of the usual apparatus of diplomatic negotiation.

The unfortunate King of Prussia was invited to appear at Tilsit; but, complying with this invitation, was admitted to no share of the intimacy of Napoleon. The conqueror studiously, and on every occasion, marked the difference between his sentiments respecting this prince and the young and powerful sovereign, for whose sake alone any shadow of royalty was to be conceded to the fallen house of Brandenburg. The beautiful and fascinating queen also arrived at Tilsit; but she was treated even more coldly and harshly than her husband. Involuntary tears rushed from her eyes as she submitted to the contemptuous civilities of Napoleon. His behaviour to this admirable person rekindled with new fervour the wrath and hatred of every Prussian bosom; and her death, following soon afterwards, and universally attributed to the cruel laceration which all her feelings as a woman and a queen had undergone, was treasured as a last injury, demanding, at whatever hazard, a terrible expiation.

The Treaty of Tilsit, to which, as the document itself bore testimony, the King of Prussia was admitted as a party solely by reason of Napoleon's "esteem for the Emperor of Russia," was ratified on the 7th July. Napoleon restored, by this act, to Frederick William, Ancient Prussia, and the French conquests in Upper Saxony--the King agreeing to adopt "the continental system," in other words, to be henceforth the vassal of the conqueror. The Polish provinces of Prussia were erected into a separate principality, styled "the Grand Duchy of Warsaw," and bestowed on the Elector of Saxony; with the exception, however, of some territories assigned to Russia, and of Dantzick, which was declared a free city, to be garrisoned by French troops until the ratification of a maritime peace. The Prussian dominions in Lower Saxony and on the Rhine, with Hanover, Hesse-Cassel, and various other small states, formed a new kingdom of Westphalia, of which Jerome Buonaparte, Napoleon's youngest brother, was recognised as King; Jerome having at length made his peace with his brother by repudiating his wife, an American lady of the name of Patterson, and consenting to a new alliance, more consonant with the views of the Emperor, with a daughter of the King of Wirtemberg. The Elector of Saxony was recognised as another King of Napoleon's creation; Joseph Buonaparte as King of Naples; and Louis, of Holland. Finally, Russia accepted the mediation of France for a peace with Turkey, and France that of Russia for a peace with England.

Such were the public articles of the peace of Tilsit; but it contained secret articles besides; and of these the English government were, ere long, fortunate enough to ascertain the import.

The British cabinet had undergone a complete change in March, 1807--the management of affairs passing from the friends and heirs of Mr. Fox into the hands of Mr. Perceval and other statesmen of the school of Pitt. The unhappy conduct of the war had rendered the preceding government eminently unpopular; and the measures of the new one assumed from the beginning a character of greater energy. But the orders which had been given must be fulfilled; and the councils of 1806 bequeathed a fatal legacy in the disastrous expeditions of 1807. Lord Granville Leveson Gower[57] (the minister at St. Petersburg) was ere this time prepared to offer to the Czar such subsidies as he had in vain expected when preparing for the campaign of Poland; but it was too late to retrieve the error of the preceding cabinet; and the English ambassador, being unable to break off the negotiations at Tilsit, was compelled to bestow all his efforts on penetrating the secrets of the compact wherein they ended.

The result of his exertions was the complete assurance of the government of St. James's, that the Emperor of Russia had adopted the alliance of Napoleon to an extent far beyond what appeared on the face of the treaty of the 7th July; that he had agreed not only to lay English commerce, in case his mediation for a peace should fail, under the same ban with that of the decrees of Berlin, but to place himself at the head of a general confederation of the Northern Maritime Powers against the naval supremacy of England--in other words, resign his own fleets, with those of Denmark, to the service of Napoleon. In requital of this obligation the French Emperor unquestionably agreed to permit the Czar to conquer Finland from Sweden--thereby adding immeasurably to the security of St. Petersburg. On the other hand it is almost as impossible to doubt that Alexander pledged himself not to interfere with those ambitious designs as to the Spanish Peninsula, which Napoleon was ere long to develop, and which were destined ultimately to work his ruin.

In a word, there seems to be little doubt that Napoleon broached at Tilsit the dazzling scheme of dividing the European world virtually between the two great monarchs of France and Russia: and that the Czar, provided he were willing to look on, while his Imperial brother of the West subjected Spain, Portugal and England to his yoke, was induced to count on equal forbearance, whatever schemes he might venture on for his own aggrandisement, at the expense of the smaller states of the North of Europe, and, above all, of the Ottoman Porte.

[Footnote 56: Kosciusko himself subsequently disavowed any knowledge of the production.]

[Footnote 57: Afterwards first Earl Granville.]

CHAPTER XXII

British Expedition to Copenhagen--Coalition of France, Austria, Prussia, and Russia, against English Commerce--Internal affairs of France--The Administration of Napoleon--his Council of State--Court--Code--Public Works--Manufactures--Taxes--Military Organisation--The Conscription.

Napoleon, having left strong garrisons in the maritime cities of Poland and Northern Germany, returned to Paris in August, and was received by the Senate and other public bodies with all the triumph and excess of adulation. The Swedish King abandoned Pomerania immediately on hearing of the treaty of Tilsit. In effect the authority of the Emperor appeared now to be consolidated over the whole continent of Europe. He had reached indeed the pinnacle of his power and pride;--henceforth he was to descend; urged downwards, step by step, by the reckless audacity of ambition and the gathering weight of guilt.

The English government, being satisfied that the naval force of Denmark was about to be employed for the purposes of Napoleon, determined to anticipate him, while it was yet time, and to send into the Baltic such a fleet as should at once convince the court of Copenhagen that resistance must be vain, and so bring about the surrender of the vessels of war (to be retained by England, not in property, but in pledge until the conclusion of a general peace), without any loss of life or compromise of honour. Twenty-seven sail of the line, carrying a considerable body of troops under the orders of Earl Cathcart, appeared before the capital of Denmark in the middle of August, and found the government wholly unprepared for defence. The high spirit of the Crown Prince, however, revolted against yielding to a demand which imperious necessity alone could have rendered justifiable on the part of England: nor, unfortunately, were these scruples overcome until the Danish troops had suffered severely in an action against the British, and the capital itself had been bombarded during three days, in which many public buildings, churches and libraries perished, and the private population sustained heavy loss both of life and property. The fleet being at length surrendered, the English withdrew with it in safety, and the rage of Napoleon--ill disguised in lofty philippics about the violations of the rights and privileges of independent nations--betrayed how completely he had calculated on the use of this marine, and how little he had anticipated a movement of such vigour from the cabinet of St. James's.

The Emperor of Russia is said to have signified, through a confidential channel, that, though for the present he found himself compelled to temporise, he approved and admired the procedure of the English government. If this be true, however, his public and open conduct bore a very different appearance. The British ambassador was dismissed from St. Petersburg, and a general coalition of Russia, Austria, Prussia, and Denmark, against the commerce of England being speedily afterwards formed, the decrees of Berlin--still further strengthened by other decrees, issued by Napoleon on the 7th December, 1806, at Milan--were in fact announced as part and parcel of the universal law of the continent. Alexander of Russia marched a large army into Finland, and took possession of that great Swedish province--the promised booty of Tilsit. His fleet in the Mediterranean gained a signal victory over the Turks, and terms of amity between the courts of St. Petersburg and Constantinople were at length arranged under the mediation or dictation of Napoleon. Everything seemed to point to a state of universal tranquillity or submission throughout the continent, and to a steady devotion of all the resources of the European monarchies to the service of the French Emperor and the destruction of his last and greatest enemy.

That enemy was ere long, in consequence of a new and unforeseen explosion of guilty ambition, to possess the means of rekindling the continental war, of distracting the alliances of Napoleon, and ultimately of ruining the power which, for the present, appeared irresistible. But a short interval of tranquillity ensued: and we may avail ourselves of the opportunity to recur for a moment to the internal administration of French affairs under the Imperial Government, as now finally organised.

Buonaparte, shortly after the peace of Tilsit, abolished _the Tribunate_; and there remained, as the last shadows of assemblies having any political influence, the Legislative Senate and the Council of State. The former of these bodies was early reduced to a mere instrument for recording the imperial decrees; the latter consisted of such persons as Napoleon chose to invest for the time with the privilege of being summoned to the palace, when it pleased him to hear the opinions of others as to measures originating in his own mind, or suggested to him by his ministers. He appears to have, on many occasions, permitted these counsellors to speak their sentiments frankly and fully, although differing from himself; but there were looks and gestures which sufficiently indicated the limits of this toleration, and which persons, owing their lucrative appointment to his mere pleasure, and liable to lose it at his nod, were not likely to transgress. They spoke openly and honestly only on topics in which their master's feelings were not much concerned.

His favourite saying during the continuance of his power was, "I am the State;" and in the exile of St. Helena he constantly talked of himself as having been, from necessity, the Dictator of France. In effect no despotism within many degrees so complete and rigid was every before established in a civilised and Christian country. The whole territory was divided into prefectures--each prefect being appointed by Napoleon--carefully selected for a province with which he had no domestic relations--largely paid--and entrusted with such a complete delegation of power that, in Napoleon's own language, each was in his department an Empereur ?petit pied. Each of these officers had under his entire control inferior local magistrates, holding power from him as he did from the Emperor: each had his instructions direct from Paris; each was bound by every motive of interest to serve, to the utmost of his ability, the government from which all things were derived, to be hoped for, and to be dreaded. Wherever the Emperor was, in the midst of his hottest campaigns, he examined the details of administration at home more closely than, perhaps, any other sovereign of half so great an empire did during the profoundest peace. It was said of him that his dearest amusement, when he had nothing else to do, was to solve problems in algebra or geometry. He carried this passion into every department of affairs; and having, with his own eye, detected some errors of importance in the public accounts, shortly after his administration began, there prevailed thenceforth in all the financial records of the state such clearness and accuracy as are not often exemplified in those of a large private fortune. Nothing was below his attention, and he found time for everything. The humblest functionary discharged his duty under a lively sense of the Emperor's personal superintendence; and the omnipresence of his police came in lieu, wherever politics were not touched upon, of the guarding powers of a free press, a free senate, and public opinion. Except in political cases the trial by jury was the right of every citizen. The Code Napoleon, that elaborate system of jurisprudence, in the formation of which the Emperor laboured personally along with the most eminent lawyers and enlightened men of the time, was a boon of inestimable value to France. "I shall go down to posterity" (said he, with just pride) "with the Code in my hand." It was the first uniform system of laws which the French Monarchy had ever possessed: and being drawn up with consummate skill and wisdom, it at this day forms the code not only of France, but of a great portion of Europe besides. Justice, as between man and man, was administered on sound and fixed principles, and by unimpeached tribunals. The arbitrary Commission Courts of Napoleon interfered with nothing but offences, real or alleged, against his authority.

The Clergy were, as we have seen, appointed universally under the direction of Government: they were also its direct stipendiaries; hence nothing could be more complete than their subjection to its pleasure. Education became a part of the regular business of the state; all the schools and colleges being placed under the immediate care of one of Napoleon's ministers--all prizes and bursaries bestowed by the government--and the whole system so arranged, that it was hardly possible for any youth who exhibited remarkable talents to avoid the temptations to a military career, which on every side surrounded him. The chief distinctions and emoluments were everywhere reserved for those who excelled in accomplishments likely to be serviceable in war: and the Lyceums, or schools set expressly apart for military students, were invested with numberless attractions, scarcely to be resisted by a young imagination. The army, as it was the sole basis of Napoleon's power, was also at all times the primary object of his thoughts. Every institution of the state was subservient and administered to it, and none more efficaciously than the imperial system of education.

The ranks of the army, however, were filled during the whole reign of Napoleon by compulsion. The conscription law of 1798 acquired under him the character of a settled and regular part of the national system; and its oppressive influence was such as never before exhausted, through a long term of years, the best energies of a great and civilised people. Every male in France, under the age of twenty-five, was liable to be called on to serve in the ranks; and the regulations as to the procuring of substitutes were so narrow, that young men of the best families were continually forced to comply, in their own persons, with the stern requisition. The first conscription list for the year included all under the age of twenty-one; and the result of the ballot within this class amounted to nearly 80,000 names. These were first called on: but if the service of the Emperor demanded further supply, the lists of those aged twenty-two, twenty-three, twenty-four, and twenty-five, were successively resorted to. There was no exemption for any one who seemed able to bear arms. The only child of his parents, the young husband and father, were forced, like any others, to abandon fireside, profession, all the ties and all the hopes of life, on a moment's notice: and there is nothing in the history of modern Europe so remarkable, as that the French people should have submitted, during sixteen years, to the constant operation of a despotic law, which thus sapped all the foundations of social happiness, and condemned the rising hopes of the nation to bleed and die by millions in distant wars, undertaken solely for the gratification of one man's insatiable ambition. On the other hand, it is not to be denied that the great majority of the conscripts, with whatever reluctance they might enter the ranks, were soon reconciled to their fate. The avenues to promotion, distinction, wealth, honour, nobility, even royal dignity, were all open before the devoted and successful soldiers of Napoleon; and the presence of so many youths of good condition and education, among the ranks of the private soldiery, could not fail, first, to render the situation immeasurably less irksome than it otherwise could have been to each individual of the class, and secondly, to elevate the standard of manners and acquirements among the soldiery generally. There never was an army in whose ranks intelligence so largely abounded, nor in which so many officers of the highest rank had originally carried a musket.

The taxation rendered necessary by the constant wars of Napoleon was great; and the utter destruction of the foreign commerce and marine of France, which the naval supremacy of England effected, made the burden the more intolerable for various important classes of the community. On the other hand the taxes were levied fairly on the whole population, which presented a blessed contrast to the system of the old regime; and the vast extension and improvement of agriculture consequent on the division of the great estates at the Revolution, enabled the nation, at large to meet the calls of the government with much less difficulty than could have been anticipated at any former period of French history. Napoleon's great public works, too, though undertaken chiefly for the purpose of gratifying his own vanity and that of the nation, could not be executed without furnishing subsistence to vast bodies of the labouring poor, and were thus serviceable to more important ends. From his vain attempts to supply the want of English manufactured goods and colonial produce, by new establishments and inventions (such especially as that of manufacturing a substitute for sugar out of beetroot), partial good, in like manner, resulted.

The evils of the conscription, of a heavy taxation, of an inquisitorial police, and of a totally enslaved press--these, and all other evils attendant on this elaborate system of military despotism, were endured for so many years chiefly in consequence of the skill with which Napoleon, according to his own favourite language, knew "to play on the imagination," and gratify the vanity of the French people. In the splendour of his victories, in the magnificence of his roads, bridges, aqueducts, and other monuments, in the general pre-eminence to which the nation seemed to be raised through the genius of its chief, compensation was found for all financial burdens, consolations for domestic calamities, and an equivalent for that liberty in whose name the Tyrant had achieved his first glories. But it must not be omitted that Napoleon, in every department of his government, made it his first rule to employ the men best fitted, in his mind, to do honour to his service by their talents and diligence; and that he thus attached to himself, throughout the whole of his empire as well as in his army, the hopes and the influence of those whose personal voices were most likely to control the opinions of society.

He gratified the French nation by adorning the capital, and by displaying in the Tuileries a court as elaborately magnificent as that of Louis XIV. himself. The old nobility, returning from their exile, mingled in those proud halls with the heroes of the revolutionary campaigns; and over all the ceremonial of these stately festivities Josephine presided with the grace and elegance of one born to be a queen. In the midst of the pomp and splendour of a court, in whose antechambers kings jostled each other, Napoleon himself preserved the soldier-like simplicity of his original dress and manners. The great Emperor continued throughout to labour more diligently than any subaltern in office. He devoted himself wholly to the ambition to which he compelled all others to contribute.

Napoleon, as Emperor, had little time for social pleasures. His personal friends were few; his days were given to labour, and his nights to study. If he was not with his army in the field, he traversed the provinces, examining with his own eyes into the minutest details of local arrangement; and even from the centre of his camp he was continually issuing edicts which showed the accuracy of his observation during these journeys, and his anxiety to promote by any means, consistent with his great purpose, the welfare of some French district, town, or even village.

The manners of the Court were at least decent. Napoleon occasionally indulged himself in amours unworthy of his character and tormenting to his wife; but he never suffered any other female to possess influence over his mind, nor insulted public opinion by any approach to that system of unveiled debauchery which had, during whole ages, disgraced the Bourbon Court, and undermined their throne.

CHAPTER XXIII

Relations of Napoleon with Spain--Treaty of Fontainebleau--Junot marches to Portugal--Flight of the Braganzas to Brazil--French troops proceed into Spain--Dissensions in the Court--Both parties appeal to Napoleon--Murat occupies Madrid--Charles and Ferdinand abdicate at Bayonne--Joseph Buonaparte crowned King of Spain.

After the ratification of the treaty of Tilsit, Napoleon, returning as we have seen to Paris, devoted all his energies to the perfect establishment of "the continental system." Something has already been said as to the difficulties which this attempt involved: in truth it was a contest between the despotic will of Buonaparte, and the interests and habits, not only of every sovereign in his alliance, but of every private individual on the continent; and it was therefore actually impossible that the imperial policy should not be baffled. The Russian government was never, probably, friendly to a system which, from the nature of the national produce and resources, must, if persisted in for any considerable time, have inflicted irreparable injury on the finances of the landholders, reduced the public establishments, and sunk the effective power of the state. In that quarter, therefore, Napoleon soon found that, notwithstanding all the professions of personal devotion which the young Czar continued, perhaps sincerely, to make, his favourite scheme was systematically violated: but the distance and strength of Russia prevented him from, for the present, pushing his complaints to extremity. The Spanish peninsula lay nearer him, and the vast extent to which the prohibited manufactures and colonial produce of England found their way into every district of that country, and especially of Portugal, and thence through the hands of whole legions of audacious smugglers, into France itself, ere long fixed his attention and resentment. In truth, a proclamation, issued at Madrid shortly before the battle of Jena, and suddenly recalled on the intelligence of that great victory, had prepared the Emperor to regard with keen suspicion the conduct of the Spanish Court, and to trace every violation of his system to its deliberate and hostile connivance.

The court presented in itself the lively image of a divided and degraded nation. The King, old and almost incredibly imbecile, was ruled absolutely by his Queen, a woman audaciously unprincipled, whose strong and wicked passions again were entirely under the influence of Manuel Godoy, "Prince of the Peace," raised, by her guilty love, from the station of a private guardsman, to precedence above all the grandees of Spain, a matrimonial connection with the royal house, and the supreme conduct of affairs. She, her paramour, and the degraded King, were held in contempt and hatred by a powerful party, at the head of whom were the Canon Escoiquiz, the Duke del Infantado, and Ferdinand, Prince of Asturias, heir of the throne. The scenes of dissension which filled the palace and court were scandalous beyond all contemporary example: and, the strength of the two parties vibrating in the scale, according as corrupt calculators looked to the extent of Godoy's present power, or to the probability of Ferdinand's accession, the eyes of both were turned to the hazardous facility of striking a balance by calling in support from the Tuileries. Napoleon, on his part, regarding the rival factions with equal scorn, flattered himself that, in their common fears and baseness, he should find the means of ultimately reducing the whole Peninsula to complete submission under his own yoke.

The secret history of the intrigues of 1807, between the French Court and the rival parties in Spain, has not yet been clearly exposed; nor is it likely to be so while most of the chief agents survive. According to Napoleon the first proposal for conquering Portugal by the united arms of France and Spain, and dividing that monarchy into three separate prizes, of which one should fall to the disposition of France, a second to the Spanish King, and a third reward the personal exertions of Godoy, came not from him, but from the Spanish minister. It was unlikely that Napoleon should have given any other account of the matter. The suggestion has been attributed, by every Spanish authority, to the Emperor; and it is difficult to doubt that such was the fact. The treaty, in which the unprincipled design took complete form, was ratified at Fontainebleau on the 29th October, 1807, and accompanied by a convention, which provided for the immediate invasion of Portugal by a force of 28,000 French soldiers, under the orders of Junot, and of 27,000 Spaniards; while a reserve of 40,000 French troops were to be assembled at Bayonne, ready to take the field by the end of November, in case England should land an army for the defence of Portugal, or the people of that devoted country presume to meet Junot by a national insurrection.

Junot forthwith commenced his march through Spain, where the French soldiery were received everywhere with coldness and suspicion, but nowhere by any hostile movement of the people. He would have halted at Salamanca to organise his army, which consisted mostly of young conscripts, but Napoleon's policy outmarched his General's schemes, and the troops were, in consequence of a peremptory order from Paris, poured into Portugal in the latter part of November. Godoy's contingent of Spaniards appeared there also, and placed themselves under Junot's command. Their numbers overawed the population, and they advanced, unopposed, towards the capital--Junot's most eager desire being to secure the persons of the Prince Regent and the royal family. The feeble government, meantime, having made, one by one, every degrading submission which France dictated, having expelled the British factory and the British minister, confiscated all English property, and shut the ports against all English vessels, became convinced at length that no measures of subserviency could avert the doom which Napoleon had fulminated. A Moniteur, proclaiming that "the House of Braganza had ceased to reign," reached Lisbon. The Prince Regent re-opened his communication with the English admiral off the Tagus (Sir Sydney Smith) and the lately expelled ambassador (Lord Strangford), and being assured of their protection, embarked on the 27th of November, and sailed for the Brazils on the 29th, only a few hours before Junot made his appearance at the gates of Lisbon. The disgust with which the Portuguese people regarded his flight, the cowardly termination, as they might not unnaturally regard it, of a long course of meanness, was eminently useful to the invader. With the exception of one trivial insurrection, when the insolent conqueror took down the Portuguese arms and set up those of Napoleon in their place, several months passed in apparent tranquillity; and these were skilfully employed by the General in perfecting the discipline of his conscripts, improving the fortifications of the coast, and making such a disposal of his force as might best guard the country from any military demonstration on the part of England.

Napoleon thus saw Portugal in his grasp: but that he had all along considered as a point of minor importance, and he had accordingly availed himself of the utmost concessions of the treaty of Fontainebleau, without waiting for any insurrection of the Portuguese, or English debarkation on their territory. His army of reserve, in number far exceeding the 40,000 men named in the treaty, had already passed the Pyrenees, in two bodies, under

Dupont and Moncey, and were advancing slowly, but steadily, into the heart of Spain. Nay, without even the pretext of being mentioned in the treaty, another French army of 12,000, under Duhesme, had penetrated through the eastern Pyrenees, and being received as friends among the unsuspecting garrisons, obtained possession of Barcelona, Pampeluna, and St. Sebastian, and the other fortified places in the north of Spain, by a succession of treacherous artifices, to which the history of civilised nations presents no parallel. The armies then pushed forwards, and the chief roads leading from the French frontiers to Madrid were entirely in their possession.

It seems impossible that such daring movements should not have awakened the darkest suspicions at Madrid; yet the royal family, overlooking the common danger about to overwhelm them and their country, continued, during three eventful months, to waste what energies they possessed in petty conspiracies, domestic broils, and, incredible as the tale will hereafter appear, in the meanest diplomatic intrigues with the court of France. The Prince of Asturias solicited the honour of a wife from the House of Napoleon. The old King, or rather Godoy, invoked anew the assistance of the Emperor against the treasonable, nay (for to such extremities went their mutual accusations), the parricidal plots of the heir-apparent. Buonaparte listened to both parties, vouchsafed no direct answer to either, and continued to direct the onward movement of those stern arbiters, who were ere long to decide the question. A sudden panic at length seized the King or his minister, and the court, then at Aranjuez, prepared to retire to Seville, and, sailing from thence to America, seek safety, after the example of the House of Braganza, in the work of whose European ruin they had so lately been accomplices. The servants of the Prince of Asturias, on perceiving the preparations for this flight, commenced a tumult, in which the populace of Aranjuez readily joined, and which was only pacified (for the moment) by a royal declaration that no flight was contemplated. On the 18th of March, 1808, the day following, a scene of like violence took place in the capital itself. The house of Godoy in Madrid was sacked. The favourite himself was assaulted at Aranjuez, on the 19th; with great difficulty saved his life by the intervention of the royal guards; and was placed under arrest. Terrified by what he saw at Aranjuez, and heard from Madrid, Charles IV. abdicated the throne; and on the 20th, Ferdinand, his son, was proclaimed King of Madrid, amidst a tumult of popular applause. Murat, Grand Duke of Berg, had before this assumed the chief command of all the French troops in Spain; and hearing of the extremities to which the court factions had gone, he now moved rapidly on Madrid, surrounded that capital with 30,000 men, and took possession of it in person, at the head of 10,000 more, on the 23rd of March. Charles IV. meantime despatched messengers both to Napoleon and Murat, asserting that his abdication had been involuntary, and invoking their assistance against his son. Ferdinand, entering Madrid on the 24th, found the French general in possession of the capital, and in vain claimed his recognition as king. Murat accepted the sword of Francis I., which, amidst other adulations, Ferdinand offered to him; but pertinaciously declined taking any part in the decision of the great question, which demanded, as he said, the fiat of Napoleon.

The Emperor heard with much regret of the precipitancy with which his lieutenant had occupied Madrid--for his clear mind had foreseen ere now the imminent hazard of trampling too rudely on the jealous pride of the Spaniards; and the events of the 17th, 18th, and 19th March were well qualified to confirm his impression, that although all sense of dignity and decorum might be extinguished in the court, the ancient elements of national honour still remained, ready to be called into action, among the body of the people. He, therefore, sent Savary, in whose practised cunning and duplicity he hoped to find a remedy for the military rashness of Murat, to assume the chief direction of affairs at Madrid; and the rumour was actively spread, that the Emperor was about to appear there in person without delay.

Madrid occupied and begirt by forty thousand armed strangers, his title unrecognised by Murat, his weak understanding and tumultuous passions worked upon incessantly by the malicious craft of Savary, Ferdinand was at length persuaded, that his best chance of securing the aid and protection of Napoleon lay in advancing to meet him on his way to the capital, and striving to gain his ear before the emissaries of Godoy should be able to fill it with their reclamations. Savary eagerly offered to accompany him on this fatal journey, which began on the 10th of April. The infatuated Ferdinand had been taught to believe that he should find Buonaparte at Burgos; not meeting him there, he was tempted to pursue his journey as far as Vittoria: and from thence, in spite of the populace, who, more sagacious than their prince, cut the traces of his carriage, he was, by a repetition of the same treacherous arguments, induced to proceed stage by stage, and at length to pass the frontier and present himself at Bayonne, where the arbiter of his fate lay anxiously expecting this consummation of his almost incredible folly. He arrived there on the 20th of April--was received by Napoleon with courtesy, entertained at dinner at the imperial table, and the same evening informed by Savary that his doom was sealed--that the Bourbon dynasty had ceased to reign in Spain, and that his personal safety must depend on the readiness with which he should resign all his pretensions into the hands of Buonaparte.

He, meanwhile, as soon as he was aware that Ferdinand had actually set out from Madrid, had ordered Murat to find the means of causing the old King, the Queen, and Godoy to repair also to Bayonne; nor does it appear that his lieutenant had any difficulty in persuading these personages that such was the course of conduct most in accordance with their interests. They reached Bayonne on the 4th of May, and Napoleon, confronting the parents and the son on the 5th, witnessed a scene in which the profligate rancour of their domestic feuds reached extremities hardly to have been contemplated by the wildest imagination. The flagitious Queen did not, it is said and believed, hesitate to signify to her son that the King was not his father--and this in the presence of that King and of Napoleon. Could crime justify crime--could the fiendish lusts and hatreds of a degenerate race offer any excuse for the deliberate guilt of a masculine genius, the conduct of this abject court might have apologised for the policy which it perhaps tempted the pampered ambition of Napoleon to commence, and which it now encouraged him to consummate by an act of suicidal violence.

Charles IV. resigned the Crown of Spain for himself and his heirs, accepting in return from the hands of Napoleon a safe retreat in Italy and a large pension. Godoy, who had entered into the fatal negotiation of Fontainebleau, with the hope and the promise of an independent sovereignty carved out of the Portuguese dominions, was pensioned off in like manner, and ordered to partake the Italian exile of his patrons. A few days afterwards, Ferdinand VII., being desired to choose at length between compliance and death, followed the example of his father, and executed a similar act of resignation. Napoleon congratulated himself on having added Spain and the Indies to his empire, without any cost either of blood or of treasure; and the French people, dazzled by the apparent splendour of the acquisition, overlooked, if there be any faith in public addresses and festivals, the enormous guilt by which it had been achieved. But ere the ink with which the Spanish Bourbons signed away their birthright was dry, there came tidings to Bayonne which might well disturb the proud day-dreams of the spoliator, and the confidence of his worshippers.

Not that Napoleon had failed to measure from the beginning the mighty dangers which surrounded his audacious design. He had been warned of them in the strongest manner by Talleyrand, and even by Fouche nay, he had himself written to rebuke the headlong haste of Murat in occupying the Spanish capital--to urge on him the necessity of conciliating the people, by preserving the show of respect for their national authorities and institutions-- to represent the imminent hazard of permitting the Duke del Infantado to strengthen and extend his party in Madrid--and concluding with those ominous words: _Remember, if war breaks out, all is lost_.

Ferdinand, before he left Madrid, invested a council of regency with the sovereign power, his uncle, Don Antonio, being president, and Murat one of the members. Murat's assumption of the authority thus conferred, the departure of Ferdinand, the liberation and departure of the detested Godoy, the flight of the old King--these occurrences produced their natural effects on the popular mind. A dark suspicion that France meditated the destruction of the national independence, began to spread; and, on the 2nd of May, when it transpired that preparations were making for the journey of Don Antonio also, the general rage at last burst out. A crowd collected round the carriage meant, as they concluded, to convey the last of the royal family out of Spain; the traces were cut; the imprecations against the French were furious. Colonel La Grange, Murat's aide-de-camp, happening to appear on the spot, was cruelly maltreated. In a moment the whole capital was in an uproar: the French soldiery were assaulted everywhere--about 700 were slain. The mob attacked the hospital--the sick and their attendants rushed out and defended it. The French cavalry, hearing the tumult, entered the city by the gate of Alcala a column of 3000 infantry from the other side by the street Ancha de Bernardo. Some Spanish officers headed the mob, and fired on the soldiery in the streets of Maravelles: a bloody massacre ensued: many hundreds were made prisoners: the troops, sweeping the streets from end to end, released their comrades; and, to all appearance, tranquillity was restored ere nightfall. During the darkness, however, the peasantry flocked in armed from the neighbouring country: and, being met at the gates by the irritated soldiery, not a few more were killed, wounded, and made prisoners. Murat ordered all the prisoners to be tried by a military commission, which doomed them to instant death. It is disputed whether the more deliberate guilt of carrying the sentence into execution lies with the commander-in-chief himself, or with Grouchy; it is certain that a considerable number of Spaniards--the English authority most friendly to the French cause admits ninety-five[58]--were butchered in cold blood on the 3rd of May.

This commotion had been preceded by a brief insurrection, easily suppressed and not unlikely to be soon forgotten, on the 23rd of April, at Toledo. The events in the capital were of a more decisive character, and the amount of the bloodshed, in itself great, was much exaggerated in the reports which flew, like wildfire, throughout the Peninsula--for the French were as eager to overawe the provincial Spaniards, by conveying an overcharged impression of the consequences of resistance, as their enemies in Madrid were to rouse the general indignation, by heightened details of the ferocity of the invaders and the sternness of their own devotion. In almost every town of Spain, and almost simultaneously, the flame of patriotic resentment broke out in the terrible form of assassination. The French residents were slaughtered without mercy: the supposed partisans of Napoleon and Godoy (not a few men of worth being causelessly confounded in their fate) were sacrificed in the first tumult of popular rage. At Cadiz, Seville, Carthagena, above all in Valencia, the streets ran red with blood. The dark and vindictive temper of the Spaniards covered the land with scenes, on the details of which it is shocking to dwell. The French soldiery, hemmed in, insulted, and whenever they could be found separately, sacrificed--often with every circumstance of savage torture--retorted by equal barbarity whenever they had the means. Popular bodies (juntas) assumed the conduct of affairs in most of the cities and provinces, renounced the yoke of France, reproclaimed Ferdinand king, and at the maritime stations of chief importance entered into communication with the English fleets, from whom they failed not to receive pecuniary supplies, and every encouragement to proceed in their measures. Deputies were sent to England without delay; and welcomed there with the utmost enthusiasm of sympathy and admiration. England could both speak and act openly. Throughout the whole of the enslaved continent the news of the Spanish insurrection was brooded over with a sullen joy.

Napoleon received the intelligence with alarm; but he had already gone too far to retract without disturbing the magical influence of his reputation. He, moreover, was willing to flatter himself that the lower population of Spain alone took an active part in these transactions; that the nobility, whose degradation he could hardly over-estimate, would abide by his voice; in a word, that with 80,000 troops in Spain, besides Junot's army in Portugal, he possessed the means of suppressing the tumult after the first effervescence should have escaped. He proceeded, therefore, to act precisely as if no insurrection had occurred. Tranquillity being re-established in Madrid, the Council of Castile were convoked, and commanded to elect a new sovereign: their choice had of course been settled beforehand: it fell on Joseph Buonaparte, King of Naples; and ere it was announced, that personage was already on his way to Bayonne. Ninety-five Notables of Spain met him in that town; and swore fealty to him and a new Constitution, the manufacture of course of Napoleon. Joseph, on entering Spain, was met by unequivocal symptoms of scorn and hatred:--nay, one great battle had already been fought between the French and the patriots:--but, the main road being strongly occupied throughout with his brother's troops, he reached Madrid in safety.

Lucien Buonaparte, it is understood, received the first offer of this crown; but he did not envy the condition of his brother's royal vassals, and declined the dangerous honour. Murat had expected it, and much resented his disappointment; but Napoleon did not consider him as possessed of the requisite prudence, and he was forced to accept the succession to the vacant throne of Naples.

Joseph had become not unpopular in Naples, and being a peaceful man, would gladly have remained in that humbler kingdom; but Napoleon no more consulted the private wishes of his subaltern princes on such occasions, than he did those of his generals in the arrangements of a campaign.

On the 24th of July (says Colonel Napier), "Joseph was proclaimed King of Spain and the Indies, with all the solemnities usual upon such occasions; not hesitating to declare himself the enemy of eleven millions of people, the object of a whole nation's hatred; calling, with a strange accent, from the midst of foreign bands, upon that fierce and haughty race to accept of a constitution which they did not understand, and which few of them had even heard of; his only hope of success resting on the strength of his brother's arms; his claims on the consent of an imbecile monarch and the weakness of a few pusillanimous nobles, in contempt of the rights of millions now arming to oppose him."

CHAPTER XXIV

Insurrection of the Spaniards and Portuguese--Their Alliance with England--Battle of Riosecco--Joseph enters Madrid--First Siege of Zaragossa--Dupont's March into Andalusia--The Battle of Baylen--Dupont Surrenders--Joseph quits Madrid--Situation of Junot--Arrival of Sir Arthur Wellesley--Battle of Rorie--Battle of Vimiero--Convention of Cintra.

On the 4th of July the King of England addressed his Parliament on the subject which then fixed the universal enthusiasm of his people. "I view" (said he) "with the liveliest interest the loyal and determined spirit manifested in resisting the violence and perfidy with which the dearest rights of the Spanish nation have been assailed. The kingdom thus nobly struggling against the usurpation and tyranny of France, can no longer be considered as the enemy of Great Britain, but is recognised by me as a natural friend and ally." It has been already mentioned that the British commanders in the neighbourhood of Spain did not wait for orders from home to espouse openly the cause of the insurgent nation. The Spanish prisoners of war were forthwith released, clothed, equipped, and sent back to their country. Supplies of arms and money were liberally transmitted thither; and, Portugal catching the flame and bursting into general insurrection also, a formal treaty of alliance, offensive and defensive, was soon concluded between England and the two kingdoms of the Peninsula.

This insurrection furnished Great Britain with what she had not yet possessed during the war, a favourable theatre whereon to oppose the full strength of her empire to the arms of Napoleon; and the opportunity was embraced with zeal, though for some time but little skill appeared in the manner of using it. The Emperor, on the other hand, observed with surprise and rage the energy of the Spaniards, and not doubting that England would hasten to their aid, bent every effort to consummate his flagitious purpose. "Thus" (says a distinguished writer) "the two leading nations of the world were brought into contact at a moment when both were disturbed by angry passions, eager for great events, and possessed of surprising power."[59]

Napoleon, from the extent and population of his empire, under the operation of the Conscription Code was enabled to maintain an army 500,000 strong; but his relations with those powers on the continent whom he had not entirely subdued were of the most unstable character, and even the states which he had formally united to France were, without exception, pregnant with the elements of disaffection. It was therefore impossible for him to concentrate the whole of his gigantic strength on the soil of Spain. His troops, moreover, being drawn from a multitude of different countries and tongues, could not be united in heart or in discipline like the soldiers of a purely national army. On the other hand, the military genius at his command has never been surpassed in any age or country: his officers were accustomed to victory, and his own reputation exerted a magical influence over both friends and foes. The pecuniary resources of the vast empire were great, and they were managed so skilfully by Buonaparte that the supplies were raised within the year, and in a metallic currency.

His ancient enemy was omnipotent at sea; and if the character of her armies stood at the moment much lower both at home and abroad than it ever deserved to do, this was a mistake which one well-organised campaign was likely to extinguish. England possessed at this time a population of twenty millions, united in the spirit of loyalty and regarding the Spanish cause as just, noble and sacred: a standing army of 200,000 of the best troops in the world, an immense recruiting establishment, and a system of militia which enabled her to swell her muster to any limit. Her colonies occupied a large share of this army; but there remained at her immediate command a force at least equal to that with which Buonaparte had conquered Austria and Prussia. Her credit was unbounded; and her commerce not only supplied means of information altogether unrivalled, but secured for her the secret goodwill of whole classes in every country. England possessed Generals worthy to cope with the best of Buonaparte's Marshals, and in the hour of need discovered that she possessed one capable of confronting, and of conquering, the great Emperor himself. Finally, she possessed the incalculable advantage of warring on the side of justice and freedom, against an usurper, whose crimes were on the same gigantic scale with his genius. The remembrance of their leader's perfidy weighed heavily on the moral strength of the French army throughout the approaching contest; while a proud conviction that their cause was the right sustained the hearts of the English.

Upon them, ultimately, the chief burden and the chief glory of the war devolved: yet justice will ever be done to the virtuous exertions of their allies of the Peninsula. At the moment when the insurrection occurred, 20,000 Spanish troops were in Portugal under the orders of Junot; 15,000 more, under the Marquis de Romana, were serving Napoleon in Holstein. There remained 40,000 Spanish regulars, 11,000 Swiss, and 30,000 militia; but of the best of these the discipline, when compared with French or English armies, was contemptible. The nobility, to whose order the chief officers belonged, were divided in their sentiments--perhaps the greater number inclined to the interests of Joseph. Above all, the troops were scattered, in small sections, over the face of the whole country, and there was no probability that any one regular army should be able to muster so strong as to withstand the efforts of a mere fragment of the French force already established within the kingdom. The fleets of Spain had been destroyed in the war with England: her commerce and revenues had been mortally wounded by the alliance with France and the maladministration of Godoy. Ferdinand was detained a prisoner in France. There was no natural leader or chief, around whom the whole energies of the nation might be expected to rally. It was amidst such adverse circumstances that the Spanish people rose everywhere, smarting under intolerable wrongs, against a French army, already 80,000 strong, in possession of half the fortresses of the country, and in perfect communication with the mighty resources of Napoleon.

There are authors who still delight to undervalue the motives of this great national movement; according to whom the commercial classes rose chiefly, if not solely, from their resentment of the pecuniary losses inflicted on them by Godoy's alliance with the author of the "continental system"; the priesthood because Godoy had impoverished the church, and they feared that a Buonapartean government would pursue the same course to a much greater extent; the peasantry because their priests commanded them. All these influences unquestionably operated, and all strongly; but who can believe in the absence of others infinitely above these, and common to all the Spaniards who, during six years, fought and bled, and saw their towns ruined and their soil a waste, that they might vindicate their birthright, the independence of their nation? Nor can similar praise be refused to the great majority of the Portuguese. Napoleon summoned a body of the nobles of that kingdom also to meet him early in the year at Bayonne: they obeyed, and being addressed by the haughty usurper in person, resisted all his efforts to cajole them into an imitation of the Spanish Notables, who at the same time and place accepted Joseph for their King. They were in consequence retained as prisoners in France during the war which followed; but their fate operated as a new stimulus upon the general feeling of their countrymen at home, already well prepared for insurrection by the brutal oppression of Junot.

The Spanish arms were at first exposed to many reverses; the rawness of their levies, and the insulated nature of their movements, being disadvantages of which it was not difficult for the experienced Generals and overpowering numbers of the French to reap a full and bloody harvest. After various petty skirmishes, in which the insurgents of Arragon were worsted by Lefebre Desnouettes, and those of Navarre and Biscay by Bessieres, the latter officer came upon the united armies of Castile, Leon and Galicia, commanded by the Generals Cuesta and Blake, on the 14th of July, at Riosecco, and defeated them in a desperate action, in which not less than 20,000 Spaniards died. This calamitous battle it was which opened the gates of Madrid to the intrusive king--whose arrival in that capital on the 20th of the same month has already been mentioned.

But Joseph was not destined to remain long in Madrid: the fortune of war, after the great day of Riosecco, was everywhere on the side of the patriots. Duhesme, who had so treacherously possessed himself of Barcelona and Figueras, found himself surrounded by the Catalonian mountaineers, who, after various affairs, in which much blood was shed on both sides, compelled him to shut himself up in Barcelona. Marshal Moncey conducted another large division of the French towards Valencia, and was to have been further reinforced by a detachment from Duhesme. The course of events in Catalonia prevented Duhesme from affording any such assistance; and the inhabitants of Valencia, male and female, rising en masse, and headed by their clergy, manned their walls with such determined resolution, that the French marshal was at length compelled to retreat. He fell back upon the main body, under Bessieres, but did not effect a conjunction with them until his troops had suffered miserably in their march through an extensive district, in which every inhabitant was a watchful enemy.

A far more signal catastrophe had befallen another powerful _corps d'arms_, under General Dupont, which marched from Madrid towards the south, with the view of suppressing all symptoms of insurrection in that quarter, and, especially, of securing the great naval station of Cadiz, where a French squadron lay, watched, as usual, by the English. Dupont's force was increased as he advanced, till it amounted to 20,000 men; and with these he took possession of Baylen and La Carolina, in Andalusia, and stormed Jaen. But before he could make these acquisitions, the citizens of Cadiz had universally taken the patriot side; the commander of the French vessels had been forced to surrender them; and the place, having opened a communication with the English fleet, assumed a posture of determined defence. General Casteas, the Spanish commander in that province, meanwhile, having held back from battle until his raw troops should have had time to be disciplined, began at length to threaten the position of the French. Jaen was attacked by him with such vigour, that Dupont was fain to evacuate it, and fall back to Baylen, where his troops soon suffered severe privations, the peasantry being in arms all around them, and the supply of food becoming from day to day more difficult. On the 16th of July, Dupont was attacked at Baylen by Casteas, who knew from an intercepted despatch the extent of his enemy's distress: the French were beaten, and driven as far as Menjibar. They returned on the 18th, and attempted to recover Baylen; but, after a long and desperate battle, in which 3000 of the French were killed, Dupont, perceiving that the Spaniards were gathering all around in numbers not to be resisted, proposed to capitulate. In effect, he and 20,000 soldiers laid down their arms at Baylen, on condition that they should be transported in safety into France. The Spaniards broke this convention, and detained them as prisoners--thus, foolishly as well a wickedly, imitating the perfidy of Napoleon's own conduct to Spain. This battle and capitulation of Baylen were termed by the Emperor himself the Caudine forks of the French army. He attributed the disaster to treachery on the part of Dupont: it was the result of the rashness of the expedition, and the incompetency of the conductor. The richest part of Spain was freed wholly of the invaders: the light troops of Casteas pushed on, and swept the country before them; and within ten days, King Joseph perceived the necessity of quitting Madrid, and removed his headquarters to Vittoria.

In the meantime Lefebre Desnouettes, whose early success in Arragon has been alluded to, was occupied with the siege of Zaragossa--the inhabitants of which city had risen in the first outbreak, and prepared to defend their walls to the last extremity. Don Jose Palafox, a young nobleman of no great talents, who had made his escape from Bayonne, was invested with the command; but the real leaders were the priests and some of the private citizens, who selected him for the prominent place as belonging to a family of eminent distinction in their kingdom, but in effect considered and used him as their tool. Some Spanish and Walloon regiments, who had formed the garrisons of strong places treacherously seized by the enemy before the war commenced, had united with Palafox, and various bloody skirmishes had occurred--ere the French general was enabled to shut them up in Zaragossa and form the siege. The importance of success in this enterprise was momentous, especially after the failure of Moncey at Valencia. Napoleon himself early saw, that if the Valencians should be able to form an union with the Arragonese at Zaragossa, the situation of the Catalonian insurgents on the one side would be prodigiously strengthened; while, on the other hand, the armies of Leon and Galicia (whose coasts offered the means of continual communication with England) would conduct their operations in the immediate vicinity of the only great road left open between Madrid and Bayonne--the route by Burgos. He therefore had instructed Savary to consider Zaragossa as an object of the very highest importance; but the corps of Lefebre was not strengthened as the Emperor would have wished it to be, ere he sat down before Zaragossa. The siege was pressed with the utmost vigour; but the immortal heroism of the citizens baffled all the valour of the French. There were no regular works worthy of notice: but the old Moorish walls, not above eight or ten feet in height, and some extensive monastic buildings in the outskirts of the city, being manned by crowds of determined men, whose wives and daughters looked on, nay, mingled boldly in their defence--the besiegers were held at bay week after week, and saw their ranks thinned in continual assaults without being able to secure any adequate advantage. Famine came and disease in its train, to aggravate the sufferings of the townspeople; but they would listen to no suggestions but those of the same proud spirit in which they had begun. The French at length gained possession of the great convent of St. Engracia, and thus established themselves within the town itself: their general then sent to Palafox this brief summons: "Headquarters, Santa Engracia--Capitulation"; but he received for answer: "Headquarters, Zaragossa--War to the knife." The battle was maintained literally from street to street, from house to house, and from chamber to chamber. Men and women fought side by side, amidst flames and carnage; until Lefebre received the news of Baylen, and having wasted two months in his enterprise, abandoned it abruptly, lest he should find himself insulated amidst the general retreat of the French armies. Such was the first of the two famous sieges of Zaragossa.

The English government meanwhile had begun their preparations for interfering effectually in the affairs of the Peninsula. They had despatched one body of troops to the support of Casteas in Andalusia; but these did not reach the south of Spain until their assistance was rendered unnecessary by the surrender of Dupont at Baylen. A more considerable force, amounting to 10,000, sailed early in June, from Cork, for Coru, under the command of the Honourable Sir Arthur Wellesley. This armament, originally designed to co-operate with another from India in a great attack on Mexico, had its destination altered the moment the Spanish Insurrection was announced. Sir Arthur, being permitted to land at what point of the Peninsula he should judge most advantageous for the general cause, was soon satisfied that Portugal ought to be the first scene of his operations, and accordingly lost no time in opening a communication with the patriots, who had taken possession of Oporto. Here the troops which had been designed to aid Casteas joined him. Thus strengthened, and well informed of the state of the French armies in Spain, Sir Arthur resolved to effect a landing and attack Junot while circumstances seemed to indicate no chance of his being reinforced by Bessieres.

It is, perhaps, an evil unavoidable in the institutions of an old and settled government, that men rarely, very rarely, unless they possess the advantages of illustrious birth and connection, can hope to be placed in situations of the highest importance until they have passed the prime vigour of their days. Sir Arthur Wellesley, fortunately for England and for Europe, commenced life under circumstances eminently favourable for the early development and recognition of his great talents. To his brother, the Marquis Wellesley's rank as Governor-General of India, he owed the opportunity of conducting our armies in the East at a time of life when, if of inferior birth, he could hardly have commanded a battalion; and the magnificent campaign of Assaye so established his reputation, that shortly after his return to Europe he was entrusted without hesitation with the armament assembled at Cork.

It was on the 8th of August, 1808--a day ever memorable in the history of Britain--that Sir Arthur Wellesley effected his debarkation in the bay of Mondego. He immediately commenced his march towards Lisbon, and on the 17th came up with the enemy under General Laborde, strongly posted on an eminence near Rorie. The French contested their ground gallantly, but were driven from it at the point of the bayonet, and compelled to retreat. The British General, having hardly any cavalry, was unable to pursue them so closely as he otherwise would have done: and Laborde succeeded in joining his shattered division to the rest of the French forces in Portugal. Junot (recently created Duke of Abrantes) now took the command in person; and finding himself at the head of full 24,000 troops, while the English army were greatly inferior in numbers, and miserably supplied with cavalry and artillery, he did not hesitate to assume the offensive. On the 21st of August he attacked Sir Arthur at Vimiero. In the language of the English General's despatch, "a most desperate contest ensued"; and the result was "a signal defeat," Junot, having lost thirteen cannon and more than two thousand men, immediately fell back upon Lisbon, where his position was protected by the strong defile of the Torres Vedras.

This retreat would not have been accomplished without much more fighting, had Sir Arthur Wellesley been permitted to follow up his victory, according to the dictates of his own understanding and the enthusiastic wishes of his army. But just as the battle was about to begin, Sir Harry Burrard, an old officer of superior rank, unfortunately entitled to assume the chief command, arrived on the field. Finding that Sir Arthur had made all his dispositions, General Burrard handsomely declined interfering until the fortune of the day should be decided; but he took the command as soon as the victory was won, and more cautiously than wisely, prevented the army from instantly advancing, as Sir Arthur Wellesley proposed, upon the coast road towards Mafra, and thus endeavouring to intercept the retreat of Junot upon Lisbon. Sir Harry, having made this unhappy use of his command, was, the very next day, superseded in his turn by Sir Hew Dalrymple, the Governor of Gibraltar; another veteran more disposed to imitate the prudence of Burrard than the daring of Wellesley.

Shortly after the third general had taken the command, Junot sent Kellerman to demand a truce, and propose a convention for the evacuation of Portugal by the troops under his orders. Dalrymple received Kellerman with more eagerness of civility than became the chief of a victorious army, and forthwith granted the desired armistice. Junot offered to surrender his magazine, stores, and armed vessels, provided the British would disembark his soldiers, with their arms, at any French port between Rochefort and L'Orient, and permit them to take with them their private property; and

Dalrymple did not hesitate to agree to these terms, although Sir John Moore arrived off the coast with a reinforcement of 10,000 men during the progress of the negotiation. The famous "Convention of Cintra" (most absurdly so named, as it was in fact concluded thirty miles from Cintra) was signed accordingly on the 30th of August; and the French army wholly evacuated Portugal in the manner provided for. The English people heard with indignation that the spoilers of Portugal had been suffered to escape on such terms; and the article concerning private property gave especial offence, as under that cover the French removed with them a large share of the plunder which they had amassed by merciless violence and rapacity during their occupation of the Portuguese territories. A parliamentary investigation was followed by a court-martial, which acquitted Dalrymple. In truth it seems now to be admitted, by competent judges, that after Burrard had interfered so as to prevent Wellesley from instantly following up the success of Vimiero, and so enabled Junot to re-occupy Lisbon and secure the pass of the Torres Vedras, it would have been imprudent to decline the terms proffered by a repelled, but still powerful enemy--who, if driven to extremities, could hardly fail to prolong the war, until Napoleon should be able to send him additional forces from Spain. Meanwhile Portugal was free from the presence of her enemies; England had obtained a permanent footing within the Peninsula; what was of still higher moment, the character of the British army was raised not only abroad, but at home; and had the two insurgent nations availed themselves, as they ought to have done, of the resources which their great ally placed at their command, and conducted their own affairs with unity and strength of purpose, the deliverance of the whole peninsula might have been achieved years before that consummation actually took place.

The Portuguese, however, split into factions--under leaders whose primary objects were selfish, who rivalled each other in their absurd jealousy of England, afforded to her troops no such supplies and facilities as they had the best title to demand and expect, and wasted their time in petty political intrigues, instead of devoting every energy to the organisation of an efficient army, and improving the defences of their naturally strong frontier. The Spaniards conducted themselves with even more signal imprudence. For months each provincial junta seemed to prefer the continuance of its own authority to the obvious necessity of merging all their powers in some central body, capable of controlling and directing the whole force of the nation; and after a supreme junta was at last established in Madrid, its orders were continually disputed and disobeyed--so that in effect there was no national government. Equally disgraceful jealousies among the generals prevented the armies from being placed under one supreme chief, responsible for the combination of all their movements. In place of this it was with difficulty that the various independent generals could be prevailed on even to meet at Madrid, and agree to the outline of a joint campaign; and that outline seemed to have no recommendation except that its gross military defects held out to each member of the Council the prospect of being able to act without communication, for good or for evil, with any of the others. The consequences of these shameful follies were calamitous: and but for events which could not have been foreseen, must have proved fatal: for the gigantic resources of the common enemy were about to be set in motion by Napoleon himself; who, on hearing of the reverses of Dupont, Lefebre, and Junot, perceived too clearly that the affairs of the Peninsula demanded a keener eye and a firmer hand than his brother's.

[Footnote 59: Col. Napier, chap. i.]

CHAPTER XXV

Napoleon at Erfurt--At Paris--Arrives at Vittoria--Disposition of the French and Spanish Armies--Successes of Soult--Passage of the Somosierra--Surrender of Madrid--Sir John Moore's Campaign--his Retreat--Battle of Coru--Death of Moore--Napoleon leaves Spain.

Three Spanish armies, each unfortunately under an independent chief, were at length in motion: their nominal strength was 130,000 men; in reality they never exceeded 100,000. Had they been combined under an able general, they might have assaulted the French army, now not exceeding 60,000, with every likelihood of success; for the position first taken up by King Joseph, after his retreat into the north, was very defective; but the Spaniards chose their basis of operations so absurdly, and were so dilatory afterwards, that Napoleon had time both to rectify Joseph's blunders and to reinforce his legions effectually, before they were able to achieve any considerable advantage.

Blake, who commanded on the west, extended his line from Burgos to Bilboa; Palafox, on the east, lay between Zaragossa and Sanguessa; Casteas, general of the central army, had his headquarters at Soria. The three armies thus lay in a long and feeble crescent, of which the horns were pushed towards the French frontier; while the enemy, resting on three strong fortresses, remained on the defensive until the Emperor should pour new forces through the passes of the Pyrenees. It was expected that the English army in Portugal would forthwith advance, and put themselves in communication either with Blake or with Casteas; and had this junction occurred soon after the battle of Virniero, the result might have been decisive: but Wellesley was recalled to London to bear witness on the trial of Dalrymple; and Sir John Moore, who then assumed the command, received neither such supplies as were necessary for any great movement, nor any clear and authentic intelligence from the authorities of Madrid, nor finally any distinct orders from his own government--until the favourable moment had gone by. In effect, Napoleon's gigantic reinforcements had begun to show themselves within the Spanish frontier, a week before the English general was in a condition to commence his march.

The Emperor, enraged at the first positive disgraces which had ever befallen his arms, and foreseeing that unless the Spanish insurrection were crushed ere the Patriots had time to form a regular government and to organise their armies, the succours of England, and the growing discontents of Germany, might invest the task with insurmountable difficulties, determined to cross the Pyrenees in person, at the head of a force capable of sweeping the whole Peninsula clear before him "at one fell swoop." Hitherto no mention of the unfortunate occurrences in Spain had been made in any public act of his government, or suffered to transpire in any of the French journals. It was now necessary to break this haughty silence. The Emperor announced accordingly that the peasants of Spain had rebelled against their King; that treachery had caused the ruin of one corps of his army; and that another had been forced, by the English, to evacuate Portugal: demanding two new conscriptions, each of 80,000 men--which were of course granted without hesitation. Recruiting his camps on the German side, and in Italy, with these new levies, he now ordered his veteran troops, to the amount of 200,000, including a vast and brilliant cavalry, and a large body of the Imperial Guards, to be drafted from those frontiers, and marched through France towards Spain. As these warlike columns passed through Paris, Napoleon addressed to them one of those orations which never failed to swell the resolution and pride of his soldiery on the eve of some great enterprise. "Comrades," said he, "after triumphing on the banks of the Danube and the Vistula, with rapid steps you have passed through Germany. This day, without a moment of repose, I command you to traverse France. Soldiers, I have need of you. The hideous presence of the leopard contaminates the peninsula of Spain and Portugal. In terror he must fly before you. Let us bear our triumphant eagles to the Pillars of Hercules: there also we have injuries to avenge. Soldiers! you have surpassed the renown of modern armies; but have you yet equalled the glory of those Romans, who, in one and the same campaign, were victorious on the Rhine, and the Euphrates, in Illyria and on the Tagus? A long peace, a lasting prosperity, shall be the reward of your labours. A real Frenchman could not, should not rest, until the seas are free and open to all. Soldiers, what you have done, and what you are about to do, for the happiness of the French people and for my glory, shall be eternal in my heart!"

Having thus dismissed his troops on their way, Buonaparte himself travelled rapidly to Erfurt, where he had invited the Emperor Alexander to confer with him. It was most needful that before he went to Spain himself, he should ascertain the safety of his empire on the other side; and there was much in the state of Germany that might well give rise to serious apprehensions. Austria was strengthening her military establishment to a vast extent, and had, by a recent law, acquired the means of drawing on her population unlimitedly, after the method of Napoleon's own conscription code. She professed pacific intentions towards France, and intimated that her preparations were designed for the protection of her Turkish frontier; but the Emperor Francis positively declined to acknowledge Joseph Buonaparte as King of Spain; and this refusal was quite sufficient for Napoleon. In Prussia, meantime, and indeed all over Germany, a spirit of deep and settled enmity was manifesting itself in the shape of patriotic clubs (the chief being called the Tugend bund, or Alliance of Virtue), which included the young and the daring of every class, and threatened, at no distant period, to convulse the whole fabric of society with the one purpose of clearing the national soil of its foreign oppressors. Napoleon affected to deride, but secretly estimated at its true importance, the danger of such associations, if permitted to take firm root among a people so numerous, so enthusiastic, and so gallant. Lastly, there is every reason to believe that, cordial as the Czar's friendship had seemed to be at Tilsit, Buonaparte appreciated the unpopularity of his "continental system" in Russia, and the power of the aristocracy there, far too accurately, not to entertain some suspicion that Alexander himself might be compelled to take the field against him, should England succeed in persuading Austria and Germany to rise in arms during his own absence in Spain. For these reasons he had requested the Czar's presence at Erfurt; and this conference was apparently as satisfactory to either as that of Tilsit had been. They addressed a joint letter to the King of England, proposing once more a general peace; but as they both refused to acknowledge any authority in Spain save that of King Joseph, the answer was of course in the negative. Buonaparte, however, had obtained his object when he thus exhibited the Czar and himself as firmly allied. He perceived clearly that Austria was determined on another campaign; gave orders for concentrating and increasing his own armies, accordingly, both in Germany and Italy; and-- trusting to the decision and rapidity of his own movements, and the comparative slowness of his ancient enemy--dared to judge that he might still bring matters to an issue in Spain, before his presence should be absolutely necessary beyond the Rhine.

On the 14th of October the conferences of Erfurt terminated; on the 24th Napoleon was present at the opening of the Legislative Session in Paris; two days after he left that capital, and reached Bayonne on the 3rd of November, where he remained, directing the movements of the last columns of his advancing army, until the morning of the 8th. He arrived at Vittoria the same evening: the civil and military authorities met him at the gates of the town, and would have conducted him to a house prepared for his reception, but he leapt from his horse, entered the first inn that he observed, and calling for maps and a detailed report of the position of all the armies, French and Spanish, proceeded instantly to draw up his plan for the prosecution of the war. Within two hours he had completed his task. Soult, who had accompanied him from Paris, and whom he ordered to take the command of Bessieres' corps, set off on the instant, reached Briviesca, where its headquarters were, at daybreak on the 9th, and within a few hours the whole machinery was once more in motion.

Napoleon had, early in October, signified to Joseph that the French cause in Spain, would always be favoured by acting on the offensive, and his disapproval of the extent to which the King had retreated had not been heard in vain. General Blake's army had already been brought to action, and defeated disastrously by Moncey, at Espinosa; from which point Blake had most injudiciously retreated towards Reynosa, instead of Burgos, where another army, meant to support his right, had assembled under the orders of the Count de Belvedere.

Soult now poured down his columns on the plains of Burgos. Belvedere was defeated by him at Gomenal even more easily than Blake had been at Espinosa. The latter, again defeated by the indefatigable Soult, at Reynosa, was obliged to take refuge, with what hardly could be called even the skeleton of an army, in the seaport of St. Ander. Thus the whole of the Spanish left was dissipated; and the French right remained at liberty to march onwards at their pleasure.

Palafox meanwhile had effected at length a junction with Casteas; and the combined Spanish armies of the centre and the east awaited the French attack, on the 22nd of November, at Tudela. The disaster here was still more complete. Casteas and Palafox separated in the moment of overthrow; the former escaping to Calatayud with the wreck of his troops, while the latter made his way once more to Zaragossa.

Napoleon now saw the main way to Madrid open before him--except that some forces were said to be posted at the strong defile of the Somosierra, within ten miles of the capital; while Soult, continuing his march by Carrion and Valladolid, could at once keep in check the English, in case they were still so daring as to advance from Portugal, and outflank the Somosierra, in case the mountains should be so defended as to bar the Emperor's approach in that direction to Madrid. Palafox was pursued, and soon shut up in Zaragossa by Lannes. That heroic city on the east, the British army on the west, and Madrid in front, were the only far-separated points on which any show of opposition was still to be traced--from the frontiers of France to those of Portugal, from the sea coast to the Tagus.

Napoleon, with his guards and the first division, marched towards Madrid. His vanguard reached the foot of the Somosierra chain on the 30th of November, and found that a corps of 12,000 men had been assembled for the defence of the pass, under General St. Juan. No stronger position could well be fancied than that of the Spaniards: the defile was narrow, and excessively steep, and the road completely swept by sixteen pieces of artillery. At daybreak, on the 1st of December, the French began their attempt to turn the flanks of St. Juan: three battalions scattered themselves over the opposite sides of the defile, and a warm skirmishing fire had begun. At this moment Buonaparte came up. He rode into the mouth of the pass, surveyed the scene for an instant, perceived that his infantry were making no progress, and at once conceived the daring idea of causing his Polish lancers to charge right up the causeway in face of the battery. The smoke of the skirmishers on the hill-sides mingled with the thick fogs and vapours of the morning, and under this veil the brave Krazinski led his troopers impetuously up the ascent. The Spanish infantry fired as they passed them, threw down their arms, abandoned their entrenchments, and fled. The Poles speared the gunners, and took possession of the cannon. The Spaniards continued their flight in such disorder that they were at last fain to quit the road to Madrid, and escape in the direction, some of Segovia, others of Talaveyra. On the morning of the 2nd, three divisions of French cavalry made their appearance on the high ground to the north-west of the capital.

During eight days the inhabitants had been preparing the means of resistance. A local and military junta had been invested with authority to conduct the defence. Six thousand regular troops were in the town, and crowds of the citizens and of the peasantry of the adjoining country were in arms along with them. The pavement had been taken up, the streets barricadoed, the houses on the outskirts loopholed, and the Retiro, a large but weak edifice, occupied by a strong garrison. Terrible violence prevailed-- many persons suspected of adhering to the side of the French were assassinated; the bells of churches and convents rung incessantly; ferocious bands paraded the streets day and night: and at the moment when the enemy's cavalry appeared, the universal uproar seemed to announce that he was about to find a new and a greater Zaragossa in Madrid.

The town was summoned at noon; and the officer employed would have been massacred by the mob but for the interference of the Spanish regulars. Napoleon waited until his infantry and artillery came up in the evening, and then the place was invested on one side. "The night was clear and bright" (says Napier); "the French camp was silent and watchful; but the noise of tumult was heard from every quarter of the city, as if some mighty beast was struggling and howling in the toils." At midnight the city was again summoned; and the answer being still defiance, the batteries began to open. In the course of the day the Retiro was stormed, and the immense palace of the Dukes of Medina Celi, which commands one side of the town, seized also.

Terror now began to prevail within; and shortly after the city was summoned, for the third time, Don Thomas Morla, the governor, came out to demand a suspension of arms. Napoleon received him with anger, and rebuked him for the violation of the capitulation at Baylen. "Injustice and bad faith," said he, "always recoil on those who are guilty of them." Many an honester Spaniard was obliged to listen in silence to such words from the negotiator of Fontainebleau and Bayonne.

Morla was a coward, and there is no doubt a traitor also. On returning to the town he urged the necessity of instantly capitulating; and most of those in authority took a similar part, except Castellas, the commander of the regular troops. The peasantry and citizens kept firing on the French outposts during the night; but Castellas, perceiving that the civil rulers were all against further resistance, withdrew his troops and sixteen cannon in safety. At eight in the morning of the 4th, Madrid surrendered. The Spaniards were disarmed, and the town filled with the French army. Napoleon took up his residence at Chamartin, a country house four miles off. In a few days tranquillity seemed completely re-established. The French soldiery observed excellent discipline: the shops were re-opened, and the theatres frequented as usual. Such is in most cases the enthusiasm of a great city!

Napoleon now exercised all the rights of a conqueror. He issued edicts abolishing the Inquisition, all feudal rights, and all particular jurisdictions; regulating the number of monks; increasing, at the expense of the monastic establishments, the stipends of the parochial clergy; and proclaiming a general amnesty, with only ten exceptions. He received a deputation of the chief inhabitants, who came to signify their desire to see Joseph among them again. His answer was, that Spain was his own by right of conquest; that he could easily rule it by viceroys, but that if they chose to assemble in their churches, priests and people, and swear allegiance to Joseph, he was not indisposed to listen to their request.

This was a secondary matter: meantime the Emperor was making his dispositions for the completion of his conquest. His plan was to invade forthwith Andalusia, Valencia and Galicia, by his lieutenants, and to march in person to Lisbon. Nor was this vast plan beyond his means; for he had at that moment 255,000 men, 50,000 horses, and 100 pieces of field artillery, actually ready for immediate service in Spain: while 80,000 men and 100 cannon, besides, were in reserve, all on the south side of the Pyrenees. To oppose this gigantic force there were a few poor defeated corps of Spaniards, widely separated from each other, and flying already before mere detachments: Seville, whose local junta had once more assumed the nominal sovereignty, and guarded in front by a feeble corps in the Sierra Morena; Valencia, without a regular garrison; Zaragossa, closely invested, and resisting once more with heroic determination; and the British army under Sir John Moore. The moment Napoleon was informed that Moore had advanced into Spain, he abandoned every other consideration, and resolved in person to march and overwhelm him.

The English general had, as we have already seen, been prevented by circumstances over which he could have no control, from commencing his campaign so early as he desired, and as the situation of the Spanish armies, whom he was meant to support, demanded. At length, however, he put his troops, 20,000 in number, into motion, and advanced in the direction of Salamanca; while a separate British corps of 13,000, under Sir David Baird, recently landed at Coru, had orders to march through Galicia, and effect a junction with Moore either at Salamanca or Valladolid. The object of the British was of course to support the Spanish armies of Blake and Belvedere in their defence: but owing to the delays and blundering intelligence already alluded to, these armies were in a hopeless condition before Sir John Moore's march began.

The news of the decisive defeat of Casteas, at Tudela, satisfied Moore that the original purpose of his march was now out of the question; but, having at length effected a junction with Baird, he felt extreme unwillingness to retreat without attempting something. He continued to receive from Madrid the most solemn assurances that the resistance of the capital would be desperate: and, with more generosity than prudence, resolved to attack Soult, then posted behind the Carrion. In doing so he fancied it possible that he should defeat an important branch of the enemy's force, intercept the communications of the Emperor's left flank, give Romana time to re-organise an army in Galicia, create a formidable diversion in favour of the south of Spain, if not of Madrid--and, at worst, secure for himself a safe retreat upon Coru; from which port his troops might be sent round without difficulty to Seville, to take part in the defence of that part of the Peninsula which was yet unbroken and the seat of the actual government.

But Buonaparte, hearing on the 20th of December of the advance of Moore, instantly put himself at the head of 50,000 men, and marched with incredible rapidity, with the view of intercepting his communications with Portugal, and in short hemming him in between himself and Soult. Moore no sooner heard that Napoleon was approaching, than he perceived the necessity of an immediate retreat; and he commenced accordingly a most calamitous one through the naked mountains of Galicia, in which his troops maintained their character for bravery, rallying with zeal whenever the French threatened their rear, but displayed a lamentable want of discipline in all other part of their conduct. The weather was tempestuous; the roads miserable; the commissariat utterly defective; and the very notion of retreat broke the high spirits of the soldiery. They ill-treated the inhabitants, drank whatever strong liquors they could obtain, straggled from their ranks, and in short lost the appearance of an army except when the trumpet warned them that they might expect the French charge. Soult hung close on their rear until they reached Coru; and Moore perceived that it would be impossible to embark without either a convention or a battle. He chose the braver alternative. The French were repelled gallantly; and the British were permitted to embark without further molestation. In the moment of victory (January 16, 1809) Sir John Moore fell, mortally wounded by a cannon-shot: his men buried him in his cloak; and the French, in testimony of their admiration of his gallantry, erected a monument over his remains.

Napoleon came up with the troops in pursuit of Moore at Benevente, on the 29th of December, and enjoyed for a moment the spectacle of an English army in full retreat. He saw that Moore was no longer worthy of his own attention, and entrusted the consummation of his ruin to Soult.

It excited universal surprise that the Emperor did not immediately return from Benevente to Madrid, to complete and consolidate his Spanish conquest. He, however, proceeded, not towards Madrid, but Paris; and this with his utmost speed,--riding on post-horses, on one occasion, not less than seventy-five English miles in five hours and a half. The cause of this sudden change of purpose, and extraordinary haste, was a sufficient one; and it ere long transpired.

CHAPTER XXVI

Austria declares War--Napoleon heads his army in Germany--Battles of Landshut and Eckmuhl--Ratisbonne taken--Napoleon in Vienna--Hostilities in Italy, Hungary, Poland, the North of Germany, and the Tyrol--Battle of Raab--Battle of Wagram--Armistice with Austria.... Progress of the War in the Peninsula, Battle of Talaveyra--English Expedition to Walcheren.... Seizure of Rome and arrest of the Pope.... Treaty of Schoenbrunn.

Napoleon had foreseen that Austria, hardly dissembling her aversion to the "continental system," and openly refusing to acknowledge Joseph as King of Spain, would avail herself of the insurrection of that country, necessarily followed by the march of a great French army across the Pyrenees, as affording a favourable opportunity for once more taking arms, in the hope of recovering what she had lost in the campaign of Austerlitz. His minister, Talleyrand, had, during his absence, made every effort to conciliate the Emperor Francis; but the warlike preparations throughout the Austrian dominions proceeded with increasing vigour--and Napoleon received such intelligence ere he witnessed the retreat of Moore, that he immediately countermanded the march of such of his troops as had not yet reached the Pyrenees,--wrote (from Valladolid) to the princes of the Rhenish league, ordering them to hold their contingents in readiness--and travelled to Paris with extraordinary haste. He reached his capital on the 22nd of January; renewed the negotiations with Vienna; and, in the meantime, recruited and concentrated his armies on the German side--thus adjourning, and as it turned out for ever, the completion of the Spanish conquest.

On the 6th of April, Austria declared war; and on the 9th, the Archduke Charles, Generalissimo of armies which are said to have been recruited, at this period, to the amount of nearly 500,000 men, crossed the Inn at the head of six corps, each consisting of 30,000; while the Archduke John marched with two other divisions towards Italy, by the way of Carinthia; and the Archduke Ferdinand assumed the command of a ninth corps in Galicia, to make head against Russia, in case that power should be forced or tempted by Napoleon to take part in the struggle. Napoleon, having so great an army in Spain, could not hope to oppose numbers such as these to the Austrians; but he trusted to the rapid combinations which had so often enabled him to baffle the same enemy; and the instant he ascertained that Bavaria was invaded by the Archduke Charles, he proceeded, without guards, without equipage, accompanied solely by the faithful Josephine, to Frankfort, and thence to Strasbourg. He assumed the command on the 13th, and immediately formed the plan of his campaign.

He found the two wings of his army, the one under Massena, the other under Davoust, at such a distance from the centre that, if the Austrians had seized the opportunity, the consequences might have been fatal. On the 17th of April, he commanded Davoust and Massena to march simultaneously towards a position in front, and then pushed forward the centre, in person, to the same point. The Archduke Lewis, who commanded two Austrian divisions in advance, was thus hemmed in unexpectedly by three armies, moving at once from three different points; defeated and driven back, at Abensberg, on the 20th; and utterly routed, at Landshut, on the 21st. Here the Archduke lost 9000 men, thirty guns, and all his stores.

Next day Buonaparte executed a variety of movements, considered as among the most admirable displays of his science, by means of which he brought his whole force, by different routes, at one and the same moment upon the position of the Archduke Charles. That prince was strongly posted at Eckmuhl, with full 100,000 men. Napoleon charged him at two in the afternoon; the battle was stern and lasted till nightfall, but it ended in a complete overthrow. The Austrians, besides their loss in the field, left in Napoleon's hands 20,000 prisoners, fifteen colours, and the greater part of their artillery; and retreated in utter disorder upon Ratisbonne. The Archduke made an attempt to rally his troops and defend that city, on the 23rd; but the French stormed the walls and drove the Austrians through the streets: and their general immediately retreated into Bohemia: thus; in effect, abandoning Vienna to the mercy of his conqueror.

Napoleon was wounded in the foot during the storming of Ratisbonne, and for a moment the troops crowded round him in great alarm; but he scarcely waited to have his wound dressed, threw himself again on horseback, and restored confidence by riding along the lines.

Thus, in five days, in spite of inferiority of numbers, and of the unfavourable manner in which his lieutenants had distributed an inferior force, by the sole energy of his genius did the Emperor triumph over the main force of his opponent.

He reviewed his army on the 24th, distributing rewards of all sorts with a lavish hand, and, among others, bestowing the title of Duke of Eckmuhl on Davoust; and forthwith commenced his march upon Vienna. The corps defeated at Landshut had retreated in that direction, and being considerably recruited, made some show of obstructing his progress; but they were defeated again and totally broken at Ehrensberg, on the 3rd of May, by Massena, and on the 9th Napoleon appeared before the walls of the capital. The Emperor had already quitted it, with all his family, except his daughter, the Archduchess Maria Louisa, who was confined to her chamber by illness. The Archduke Maximilian, with the regular garrison of 10,000 men, evacuated it on Napoleon's approach; and though the inhabitants had prepared for a vigorous resistance, the bombardment soon convinced them that it was hopeless. It perhaps deserves to be mentioned, that on learning the situation of the sick princess, Buonaparte instantly commanded that no fire should be directed towards that part of the town. On the 10th a capitulation was signed, the French troops took possession of the city, and Napoleon once more established his headquarters in the imperial palace of Schoenbrunn.

In the meantime, the Archduke Ferdinand had commenced the war in Poland, and obtaining the advantage in several affairs, taken possession of Warsaw; but the news of Eckmuhl recalled this division to the support of the main army, under the Archduke Charles; and the Russian troops not only retook Warsaw, but occupied the whole of the Austro-Polish provinces. Alexander, however, showed no disposition to push the war with vigour, or to advance into Germany for the support of Napoleon. In Italy, in like manner, the Archduke John had at first been successful. But after defeating Eugene Beauharnois, Napoleon's viceroy, and taking possession of Padua and Vicenza, this prince also was summoned to retrace his steps, in consequence of the catastrophe at Eckmuhl. Eugene pursued him into Hungary, and defeated him in a great battle at Raab. Colonel Schill, the Prussian partisan already mentioned, had availed himself of the concentration of Napoleon's troops for the Austrian campaign, to take up arms, though without any authority from his sovereign, in the hope that the national resentment would burst out in an universal insurrection; and the Duke of Brunswick, son to him who was mortally wounded at Jena, had also appeared in Lusatia, and invited all true Germans to imitate the heroic conduct of the Spaniards. These occurrences threatened a general burst of war wherever the Tugend-bund and other patriotic associations had for some time been strongly influencing the popular mind. The battle of Eckmuhl, however, diffused new awe all over the north of Germany. The troops of Saxony checked the Duke of Brunswick's progress, and Schill's heroic band were at last shut up in Stralsund, where their leader perished in a sortie; thus, and only thus, escaping the vengeance of Napoleon.

Among the mountains of the Tyrol, the native zeal of a few hardy peasants achieved more than all the mighty population of Germany. This ancient province of the house of Austria had been, in sinful violation of all the rights of mankind, transferred to the hated yoke of Bavaria, by the treaty of Presburg. The mountaineers no sooner heard that their rightful sovereign was once more in arms against Napoleon, than they rose (early in April), under the guidance of Hofer, a gallant peasant, seized the strong passes of their country, and, in the course of four days, made every French and Bavarian soldier quartered among them a prisoner,--with the exception of the garrison of the fortress of Kufstein. Napoleon caused Lefebre to march into the country with his division; but Hofer posted his followers on the edge of precipices, from which they fired on the French columns with the skill of practised marksmen, and rolled down torrents of stones with such effect, that Lefebre was compelled to retreat. Austria, however, having enough of work at home, could not afford to sustain the efforts of these heroic peasants by any detachment of regular troops. On the retirement of Lefebre, they issued from their hills and wasted the neighbouring territory of Bavaria; but the general issue of the campaign left them at the mercy of Napoleon, who suppressed the insurrection, finally, by overwhelming numbers, and avenged it by massacring Hofer and all who had taken a prominent part in the cause of freedom.

These popular movements, however, could not be regarded with indifference by him who had witnessed and appreciated the character of the Spanish insurrection. Napoleon well knew, that unless he concluded the main contest soon, the spirit of Schill and Hofer would kindle a general flame from the Rhine to the Elbe; and he therefore desired fervently that the Austrian generalissimo might be tempted to quit the fastnesses of Bohemia, and try once more the fortune of a battle.

The Archduke, having re-established the order and recruited the numbers of his army, had anticipated these wishes of his enemy, and was already posted on the opposite bank of the Danube, which river, being greatly swollen, and all the bridges destroyed, seemed to divide the two camps, as by an impassable barrier.

Napoleon determined to pass it; and after an unsuccessful attempt at Nussdorff, met with better fortune at Ebersdorff, where the river is broad and intersected by a number of low and woody islands, the largest of which bears the name of Lobau. On these islands Napoleon established the greater part of his army, on the 19th of May, and on the following day made good his passage, by means of a bridge of boats, to the left bank of the Danube; where he took possession of the villages of Asperne and Essling, with so little show of opposition, that it became evident the Archduke wished the inevitable battle to take place with the river between his enemy and Vienna.

On the 21st, at daybreak, the Archduke appeared on a rising ground, separated from the French position by an extensive plain; his whole force divided into five heavy columns, and protected by not less than 200 pieces of artillery. The battle began at four p.m., with a furious assault on the village of Asperne; which was taken and retaken several times, and remained at nightfall in the occupation, partly of the French, and partly of the assailants, who had established themselves in the church and churchyard. Essling sustained three attacks also; but there the French remained in complete possession. Night interrupted the action; the Austrians exulting in their partial success; Napoleon surprised that he should not have been wholly victorious. On either side the carnage had been terrible, and the pathways of the villages were literally choked with the dead.

Next morning the battle recommenced with equal fury; the French recovered the church of Asperne; but the Austrian right wing renewed their assaults on that point with more and more vigour, and in such numbers, that Napoleon guessed the centre and left had been weakened for the purpose of strengthening the right. Upon this he instantly moved such masses, en 閏 helon, on the Austrian centre, that the Archduke's line was shaken; and for a moment it seemed as if victory was secure.

At this critical moment, by means of Austrian fireships suddenly sent down the swollen and rapid river, the bridge connecting the island of Lobau with the right bank was wholly swept away. Buonaparte perceived that if he wished to preserve his communications with the right of the Danube, where his reserve still lay, he must instantly fall back on Lobau; and no sooner did his troops commence their backward movement, than the Austrians recovered their order and zeal, charged in turn and finally made themselves masters of Asperne. Essling, where Massena commanded, held firm, and under the protection of that village and numerous batteries erected near it, Napoleon succeeded in withdrawing his whole force during the night. On the morning of the 23rd the French were cooped up in Lobau and the adjacant islands--Asperne, Essling, the whole left bank of the river, remaining in the possession of the Austrians. On either side a great victory was claimed; and with equal injustice. But the situation of the French Emperor was imminently hazardous: he was separated from Davoust and his reserve; and had the enemy either attacked him in the islands, or passed the river higher up, and so overwhelmed Davoust and relieved Vienna, the results might have been fatal. But the Archduke's loss in these two days had been great; and, in place of risking any offensive movement, he contented himself with strengthening the position of Asperne and Essling, and awaiting quietly the moment when his enemy should choose to attempt once more the passage to the left bank, and the re-occupation of these hardly contested villages.

Napoleon availed himself of this pause with his usual skill. That he had been checked was true, and that the news would be heard with enthusiasm through Germany he well knew. It was necessary to revive the tarnished magic of his name by another decisive battle: and he made every exertion to prepare for it. Some weeks, however, elapsed ere he ventured to resume the offensive. On the 4th of July he had at last re-established thoroughly his communication with the right bank, and arranged the means of passing to the left at a point where the Archduke had made hardly any preparation for receiving him. The Austrians, having rashly calculated that Asperne and Essling must needs be the objects of the next contest as of the preceding, were taken almost unawares by his appearance in another quarter. They changed their line on the instant; and occupied a position, the centre and key of which was the little town of Wagram.

Here, on the 6th of July, the final and decisive battle was fought. The Archduke had extended his line over too wide a space; and this old error enabled Napoleon to ruin him by his old device of pouring the full shock of his strength on the centre. The action was long and bloody: at its close there remained 20,000 prisoners, besides all the artillery and baggage, in the hands of Napoleon. The Archduke fled in great confusion as far as Znaim, in Moravia. The Imperial Council perceived that further resistance was vain: an armistice was agreed to at Znaim; and Napoleon, returning to Schoenbrunn, continued occupied with the negotiation until October.

In this fierce campaign none more distinguished himself than Lannes, Duke of Montebello. At Ratisbonne he headed in person the storming party, exclaiming, "Soldiers, your general has not forgotten that he was once a grenadier." At the battle of Asperne his exertions were extraordinary. He was struck, towards the close of the day, by a cannon-shot, which carried off both his legs. The surgeons, on examining the wound, declared it mortal. He answered them with angry imprecations, and called with frantic vehemence for the Emperor. Napoleon came up, and witnessed the agonies of the dying marshal, who blasphemed heaven and earth that he should be denied to see the end of the campaign. Thus fell Lannes, whom, for his romantic valour, the French soldiery delighted to call the Roland of the camp.

The war, meanwhile, had been pursued with mixed fortune in the Peninsula. Zaragossa, after sustaining another siege with fortitude not unworthy of the first, was at length compelled to surrender in the month of February. Sir Arthur Wellesley, being restored to the command of the British army in Portugal, landed at Lisbon on the 22nd of April, and immediately marched upon Oporto, which Soult had occupied early in the year. Soult was defeated under the walls of the town, and forthwith began his retreat towards Galicia, which he effected under circumstances as miserable as had attended Sir John Moore's march on Coru in the preceding campaign. Sir Arthur was prevented from urging the pursuit of Soult by the intelligence that Marshal Victor was laying Andalusia waste, being opposed only by Cuesta, a bigoted old general, and an army which had lost heart by repeated disasters. The English leader perceived that if he marched into Galicia, Victor must possess the means of instantly re-occupying Portugal; and resolved, in place of following Soult, to advance towards this more formidable enemy. He effected a junction with Cuesta at Oropesa, on the 20th of July, and marched along the Tagus towards the position of Victor. He, however, having a force at least double that of Wellesley, assumed the offensive, and attacked the allies, on the 28th, at Talaveyra de la Reyna. The battle ended in the total defeat and repulsion of

Victor; but Wellesley found it impossible to advance further into Spain, because Ney, Soult and Mortier were assembling their divisions, with the view of coming between him and Portugal. The English retired, therefore, to Badajos, and thence to the Portuguese frontier.

On the eastern side of the Peninsula, Blake, advancing with the view of recovering Zaragossa, was met on the 19th of June by Marshal Suchet, Duke of Albufera, and totally routed. The central Spanish army, under Ariezaga, attempted, with equal ill-fortune, to relieve Madrid. King Joseph, accompanied by Soult, Victor, and Mortier, met them on the 19th November, and broke them utterly. In December Girona surrendered to Augereau; and the intrusive King appeared to be in possession of far the greater part of Spain. But his command extended no further than the actual presence of his brother's legions. Wherever they were posted, all was submission; beyond their lines the country remained as hostile as ever. The soldiery of the defeated armies dispersed themselves in small bands, watching every opportunity to surprise detachments and cut off supplies; and, in spite of all their victories, the situation of the invaders became every hour more embarrassing. In Portugal, meanwhile, the English general (created Lord Wellington after the battle of Talaveyra) was gradually organising a native force not unworthy of acting under his banners; and on that side it was obvious that, unless Napoleon made some extraordinary exertions, the French cause was wholly undone.

Portugal was safe; and the character of the British army had been raised by another splendid victory in Spain; but these were trivial advantages compared with what Lord Wellington might have achieved, had his government placed him, as they could easily have done, at the head of an army of 80,000 or 100,000 men, while Napoleon was occupied with the campaign of Essling and Wagram. Instead of strengthening Wellington's hands in an efficient manner, the English cabinet sent 40,000 troops, under the command of the Earl of Chatham, an indolent or incompetent general, to seize the isle of Walcheren, and destroy the shipping and works at the mouth of the Scheld; nor was this ill-judged expedition despatched from Britain until the first of August, three weeks after the decisive battle of Wagram had been fought and won. Lord Chatham took Flushing, and fixed his headquarters at Middleburg; but Bernadotte (Prince of Ponte Corvo) put Antwerp into such a state of defence that the plan of besieging that city was, ere long, abandoned.

A pestilence, meantime, raged among the marches of Walcheren; the English soldiers were dying by thousands. The news of the armistice of Znaim arrived; and Lord Chatham abandoned his conquests. A mere skeleton of his army returned to their own country, from the most disastrous expedition which England had undertaken since that of Carthagena, seventy years before.

The announcement of the armistice with Austria put an end, in effect, to all hostile demonstrations on the continent, the Peninsula alone excepted. The brave Schill (as has already been said) was happy enough to fall in the field: his followers, being at last compelled to surrender at Stralsund, were treated as rebels, and died with the constancy of patriots. The Duke of Brunswick, who had by this time obtained considerable successes in Franconia, found himself abandoned, in like manner, to the undivided strength of Napoleon. At the head of a few regiments, whose black uniform announced their devotion to the one purpose of avenging their former sovereign, the Duke succeeded in cutting his way to the Baltic, where some English vessels received him. Germany, in apparent tranquillity, awaited the result of the negotiations of Vienna.

Napoleon, a few days after he returned from Moravia to Schoenbrunn, escaped narrowly the dagger of a young man, who rushed upon him in the midst of all his staff, at a grand review of the Imperial Guard. Berthier and Rapp threw themselves upon him, and disarmed him at the moment when his knife was about to enter the Emperor's body. Napoleon demanded what motive had actuated the assassin. "What injury," said he, "have I done to you?" "To me, personally, none," answered the youth, "but you are the oppressor of my country, the tyrant of the world; and to have put you to death would have been the highest glory of a man of honour." This enthusiastic youth, by name Stabbs, son of a clergyman of Erfurt, was, justly-- no doubt--condemned to death, and he suffered with the calmness of a martyr.

Buonaparte led at Schoenbrunn nearly the same course of life to which he was accustomed at the Tuileries; seldom appearing in public; occupied incessantly with his ministers and generals. The length to which the negotiations with Austria were protracted excited much wonder; but he had other business on hand besides his treaty with the Emperor Francis, and that treaty had taken a very unexpected shape.

It was during his residence at Schoenbrunn that a quarrel, of no short standing, with the Pope reached its crisis. The very language of the Consular Concordat sufficiently indicated the reluctance and pain with which the head of the Romish church acquiesced in the arrangements devised by Buonaparte, for the ecclesiastical settlement of France; and the subsequent course of events, but especially in Italy and in Spain, could hardly fail to aggravate those unpleasant feelings. In Spain and in Portugal, the resistance to French treachery and violence was mainly conducted by the priesthood; and the Pope could not contemplate their exertions without sympathy and favour. In Italy, meantime, the French Emperor had made himself master of Naples, and of all the territories lying to the north of the papal states; in a word, the whole of the peninsula was his, excepting only that, narrow central stripe which still acknowledged the temporal sovereignty of the Roman Pontiff. This state of things was necessarily followed by incessant efforts on the part of Napoleon to procure from the Pope a hearty acquiescence in the system of the Berlin and Milan decrees; and thus far he at length prevailed. But when he went on to demand that his holiness should take an active part in the war against England, he was met by a steady refusal. Irritated by this opposition, and, perhaps, still more by his suspicion that the patriots of the Spanish Peninsula received secret support from the Vatican, Buonaparte did not hesitate to issue a decree in the following words: "Whereas the temporal sovereign of Rome has refused to make war against England, and the interests of the two kingdoms of Italy and Naples ought not to be intercepted by a hostile power; and whereas the donation of Charlemagne, _our illustrious predecessor_, of the countries which form the Holy See, was for the good of Christianity, and not for that of the _enemies of our holy religion_, we, therefore, decree that the duchies of Urbino, Ancona, Macerata, and Camarino, be for ever united to the kingdom of Italy."

The seaports of the papal territory were forthwith occupied by French troops, but Pius remained for some time in undisturbed possession of Rome itself. On his return from Spain, however, Napoleon determined to complete his work in Italy, ere he should begin the inevitable campaign with Austria. General Miollis, therefore, took military possession of Rome in February, 1809; the Pope, however, still remaining in the Vatican, and attended there as usual by his own guards.

On the 17th of May, Napoleon issued, from Vienna, his final decree declaring the temporal sovereignty of the Pope to be wholly at an end, incorporating Rome with the French empire, and declaring it to be his second city; settling a pension on the holy father in his spiritual capacity--and appointing a committee of administration for the civil government of Rome. The Pope, on receiving the Parisian senatus-consultum, ratifying this imperial rescript, instantly fulminated a bull of excommunication against Napoleon. Shortly after some unauthentic news from Germany inspired new hopes into the adherents of the Pontiff; and, disturbances breaking out, Miollis, on pretence that a life sacred in the eyes of all Christians might be endangered, arrested Pius in his palace at midnight, and forthwith despatched him under a strong escort to Savona.

The intelligence of this decisive step reached Napoleon soon after the battle of Wagram, and he was inclined to disapprove of the conduct of Miollis as too precipitate. It was now, however, impossible to recede; the Pope was ordered to be conveyed across the Alps to Grenoble. But his reception there was more reverential than Napoleon had anticipated, and he was soon reconducted to Savona.

This business would, in any other period, have been sufficient to set all Catholic Europe in a flame; and even now Buonaparte well knew that his conduct could not fail to nourish and support the feelings arrayed against him openly in Spain and in Southern Germany, and suppressed, not extinguished, in the breasts of a great party of the French clergy at home. He made, therefore, many efforts to procure from the Pope some formal relinquishment of his temporal claims--but Pius VII. remained unshaken; and the negotiation at length terminated in the removal of His Holiness to Fontainebleau, where he continued a prisoner, though treated personally with respect, and even magnificence, during more than three years:--until, in the general darkening of his own fortunes, the imperial jailer was compelled to adopt another line of conduct.

The treaty with Austria was at last signed at Schoenbrunn on the 14th of October. The Emperor Francis purchased peace by the cession of Salzburg, and a part of Upper Austria, to the Confederation of the Rhine; of part of Bohemia to the King of Saxony, and of Cracow and western Galicia to the same Prince, as Grand Duke of Warsaw; of part of eastern Galicia to the Czar;

and to France herself, of Trieste, Carniola, Fruili, Villach, and some part of Croatia and Dalmatia. By this act, Austria gave up in all territory to the amount of 45,000 square miles, with a population of nearly four millions; and Napoleon, besides gratifying his vassals and allies, had completed the connection of the kingdom of Italy with his Illyrian possessions, obtained the whole coasts of the Adriatic, and deprived Austria of her last seaport. Yet, when compared with the signal triumphs of the campaign of Wagram, the terms on which the conqueror signed the peace were universally looked upon as remarkable for moderation; and he claimed merit with the Emperor of Russia on the score of having spared Austria in deference to his personal intercession.

Buonaparte quitted Vienna on the 16th of October; was congratulated by the public bodies of Paris, on the 14th of November, as "the greatest of heroes, who never achieved victories but for the happiness of the world"; and soon after, by one of the most extraordinary steps of his personal history, furnished abundant explanation of the motives which had guided his diplomacy at Schoenbrunn.

CHAPTER XXVII

Napoleon divorces Josephine--Marries the Archduchess Maria Louisa--Deposes Louis Buonaparte--Annexes Holland and the whole Coast of Germany to France--Revolution in Sweden--Bernadotte elected Crown Prince of Sweden--Progress of the War in the Peninsula--Battle of Busaco--Lord Wellington retreats to the Lines of Torres Vedras.

The treacherous invasion of Spain, and the imprisonment of the Pope, were but the first of a series of grand political errors, destined to sap the foundations of this apparently irresistible power. On his return to Paris, Napoleon proudly proclaimed to his senate, that no enemy opposed him throughout the continent of Europe--except only a few fugitive-bands of Spanish rebels, and "the English leopard"[60] in Portugal, whom ere long he would cause to be chased into the sea. In the meantime, the Pensinula was too insignificant an object to demand either his own presence, or much of their concern: the general welfare of the empire called on them to fix their attention on a subject of a very different nature; namely, the situation of the imperial family. "I and my house," said Napoleon, "will ever be found ready to sacrifice everything, even our own dearest ties and feeling, to the welfare of the French people."

This was the first public intimation of a measure which had for a considerable period occupied much of Napoleon's thoughts, and which, regarded at the time (almost universally) as the very master-stroke of his policy, proved in the issue no mean element of his ruin.

Josephine had loved Napoleon, and been beloved passionately by him in his youth. She had shared his humbler fortune; by her connections in Paris, and especially by her skilful conduct during his Egyptian expedition, and immediately afterwards, she had most materially assisted him in the attainment of the sovereign dignity: she had subsequently adorned his court, and gratified his pride, by the elegance of her manners, and won to herself the attachment of his people, by her sincere good nature and active benevolence. Her power over him was known to be great, and no one ever doubted but that it had uniformly been exerted on the side of mercy. She was considered as the good angel who, more frequently and effectually than any influence besides, interfered to soothe the fierce passions and temper the violent acts of her lord. Her devotion to him was perfect: she partook his labours as far as he would permit her to do so, submitted to all his caprices, and, with a dark presentiment that his ambition would one day cast her aside, continued to centre the whole of her existence in the contemplation of his glory.

Long before Napoleon assumed the imperial title, his hopes of offspring from this union were at an end; and, at least from the hour in which his authority was declared to be hereditary, Josephine must have begun to suspect that, in his case also, the ties of domestic life might be sacrificed to those views of political advantage, which had so often dissolved the marriages of princes. For a moment she seems to have flattered herself that Napoleon would be contented to adopt her son: and Eugene, as we have seen, was indeed announced, at the period of his alliance with the royal family of Bavaria, as the successor to the throne of Italy, in case his father-in-law should leave no second son to inherit it. Louis Buonaparte afterwards wedded Hortense de Beauharnois, and an infant son, the only pledge of their ill-assorted union, became so much the favourite of Napoleon, that Josephine, as well as others, regarded this boy as the heir of France. But the child died early; and the Emperor began to familiarise himself with the idea of dissolving his own marriage.

There is now no doubt that, as early as the conferences of Tilsit, the scheme of such a connection with the imperial family of Russia was broached; and as little that Alexander treated the proposal with coldness, in consequence of the insuperable aversion with which the empress-mother (a princess whose influence was always commanding) persisted in regarding the character of Buonaparte. At Erfurt this matter was once more touched upon; and a second rejection of his personal alliance was probably the chief of not a few incidents at that meeting, which satisfied Napoleon as to the uncertain condition of his relations with the Russian court. Then, however, he had abundant reasons for dissembling his displeasure: and the pretext of difficulties arising from difference of religion was permitted to pass.

Fouchewas one of the first to penetrate the secret thoughts of Buonaparte: and he, with audacity equal to his cunning, ventured to take on himself the dangerous office of sounding the Empress as to this most delicate of all subjects. One evening, before Napoleon left Paris on his unhallowed expedition to Spain, the minister of police drew Josephine aside into a corner of her saloon, and, after a preface of abundant commonplaces, touching the necessities of the empire and the painful position of the Emperor, asked her in plain terms whether she were not capable of sacrificing all private feelings to these? Josephine heard him with at least the appearance of utter surprise, ordered him to quit her presence, and went immediately to demand of Napoleon whether the minister had had any authority for this proceeding. The Emperor answered in the negative, and with high demonstrations of displeasure: but when Josephine went on to ask the dismissal of Fouche as the only fit punishment for so great an outrage, he refused to comply. He remained steadfast, in spite of the urgencies and lamentations of an insulted woman; and from that hour Josephine must have felt that her fate was fixed.

The apartments of Napoleon, and those of his wife, which were immediately over them, at the Tuileries, had communication by means of a private staircase; and it was the custom of the Emperor himself to signify, by a tap on the door of Josephine's sitting-room, his desire to converse with her in his cabinet below. In the days of their cordial union the signal was often made, most commonly in the evening, and it was not unusual for them to remain shut up together in conversation for hours. Soon after his return from Schoenbrunn, the ladies in attendance began to remark that the Emperor's knock was heard more frequently than it had ever used to be, that their mistress seemed to listen for it at certain hours with a new and painful anxiety, and that she did not obey the signal with her accustomed alacrity. One evening Napoleon surprised them by carrying Josephine into the midst of them, pale, apparently lifeless. She was but awaking from a long swoon into which she had fallen on hearing him at last pronounce the decree which terminated their connection.

This was on the 5th of December. On the 15th the Emperor summoned his council, and announced to them, that at the expense of all his personal feelings, he, devoted wholly to the welfare of the state, had resolved to separate himself from his most dear consort. Josephine then appeared among them, and, not without tears, expressed her acquiescence in the decree. The council, after haranguing the imperial spouses on the nobleness of their mutual sacrifice, accepted and ratified the dissolution of the marriage. The title of Empress was to continue with Josephine for life, and a pension of two millions of francs (to which Napoleon afterwards added a third million from his privy purse) was allotted to her. She retired from the Tuileries, residing thenceforth mostly at the villa of Malmaison; and in the course of a few weeks it was signified that Napoleon had demanded the hand of the Archduchess Maria Louisa, daughter to the Emperor Francis, the same youthful princess who has been mentioned as remaining in Vienna, on account of illness, during the second occupation of that capital.

Having given her hand, at Vienna, to Berthier, who had the honour to represent the person of his master, the young archduchess came into France in March, 1810. On the 28th, as her carriage was proceeding towards Soissons, Napoleon rode up to it, in a plain dress, altogether unattended; and, at once breaking through all the etiquettes of such occasions, introduced himself to his bride. She had never seen his person till then, and it is said that her first exclamation was, "Your majesty's pictures have not done you justice." Buonaparte was at this time forty years of age; his countenance had acquired a certain fulness, and that statue-like calmness of expression with which posterity will always be familiar; but his figure betrayed as yet nothing more than a tendency towards corpulence. He was considered as a handsomer man at this period than he had been in her earlier days. They spent the evening at the chateau of Compiegne, and were remarried, on the 2nd of April, at Paris, amidst every circumstance of splendour. Among other imperial gallantries, Napoleon had provided a set of apartments at the Tuileries in which, down to the minutest article of furniture, Maria-Louisa found a facsimile of those which she had been accustomed to occupy in her father's palace of Schoenbrunn. For some time he seemed to devote himself, like a mere lover, to the society of his new partner; and was really, according to his own account at St. Helena, enchanted with the contrast which her youthful simplicity of character and manners presented to the finished and elaborate graces of Josephine. Of the uniform attachment and affection of both his wives, he spoke afterwards with equal praises. But he in vain endeavoured to prevail on Maria-Louisa to make a personal acquaintance with her predecessor; and, at length, found it necessary to give up his own visits to Malmaison, which for a time were not unfrequent.

Napoleon, in his exile, said that "the Spanish ulcer" and the Austrian match were the two main causes of his ruin;--and they both contributed to it largely, though by no means equally. His alliance with the haughtiest of the old sovereign houses gave deep offence indeed to that great party in France, who, though willing to submit to a Dictator, still loathed the name of hereditary monarchy. Nothing, perhaps, could have shocked those men more grievously than to see the victorious heir and representative of their revolution seeking to mix his blood with that of its inveterate enemies, and making himself free, as it were, of what they had been accustomed to call the old-established "corporation of tyrants." Another, and, it is to be hoped, as large a class of his subjects, were disgusted with his abandonment of the wife of his youth, for the sake of gratifying his vanity and ambition. There were also, we may easily believe, not a few royalists of the old school who had hitherto acquiesced in his sway the more easily, because he seemed destined to die childless, and in a contest for the throne of France, they flattered themselves the legitimate heir of the monarchy might outweigh any of his remoter kindred. And, lastly, it is not improvable that some of Napoleon's marshals had accustomed themselves to dream of events such as occurred on the death of Alexander the Great. But making all allowance for these exceptions, it is hardly possible to doubt that a vast proportion of the upper classes of society in France must have been disposed to hail the Emperor's alliance with the house of Austria, as a pledge of his desire to adopt, henceforth, a more moderate line of policy as to his foreign relations; or that his throne must have been strengthened in the eyes of the nation at large by the prospect--soon realised--of a son of his own blood to fill it after him. Napoleon's own opinion was, that the error lay, not in seeking a bride of imperial birth, but in choosing her at Vienna. Had he persisted in his demands, the Czar, he doubted not, would have granted him his sister; the proud dreams of Tilsit would have been realised, and Paris and St. Petersburg become the only two capitals of Europe.

The Emperor's new marriage was speedily followed by another event, which showed how little the ordinary ties and feelings of domestic life now weighed with him in the scale against ambition. His brother Louis, a weak, but benevolent man, had in vain been cautioned by Napoleon, on his promotion to the Dutch throne, that, in his administration of this subaltern monarchy, "the first object of his care must ever be _the Emperor, the second France, and the third Holland_." Louis, surrounded by native ministers, men of great talents and experience, and enlightened lovers of their country, had his sympathies ere long enlisted on the side of those whom he might be pardoned for wishing to consider as really his subjects. His queen, on the other hand, the daughter of Josephine, and the favourite of Napoleon, made her court, as far as she could, a French one, and was popularly regarded as heading the party who looked in all things to the Tuileries. The meek-spirited Louis, thwarted by this intriguing woman, and grossly insulted by his brother, struggled for some time with the difficulties of his situation; but his patience availed nothing: his supposed connivance at the violations of the Berlin and Milan decrees, in the same proportion as it tended to raise him more and more in the affections of the Dutch, fixed and heightened the displeasure of Napoleon. He was at length summoned to Paris, and without a moment's hesitation obeyed. On arriving there he took up his residence in the house of his mother, and next morning found himself a prisoner. Having abdicated his throne, Louis retired to Gratz, in Styria, and to that private mode of life for which his character fitted him: his name continues to be affectionately remembered in Holland. His beautiful wife, despite the fall of her mother, chose to fix her residence in Paris, where she once more shone the brightest ornament of the court. On the 9th of July, 1810, the kingdom of Holland was formally annexed to the French empire; Amsterdam taking rank among the cities next after Rome.

In pursuance of the same stern resolution to allow no consideration to interfere with the complete and effectual establishment of the "continental system," Buonaparte shortly afterwards annexed the Hanse towns, Oldenburg, and the whole sea-coast of Germany, from the frontier of Holland to that of Denmark, to the French empire. The King of Prussia was as yet in no condition to remonstrate against this new act of rapacity: opposition from any other German state was wholly out of the question.

In truth there had been, for several years, but one power in the North of Europe at once decidedly adverse in spirit, and in any degree independent; and now, to all appearance, this last exception also was removed. Gustavus IV., King of Sweden, had persisted in his original hatred of the French Revolution, and of Buonaparte, in opposition to a powerful party in that country, who considered the conduct of their sovereign, in standing out against so gigantic an enemy, as mere obstinacy--in fact as insane. In consequence of his pertinacious refusal to submit to the supreme will of Napoleon, the Pomeranian provinces and Finland had been lost to the kingdom. The monarch's personal behaviour unfortunately was so extravagant as to furnish some grounds for suspecting him of mental aberration. He was arrested in his palace, and, an act of abdication for himself and his children being extorted, deposed: his uncle, the Duke of Sudermania, was called to the throne in his room, as Charles XIII.; and, amicable relations being soon established between the Courts of Stockholm and the Tuileries, Pomerania was restored, and the English flag and commerce banished from the ports of Sweden in December, 1809.

In May, 1810, the Prince of Augustenburg, who had been recognised as heir to Charles XIII., died suddenly: and the choice of a successor was, according to the Constitution of Sweden, to depend on the vote of the Diet, which assembled accordingly as Orebro, in the month of August following.

The royal house (except the immediate line of the deposed king) being extinct, many candidates were proposed; and among others the King of Denmark and Norway, upon whom, in true policy, the choice should have fallen, as in that case a state capable of balancing the power of Russia on the Baltic might have been consolidated. But the eyes of men were turned almost exclusively at this time to Napoleon; and in the hope of securing his friendship and protection, the succession was at last proposed to Marshal Bernadotte, Prince of Ponte Corvo, and brother-in-law to Joseph Buonaparte, as married to that Mademoiselle Clery, who in early days had received

Napoleon's own addresses. The Marshal had gained goodwill by his moderation and justice, when entrusted with the government of Hanover and Swedish Pomerania, after these countries fell into the hands of the French in consequence of the campaign of 1806-7. His military reputation was high; there was no stain on his private character: and there was one circumstance especially in his favour, that he had been bred a Protestant, and might therefore be expected to conform, without scruple, to the established church of Sweden. But the chief recommendation was, without doubt, the belief of the Swedish Diet that Bernadotte stood in the first rank of Napoleon's favour.

Napoleon, however, had never forgiven Bernadotte for his refusal to act on his side on the 18th Brumaire. He thenceforth considered this great soldier of the Republic as one who might serve the Emperor well, because in doing so he served France, but who looked to himself with none of those feelings of personal devotion which could alone entitle a subject to his favour. Bernadotte had been distinguished in the army before Napoleon himself appeared on the great theatre of events; he could never be classed with those who had earned all their distinction and pre-eminence under the banners of the Emperor; he had an existence separate and his own; he had stood aloof at the great and decisive crisis of Napoleon's fate; he might be entrusted and employed afterwards--he could never be loved. The proposal of the Diet, therefore, was the reverse of agreeable to him whose favour it was expressly designed to conciliate. Bernadotte, however, was powerful in the esteem of a great party in the French army, as well as among the old republicans of the state: to have interfered against him would have been to kindle high wrath and hatred among all those officers who belonged to the ante-Buonapartean period; and, on the other hand, to oppose the free-will of the Swedes would have appeared extraordinary conduct indeed on the part of a sovereign who studiously represented himself as owing everything to the free-will of the French. Sweden, finally, was still an independent state; and the events of the Peninsula were likely to impress the Emperor with a lively sense of the dangers of exciting a spirit of national aversion at the other extremity of Europe. Napoleon consented to the acceptance of the proffered dignity by Bernadotte. The Marshal was called on to sign a declaration, before he left Paris, that he would never bear arms against France. He rejected this condition as incompatible with the connexion which Napoleon himself had just sanctioned him in forming with another state, and said he was sure the suggestion came not from the Emperor, who knew what were the duties of a sovereign, but from some lawyer. Napoleon frowned darkly, and answered with an air of embarrassment, "Go; our destinies are about to be fulfilled." Bernadotte said he had not heard his words distinctly: Napoleon repeated them; and they parted. Bernadotte was received with an enthusiastic welcome in Stockholm; and, notwithstanding the unpleasant circumstances under which Napoleon had dismissed him, the French alliance continued to be maintained. The private history of the transaction was not likely to be divulged at the time; and the natural as well as universal notion was, that Sweden, governed in effect by Marshal Bernadotte as crown prince, had become almost as mere a dependence of France as Naples under King Joachim Murat, or Westphalia under King Jerome Buonaparte.

The war, meanwhile, continued without interruption in the Peninsula; whither, but for his marriage, Napoleon would certainly have repaired in person after the peace of Schoenbrunn left him at ease on his German frontier. Although the new alliance had charms enough to detain him in France, it by no means withdrew his attention from the state of that fair kingdom which still mocked Joseph with the shadow of a crown. In the open field, indeed, the French appeared everywhere triumphant, except only where the British force from Portugal interfered, and in almost every district of Spain the fortresses were in their hands; yet the spirit of the people remained wholly unsubdued. The invaders could not count an inch of soil their own beyond their outposts. Their troops continued to be harassed and thinned by the indomitable guerillas or partisan companies; and, even in the immediate neighbourhood of their strongest garrisons, the people assembled to vote for representatives in the Cortes, which had at last been summoned to meet in Cadiz, there to settle the national government, during the King's absence, on a regular footing.

The battle left the central part of Spain wholly undefended; and Soult, Victor and Mortier, forcing the passes of the Sierra Morena, made themselves masters, early in the year of Jaen, Cordova, Grenada, Malaga, and Seville itself. Cadiz, to which the Central Junta had ere this retired, was now garrisoned by a large Spanish force, including the army of Estremadura, under the Duke D'Albuquerque, and a considerable detachment of English troops from Gibraltar; and Soult sat down before the place in form. Could he have taken Cadiz, no fortress of importance would have remained with the patriots in the south of Spain: but the strength of the situation and the ready access to the sea and Gibraltar, rendered all his efforts vain.

On the eastern side of Spain Suchet defeated the Spanish General O'Donnell under the walls of Ostalric; and took afterwards that town, Lerida, Mequineza, and Tortosa. But Valencia once more repelled the invaders. After a bloody sally of the inhabitants Suchet withdrew from before the walls.

It was on the Portuguese side, however, that the events of most importance occurred. It was there that the disgraces of Vimiero and Talaveyra must be avenged; and there accordingly Napoleon had directed his chief force to be set in motion. Massena (Prince of Essling), second only to himself in reputation, took the command, early in the season, of "the army of Portugal," at least 100,000 strong, and whose commission it was to drive the English leopards, and the Seapoy General (as, ignorant of the future, Buonaparte at this time called Wellington) into the sea. To this gigantic army that leader could oppose at most 20,000 British troops; but 30,000 Portuguese had by this time been so well trained by General Beresford, that they were held not unworthy of fighting by the side of Englishmen. Still Lord Wellington's whole force was barely half that of Massena: and his operations were necessarily confined to the defensive. He had no means to prevent the French Marshal from taking Oviedo and Ciudad Rodrigo--almost in his sight; but commenced his retreat, and conducted it with a coolness and precision which not a little disconcerted the pursuers. They at length ventured to attack the English on their march. On the 27th September, 1810, they charged in five columns, on the heights of Busaco, and were driven back with such terrible carnage that no further assault was threatened. Massena kept advancing, step by step, as Wellington withdrew, not doubting that his enemy would embark as soon as he reached Lisbon, and leave him in quiet possession of that capital and the rich country around. His surprise was great when Lord Wellington at last halted on the lines of the Torres Vedras, which had by this time been so strengthened, that even in inferior hands they might have been considered impregnable.

This formidable position, extending about twelve leagues between the sea and the Tagus, placed the port of Lisbon and the adjacent territory in the secure possession of the English general. Massena might flatter his master with the announcement that he was besieging Lisbon; but in reality his own army very soon suffered all the inconveniences and privations of a besieged garrison. The country around him had been laid waste: every Portuguese peasant was a deadly enemy. To advance was impossible, and there was infinite difficulty in keeping his communications open behind. Thus, during many months, the two armies lay face to face in inaction.

[Footnote 60: The leopards had been changed into lions in the English shield five hundred years before this! To such small matters could Buonaparte's rancour stoop.]

CHAPTER XXVIII

Events of the year 1811--Birth of the King of Rome--Disgrace of Fouche-Discontents in France--Relations with Russia--Licence System--Napoleon prepares for War with Russia--The Campaign in the Peninsula--Massena's Retreat--Battle of Fuentes d'Onor--Lord Wellington blockades Ciudad Rodrigo--Retreats--Joseph wishes to Abdicate.

On the 20th of April, 1811, Napoleon's wishes were crowned by the birth of a son. The birth was a difficult one, and the nerves of the medical attendant were shaken. "She is but a woman," said the Emperor, who was present: "treat her as you would a Bourgeoise of the Rue St. Denis." The accoucheur at a subsequent moment withdrew Napoleon from the couch, and demanded whether, in case one life must be sacrificed, he should prefer the mother's or the child's. "The mother's," he answered; "it is her right!" At length the child appeared, but without any sign of life. After the lapse of some minutes a feeble cry was heard, and Napoleon entering the ante-chamber in which the high functionaries of the state were assembled, announced the event in these words: "It is a King of Rome."

The birth of the heir of Napoleon was received with as many demonstrations of loyal enthusiasm as had ever attended that of a Dauphin; yet, from what has been said as to the light in which various parties of men in France from the beginning viewed the Austrian alliance, it may be sufficiently inferred that the joy on this occasion was far from universal. The royalists considered the event as fatal to the last hopes of the Bourbons; the ambitious generals despaired of any future dismemberment of the empire: the old republicans, who had endured Buonaparte's despotic power as the progeny of the revolution, looked forward with deep disgust to the rule of a dynasty proud of sharing the blood of the haughtiest of all the royal houses of Europe, and consequently more likely to make common cause with the little band of hereditary sovereigns than with the people. Finally, the title, "King of Rome," put an end to the fond hopes of the Italians, who had been taught by Napoleon to expect that, after his death, their country should possess a government separate from France; nor could the same title fail to excite some bitter feelings in the Austrian court, whose heir-apparent under the old empire had been styled commonly "The King of the Romans." For the present, however, both at home and abroad, the event was naturally looked on as adding much strength to the throne of Napoleon.

He, thus called on to review with new seriousness the whole condition and prospects of his empire, appears to have felt very distinctly that neither could be secure, unless an end were, by some means, put to the war with England. However he might permit himself to sneer at his great enemy in his public addresses from the throne, and in his bulletins, Napoleon had too much strength of mind not to despise those who, in any of their private communications, had the meanness to affect acquiescence in such views. When Denon brought him, after the battle of Wagram, the design of a medal representing an eagle strangling a leopard, Buonaparte rebuked and dismissed the flatterer. "What," said he, "strangling the leopard! There is not a spot of the sea on which the eagle dares show himself. This is base adulation. It would have been nearer the truth to represent the eagle as choked by the leopard."

He sent a private messenger to London to ascertain from personal communication with the Marquess Wellesley, then minister for foreign affairs, on what terms the English government would consent to open a formal negotiation; but this attempt was baffled by a singular circumstance. Fouche having derived new audacity from the results of his extraordinary conversation with Josephine, on the subject of the divorce, had ventured to send a dependent of his own to London, for the purpose of sounding Lord Wellesley on the question of preliminaries; not doubting that could he give distinct information on this head to his master, without having in any degree compromised the imperial dignity, the service would be considered as most valuable. But Lord Wellesley, beset, at the same time, and on the same very delicate topic, by two different persons, neither of whom produced any proper credentials, and who denied all knowledge of each other, conceived, very naturally, that they were mere adventurers if not spies, and at once broke off his communications with both. Napoleon, on discovering this intrigue, summoned Foucheto his presence. "So, sir," said he, "I find you make peace and war without consulting me." He was dismissed from the ministry of police, and sent into an honourable banishment, as Governor of Rome. Fouches presumption had been great: but long ere now Napoleon was weary, not of him only, but of Talleyrand, and indeed of all those ministers who, having reached eminent stations before he himself acquired the supreme power, preserved, in their manner of transacting business, and especially of offering advice, any traces of that period in which Frenchmen flattered themselves they were free. The warnings which he had received, when about to commence his atrocious proceedings against Spain, were remembered with the higher resentment, as the course of events in that country, month after month, and year after year, confirmed the accuracy of the foresight which he had contemned. This haughty spirit could not endure the presence of the man who could be supposed to fancy that even on one point, he had the better of his master.

The disgrace of Fouchewas certainly a very unpopular measure. The immediate cause of it could not be divulged, and the minister was considered as having fallen a sacrifice to the honesty of his remonstrances on the Spanish invasion and the increased rigour of the Emperor's domestic administration. It was about this time that, in addition to the castle of Vincennes, nine new state-prisons were established in France; and the number of persons confined in these receptacles, on warrants signed by the Emperor and his slavish privy council, far exceeded those condemned to similar usage in any recent period of the Bourbon monarchy, under the lettres de cachet of the sovereign. These were proofs, not to be mistaken, of the growth of political disaffection. In truth the "continental system," the terrible waste of life occasioned by the late campaigns in Poland and Austria, and the constant demands, both on the treasure and the blood of France, rendered necessary by the apparently interminable war in the Peninsula--these were evils which could not exist without alienating the hearts of the people. The police filled the ears of the Emperor with reports of men's private conversation. Citizens were daily removed from their families, and buried in remote and inaccessible dungeons, for no reason but that they had dared to speak what the immense majority of their neighbours thought. His quarrels with Lucien, who had contracted a marriage unsuitable, in the Emperor's opinion, to his rank, were so indecently violent, that that ablest of his brothers at length sought a refuge in England, where he remained during several years. The total slavery of the press, its audacious lies, and more audacious silence, insulted the common sense of all men. Disaffection was secretly, but rapidly, eating into the heart of his power; and yet, as if blinded to all consequences by some angry infliction of heaven, the irritable ambition of Napoleon was already tempting another great foreign enemy into the field.

When the Emperor of Russia was informed of Buonaparte's approaching nuptials with the Austrian princess, his first exclamation was, "Then the next thing will be to drive us back into our forests." In truth the conferences of Erfurt had but skinned over a wound, which nothing could have cured but a total alteration of Napoleon's policy. The Russian nation suffered so much from the "continental system," that the sovereign soon found himself compelled to relax the decrees drawn up at Tilsit in the spirit of those of Berlin and Milan. Certain harbours were opened partially for the admission of colonial produce, and the export of native productions; and there ensued a series of indignant reclamations on the part of Napoleon, and haughty evasions on that of the Czar, which, ere long, satisfied all near observers that Russia would not be slow to avail herself of any favourable opportunity of once more appealing to arms. The Spanish insurrection, backed by the victories of Lord Wellington, must have roused alike the hope and the pride of a young and ambitious prince, placed at the head of so great a nation; the inference naturally drawn from Napoleon's marriage into the house of Austria was, that the whole power of that monarchy would, henceforth, act in unison with his views--in other words, that were the Peninsula once thoroughly subdued, the whole of Western Europe would be at his command, for any service he might please to dictate. It would have been astonishing if, under such circumstances, the ministers of Alexander had not desired to bring their disputes with Paris to a close, before Napoleon should have leisure to consummate the conquest of Spain.

During the summer of 1811, then, the relations of these two governments were becoming every day more dubious; and when, towards the close of it, the Emperor of Austria published a rescript, granting a free passage through his territories to the troops of his son-in-law, England, ever watchful of the movements of her great enemy, perceived clearly that she was about to have an ally.

From the moment in which the Russian government began to reclaim seriously against certain parts of his conduct, Buonaparte increased by degrees his military force in the north of Germany and the Grand Duchy of Warsaw, and advanced considerable bodies of troops nearer and nearer to the Czar's Polish frontier. These preparations were met by some similar movements on the other side; yet, during many months, the hope of terminating the differences by negotiation was not abandoned. The Russian complaints, at length, assumed a regular shape, and embraced three distinct heads, viz.:--

First, the extension of the territories of the Duchy of Warsaw, under the treaty of Schoenbrunn. This alarmed the court of St. Petersburg, by reviving the notion of Polish independence, and Buonaparte was in vain urged to give his public guarantee that no national government should be re-established in the dismembered kingdom:

Second, the annexation of the Duchy of Oldenburg to the French empire, by that edict of Napoleon which proclaimed his seizure of the whole sea-coast of Germany, between Holland and the Baltic. Oldenburg, the hereditary territory of the Emperor Alexander's brother-in-law, had been expressly guaranteed to that prince by the treaty of Tilsit. Napoleon was asked to indemnify the ejected duke by the cession of Dantzick, or some other territory in the neighbourhood of the Grand Duchy of Warsaw; but this he declined, though he professed his willingness to give some compensation elsewhere:

Thirdly, the Czar alleged, and most truly, that the state of his country made it altogether necessary that the regulations of the "continental system" should be dispensed with in his instance, and declared that he could no longer submit to see the commerce of an independent empire trammelled for the purpose of serving the policy of a foreign power. Buonaparte admitted that it might be necessary to modify the system complained of, and expressed his belief that it would be found possible to devise some middle course, by which the commercial interests of France and Russia might be reconciled. His meaning probably was, that, if their other differences could be arranged, this part of the dispute might be settled by admitting the Czar to adopt, to a certain extent, in the north of Europe, a device which he himself had already had recourse to on a large scale, for counteracting the baneful effects of his own favourite system, in his own immediate territories. Napoleon had soon discovered that, to exclude English goods and colonial produce entirely, was actually impossible; and seeing that, either with or without his assent, the decrees of Berlin and Milan would, in one way or other, continue to be violated, it occurred to him that he might at least engross the greater part of the profits of the forbidden traffic himself. This he accomplished by the establishment of a system of custom-house regulations, under which persons desirous to import English produce into France might purchase the imperial licence for so doing. A very considerable relaxation in the pernicious influence of the Berlin code was the result of this device; and a proportional increase of the Emperor's revenue attended it. In after-days, however, he always spoke of this licence-system as one of the few great mistakes of his administration. Some petty riots among the manufacturing population of the county of Derby were magnified in his eyes into symptoms of an approaching revolution in England; the consequence, as he flattered himself, of the misery inflicted on his great enemy by the "continental system"; and to the end he continued to think that, had he resisted the temptation to enrich his own exchequer by the produce of licences, such must have been the ultimate issue of his original scheme. It was, however, by admitting Alexander to a share in the pecuniary advantages of the licence-system, that he seems to have thought the commercial part of his dispute with Russia might be accommodated.

And, indeed, had there been no cause of quarrel between these powers, except what appeared on the face of their negotiations, it is hardly to be doubted that an accommodation might have been effected. The simple truth was, that the Czar, from the hour of Maria Louisa's marriage, felt a perfect conviction that the diminution of the Russian power in the north of Europe would form the next great object of Napoleon's ambition. His subsequent proceedings, in regard to Holland, Oldenburg, and other territories, and the distribution of his troops, in Pomerania and Poland, could not fail to strengthen Alexander in this view of the case; and if war must come, there could be no question as to the policy of bringing it on before Austria had entirely recovered from the effects of the campaign of Wagram, and, above all, while the Peninsula continued to occupy 200,000 of Buonaparte's troops.

Before we return to the war in Portugal (the details of which belong to the history of Wellington, rather than of Napoleon), we may here notice very briefly one or two circumstances connected with the exiled family of Spain. It affords a melancholy picture of the degradation of the old king and queen, that these personages voluntarily travelled to Paris for the purpose of mingling in the crowd of courtiers congratulating their deceiver and spoiler on the birth of the king of Rome. Their daughter, the queen of Etruria, appears to have been the least degenerate of the race; and she accordingly met with the cruellest treatment from the hand which her parents were thus mean enough to kiss. She had been deprived of her kingdom at the period of the shameful scenes of Bayonne in 1807, on pretext that that kingdom would afford the most suitable indemnification for her brother Ferdinand on his cession to Buonaparte of his rights in Spain, and with the promise of being provided for elsewhere. This promise to the sister was no more thought of afterwards than the original scheme for the indemnification of the brother. Tuscany became a French department. Ferdinand was sent a prisoner to the castle of Valeney--a seat of Talleyrand--and she, after remaining for some time with her parents, took up her residence, as a private person, under surveillance, at Nice. Alarmed by the severity with which the police watched her, the queen at length made an attempt to escape to England. Her agents were discovered, tried by a military commission, and shot; and the unfortunate lady herself confined in a Roman monastery. A plan for the liberation of Ferdinand was about the same time detected by the emissaries of the French police: the real agent being arrested, a pretender, assuming his name and credentials, made his way into Valeney, but Ferdinand was either too cunning, or too timid to incur this danger; revealing to his jailers the proposals of the stranger, he escaped the snare laid for him, and thus cheated Napoleon of a pretext for removing him also to some Italian cell.

During four months after Wellington's famous retreat terminated in his occupation of the lines of Torres Vedras, Massena lay encamped before that position, in vain practising every artifice which consummate skill could suggest for the purpose of drawing the British army back into the field. He attempted to turn first the one flank of the position and then the other; but at either point he found his antagonist's preparations perfect. Meantime his communication with Spain was becoming every day more and more difficult, and the enmity of the peasantry was so inveterate that his troops began to suffer much from the want of provisions. Massena at length found himself compelled to retreat; and, if he executed the military movement with masterly ability, he for ever disgraced his name by the horrible licence which he permitted to his soldiery. Every crime of which man is capable--every brutality which can dishonour rational beings--must be recorded in the narrative of that fearful march. Age, rank, sex, character, were alike contemned; it seemed as if, maddened with a devilish rage, these ferocious bands were resolved to ruin the country which they could not possess, and to exterminate, as far as was in their power, the population which they could neither conciliate nor subdue.

Lord Wellington followed hard on their footsteps until they were beyond the Portuguese frontier; within it they had left only one garrison--at Almeida, and of this town the siege was immediately formed; while the British general himself invested the strong Spanish city and fortress of Ciudad Rodrigo. But Massena, on regaining communication with the French armies in Castile, swelled his numbers so much, that he ventured to resume the offensive. Lord Wellington could not maintain the siege of Ciudad Rodrigo in the face of such an army as Massena had now assembled; but when the marshal indicated his wishes to bring on battle, he disdained to decline the invitation. The armies met at Fuentes d'Onor, on the 5th May 1811, and the French were once more defeated. The garrison of Almeida contrived to escape across the frontier, before the siege, which had been interrupted, could be renewed. Portugal remained in a miserable state of exhaustion indeed, but altogether delivered of her invaders; and Napoleon, as if resolved that each of his marshals in succession should have the opportunity of measuring himself against Wellington, now sent Marmont to displace Massena.

Soult meanwhile had advanced on the southern frontier of Portugal from Estremadura, and obtained possession of Badajos, under circumstances which Lord Wellington considered as highly disgraceful to the Spanish garrison of that important place, and the armies which ought to have been ready to cover it. On the other hand, an English corps, under General Graham, sallied out of Cadiz, and were victorious in a brilliant affair on the heights of Barossa, in front of that besieged city.

As concerned the Spanish armies, the superiority of the French had been abundantly maintained during this campaign; and it might still be said that King Joseph was in military possession of all but some fragments of his kingdom. But the influence of the English victories was by no means limited to the Portuguese, whose territory they had delivered. They breathed new ardour into the Spanish people: the Guerilla warfare, trampled down in one spot only to start up in fifty others, raged more and more widely, as well as fiercely, over the surface of the country: the French troops lost more lives in this incessant struggle, wherein no glory could be achieved, than in any similar period spent in a regular campaign; and Joseph Buonaparte, while the question of peace or war with Russia was yet undecided, became so weary of his situation, that he earnestly entreated Napoleon to place the crown of Spain on some other head.

Such were the circumstances under which the eventful year 1812 began.

CHAPTER XXIX

Capture of Ciudad Rodrigo--and of Badajos--Battle of Salamanca--State of Napoleon's Foreign Relations--His Military Resources--Napoleon at Dresden--Rupture with Russia--Napoleon's conduct to the Poles--Distribution of the Armies--Passage of the Niemen--Napoleon at Wilna.

Lord Wellington had now complete possession of Portugal; and lay on the frontiers of that kingdom, ready to act on the offensive within Spain, whenever the distribution of the French armies should seem to offer a fit opportunity. Learning that Marmont had sent considerable reinforcements to Suchet, in Valencia, he resolved to advance and once more besiege Ciudad Rodrigo. He re-appeared before that strong fortress on the 8th of January 1812, and carried it by storm on the 19th, four days before Marmont could collect a force adequate for its relief. He instantly repaired the fortifications, entrusted the place to a Spanish garrison, and repaired in person to the southern part of the Portuguese frontier, which required his attention in consequence of that miserable misconduct of the Spaniards which had enabled the French to make themselves masters of Badajos in the preceding year. He appeared before that city on the 16th March, and in twenty days took it also. The loss of life on both sides, in these rapid sieges, was very great; but they were gained by a general at the head of at most 50,000 men, in despite of an enemy mustering full 80,000; and the results were of the first importance to the English cause. Marmont, on hearing of the fall of the second fortress, immediately retreated from the neighbourhood of Ciudad Rodrigo, which he had made a vain attempt to regain; and Soult, who had arrived from before Cadiz just in time to see the British flag mounted on the towers of Badajos, retired in like manner. The English general hastened to make the best use of his advantage, by breaking up the only bridge by which Marmont and Soult could now communicate; and, having effected this object early in May, marched in June to Salamanca, took the forts there, and 800 prisoners, and--Marmont retiring as he advanced--hung on his rear until he reached the Douro.

Marmont was now joined by Bonnet's army from Asturias, and thus once more recovered a decided superiority in numbers. Wellington accordingly retired in his turn; and for some days the two hostile armies moved in parallel lines, often within half cannon shot, each waiting for some mistake of which advantage might be taken. The weather was all the while intensely hot; numbers fainted on the march; and when any rivulet was in view, it was difficult to keep the men in their ranks. On the evening of the 21st of July, Wellington and Marmont lay in full view of each other, on two opposite rising grounds near Salamanca; a great storm of thunder and rain came on, and during the whole night the sky was bright with lightning. Wellington was at table when he received intelligence that his adversary was extending his left,--with the purpose of coming between him and Ciudad Rodrigo. He rose in haste, exclaiming, "Marmont's good genius has forsaken him," and was instantly on horseback. The great battle of Salamanca was fought on the 22nd of July. The French were attacked on the point which Marmont's movement leftwards had weakened, and sustained a signal defeat. The commander-in-chief himself lost an arm: 7000 prisoners, eleven guns, and two eagles were taken; and it was only the coming on of night that saved the army from utter destruction. Wellington pursued the flying enemy as far as Valladolid, and then, re-crossing the Douro, marched upon Madrid. King Joseph fled once more at his approach, and the English were received with enthusiasm in the capital of Spain.

Lord Wellington had thus ventured to place himself in the heart of Spain, with, at most, 60,000 men, well-knowing that the French armies in the Peninsula still mustered at the least 150,000 in the expectation that so spirited a movement, coming after the glorious successes of Ciudad Rodrigo, Badajos, and Salamanca, would effectually stimulate the Spanish generals. Ballasteros in particular, he doubted not, would at least take care to occupy all the attention of Soult, and prevent that able leader from advancing out of the south. But the Spaniard's egregious pride took fire at the notion of being directed by an Englishman, and he suffered Soult to break up the siege of Cadiz, and retire with all his army undisturbed towards the Sierra Morena. Lord Wellington, incensed at this folly, was constrained to divide his army. Leaving half at Madrid under Sir R. Hill, to check Soult, he himself marched with the other for Burgos, by taking which great city he judged he should have it in his power to overawe effectually the remains of the army of Marmont. He invested Burgos accordingly on the 19th of September, and continued the siege during five weeks, until Soult, with a superior force, began to threaten Hill, and (Marmont's successor) Clausel, having also received great reinforcements, appeared ready to resume the offensive. Lord Wellington then abandoned the siege of Burgos and commenced his retreat. He was joined in the course of it by Hill, and Soult and Clausel then effected their junction also, in his rear--their troops being nearly double his numbers. He retired leisurely and deliberately as far as Ciudad Rodrigo--and thus closed the Peninsular campaign of 1812. But in sketching its progress we have lost sight for a moment of the still mightier movements in which Napoleon was personally engaged upon another scene of action.

It has already been mentioned, that before the year 1811 reached its close, the approach of a rupture with Russia was sufficiently indicated in an edict of the Emperor of Austria, granting a free passage through his territories to the armies of his son-in-law. However, during several months following, the negotiations between the Czar and Napoleon continued; and more than once there appeared considerable likelihood of their finding an amicable termination. The tidings of Lord Wellington's successes at Ciudad Rodrigo and Badajos were calculated to temper the ardour of Buonaparte's presumption; and for a moment he seems to have felt the necessity of bringing the affairs of the Peninsula to a point, ere he should venture to involve himself in another warfare. He, in effect, opened a communication with the English government, when the fall of Badajos was announced to him; but before the negotiation had proceeded many steps, his pride returned on him in its original obstinacy, and the renewed demand, that Joseph should be recognised as King of Spain, abruptly closed the intercourse of the diplomatists.

Such being the state of the Peninsula, and all hope of an accommodation with England at an end, it might have been expected that Napoleon would have spared no effort to accommodate his differences with Russia, or, if a struggle must come, to prepare for it, by placing his relations with the other powers, capable of interfering on one side or the other, on a footing favourable to himself. But here also the haughty temper, which adversity itself could never bend, formed an insurmountable and fatal obstacle. To gain the cordial friendship of Sweden was obviously, from the geographical position of that country, and the high military talents of Bernadotte, an object of the most urgent importance; yet the Crown Prince, instead of being treated with as the head of an independent state, was personally insulted by the French resident at Stockholm, who, in Bernadotte's own language, "demeaned himself on every occasion as if he had been a Roman proconsul, dictating absolutely in a province." In his anxiety to avoid a rupture, Bernadotte at length agreed to enforce the "continental system," and to proclaim war against England. But these concessions, instead of producing hearty goodwill, had a directly contrary effect. England, considering Sweden as an involuntary enemy, disdained to make any attempt against her; and the adoption of the anti-commercial edicts of Napoleon was followed by a multiplicity of collisions between the Swedish coasters and the Imperial douaniers, out of which arose legal questions without number. These, in most cases, were terminated at Paris, with summary injustice, and the provocations and reclamations of Bernadotte multiplied daily. Amazed that one who had served under his banners should dare to dispute his will, Napoleon suffered himself to speak openly of causing Bernadotte to finish his Swedish studies in Vincennes. Nay, he condescended to organise a conspiracy for the purpose of putting this threat into execution. The Crown Prince escaped, through the zeal of a private friend at Paris, the imminent danger of being carried off after the fashion of the D'Enghiens and the Rumbolds: and thenceforth his part was fixed.

On the other flank of the Czar's dominion--his hereditary enemy, the Grand Seignior, was at this time actually at war with him. Napoleon had neglected his relations with Constantinople for some years past; but he now perceived the importance of keeping this quarrel alive, and employed his agents to stimulate the Grand Seignior to take the field in person at the head of 100,000 men, for the purpose of co-operating with himself in a general invasion of the Russian empire. But here he encountered a new and an unforeseen difficulty. Lord Castlereagh, the English minister for foreign affairs, succeeded in convincing the Porte, that, if Russia were once subdued, there would remain no power in Europe capable of shielding her against the universal ambition of Napoleon. And wisely considering this prospective danger as immeasurably more important than any immediate advantage which she could possibly reap from the humiliation of her old rival, the Porte commenced a negotiation, which, exactly at the most critical moment (as we shall see hereafter) ended in a peace with Russia.

The whole forces of Italy--Switzerland, Bavaria, and the princes of the Rhenish League,--including the Elector of Saxony,--were at Napoleon's disposal. Denmark hated England too much to have leisure for fear of him. Prussia, surrounded and studded with French garrisons, was more than ever hostile to France; and the king was willing, in spite of all that he had suffered, to throw himself at once into the arms of Russia. But this must have inferred his immediate and total ruin, unless the Czar chose to march at once into Germany. Such a movement was wholly inconsistent with the plan of operations contemplated, in case of a war with Buonaparte, by the military advisers of Alexander; and Frederick William saw himself compelled to place 20,000 troops, the poor relics of his army, at the disposal of the common oppressor.

Austria was bound by treaty to assist Napoleon with 30,000 men, whenever he chose to demand them; but this same treaty included Buonaparte's guarantee of Austria's Polish provinces. Could he have got rid of this pledge, he distinctly perceived the advantages which he might derive from the enthusiasm of the Poles; to proclaim their independence would have been, he well knew, to array a whole gallant nation under his banners; and of such objections to their independence as might be started by his own creature, the Grand Duke of Warsaw, he made little account. But Austria would not consent to give up his guarantee of Galicia, unless he consented to yield back the Illyrian territory which she had lost at Schoenbrunn; and this was a condition to which Napoleon would not for a moment listen. He would take whatever he could gain by force or by art; but he would sacrifice nothing. The evil consequences of this piece of obstinacy were twofold. Austria remained an ally indeed, but at best a cold one; and the opportunity of placing the whole of Poland in insurrection, between him and the Czar, was for ever lost.

But if Napoleon, in the fulness of his presumption, thus neglected or scorned the timely conciliation of foreign powers-some of whom he might have arrayed heartily on his side, and others at least retained neutral-he certainly omitted nothing as to the preparation of the military forces of his own empire. Before yet all hopes of an accommodation with St. Petersburg where at an end, he demanded and obtained two new conscriptions in France; and moreover established a law by which he was enabled to call out 100,000 men at a time, of those whom the conscriptions had spared, for service at home. This limitation of their service he soon disregarded; and in effect the new system-that of the Ban, as he affected to call it-became a mere extension of the old scheme. The amount of the French army at the period in question (exclusive of the Ban) is calculated at 850,000 men; the army of the kingdom of Italy mustered 50,000; that of Naples, 30,000; that of the Grand Duchy of Warsaw, 60,000; the Bavarian, 40,000; the Westphalian, 30,000; the Saxon, 30,000; Wirtemberg, 15,000; Baden, 9,000; and the minor powers of the Rhenish League, 23,000. Of these armies Napoleon had the entire control. In addition, Austria was bound to furnish him with 30,000, and Prussia with 20,000 auxiliaries. The sum-total is 1,187,000. Deducting 387,000--a large allowance for hospitals, furloughs, and incomplete regiments-there remained 800,000 effective men at his immediate command. The Spanish peninsula might perhaps occupy, even now, 150,000; but still Napoleon could bring into the field against Russia, in case all negotiation failed, an army of 650,000 men; numbers such as Alexander could have no chance of equalling; numbers such as had never before followed an European banner.

Notwithstanding all this display of military strength, the French statesmen who had in former days possessed the highest place in the Emperor's confidence, and who had been shaken in his favour by their bold prophecies of the result of his attempts on Spain and Portugal, did not hesitate to come forward on this new occasion, and offer warnings, for which the course of events in the Peninsula might have been expected to procure a patient hearing. Talleyrand, still in office, exhausted all his efforts in vain. Fouche who on pretence of ill health had thrown up his Roman government, and was now resident at his country seat near Paris, drew up a memorial, in which the probable consequences of a march into Russia were detailed with masterly skill and eloquence; and demanded an audience of the Emperor, that he might present it in person. Napoleon, whose police now watched no one so closely as their former chief, was prepared for this. He received Fouchewith an air of cool indifference. "I am no stranger to your errand," said he. "The war with Russia pleases you as little as that of Spain." Foucheanswered, that he hoped to be pardoned for having drawn up some reflections on so important a crisis. "It is no crisis at all," resumed Buonaparte, "but a mere war of politics. Spain falls whenever I have destroyed the English influence at St. Petersburg. I have 800,000 soldiers in readiness: with such an army I consider Europe as an old prostitute, who must obey my pleasure. Did not you yourself once tell me that the word impossible is not French? You grandees are now too rich, and though you pretend to be anxious about my interests, you are only thinking of what might happen to yourselves in case of my death, and the dismemberment of my empire. I regulate my conduct much more by the sentiments of my army than by yours. Is it my fault that the height of power which I have attained compels me to ascend to the dictatorship of the world? My destiny is not yet accomplished-the picture exists as yet only in outline. There must be one code, one court of appeal, and one coinage for all Europe. The states of Europe must be melted into one nation, and Paris be its capital." It deserves to be mentioned that neither the statesman thus contemptuously dismissed, nor any of his brethren, ever even alluded to the injustice of making war on Russia for the mere gratification of ambition. Their arguments were all drawn from the extent of Alexander's resources-his 400,000 regulars, and 50,000 Cossacks, already known to be in arms-and the enormous population on which he had the means of drawing for recruits; the enthusiastic national feelings of the Muscovites; the distance of their country; the severity of their climate; the opportunity which such a war would afford to England of urging her successes in Spain; and the chance of Germany rising in insurrection in case of any reverses.

There was, however, one person who appealed to the Emperor on other grounds. His uncle, the Cardinal Fesch, had been greatly afflicted by the treatment of the Pope, and he contemplated this new war with dread, as likely to bring down the vengeance of Heaven on the head of one who had dared to trample on its vicegerent. He besought Napoleon not to provoke at once the wrath of man and the fury of the elements; and expressed his belief that he must one day sink under the weight of that universal hatred with which his actions were surrounding his throne. Buonaparte led the churchman to the window, opened it, and pointing upwards, said, "Do you see yonder star?" "No, sire," replied the Cardinal. "But I see it," answered Napoleon; and abruptly dismissed him.

Trusting to this star, on which one spot of fatal dimness had already gathered, Napoleon, without waiting for any formal rupture with the Russian diplomatists at Paris, now directed the march of very great bodies of troops into Prussia and the Grand Duchy of Warsaw. Alexander's minister was ordered, in the beginning of April, to demand the withdrawal of these troops, together with the evacuation of the fortresses in Pomerania, in case the French government still entertained a wish to negotiate. Buonaparte instantly replied that he was not accustomed to regulate the distribution of his forces by the suggestions of a foreign power. The ambassador demanded his passports, and quitted Paris.

On the 9th of May, Napoleon left Paris with his Empress, and arrived on the 16th at Dresden, where the Emperor of Austria, the Kings of Prussia, Naples, Wirtemberg, and Westphalia, and almost every German sovereign of inferior rank, had been invited, or commanded, to met him. He had sent to request the Czar also to appear in this brilliant assemblage, as affording a last chance of an amicable arrangement; but the messenger could not obtain admission to Alexander's presence.

Buonaparte continued for some days to play the part of undisputed master amidst this congregation of royalties. He at once assumed for himself and his wife precedence over the Emperor and Empress of Austria; and, in the blaze of successive festivals, the King of Saxony appeared but as some chamberlain, or master of the ceremonies, to his imperious guest.

Having sufficiently indicated to his allies and vassals the conduct which they were respectively to adopt, in case the war should break out, Napoleon, already weary of his splendid idleness, sent on the Abb?de Pradt to Warsaw, to prepare for his reception among the Poles, dismissed Maria Louisa on her return to Paris, and broke up the Court in which he had, for the last time, figured as "the King of Kings." Marshal Ney, with one great division of the army, had already passed the Vistula; Junot, with another, occupied both sides of the Oder. The Czar was known to be at Wilna, his Lithuanian capital, there collecting the forces of his immense empire, and entrusting the general arrangements of the approaching campaign to Marshal Barclay de Tolly.[61] The season was advancing; and it was time that the question of peace or war should be forced to a decision.

Napoleon arrived at Dantzick on the 7th of June; and during the fortnight which ensued, it was known that the final communications between him and Alexander were taking place. The attention of mankind was never more entirely fixed on one spot than it was, during these fourteen days, upon Dantzick. On the 22nd, Buonaparte broke silence in a bulletin. "Soldiers," said he, "Russia is dragged on by her fate: her destiny must be accomplished. Let us march! let us cross the Niemen: let us carry war into her territories. Our second campaign of Poland will be as glorious as our first: but our second peace shall carry with it its own guarantee: it shall put an end for ever to that haughty influence which Russia has exercised for fifty years on the affairs of Europe." The address, in which the Czar announced the termination of his negotiations, was in a far different tone. After stating the innumerable efforts he had made to preserve peace, without losing for Russia the character of an independent state, he invoked the aid of Almighty Providence as "the witness and the defender of the true cause;" and concluded in these words--"Soldiers, you fight for your religion, your liberty, and your native land. Your Emperor is amongst you; and God is the enemy of the aggressor."

Buonaparte reviewed the greater part of his troops on the field of Friedland; and having assured them of still more splendid victories over the same enemy, issued his final orders to the chief officers of his vast army. Hitherto the Poles had had no certain intelligence of the object which Napoleon proposed to himself. As soon as no doubt remained on that score, the Diet at Warsaw sent both to him and to the King of Saxony, to announce their resolution to seize this opportunity of re-establishing the ancient national independence of their dismembered country. We have already mentioned the circumstance which compelled the Emperor to receive this message with coldness. He was forced to acknowledge that he had guaranteed to Austria the whole of her Polish provinces. It was therefore impossible for him to take part in the re-establishment of Old Poland: "Nevertheless," added he, with audacious craft, "I admire your efforts; I even authorise them. Persist; and it is to be hoped your wishes will be crowned with success."

This answer effectually damped the ardour of the Poles; and thenceforth, with a few exceptions, the eminent and influential men of the nation were mere observers of the war. If any doubt as to Napoleon's treachery could have remained after his answer to the Diet, it must have been wholly removed when the plan of his campaign transpired, and the Austrian auxiliaries were known to be stationed on the right of his whole line. On them, as it seemed, the march through Volhynia was thus devolved, and no clearer proof could have been afforded that it was Napoleon's desire to repress every symptom of a national insurrection in Lithuania. The inhabitants, had French soldiers come amongst them, might have been expected to rise in enthusiasm; the white uniform of Austria was known to be hateful in their eyes, in the same degree, and for precisely the same reason, as the Russian green.

The disposition of the French army when the campaign commenced was as follows:--The left wing, commanded by Macdonald, and amounting to 30,000 men, had orders to march through Courland, with the view of, if possible, outflanking the Russian right, and gaining possession of the sea coast, in the direction of Riga. The right wing, composed almost wholly of the Austrians, 30,000 in number, and commanded by Schwartzenberg, were stationed, as has been already mentioned, on the Volhynian frontier. Between these moved the various corps forming the grand central army, under the general superintendence of Napoleon himself, viz. those of Davoust, Ney, the King of Westphalia, the Viceroy of Italy, Poniatowski, Junot and Victor; and in numbers not falling below 250,000. The communication of the centre and left was maintained by the corps of Oudinot, and that of the centre and the extreme right by the corps of Regnier, who had with him the Saxon auxiliaries and the Polish legion of Dombrowski. The chief command of the whole cavalry of the host was assigned to Murat, King of Naples; but he was in person at the headquarters of the Emperor, having immediately under his order three divisions of horse, those of Grouchy, Montbrun, and Nansouty. Augereau with his division was to remain in the north of Germany, to overawe Berlin and protect the communications with France.

A glance at the map will show that Napoleon's base of operations extended over full one hundred leagues; and that the heads of his various columns were so distributed, that the Russians could not guess whether St. Petersburg or Moscow formed the main object of his march.

The Russian main army, under Barclay de Tolly himself, had its headquarters at Wilna; and consisted, at the opening of the campaign, of 120,000. Considerably to the left lay "the second army," as it was called, of 80,000, under Bagrathion; with whom were Platoff and 12,000 of his Cossacks; while, at the extreme of that wing, "the army of Volhynia," 20,000 strong, commanded by Tormazoff, watched Schwartzenberg. On the right of Barclay de Tolly was Witgenstein with 30,000, and between these again and the sea, the corps of Essen, not more than 10,000 strong. Behind the whole line two armies of reserve were rapidly forming at Novgorod and Smolensko; each, probably, of about 20,000 men. The Russians actually on the field at the opening of the campaign were, then, as nearly as can be computed, in number 260,000; while Napoleon was prepared to cross the Niemen at the head of at least 470,000 men.

On the Russian side the plan of the campaign had been settled ere now; it was entirely defensive. Taught by the events of the former war in Poland, and of that which had already fixed the reputation of Wellington in the Peninsula, the Czar was resolved, from the beginning, to draw Buonaparte if possible into the heart of his own country ere he gave him battle. The various divisions of the Russian force had orders to fall back leisurely as the enemy advanced, destroying whatever they could not remove along with them, and halting only at certain points, where intrenched camps had already been formed for their reception. The difficulty of feeding half a million of men in a country deliberately wasted beforehand, and separated by so great a space from Germany, to say nothing of France, was sure to increase with every hour and every step; and Alexander's great object was to husband his own strength until the Polar winter should set in around the strangers, and bring the miseries which he thus foresaw to a crisis. Napoleon, on the other hand, had calculated on being met by the Russians at, or even in advance of, their frontier (as he had been by the Austrians in the campaigns of Austerlitz and Wagram, and by the Prussians in that of Jena); of gaining a great battle; marching immediately either to St. Petersburg or to Moscow--and dictating a peace, after the fashion of Presburg or Schoenbrunn, within the walls of one of the Czar's own palaces.

On the 24th of June, the grand imperial army, consolidated into three masses, began their passage of the Niemen; the King of Westphalia at Grodno; the Viceroy Eugene at Pilony, and Napoleon himself near Kowno. The emperor rode on in front of his army to reconnoitre the banks; his horse stumbled, and he fell to the ground. "A bad omen--a Roman would return," exclaimed some one; it is not certain whether Buonaparte himself or one of his attendants. The first party that crossed were challenged by a single Cossack. "For what purpose," said he, "do you enter the Russian country?"

"To beat you and take Wilna," answered the advanced guard. The sentinel struck spurs to his horse, and disappeared in the forest. There came on at the same moment a tremendous thunder-storm. Thus began the fatal invasion.

No opposition awaited these enormous hosts as they traversed the plains of Lithuania. Alexander withdrew his armies deliberately as they advanced. The capital itself, Wilna, was evacuated two days before they came in sight of it; and Napoleon took up his quarters there on the 28th of June. But it was found that all the magazines, which Buonaparte had counted on seizing, had been burnt before the Russians withdrew, and the imperial bulletins began already to denounce the "barbarous method" in which the enemy seemed resolved to conduct his defence.

It was noticed in an early part of this narrative that Napoleon's plan of warfare could hardly have been carried into execution on a great scale, unless by permitting the troops to subsist on plunder; and we have seen through how many campaigns the marauding system was adopted without producing any serious inconvenience to the French. Buonaparte, however, had learned from Spain and Portugal how difficult it is for soldiers to find food in these ways, provided the population around them be really united in hostility against them. He had further considered the vast distance at which a war with Russia must needs be carried on, and the natural poverty of most of the Czar's provinces, and came to the resolution of departing on this occasion from his old system. In a word, months before he left Paris, he had given orders for preparing immense quantities of provisions of all kinds, to be conveyed along with his gigantic host, and render him independent of the countries which might form the theatre of his operations. The destruction of the magazines at Wilna was sufficient indication that the Emperor had judged well in ordering his commissariat to be placed on an efficient footing; and his attention was naturally directed to ascertaining, ere he advanced further, in how much his directions as to this matter had been fulfilled. He remained twenty days at Wilna--a pause altogether extraordinary in a Buonapartean campaign, and which can only be accounted for by his anxiety on this head. The result of his inquiries was most unsatisfactory. The prodigious extent of the contracts into which his war-minister had entered was adequate to the occasion; but the movement of such enormous trains of cattle and waggons as these contracts provided for must, under any circumstances, have been tedious, and in some degree uncertain. In this case they were entered into either by French traders, who, in consequence of Buonaparte's own practice in preceding campaigns, could have slender experience of the method of supplying a great army in the field; by Germans, who regarded the French Emperor as the enemy of the world, and served him accordingly with reluctance; or finally, by Polish Jews--a race of inveterate smugglers, and consequently of inveterate swindlers.

The result was, that after spending three weeks at Wilna, the Emperor found himself under the necessity, either of laying aside his invasion for another year, or of urging it in the face of every difficulty which he had foreseen, and, moreover, of that presented by a commissariat less effective by two-thirds than he had calculated on.

[Footnote 61: This officer had been born and educated in Germany. He was descended from an ancient Scottish family, exiled for adherence to the Stuarts, in 1715.]

CHAPTER XXX

Russia makes Peace with England, with Sweden, and with Turkey--Internal preparations--Napoleon leaves Wilna--The Dwina--Bagrathion's Movements--Battle of Smolensko--Battle of Borodino--Napoleon enters Moscow--Constancy and Enthusiasm of the Russians--Conduct of Rostophchin--The burning of Moscow--Kutusoff refuses to Treat.

While Napoleon was detained in the capital of Lithuania by the confusion and slowness which marked almost every department of his commissariat at this great crisis, the enemy employed the unexpected pause to the best advantage. The Czar signed treaties of strict alliance with England, Sweden, and the Spanish Cortes, in the middle of July; and the negotiation with Turkey was urged, under the mediation of England, so effectually, that a peace with that Power also was proclaimed early in August. By these means Alexander was enabled to withdraw whatever troops he had been maintaining on the two flanks of his European dominions, and bring them all to the assistance of his main army. Admiral Tchichagoff, at the head of 50,000 soldiers, hitherto opposed to the Turks on the side of Moldavia, marched towards the left wing of Barclay de Tolly's force; and the right, which had gradually retired until it reached a strong camp formed on the river Dwina, was reinforced from

Finland, though not so largely. The enthusiasm of the Russian nation appeared in the extraordinary rapidity with which supplies of every kind were poured at the feet of the Czar. From every quarter he received voluntary offers of men, of money, of whatever might assist in the prosecution of the war. The Grand Duchess, whose hand Napoleon had solicited, set the example by raising a regiment on her estate. Moscow offered to equip and arm 80,000 men. Platoff, the veteran hetman of the Cossacks, promised his only daughter and 200,000 roubles to the man by whose hand Buonaparte should fall. Noblemen everywhere raised troops, and displayed their patriotism by serving in the ranks themselves, and entrusting the command to experienced officers, chosen by the government. The peasantry participated in the general enthusiasm, and flocked in from every province, demanding arms and training. Two hundred thousand militiamen were called out, and in separate divisions began their march upon the camp.

Napoleon, having done whatever lay in his power to remedy the disorders of his commissariat--and this, after all, does not appear to have been much--at length reappeared in the field. He had now determined to make St. Petersburg his mark: he counted much on the effects which a triumphal entry into the capital would produce throughout the country; and the fleet at Cronstadt was in itself a prize of the utmost importance. He directed, therefore, all his efforts towards the Dwina, where the Russian commander-in-chief had now halted on extensive intrenchments, and Riga. This town, however, was now defended, not only by Essen, but by the English sailors of Admiral Martin's fleet, and resisted effectually; and, to the confusion of Napoleon, he was repelled in three successive attempts to force Barclay's camp at Dunaburg.

He upon this changed his plan of operations, and resolving to march, not for Petersburg, but for Moscow, threw forward the centre of his army, under Davoust, with the view of turning Barclay's position, and cutting off his communications with Bagrathion. That general was compelled by this movement to pass the Dnieper (or Borysthenes); and Barclay, on perceiving the object of Davoust's march, broke up from the camp on the Dwina, and retired upon Vitepsk, where he hoped to be joined by Bagrathion. Davoust, however, brought Bagrathion to action near Mohilow, on the 23rd of July; and as the French remained in possession of that town at the end of the day, the Russians found themselves under the necessity of altering the line of their retreat. Bagrathion informed Barclay that he was now marching, not on Vitepsk, but on Smolensko, and the commander-in-chief felt the necessity of abandoning Vitepsk also. During three days (the 25th, 26th, and 27th of July), his troops were engaged with the French at Vitepsk; and, though Napoleon's bulletins announced three splendid victories, the result was that the Russians left their position in admirable order, and retired altogether unmolested on the proposed point of junction. Meantime Regnier, on the right wing, and Oudinot, on the left, were defeated; the former by Tormazoff, the latter by Witgenstein, both with severe loss. The Emperor halted at Vitepsk for several days; "his troops," as the bulletins admitted, "requiring refreshment." The Russian plan of defence was already ascertained--and alarming. The country was laid utterly desolate wherever they retired; every village was burned ere they quitted it: the enthusiastic peasantry withdrew with the army and swelled its ranks.

 Napoleon quitted Vitepsk on the 8th of August, and after a partial engagement at Krasnoi on the 14th, came in sight of Smolensko, on the 16th. The first and second armies of the Czar (Bagrathion having at length effected his junction with Barclay), lay behind the river which flows at the back of this town; but it was occupied in great force. Three times did Buonaparte attack it, and three times he was repulsed. During the night the garrison withdrew, and joined the army across the river--but before they went they committed the city to the flames, and, the buildings being chiefly of wood, the conflagration, according to the French bulletin, "resembled in its fury an eruption of Vesuvius." "Never" (continues the same bulletin) "was war conducted with such inhumanity: the Russians treat their own country as if it were that of an enemy." Such was indeed their resolution. They had no desire that the invader should establish himself in winter quarters at Smolensko. With the exception of some trivial skirmishes, they retreated unmolested from Smolensko to Dorogobuz, and thence on Viasma; halting at each of these towns, and deliberately burning them in the face of the enemy.

 It now, however, began to be difficult in the extreme to prevail on the Russian soldiery to continue their retreat. They had consented to retire in the beginning solely because they were assured that such was the will of their Father--as they affectionately call their sovereign; but reinforcements were now joining them daily from the interior, and the skirmishes which had occurred had so inflamed their spirits, that it seemed impossible to restrain them much longer. At this period also, Barclay was appointed to the war-ministry at St. Petersburg, and Kutusoff, who assumed the command in his stead, was supposed to doubt whether the system of retreat had not been far enough persisted in. The new general at length resolved to comply with the clamorous entreaties of his troops, and fixed on a strong position between Borodino and Moskwa, on the high road to Moscow, where he determined to await the attack of Napoleon. It was at Gjatz that the Emperor was informed of Kutusoff's arrival, and of the universal belief that the Czar had at length consented to run the hazard of a great battle. A little further on a Russian officer, on some pretext, appeared with a flag of truce; his real errand being, no doubt, to witness the state of the invader's camp. Being brought into Napoleon's presence this man was asked, "What he should find between Viasma and Moscow?" He answered, "Pultowa."

On the 5th of September, Napoleon came in sight of the position of Kutusoff, and succeeded in carrying a redoubt in front of it. All the 6th the two armies lay in presence of each other, preparing for the contest. The Russians were posted on an elevated plain; having a wood on their right flank, their left on one of the villages, and a deep ravine, the bed of a small stream, in their front. Extensive field-works covered every more accessible point of this naturally very strong ground; and in the centre of the whole line, a gentle eminence was crowned by an enormous battery, serving as a species of citadel. The Russian army were 120,000 in numbers; nor had Napoleon a greater force in readiness for his attack. In artillery also the armies were equal. It is supposed that each had 500 guns in the field. Buonaparte addressed his troops in his usual style of language: "Soldiers! here is the battle you have longed for; it is necessary, for it brings us plenty, good winter-quarters, and a safe return to France. Behave yourselves so that posterity may say of each of you, He was in that great battle beneath the walls of Moscow."

In the Russian camp, meanwhile, the clergy appeared in their richest vestments, and displaying their holiest images, called on the men to merit Paradise by devoting themselves in the cause of their country. The soldiers answered with shouts which were audible throughout all the enemy's lines.

At four o'clock in the morning of the 7th, the French advanced under cover of a thick fog, and assaulted at once the centre, the right, and the left of the position. Such was the impetuosity of the charge that they drove the Russians from their redoubts; but this was but for a moment. They rallied under the very line of their enemy's fire, and instantly re-advanced. Peasants who, till that hour, had never seen war, and who still wore their usual rustic dress, distinguished only by a cross sewed on it in front, threw themselves into the thickest of the combat. As they fell, others rushed on and filled their places. Some idea may be formed of the obstinacy of the contest from the fact, that of one division of the Russians which mustered 30,000 in the morning, only 8000 survived. These men had fought in close order, and unshaken, under the fire of eighty pieces of artillery. The result of this terrible day was, that Buonaparte withdrew his troops and abandoned all hope of forcing his way through the Russians. In no contest by many degrees so desperate had he hitherto been engaged. Night found either army on the ground they had occupied at daybreak. The number of guns and prisoners taken by the French and the Russians was about equal; and of either host there had fallen not less than 40,000 men. Some accounts raise the gross number of the slain to 100,000. Such was the victory in honour of which Napoleon created Marshal Ney Prince of Moskwa.

Buonaparte, when advised by his generals, towards the conclusion of the day, to bring forward his own guard and hazard one final attack at their head, answered, "And if my guard fail, what means should I have for renewing the battle to-morrow?" The Russian commander, on the other hand, appears to have spared nothing to prolong the contest.--During the night after, his cavalry made several attempts to break into the enemy's lines; and it was only on receiving the reports of his regimental officers in the morning, that Kutusoff perceived the necessity of retiring until he should be further recruited. His army was the mainstay of his country: on its utter dissolution his master might have found it very difficult to form another; but while it remained perfect in its organisation, the patriotic population of the empire were sure to fill up readily every vacancy in its ranks. Having ascertained then the extent of his loss, and buried his dead (among whom was the gallant Bagrathion) with great solemnity,--the Russian slowly and calmly withdrew from his intrenchments, and marched on Mojaisk. Napoleon was so fortunate as to be joined exactly at this time by two fresh divisions from Smolensko, which nearly restored his muster to what it had been when the battle began; and, thus reinforced, commanded the pursuit to be vigorously urged. On the 9th, the French van came in sight of the Russian rear again, and Buonaparte prepared for battle. But next morning Kutusoff had masked his march so effectually, by scattering clouds of Cossacks in every direction around the French, that down to the 12th the invader remained uncertain whether he had retreated on Kalouga, or directly to the capital. The latter he, at length, found to be the case; and on the 14th of September Napoleon reached the Hill of Salvation; so named because from that eminence the Russian traveller obtains his first view of the ancient metropolis, affectionately called "Mother Moscow," and hardly less sacred in his eyes than Jerusalem. The soldiery beheld with joy and exultation the magnificent extent of the place; its mixture of Gothic steeples and Oriental domes; the vast and splendid mansions of the haughty boyards, embosomed in trees; and, high over all the rest, the huge towers of the Kremlin, at once the palace and the citadel of the old Czars. The cry of "Moscow! Moscow!" ran through the lines. Napoleon himself reined in his horse and exclaimed, "Behold at last that celebrated city!" He added, after a brief pause, "it was time."

Buonaparte had not gazed long on this great capital ere it struck him as something remarkable that no smoke issued from the chimneys. Neither appeared there any military on the battlements of the old walls and towers. There reached him neither message of defiance, nor any deputation of citizens to present the keys of their town, and recommend it and themselves to his protection. He was yet marvelling what these strange circumstances could mean, when Murat, who commanded in the van, and had pushed on to the gates, came back and informed him that he had held a parley with Milarodowitch, the general of the Russian rear-guard, and that, unless two hours were granted for the safe withdrawing of his troops, he would at once set fire to Moscow. Napoleon immediately granted the armistice. The two hours elapsed, and still no procession of nobles or magistrates made its appearance.

On entering the city the French found it deserted by all but the very lowest and most wretched of its vast population. They soon spread themselves over its innumerable streets, and commenced the work of pillage. The magnificent palaces of the Russian boyards, the bazaars of the merchants, churches and convents, and public buildings of every description, swarmed with their numbers.

The meanest soldier clothed himself in silk and furs, and drank at his pleasure the costliest wines. Napoleon, perplexed at the abandonment of so great a city, had some difficulty in keeping together 30,000 men under Murat, who followed Milarodowitch, and watched the walls on that side.

The Emperor, who had retired to rest in a suburban palace, was awakened at midnight by the cry of fire. The chief market-place was in flames; and some hours elapsed before they could be extinguished by the exertions of the soldiery. While the fire still blazed, Napoleon established his quarters in the Kremlin, and wrote, by that fatal light, a letter to the Czar, containing proposals for peace. The letter was committed to a prisoner of rank; no answer ever reached Buonaparte.

Next morning found the fire extinguished, and the French officers were busied throughout the day in selecting houses for their residence. The flames, however, burst out again as night set in, and under circumstances which might well fill the mind of the invaders with astonishment and with alarm. Various detached parts of the city appeared to be at once on fire; combustibles and matches were discovered in different places as laid deliberately; the water-pipes were cut: the wind changed three times in the course of the night, and the flames always broke out again with new vigour in the quarter from which the prevailing breeze blew right on the Kremlin. It was sufficiently plain that Rostophchin, governor of Moscow, had adopted the same plan of resistance in which Smolensko had already been sacrificed; and his agents, whenever they fell into the hands of the French, were massacred without mercy.

A French adventurer, who had been resident for some time in Moscow, gave an account of Rostophchin's conduct in quitting the city, which might have prepared Napoleon for some such catastrophe. This person, on hearing of the approach of his countrymen, had used some expressions which entitled him to a place in the prisons of Moscow. The day before Buonaparte entered it, Rostophchin held a last court of justice. This Frenchman, and a disaffected Russian, were brought before him. The latter's guilt having been clearly proved, the governor, understanding his father was in court, said he granted some minutes to the old man to converse with and bless his son. "Shall I give my blessing to a rebel?" cried the aged parent--"I hereby give him my curse." Rostophchin ordered the culprit to be executed, and then turning to the Frenchman, said, "Your preference of your own people was natural. Take your liberty. There was but one Russian traitor, and you have witnessed his death." The governor then set all the malefactors in the numerous jails of Moscow at liberty, and, abandoning the city to them, withdrew at the head of the inhabitants, who had for some time been preparing the means of retreat at his suggestion.

Such was the story of the Frenchman; and every hour brought some new confirmation of the relentless determination of Rostophchin's countrymen. Some peasants, brought in from the neighbouring country, were branded on the arm with the letter N. One of them understanding that this marked him as the property and adherent of Napoleon, instantly seized an axe and chopped off his limb. Twelve slaves of Count Woronzow were taken together and commanded to enlist in the French service, or suffer death; four of the men folded their arms in silence, and so died. The French officer in command spared the rest. Such were the anecdotes which reached Napoleon as he surveyed, from the battlements of the Kremlin, the raging sea of fire which now swept the capital, east, west, north, and south. During four days the conflagration endured, and four-fifths of the city were wholly consumed. "Palaces and temples," says the Russian author, Karamsin, "monuments of art and miracles of luxury, the remains of ages long since past, and the creations of yesterday, the tombs of ancestors, and the cradles of children, were indiscriminately destroyed. Nothing was left of Moscow save the memory of her people, and their deep resolution to avenge her fall."

During two days Napoleon witnessed from the Kremlin the spread of this fearful devastation, and, in spite of continual showers of sparks and brands, refused to listen to those who counselled retreat. On the third night, the equinoctial gale rose, the Kremlin itself took fire, and it became doubtful whether it would be possible for him to withdraw in safety; and then he at length rode out of Moscow, through streets in many parts arched over with flames, and buried, where this was not the case, in one dense mantle of smoke. "These are indeed Scythians," said Napoleon. He halted, and fixed his headquarters at Petrowsky, a country palace of the Czar, about a league distant. But he could not withdraw his eyes from the rueful spectacle which the burning city presented, and from time to time repeated the same words, "This bodes great misfortune."

On the 20th, the flames being at length subdued or exhausted, Napoleon returned to the Kremlin, well aware how mighty a calamity had befallen him, but still flattering himself that the resolution of the enemy would give way on learning the destruction of their ancient and sacred metropolis. The poor remains of the enormous city still furnished tolerable lodgings for his army: of provisions there was as yet abundance; and the invaders, like true Frenchmen, fitted up a theatre, and witnessed plays acted by performers sent from France; while the Emperor himself exhibited his equanimity by dating a decree, regulating the affairs of the Theatre Francis at Paris, from "the imperial headquarters in the Kremlin." His anxiety to show the French that, even during his hottest campaigns, his mind continued to be occupied with them and their domestic administration has already been alluded to. There was audacious quackery in a stage rescript from Moscow.

Day passed after day and still there came no answer from Alexander: Buonaparte's situation was becoming hourly more difficult. The news of the great battle of Salamanca had already reached him: the rumour of some distant disaster could not be prevented from spreading among the soldiery. Nearer him, the two flanks of his mighty host had been alike unsuccessful. The united army of Tormazoff and Tchichagoff, on the south, and that of Witgenstein, on the north, had obtained decided advantages over the French generals respectively opposed to them, and now threatened to close in between Napoleon's central columns and the magazines in Poland. Witzingerode was at the head of a formidable force on the road to St. Petersburg; and to the south-west of Moscow lay Kutusoff, on a very strong position, with an army to which every hour brought whole bands of enthusiastic recruits. On every side there was danger; the whole forces of Russia appeared to be gathering around him. Meantime the season was far advanced; the stern winter of the north was at hand; and the determined hostility of the peasantry prevented the smallest supplies of provision from being introduced into the capital. Had the citizens remained there, the means of subsistence would of course have continued to be forwarded in the usual methods from the provinces; but neither boat nor sledge was put in motion after it was known that Moscow contained no population but the French. The stores, at first sight so ample, within the city itself, had already begun to fail: the common soldiers had rich wines and liqueurs in abundance, but no meat except horse-flesh, and no bread. Daru gave the Emperor what the latter called "a lion's counsel"; to draw in all his detachments, convert Moscow into an intrenched camp, kill and salt every horse, and trust to foraging parties for the rest--in a word, to lay aside all thoughts of keeping up communication with France, or Germany, or even Poland; and issue forth from Moscow, with his army entire and refreshed, in the commencement of the spring. But Napoleon had excellent reasons for suspecting that were he and his army cut off from all communication, during six months, with what they had left behind them, the Prussians, the Austrians, his Rhenish vassals themselves, might throw off the yoke: while, on the other hand, the Russians could hardly fail, in the course of so many months, to accumulate, in their own country, a force before which his isolated army, on re-issuing from their winter quarters, would appear a mere speck.

Napoleon at length sent Count Lauriston to the headquarters of Kutusoff, with another letter to Alexander, which the Count was to deliver in person. Kutusoff received the Frenchman in the midst of all his generals, and answered with such civility that the envoy doubted not of success. The end, however, was that the Russian professed himself altogether unable to entertain any negotiation, or even to sanction the journey of any French messenger--such being, he said, the last and most express orders of his Prince. He offered to send on Napoleon's letter to St. Petersburg, by one of his own aides-de-camp; and to this Lauriston was obliged to agree. This interview occurred on the 6th of October: no answer from St. Petersburg could be expected sooner than the 26th. There had already been one fall of snow. To retreat after having a second time written to the Czar, would appear like the confession of inability to remain. The difficulties and dangers attendant on a longer sojourn in the ruined capital have already been mentioned; and they were increasing with fearful rapidity every hour. It was under such circumstances that Napoleon lingered on in the Kremlin until the 19th of October; and it seems probable that he would have lingered even more days there, had he not received the tidings of a new reverse, near at hand, and which effectually stirred him. His attendants have not hesitated to say that, from the time when he entered Russia, his mind had seemed to be in a state of indecision and lethargy, when compared with what they had been accustomed to witness in previous campaigns. From this hour his decision and activity (if indeed they had ever been obscured) appear to have been displayed abundantly.

Murat had, without Napoleon's command, and indeed in opposition to his wishes, established a strange species of armistice with Kutusoff, under articles which provided that three hours' notice must precede any regular affair between the two armies confronted to each other, but allowed the petty warfare of the Cossacks and other light troops to proceed without interruption on either flank. This suited Kutusoff's purpose; for it in effect left him in full possession of the means to avoid a general action until he chose to hazard one, and yet offered no interruption to the measures by which he and his nation were deliberately and systematically straitening the supplies of the invader. Napoleon alleged that Murat had entered on the compact from the desire of gratifying his own vanity, by galloping about on a neutral ground, and attracting the admiration of both armies, but especially of the Cossacks, by his horsemanship, and the brilliant, if not fantastic, dresses in which it was at all times his delight to exhibit his fine person. But King Joachim never displayed his foppery so willingly as on the field of battle: he committed only, on a smaller scale, the same error which detained his master in the Kremlin.

CHAPTER XXXI

Napoleon quits Moscow--Battles of Vincovo and Malo-Yaraslovetz--Retreat on Verreia--and Smolensko--Repeated Defeats and Sufferings of the French--Smolensko--Krasnoi--Passage of the Beresina--Smorgonie--Napoleon quits the Army--his arrival at Warsaw--at Dresden--in Paris.

The armistice, such as it was, between Joachim and Kutusoff, was broken through so soon as the latter had sufficiently disciplined the new recruits who had crowded to his standard from every region of the empire. Murat then received considerable reinforcements from Moscow, together with Napoleon's commands to gain possession, if possible, of one of the roads leading to Kalouga. There, and at Toula, the chief magazines of the Russian army were known to be established; and, moreover, by retiring in that direction towards Poland, (should a retreat finally be found necessary,) Napoleon counted on the additional and far greater advantage of traversing a country hitherto unwasted.

The King of Naples, accordingly, pushed his light troops over a new district; and had the mortification to find the Russian system of defence persevered in wherever he advanced. The splendid country house of Rostophchin was burnt to the ground, ere the French reached it; and the following letter, affixed to its gates, breathed the same spirit which had dared to sacrifice Moscow:--"I have for eight years embellished this residence, and lived happily in it with my family. The inhabitants of the estate, in number 1720, quitted it at your approach; and I set fire to my house, that it may not be polluted with your presence."

Kutusoff was no longer disposed to witness in inaction the progress of Murat. He divined that Napoleon must at last be convinced of the necessity of abandoning Moscow, and determined that at all events he should not make his retreat in the direction of Kalouga. General Bennigsen was ordered to attack Murat, on the 18th October, at Vincovo: and the result was decidedly in favour of the Russians, in whose hands there remained nearly 3000 prisoners, and forty pieces of artillery. The cannonade was heard at the Kremlin; and no sooner did the issue of the day reach Napoleon, than he made up his mind to march his whole army to the support of the King of Naples. That same evening, several divisions were put in motion; he himself, at the head of others, left Moscow on the 19th; and the metropolis was wholly evacuated on the morning of the 22nd. Russian troops entered it immediately afterwards, in time to preserve the Kremlin, which had been undermined and attempted to be blown up in a last access of rage; and within a few hours, so completely had the patriotic peasants baffled Napoleon, the town swarmed with people, and all the market-places were crowded with every species of provision. The Emperor's bulletins announced that "Moscow had been found not to be a good military position,"--that it was "necessary for the army to breathe on a wider space." The precipitancy, however, with which the French retired was such that they left their sick and wounded to the mercy of the Russians; and yet thousands of waggons, laden with the spoil of Moscow, attended and encumbered their march.

Kutusoff now perceived that he had to expect the attack of a greater than Murat. The Russian general occupied a position at Taroutino, on the old road to Kalouga (the central one of three nearly parallel routes), so strong by nature, and so improved by art, that Napoleon judged it hopeless to attack him there. He therefore made a lateral movement, and pushed on by the western road--meaning, after he had passed Taroutino, to strike back again into the central one, and so interpose himself between Kutusoff and Kalouga. The old Russian, however, penetrated this plan; and instantly, by a manoeuvre of precisely the same kind--marching to the eastward, and thence back to the centre again,--baffled it. The French van, having executed the first part of their orders, and regained the middle road in the rear of Taroutino, advanced without opposition as far as Malo-Yaraslovetz, and occupied that town. But at midnight they were assaulted furiously within it, and driven back across the river Louja, where the leading divisions of the army bivouacked. Early in the morning the French retook Malo-Yaraslovetz at the point of the bayonet, and the greater part of the day was spent in a succession of obstinate contests, in the course of which the town five times changed masters. In the evening, Napoleon came up with his main body. He found his troops, indeed, in possession of the place; but beyond it, his generals informed him, Kutusoff and his whole army were now posted, and this on a position at least as strong as that of Taroutino, which he himself had considered unassailable.

The Emperor's headquarters were in the wretched and filthy hut of a poor weaver, and here an angry debate ensued between Murat and Davoust; the former of whom urged the necessity of instantly attacking the Russian, while the latter pronounced such an attempt to be worthy of a madman. The Emperor heard them in gloomy silence, and declared that he would judge for himself in the morning. He dismissed them all, and, if Segur may be believed, spent the night in great agitation; now rising, now lying down again-- incessantly calling out--yet refusing to admit anyone within a temporary screen of cloth which concealed his person from the eyes of his attendants. This was the first occasion on which Buonaparte betrayed in his demeanour that dark presentiment which had settled on his mind ever since he beheld the flames of Moscow.

At daybreak he passed the Louja with a few attendants, for the purpose of reconnoitring Kutusoff's position. He had scarcely crossed the bridge, when a party of Platoff's Cossacks, galloping furiously, and sweeping some scattered companies of the French before them, came full upon the Emperor and his suite. Napoleon was urged to seek safety in flight; but he drew his sword and took post on the bank by the way-side. The wild spearmen, intent on booty, plunged on immediately below him, and, after stripping some soldiers, retired again at full speed to their Pulk, without having observed the inestimable prize. The Emperor watched their retreat, and continued his reconnaissance. It satisfied him that Davoust had judged rightly.

He made another effort to force a passage southwards at Medyn; but here also he was repelled, and forced to abandon the attempt. Meantime the army which had occupied Moscow begun to send forth its Cossacks on his rear. In a word, it became apparent that if the retreat were to be urged, it must now be in the direction of Verreia and Smolensko; that is, through the same provinces which had been entirely wasted in the earlier part of the campaign.

Kutusoff, whether merely overpowered for the moment with that vague sentiment which Buonaparte's name had hitherto been accustomed to inspire, or that he knew of a still better position nearer Kalouga, was, in fact, retiring from his strong ground behind Malo-Yaraslovetz, at the moment when the French began to break up from the Louja. No sooner, however, was that movement known, than the Russian penetrated the extent of his adversary's embarrassments; and Platoff, with the Cossacks, received orders to hang close on the French rear--while Milarodowitch, with 18,000 men, pushed directly on Viasma; and the main army taking a parallel, and a shorter, though less practicable route, marched also with the view of watching the retreat on Smolensko.

As Buonaparte was about to leave Verreia, General Witzingerode was brought a prisoner into his presence. This officer had advanced to the Kremlin, ere it was abandoned, with a flag of truce, for the purpose of entering into some arrangements concerning the French wounded; and it is to be supposed, of dissuading the departing garrison from destroying the citadel. He was, however, placed instantly under arrest, and hurried away with the enemy's march. Napoleon, whose temper was by this time embittered into ungovernable rage, charged the General with being the leader of the Cossacks, and threatened to have him shot, on the instant, as a brigand. Witzingerode replied, that "he commanded not the Cossacks, but a part of the regular army; and that, in the character of a Russian soldier, he was at all times prepared for a French bullet." Napoleon, now ascertaining the name, country, and rank of his prisoner, pursued in these angry ejaculations: "Who are you? A man without a country--You have ever been my enemy--You were in the Austrian's ranks at Austerlitz--I now find you in the Russian! Nevertheless, you are a native of the Confederation of the Rhine--therefore my subject--and a rebel.--Seize him, gens-d'armes! Let the traitor be brought to trial." The Emperor's attendants were wise enough to foresee the effects of such violence, if persisted in: they interposed, and Witzingerode was sent on as a prisoner of war towards Smolensko.[62]

On the 28th of October, Napoleon himself, with 6000 chosen horse, began his journey towards Smolensko; the care of bringing up the main body being given to Beauharnois, while Ney commanded the rear. From the commencement of this march, hardly a day elapsed in which some new calamity did not befall those hitherto invincible legions. The Cossacks of Platoff came on one division at Kolotsk, near Borodino, on the 1st of November, and gave them a total defeat. A second division was attacked on the day after, and with nearly equal success, by the irregular troops of Count Orloff Denizoff. On the 3rd, Milarodowitch reached the main road near Viasma, and after routing Ney, Davoust, and Beauharnois, drove them through the town, which he entered with drums beating and colours flying, and making a passage for the rest of the army over the dead bodies of the enemy. Beauharnois, after this, separated his division from the rest, and endeavoured to push for Vitepsk, by the way of Douchowtchina, and Platoff followed him, while Milarodowitch continued the pursuit on the main road. The separation of troops so pressed is a sufficient proof that they were already suffering severely for want of food; but their miseries were about to be heightened by the arrival of a new enemy. On the 6th of November, the Russian winter fairly set in; and thenceforth, between the heavy columns of regular troops which on every side watched and threatened them, the continued assaults of the Cossacks who hung around them in clouds by day and by night, rushing on every detached party, disturbing every bivouack, breaking up bridges before, and destroying every straggler behind them, and the terrible severity of the climate, the frost, the snow, the wind--the sufferings of this once magnificent army were such as to baffle all description.

The accounts of the Russian authorities, of the French eye-witnesses who have since told this story, and, it must be added, of the Emperor's own celebrated "twenty-ninth bulletin," are in harmony with each other. The enormous train of artillery which Napoleon had insisted on bringing away from Moscow was soon diminished; and the roads were blocked up with the spoils of the city, abandoned of necessity as the means of transport failed. The horses, having been ill-fed for months, were altogether unable to resist the united effects of cold and fatigue. They sank and stiffened by hundreds and by thousands. The starving soldiery slew others of these animals, that they might drink their warm blood, and wrap themselves in their yet reeking skins. The discipline of these miserable bands vanished. Ney was indeed able to keep together some battalions of the rear guard, and present a bold aspect to the pursuers--the marshal himself not disdaining to bear a firelock, and share the meanest fatigues of his followers; but elsewhere there remained hardly the shadow of military order. Small and detached bodies of men moved, like soldiers, on the highway--the immense majority dispersed themselves over the ice and snow which equalised the surface of the fields on either side, and there sustained from time to time the rapid and merciless charge of the Cossacks.

Beauharnois, meantime, discovered before he had advanced far on his separate route, that Witgenstein, having defeated successively St. Cyr and Victor on the Dwina, was already in possession of Vitepsk. The viceroy therefore was compelled to turn back towards the Smolensko road. Platoff turned with him, and brought him once more to action, "killing many," said the Hetman's despatch, "but making few prisoners." The army of Italy, if it could still be called an army, mingled with the few troops who still preserved some show of order under Ney, before they came in sight of Smolensko, and communicated to them their own terror and confusion.

Meanwhile the Russian "army of Volhynia," after it was strengthened by the arrival of Tchichagoff from the Danube, had been able (as we have already hinted) to bear down all the opposition of Schwartzenberg and Regnier; had driven their forces before them, and taken possession of Napoleon's great depot, Minsk, from which they might hope ere long to communicate with Witgenstein. The armies of Witgenstein and Tchichagoff, then, were about to be in communication with each other, and in possession of those points at which Napoleon was most likely to attempt his escape from Smolensko, into Poland; while the main army itself, having advanced side by side with the French, was now stationed to the south-west of Smolensko, in readiness to break the enemy's march whenever Kutusoff should choose; Milarodowitch, finally, and Platoff, were hanging close behind, and thinning every hour the miserable bands who had no longer heart, nor, for the most part, arms of any kind wherewith to resist them. But the whole extent of these misfortunes was not known to any one of the French generals, nor even to Napoleon himself, at the time when Beauharnois and Ney at length entered Smolensko.

The name of that town had hitherto been the only spell that preserved any hope within the soldiers of the retreat. There, they had been told, they should find food, clothing, and supplies of all sorts: and there, being once more assembled under the eye of the Emperor, speedily reassume an aspect, such as none of the northern barbarians would dare to brave.

But these expectations were cruelly belied. Smolensko had been, as we have seen, almost entirely destroyed by the Russians in the early part of the campaign. Its ruined walls afforded only a scanty shelter to the famished and shivering fugitives; and the provisions assembled there were so inadequate to the demands of the case, that after the lapse of a few days, Buonaparte found himself under the necessity of once more renewing his disastrous march. He had, as yet, received no intelligence of the capture of Minsk by Tchichagoff. It was in that direction, accordingly, that he resolved to force his passage into Poland.

Although the grand army had mustered 120,000 when it left Moscow, and the fragments of various divisions besides had met the Emperor at Smolensko, it was with great difficulty that 40,000 men could now be brought together in anything like fighting condition. These Napoleon divided into four columns, nearly equal in numbers: of the first, which included 6000 of the imperial guard, he himself took the command, and marched with it towards Krasnoi, the first town on the way to Minsk: the second corps was that of Eugene Beauharnois; the third, Davoust's; and the fourth, destined for the perilous service of the rear, and accordingly strengthened with 3000 of the guard, was entrusted to the heroic guidance of Ney. The Emperor left Smolensko on the 13th of November, having ordered that the other corps should follow him on the 14th, 15th, and 16th, respectively; thus interposing a day's march between every two divisions.

It is not to be questioned that Napoleon, in thus arranging his march, was influenced by the pressing difficulty of finding provisions, and also by the enfeebled condition of the greater part of his remaining troops. The division of his force, however, was so complete, that had he been opposed by a general adequate to the occasion, his total and immediate ruin could hardly have been avoided. But Kutusoff appears to have exhausted the better part of his daring at Borodino, and thenceforth to have adhered to the plan of avoiding battle--originally wise and necessary--with a pertinacity savouring of superstition. It must be admitted, that hitherto, in suffering the climate to waste his enemy's numbers, and merely heightening the misery of the elemental war by his clouds of Cossacks, and occasional assaults of other light troops, he had reaped almost every advantage which could have resulted from another course. But the army of Napoleon had been already reduced to a very small fragment of its original strength; and even that fragment was now split into four divisions, against any one of which it would have been easy to concentrate a force overwhelmingly superior. It seems to be generally accepted that the name of Napoleon saved whatever part of his host finally escaped from the territory of Russia; in a word, that had Kutusoff been able to shake off that awe which had been the growth of a hundred victories, the Emperor himself must have either died on some bloody field between Smolensko and the Beresina, or revisited, as a prisoner, the interior of the country which, three months before, he had invaded at the head of half a million of warriors.

He himself, with his column, reached Krasnoi unmolested, although the whole of the Russian army, moving on a parallel road, were in full observation of his march. Eugene, who followed him, was, however, intercepted on his way by Milarodowitch, and after sustaining the contest gallantly against very disproportionate numbers, and a terrible cannonade, was at length saved only by the fall of night. During the darkness, the Viceroy executed a long and hazardous detour, and joined the Emperor in Krasnoi, on the 17th. On this night-march they fell in with the videttes of another of Kutusoff's columns, and owed their preservation to the quickness of a Polish soldier, who answered the challenge in Russian. The loss, however, had been severe; the two leading divisions, now united in Krasnoi, mustered scarcely 15,000.

Napoleon was most anxious to secure the passage of the Dnieper at Liady, and immediately gave Eugene the command of the van, with orders to march on this point; but he was warned by the losses which his son-in-law had undergone, of the absolute necessity of waiting at Krasnoi until Davoust and Ney should be able to come up with him. He determined, therefore, to abide, with 6000 of the guard, and another corps of 5000, whatever numbers Kutusoff might please to bring against him. He drew his sword, and said, "I have long enough played the Emperor--I must be the general once more."

In vain was Kutusoff urged to seize this opportunity of pouring an irresistible force on the French position. The veteran commanded a cannonade--and, as he had 100 pieces of artillery well placed, the ranks of the enemy were thinned considerably. But, excepting one or two isolated charges of cavalry, he adventured on no closer collision; and Napoleon held his ground, in face of all that host, until nightfall, when Davoust's division, surrounded and pursued by innumerable Cossacks, at length were enabled to rally once more around his headquarters.

He had the mortification to learn, however, that Ney was probably still in Smolensko, and that a Russian force had marched on towards Liady, with the design of again intercepting Eugene. The Emperor, therefore, once more divided his numbers--pushed on in person to support Beauharnois and secure Liady--and left Davoust and Mortier to hold out as long as possible at Krasnoi, in the hope of being there joined by Ney. Long, however, before that gallant chief could reach this point, the Russians, as if the absence of Napoleon had at once restored all their energy, rushed down and forced on Davoust and Mortier, the battle which the Emperor had in vain solicited. On that fatal field the French left forty-five cannon and 6000 prisoners, besides the slain and the wounded. The remainder with difficulty effected their escape to Liady, where Napoleon once more received them, and crossed the Dnieper.

Ney, meanwhile, having in execution of his master's parting injunctions blown up whatever remained of the walls and towers of Smolensko, at length set his rear-guard in motion, and advanced to Krasnoi, without being harassed by any except Platoff, whose Cossacks entered Smolensko ere he could wholly abandon it. The field strewn with many thousand corpses, informed him sufficiently that a new disaster had befallen the fated army. Yet he continued to advance on the footsteps of those who had thus shattered Davoust and Mortier, and met with no considerable interruption until he reached the ravine in which the rivulet Losmina has its channel. A thick mist lay on the ground, and Ney was almost on the brink of the ravine, before he perceived that it was manned throughout by Russians, while the opposite banks displayed a long line of batteries deliberately arranged, and all the hills behind were covered with troops.

A Russian officer appeared and summoned Ney to capitulate. "A mareschal of France never surrenders," was his intrepid answer; and immediately the batteries, distant only 250 yards, opened a tremendous storm of grape shot. Ney, nevertheless, had the hardihood to plunge into the ravine, clear a passage over the stream, and charge the Russians at their guns. His small band were repelled with fearful slaughter; but he renewed his efforts from time to time during the day, and at night, though with numbers much diminished, still occupied his original position in the face of a whole army interposed between him and Napoleon.

The Emperor had by this time given up all hope of ever again seeing anything of his rear-column. But during the ensuing night, Ney effected his escape; nor does the history of war present many such examples of apparently insuperable difficulties overcome by the union of skill and valour. The marshal broke up his bivouac at midnight, and marched back from the Losmina, until he came on another stream, which he concluded must flow also into the Dnieper. He followed this guide, and at length reached the great river at the place where it was frozen over, though so thinly, that the ice bent and crackled beneath the feet of the men, who crossed it in single files. The waggons laden with the wounded, and what great guns were still with Ney, were too heavy for this frail bridge. They attempted the passage at different points, and one after another went down, amidst the shrieks of the dying and the groans of the onlookers. The Cossacks had by this time gathered hard behind, and swept up many stragglers, besides the sick. But Ney had achieved his great object: and on the 20th, he, with his small and devoted band, joined the Emperor once more at Orcsa. Napoleon received him in his arms, hailed him as "the bravest of the brave," and declared that he would have given all his treasures to be assured of his safety.

The Emperor was once more at the head of his united "grand army"; but the name was ere now become a jest. Between Smolensko and the Dnieper the Russians had taken 228 guns, and 26,000 prisoners; and, in a word, having mustered 40,000 effective men at leaving Smolensko, Napoleon could count only 12,000 after Ney joined him at Orcsa. Of these there were but 150 cavalry; and, to remedy this defect, officers still in possession of horses, to the number of 500, were now formed into a "sacred band," as it was called, for immediate attendance on the Emperor's person. The small fragment of his once gigantic force had no sooner recovered something like the order of discipline, than it was again set in motion.

But scarcely had the Emperor passed the Dnieper, when he received the tidings of the fall of Minsk, and the subsequent retreat of Schwartzenberg towards Warsaw. It was, therefore, necessary, to alter his plan, and force a passage into Poland to the northward of that great dep 魅. It was necessary, moreover, to do this without loss of time, for the Emperor well knew that Witgenstein had been as successful on his right flank, as Tchichagoff on his left; and that these generals might soon be, if they already were not, in communication with each other, and ready to unite all their forces for the defence of the next great river on his route--the Beresina.

Napoleon had hardly resolved to attempt the passage of this river at Borizoff, ere, to renew all his perplexities, he received intelligence that Witgenstein had defeated Dombrowski there, and retained possession of the town and bridge. Victor and Oudinot, indeed, advanced immediately to succour Dombrowski, and re-took Borizoff; but Witgenstein burnt the bridge before he re-crossed the Beresina. Imperfect as Victor's success was, Napoleon did not hear of it immediately. He determined to pass the Beresina higher up, at Studzianska, and forthwith threw himself into the huge forests which border that river, adopting every stratagem by which his enemies could be puzzled as to the immediate object of his march.

His 12,000 men, brave and determined, but no longer preserving in their dress, nor, unless when the trumpet blew, in their demeanour, a soldier-like appearance, were winding their way amidst these dark woods, when suddenly the air around them was filled with sounds which could only proceed from the march of some far greater host. They were preparing for the worst, when they found themselves in presence of the advanced guard of the united army of Victor and Oudinot, who had, indeed, been defeated by Witgenstein, but still mustered 50,000 men, completely equipped and hardly shaken in discipline. With what feelings must these troops have surveyed the miserable half-starved and half-clad remains of that "grand army," their own detachment from whose banners had, some few short months before, filled every bosom among them with regret!

Having melted the poor relics of his Moscow army into these battalions, Napoleon now continued his march on Studzianska; employing, however, all his wit to confirm Tchichagoff in the notion that he meant to pass the Beresina at a different place,--and this with so much success, that Tchaplitz, with the Russian rear-guard, abandoned a strong position, commanding the river, during the very night which preceded his appearance there. Two bridges were erected, and Oudinot had passed over before Tchaplitz perceived his mistake, and returned again toward Studzianska.

Discovering that the passage had already begun, and that in consequence of the narrowness of the only two bridges, it must needs proceed slowly, Tchichagoff and Witgenstein now arranged a joint plan of attack. The latter once more passed to the eastern bank of the river, and, having wholly cut off one division of 7000, under Partonneux, not far from Borizoff, proceeded towards Studzianska. Platoff and his indefatigable Cossacks joined Witgenstein on this march, and they arrived long before the rear-guard of Napoleon could pass the river. But the operations on the other side of the Beresina were far less zealously or skilfully conducted. Tchichagoff was in vain urged to support effectually Tchaplitz; who attacked the French that had passed, and being repelled by Oudinot, left them in unmolested possession, not only of the bridges on the Beresina, but of a long train of wooden causeways, extending for miles beyond the river, over deep and dangerous morasses, and which being composed of old dry timber, would have required, says Segur, "to destroy them utterly, but a few sparks from the Cossacks' tobacco pipes."

In spite of this neglect, and of the altogether extraordinary conduct of Kutusoff, who still persisted in marching on a line parallel with Napoleon, and refusing to hazard any more assaults, the passage of the Beresina was one of the most fearful scenes recorded in the annals of war. Victor, with the rear-division, consisting of 8000 men, was still on the eastern side--when Witgenstein and Platoff appeared on the heights above. The still numerous retainers of the camp, crowds of sick, wounded, and women, and the greater part of the artillery, were in the same situation. When the Russian cannon began to open upon this multitude, crammed together near the bank, and each anxiously expecting the turn to pass, a shriek of utter terror ran through them, and men, women, horses, and waggons rushed at once, pell-mell, upon the bridges. The larger of these, intended solely for waggons and cannon, ere long broke down, precipitating all that were upon it into the dark and half-frozen stream. The scream that rose at this moment, says one that heard it, "did not leave my ears for weeks; it was heard clear and loud over the hurrahs of the Cossacks, and all the roar of artillery." The remaining bridge was now the only resource, and all indiscriminately endeavoured to gain a footing on it. Squeezed, trampled, forced over the ledges, cut down by each other, and torn by the incessant shower of Russian cannonade, they fell and died in thousands. Victor stood his ground bravely until late in the evening, and then conducted his division over the bridge. There still remained behind a great number of the irregular attendants, besides those soldiers who had been wounded during the battle, and guns and baggage-carts enough to cover a large meadow. The French now fired the bridge, and all these were abandoned to their fate. The Russian account states, that when the Beresina thawed after that winter's frost, 36,000 bodies were found in its bed.

Tchaplitz was soon joined in his pursuit of the survivors by Witgenstein and Platoff, and nothing could have saved Napoleon but the unexpected arrival of a fresh division under Maison, sent forwards from Poland by Maret, Duke of Bassano.

But the severity of the winter began now to be intense, and the sufferings of the army thus recruited were such, that discipline ere long disappeared, except among a few thousands of hardy veterans, over whose spirits the Emperor and Ney preserved some influence. The assaults of the Cossacks continued as before: the troops often performed their march by night, by the light of torches, in the hope of escaping their merciless pursuers. When they halted, they fell asleep in hundreds to wake no more. Their enemies found them frozen to death around the ashes of their watch-fires. It is said, among other horrors, that more than once they found poor famished wretches endeavouring to broil the flesh of their dead comrades. On scenes so fearful the veil must not be entirely dropt. Such is the price at which ambition does not hesitate to purchase even the chance of what the world has not yet ceased to call glory!

The haughty and imperious spirit of Napoleon sank not under all these miseries. He affected, in so far as was possible, not to see them. He still issued his orders as if his army, in all its divisions, were entire, and sent bulletins to Paris announcing a succession of victories. When his officers came to inform him of some new calamity, he dismissed them abruptly, saying, "Why will you disturb my tranquillity? I desire to know no particulars. Why will you deprive me of my tranquillity?"

On the 3rd of December he reached Malodeczno, and announced to his marshals that the news he had received from Paris, and the uncertain nature of his relations with some of his allies, rendered it indispensable for him to quit his army without further delay. They were now, he said, almost within sight of Poland; they would find plenty of everything at Wilna. It was his business to prepare at home the means of opening the next campaign in a manner worthy of the great nation. At Smorgoni, on the 5th, the garrison of Wilna met him; and then, having entrusted to these fresh troops the protection of the rear, and given the chief command to Murat, he finally bade adieu to the relics of his host. He set off at midnight in a traineau, accompanied by Caulaincourt, whose name he assumed: two other vehicles of the same kind followed, containing two officers of rank, Rustan the Emperor's favourite Mameluke, and one domestic besides.

Having narrowly escaped being taken by a party of irregular Russians at Youpranoni, Napoleon reached Warsaw at nightfall, on the 10th of December. His ambassador there, the Abb?de Pradt, who had as yet heard no distinct accounts of the progress of events, was unexpectedly visited by Caulaincourt, who abruptly informed him that the grand army was no more. The Abb?accompanied Caulaincourt to an obscure inn, where the Emperor, wrapped in a fur cloak, was walking up and down rapidly, beside a newly-lit fire. He was received with an air of gaiety, which for a moment disconcerted him; and proceeded to mention that the inhabitants of the Grand Duchy were beginning to show symptoms of disaffection, and even of a desire to reconcile themselves with the Prussians, under whose yoke they feared they were destined to return. The Abb?expressed his own satisfaction that the Emperor had escaped from so many dangers. "Dangers," cried Napoleon, "there were none--I have beat the Russians in every battle--I live but in dangers--it is for kings of Cockaigne to sit at home at ease. My army is in a superb condition still--it will be recruited at leisure at Wilna, and I go to bring up 300,000 men more from France. I quit my army with regret, but I must watch Austria and Prussia, and I have more weight on my throne than at headquarters. The Russians will be rendered foolhardy by their successes--I shall beat them in a battle or two on the Oder, and be on the Niemen again within a month." This harangue, utterly contradictory throughout, he began and ended with a favourite phrase--"Monsieur L'Ambassadeur, from the sublime to the ridiculous there is but a step."

Resuming his incognito and his journey, Napoleon reached Dresden on the evening of the 14th December, where the King of Saxony visited him secretly at his inn, and renewed his assurances of fidelity. He arrived at the Tuileries on the 18th, late at night, after the Empress had retired to rest. He entered the ante-chamber, to the confusion of her attendants, who at length recognised him with a cry that roused Maria Louisa from her slumbers; and Napoleon was welcomed with all the warmth of undiminished affection.

The army, whom its chief had thus abandoned, pursued meanwhile that miserable march, of which every day augmented the disorder. The garrison of Wilna and Maison's corps, united to those who escaped across the Beresina, might number in all 80,000. Before Murat reached Wilna, 40,000 of these had either died or fallen alive into the hands of their unrelenting pursuers. In that city there were abundant magazines of every kind, and the few who had as yet preserved some appearance of order, together with the multitudes of broken stragglers, rushed in confusion into the place, in the hope of at length resting from their toils, and eating and drinking, for at least one day, in peace. Strong men were observed weeping with joy at the sight of a loaf of bread. But scarcely had they received their rations, ere the well-known hurrah of Platoff rung once more in their ears. They fled once more, with such of their baggage as could be most easily got into motion; but many fell beneath the spears of the Cossacks, and not a few, it is said, were butchered deliberately in the moment of their perplexity by their Lithuanian hosts, the same Polish Jews who had already inflicted such irreparable injury on the whole army, by their non-observance of their contracts. Shortly after, a waggon laden with coin was overturned on the road, and the soldiers, laying aside all attention to their officers, began to plunder the rich spoil. The Cossacks came up--but there was enough for all, and friend and foe pillaged the imperial treasure, in company, for once, without strife. It deserves to be recorded that some soldiers of the imperial guard restored the money which fell to their share on this occasion, when the weary march at length reached its end.

They passed the Niemen at Kowno; and the Russians did not pursue them into the Prussian territory. At the time when they escaped finally from Poland, there were about 1000 in arms, and perhaps 20,000 more, utterly broken, dispersed, and demoralised.

Schwartzenberg, the general of the Austrian auxiliaries, on learning the departure of Napoleon, formed an armistice with the Russians, and retired by degrees into his own prince's territory. These allies had shown little zeal in any part of the campaign; and their conduct seems to have been appreciated by the Russians accordingly.

In Courland, on the left flank of the French retreat, there remained the separate corps of Macdonald, who had with him 20,000 Prussians and 10,000 Bavarians and other Germans. These Prussians had been sent on this detached service in just apprehension of their coldness to the invader's cause. Macdonald, on learning the utter ruin of the main army, commenced his march upon Tilsit. On reaching that place D'York, the commander of the Prussians, refused any longer to obey the marshal's orders, and separated his men entirely--thus taking on himself the responsibility of disobeying the letter of his sovereign's commands, and anticipating that general burst of national hatred which, as all men perceived, could not much longer be deferred.

To the great honour, however, of the Prussian people, the wearied relics of Napoleon's grand army were received in the country which, in the days of their prosperity, they had so wantonly insulted, if not with friendship, at least, with compassion. They took up their quarters, and remained for a time unmolested, in and near Konigsberg.

Thus ended the invasion of Russia. There had been slain in battle, on the side of Napoleon, 125,000 men. Fatigue, hunger, and cold, had caused the death of 132,000! and the Russians had taken of prisoners 193,000--including forty-eight generals and 3000 regimental officers. The total loss was, therefore, 450,000 men. The eagles and standards left in the enemy's hands were seventy-five in number, and the pieces of cannon nearly one thousand.

Exclusive of the Austrian and Prussian auxiliaries, there remained of all the enormous host which Napoleon set in motion in August about 40,000 men; and of these not 10,000 were of the French nation.

[Footnote 62: He was rescued in Poland by a party of Cossacks.]

CHAPTER XXXII

Conspiracy of Mallet--Napoleon's reception in Paris--his Military Preparations--Prussia declares War--Austria negotiates with Napoleon--Bernadette appears in Germany--The Russians advance into Silesia--Napoleon heads his Army in Saxony--Battle of Lutzen--Battle of Bautzen.

Some allusion has already been made to the news of a political disturbance in Paris, which reached Napoleon during his retreat from Moscow, and quickened his final abandonment of the army. The occurrence in question was the daring conspiracy headed by General Mallet. This officer, one of the ancient noblesse, had been placed in confinement in 1808, in consequence of his connection with a society called the Philadelphes, which seems to have sprung up within the French army, at the time when Napoleon seized the supreme power, and which had for its immediate object his deposition--while some of the members contemplated the restoration of a republican government, and others, of whom Mallet was one, the recall of the royal family of Bourbon. The people of Paris had for some weeks received no official intelligence from the grand army, and rumours of some awful catastrophe were rife among all classes, when Mallet conceived the daring project of forging a senatus-consultum, announcing the fall of Napoleon in a great battle in Russia, and appointing a provisional government. Having executed this forgery, the general escaped from his prison, and appeared in full uniform, attended by a corporal dressed as an aide-de-camp, at midnight, on the 22nd of October 1812, at the gates of the Minims barracks, then tenanted by some new and raw levies. The audacity with which he claimed the obedience of these men to the senatorial decree overawed them. He assumed the command, and on the instant arrested by their means Savary, minister of police, and some others of the principal functionaries in the capital. General Hullin, the military governor, was summoned and hesitated; at that moment the officer of police, from whose keeping Mallet had escaped, recognised him, and he was immediately resisted, disarmed, and confined. The whole affair was over in the course of a few hours, but the fact that so wild a scheme should have been so nearly successful was sufficiently alarming. The ease and indifference with which a considerable body of armed men, in the very heart of Paris, had transferred their services to a new authority, proclaimed by a stranger, made Napoleon consider with suspicion the basis of his power. And ignorant to what extent the conspiracy had actually gone, he heard with additional alarm, that no fewer than twenty-four persons, including the leader, had been condemned to death. Of so many he was willing to believe that some at least had been mere dupes, and apprehended that so much bloodshed might create a violent revulsion of public feeling. The Parisians beheld the execution of these men with as much indifference as their bold attempt; but of this Napoleon was ignorant, until he reached the Tuileries.

His arrival, preceded as it had been by the twenty-ninth bulletin, in which the veil was at last lifted from the fatal events of the campaign, restored for the moment the appearances of composure, amidst a population of which almost every family had lost a son or a brother. Such was the influence that still clung to his name. The Emperor was safe. However great the present calamity, hope remained. The elements, as they were taught to believe, had not merely quickened and increased, but wholly occasioned the reverses of the army. The Russian winter was the only enemy that had been able to triumph over his genius, and the valour of Frenchmen. The senate, the magistrates, all those public bodies and functionaries who had the means of approaching the throne, now crowded to its footsteps with addresses full of adulation yet more audacious than they had ever before ventured on. Tho voice of applause, congratulation, and confidence, re-echoed from every quarter, drowned the whispers of suspicion, resentment, and natural sorrow. Every department of the public service appeared to be animated with a spirit of tenfold activity. New conscriptions were called for and yielded. Regiments arrived from Spain and from Italy. Every arsenal resounded with the preparation of new artillery--thousands of horses were impressed in every province. Ere many weeks had elapsed. Napoleon found himself once more in a condition to take the field with not less than 350,000 soldiers. Such was the effect of his new appeal to the national feelings of this great and gallant people.

Meanwhile the French garrisons dispersed over the Prussian territory were wholly incompetent to overawe that oppressed and insulted nation, now burning with the settled thirst and the long-deferred hope of vengeance. The king interposed, indeed, his authority to protect the soldiers of Napoleon from popular violence; but it presently became manifest that their safety must depend on their concentrating themselves in a small number of fortified places; and that even if Frederick William had been cordially anxious to preserve his alliance with France, it would soon be impossible for him to resist the unanimous wishes of his people. Murat was already weary of his command. He found himself thwarted and controlled by the other generals, none of whom respected his authority; and one of whom, when he happened to speak of himself in the same breath with the sovereigns of Austria and

Prussia, answered without ceremony, "You must remember that these are kings by the grace of God, by descent, and by custom; whereas you are only a king by the grace of Napoleon, and through the expenditure of French blood." Murat was moreover jealous of the extent to which his queen was understood to be playing the sovereign in Naples, and he threw up his command; being succeeded by Eugene Beauharnois, and insulted anew by Napoleon himself, in a general order which announced this change, and alleged as its causes, the superior military skill of the viceroy, and his possession of "the full confidence of the Emperor." Eugene succeeded to the command at the moment when it was obvious that Frederick William could no longer, even if he would, repress the universal enthusiasm of his people. On the 31st of January, the King made his escape to Breslau, in which neighbourhood no French were garrisoned, erected his standard, and called on the nation to rise in arms. Whereon Eugene retired to Magdeburg, and shut himself up in that great fortress, with as many troops as he could assemble to the west of the Elbe.

Six years had elapsed since the fatal day of Jena; and, in spite of all the watchfulness of Napoleon's tyranny, the Prussian nation had recovered in a great measure its energies. The people now answered the call of their beloved prince, as with the heart and voice of one man. Youths of all ranks, the highest and the lowest, flocked indiscriminately to the standard: the students of the universities formed themselves into battalions, at the head of which, in many instances, their teachers marched. The women flung their trinkets into the king's treasure--the gentlemen melted their plate--England poured in her gold with a lavish hand. The rapidity with which discipline was established among the great levies thus assembled, excited universal astonishment. It spoke the intense and perfect zeal with which a people, naturally warlike, had devoted themselves to the sacred cause of independence. The Emperor of Russia was no sooner aware of this great movement, than he resolved to advance into Silesia. Having masked several French garrisons in Prussian Poland, and taken others, he pushed on with his main army to support Frederick William. There was some risk in leaving a considerable number of hostile fortresses behind him and his own frontier; but this he encountered cheerfully, rather than permit the Prussians to stand alone in the first onset of Napoleon, of whose extensive preparations all Europe was well aware. The two sovereigns, long attached to each other by the warmest feelings of personal friendship, though of late compelled by the iron force of circumstances to put on the disguise of hostility, met at Breslau on the 15th of March. Tears rushed down the cheeks of Frederick William, as he fell into the arms of Alexander--"Wipe them," said the Czar; "they are the last that Napoleon shall ever cause you to shed."

The aged Kutusoff having died, the command of the Russian army was now given to Witgenstein; while that of the Prussians was entrusted to a leader, whose name was hailed as the sure pledge of unremitting activity and indomitable perseverance. This was Blucher, an officer originally trained under the great Frederick, whose exemplary conduct after the battle of Jena has already been mentioned. The brave old man had, since that catastrophe, lived in utter retirement. The soldiery had long before bestowed on him the nom-de-guerre of Marshal Forwards, and they heard of his appointment with universal delight. Addicted to drinking, smoking, and gambling, and little conversant with the higher branches of war as an art, Blucher was at first despised by Napoleon. But his technical deficiencies were abundantly supplied by the skill of Scharnforst, and afterwards of Gneisenau; and he himself possessed such influence over the minds of his men in the day of action, and was sure to rally them so rapidly after defeat, and to urge them on so keenly when fortune was more favourable, that ere long the Emperor was forced to confess that no one gave him so much trouble as that "debauched old dragoon." Blucher hated the very names of France and Buonaparte with a perfect hatred; and, once more permitted to draw his sword, he swore never to sheathe it until the revenge of Prussia was complete.

The Crown Prince of Sweden landed with 35,000 men at Stralsund, and advanced through Mecklenburg, while the sovereigns of Russia and Prussia were concentrating their armies in Silesia. It was announced and expected that German troops would join Bernadotte, so as to enable him to open the campaign on the lower Elbe with a separate army of 100,000. Lord Wellington was about to advance once more into Spain, with his victorious veterans. Three great armies, two of which might easily communicate with each other, were thus taking the field against him at once; and yet, such was Napoleon's pride or obstinacy, that he would make no sacrifice whatever to secure the assistance of Austria. He still adhered to his resolution of entering into no general peace which should not recognise Joseph as King of Spain; and refused absolutely to listen to any proposals which included the cession either of Illyria or the Tyrol. Ere he once more left Paris, he named Maria Louisa Regent in his absence; but this was a circumstance not likely to have much weight with the wavering counsels of the Austrian.

While Napoleon's military preparations were in progress, he made an effort to conciliate that large party of his subjects, who had hitherto looked on him with coldness as the oppressor of the head of the Catholic church. During his absence in Russia, the Pope had been removed once more to Fontainebleau, where he now occupied apartments in the palace, under strict surveillance of the police. The Emperor presented himself suddenly in his hunter's dress before the holy father on the 13th of January; and exerted his talents with such success, that preliminary articles of a new concordat were at length drawn up. But in his eagerness to produce a favourable impression on the Catholic public, Napoleon published these preliminary articles, as if they had formed a definite and ratified treaty; and Pius, indignant at this conduct, which he considered as equally false and irreverent, immediately announced his resolution to carry the negotiation no further.

The Pope, however, was the only man in France who as yet durst openly confront the rage of Buonaparte. As the time when he was expected to assume once more the command of his army in the field drew near, the addresses of his apparently devoted subjects increased in numbers, and still more in the extravagance of their adulations.

Napoleon quitted Paris in the middle of April, and on the 18th reached the banks of the Saale; where the troops he had been mustering and organising in France had now been joined by Eugene Beauharnois and the garrison of Magdeburg. The Czar and his Prussian ally were known to be at Dresden; and it soon appeared that, while they meditated a march westwards on Leipsig, the French intended to move eastwards with the view of securing the possession of that great city. Of the armies thus about to meet each other's shock in the heart of Saxony, there is no doubt that Buonaparte's was considerably the more numerous. His activity had been worthy of his reputation; and a host nearly 200,000 strong was already concentrated for action, while reserves to nearly a similar extent were gradually forming behind him on the Rhine. The Russians had not as yet pushed forward more than half their disposable troops beyond the Vistula--wherever the blame lay, such was the fact; the Prussians, unanimous as their patriotism was, had had only three months to reorganise their establishments. Under such circumstances, the advance of the allies beyond the Elbe, could only have proceeded from their ardent wish to stimulate the spirit of insurrection in the kingdom of Saxony and the neighbouring states. It was obviously Napoleon's interest to bring them to action while their numbers were thus unequal, and ere the sole object of their hazardous advance could be realised.

The armies met sooner than he had ventured to hope, on the first of May, near the town of Lutzen, celebrated already as the scene of the battle in which King Gustavus Adolphus died. The allies crossed the Elster suddenly, under the cover of a thick morning fog, and attacked the left flank of the French, who had been advancing in column, and who thus commenced the action under heavy disadvantages. But the Emperor so skilfully altered the arrangement of his army, that, ere the day closed, the allies were more afraid of being enclosed to their ruin within his two wings, than hopeful of being able to cut through and destroy that part of his force which they had originally charged and weakened, and which had now become his centre. Night interrupted the conflict. They retreated next morning, leaving Napoleon in possession of the field. But here the advantage stopped. The slain of the one army were not more numerous than those of the other; and the allies, convinced of their mistake, but neither broken nor discouraged, fell back leisurely on Leipsig, thence on Dresden, and finally across the Elbe to Bautzen, without leaving either prisoners or guns in the hands of the French. The victory of Lutzen was blazoned abroad, as having restored all its glory to the eagle of Napoleon; but he clearly perceived that the days were no more in which a single battle determined the fate of a campaign, and an empire. It was at Lutzen that Marshal Bessieres died.

Napoleon entered Dresden on the 6th, and on the 12th was joined there by the King of Saxony, who certainly had been individually a gainer by his alliance, and who still adhered to it, in opposition to the wishes both of his people and his army. The Saxon troops, who had been wavering, once more submitted to act in concert with the French; and Hamburg, which city had partaken in the movement of Prussia, and all the country to the left of the Elbe, fell back, for the moment, into their hands. The cruelty with which the defection of Hamburg, in particular, was now revenged on the inhabitants by Marshal Davoust, has consigned to lasting abhorrence the name of that able but heartless satellite of Napoleon. All the atrocities of Junot and Massena, in

Portugal, in 1808 and 1809, were equalled on the banks of the Elbe, by Davoust, in the summer of 1813.

While the Emperor paused at Dresden, Ney made various demonstrations in the direction of Berlin, with the view of inducing the allies to quit Bautzen; but it soon became manifest that they had resolved to sacrifice the Prussian capital, if it were necessary, rather than forego their position; by adhering to which they well knew Buonaparte must ultimately be compelled to carry his main force into a difficult and mountainous country, in place of acting in the open plains of Saxony and Brandenburg. They were, moreover, desirous to remain in the neighbourhood of Bohemia for another reason. The Austrian Emperor had again renewed his negotiation with Napoleon; urging him to accept his mediation for the conclusion of a general peace, and at the same time giving him to understand that such a peace could not be obtained, unless he would consent to be satisfied with the frontier of the Rhine, and restore effectively the independence of the German nation. Napoleon's conferences with Bubna, the Austrian envoy, were frequent and long; but they ended where they began. He was well aware, however, that the Emperor Francis was increasing his military establishment largely, and that a great body of troops was already concentrated behind the mountainous frontier of Bohemia. He could not but see that Austria regarded herself as enabled and entitled to turn the scale on whichsoever side she might choose; and he determined to crush the army which had retreated from Lutzen, ere the ceremonious cabinet of Vienna should have time to come to a distinct understanding with the headquarters of Alexander and Frederick William. Victory, he clearly saw, could alone serve his interests with the Austrian.

Having replaced by woodwork some arches of the magnificent bridge over the Elbe, at Dresden, which the allies had blown up on their retreat, Napoleon now moved towards Bautzen, and came in sight of the position on the morning of the 21st of May. Its strength was obviously great. In their front was the river Spree: wooded hills supported their right, and eminences well fortified their left. The action began with an attempt to turn their right, but Barclay de Tolly anticipated this movement, and repelled it with such vigour, that a whole column of 7000 dispersed and fled into the hills of Bohemia for safety. The Emperor then determined to pass the Spree in front of the enemy, and they permitted him to do so, rather than come down from their position. He took up his quarters in the town of Bautzen, and his whole army bivouacked in presence of the allies. The battle was resumed at daybreak on the 22nd; when Ney on the right, and Oudinot on the left, attempted simultaneously to turn the flanks of the position; while Soult and Napoleon himself directed charge after charge on the centre. During four hours the struggle was maintained with unflinching obstinacy; the wooded heights, where Blucher commanded, had been taken and retaken several times--the bloodshed, on either side, had been terrible--ere, the situation of both flanks being apparent, the allies perceived the necessity either of retiring, or of continuing the fight against superior numbers on disadvantageous ground. They withdrew accordingly; but still with all the deliberate coolness of a parade: halting at every favourable spot, and renewing their cannonade. "What," exclaimed Napoleon, "no results! not a gun! not a prisoner!--these people will not leave me so much as a nail." During the whole day he urged the pursuit with impetuous rage, reproaching even his chosen generals as "creeping scoundrels," and exposing his own person in the very hottest of the fire. By his side was Duroc, the grand master of the palace, his dearest--many said, ere now, his only friend. Bruyeres, another old associate of the Italian wars, was struck down in their view. "Duroc," whispered Napoleon, "fortune has a spite at us this day." A few minutes afterwards, Duroc himself was mortally wounded. The Emperor instantly ordered a halt, and remained all the afternoon in front of his tent, surrounded by the guard, who did not witness his affliction without tears. From this time he would listen to no reports or suggestions.--"Everything to-morrow," was his invariable answer. He stood by Duroc while he died; drew up with his own hand an epitaph to be placed over his remains by the pastor of the place, who received 200 napoleons to defray the expense of a fitting monument; and issued also a decree in favour of his departed friend's children. Thus closed the 22nd. The allies being strongly posted during most of the day, had suffered less than the French; the latter had lost 15,000, the former 10,000 men.

They continued their retreat into Upper Silesia; and Buonaparte advanced to Breslau, and released the garrison of Glogau. Meanwhile the Austrian having watched these indecisive though bloody fields, once more renewed his offers of mediation. The sovereigns of Russia and Prussia expressed great willingness to accept it; and Napoleon also appears to have been sincerely desirous for the moment of bringing his disputes to a peaceful termination. He agreed to an armistice, and in arranging its conditions agreed to fall back out of Silesia; thus enabling the allied princes to re-open communications with Berlin. The lines of country to be occupied by the armies, respectively, during the truce, were at length settled, and it was signed on the 1st of June. The French Emperor then returned to Dresden, and a general congress of diplomatists prepared to meet at Prague.

CHAPTER XXXIII

Napoleon's Interview with Metternich--Advice of his Ministers and Generals--Intelligence from Spain--Battle of Vittoria--Congress of Prague Dissolved--Austria declares War--Battle of Dresden--Death of Moreau--Battle of Culm--Surrender of Vandamme--Battles of Grossbeeren, Wahlstadt, and Dennewitz--Napoleon retires from the Elbe--The Battle of Leipsig--The Battle of Hanau--The Allies on the Rhine.

England alone refused to send any representative to Prague, alleging that Buonaparte had as yet signified no disposition to recede from his pretensions on Spain, and that he had consented to the armistice with the sole view of gaining time for political intrigue and further military preparation. It may be doubted whether any of the allied powers who took part in the congress did so with much hope that the disputes with Napoleon could find a peaceful end. His recent successes were to the general view dazzling, however in reality unproductive, and must have been supposed to quicken the flame of his pride. But it was of the utmost importance to gain time for the advance of Bernadotte; for the arrival of new reinforcements from Russia; for the completion of the Prussian organisation; and, above all, for determining the policy of Vienna.

Metternich, the Austrian minister, repaired in person to Dresden; and, while inferior diplomatists wasted time in endless discussions at Prague, one interview between him and Napoleon brought the whole question to a definite issue. The Emperor had hitherto seen in Metternich only a smooth and elegant courtier, and he expected to bear him down by military violence and rudeness. He assumed at once that Austria had no wish but to drive a good bargain for herself, and asked broadly, _What is your price? Will Illyria satisfy you? I only wish you to be neutral--I can deal with these Russians and Prussians single-handed._ Metternich stated plainly that the time in which Austria could be neutral was past; that the situation of Europe at large must be considered. Napoleon insinuated that he would be happy to dismember Prussia, and give half her territories to Austria. Metternich replied that his government was resolved to be gained by no share in the spoils of others; that events had proved the impossibility of a steadfast peace, unless the sovereigns of the continent were restored to the rank of independence; in a word, that the Rhenish Confederacy must be broken up; that France must be contented with the boundary of the Rhine, and pretend no longer to maintain her usurped and unnatural influence in Germany. Napoleon replied by a gross personal insult: _Come, Metternich, said he, tell me honestly how much the English have given you to take their part against me?_

The Austrian court at length sent a formal document, containing its ultimatum: the tenor of which Metternich had sufficiently indicated in this conversation. Talleyrand and Fouche who had now arrived from Paris, urged the Emperor to accede to the proffered terms. They represented to him the madness of rousing all Europe to conspire for his destruction, and insinuated that the progress of discontent was rapid in France itself. Their arguments were backed by intelligence of the most disastrous character from Spain. Wellington, on perceiving that Napoleon had somewhat weakened his armies in that country, when preparing for his Saxon campaign, had once more advanced from the Portuguese frontier. He was now in possession of the supreme authority over the Spanish armies, as well as the Portuguese and English, and had appeared in greater force than ever. The French line of defences on the Douro had been turned and abandoned: their armies had concentrated to withstand him at Vittoria, and there, on the 21st of June, Joseph and Marshal Jourdan had sustained a total defeat. The "Intrusive King" was now retreating towards the Pyrenees, chased from post to post by an enemy who, as it seemed, bade fair to terminate his campaign by an invasion of the south-western provinces of France. Napoleon was urged by his military, as well as political advisers, to appreciate duly the crisis which his affairs had reached. Berthier, and indeed almost all the generals on whose opinions he had been accustomed to place reliance, concurred in pressing him either to make peace on the terms proposed, or to draw in his garrisons on the Oder and Elbe, whereby he would strengthen his army with 50,000 veterans, and retire to the Rhine. There, they said, with such a force assembled on such a river, and with all the resources of France behind him, he might bid defiance to the united armies of Europe, and, at worst, obtain a peace that would leave him in secure tenure of a nobler dominion than any of the kings, his predecessors, had ever hoped to possess. Ten battles lost, said he, _would not sink me lower than you would have me to place myself by my own voluntary act; but one battle gained enables me to seize Berlin and Breslau, and make peace on terms compatible with my glory._ He proceeded to insult both ministers and generals by insinuations that they were actuated by selfish motives; complained haughtily that they seemed disposed to draw distinctions between the country and the sovereign; and ended by announcing that he did not wish for any plans of theirs, but their service in the execution of his.

Thus blinded by arrogance and self-confidence, and incapable of weighing any other considerations against what he considered as the essence of his personal glory, Napoleon refused to abate one iota of his pretensions--until it was too late. Then, indeed, whether more accurate intelligence from Spain had reached him, or the accounts of those who had been watching the unremitting preparations of the allies in his neighbourhood, had at length found due weight--then, indeed, he did show some symptoms of concession. A courier arrived at Prague with a note, in which he signified his willingness to accede to a considerable number of the Austrian stipulations. But this was on the 11th of August. The day preceding was that on which, by the agreement, the armistice was to end. On that day Austria had to sign an alliance, offensive and defensive, with Russia and Prussia. On the night between the 10th and 11th, rockets answering rockets, from height to height along the frontiers of Bohemia and Silesia, had announced to all the armies of the allies this accession of strength and the immediate recommencement of hostilities.

On neither side had the pending negotiation been permitted for a moment to interrupt or slacken military preparation. Napoleon had sent Beauharnois into Italy, to be ready in case of any Austrian demonstration in that quarter; and General Wrede, with the Bavarian army, guarded his rear. An Austrian army, 60,000 strong, was now ready to pass the Alps; and, to watch Wrede, another corps of 40,000, under the Prince of Reuss, had taken their station. These were minor arrangements. The forces now assembled around Napoleon himself were full 250,000 in number, and disposed as follows: Macdonald lay with 100,000 at Buntzlaw, on the border of Silesia; another corps of 50,000 had their headquarters at Zittau, in Lusatia; St. Cyr, with 20,000, was at Pirna, on the great pass from Bohemia; Oudinot at Leipsig, with 60,000; while with the Emperor himself at Dresden remained 25,000 of the imperial guard, the flower of France. The reader, on referring to the map, will perceive that these corps were so distributed as to present a formidable front on every point where it was likely the allies should hazard an attack, and, moreover, so that Napoleon could speedily reinforce any threatened position with his reserve from Dresden. For the armies to be opposed were thus situated:--Behind the Erzgebirge, or Metallic Mountains, and having their headquarters at Prague, lay _The Grand Army of the Allies_ (consisting of 120,000 Austrians and 80,000 Russians and Prussians), commanded in chief by the Austrian general Schwartzenberg. The French corps at Zittau and Pirna were prepared to encounter these, should they attempt to force their way into Saxony, either on the right or the left of the Elbe. The Second Army of the Allies (consisting of 80,000 Russians and Prussians), called the _Army of Silesia_, and commanded by Blucher, lay in advance at Breslau. The French corps at Zittau and Buntzlau were in communication, and could confront Blucher wherever he might attempt to approach the Elbe. Lastly the Crown Prince of Sweden was at Berlin, with 30,000 of his own troops, and 60,000 Russians and Prussians, Oudinot and Macdonald were so stationed that he could not approach the upper valley of the Elbe without encountering one or other of them, and they also had the means of mutual communication and support. The French had garrisons at Wittemberg, Magdeburg, and elsewhere on the Elbe; and between the main armies of the Allies were various flying corps of Russian and Prussian light troops.

On the whole, Dresden formed the centre of a comparatively small circle, completely occupied by the French; while the Allies might be considered as lying on part of a much wider circle beyond them. Napoleon had evidently arranged his troops with a view of provoking his enemies to make isolated assaults, and so beating them in detail. But he was now opposed by generals well acquainted with his system of tactics, and who had accordingly prepared a counter-scheme expressly calculated to baffle the plan of arrangements on which he had reckoned. The commanders of the three allied armies agreed-- that whosoever of them should be first assailed or pressed by the French, should on no account accept battle, but retreat; thus tempting Napoleon in person to follow, leaving Dresden open to the assault of some other great branch of their confederacy, and so enabling them at once to seize all his magazines, to break the communications between the remaining divisions of his army, and interpose a hostile force in the rear of them all--between the Elbe and the Rhine. The plan of the Allies is supposed to have been drawn up by two generals who thoroughly understood the military system of Napoleon--Bernadotte, the Crown Prince of Sweden and Moreau; who had some time ere this accepted the invitation of the Emperor Alexander, and returned from his American exile, to take part in the war--which now, in the opinion of many Frenchmen, had for its object the emancipation of France itself, as well as of the other countries of Europe. The conduct of Moreau, in placing himself in the ranks of the Allies, will be praised or condemned, according as men judge him to have been swayed by patriotic motives, or by those of personal resentment and ambition. There can be no question that his arrival brought a great accession of military skill to their counsels.

Blucher made the first movement; and no sooner did Napoleon understand that he was threatening the position of Macdonald than he quitted Dresden (15th August) with his guard and a powerful force of cavalry, and proceeded to the support of his lieutenant. The Prussian adhered faithfully to the general plan, and retired across the Katsbach, in the face of his enemies. Napoleon was still pursuing him in the direction of the Neiss and Breslau, when he was informed that Schwartzenberg had rushed down from the Bohemian hills. He instantly abandoned Blucher to the care of Macdonald, and sent his guards back to Dresden, whither he himself also began his journey early on the 23rd.

Having driven St. Cyr, and his 20,000 men, before him, Schwartzenberg (with whom were the Sovereigns of Russia and Prussia in person) made his appearance on the heights to the south of the Saxon capital, on the 25th. The army of St. Cyr had thrown themselves into the city, and it was now surrounded with fortifications of considerable strength. Yet had this vast host attacked it at once, there is every reason to believe it must have fallen before Napoleon could have returned from Silesia. They delayed, for whatever reason, until daybreak on the 26th; and then assailed Dresden in six columns, each more numerous than its garrison. St. Cyr already began to despair, when the imperial guard made their appearance crossing the bridge from the Eastern side of the Elbe, and in the midst of them Napoleon. A German author[63] says: "It was then that, for the first time, I beheld his face. He came on with the eye of a tyrant, and the voice of a lion, urging his breathless and eager soldiers." Two sallies were on the instant executed by these troops, hot as they were from their long and toilsome march. The Allies were driven back for some space. Night set in, and the two armies remained in presence till the morning. Then, amidst a fierce storm of wind and rain, Napoleon renewed the battle. 200,000 men (such had been the rapid decision of his orders to his various generals) were now gathered round him, and he poured them out with such skill, on either flank of the enemy's line that ere the close of the day, they were forced to withdraw altogether from their attempt. Ney and Murat on the left flank, and Vandamme on the right (at Pirna), had taken possession of the two chief roads into Bohemia, and in consequence they were compelled to retreat by the comparatively difficult country paths between. On either side 8000 men had been slain or wounded; but with the French there remained from 15 to 20,000 prisoners, and twenty-six cannon; and the ablest of all the enemy's generals had fallen.

Early in the day Buonaparte himself ordered some half-dozen cannon to be fired at once upon a group, apparently of reconnoitring officers, and this was followed by a movement which was thought to indicate that some personage of importance had been wounded. A peasant came in the evening, and brought with him a bloody boot and a greyhound, both the property, he said, of the great man who was no more: the name on the collar was Moreau. Both his legs had been shot off. He continued to smoke a cigar while they were amputated and dressed, in the presence of Alexander, and died shortly after; thus, if he had erred, paying the early forfeit of his errors.

But Fortune had only revisited the banners of her ancient favourite with a momentary gleam of sunshine. The fatigues he had undergone between the 15th and the 28th of August would have broken any other frame, and they, for the time, weakened his. It is said that a mess of mutton and garlic, the only food he had tasted on the 26th, had besides deranged his stomach. Unable to remain with the columns in the rear of Schwartzenberg, he returned to Dresden weary and sick; and thenceforth evil tidings awaited him.

Vandamme continued the pursuit on the Pirna road. Seduced by the enormous prize which lay before him at Toeplitz, where the chief magazines of the Allies had been established, and on which all their broken columns were now endeavouring to reassemble, this rude and hot-headed soldier incautiously advanced beyond the wooded heights of Peterswald into the valley of Culm. A Russian corps suddenly turned on him, and formed in line of battle. Their General, Count D'Osterman, assured them that the life of "their Father" depended on their steadfastness; and no effort could shake them.

The battle continued till night, when Vandamme ought undoubtedly to have retired to Peterswald. He lingered till the morning of the 30th;--when behind him, on those very heights, appeared the Prussian corps of Kleist, who had been wandering and lost their way amidst the forests. The French rushed up the hill in despair, thinking they were intercepted by design. The Prussians, on their part, doubted not that some other division of Napoleon's force was hard behind them, and rushed down--with the same fear, and the same impetuosity. The Russians advanced and completed the disarray. The field was covered with dead: Vandamme and nearly 8000 men laid down their arms. Many eagles were taken--the rest of the army dispersed in utter confusion among the hills.

This news reached Napoleon still sick at Dresden. "Such," said he to Murat, "is the fortune of war--high in the morning--low ere night. Between triumph and ruin there intervenes but a step." A map lay stretched on the table before him; he took his compasses, and measuring distances on it with an idle hand, repeated the lines of one of his favourite poets.

Hard on the tidings of Culm followed others of the same complexion. No sooner did Blucher perceive that Napoleon had retired from Silesia, than he resumed the offensive, and descended from the position he had taken up at Jauer. He encountered Macdonald, who was by no means prepared for this boldness, on the plains between Wahlstadt and the river Katsbach, on the 26th of August, and after a hard fought day gained a complete victory.[64] The French lost 15,000 men and 100 guns, and fell back on Dresden. Oudinot, meanwhile, had advanced from Leipsig towards Berlin, with the view of preventing Bernadotte from effecting a junction with Blucher, or overwhelming the French garrisons lower down the Elbe. The Crown Prince, however, met and defeated him at Grossbeeren, on the 23rd of August; took Luckau, where 1000 men were in garrison, on the 28th; and continued to advance towards Wittemberg, under the walls of which city Oudinot at length concentrated all his forces. Napoleon, perceiving the importance of this point, sent Ney with new troops, and gave him the chief command, with strict orders to force his way to Berlin; so placing Bernadotte between the Leipsig army and himself at Dresden. Ney endeavoured to pass the Swedes without a battle, but failed in this attempt. A general action was forced on him on the 7th of September, at Dennewitz. He also was wholly defeated; 10,000 prisoners and forty-six guns remained in the hands of Bernadotte; and Ney retreated in confusion upon Torgau.

Napoleon had now recovered his health and activity; and the exertions which he made at this period were never surpassed, even by himself. On the 3rd of September he was in quest of Blucher, who had now advanced near to the Elbe; but the Prussian retired and baffled him as before. Returning to Dresden he received the news of Dennewitz, and immediately afterwards heard that Witgenstein had a second time descended towards Pirna. He flew thither on the instant; the Russian also gave way, according to the general plan of the campaign; and Buonaparte once more returned to Dresden on the 12th. Again he was told that Blucher, on the one side, and Witgenstein on the other, were availing themselves of his absence, and advancing. He once more returned to Pirna: a third time the Russian retired. Napoleon followed him as far as Peterswald, and, having contemplated with his own eyes the scene of Vandamme's catastrophe, once more returned to his centre-point.

Not all Ney's exertions could prevent Bernadotte and Blucher from at length effecting their junction to the west of the Elbe. The Marshal, having witnessed the combination of these armies, retreated to Leipsig. Napoleon ordered Regnier and Bertrand to march suddenly from Dresden on Berlin, in the hope of recalling Blucher; but the veteran persisted. Meantime Schwartzenberg was found to be skirting round the hills to the westward, as if for the purpose of joining Blucher and Bernadotte, in the neighbourhood of Leipsig. It became manifest to all that Dresden had ceased to be the key of Napoleon's defence: yet he clung to the Elbe, as he had done to the Kremlin.

He lingered at Dresden at least three weeks after all rational hope of holding that river was gone; and even at the last, when he perceived the necessity of transferring his person to Leipsig, he could not be persuaded to call in his garrisons scattered down the valley, which he still hoped some turn of events would enable him to revisit in triumph.

Towards Leipsig, however, as on a common centre, the forces of France, and all her enemies, were now at length converging. Napoleon reached that venerable city on the 15th of October, and almost immediately the heads of Schwartzenberg's columns began to appear towards the south. It was necessary to prepare on the northern side also, in case Bernadotte and Blucher should appear ere the grand army was disposed of; and, lastly, it was necessary to secure effectually the ground to the west of Leipsig;--a series of marshy meadows interfused with the numerous branches of the Pleiss and the Elster, through which lies the only road to France. Napoleon having made all his preparations, reconnoitred every outpost in person, and distributed eagles, in great form, to some new regiments which had just joined him. The ceremonial was splendid: the soldiers knelt before the Emperor, and in presence of all the line: military mass was performed, and the young warriors swore to die rather than witness the dishonour of France. Upon this scene the sun descended; and with it the star of Napoleon went down for ever.

At midnight three rockets, emitting a brilliant white light, sprung into the heavens to the south of the city; these marked the position on which Schwartzenberg (having now with him the Emperor of Austria, as well as Alexander and Frederick William) had fixed his headquarters. They were answered by four rockets of a deep red colour, ascending on the instant from the northern horizon; and Napoleon doubted not that he was to sustain on the morrow the assault of Blucher and Bernadotte, as well as of the grand army of the Allies. Blucher was indeed ready to co-operate with Schwartzenberg; and though the Crown Prince had not yet reached his ground, the numerical superiority of the enemy was very great. Buonaparte had with him, to defend the line of villages to the south and north of Leipsig, 136,000 men; while, even in the absence of Bernadotte, who might be hourly looked for, the Allies mustered not less than 230,000.

The battle commenced on the southern side, at daybreak of the 16th. The Allies charged the French line there six times in succession, and were as often repelled. Napoleon then charged in his turn, and with such effect, that Murat's cavalry were at one time in possession of a great gap between the two wings of the enemy. The Cossacks of the Russian imperial guard, however, encountered the French horse, and pushed them back again. The combat raged without intermission until nightfall: three cannon shots, discharged at the extremity of either line, then marked as if preconcertedly, the pause of battle; and both armies bivouacked exactly where the morning light had found them. Such was the issue on the south, where Napoleon himself commanded. Marmont, his lieutenant on the northern side, had been less fortunate. Blucher attacked him with a vast superiority of numbers: nothing could be more obstinate than his defence; but he lost many prisoners and guns, was driven from his original ground, and occupied, when the day closed, a new line of positions, much nearer the walls of the city.

Gallant as the behaviour of his troops had been, the result satisfied Napoleon that he must finally retreat from Leipsig; and he now made a sincere effort to obtain peace. General Mehrfeldt, the same Austrian officer who had come to his headquarters after the battle of Austerlitz, to pray for an armistice on the part of the Emperor Francis, had been made prisoner in the course of the day, and Napoleon resolved to employ him as his messenger. Mehrfeldt informed him that the King of Bavaria had at length acceded to the alliance. This intelligence added to his perplexities, already sufficiently great, the prospect of finding a new enemy stationed on the line of his march to France. He entreated the Austrian to request for him the personal intercession of Francis. "I will renounce Poland and Illyria," said he, "Holland, the Hanse Towns, and Spain. I will consent to lose the sovereignty of the kingdom of Italy, provided that state remain as an independent one-- and I will evacuate all Germany. Adieu! Count Mehrfeldt, when on my part you name the word armistice to the two Emperors, I doubt not the sound will awaken many recollections."

It was now too late: the Allied Princes had sworn to each other to entertain no treaty while one French soldier remained on the Eastern side of the Rhine. Napoleon received no answer to his message; and prepared for the difficult task of retreating with 100,000 men, through a crowded town, in presence of an enemy already twice as numerous, and in early expectation of being joined by a third great and victorious army.

During the 17th the battle was not renewed, except by a distant and partial cannonade. The Allies were resolved to have the support of Bernadotte in the decisive contest.

At eight in the morning of the 18th it began, and continued until nightfall without intermission. Buonaparte had contracted on the south, as well as on the north, the circuit of his defence; and never was his generalship, or the gallantry of his troops, more brilliantly displayed than throughout this terrible day. Calm and collected, the Emperor again presided in person on the southern side, and again, where he was present, in spite of the vast superiority of the enemy's numbers, the French maintained their ground to the end. On the north, the arrival of Bernadotte enabled Blucher to push his advantages with irresistible effect; and the situation of Marmont and Ney (now also stationed on that side) was further perplexed by the shameful defection of 10,000 Saxons, who went over with all their artillery to the enemy, in the very midst of the battle. The two marshals, therefore, were compelled to retire from point to point, and at nightfall lay almost close to the walls of Leipsig. Three cannon shot, as before, marked the general termination of the battle.

The loss on either side had been great. Napoleon's army consisted chiefly of very young men--many were merely boys--the produce of his forestalled conscriptions: yet they fought as bravely as the guard. The behaviour of the Germans, on the other hand, at length considering their freedom and independence as hanging on the fortune of a single field, had been answerable to the deep enthusiasm of that thoughtful people. The burghers of Leipsig surveyed from their towers and steeples one of the longest, sternest, and bloodiest of battles: and the situation of the King of Saxony, who remained all the while in the heart of his ancient city, may be imagined.

Napoleon gave orders at midnight for the commencement of the inevitable retreat; and while the darkness lasted, the troops continued to file through the town, and across the two bridges, over the Pleisse, beyond its walls. One of these bridges was a temporary fabric, and it broke down ere daylight came to show to the enemy the movement of the French. The confusion necessarily accompanying the march of a whole army, through narrow streets and upon a single bridge, was fearful. The Allies stormed at the gates on either side, and, but for the heroism of Macdonald and Poniatowski, to whom Napoleon entrusted the defence of the suburbs, it is doubted whether he himself could have escaped in safety. At nine in the morning of the 19th, he bade farewell for ever to the King of Saxony, who remained to make what terms he could with the allied sovereigns. The battle was ere then raging all round the walls.

At eleven o'clock the Allies had gathered close to the bridge from either wing; and the walls over against it had been entrusted to Saxons, who now, like their brethren of the day before, turned their fire on the French. The officer to whom Napoleon had committed the task of blowing up the bridge, when the advance of the enemy should render this necessary, conceived that the time was come, and set fire to his train. The crowd of men, urging each other on the point of safety, could not at once be stopped. Soldiers and horses, cannons and wains, rolled headlong into the deep though narrow river; which renewed, though on a smaller scale, the horrors of the Beresina. Marshal Macdonald swam the stream in safety: the gallant Poniatowski, the hope and pride of Poland, had been twice wounded ere he plunged his horse into the current, and he sank to rise no more. Twenty-five thousand Frenchmen, the means of escape entirely cut off, laid down their arms within the city. Four Princes, each entering at the head of his own victorious army, met at noon in the great market-place at Leipsig: and all the exultation of that solemn hour would have been partaken by the inhabitants, but for the fate of their own sovereign, personally esteemed and beloved, who now vainly entreated to be admitted to the presence of the conquerors, and was sent forthwith as a prisoner of war to Berlin.

Napoleon, in killed, wounded, and prisoners, lost at Leipsig at least 50,000 men.

The retreat of the French through Saxony was accompanied with every disaster which a hostile peasantry, narrowness of supplies, and the persevering pursuit of the Cossacks and other light troops could inflict on a disordered and disheartened mass of men. The soldiers moved on, while under the eye of Napoleon, in gloomy silence: wherever he was not present, they set every rule of discipline at nought, and were guilty of the most frightful excesses. The Emperor conducted himself as became a great mind amidst great misfortunes. He appeared at all times calm and self-possessed; receiving, every day that he advanced, new tidings of evil.

He halted for two days at Erfurt, where extensive magazines had been established, employing all his energies in the restoration of discipline: and would have remained longer, had he not learned that the victors of Leipsig were making progress on either flank of his march, while the Bavarians (so recently his allies), reinforced by some Austrian divisions, were moving rapidly to take post between him and the Rhine. He resumed his march, therefore, on the 25th. It was here that Murat quitted the army. Notwithstanding the unpleasant circumstances under which he had retired to Naples in January, Joachim had reappeared when the Emperor fixed his headquarters at Dresden in the summer, and served with his usual gallantry throughout the rest of the campaign. The state of Italy now demanded his presence; and the two brothers-in-law, after all their differences, embraced each other warmly and repeatedly at parting--as if under a mutual presentiment that they were parting to meet no more.

The Austro-Bavarians had taken up a position amidst the woods near Hanau before the Emperor approached the Mayne. He came up with them in the morning of the 30th, and his troops charged on the instant with the fury of desperation. Buonaparte cut his way through ere nightfall; and Marmont, with the rear, had equal success on the 31st. In these actions there fell 6000 of the French; but the enemy had 10,000 killed or wounded, and lost 4000 prisoners, and these losses would have been far greater but for the ready wit of a patriotic miller, who, watching the tide of battle, suddenly let the water into his mill-stream, and thus interposed a seasonable obstacle between the French cavalry and some German infantry, whom they had been driving before them; a service which the King of Prussia subsequently rewarded with munificence.

The pursuit on the road which Napoleon adopted had been entrusted to the Austrians, who urged it with far less vigour than the Prussians under the fiery guidance of Blucher would probably have exerted. No considerable annoyance, therefore, succeeded to the battle of Hanau. The relics of the French host at length passed the Rhine; and the Emperor having quitted them at Mentz, arrived in Paris on the 9th of November.

The armies of Austria and Prussia at length halted on the Rhine. To the Germans of every age this great river has been the object of an affection and reverence scarcely inferior to that with which an Egyptian contemplates the Nile, or the Indian his Ganges. When these brave bands having achieved the rescue of their native soil, came in sight of this its ancient landmark, the burden of an hundred songs, they knelt, and shouted the Rhine! the Rhine! as with the heart and voice of one man. They that were behind rushed on, hearing the cry, in expectation of another battle.

[Footnote 63: Hoffman's Account of his own Life.]

[Footnote 64: Blucher was created Prince of Wahlstadt.]

CHAPTER XXXIV

Declaration of the Allies at Frankfort--Revolution of Holland--Liberation of the Pope and Ferdinand VII.--Obstinacy of Napoleon--His Military Preparations--Dissolution of the Legislative Senate.

Of the events which crowded upon each other in the space of a few weeks after the overthrow of Leipsig, any one would in times less extraordinary have been sufficient to form an epoch in history. Having once reached the summit of his greatness, the long-favoured child of fortune was destined to sink even more rapidly than he had ascended. Every day added some new alliance to the camp of his foreign enemies; and every hour that passed brought with it clearer indications that the French nation (considered apart from the army) were weary utterly of the very names of War, and Ambition, and Napoleon.

The fabric of his German empire crumbled into nothing, as at the spell of a magician. Hanover returned to the dominion of its rightful sovereign immediately. Brunswick, Hesse, and the other states which had formed Jerome's kingdom of Westphalia, followed the same example. The Confederation of the Rhine was dissolved for ever; and the princes who had adhered to that league were permitted to expiate their, in most cases involuntary, error, by now bringing a year's revenue and a double conscription to the banner of the Allies. Bernadotte turned from Leipsig to reduce the garrisons which Napoleon, in the rashness of his presumption, had disdained to call in, even when compelled to evacuate Dresden; and one by one they fell, though in most cases--particularly at Dantzick, Wirtemberg, and Hamburg--the resistance was obstinate and long. The Crown Prince--having witnessed the reduction of some of these fortresses, and entrusted the siege of the others to his lieutenants--invaded Denmark, and the government of that country perceived the necessity of acceding to the European alliance, by whatever fine its long adhesion to Napoleon might be expiated. The treaty was concluded at Kiel, on the 14th of January, 1814. Sweden yielded Pomerania to Denmark; Denmark gave up Norway to Sweden; and 10,000 Danish troops having joined his standard, Bernadotte then turned his face towards the Netherlands.

In Holland, no sooner had the story of Leipsig reached it than a complete, though bloodless revolution was effected. The cry of _orange boven_, "up with the orange," burst simultaneously from every part of the country: the French governors, yielding to a power which they perceived the absurdity of attempting to resist, retired on the instant, and the long-exiled Stadtholder, the Prince of Orange, returning in triumph from England, assumed the administration of affairs in November, 1813. A few French garrisons remained shut up in strong places, of which the most important was Bergen-op-Zoom; and Bernadotte now co-operated with the Russian corps of Witzingerode, the Prussians of Bulow, and a British force of 10,000, under Sir T. Graham,[65] with the view of completing the deliverance of Holland; which was ere long effected, with the exception of Bergen-op-Zoom, from whose walls the English were repulsed with dreadful slaughter.

On the side of Italy the aspect of affairs was almost as dark. General Hiller, having conducted an Austrian army through the Tyrol, as soon as the decision of his government was taken, had defeated Eugene Beauharnois, and driven him behind the Adige. The Croats, the Tyrolese, all the Illyrians were rising, and--so far from giving aid in the defence of the French soil--it was manifest that the Viceroy could hardly hope to maintain himself much longer in Lombardy. An English naval force had already taken Trieste: the Adriatic was free; and, to complete Napoleon's perplexity as to this quarter, it was no longer a secret that Murat, his brother-in-law, his creature, was negotiating with Austria, and willing, provided that Naples were guaranteed to him, to array the force of that state also on the side of the confederacy.

As little comfort could Buonaparte derive if he turned to the Pyrenees. He had sent Soult thither from Dresden, to retrieve if possible the fortunes of the army defeated in June at Vittoria; and that most able general, with considerable reinforcements, had entered Spain, and attempted to relieve the siege of Pamplona--of which strong place, as well as St. Sebastian Lord Wellington had resolved to be master before he should pass the French frontier with his victorious army. But Soult also had been twice defeated; the fortresses had fallen: except a detached, and now useless force under Suchet in Catalonia, there remained no longer a single French soldier in Spain. The Peninsula had at length been delivered by the genius of Wellington; and his army were cantoned within the territory of France ere the close of the campaign. Such were the tidings which reached Napoleon from his Italian and Spanish frontiers, at the very moment when it was necessary for him to make head against the Russians, the Austrians, and the Germans, chiefly armed and supplied at the expense of England, and now rapidly concentrating in three great masses on different points of the valley of the Rhine.

Nor were even these the worst tidings. Two parties, of which one had not of late years attracted much public notice, and the other had as long wanted efficient leaders, were well-known ere now to be labouring throughout France, though not as yet in conjunction, for one common purpose--the deposition of Buonaparte. The royalists had recovered a great share of their ancient influence in the society of Paris, even before the disasters of the Russian expedition. The exiled Bourbon had found means to distribute proclamations early in 1813: his agents had ever since been exerting themselves indefatigably, both in Paris and in the provinces, especially in those of the west. The Mayor of Bourdeaux (Lynch) was at the head of a loyal association, comprehending the chief inhabitants of that great city, and already in communication with the Marquess of Wellington, who, however, felt it his duty to check them on this occasion, lest the progress of events should render their efforts fruitless to Louis, and fatal to themselves. La Roche Jacquelein (a name already so illustrious in La Vende) had once more prepared that faithful province for insurrection. Saintonge had been organised by the Abb?Jaqualt; Perigord by Messieurs de la Roche Aymon; and in the countries about Nantes, Angers, and Orleans, great bands, consisting partly of Buonaparte's own refractory conscripts, were in training under the Counts De L'Orge, D'Antichamp, and Suzannet. The royalist gentlemen of Touraine, to the number of 1000, were headed by the Duke of Duras; those of Brittany were mustering around Count Vittray, and various chieftains of the old Chouans; and Cadoudal, brother to Georges, was among the peasantry of Varnes. These names, most of them well-known in the early period of the Revolution, are of themselves sufficient to show how effectually the Buonapartean government had endeavoured, during thirteen years, to extinguish the old fire of loyalty. It had all the while glowed under the ashes, and it was now ready to burst forth shining and bright. The Bourbon princes watched the course of events with eager hope. The Duke of Berri was already in Jersey, Monsieur (now Charles X.) in the Netherlands, and the Duke D'Angouleme about to make his appearance at the headquarters of Wellington, in Bearn, the cradle of his race. The republicans, meanwhile,-- those enthusiasts of the Revolution who had in the beginning considered Buonaparte's consulate as a dictatorship forced on France by the necessities of the time, and to be got rid of as soon as opportunity should serve--and who had long since been wholly alienated from him, by his assumption of the imperial dignity, his creation of orders and nobles, his alliance with the House of Austria, and the complete despotism of his internal government--these men had observed, with hardly less delight than the royalists, that succession of reverses which darkens the story of the two last campaigns. Finally, not a few of Napoleon's own ministers and generals, irritated by his personal violence, and hopeless of breathing in peace while that fierce and insatiable spirit continued at the head of affairs, were well prepared to take a part in his overthrow; nor was it long ere all these internal enemies, at whatever distance their principles and motives might have seemed to place them from each other, were content to overlook their differences and work together. Talleyrand, there can be little doubt, and others only second to him in influence, were in communication with the Bourbons, before the Allies crossed the Rhine. Ere then, said Napoleon at St. Helena, _I felt the reins slipping from my hands_.

The allied princes issued, at Frankfort on the Mayne, a manifesto, the firm and temperate language of which was calculated to make a strong impression in France, as well as elsewhere. The sovereigns announced their belief that it was for the interest of Europe that France should continue to be a powerful state, and their willingness to concede to her, even now, greater extent of territory than the Bourbon kings had ever claimed--the boundaries, namely, of the Rhine, the Alps, and the Pyrenees. Their sole object in invading France was to put an end to the authority which Napoleon had usurped over other nations. They disclaimed any wish to interfere with the internal government-- it was the right of the nation to arrange that as they pleased; the hostility of Europe was against, not France, but Napoleon--and even as to Napoleon, against not his person, but his system. The same terms were tendered to Napoleon himself, through M. de St. Aignan, one of his own ministers, who happened to have fallen into the hands of the Allies at Weimar; and his answer was such that diplomatists from all the belligerent powers forthwith assembled at Manheim;--Lord Aberdeen appearing on the part of the government of England--a circumstance of itself sufficient to give to these new conferences a character of greater promise than had attended any of recent date.

But although Napoleon authorised Caulaincourt to commence this negotiation on his behalf, it was very soon manifest that he did so merely, as before, for the purpose of gaining time. His military preparations were urged with unremitting energy. New conscriptions were called for, and granted: every arsenal resounded with the fabrication of arms: and all the taxes were at once doubled by an imperial decree. The enslaved press proclaimed that the national ardour was thoroughly stirred, and with its thousand voices reminded the Allies of the effects of the Duke of Brunswick's proclamation when about to touch the sacred soil of France in 1793.

But the enthusiasm of the revolutionary period was long since gone by. In vain did Napoleon send special agents through the departments, calling on Frenchmen of all classes to rise in arms for the protection of the soil. Coldness, languor, distrust met them almost everywhere. The numerical results even of the conscription-levy were far under what they should have been; and of those who did enrol themselves, multitudes daily deserted, and not a few took part with those royalist bands who were, as we have already seen, mustering and training zealously in almost every district that was either strong by nature, or remote from the great military establishments of Buonaparte. Nay, even the Legislative Senate, so long the silent and submissive slaves of all his imperial mandates, now dared to testify some sympathy with the feelings of the people, whom, in theory at least, they were supposed to represent. This was a novelty for which Napoleon had not been prepared, and he received it in a manner little likely to conciliate the attachment of wavering men. They ventured to hint that ancient France would remain to him, even if he accepted the proposals of the Allies, and that Louis XIV., when he desired to rouse the French people in his behalf in a moment of somewhat similar disaster, had not disdained to detail openly the sincere efforts which he had made to obtain an honourable peace. "Shame on you!" cried the Emperor, "Wellington has entered the south, the Russian menace the northern frontier, the Prussians, Austrians, and Bavarians, the eastern. Shame! Wellington is in France, and we have not risen en masse to drive him back! All my Allies have deserted--the Bavarian has betrayed me. No peace till we have burned Munich! I demand a levy of 300,000 men--with this and what I already have, I shall see a million in arms. I will form a camp of 100,000 at Bourdeaux; another at Mentz; a third at Lyons. But I must have grown men--these boys serve only to encumber the hospitals and the road-sides.... Abandon Holland! sooner yield it back to the sea! Senators, an impulse must be given--all must march--you are fathers of families--the heads of the nation--you must set the example. Peace! I hear of nothing but peace when all around should echo to the cry of war." The senate, nevertheless, drew up and presented a report which renewed his wrath. He reproached them openly with desiring to purchase inglorious ease for themselves at the expense of his honour. _I am the state, said he, repeating a favourite expression: What is the throne?--a bit of wood gilded and covered with velvet--I am the state--I alone am here the representative of the people. Even if I had done wrong you should not have reproached me in public--people wash their dirty linen at home. France has more need of me than I of France._

Having uttered these furious words, Napoleon repaired to his council of state, and there denounced the legislative senate, as composed of one part of traitors and eleven of dupes. In place of assisting, said he, _they impede me. Our attitude alone could have repelled the enemy--they invite him. We should have presented a front of brass--they lay open wounds to his view. I will not suffer their report to be printed. They have not done their duty, but I will do mine--I dissolve the Legislative Senate_. And the Emperor did accordingly issue his decree, proroguing indefinitely that assembly, the last feeble shadow of popular representation in France.

The greatest confusion already began to pervade almost every department of the public service. The orders of the government were more peremptory than ever, and they were hourly more neglected. Whole bands of conscripts, guilty of endeavouring to escape, were tried by military commissions and decimated. Even close to the barriers of Paris such executions were constantly going on; and all in vain. The general feeling was that of sullen indifference. Hireling musicians paraded the streets, singing fine-new ballads in honour of the Emperor, to a long-forgotten tune ; the passengers gathered round them, and drowned the strains in hooting and laughter. In every saloon discussions such as the police had long suppressed were urged without ceremony. _This will not continue; the cord is too much stretched--it will soon be over_; such was the universal language. Talleyrand, hearing an officer express his alarm and astonishment, made answer in words which have passed into a proverb:--It is the beginning of the end.

During this uneasy pause, Napoleon at last dismissed his venerable prisoner of Fontainebleau. It is not unlikely that, in the altered state of Italy, he thought the arrival of the Pope might tend to produce some dissension among his enemies in that quarter; and, in effect, when Pius reached Rome, he found the capital of the Catholic world in the hands of Murat, who had ere then concluded his treaty with Francis, and was advancing into the north of Italy, in the view of co-operating in the campaign against Beauharnois, with the Austrians on the one side, and on the other, with an English force recently landed at Leghorn, under Lord William Bentinck.

He also unlocked the gates of Valeney on Ferdinand of Spain; and, without doubt, the letter, in which he announced this intention to his injured victim, will ever be recorded among the prime instances of his audacity. He informed Ferdinand that the English were spreading _jacobin principles_ in Spain, and attacking the foundations of the throne, the aristocracy, and the church; and that he, therefore, was anxious to see him at the head of affairs in the kingdom, provided he would expel the English, and re-establish its relations with France, on the footing of the peace which gave Godoy his title. Ferdinand durst not execute any treaty without consulting the Cortes. They disdained to treat at all with Napoleon. He then liberated the King unconditionally; and after five years' captivity, Ferdinand re-entered Spain, amidst the all but universal acclamations of a nation, who had bled at every pore in his cause, and whom his government was destined ere long to satisfy that they had bled in vain. Napoleon, no doubt, understood well what sort of a present he was conferring on the Spaniards when he restored Ferdinand, and probably calculated that his arrival would fill the country with civil tumults, sufficient to paralyse its arm for foreign war. And--had the King returned but a year earlier--such, in all likelihood, would have been the consequence. Once more Napoleon was too late in doing good that evil might follow.

For some time, thanks to the slavery of the Parisian press, the population of the capital remained in ignorance as to the proceedings of the Allies on the Rhine. Indeed--such was still the influence of the Emperor's military reputation--the inhabitants of the French provinces on that frontier, continued to believe it impossible that any foreign army should dare to invade their soil, until they that had ears to hear, and eyes to see, were perforce undeceived. Schwartzenberg, with the Grand Army, at length crossed the Rhine, between Basle and Schaffhausen, on the 20th of December, and disregarding the claim of the Swiss to preserve neutrality, advanced through that territory unopposed, and began to show themselves in Franche-Comt? in Burgundy, even to the gates of Dijon. On the 1st of

January, 1814, the Silesian Army, under Blucher, crossed the river at various points between Rastadt and Coblentz; and shortly after, the Army of the North, commanded by Witzingerode and Bulow (for Bernadotte declined having any part in the actual invasion of France) began to penetrate the frontier of the Netherlands. The wealthier inhabitants of the invaded provinces escaped to Paris, bearing with them these tidings; the English of Verdun were seen traversing the capital on their route to more distant quarters; the state prisoners of Vincennes itself, under the walls of Paris, were removed. The secret, in a word, could no longer be kept. It was known to every one that the Pyrenees had been crossed by Wellington, and the Rhine by three mighty hosts, amounting together to 300,000 men, and including representatives of every tongue and tribe, from the Germans of Westphalia to the wildest barbarians of Tartary. Persons of condition despatched their plate and valuables to places at a distance from the capital; many whole families removed daily; and the citizens of Paris were openly engaged in laying up stores of flour and salted provisions, in contemplation of a siege.

The violation of the Swiss territory was in itself indefensible; but he who had so often disdained all rules of that kind in his own person, who had seized D'Enghien, who had traversed Bareuth, could hardly hope to be listened to when he complained of Schwartzenberg's proceeding. The allied generals, moreover, proclaimed everywhere as they advanced, that they came as the friends not the enemies of the French nation, and that any of the peasantry who took up arms to oppose them must be content to abide the treatment of brigands. This assuredly was a flagrant outrage against the most sacred and inalienable rights of mankind: but Napoleon had set the fatal example himself in Lombardy, and followed it without a blush, in Egypt, in Germany, in Spain, in Portugal, and but yesterday in Russia. Here also, therefore, his reclamations moved no feeling favourable to himself; and the time was gone by when the French people would have been ready to take fire at so lawless an aggression upon their national rights:--these Napoleon's tyranny had trampled down ere strangers dared to insult them. There were some few scattered instances of resistance; but in general, the first advance of the Allies was regarded with indifference; and it was only at a later period, when the invading generals were no longer able to maintain strict discipline among their barbarous hordes of horsemen, then scattered over a wide extent of country, that the sense of individual suffering afforded even a glimpse of hope to Napoleon, and those who, like him, were eager to oppose a national insurrection to the allied march.

Meantime, nearer and nearer every day the torrent of invasion rolled on--sweeping before it, from post to post, the various corps which had been left to watch the Rhine. Marmont, Mortier, Victor, and Ney, commanding in all about 50,000 men, retired of necessity before the enemy. It had been considered as certain that much time must be occupied with the besieging of the great fortresses on the Rhenish frontier. But it was now apparent that the Allies had resolved to carry the war into the interior, without waiting for the reduction of these formidable outworks. Their numbers were such that they could afford to mask them, and still pass on with hosts overwhelmingly superior to all those of Napoleon's lieutenants. These withdrew, and with them, and behind them, came crowds of the rustic population possessing any means of transport. Carts and waggons, crammed with terrified women and children, thronged every avenue to the capital. It was at last necessary that the Emperor should break silence to the Parisians, and re-appear in the field.

The invasion of France, however, rallied around Napoleon some persons of eminence who had long hung aloof from him. Carnot in particular, who, ever since he opposed the assumption of the imperial title, had remained in retirement, came forward to offer his sword in what he now considered as the cause of his country. Nor did Buonaparte fail to receive such proposals as they deserved. He immediately sent his old enemy to command the great city and fortress of Antwerp; and similar instances of manly confidence might be mentioned to his honour.

On the 22nd of January the first official news of the invasion appeared; the Moniteur announced that Schwartzenberg had entered Switzerland on the 20th of December, and that Blucher also had crossed the Rhine on the first day of the year; thus confessing openly the deliberate deceit of its previous silence. The next morning, being Sunday, the officers of the National Guard were summoned to the Tuileries. They lined the Saloon of the Marshals, to the number of 900, altogether ignorant of the purpose for which they had been convoked. The Emperor took his station in the centre of the hall; and immediately afterwards the Empress with the King of Rome (carried in the arms of Countess Montesquiou), appeared at his side. "Gentlemen," said Napoleon, "France is invaded; I go to put myself at the head of my troops, and, with God's help and their valour, I hope soon to drive the enemy beyond the frontier." Here he took Maria Louisa in one hand and her son in the other, and continued--"But if they should approach the capital, I confide to the National Guard the Empress and the King of Rome"--then correcting himself, he said in a tone of strong emotion--"_my wife and my child_." Several officers stepped from their places and approached him; and tears were visible on the cheeks even of those who were known to be no worshippers of the Emperor, or hearty supporters of his cause.

A Frenchman can rarely resist a scene: and such this was considered, and laughed at accordingly, ere next morning. It is, nevertheless, difficult to refuse sympathy to the chief actor. Buonaparte was sincerely attached to Maria Louisa, though he treated her rather with a parental tenderness than like a lover; and his affection for his son was the warmest passion in his heart, unless, indeed, we must except his pride and his ambition, both of which may be well supposed to have merged for a moment in the feeling which shook his voice.

[Footnote 65: Now Lord Lynedoch.]

CHAPTER XXXV

The Campaign of France--Battles of Brienne and La Rothiere--Expedition of the Marne--Battles of Nangis and Montereau--Schwartzenberg Retreats--Napoleon again marches against Blucher--Attacks Soissons and is Repulsed--Battles of Craonne and Laon--Napoleon at Rheims--His Perplexities--He Marches to St. Dizier.

Napoleon spent part of the 24th of January in reviewing troops in the courtyard of the Tuileries, in the midst of a fall of snow, which must have called up ominous recollections, and at three in the morning of the 25th, once more left his capital. He had again appointed Maria Louisa Regent, placed his brother Joseph at the head of her council, and given orders for raising military defences around Paris, and for converting many public buildings into hospitals. He set off in visible dejection; but recovered all his energy on reaching once more the congenial atmosphere of arms.

He arrived at Chalons ere midnight; and found that Schwartzenberg and

Blucher, having severally passed through Franche-Comt?and Lorraine, were now occupying--the former with 97,000 men, the latter with 40,000--an almost complete line between the Marne and the Seine. Blucher was in his own neighbourhood, and he immediately resolved to attack the right of the Silesian army, which was pushing down the valley of the Marne, while its centre kept the parallel course of the Aube, ere the Prussian marshal could concentrate all his own strength, far less be adequately supported from the side of Schwartzenberg, who was advancing down the Seine towards Bar. A sharp skirmish took place accordingly on the 27th at St. Dizier; and Blucher, warned of Napoleon's arrival, lost no time in calling in his detachments, and taking a post of defence at Brienne-le-Chateau on the Aube--the same town where Buonaparte had received his military education. Could Napoleon force him from the Aube, it was evident that the French would be enabled to interpose themselves effectually between the two armies of the Allies: and it was most necessary to divide the enemy's strength, for after all his exertions, Napoleon had been able to add only 20,000 good troops to the 50,000 who had been retiring before the allied columns from the course of the Rhine.

Napoleon, therefore, marched through a thick forest upon the scene of his youthful studies, and appeared there on the 29th:--having moved so rapidly that Blucher was at dinner in the chateau, when the French thundered at his gates, and with difficulty escaped to the rear through a postern--actually leading his horse down a stair. The Russians, however, under Alsusieff, maintained their place in the town courageously; and, some Cossacks throwing themselves upon the rear of the French, the Emperor himself was involved in the mel 閑, drew his sword, and fought like a private dragoon. General Gourgaud shot a Cossack when in the act of thrusting his spear at Napoleon's back. The town of Brienne was burnt to the ground; Alsusieff was made prisoner; Lefebre Desnouettes died; and there was considerable slaughter on both sides; but the affair had no result of importance. Blucher retired but a little further up the Aube, and posted himself at La Rothiere, where Schwartzenberg, warned by the cannonade, hastened to co-operate with him.

Napoleon said at St. Helena, that during the charge of the Cossacks at Brienne, he recognised a particular tree, under which, when a boy, he used to sit and read the Jerusalem Delivered of Tasso. The field had been, in those days, part of the exercise ground of the students, and the chateau, whence

Blucher escaped so narrowly, their lodging. How strange must have been the feelings of the man who, having but yesterday planted his eagles on the Kremlin, now opened his fifteenth campaign amidst the scenes of his own earliest recollections--of the days in which he had never dreamt of empire!

On the first of February Blucher, in his turn, assumed the offensive, assaulting the French position in his front at once on three several points. The battle lasted all day, and ended in the defeat of the French, who, with the loss of 4000 prisoners and seventy-three guns, escaped from the field in such disorder, that, according to Napoleon's own avowal at St. Helena, he had serious thoughts of putting an end to the war by voluntarily resigning the crown to the heir of the Bourbons. However this may have been, while the division of Marmont retired down the Aube before Blucher, Napoleon himself struck across the country to Troyes, which there was every reason to fear must be immediately occupied by Schwartzenberg; and was there joined by a considerable body of his own guard, in high order and spirits, whose appearance restored, in a great measure, the confidence of the troops beaten at La Rothiere.

On the 3rd, he received at Troyes a despatch from Caulaincourt, informing him that Lord Castlereagh, the English Secretary of State for Foreign Affairs, had arrived at the headquarters of the Allies--that negotiations were to be resumed the morning after at Chatillon--(now in the rear of the armies), and beseeching him to intimate distinctly at what price he was now willing to purchase peace. Napoleon replied, by granting Caulaincourt full powers to do everything necessary "to keep the negotiation alive, and save the capital." But the Duke of Vicenza durst not act immediately on a document so loosely worded, and sent back once more to beg for a specific detail of the Emperor's purposes. Napoleon had his headquarters at Nogent, on the Seine, some leagues below Troyes, when the despatch reached him, on the evening of the 8th of February; and his counsellors unanimously urged him to make use of this, probably last, opportunity. They at length prevailed on him to agree to abandon Belgium, the left of the Rhine, Italy, and Piedmont. But in the night after the consultation, and before the ultimatum received his signature, Napoleon received information which quite altered his views. He learned that Blucher, instead of continuing his march down the Aube, and in communication with Schwartzenberg on the Seine, had transferred his whole army to the Marne, and was now advancing towards Paris by the Montmirail road. That the Allies, after experiencing the effects of disunion at Brienne, and those of conjunction at La Rothiere, should have almost in the moment of victory again resolved on separating their forces, is a circumstance which no writer has as yet explained in any satisfactory manner. The blunder was great; yet in the end its consequences were disastrous, not to those who committed, but to him whose eagle-eye detected it, and who could not resist the temptation which it presented, to make one warlike effort more. Buonaparte, in a word, refused to sign the despatch on the morning of the 9th; and having left Bourmont at Nogent, with a small force to defend the bridge over the Seine, and Oudinot with another, for the same purpose, at the next bridge in descending the river, namely, that of Bray, immediately commenced his march with the main body of his army upon Sezanne.

It was the depth of winter--the cross-roads on which they moved were in the most frightful condition, insomuch that had not the zealous Mayor of Barbonne collected 500 horses, and come to their assistance, they must have been forced to leave all their artillery in a slough near that town; yet this determined band marched nearly forty miles ere they halted with the dark. Next morning they proceeded with equal alacrity, and at length debouched on the road by which Blucher's army was advancing, at Champaubert. Alsusieff and the central division were passing, when Napoleon unexpectedly appeared at this point, and were altogether unable to resist his onset. They dispersed in confusion with great loss, and fled towards the Marne. Meantime the van of the same army, commanded by Sacken, who were advancing on La Fert? and the division of D'York, already in sight of Meaux, turned on hearing the cannonade of Champaubert, and countermarched with the view of supporting Alsusieff. They shared the fate of the centre, and having been severely handled at Montmirail, escaped across the Marne at Chateau-Tierry; thus leaving Blucher and the rear division alone to abide the attack of Napoleon's entire force between the Marne and the Aube. The Prussian marshal, advancing rapidly in consequence of the firing of these battles, found himself all at once in presence of an army flushed with victory, vastly superior in numbers, and well provided with cavalry, of which he had almost none. He retired in alternate squares, sustaining all day the charges of the French, with much loss of life, but with no disorder; and at length cut his way, at Etoges, through a column of heavy horse, sent round to intercept him, and drawn up on the causeway. Blucher himself was, in the course of this day, obliged to fight hand to hand like a private soldier. His retreat was masterly, and he finally crossed the Marne at Chalons.

Such was Napoleon's celebrated "Expedition of the Marne." In five days his arms had been three times successful. He had shattered and dispersed (as he thought effectually) the Silesian army, and above all, recovered the spirits of his own soldiery. A column of 7000 Prussian prisoners, with a considerable number of guns and standards, at length satisfied the Parisians that Victory had not entirely forsworn her old favourite. Thus far all was well; and had Napoleon, from the field which thus raised the courage of his troops, and revived the confidence of his capital, despatched authority to Caulaincourt to conclude the treaty on the terms before described--the victor of Montmirail might have kept the throne of France. But his own presumption was rekindled by the same success which dazzled inferior eyes--and Napoleon wrote on the instant to his representative at Chatillon, that he might now assume "an attitude less humble." This error proved fatal.

Scarcely had the Parisians seen the prisoners from Montmirail marched along their boulevards, before they heard that the Cossacks were in possession of Fontainebleau. Napoleon had left, as was mentioned, small divisions of his army to guard the bridges over the Seine at Nogent and Bray. The enemy, however, soon discovered that the Emperor and his chief force were no longer in that quarter, and--while he was beating Alsusieff, Sacken, and Blucher--had made good the passage of the Seine, at three different points, at Nogent, at Bray, and still further down, at Montereau, driving the discomfited guardians of these important places before them. Schwartzenberg had already his headquarters at Nangis, and was obviously resolved to reach Paris, if possible, while Napoleon was on the Marne. The light troops of the grand allied army were scattering confusion on both sides of the Seine--and one party of them were so near the capital as Fontainebleau.

Buonaparte instantly committed to Marmont and Mortier the care of watching the Chalons road and the remains of Blucher's army, and marched with his main body on Meaux, where he received (15th February) the welcome reinforcement of 20,000 veterans from Spain, commanded by Grouchy. On the 16th, Victor and Oudinot were engaged with the van of Schwartzenberg, on the plains of Guignes, when the Emperor arrived to their assistance. The enemy immediately drew back, and concentrated his strength at Nangis. Napoleon attacked that position on the morning of the 17th, and with such effect, that the allies retreated after considerable loss, though not in disorder, on the bridges in their rear.

They halted, however, at Montereau, and Victor, who commanded the pursuers on that route, failed in dislodging them. Napoleon resented this as a heinous error, and coming up on the morning of the 18th, rebuked him in terms of violent wrath, and formally dismissed him from the service. The Marshal, tears streaming down his face, declared that though he had ceased to be an officer, he must still be a soldier, and would serve once more in the ranks, from which he had originally risen. The old man's son-in-law, General Chateau, had been slain the same morning. Napoleon extended his hand to him, and said he could not give him back the command of his corps d'arm 閑, which had already been assigned to another, but that he was welcome to place himself at the head of a brigade of the guard. The attack then commenced with fury, and the bridge and town of Montereau were carried. The defence was, however, long and stern, and Napoleon was seen pointing cannon with his own hand, under the heaviest of the fire. The artillerymen, delighted with witnessing this resumption of his ancient trade, were, nevertheless, alarmed at the exposure of his person, and entreated him to withdraw. He persisted in his work, answering gaily, "My children! the bullet that shall kill me is not yet cast." Pursuing his advantage, Napoleon saw the grand army continue their retreat in the direction of Troyes, and on the morning of the 22nd arrived before Mery.

The astonishment of the Emperor was great, when he found this town occupied, not by a feeble rear-guard of Schwartzenberg, but by a powerful division of Russians, commanded by Sacken, and, therefore, belonging to the apparently indestructible army of Blucher. These unexpected enemies were charged in the streets, and at length retired out of the town (which was burnt to the ground in the struggle) and thence beyond the Aube--which, in that quarter, runs nearly parallel with, and at no great distance from, the Seine. The Emperor then halted, and spent the night in a wheelwright's cottage at Chatres.

All this while the semblance, at least, of negotiation had been kept up at Chatillon. Caulaincourt, receiving no answer to that important despatch which reached Buonaparte (as has been mentioned) at Nogent, on the 8th of

February proceeded to act on the instructions dated at Troyes, on the 3rd; and, in effect, accepted the basis of the Allies. When Schwartzenberg was attacked at Nangis on the 17th, he had just received the intelligence of Caulaincourt's having signed the preliminary articles; and he, therefore, sent a messenger to ask why the Emperor, if aware of his ambassador's act, persisted in hostilities? Napoleon had ere then, as we have seen, desired Caulaincourt to assume "a less humble attitude," and instead of ratifying, as he was bound on every principle of honour and law to do, the signature which his ambassador had had full powers to affix, he returned no answer whatever to Schwartzenberg, but despatched a private letter to the Emperor of Austria, once more endeavouring to seduce him from the European league. The Emperor's reply to this despatch reached Napoleon at this hovel in Chatres: it announced his resolution on no account to abandon the general cause; but, at the same time, intimated that Francis lent no support to the Bourbonists (who were now arming in Franche-Comt?around Monsieur), and urged Napoleon to avert by concession, ere it was yet too late, total ruin from himself and his House. Buonaparte, flushed with a succession of victories, was in no temper to listen to such advice, and the Austrian envoy left his headquarters with a note, signifying that now he would not even consent to a day's armistice, unless the Allies would fall back so as to leave Antwerp in their front.

The same evening there came news from Paris, which might have been expected to disturb the pride of these imaginations. The Council of State had discussed deliberately the proposals of the Allied Powers, and, with only one dissenting voice, now entreated the Emperor to accept them. They announced to him that--while he had been driving the Austrians up the Seine--the Army of the North, the third great force of the Allies, had at length effected their juncture with Blucher; who was now, therefore, at the head of a much greater army than he had as yet commanded, and was manifestly resolved to descend directly on Paris from Chalons. Napoleon was urged anew by those about his person, to send to Chatillon and accept the basis to which Caulaincourt had agreed. He answered that he had sworn at his coronation to preserve the territory of the Republic entire, and that he could not sign this treaty without violating his oath!--and dismissed his counsellors, saying haughtily, "If I am to be scourged, let the whip at least come on me of necessity, and not through any voluntary stooping of my own."

Instead, therefore, of sending messengers of peace to Chatillon, Napoleon now thought only of the means of at once holding Schwartzenberg in check on the Seine, and returning once more to confront Blucher on the Marne. He pushed on, however, as far as Troyes, in the expectation of still terrifying the allied princes into some compromise. In this city he found that certain gentlemen had openly assumed the white cockade, the mark of the Bourbonists, during its occupation by the enemy, though without any countenance from the sovereigns. One of these gentlemen was so unfortunate as to fall into his hands, and was immediately executed.

The Emperor in vain expected new proposals from Chatillon; none such reached him at Troyes--and he recurred to his scheme of a second "Expedition of the Marne." He desired Oudinot and Macdonald, with their divisions, to manoeuvre in the direction of Schwartzenberg: and these generals commanded their troops to shout "vive l'Empereur" whenever they were within hearing of the enemy, which for a little time kept up the notion that Napoleon himself was still advancing on the road to Bar. Meanwhile he was once more marching rapidly across the country to Sezanne; at which point he received intelligence that Mortier and Marmont had been driven from Fert?sous-Jouarre by Blucher, and were in full retreat to Meaux. Meaux he considered as almost a suburb of Paris, and quickened his speed accordingly. Hurrying on, at Fert?Goucher, he was at once met and overtaken by evil tidings. Schwartzenberg, having discovered the Emperor's absence, had immediately resumed the offensive, defeated Oudinot and Macdonald at Bar, and driven them before him as far as Troyes; and Augereau, who commanded in the neighbourhood of Lyons, announced the arrival of a new and great army of the Allies in that quarter. Napoleon resumed, however, his march, and having been detained some time at Fert? in consequence of the destruction of the bridge, took the direction of Chateau-Thierry and Soissons, while Mortier and Marmont received his orders to resume the offensive in front of Meaux. He hoped, in this manner, to throw himself on the flank of Blucher's march, as he had done before at Champaubert. But the Prussian received intelligence this time of his approach; and, drawing his troops together, retired to Soissons in perfect order.

Napoleon proceeded with alacrity in the direction of Soissons, not doubting that the French garrison entrusted with the care of that town, and its bridge over the Marne, were still in possession of it, and eager, therefore, to force

Blucher into action with this formidable obstacle in his rear. But Soissons had been taken by a Russian corps, retaken by a French one, and fallen once more into the hands of the enemy, ere the Emperor came in sight of it. The Muscovite Black Eagle, floating on the towers, gave him the first intimation of this misfortune. He assaulted the place impetuously: the Russians repelled the attack; and Napoleon, learning that Blucher had filed his main body through the town, and posted himself behind the Marne, marched up the left bank of that river, and crossed it also at Bery.

A few leagues in front of this place, on the heights of Craonne, two Russian corps, those of Sacken and Witzingerode, were already in position; and the Emperor lost no time in charging them there, in the hope of destroying them ere they could unite with Blucher. The battle of Craonne began at eleven a.m. on the 7th of March, and lasted till four in the afternoon. The Russians had down to this hour withstood the utmost exertions of Ney on their right, of Victor on their left, and of Napoleon himself on their centre. The loss in slain and wounded had been about equal on both sides; no cannon, and hardly a prisoner, had been taken. The Emperor, enraged with this obstinate resistance, was preparing for a final effort, when suddenly the Russians began to retreat. He followed them; but they withdrew with the deliberation and impunity of a parade. They had been ordered to fall back on the plateau of Laon, in order to form there on the same line with Blucher, who was once more in presence, and eager to concentrate all his force for a decisive conflict.

It took place on the 9th. Napoleon found his enemy strongly posted along an elevated ridge, covered with wood, and further protected in front by a succession of terrace-walls, the enclosures of vineyards. There was a heavy mist on the lower ground, and the French were advancing up the hill ere their movement was discovered. They were met by a storm of cannonade which utterly broke their centre. On either flank of the enemy's position they then charged in succession, and with like results. On all points they were repelled, except only at the village of Athies, where Marmont had obtained some advantage. Night interrupted the contest, and the armies bivouacked in full view of each other. The Allies, in consequence of their well-covered position, had suffered comparatively little; of the French some thousands had died-- and all in vain. Napoleon was, however, resolved to renew the attack, and mounted his horse accordingly at four in the morning of the 10th. At that moment news came that Marmont's corps had just been assaulted at Athies, and so thoroughly discomfited that they were now flying in confusion towards Corbery. Notwithstanding this ominous opening, the battle in front of Laon was continued all the day. But the tide of fortune had turned, and could not be resisted. On the 11th, Napoleon commenced his retreat, having lost thirty cannon and ten thousand men.

Soissons had been evacuated by the Allies when concentrating themselves for the battle of Laon. Napoleon threw himself, therefore, into that town, and was making his best efforts to strengthen it, in expectation of the Prussian advance, when once more a messenger of evil tidings reached him. A detached Russian corps, commanded by St. Priest, a French emigrant, had seized Rheims by a coup-de-main. The possession of this city (as a glance at any good map will show) could hardly fail to re-establish Blucher's communications with Schwartzenberg--and Napoleon instantly marched thither in person, leaving Marmont to hold out as well as he could at Soissons, in case that should be the direction of Blucher's march. Buonaparte, moving with his usual rapidity, came unexpected on Rheims, and took the place by assault at midnight. St. Priest had fallen; and the bulletin announced that he met his fate by a ball from the same cannon which killed Moreau. If it were so, no one could have ascertained the fact; but Napoleon's imagination was always ready to welcome a tale that savoured of fatality.

From Rheims, where he remained for three days to refresh his unfortunate followers, he despatched at length full powers to Caulaincourt to conclude any treaty, which should secure the immediate evacuation of the old French territory, and a mutual restoration of prisoners. Maret, (Duke of Bassano,) however, wrote--by the same messenger--at much greater length; informing the plenipotentiary that the Emperor would refuse to ratify any treaty whatever--if, in the interim, events should have taken a turn in his favour. It is to be doubted whether Caulaincourt would have ventured to act, on instructions thus qualified, with the decision which the emergency required. But he was not put to the proof. The Allies had determined to negotiate no more, ere the despatch of Rheims reached him.

Throughout this crisis of his history, it is impossible to survey the rapid energy of Napoleon--his alert transitions from enemy to enemy, his fearless assaults on vastly superior numbers, his unwearied resolution, and exhaustless invention--without the highest admiration which can attend on a master of warfare. But it is equally impossible to suppress astonishment and indignation in following, or rather attempting to follow, the threads of obstinacy, duplicity, pride, and perfidy, which, during the same period, complicated, without strengthening, the tissue of his negotiations. It is only when we fix our eyes on the battles and marches of this wonderful campaign, that we can hesitate to echo the adage:--_Whom God hath doomed to destruction, he first deprives of reason._

To complete our notion of the energies of Napoleon--he had all through this, the most extraordinary of his campaigns, continued to conduct, from his perpetually changing headquarters, the civil business of his empire. He occupied himself largely with such matters during his stay at Rheims; but it was there that the last despatches from the home-department at Paris were destined to reach him; and, before he could return his answer, there came couriers upon couriers--with tidings which would have unmanned any other mind, and which filled his with perplexity. On the one side, Blucher had profited by his departure, crushed down the feeble opposition of the corps left at Soissons, and repassed the Marne. On the other hand, Schwartzenberg had detected, almost as soon as it took place, his march on Sezanne, and instantly resumed the offensive. Oudinot and Girard had been forced to give way before the immeasurably superior numbers of the Grand Army. They had been defeated with great slaughter at Bar on the Aube; and the Austrian was once more at Troyes. The Allies were, therefore, to all appearance, in full march upon Paris, both by the valley of the Marne, and by that of the Seine, at the moment when Napoleon had thought to paralyse all their movements by taking up a position between them at Rheims.

He still counted largely on the magic of his name; and even now he had hardly over-reckoned. When Schwartzenberg understood that Napoleon was at Rheims, the old terror returned, and the Austrian instantly proposed to fall back from Troyes. But there was by this time, in the camp of the allied powers, one who, though not a soldier, appreciated, far better than all those about him, that had grown grey in arms, the circumstances of the time, and the conduct which these demanded. Lord Castlereagh took upon himself the responsibility of signifying that the Grand Army might retire if the sovereigns pleased, but that if such a movement took place, the subsidies of England must be considered as at an end. This bold word determined the debate. Schwartzenberg's columns instantly resumed their march down the Seine.

Napoleon, meanwhile, had been struggling with himself; whatever line of action he might adopt was at best hazardous in the extreme. Should he hasten after Blucher on the Marne, what was to prevent Schwartzenberg from reaching Paris, ere the Silesian army, already victorious at Laon, could be once more brought to action by an inferior force? Should he throw himself on the march of Schwartzenberg, would not the fiery Prussian be at the Tuileries, long before the Austrian could be checked on the Seine? There remained a third course--namely, to push at once into the country in the rear of the Grand Army; and to this there were sundry inducements. By doing so, he might possibly--such were still the Emperor's conceptions as to the influence of his name--strike the advancing Allies, both the Austrian and the Prussian, with terror, and paralyse their movements. Were they likely to persist in their _Hurrah on Paris_ (at this period the Cossack vocabulary was in vogue), when they knew Napoleon to be posting himself between them and their own resources, and at the same time relieving and rallying around him all the garrisons of the great fortresses of the Rhine? Would not such conduct be considered as entirely out of the question by superstitious adherents to the ancient technicalities of war? Would not Schwartzenberg at least abandon the advance and turn to follow him, who still fancied that no one could dream of conquering France without having ruined Napoleon? But--even supposing that the allied powers should resist all these suggestions and proceed upon the capital--would not that great city, with Marmont and Mortier, and the national guard, be able to hold the enemy at bay for some considerable space; and, during that space, could the Emperor fail to release his garrisons on the Rhine, and so place himself once more at the head of an army capable, under his unrivalled guidance, of relieving France and ruining her invaders, by a great battle under the walls of Paris?

It must be added, in reference to Napoleon's choice among these difficulties, that ere now the continuance of the warfare had much exacerbated the feelings of the peasantry, who, for the most part, regarded its commencement with indifference. The perpetual marches and counter-marches of the armies, the assaults and burnings of towns and villages, the fierce demeanour of the justly embittered Prussians, and the native barbarism of the Russians, had spread devastation and horror through some of the fairest provinces of France. The desolation was such that wolves and other beasts of prey appeared, in numbers which recalled the ages of the unbroken forest, amidst the vineyards and gardens of Champagne. All who could command the means of flight had escaped; of those that remained there were few who had not, during three months, suffered painful privations, seen their cottages occupied by savage strangers, and their streams running red with the blood of their countrymen. The consequence was that the peasantry on the theatre of the war, and behind it, were now in a state of high excitement. Might not the Emperor, by throwing himself and his sorely diminished, but still formidable, band of veterans among them, give the finishing impulse, and realise at length his fond hope of a national insurrection?

While Napoleon was thus tossed in anxiety by what means to avert, if it were yet possible, from Paris, the visitation of those mighty armies, against whom energies, such as he alone possessed, had been exerted in vain--the capital showed small symptoms of sympathising with him. The newspapers had announced nothing but victories; but the truth could not fail to penetrate in spite of all this treachery. The streets were daily traversed by new crowds of provincialists, driven or terrified from their dwellings. Every hospital, and many public buildings besides, were crammed with wounded soldiers; and the number of dead bodies, continually floating down the Seine was so great, that the meanest of the populace durst no longer make use of the water. As one conclusive token of the universal distrust, it may be mentioned that, whereas in usual times the amount of taxes paid daily into the exchequer at Paris is about ?000, the average, after the 1st of March, did not exceed ?5. It was Savary's business to despatch a full account of the state of the city every night to headquarters;--and he did not hesitate to inform the Emperor that the machinery of government was clogged in every wheel, and that the necessity of purchasing peace, by abandoning him, was the common burden of conversation.

Meantime, to swell the cup of his anxieties, there reached him new intelligence of the most alarming character from the south-western provinces, invaded by Lord Wellington. That victorious general had driven Soult before him through the Pays de Gaves (the tract of strong country broken by the torrents descending from the Pyrenees); defeated him in another great battle at Orthes; and was now pursuing him in the direction of Toulouse. Nor was even this the worst: the English had been received more like friends than enemies by the French; their camp was far better served with provisions than that of Soult; and lastly, Bourdeaux had risen openly in the cause of Louis. The white flag was floating on every tower of the third city in France, and the Duke D'Angouleme was administering all the offices of government, in the midst of a population who had welcomed him with the enthusiasm of old loyalty.

It was amidst such circumstances that Napoleon at length decided on throwing himself on the rear of the Allies. They were for some time quite uncertain of his movements after he quitted Rheims, until an intercepted letter to Maria Louisa informed them that he was at St. Dizier.

CHAPTER XXXVI

The Allies approach Paris--Maria Louisa retires to Blois--Marmont and Mortier occupy the Heights of Montmartre--They are defeated--King Joseph escapes--Marmont capitulates--the Allies enter Paris--Napoleon at Fontainebleau--His abdication.

Napoleon continued for several days to manoeuvre on the country beyond St. Dizier. Having thus seized the roads by which the Grand Army had advanced, he took prisoners many persons of distinction on their way to its headquarters--and at one time the Emperor of Austria himself escaped most narrowly a party of French hussars. Meanwhile petty skirmishes were ever and anon occurring between Napoleon's rear-guard and Austrians, whom he took for the van-guard of Schwartzenberg. They were, however, detached troops, chiefly horse, left expressly to hang on his march, and cheat him into this belief. The Grand Army was proceeding rapidly down the Seine; while Blucher, having repeatedly beaten Marmont and Mortier, was already within sight of Meaux.

It has been mentioned that Napoleon, ere he commenced his campaign, directed some fortifications to be thrown up on the side of Paris nearest to the invading armies. His brother Joseph, however, was, as Spain had witnessed, neither an active nor a skilful soldier; and the civil government of this tempestuous capital appears to have been more than enough to employ what energies he possessed. The outworks executed during the campaign were few and inconsiderable; and to occupy them, there were now but 8000 fresh regulars, the discomfited divisions of Marmont and Mortier, and the

National Guard of the metropolis. This last corps had 30,000 names on its roll: but such had been the manifestations of public feeling, that the Emperor's lieutenants had not dared to furnish more than a third of these with firearms: the others had only pikes: and every hour increased the doubts of the Regency-council whether any considerable portion of these men--who were chiefly, in fact, the shopkeepers of Paris--would consent to shed their blood in this cause.

Meanwhile the royalists within the city had been watching the progress of events with eagerness and exultation. Talleyrand was ere now in close communication with them, and employing all the resources of his talents to prevail on them to couple their demand for the heir of the Bourbons, with such assertions of their belief that that dynasty ought never to be re-established otherwise than on a constitutional basis, as might draw over to their side the more moderate of the republicans. Nor had these efforts been unsuccessful. Various deputations from the royalists had found their way to the headquarters, both of Blucher and Schwartzenberg, before the middle of March, and expressed sentiments of this nature. As yet, however, none of the Allies had ventured to encourage directly the hopes of the Bourbon party. They persisted in asserting their resolution to let the French nation judge for themselves under what government they should live; and to take no part in their civil feuds. Talleyrand himself was in correspondence with the Czar; but, in his letters, he, as far as is known, confined himself to urging the advance of the armies. A billet from him was delivered to Alexander just before the final rush on Paris begun: it was in these words--"You venture nothing, when you may safely venture everything--venture once more."

De Pradt, and many other of those statesmen whom Napoleon, in latter days, had disgraced or disobliged, were, ere this time, labouring diligently in the same service. It must be admitted that he, like the falling Persian, was

"Deserted in his utmost need By those his former bounty fed;"

but he had brought himself to this extremity by his scorn of their counsels; nor even at the eleventh hour did his proud heart dream of recalling confidence, by the confession of error.

On the 26th of March, the distant roaring of artillery was heard at intervals on the boulevards of Paris; and the alarm began to be violent. On the 27th (Sunday) Joseph Buonaparte held a review in the Place Carousel; and the day being fine, and the uniforms mostly new, the confidence of the spectators rose, and the newspapers expressed their wishes that the enemy could but behold what forces were ready to meet and destroy them. That same evening the Allies passed the Marne at various points; at three in the morning of the 28th, they took Meaux; and at daybreak, "the terrified population of the country between Meaux and Paris came pouring into the capital," says an eye-witness, "with their aged, infirm, children, cats, dogs, live-stock, corn, hay, and household goods of every description. The boulevards were crowded with waggons, carts, and carriages thus laden, to which cattle were tied, and the whole surrounded with women." The regular troops now marched out of the town, leaving all the barriers in charge of the National Guard. The confusion that prevailed everywhere was indescribable.

On the 29th, the Empress, her son, and most of the members of the Council of State, set off, attended by 700 soldiers, for Rambouillet--from which they continued their journey to Blois--and in their train went fifteen waggons laden with plate and coin from the vaults of the Tuileries. The spectators looked on their departure in gloomy silence: and King Joseph published the following proclamation; "Citizens of Paris! A hostile column has descended on Meaux. It advances; but the Emperor follows close behind, at the head of a victorious army. The Council of Regency has provided for the safety of the Empress and the King of Rome. I remain with you. Let us arm ourselves to defend this city, its monuments, its riches, our wives, our children--all that is dear to us. Let this vast capital become a camp for some moments; and let the enemy find his shame under the walls which he hopes to overleap in triumph. The Emperor marches to our succour. Second him by a short and vigorous resistance, and preserve the honour of France." No feeling favourable to Napoleon was stirred by this appeal. The boulevards continued to be thronged with multitudes of people; but the most part received the proclamation with indifference--not a few with murmurs. Some officers urged Savary to have the streets unpaved, and persuade the people to arm themselves with the stones, and prepare for a defence such as that of Zaragossa. He answered, shaking his head, "the thing cannot be done."

All day, waggons of biscuit and ammunition were rolling through the town; wounded soldiers came limping to the barriers; and the Seine heaved thicker and thicker with the carcases of horses and men. That night, for once, the theatres were deserted.

On the 30th, the Allies fought and won the final battle. The French occupied the whole range of heights from the Marne at Charenton, to the Seine beyond St. Denis; and the Austrians began the attack about eleven o'clock, towards the former of these points, while nearly in the midst between them, a charge was made by the Russians on Pantin and Belleville. The Prussians, who were posted over against the heights of Montmartre, did not come into action so early in the day. The French troops of the line were stationed everywhere in the front, and commanded by Marmont and Mortier. Those battalions of the National Guard, whose spirit could be trusted, and who were adequately armed, took their orders from Moncey, and formed a second line of defence. The scholars of the Polytechnic School volunteered to serve at the great guns, and the artillery was, though not numerous, well arranged, and in gallant hands.

The French defence, in spite of all the previous disasters, and of the enormous superiority of the enemy's numbers, was most brave: but by two o'clock the Allies had completely beaten them at all points, except only at Montmartre, where they were rapidly making progress. Marmont then sent several aides-de-camp to request an armistice, and offer a capitulation. One only of his messengers appears to have reached the headquarters of the sovereigns--and both the Czar and King of Prussia immediately professed their willingness to spare the city, provided the regular troops would evacuate it. Blucher, meanwhile, continued pressing on at Montmartre, and shortly after four, the victory being completed in that direction, the French cannon were turned on the city, and shot and shells began to spread destruction within its walls. The capitulation was drawn up at five o'clock, close to the barrier St. Denis.

King Joseph showed himself on horseback among the troops early in the morning; but was not visible after the attack began. At one o'clock he received a message from Marmont, requesting reinforcements. "Where am I to find them?" answered he--"is your horse a good one?" The aide-de-camp answered in the affirmative. "Then follow me," said Joseph; and without further ceremony began his journey to Blois.[66]

We must now turn to Napoleon. It was not until the 27th that he distinctly ascertained the fact of both the allied armies having marched directly on Paris. He instantly resolved to hasten after them, in hopes to arrive on their rear, ere yet they had mastered the heights of Montmartre; nor did his troops refuse to rush forward once more at his bidding. He had to go round by Doulevent and Troyes, because the direct route was utterly wasted, and could not furnish food for his men. At Doulevent he received a billet from La Vallette, his Post-Master General, in these terms: "The partisans of the stranger are making head, seconded by secret intrigues. The presence of the Emperor is indispensable--if he desires to prevent his capital from being delivered to the enemy. There is not a moment to be lost." Urging his advance accordingly with renewed eagerness--Buonaparte reached Troyes on the night of the 29th--his men having marched fifteen leagues since the daybreak. On the 30th, Macdonald in vain attempted to convince him that the fate of Paris must have been decided ere he could reach it, and advised him to march without further delay so as to form a conjunction with Augereau. "In that case," said the marshal, "we may unite and repose our troops, and yet give the enemy battle on a chosen field. If Providence has decreed our last hour, we shall, at least, die with honour, instead of being dispersed, pillaged, and slaughtered by Cossacks." Napoleon was deaf to all such counsel. He continued to advance. Finding the road beyond Troyes quite clear, he threw himself into a postchaise, and travelled on before his army at full speed, with hardly any attendance. At Villeneuve L'Archeveque he mounted on horseback, and galloping without a pause, reached Fontainebleau late in the night. He there ordered a carriage, and taking Caulaincourt and Berthier into it, drove on towards Paris. Nothing could shake his belief that he was yet in time--until, while he was changing horses at La Cour de France, but a few miles from Paris, General Belliard came up, at the head of a column of cavalry--weary and dejected men, marching towards Fontainebleau, in consequence of the provisions of Marmont's capitulation, from the fatal field of Montmartre.

Even then Napoleon refused to halt. Leaping from his carriage, he began: "What means this? Why here with your cavalry, Belliard? And where are the enemy? Where are my wife and my boy? Where Marmont? Where Mortier?" Belliard walking by his side, told him the events of the day. He called out for his carriage--and insisted on continuing his journey. The general in vain informed him that there was no longer an army in Paris; that the regulars were all coming behind, and that neither they nor he himself, having left the city in consequence of a convention, could possibly return to it. The Emperor still demanded his carriage, and bade Belliard turn with the cavalry and follow him. "Come," said he, "we must to Paris--nothing goes aright when I am away--they do nothing but blunder." He strode on, crying, "You should have held out longer--you should have raised Paris--they cannot like the Cossacks--they would surely have defended their walls--Go! go! I see every one has lost his senses. This comes of employing fools and cowards." With such exclamations Buonaparte hurried onwards, dragging Belliard with him, until they were met, a mile from La Cour de France, by the first of the retreating infantry. Their commander, General Curial, gave the same answers as Belliard. "In proceeding to Paris," said he, "you rush on death or captivity." Perceiving at length that the hand of necessity was on him, the Emperor then abandoned his design. He sank at once into perfect composure; gave orders that the troops, as they arrived, should draw up behind the little river Essonne; despatched Caulaincourt to Paris, with authority to accept whatever terms the Allied Sovereigns might be pleased to offer; and turned again towards Fontainebleau.

It was still dark when Napoleon reached once more that venerable castle. He retired to rest immediately; not, however, in any of the state-rooms which he had been accustomed to occupy, but in a smaller apartment, in a different and more sequestered part of the building.

The Duke of Vicenza reached the Czar's quarters at Pantin early in the morning of the 31st, while he was yet asleep; and recognised, amidst the crowd in the ante-chamber, a deputation from the municipality of Paris, who were waiting to present the keys of the city, and invoke the protection of the conqueror. As soon as Alexander awoke, these functionaries were admitted to his presence, and experienced a most courteous reception. The Czar repeated his favourite expression, that he had but one enemy in France: and promised that the capital, and all within it, should be treated with perfect consideration. Caulaincourt then found his way to Alexander--but he was dismissed immediately. The countenance of the envoy announced, as he came out, that he considered the fate of his master as decided; nor, if he had preserved any hope, could it have failed to expire when he learned that Alexander had already sent to Talleyrand, requesting him on no account to quit the capital, and proposing to take up his own residence in his hotel.

Nesselrode, the Russian minister, who received the municipal deputation ere the Czar awoke, entered freely into conversation with the gentleman at their head, M. Laborde. That person, being questioned as to the state of public feeling, answered that there were three parties: the army, who still adhered to Buonaparte; the republicans, who wished for his deposition, but would not object to the King of Rome being recognised as Emperor, provided a liberal constitution were established, and the regency placed in fit hands; and finally, the old nobility and the saloons of Paris, who were united in desiring the restoration of the Bourbons. "But at the Prince of Benevento's," said Laborde, "the Emperor will best acquire a knowledge of all this--it is there that our chief statesmen assemble habitually." This conversation is supposed to have fixed Alexander's choice of a residence; and as we have already seen that Talleyrand was ere now committed in the cause of Louis, the result of this choice may be anticipated.

The history of what La Vallette had called "the secret intrigues with the stranger" has not yet been cleared up--nor is it likely to be so for some time. If there was one of the Allied Princes on whose disposition to spare himself, or at least his family, Napoleon might have been supposed to count,--it must have been the Emperor of Austria; and yet, at daybreak this very morning, a proclamation was tossed in thousands over the barriers of Paris, in which several phrases occurred, not to be reconciled with any other notion than that he and all the Allies agreed in favouring the restoration of the Bourbons, ere any part of their forces entered the capital. This document spoke of the anxiety of "the sovereigns" to see the establishment of "a salutary authority in France": of the opportunity offered to the Parisians of "accelerating the peace of the world"; of the "conduct of Bordeaux" as affording "an example of the method in which foreign war and civil discord might find a common termination"; it concluded thus: "It is in these sentiments that Europe in arms before your walls addresses herself to you. Hasten then to respond to the confidence which she reposes in your love for your country, and in your wisdom;" and was signed "SCHWARTZENBERG, Commander-in-Chief of the Allied Armies."

There was a circumstance of another kind which assisted in stimulating the hopes and swelling the adherents of the royal cause. The Allies had, in the early part of the campaign, experienced evil from the multiplicity of uniforms worn among the troops of so many nations and tongues, and the likeness which some of the dresses, the German especially, bore to those of the French. The invading soldiers had latterly adopted the practice of binding pieces of white linen round their left arms; and this token, though possibly meant only to enable the strangers to recognise each other, was not likely to be observed with indifference by the Parisians, among whom the Bourbonists had already begun to wear openly the white cockade.

Finally, a vivid sensation was excited in Paris at this critical moment by the publication of Chateaubriand's celebrated tract, entitled "Of Buonaparte and of the Bourbons." The first symptom of freedom in the long enslaved press of Paris was not likely, whatever it might be, to meet with an unfriendly reception; but this effusion of one of the most popular writers of the time (though composed in a style not suited to sober English tastes) was admirably adapted to produce a powerful effect, at such a moment of doubt and hesitation, on the people to whom it was addressed.

The agents of Buonaparte had not been idle during the 30th: they had appealed to the passions of those wretched classes of society who had been the willing instruments of all the horrible violence of the revolution, and among whom the name of Bourbon was still detested; nor without considerable effect. The crowds of filthy outcasts who emerged from their lanes and cellars, and thronged some of the public places during the battle, were regarded with equal alarm by all the decent part of the population, however divided in political sentiments. But the battle ended ere they could be brought to venture on any combined movement; and when the defeated soldiery began to file in silence and dejection through the streets, the mob lost courage, and retreated also in dismay to the obscure abodes of their misery and vice.

The royalists welcomed with exultation the dawn of the 31st. Together with the proclamation of Schwartzenberg, they circulated one of Monsieur, and another of Louis XVIII. himself; and some of the leading gentlemen of the party, the Montmorencys, the Noailles, the Rohans, the Rochefoucalds, the Polignacs, the Chateaubriands, were early on horseback in the streets; which they paraded without interruption from any, either of the civil authorities, or of the National Guard, decorated with the symbols of their cause, and appealing with eloquence to the feelings of the onlookers. As yet, however, they were only listened to. The mass of the people were altogether uncertain what the end was to be: and, in the language of the chief orator himself, M. Sosthenes de Rochefoucald, "the silence was most dismal." At noon the first of the Allied troops began to pass the barrier and enter the city. The royalist cavaliers met them; but though many officers observing the white cockade exclaimed "la belle decoration!" the generals refused to say anything which might commit their sovereigns. Some ladies of rank, however, now appeared to take their part in the scene; and when these fair hands were seen tearing their dresses to make white cockades, the flame of their enthusiasm began to spread. Various pickets of the National Guard had plucked the tricolor badge from their caps, and assumed the white, ere many of the Allies passed the gates.

At noon, as has been mentioned, this triumphal procession began, and it lasted for several hours. The show was splendid; 50,000 troops, horse, foot, and artillery, all in the highest order and condition, marched along the boulevards; and in the midst appeared the youthful Czar and the King of Prussia, followed by a dazzling suite of princes, ambassadors, and generals. The crowd was so great that their motion, always slow, was sometimes suspended. The courteous looks and manners of all the strangers--but especially the affable and condescending air of Alexander, were observed at first with surprise; as the cavalcade passed on, and the crowd thickened, the feelings of the populace rose from wonder to delight, and ended in contagious and irresistible rapture. No sovereigns entering their native capitals were ever received with more enthusiastic plaudits; and still, at every step, the shouts of _Vive L'Empereur Alexandre!--Vive le Roi de Prusse!_ were more and more loudly mingled with the long-forgotten echoes of Vive le Roi!--_Vive Louis XVIII.--Vivent les Bourbons!_

The monarchs at last halted, dismissed their soldiers to quarters in the city, saw Platoff and his Cossacks establish their bivouack in the Champs Elyseess, and retired to the residences prepared for them; that of Alexander being, as we have mentioned above, in the hotel of Talleyrand.

While the Czar was discussing with this wily veteran, and a few other French statesmen of the first class, summoned at his request, the state of public opinion, and the strength of the contending parties--the population of Paris continued lost in surprise and admiration, at the sudden march of events, the altogether unexpected amount of the troops of the Allies--(for they that had figured in the triumphal procession were, it now appeared, from the occupation of all the environs, but a fragment of the whole)--and above all, perhaps--such is the theatric taste of this people--the countless varieties of lineament and costume observable among the warlike bands lounging and parading about their streets and gardens. The capital wore the semblance of some enormous masquerade. Circassian noblemen in complete mail, and wild Bashkirs with bows and arrows, were there. All ages, as well as countries, seemed to have sent their representatives to stalk as victors amidst the nation which but yesterday had claimed glory above the dreams of antiquity, and the undisputed mastery of the European world.

The council at the hotel of Talleyrand did not protract its sitting. Alexander and Frederick William, urged by all their assessors to re-establish the House of Bourbon, still hesitated. "It is but a few days ago," said the Czar, "since a column of 5 or 6000 new troops suffered themselves to be cut in pieces before my eyes, when a single cry of Vive le Roi would have saved them." De Pradt answered, "Such things will go as long as you continue to treat with Buonaparte--even although at this moment he has a halter round his neck." The Czar did not understand this last illusion; it was explained to him that the Parisians were busy in pulling down Napoleon's statue from the top of the great pillar in the Place Vendome. Talleyrand now suggested that the Conservative Senate should be convoked, and required to nominate a provisional government, the members of which should have power to arrange a constitution. And to this the sovereigns assented. Alexander signed forthwith a proclamation asserting the resolution of the Allies to "treat no more with Napoleon Buonaparte, or any of his family." Talleyrand had a printer in waiting, and the document was immediately published, with this significant affix, "Michaud, Printer to the King." If any doubt could have remained after this, it must be supposed to have ceased at nine the same evening, when the royalist gentry once more assembled, sent a second deputation to Alexander, and were (the Czar himself having retired to rest) received, and answered in these words, by his minister Nesselrode:--"I have just left the Emperor, and it is in his name that I speak. Return to your assembly, and announce to all the French, that, touched with the cries he has heard this morning, and the wishes since so earnestly expressed to him, his Majesty is about to restore the crown to him to whom alone it belongs. Louis XVIII. will immediately ascend his throne."

And yet it is by no means clear that even at the time when this apparently most solemn declaration was uttered, the resolution of the Allies had been unalterably taken. Nesselrode personally inclined to a regency, and preserving the crown to the King of Rome; nor is it to be doubted that that scheme, if at all practicable, would have been preferred by the Emperor of Austria. But the Frenchmen who had once committed themselves against Napoleon could not be persuaded but that his influence would revive, to their own ruin, under any Buonapartean administration; and the events of the two succeeding days were decisive. The Municipal Council met, and proclaimed that the throne was empty. This bold act is supposed to have determined the Conservative Senate. On the 1st of April that body also assembled, and named a provisional government, with Talleyrand for its head. The deposition of Napoleon was forthwith put to the vote, and carried without even one dissentient voice. On the 2nd the Legislative Senate, angrily dispersed in January, were in like manner convoked; and they too ratified the decrees proposed by the Conservative. On the 3rd the senatus-consultum was published, and myriads of hands were busy in every corner of the city pulling down the statues and pictures, and effacing the arms and initials of Napoleon. Meantime the Allied Princes appointed military governors of Paris, were visible daily at processions and festivals, and received, night after night, in the theatres, the tumultuous applause of the most inconstant of peoples.

It was in the night between the 2nd and the 3rd that Caulaincourt returned from his mission to Fontainebleau, and informed Napoleon of the events which he had witnessed; he added, that the Allies had not yet, in his opinion, made up their minds to resist the scheme of a regency, but that he was commissioned to say nothing could be arranged, as to ulterior questions, until he, the Emperor, had formally abdicated his throne. The Marshals assembled at Fontainebleau seem, on hearing this intelligence, to have resolved unanimously that they would take no further part in the war; but Napoleon himself was not yet prepared to give up all without a struggle. The next day, the 4th of April, he reviewed some of his troops, harangued them on "the treasonable proceedings in the capital," announced his intention of instantly marching thither, and was answered by enthusiastic shouts of "Paris! Paris!" He, on this, conceiving himself to be secure of the attachment of his soldiery, gave orders for advancing headquarters to Essonne. With the troops which had filed through Paris, under Marmont's convention, and those which had followed himself from Troyes, nearly 50,000 men were once more assembled around Fontainebleau; and with such support Napoleon was not yet so humbled as to fear hazarding a blow, despite all the numerical superiority of the Allies.

When, however, he retired to the chateau, after the review, he was followed by his Marshals, and respectfully, but firmly, informed, that if he refused to negotiate on the basis of his personal abdication, and persisted in risking an attack on Paris, they would not accompany him. He paused for a moment in silence--and a long debate ensued. The statements and arguments which he heard finally prevailed; and Napoleon drew up, and signed, in language worthy of the solemn occasion, this act:--

The Allied powers having proclaimed that the Emperor Napoleon is the sole obstacle to the re-establishment of peace in Europe, he, faithful to his oath, declares that he is ready to descend from the throne, to quit France, and even to relinquish life, for the good of his country; which is inseparable from the rights of his Son, from those of the Regency in the person of the Empress, and from the maintenance of the laws of the Empire. Done at our Palace of Fontainebleau, April the 4th, 1814. NAPOLEON.

Buonaparte appointed Caulaincourt to bear this document to Paris on his behalf; and the Marshals proposed that Ney should accompany him as their representative. It was suggested that Marmont also should form part of the deputation; but he was in command of the advanced division at Essonne, and Macdonald was named in his stead. These officers now desired to know on what stipulations, as concerned the Emperor personally, they were to insist. "On none," he answered; "obtain the best terms you can for France--for myself I ask nothing."

Hitherto nothing could be more composed or dignified than his demeanour. He now threw himself on a sofa, hid his countenance for some minutes, and then starting up with that smile which had so often kindled every heart around him into the flame of onset, exclaimed--"Let us march, my comrades; let us take the field once more."

The answer was silence and some tears; and he, also in silence, dismissed the messengers and the assemblage.

Caulaincourt, Ney and Macdonald immediately commenced their journey; and on reaching Essonne received intelligence which quickened their speed. Victor, and many other officers of the first rank, not admitted to the council at Fontainebleau, and considering the events of the two preceding days in the capital as decisive, had already sent in their adhesion to the provisional government; and Marmont, the commander of Napoleon's division in advance, had not only taken the same step for himself personally, but entered into a separate convention the night before, under which it had been settled that he should forthwith march his troops within the lines of the allied armies. The Marshals of the mission entreated Marmont to suspend his purpose, and repair with themselves to Paris. He complied; and on arriving in the capital they found themselves surrounded on all sides with the shouts of _Vive le Roi_! Such sounds accompanied them to the hotel Talleyrand, where they were forthwith admitted to the presence of the Czar. The act of abdication was produced; and Alexander expressed his surprise that it should have contained no stipulations for Napoleon personally; "but I have been his friend," said he, "and I will willingly be his advocate. I propose that he should retain his imperial title, with the sovereignty of Elba or some other island."

When Buonaparte's envoys retired from the Autocrat's presence, it still remained doubtful whether the abdication would be accepted in its present form, or the Allies would insist on an unconditional surrender. There came tidings almost on the instant which determined the question. Napoleon had, shortly after the mission left him, sent orders to General Souham, who commanded at Essonne in the absence of Marmont, to repair to his presence at Fontainebleau. Souham, who, like all the upper officers of Marmont's corps (with but two exceptions), approved of the convention of the 3rd, was alarmed on receiving this message. His brethren, being summoned to council, participated in his fears; and the resolution was taken to put the convention at once in execution. The troops were wholly ignorant of what was intended, when they commenced their march at five in the morning of the 5th; and for the first time suspected the secret views of their chiefs, when they found themselves in the midst of the allied lines, and watched on all sides by overwhelming numbers, in the neighbourhood of Versailles. A violent commotion ensued; some blood was shed; but the necessity of submission was so obvious, that ere long they resumed the appearance of order, and were cantoned in quiet in the midst of the strangers.

This piece of intelligence was followed by more of the like complexion. Officers of all ranks began to abandon the camp at Fontainebleau, find present themselves to swear allegiance to the new government. Talleyrand said wittily when some one called Marmont a traitor, "his watch only went a little faster than the others."

At length the allied princes signified their resolution to accept of nothing but an unconditional abdication; making the marshals, however, the bearers of their unanimous accession to the proposals of Alexander in favour of Napoleon and his House; which, as finally shaped, were these:--

1st, The imperial title to be preserved by Napoleon, with the free sovereignty of Elba, guards, and a navy suitable to the extent of that island, a pension from France of six millions of francs annually: 2nd, The Duchies of Parma, Placentia and Guastalla to be granted in sovereignty to Maria Louisa and her heirs: and 3rd, Two millions and a half of francs annually to be paid, by the French government, in pensions to Josephine and the other members of the Buonaparte family.

Napoleon, on hearing the consequences of Marmont's defection, exclaimed, "Ungrateful man! but I pity him more than myself." Every hour thenceforth he was destined to meet similar mortifications. Berthier, his chosen and trusted friend, asked leave to go on private business to Paris, adding that he would return in a few hours. The Emperor consented; and, as he left the apartment, whispered with a smile, "He will return no more." What Napoleon felt even more painfully, was the unceremonious departure of his favourite Mameluke, Rustan.

Ere the Marshals returned from Paris he reviewed his guard again, and it was obvious to those about him that he still hankered after the chances of another field. We may imagine that his thoughts were like those of the Scottish usurper:--

"I have lived long enough: my May of life Is fallen into the sear, the yellow leaf.... Come, put mine armour on; give me my staff. ... The Thanes fly from me."

He sometimes meditated a march southwards, collecting on his way the armies of Augereau and Soult, and re-opening the campaign as circumstances might recommend, behind either the Loire or the Alps. At other times the chance of yet rousing the population of Paris recurred to his imagination. Amidst these dreams, of which every minute more clearly showed the vanity, Napoleon received the ultimatum of the invading powers. He hesitated and pondered long ere he would sign his acceptance of it. The group of his personal followers had been sorely thinned; and the armies of the Allies, gradually pushing forward from Paris, had nearly surrounded Fontainebleau, when he at length (on the 11th of April) abandoned all hope, and executed an instrument, formally "renouncing for himself and his heirs the thrones of France and of Italy."

Even after signing this document, and delivering it to Caulaincourt, he made a last effort to rouse the spirits of the chief officers still around his person. They, as the Marshals had done on the 4th, heard his appeals in silence; and the Duke of Vicenza, though repeatedly commanded to give him back the act of abdication, refused to do so. It is generally believed that, during the night which ensued, Napoleon's meditations were, once more, like those of the falling Macbeth:--

"There is no flying hence, nor tarrying here. I 'gin to be weary o' the sun."--

Whether the story, very circumstantially told, of his having swallowed poison on that night, be true, we have no means of deciding. It is certain that he underwent a violent paroxysm of illness, sank into a death-like stupor, and awoke in extreme feebleness, lassitude, and dejection; in which condition several days were passed.

Napoleon remained long enough at Fontainebleau to hear of the restoration of the Bourbon Monarchy, and the triumphant entrance of the Count d'Artois (now Charles X.) into Paris, as Lieutenant for his brother, Louis XVIII.; and of another event, which ought to have given him greater affliction. Immediately on the formation of the provisional government, messengers had been sent from Paris to arrest the progress of hostilities between Soult and Wellington. But, wherever the blame of intercepting and holding back these tidings may have lain, the English General received no intelligence of the kind until, pursuing his career of success, he had fought another great and bloody battle, and achieved another glorious victory, beneath the walls of Toulouse. This unfortunate, because utterly needless, battle, occurred on the 11th of April. On the 14th the news of the fall of Paris reached Lord Wellington; and, Soult soon afterwards signifying his adhesion to the new government, his conqueror proceeded to take part in the final negotiations of the Allies at Paris.

It was on the 20th of April that Napoleon once more called his officers about him, and signified that they were summoned to receive his last adieus. Several of the marshals and others who had some time before sworn fealty to the king, were present. "Louis," said he, "has talents and means: he is old and infirm; and will not, I think, choose to give a bad name to his reign. If he is wise, he will occupy my bed, and only change the sheets. But he must treat the army well, and take care not to look back on the past, or his time will be brief. For you, gentlemen, I am no longer to be with you;--you have another government; and it will become you to attach yourselves to it frankly, and serve it as faithfully as you have served me."

He now desired that the relics of his imperial guard might be drawn up in the courtyard of the castle. He advanced to them on horseback; and tears dropped from his eyes as he dismounted in the midst. "All Europe," said Napoleon, "has armed against me. France herself has deserted me, and chosen another dynasty. I might, with my soldiers, have maintained a civil war for years--but it would have rendered France unhappy. Be faithful to the new sovereign whom your country has chosen. Do not lament my fate: I shall always be happy while I know that you are so. I could have died--nothing was easier--but I will always follow the path of honour. I will record with my pen the deeds we have done together. I cannot embrace you all" (he continued, taking the commanding officer in his arms)--"but I embrace your general. Bring hither the eagle. Beloved eagle! may the kisses I bestow on you long resound in the hearts of the brave; farewell, my children--farewell, my brave companions--surround me once more--farewell!"

Amidst the silent but profound grief of these brave men, submitting like himself to the irresistible force of events, Napoleon placed himself in his carriage, and drove rapidly from Fontainebleau.

Of all that lamented the fall of this extraordinary man, no one shed bitterer tears than the neglected wife of his youth. Josephine had fled from Paris on the approach of the Allies; but being assured of the friendly protection of Alexander, returned to Malmaison ere Napoleon quitted Fontainebleau. The Czar visited her frequently, and endeavoured to soothe her affliction. But the ruin of "her Achilles," "her Cid" (as she now once more, in the day of misery, called Buonaparte), had entered deep into her heart. She sickened and died before the Allies left France.

Maria Louisa, meanwhile, and her son, were taken under the personal protection of the Emperor of Austria, and had begun their journey to Vienna some time before the fallen "Child of Destiny" reached Elba.

[Footnote 66: An English d 闺 enu, who was then in Paris, says: "During the battle, the Boulevard des Italiens and the Caff?Tortoni were thronged with fashionable loungers of both sexes, sitting as usual on the chairs placed there, and appearing almost uninterested spectators of the number of wounded French brought in. The officers were carried on mattresses. About two o'clock a general cry of sauve qui peut was heard on the boulevards, from the Porte St. Martin to Les Italiens; this caused a general and confused flight, which spread like the undulations of a wave, even beyond the Pont Neuf.... During the whole of the battle wounded soldiers crawled into the streets, and lay down to die on the pavement.... The Moniteur of this day was a full sheet; but no notice was taken of the war, or the army. Four columns were occupied by an article on the dramatic works of Denis, and three with a dissertation on the existence of Troy."--Memorable Events in Paris in 1814, p. 93.]

CHAPTER XXXVII

Napoleon's Journey to Frejus--Voyage to Elba--his conduct and occupations there--Discontents in France--Return of Prisoners of War--Jealousy of the Army--Union of the Jacobins and Buonapartists--Their intrigues--Napoleon escapes from Elba.

Four commissioners, one from each of the great Allied Powers, Austria, Russia, Prussia, and England, accompanied Buonaparte on his journey. He was attended by Bertrand, Grand Master of the Palace, and some other attached friends and servants; and while fourteen carriages were conveying him and his immediate suite towards Elba, 700 infantry and about 150 cavalry of the Imperial Guard (all picked men, and all volunteers), marched in the same direction, to take on them the military duties of the exiled court.

During the earlier part of his progress Napoleon continued to be received respectfully by the civil functionaries of the different towns and departments, and with many tokens of sympathy on the part of the people; and his personal demeanour was such as it had been wont to appear in his better days. At Valence he met Augereau, whose conduct during the campaign had moved his bitterest displeasure; the interview was short--the recriminations mutual, and, for the first time perhaps, the fallen Emperor heard himself addressed in that tone of equality and indifference to which, for so many years, he had been a stranger. Thenceforth the course of his journey carried him more and more deeply into the provinces wherein his name had never been popular, and contemptuous hootings began by degrees to be succeeded by clamours of fierce resentment. On more than one occasion the crowd had threatened personal violence when the horses were changing, and he appears to have exhibited alarm such as could hardly have been expected in one so familiar with all the dangers of warfare. But civil commotions, as we have seen in the case of the revolution of Brumaire, were not contemplated by Napoleon so calmly as the tumults of the field. At this time besides he was suffering under a bodily illness, the fruit of debauchery, which acts severely on the stoutest nerves. It is admitted on all hands that he showed more of uneasiness and anxiety than accords with the notion of a heroic character. At length he disguised himself, and sometimes appearing in an Austrian uniform, at others riding on before the carriages in the garb of a courier, reached in safety the place of embarkation.

A French vessel had been sent round from Toulon to Cannes, for the purpose of conveying him to Elba; but there happened to be an English frigate also in the roads, and he preferred sailing under any flag rather than the Bourbon. His equanimity seemed perfectly re-established from the moment when he set his foot on the British deck. He conversed affably with Captain Usher and the officers; and by the ease and plainness of his manners, his intelligent curiosity as to the arrangements of the ship, and the warm eulogies which he continued to pronounce on them, and on the character of the English nation at large, he succeeded in making a very favourable impression on all the crew--with the exception of Hinton, a shrewd old boatswain, who, unmoved by all the imperial blandishments, growled, at the close of every fine speech, the same homely comment, "humbug." Saving this hard veteran, the usual language of the forecastle was, that "Buonaparte was a very good fellow after all"; and when, on finally leaving the Undaunted, he caused some 200 Napoleons to be distributed among the sailors, they "wished his honour long life, and better luck the next time."

He came within view of his new dominions on the afternoon of the 4th of May, and went ashore in disguise the same evening, in order to ascertain for himself whether the feelings of the Elbese at all resembled those of the Provencials. Finding that, on the contrary, the people considered his residence as likely to increase in every way the consequence and prosperity of their island, he returned on board the ship, and at noon, the day after, made his public entrance into the town of Porto Ferraio, amidst all possible demonstrations of welcome and respect.

The Russian and Prussian commissioners did not accompany him beyond the coast of Provence: the Austrian Baron Kholer, and the English Sir Neil Campbell, landed with Napoleon, and took up their residence at Ferraio. He continued for some time to treat both of these gentlemen with every mark of distinction, and even cordiality: made them the companions of his table and excursions; and conversed with apparent openness and candour on the past, the present, and the future. "There is but one people in the world," said he to Colonel Campbell--"the English--the rest are only so many populaces. I tried to raise the French to your level of sentiment, and failing to do so, fell of course. I am now politically dead to Europe. Let me do what I can for Elba.... It must be confessed," said he, having climbed the hill above Ferraio, from whence he could look down on the whole of his territory as on a map--"it must be confessed," said the Emperor, smiling, "that my island is very small."

The island, however, was his; and, as on the eye itself a very small object near at hand fills a much greater space than the largest which is distant, so, in the mind of Napoleon, that was always of most importance in which his personal interests happened for the time to be most concerned. The island-- mountainous and rocky, for the most part barren, and of a circumference not beyond sixty miles--was his; and the Emperor forthwith devoted to Elba the same anxious care and industry which had sufficed for the whole affairs of France, and the superintendence and control of half Europe besides. He, in less than three weeks, had explored every corner of the island, and projected more improvements of all sorts than would have occupied a long lifetime to complete. He even extended his empire by sending some dozen or two of his soldiers to take possession of a small adjacent islet, hitherto left unoccupied for fear of corsairs. He established four different residences at different corners of Elba, and was continually in motion from one to another of them. Wherever he was, in houses neither so large nor so well furnished as many English gentlemen are used to inhabit, all the etiquettes of the Tuileries were, as far as possible, adhered to; and Napoleon's eight or nine hundred veterans were reviewed as frequently and formally as if they had been the army of Austerlitz or of Moscow. His presence gave a new stimulus to the trade and industry of the islanders; the small port of Ferraio was crowded with vessels from the opposite coasts of Italy; and, such was still the power of his name, that the new flag of Elba (covered with Napoleon's bees), traversed with impunity the seas most infested with the Moorish pirates.

Buonaparte's eagerness as to architectural and other improvements was, ere long, however, checked in a manner sufficiently new to him--namely, by the want of money. The taxes of the island were summarily increased; but this gave rise to discontent among the Elbese, without replenishing at all adequately the Emperor's exchequer. Had the French government paid his pension in advance, or at least quarterly, as it fell due, even that would have borne a slender proportion to the demands of his magnificent imagination. But Napoleon received no money whatever from the Bourbon court; and his complaints on this head were unjustly and unwisely neglected. These new troubles embittered the spirit of the fallen Chief; and the first excitement of novelty being over he sank into a state of comparative indolence, and apparently of listless dejection; from which, however, he was, ere long, to be roused effectually, by the course of events in that great kingdom, almost in sight of whose shores he had been most injudiciously permitted to preserve the shadow of sovereign state.

Louis XVIII., advanced in years, gross and infirm in person, and devoted to the luxuries of the table, was, in spite of considerable talents and accomplishments, and a sincere desire to conciliate the affections, by promoting the interests, of all orders of his people, but ill-adapted for occupying, in such trying times, the throne which, even amidst all the blaze of genius and victory, Napoleon had at best found uneasy and insecure.[67] The King himself was, perhaps, less unpopular than almost any other member of his family; but it was his fatal misfortune, that while, on the whole, every day increased the bitterness of those who had never been sincerely his friends, it tended to chill the affections of the royalists who had partaken his exile, or laboured, ere success was probable, for his return.

Louis had been called to the throne by the French senate, in a decree which at the same time declared the legislative constitution, as composed of a hereditary sovereign and two houses of assembly, to be fixed and unchangeable; which confirmed the rights of all who had obtained property in consequence of the events of the Revolution, and the titles and orders conferred by Buonaparte: in a word, which summoned the Bourbon to ascend the throne of Napoleon--on condition that he should preserve that political system which Napoleon had violated. Louis, however, though he proceeded to France on this invitation, did not hesitate to date his first act in the twentieth year of his reign; and though he issued a charter, conferring, as from his own free will, every privilege which the senate claimed for themselves and the nation, this mode of commencement could not fail to give deep offence to those, not originally of his party, who had consented to his recall. These men saw, in such assumptions, the traces of those old doctrines of _divine right_, which they had through life abhorred and combated; and asked why, if all their privileges were but the gifts of the King, they might not, on any tempting opportunity, be withdrawn by the same authority? They, whose possessions and titles had all been won since the death of Louis XVI., were startled when they found, that, according to the royal doctrine, there had been no legitimate government all that time in France. The exiled nobles, meanwhile, were naturally the personal friends and companions of the restored princes: their illustrious names, and, we must add, their superior manners, could not fail to excite unpleasant feelings among the new-made dukes and counts of Buonaparte. Among themselves it was no wonder that expectations were cherished, and even avowed, of recovering gradually, if not rapidly, the estates of which the Revolution had deprived them. The churchmen, who had never gone heartily into Napoleon's ecclesiastical arrangements, sided of course with these impoverished and haughty lords; and, in a word, the first tumult of the restoration being over, the troops of the Allies withdrawn, and the memory of recent sufferings and disasters beginning to wax dim amidst the vainest and most volatile of nations, there were abundant elements of discontent afloat among all those classes who had originally approved of, or profited by, the revolution of 1792.

Of these the most powerful and dangerous remains to be noticed; and, indeed, had the Bourbons adopted judicious measures concerning _the army_, it is very probable that the alarms of the other classes now alluded to might have subsided. The Allies, in the moment of universal delight and conciliation, restored at once, and without stipulation, the whole of the prisoners who had fallen into their hands during the war. At least 150,000 veteran soldiers of Buonaparte were thus poured into France ere Louis was well-seated on the throne; men, the greater part of whom had witnessed nothing of the last disastrous campaigns; who had sustained themselves in their exile by brooding over the earlier victories in which themselves had had a part; and who now, returning fresh and vigorous to their native soil, had but one answer to every tale of misfortune which met them: "These things could never have happened had we been here."

The conquerors, in their anxiety to procure for Louis XVIII. a warm reception among the French, had been led into other mistakes, which all tended to the same issue. They had (with some exceptions on the part of Prussia) left the pictures and statues, the trophies of Napoleon's battles, untouched in the Louvre--they had not even disturbed the monuments erected in commemoration of their own disgraces. These instances of forbearance were now attributed by the fierce and haughty soldiery of Buonaparte, to the lingering influence of that terror which their own arms under his guidance had been accustomed to inspire. Lastly, the concessions to Napoleon himself of his imperial title, and an independent sovereignty almost within view of France, were interpreted in the same fashion by these habitual worshippers of his renown. The restored King, on his part, was anxious about nothing so much as to conciliate the affections of the army. With this view he kept together bands which, long accustomed to all the licence of warfare, would hardly have submitted to peace even under Napoleon himself. Even the Imperial Guard, those chosen and devoted children of the Emperor, were maintained entire on their old establishment; the Legion of Honour was continued as before; the war ministry was given to Soult, the ablest, in common estimation, of Buonaparte's surviving marshals; and the other officers of that high rank were loaded with every mark of royal consideration. But these arrangements only swelled the presumption of those whose attachment they were meant to secure. It was hardly possible that the King of France should have given no military appointments among the nobles who had partaken his exile. He gave them so few, that they, as a body, began to murmur ere the reign was a month old: but he gave enough to call up insolent reclamations among those proud legionaries, who in every royalist, beheld an emblem of the temporary humiliation of their own caste. When, without dissolving or weakening the Imperial (now Royal) Guard, he formed a body of household troops, composed of gentlemen, and entrusted them with the immediate attendance on his person and court, this was considered as a heinous insult; and when the King bestowed the cross of the Legion of Honour on persons who would have much preferred that of St. Louis, the only comment that obtained among the warriors of Austerlitz and Friedland, was, that which ascribed to the Bourbons a settled design of degrading the decoration which they had purchased with their blood.

In a word, the French soldiery remained cantoned in the country in a temper stern, gloomy, and sullen; jealous of the Prince whose bread they were eating; eager to wipe out the memory of recent disasters in new victories; and cherishing more and more deeply the notion (not perhaps unfounded) that had Napoleon not been betrayed at home, no foreigners could ever have hurled him from his throne. Nor could such sentiments fail to be partaken, more or less, by the officers of every rank who had served under Buonaparte. They felt, almost universally, that it must be the policy of the Bourbons to promote, as far as possible, others rather than themselves. And even as to those of the very highest class--could any peaceful honours compensate, to such spirits as Ney and Soult, for a revolution, that for ever shrouded in darkness the glittering prizes on which Napoleon had encouraged them to speculate? Were the comrades of Murat and Bernadotte to sit down in contentment as peers of France, among the Montmorencies and the Rohans, who considered them at the best as low-born intruders, and scorned, in private society, to acknowledge them as members of their order? If we take into account the numerous personal adherents whom the Imperial government, with all the faults of its chief, must have possessed--and the political humiliation of France, in the eyes of all Europe, as well as of the French people themselves, immediately connected with the disappearance of Napoleon--we shall have some faint conception of that mass of multifarious griefs and resentments, in the midst of which the unwieldy and inactive Louis occupied, ere long, a most unenviable throne--and on which the eagle-eyed Exile of Elba gazed with reviving hope even before the summer of 1814 had reached its close.

Ere then, as we have seen, the demeanour and conduct of Napoleon were very different from what they had been when he first took possession of his mimic empire. Ere then his mother, his sister Pauline (a woman, whose talents for intrigue equalled her personal charms), and not a few ancient and attached servants, both of his civil government and of his army, had found their way to Elba, and figured in "his little senate." Pauline made repeated voyages to Italy, and returned again. New and busy faces appeared in the circle of Porto Ferraio--and disappeared forthwith--no one knew whence they had come or whither they went; an air of bustle and of mystery pervaded the atmosphere of the place. Sir Neil Campbell found it more and more difficult to obtain access to the presence of Buonaparte--which the refusal of the English government to acknowledge the Imperial title, and this officer's consequent want of any very definite character at Elba, left him no better means of overcoming than to undertake journeys and voyages, thereby gaining a pretext for paying his respects at every departure and return. Sir Neil early suspected that some evil was hatching, and repeatedly remarked on the absurdity of withholding Napoleon's pension, thereby tempting him, as it were, to violence. But neither the reports nor the reclamations of this gentleman appear to have received that attention which they merited.

What persons in France were actually in communication on political subjects with the turbulent court of Elba, during that autumn and the following winter, is likely to remain a secret: that they were neither few nor inactive, nor unskilful, the event will sufficiently prove. The chiefs of the police and of the post-office had been removed by Louis; but the whole inferior machinery of these establishments remained untouched; and it is generally believed, that both were early and sedulously employed in the service of the new conspiracy. We have seen that Soult was commander-in-chief of the army; and it is very difficult, on considering the subsequent course of events, to doubt that he also made a systematic use of his authority with the same views, distributing and arranging the troops according to far other rules than the interests of his royal master.

Ere the autumn closed, Buonaparte granted furloughs on various pretexts to about 200 of his guardsmen; and these were forthwith scattered over France, actively disseminating the praises of their chief, and, though probably not aware how soon such an attempt was meditated, preparing the minds of their ancient comrades for considering it as by no means unlikely that he would yet once more appear in the midst of them. It is certain that a notion soon prevailed that Napoleon would revisit the soil of France in the spring of the coming year. He was toasted among the soldiery, and elsewhere also, under the soubriquet of Corporal Violet. That early flower, or a ribbon of its colour, was the symbol of rebellion, and worn openly, in the sight of the unsuspecting Bourbons.

Their security was as profound as hollow; nor was it confined to them. The representatives of all the European princes had met in Vienna, to settle finally a number of questions left undecided at the termination of the war. Talleyrand was there for France, and Wellington for England; and yet it is on all hands admitted, that no surprise was ever more sudden, complete, and universal than theirs, when on the 11th of March, 1815, a courier arrived among them with the intelligence that Napoleon Buonaparte had reared his standard in Provence.[68]

[Footnote 67: When the King first came to Paris, there appeared a caricature representing an eagle flying away from the Tuileries, and a brood of porkers entering the gate; and His Majesty was commonly called by the rabble, not Louis dix huit, but Louis Cochon (the pig), or Louis des hu 類 res (of the oysters).]

[Footnote 68: The Emperor Alexander alone preserved perfect self-possession; and, turning to the Duke of Wellington, exclaimed "Eh bien, Wellington, c'est ?vous encore une fois sauver le monde."]

CHAPTER XXXVIII

Napoleon lands at Cannes--his progress to Grenoble--Lyons--Fontainebleau--Treason of Labedoyere and Ney--Louis XVIII. retires to Ghent, and Napoleon arrives in Paris.

The evening before Napoleon sailed (February the 26th), his sister Pauline gave a ball, to which all the officers of the Elbese army were invited. A brig (the Inconstant) and six small craft, had meanwhile been prepared for the voyage, and at dead of night, without apparently any previous intimation, the soldiery were mustered by tuck of drum, and found themselves on board ere they could ask for what purpose. When the day broke, they perceived that all the officers and the Emperor himself were with them, and that they were steering for the coast of France; and it could no longer be doubtful that the scheme which had for months formed the darling object of all their hopes and dreams was about to be realised.

Sir Neil Campbell, who had been absent on an excursion to Leghorn, happened to return to Porto Ferraio almost as soon as the flotilla had quitted it. The mother and sister of Buonaparte in vain endeavoured to persuade the English officer that he had steered toward the coast of Barbary. He pursued instantly towards Provence, in the Partridge, which attended his orders, and came in sight of the fugitive armament exactly when it was too late. Ere then Napoleon had encountered almost an equal hazard. A French ship of war had crossed his path; but the Emperor made all his soldiery lie flat on the decks, and the steersman of the Inconstant, who happened to be well acquainted with the commanding officer, had received and answered the usual challenge without exciting any suspicion. Thus narrowly escaped the flotilla which carried "Caesar and his fortune."

On the 1st of March he was once more off Cannes--the same spot which had received him from Egypt, and at which he had embarked ten months before for Elba. There was no force whatever to oppose his landing; and his handful of men--500 grenadiers of the guard, 200 dragoons, and 100 Polish lancers, these last without horses, and carrying their saddles on their backs--were immediately put in motion on the road to Paris. Twenty-five grenadiers which he detached to summon Antibes were arrested on the instant by the governor of that place; but he despised this omen, and proceeded without a pause. He bivouacked that night in a plantation of olives, with all his men about him. As soon as the moon rose, the reille sounded. A labourer going thus early afield, recognised the Emperor's person, and, with a cry of joy, said he had served in the army of Italy, and would join the march. "Here is already a reinforcement," said Napoleon; and the march recommenced. Early in the morning they passed through the town of Grasse, and halted on the height beyond it--where the whole population of the place forthwith surrounded them, some cheering, the great majority looking on in perfect silence, but none offering any show of opposition. The roads were so bad in this neighbourhood, that the pieces of cannon which they had with them were obliged to be abandoned in the course of the day, but they had marched full twenty leagues ere they halted for the night at Cerenon. On the 5th,

Napoleon reached Gap. He was now in Dauphiny, called "The cradle of the Revolution," and the sullen silence of the Provencials was succeeded by popular acclamations; but still no troops had joined him--and his anxiety was great.

It was at Gap that he published his first proclamations; one "To the Army," another "To the French people," both no doubt prepared at Elba, though dated "March 1st, Gulf of Juan." The former, and more important of the two, ran in these words--"Soldiers! we have not been beaten. Two men, raised from our ranks,[69] betrayed our laurels, their country, their prince, their benefactor. In my exile I have heard your voice. I have arrived once more among you, despite all obstacles, and all perils. We ought to forget that we have been the masters of the world; but we ought never to suffer foreign interference in our affairs. Who dares pretend to be master over us? Take again the eagles which you followed at Ulm, at Austerlitz, at Jena, at Montmirail. Come and range yourselves under the banners of your old chief. Victory shall march at the charging step. The Eagle, with the national colours, shall fly from steeple to steeple--on to the towers of Notre Dame! In your old age, surrounded and honoured by your fellow-citizens, you shall be heard with respect when you recount your high deeds. You shall then say with pride--I also was one of that great army which entered twice within the walls of Vienna, which took Rome, and Berlin, and Madrid, and Moscow--and which delivered Paris from the stain printed on it by domestic treason, and the occupation of strangers."

It was between Mure and Vizele that Cambronne, who commanded his advanced guard of forty grenadiers, met suddenly a battalion sent forwards from Grenoble to arrest the march. The colonel refused to parley with Cambronne; either party halted until Napoleon himself came up. He did not hesitate for a moment. He dismounted, and advanced alone; some paces behind him came a hundred of his guard, with their arms reversed. There was perfect silence on all sides until he was within a few yards of the men. He then halted, threw open his surtout so as to show the star of the Legion of Honour, and exclaimed, "If there be among you a soldier who desires to kill his general--his Emperor--let him do it now. Here I am."--The old cry of Vive l'Empereur burst instantaneously from every lip. Napoleon threw himself among them, and taking a veteran private, covered with chevrons and medals, by the whisker, said, "Speak honestly, old Moustache, couldst thou have had the heart to kill thy Emperor?" The man dropped his ramrod into his piece to show that it was uncharged, and answered, "Judge if I could have done thee much harm--all the rest are the same." Napoleon gave the word, and the old adherents, and the new, marched together on Grenoble.

Some space ere they reached that town, Colonel Labedoyere, an officer of noble family, and who had been promoted by Louis XVIII., appeared on the road before them, at the head of his regiment, the seventh of the line. These men, and the Emperor's little column, on coming within view of each other, rushed simultaneously from their ranks, and embraced with mutual shouts of Live Napoleon! Live the Guard! Live the Seventh! Labedoyere produced an eagle, which he had kept concealed about his person, and broke open a drum which was found to be filled with tricolor cockades; these ancient ensigns were received with redoubled enthusiasm. This was the first instance of an officer of superior rank voluntarily espousing the side of the invader. The impulse thus afforded was decisive; in spite of all the efforts of General Marchand, Commandant of Grenoble, the whole of that garrison, when he approached the walls, exclaimed Vive l'Empereur! Their conduct, however, exhibited a singular spectacle. Though thus welcoming Napoleon with their voices, they would not so far disobey the governor as to throw open the gates. On the other hand no argument could prevail on them to fire on the advancing party. In the teeth of all the batteries, Buonaparte calmly planted a howitzer or two, and blew the gates open, and then, as if the spell of discipline were at once dissolved, the garrison broke from their lines, and he in an instant found himself dragged from his horse, and borne aloft on these men's shoulders towards the principal inn of the place, amidst the clamours of enthusiastic and delirious joy. Marchand remained faithful to his oath; and was dismissed without injury. Next morning the authorities of Grenoble waited on Napoleon, and tendered their homage. He reviewed his troops, now about 7000 in numbers, and on the 9th recommenced his march.

On the 10th, Buonaparte came within sight of Lyons, and was informed that Monsieur and Marshal Macdonald had arrived to take the command, barricaded the bridge of Guillotierre, and posted themselves at the head of a large force to dispute the entrance of the town. Nothing daunted with this intelligence, the column moved on, and at the bridge of Lyons, as at the gates of Grenoble, all opposition vanished when his person was recognised by the soldiery. The Prince and Macdonald were forced to retire, and Napoleon entered the second city of France in triumph. A guard of mounted gentlemen had been formed among the citizens to attend on the person of Monsieur. These were among the foremost to offer their services to the Emperor, after he reached his hotel. Surrounded by his own soldiery, and by a manufacturing population, whom the comparatively free admission of English goods after the peace of Paris had filled with fear and discontent, and who now welcomed the great enemy of England with rapturous acclamations, Napoleon could afford to reject the assistance of these faithless cavaliers. He dismissed them with contempt; but finding that one of their number had followed Monsieur until his person was out of all danger, immediately sent to that individual the cross of the Legion of Honour.

This revolution had been proceeding during more than a week, ere the gazettes of Paris ventured to make any allusion to its existence. There then appeared a royal ordonnance, proclaiming Napoleon Buonaparte _an outlaw_, and convoking on the instant the two chambers. Next day the Moniteur announced that, surrounded on all hands by faithful garrisons and a loyal population, this outlaw was already stripped of most of his followers, wandering in despair among the hills, and certain to be a prisoner within two or three days at the utmost. The Moniteur, however, was no very decisive authority in 1815, any more than in 1814; and the public mind continued full of uncertainty, as to the motives and every circumstance of this unparalleled adventure. Monsieur, meanwhile, had departed, we have seen with what success, to Lyons; the Duke of Angouleme was already at Marseilles, organising the loyal Provencials, and preparing to throw himself on Grenoble and cut off the retreat of Buonaparte; and Louis continued to receive addresses full of loyalty and devotion from the public bodies of Paris, from towns, and departments, and, above all, from the marshals, generals, and regiments who happened to be near the capital.

This while, however, the partisans of Napoleon in Paris were far more active than the royalists. They gave out everywhere that, as the proclamation from the Gulf of Juan had stated, Buonaparte was come back thoroughly cured of that ambition which had armed Europe against his throne; that he considered his act of abdication void, because the Bourbons had not accepted the crown on the terms on which it was offered, and had used their authority in a spirit, and for purposes, at variance with the feelings and the interests of the French people; that he was come to be no longer the dictator of a military despotism, but the first citizen of a nation which he had resolved to make the freest of the free; that the royal government wished to extinguish by degrees all memory of the revolution--that he was returning to consecrate once more the principles of liberty and equality, ever hateful in the eyes of the old nobility of France, and to secure the proprietors of forfeited estates against all the machinations of that dominant faction; in a word, that he was fully sensible to the extent of his past errors, both of domestic administration and of military ambition, and desirous of nothing but the opportunity of devoting, to the true welfare of peaceful France, those unrivalled talents and energies which he had been rash enough to abuse in former days. With these suggestions they mingled statements perhaps still more audacious. According to them, Napoleon had landed with the hearty approbation of the Austrian court, and would be instantly rejoined by the Empress and his son. The Czar also was friendly; even England had been sounded ere the adventure began, and showed no disposition to hazard another war for the sake of the Bourbons. The King of Prussia, indeed, remained hostile--but France was not sunk so low as to dread that state single-handed. It was no secret, ere this time, that some disputes of considerable importance had sprung up among the great powers whose representatives were assembled at Vienna; and such was the rash credulity of the Parisians, that the most extravagant exaggerations and inventions which issued from the saloon of the Duchess de St. Leu (under which name Hortense Beauharnois, wife of Louis Buonaparte, had continued to reside in Paris)--and from other circles of the same character, found, to a certain extent, credence. There was one tale which ran louder and louder from the tongue of every Buonapartist, and which royalist and republican found, day after day, new reason to believe; namely, that the army were, high and low, on the side of Napoleon; that every detachment sent to intercept him, would but swell his force; in a word, that--unless the people were to rise _en masse_--nothing could prevent the outlaw from taking possession of the Tuileries ere a fortnight more had passed over the head of Louis.

It was at Lyons, where Napoleon remained from the 10th to the 13th, that he formally resumed the functions of civil government. He published various decrees at this place; one, commanding justice to be administered everywhere in his name after the 15th; another abolishing the Chambers of the Peers and the Deputies, and summoning all the electoral colleges to meet in Paris at a Champ-de-Mai,[70] there to witness the coronation of Maria

Louisa and of her son, and settle definitively the constitution of the state; a third, ordering into banishment all whose names had not been erased from the list of emigrants prior to the abdication of Fontainebleau; a fourth, depriving all strangers and emigrants of their commissions in the army; a fifth, abolishing the order of St. Louis, and bestowing all its revenues on the Legion of Honour; and a sixth, restoring to their authority all magistrates who had been displaced by the Bourbon government. These proclamations could not be prevented from reaching Paris; and the Court, abandoning their system of denying or extenuating the extent of the impending danger, began to adopt more energetic means for its suppression.

It was now that Marshal Ney volunteered his services to take the command of a large body of troops, whose fidelity was considered sure, and who were about to be sent to Lons-le-Saunier, there to intercept and arrest the invader. Well aware of this great officer's influence in the army, Louis did not hesitate to accept his proffered assistance; and Ney, on kissing his hand at parting, swore that in the course of a week he would bring Buonaparte to his majesty's feet in a cage, like a wild beast.

On reaching Lons-le-Saunier, Ney received a letter from Napoleon, summoning him to join his standard as "the bravest of the brave." In how far he guided or followed the sentiments of his soldiery we know not, but the fact is certain, that he and they put themselves in motion forthwith, and joined the march of Buonaparte on the 17th at Auxerre. Ney, in the sequel, did not hesitate to avow that he had chosen the part of Napoleon long ere he pledged his oath to Louis; adding that the greater number of the marshals were, like himself, original members of the Elbese conspiracy. Of the latter of these assertions no other proof has hitherto been produced; and the former continues to be generally as well as mercifully discredited.

In and about the capital there still remained troops far more than sufficient in numbers to overwhelm the advancing column, and drag its chief to the feet of Louis. He entrusted the command of these battalions to one whose personal honour was as clear as his military reputation was splendid--Marshal Macdonald; and this gentleman proceeded to take post at Melun, in good hope, notwithstanding all that happened, of being duly supported in the discharge of his commission.

On the 19th, Napoleon slept once more in the chateau of Fontainebleau; on the morning of the 20th he advanced through the forest in full knowledge of Macdonald's arrangements--and he advanced alone. It was about noon that the marshal's troops, who had for some time been under arms on an eminence beyond the wood, listening, apparently with delight, to the loyal strains of Vive Henri Quatre and La Belle Gabrielle, perceived suddenly a single open carriage coming at full speed towards them from among the trees. A handful of Polish horsemen, with their lances reversed, followed the equipage. The little flat cocked hat--the grey surtout--the person of Napoleon was recognised. In an instant the men burst from their ranks, surrounded him with the cries of _Vive l'Empereur_, and trampled their white cockades in the dust.

Macdonald escaped to Paris; but his master had not awaited the issue of the last stand at Melun. Amidst the tears and lamentations of the loyal burghers of the capital, and the respectful silence of those who really wished for the success of his rival, Louis had set off from the Tuileries in the middle of the preceding night. Macdonald overtook him, and accompanied him to the frontier of the Netherlands, which he reached in safety. There had been a plan organised by Generals Lallemand and Lefevre for seizing the roads between Paris and Belgium, and intercepting the flight of the King; but Marshal Mortier had been successful in detecting and suppressing this movement.

On the evening of the 20th of March, Napoleon once more entered Paris. He came preceded and followed by the soldiery, on whom alone he had relied, and who, by whatever sacrifices, had justified his confidence. The streets were silent as the travel-worn cavalcade passed along; but all that loved the name of the cause of Napoleon were ready to receive him in the Tuileries, and he was almost stifled by the pressure of those enthusiastic adherents, who the moment he stopped, mounted him on their shoulders, and carried him so in triumph up the great staircase of the palace. He found, in the apartments which the King had just vacated, a brilliant assemblage of those who had in former times filled the most prominent places in his own councils and court: among the rest was Fouche This personage was not the only one present who had recently intrigued with the Bourbons against Buonaparte-- with as much apparent ardour, and perhaps with about as much honesty, as in other times he had ever brought to the service of the Emperor.

"Gentlemen," said Napoleon, as he walked round the circle, "it is disinterested people who have brought me back to my capital. It is the subalterns and the soldiers that have done it all. I owe everything to the people and the army."

[Footnote 69: The allusion is to Marmont's conduct at Essonne, and Augereau's hasty abandonment of Lyons when the Austrians approached it in March, 1814.]

[Footnote 70: Napoleon took the idea and name of this assembly from the history of the early Gauls.]

CHAPTER XXXIX

The Hundred Days--Declaration of the Congress at Vienna--Napoleon prepares for War--Capitulation of the Duke d'Angouleme--Insurrection of La Vend 閑--Murat advances from Naples--Is Defeated--And takes refuge in France--The Champ-de-Mai--Dissatisfaction of the Constitutionalists.

The reports so zealously circulated by the Buonapartists, that some at least of the great European powers were aware, and approved, of the meditated debarkation at Cannes--and the hopes thus nourished among the French people, that the new revolution would not disturb the peace of the world-- were very speedily at an end. The instant that the news of Napoleon's daring movement reached Vienna, the Congress published a proclamation in these words:--"By breaking the convention which established him in Elba, Buonaparte destroys the only legal title on which his existence depended. By appearing again in France, with projects of confusion and disorder, he has deprived himself of the protection of the law, and manifested to the universe that there can be neither peace nor truce with him. The powers consequently declare that Napoleon Buonaparte has placed himself without the pale of civil and social relations, and that, as an enemy and disturber of the tranquillity of the world, he has rendered himself liable to public vengeance." These sentiments underwent no change in consequence of the apparently triumphant course of Napoleon's adventure. All Europe prepared once more for war. It was evident that the usurper owed everything to the French soldiery--that body to which the treaty of Paris had at once restored 150,000 veterans, idle, and indisposed for ordinary labour--and that until this ferocious military were effectually humbled there could be no peace for the world.

A formal treaty was forthwith entered into, by which the four great powers bound themselves to maintain each of them at least 150,000 troops in arms, until Buonaparte should either be dethroned, or reduced so low as no longer to endanger the peace of Europe. The other states of the continent were to be invited to join the alliance, furnishing contingents adequate to their respective resources. The King of France was to be requested to sign the treaty also; but with reference to this article an explanatory note was affixed, by the representatives of the Prince Regent of England, denying, on the part of his royal highness, any wish to force a particular government on the people of France: and it was further stipulated that in case Britain should not furnish all the men agreed on, she should compensate by paying at the rate of ?0 per annum for every cavalry soldier, and ?0 per annum for every foot soldier under the full number. Such was the treaty of Vienna; but the zeal of the contracting parties went far beyond the preparations indicated in its terms. Napoleon was hardly re-seated on his throne ere he learned that he must in all likelihood maintain it against 300,000 Austrians, 225,000 Russians, 236,000 Prussians, an army of 150,000 men furnished by the minor states of Germany, 50,000 contributed by the government of the Netherlands, and 50,000 English, commanded by the Duke of Wellington;--in all one million eleven thousand soldiers.

His preparations to meet this gigantic confederacy began from the moment when he re-established himself in the Tuileries. Carnot became once more minister of war; and what Napoleon and he, when labouring together in the re-organisation of an army, could effect, had been abundantly manifested at the commencement of the consulate. The army cantoned in France, when Buonaparte landed at Cannes, numbered 175,000; the cavalry had been greatly reduced: and the disasters of 1812, 1813, and 1814, were visible in the miserable deficiency of military stores and arms, especially of artillery. By incredible exertions, notwithstanding the pressure of innumerable cares and anxieties of all kinds, and although the temper of the nation prevented him from having recourse to the old method of conscription--the Emperor, ere May was over, had 375,000 men in arms--including an imperial guard of 40,000 chosen veterans, in the most splendid state of equipment and discipline, a large and brilliant force of cavalry, and a train of artillery of proportional extent and excellence.

Napoleon, however, made sundry attempts to open a negotiation with the Allies--nor wanted there statesmen, even in England, to lend their best support to his reclamations. He urged three arguments in defence of his breach of the convention by which he had become sovereign of Elba: 1st, the detention of his wife and son by the court of Austria--an affair with which the king whose dominions he had invaded could have had nothing to do: 2nd, the nonpayment of his pension--a grievance which might have furnished a legitimate ground of complaining to the powers that guaranteed its punctual discharge, and which, if so complained of at the Congress of Vienna, there is no reason to doubt would have been redressed: and 3rd, the voice of the French nation, which he, according to his own statement, had but heard and obeyed. But the state of public feeling in France could not be effectually misrepresented now: and the answer that met him from every quarter was one and the same--namely, that he had ascended the throne of Louis in consequence of the treason of the army, and the intrigues of a faction, in direct opposition to the wishes of almost all the upper classes of society throughout France, and, as regarded the mass of the nation, amidst profound indifference.

Meanwhile the royalists at home had failed in all their endeavours to prevent his authority from being recognised all over France. The Duke d'Angouleme was soon surrounded by the superior numbers of General Gilly, and capitulated--on condition of being permitted to disband his followers, and embark at Cette for Spain--a convention which Napoleon did not hesitate to ratify. The Duchess of Angouleme, daughter of Louis XVI., displayed at Bourdeaux such heroism as drew from Napoleon himself the sarcastic eulogy, "She is the only man of her race;" but in spite of the loyalty of the inhabitants all her efforts were vain. The garrison was strong; they had caught the general flame; and the Princess was at length compelled to take refuge in an English frigate. The Duke of Berri repaired, on the first alarm, to La Vend 閑: but the regular troops in that faithful province were, thanks to the previous care of King Louis's war-minister, so numerous and so well posted, that this effort failed also, and the Duke escaped to England. Before March had ended, the tricolor flag was displayed on every tower of France.

Having discovered that there was no chance--if indeed he had ever contemplated one--of persuading the Emperor of Austria to restore his wife and son to him, Napoleon, ere he had been many days at the Tuileries, set on foot a scheme for carrying them off from Vienna, by a mixture of stratagem and force. There were French people in the suite of Maria Louisa who easily embarked in this plot; and forged passports, relays of horses, and all other appliances had been so well provided, that but for a single individual, who betrayed the design, there seems to have been a considerable probability of its success. On discovering this affair the Emperor of Austria dismissed the French attendants of his daughter, and caused her to discontinue the use of the arms and liveries of Napoleon, which she had hitherto retained--nay, even the imperial title itself, resuming those of her own family, and original rank as archduchess. This procedure could not be concealed at Paris, and completed the conviction of all men, that there was no hope whatever of avoiding another European war; and almost at the same time a rash expedition of Murat, which, if successful, might have materially influenced the conduct of Austria, reached its end.

  Napoleon, when at St. Helena, always persisted in denying any participation in this design of his brother-in-law; but, however this may have been, it is certain that much intercourse subsisted, during his stay at Elba, between the Queen of Naples and the female branches of the family at Porto Ferraio; nor can anyone doubt either that Murat had received some pretty distinct intimation of Napoleon's intended descent in France--or that he ventured on his movement in the confidence that this and the Emperor's would lend to each other much moral support--or that, if Joachim had prospered, Napoleon would have considered what he did as the best service that could have been rendered to himself.

  Among the subjects which, prior to Buonaparte's reappearance, occupied the Congress of Vienna, one of the chief was the conduct of Murat during the campaign of 1814. Talleyrand charged him with having, throughout, been a traitor to the cause of the Allies; and exhibited a series of intercepted letters, from him to Napoleon, in proof of this allegation. The Duke of Wellington, on the other hand, considered these documents as proving no more than that Murat had reluctantly lifted his banner against the author of his fortunes. Talleyrand had always hated Murat and despised him--(the father of the King of Naples had originally been steward in the household of the Perigords)--and persisted in urging on the Congress the danger of suffering a sovereign of

Buonaparte's family and creation to sit on the throne which belonged of right to the King of the Sicilies. The affair was still under discussion, to the mortal annoyance of the person whose interests were at stake, when Napoleon landed at Cannes. Murat resolved to rival his brother's daring; and, without further pause, marched, at the head of 50,000 men, to Rome, from which the Pope and cardinals fled precipitately at his approach. The Neapolitans then advanced into the North of Italy, scattering proclamations by which Joachim invited all true Italians to rally round him, and assist in the erection of their country into one free and independent state, with him at its head. The Austrian commander in Lombardy forthwith put his troops in motion to meet Murat. The rencontre took place at Occhiobello. The Neapolitans fled in confusion almost at the sight of the enemy; and Murat, unable to rally them, sought personal safety in a fishing vessel, which landed him near Toulon, about the end of May. Napoleon was in vain entreated to receive him at Paris. He refused, asking, with bitter scorn--if the war between France and Naples, which subsisted in 1814, had ever been terminated by treaty? Murat lingered for some time in obscurity near Toulon; and, relanding on the coast of Naples after the King of the Two Sicilies had been re-established on that throne, in the vain hope of exciting an insurrection and recovering what he had lost, was seized, tried, and executed. This vain, but high-spirited, man, met his fate with heroic fortitude; and Napoleon, at St. Helena, often said that the fortune of the world might have been changed, had there been a Murat to head the French cavalry at Waterloo.

The result of this rash expedition enabled Austria to concentrate all her Italian forces also for the meditated re-invasion of France. The Spanish army began to muster towards the passes of the Pyrenees: the Russians, Swedes, and Danes were already advancing from the north: the main armies of Austria, Bavaria, and the Rhenish princes were rapidly consolidating themselves along the Upper Rhine. Blucher was once more in command of the Prussians, in the Netherlands; and Wellington, commanding in chief the British, Hanoverians, and Belgians, had also established his headquarters at Brussels by the end of May. Every hour the clouds were thickening apace, and it became evident, that, if Napoleon remained much longer in Paris, the war would burst simultaneously on every frontier of his empire.

He had no intention to abide at home the onset of his enemies; but the situation of civil affairs was such as to embarrass him, in the prospect of departure, with difficulties which, in former days, were not used to perplex the opening of his campaigns.

Hard indeed was his task from the beginning--to conciliate to himself heartily the political faction who detested, and had assisted in overthrowing the government of the Bourbons, and this without chilling the attachment of the military, who despised these coadjutors, both as theorists and as civilians, and had welcomed Napoleon only as the certain harbinger of war, revenge, and plunder. How little his soldiery were disposed to consider him as owing anything to a civil revolution, appeared almost from the commencement of his march from Cannes. It was observed that these haughty bands moved on in contemptuous silence whenever the populace cheered his approach, and shouted _Vive l'Empereur only when there were no pequin_[71] voices to mingle in the clamour. Every act of Napoleon after he reached Paris, that was meant to conciliate the common people of the capital, was the theme of angry comment among these martial circles. Such measures as he adopted in deference to the prejudices of the old republican party, were heard of with equal contempt. The pacific language of his first proclamations was considered as a fair stratagem--and no more. To them the man was nothing but as the type of the system: they desired to hear of nothing in France but the great Caesar, and the legions to whom he owed his greatness, and who had the same right to a new career of battles, as he to his Imperial crown, at once the prize of past, and the pledge of future victories.

With the views of these spirits, eager for blood and plunder, and scornful of all liberty but the licence of the camp, Napoleon was engaged in the endeavour to reconcile the principles and prejudices of men who had assisted in rebuilding his throne, only because they put faith in the assertions of himself and his friends, that he had thoroughly repented of the despotic system on which he had formerly ruled France--that ten months of exile and reflection had convinced him how much better it was to be the first citizen of a free state, than the undisputed tyrant of half the world--in a word, that his only remaining ambition was to atone for the violence of his first reign by the mildness of his second. As a first step to fasten the goodwill of these easy believers, he, immediately on arriving in Paris, proclaimed the freedom of the press; but he soon repented of this concession. In spite of all the watchfulness, and all the briberies of his police, he could never bend to his own service the whole of this power. The pure republicans--even the pure royalists--continued to have their organs; and the daily appeals of either to the reason and the passions of a people so long strange to the exercise of such influence, otherwise than in subservience to the government of the time, whatever that might be, produced such effects, that, almost from the time in which he bestowed the boon, he was occupied with devising pretexts for its recall. He ere long caused, perhaps, more resentment by some efforts to thwart the conduct of the press, than would have resulted from the absolute prolongation of its slavery. Some even of the decrees of Lyons were hard to be reconciled with the professions of one who disclaimed any wish to interfere with the sacred right of the nation to frame its constitution for itself. But in almost every act of his government after he reached Paris, he furnished additional evidence how imperfectly his mind had divested itself of the ancient maxims. Even the edict, emancipating the press from all control, was an assumption on his part of the complete power of legislation. The same might be said of another decree, abolishing negro slavery and the slave trade, which he published shortly after: but this second measure exposed him to other comments. Who could seriously believe that at that moment of tumult, ere France was even in semblance entirely his, and while all Europe was openly arming against him, he had leisure for the affairs of the negroes? This display of philanthropy was set down universally for a stage-trick; and men quickened their eyes, lest such unsubstantial shows in the distant horizon might be designed to withdraw their attention from the foreground.

The great assemblage of Champ-de-Mai had been originally announced for the 10th of May; and its principal business as the formation of a new constitution. The meeting did not take place so early, and the task of proposing a constitutional scheme for its consideration, proved far more difficult than the Emperor had contemplated. He had the assistance, in this labour, of Carnot and Sieyes, whose names would have carried great weight with the republican party--had not both of these old jacobins and regicides accepted, on entering the Emperor's service, high rank in his peerage--a proceeding in direct violation of all the professions of their lives. He was further favoured with the aid of his brother Lucien, who, in spite of all previous misunderstandings, returned on this occasion to Paris; influenced, probably, by the same egregious vanity which made him fancy himself a poet, and hoping, under existing circumstances, to impress Napoleon with such a sense of his value as might secure him henceforth a commanding influence in the government of France. The Abb?Sieyes, and Lucien also, had had some experience ere now of Napoleon in the character of a constitution-maker. He was no longer so powerful as he had been when they formerly toiled together upon such a task: disputes arose; and the Emperor, to cut these short, and give a decisive proof of his regard for freedom of debate, soon broke up the discussion, retired from the Tuileries to the small palace called the Elysees, and there drew up the scheme which pleased himself, and which was forthwith published under the title of "Act Additional to the Constitutions of the Empire."

This title gave great offence, because it seemed to recognise many anterior enactments, wholly irreconcilable with the tenor of the document itself; and the mode of its promulgation furnished even more serious ground of objection. This constitution was, on the face of it, not a compact between the prince and the people, but the record of boons conceded by the former to the latter. In a word, all they that had condemned Louis XVIII. for his royal charter, were compelled to acknowledge that their own imperial champion of freedom was beginning his new career by a precisely similar display of presumption.

The substance of the "additional act" disappointed all those who hankered after the formal exposition of first principles; but it must be allowed that its provisions seem to include whatever is needful for the arrangement of a free representative constitution; hereditary monarchy; a hereditary peerage; a house of representatives, chosen by the people, at least once within every five years; yearly taxes, levied only by the whole legislature; responsible ministers; irremovable judges; and, in all criminal cases whatever, the trial by jury. The act, however, was published; the electoral colleges accepted of it, as they had done of all its predecessors; and it by degrees came out that the business of the Champ-de-Mai was to be--not even the discussion of the imperial scheme, but only to swear submission to its regulations, and witness a solemn distribution of eagles to those haughty bands who acknowledge no law but that of the sword.

This promised assemblage was preceded by one of the rabble of Paris, convoked in front of the Tuileries on the 17th of May, and there feasted and harangued by Napoleon--a condescension which excited lively displeasure among his soldiery. He himself looked and spoke as one thoroughly ashamed of what he had done and was doing. It had been his desire to stimulate among these people something of the old zeal of the revolutionary period, in case Paris should be once more threatened by a foreign enemy; but he had the double mortification to find that the army considered their touch as contamination, and that among themselves the name of Louis was almost as popular as his own. Even the _Dames des halles_, so conspicuous in the revolutionary tumults, screamed royalist ditties in his ear as they drank his wine; and the only hearty cheers were those of the day-labourers, who had profited by his resumption of some great public works suspended by the King's government.

The Champ-de-Mai itself, which, despite its name, fell on the 1st of June, turned out hardly a more successful exhibition. Napoleon, his brothers, and the great civil functionaries, appeared in theatric dresses, in the midst of an enormous amphitheatre, where the deputies, sent from the departments to swear allegiance to the Emperor and the "additional act," were almost lost in the military among whom the eagles were to be distributed. The enthusiasm was confined to these. The same ominous silence which prevailed at the coronation of 1804 was preserved among the people. The sun shone bright, and the roar of cannon filled every pause of the martial music. It was a brilliant spectacle; but Napoleon retired from it in visible dejection.

Three days after, the two houses met; and while that of the peers, composed of persons who all owed their rank, and most of them much besides, to Napoleon, showed every disposition to regulate their conduct by his pleasure, there appeared from the beginning a marked spirit of independence in a considerable proportion of the representative body. The Emperor's address to both was moderate and manly. He requested their support in the war which circumstances had rendered unavoidable, and professed his desire that they should consider the "additional act" and all other subjects of national interest, and suggest whatever alterations might appear to them improvements. Some debates, by no means gratifying to Napoleon, ensued; but he had no leisure for witnessing much of their proceedings. It was now needful that he should appear once more in his own element.

[Footnote 71: By this contemptuous name his soldiery designated all who had never borne arms. The word dropt once from the lips of one of Napoleon's marshals in the hearing of Talleyrand, who asked its meaning.

"Nous nommons pequin," answered the rude soldier, "tout ce qui n'est pas militaire."--"Ah!" said the cool Talleyrand--"comme nous nommons militaire tout ce qui n'est pas civil."]

CHAPTER XL

Napoleon heads his army on the Belgian frontier--Passes the Sambre at Charleroi--Defeats Blucher at Ligny--Battle of Quatre-Bras--The English fall back on a position previously selected by Wellington--THE BATTLE OF WATERLOO--Napoleon returns to Paris.

Napoleon had now, among other preparations, strongly fortified Paris and all the positions in advance of it on the Seine, the Marne and the Aube, and among the passes of the Vosgesian hills. Lyons also had been guarded by very formidable outworks. Massena, at Metz, and Suchet, on the Swiss frontier, commanded divisions which the Emperor judged sufficient to restrain Schwartzenberg for some time on the Upper Rhine: should he drive them in, the fortresses behind could hardly fail to detain him much longer. Meantime the Emperor himself had resolved to attack the most alert of his enemies, the Prussians and the English, beyond the Sambre--while the Austrians were thus held in check on the Upper Rhine, and ere the armies of the North could debouche upon Manheim, to co-operate by their right with Wellington and Blucher, and by their left with Schwartzenberg. Of the Belgian army, and even of the Belgian people, he believed himself to possess the secret goodwill, and that one victory would place the Allies in a hostile country. By some daring battle, and some such splendid success, he yet hoped to shatter the confidence of the European confederacy; nor--even had he entertained little hope of this kind--was the situation of affairs in Paris such as to recommend another protracted and defensive warfare within France. The fatal example of 1814 was too near: it behoved Napoleon to recommence operations in the style which had characterised his happier campaigns.

He left Paris on the evening of the 11th of June, exclaiming, as he entered his carriage, "I go to measure myself against Wellington." He arrived at Vervins on the 12th, and assembled and reviewed at Beaumont, on the 14th, the whole of the army which had been prepared to act immediately under his own orders. They had been carefully selected, and formed, perhaps, the most perfect force, though far from the most numerous, with which he had ever taken the field. Buonaparte saw before him 25,000 of his imperial guard, 25,000 cavalry in the highest condition, 300 pieces of artillery admirably served, and infantry of the line, almost all veterans, sufficient to swell his muster to at least 135,000 men. He reminded them that this was the anniversary of Marengo and of Friedland, and asked, "Are they and we no longer the same men? The madmen!" he continued, "a moment of prosperity has blinded them. The oppression and humiliation of the French people is beyond their power. If they enter France they will there find their tomb. Soldiers! we have forced marches, battles and dangers before us. For every Frenchman who has a heart the moment is arrived to conquer or to perish!" Such was his oration: and never was army more thoroughly imbued with the spirit of its chief.

Blucher's army numbered at this time about 100,000 men, and, extending along the line of the Sambre and the Meuse, occupied Charleroi, Namur, Givet, and Liege. They communicated on their right with the left of the Anglo-Belgian army, under Wellington, whose headquarters were at Brussels. This army was not composed, like Blucher's or Napoleon's, of troops of the same nation. The Duke had less than 35,000 English; and of these but few were veterans--the flower of his Peninsular Army having been despatched to America, to conclude a war into which the United States had forced England, on very trivial pretences, during the season of her greatest difficulties and dangers, in 1812. The King's German Legion, 8000 strong, was, however, equal to the best British force of like amount; and there were 5000 Brunswickers, headed by their gallant Duke and worthy of his guidance. The Hanoverians, exclusive of the Legion, numbered 15,000: of Nassau troops, Dutch and Belgian, commanded by the Prince of Orange, son to the sovereign of the Netherlands, there might be 17,000; but the spirit of the Belgian part of this army was, not without reason, suspected on all sides. The Duke of Wellington's motley host amounted, then, in all to 75,000 men. His first division occupied Enghien, Brain-le-Comte and Nivelles, communicating with the Prussian right at Charleroi. The second division (Lord Hill's) was cantoned in Halle, Oudenard and Gramont--where was most of the cavalry. The reserve (Sir Thomas Picton's) were at Brussels and Ghent. The English and Prussian commanders had thus arranged their troops, with the view of being able to support each other, wherever the French might hazard their assault. It could not be ascertained beforehand whether Napoleon's mark was Ghent or Brussels; even had the Allied Generals known that it was the latter city, who could inform them by which of the three great routes, of Namur, of Charleroi, or of Mons, he designed to force his passage thither? Fouche indeed, doubly and trebly dyed in treason, had, when accepting office under Napoleon, continued to maintain his correspondence with Louis at Ghent, and promised to furnish the Allies with the outline of the Emperor's plan of the campaign ere it began. But the minister of police took care that this document should not arrive until the campaign was decided.

At daybreak on Thursday, the 15th, the French drove in all the outposts on the west bank of the Sambre, and at length assaulted Charleroi; thus revealing the purpose of the Emperor; namely, to crush Blucher ere he could concentrate all his own strength, far less be supported by the advance of Wellington, and then rush at once upon Brussels. Ziethen, however, held out, though with severe loss, at Charleroi so long, that the alarm spread along the whole Prussian line; and then fell back in good order on a position between Ligny and Armand; where Blucher now awaited Napoleon's attack--at the head of the whole of his army, except the division of Bulow which had not yet come up from Liege. The scheme of beating the Prussian divisions in detail had therefore failed; but the second part of the plan, namely, that of separating them wholly from Wellington, might still succeed. With this view, while Blucher was concentrating his force about Ligny, the French held on the main road to Brussels from Charleroi; beating in some Nassau troops at Frasnes, and followed them as far as Quatre-Bras, a farmhouse, so called, because it is there that the roads from Charleroi to Brussels, and from Nivelles to Namur, cross each other.

At half-past one o'clock, p.m., of the same day (Thursday the 15th) a Prussian officer[72] of high rank arrived at Wellington's headquarters in Brussels, with the intelligence of Napoleon's decisive operations. By two o'clock orders were despatched to all the cantonments of the Duke's army, for the divisions to break up, and concentrate on the left at Quatre-Bras; his Grace's design being that his whole force should be assembled there, by eleven o'clock on the next night, Friday the 16th.

It was at first intended to put off a ball announced for the evening of Thursday, at the Duchess of Richmond's hotel in Brussels; but on reflection it seemed highly important that the population of that city should be kept as far as possible in ignorance as to the course of events, and the Duke of

Wellington desired that the ball should proceed accordingly; nay, the general officers received his commands to appear in the ball-room--each taking care to quit the apartment as quietly as possible, at ten o'clock, and proceed to join his respective division en route. This arrangement was carried into strict execution. The Duke himself retired at twelve o'clock, and left Brussels at six o'clock next morning for Quatre-Bras. The reserve quitted Brussels in the night with the most perfect silence and regularity, unnoticed by the inhabitants; and the events which had occurred were almost wholly unknown in that city, except to the military authorities, until the next day.

The Duke of Wellington conversed at the ball with various persons on the movements which had occurred; stated his calculation of the French force directed against his left, and expressed his confidence that his whole army would be up at Quatre-Bras by eleven o'clock the next night. This most extraordinary and rapid concentration of force was effected; the various divisions of the army, previously cantoned over an extent of fifty miles, were collected at Quatre-Bras, within the short space of twenty-four hours.

Napoleon, on coming up from Charleroi, about noon on the 16th, hesitated for a time whether Blucher at Ligny, or the English at Quatre-Bras, ought to form the main object of his attack. The Anglo-Belgian army was not yet concentrated--the Prussian, with the exception of one division, was: and he at length resolved to give his own personal attention to the latter. With the main strength of his army, therefore, he assaulted Blucher at three in the afternoon; and about the same time Ney, with 45,000 men, commenced seriously (for there had been skirmishes ever since daybreak) the subordinate attack on the position of Wellington.

The English General had held a conference with Blucher this morning at Bry; and settled with him the ultimate measures to be adopted under whatever course the events of the day might assume; and he now awaited the assault of Ney under many disadvantages. His troops were vastly inferior in number, and all, except a few Belgians, that were now on the field, had been marching since midnight. The enemy were comparatively fresh; and they were posted among growing corn, as high as the tallest man's shoulders, which, with an inequality of ground, enabled them to draw up a strong body of cuirassiers close to the English, and yet entirely out of their view. The 79th and 42nd regiments were thus taken by surprise, and the former would have been destroyed but for the coming up of the latter. The 42nd, formed into a square, was repeatedly broken, and as often recovered--though with terrible loss of life: for out of 800 that went into the action, only ninety-six privates and four officers returned unhurt. The divisions of Alten, Halket, Cooke, Maitland, and Byng successively arrived; and night found the English general, after a severe and bloody day, in possession of Quatre-Bras. The gallant Duke of Brunswick, fighting in the front of the line, fell almost in the beginning of the battle. The killed and wounded on the side of the Allies were 5000, and the French loss could not have been less.

Blucher fought as stern a battle, but with worse fortune. With 80,000 men he had to sustain the assault of 90,000, headed by Napoleon; and the villages of Amand and Ligny were many times taken and re-taken in the course of the day. It is said, that two of the French corps hoisted the black flag: it is certain that little quarter was either asked or given. The hatred of the French and Prussians was inflamed to the same mortal vehemence. It is said that the loss on Blucher's side was 20,000 men--and on the other 15,000--numbers, when we consider the amount of the troops engaged, all but unparalleled. However, the non-arrival of Bulow, and the successive charges of fresh divisions of the enemy, at length forced Blucher to retire. In the course of the day the brave old man had his horse shot under him, in heading a charge of cavalry, and was ridden over undetected, by both his own men and the French. He now retreated on the river Dyle, in the direction of Wavre; but contrived to mask his movements so skilfully, that Napoleon knew not until noon on the 17th what way he had taken.

The bulletins of the Emperor announced two victories of the most dazzling description as the work of the 16th. Blucher would be heard of no more, they said; and Wellington, confounded and amazed, was already within the jaws of ruin.

Napoleon, having ascertained the retreat of the Prussian, now committed the pursuit of him to Marshal Grouchy, and a corps of 32,000 men--and turned in person to Quatre-Bras, in the hope of pouring his main force, as well as Ney's, on Wellington, in a situation where it was altogether improbable he should receive any assistance from Blucher. But no sooner was the Duke aware of Blucher's march on Wavre, than he, in adherence to the common plan of the campaign, gave orders for falling back from Quatre-Bras.

He had before now been heard to say, that if ever it were his business to defend Brussels, he would choose to give battle on the field of Waterloo, in advance of the forest of Soignies; and he now retired thither--in the confidence of being joined there in the morning, ere the decisive contest should begin, by Blucher. The day was rainy, the roads were covered deep with mud, and the English soldiery are of all others most discouraged by the command to retreat. Their spirits, however, rose gallantly when, on reaching the destined field, they became aware of their leader's purpose; and, having taken up their allotted stations, they bivouacked under the storm in the sure hope of battle.

All his arrangements having been effected early in the evening of the 17th, the Duke of Wellington rode across the country to Blucher, to inform him personally that he had thus far effected the plan agreed on at Bry, and express his hope to be supported on the morrow by two Prussian divisions. The veteran replied, that he would leave a single corps to hold Grouchy at bay as well as they could, and march himself with the rest of his army upon Waterloo; and Wellington immediately returned to his post.[73] The cross roads between Wavre and Mont St. Jean were in a horrid condition; the rain fell in torrents, and Grouchy had 32,000 men to attack Thielman's single division, left at Wavre. Blucher's march, however, began; and if it occupied longer time than had been anticipated, the fault was none of his.

The position of the Duke of Wellington was before the village of Mont St. Jean, about a mile and a half in advance of the small town of Waterloo, on a rising ground, having a gentle and regular declivity before it--beyond this a plain of about a mile in breadth--and then the opposite heights of La Belle Alliance, on which the enemy would of course form their line. The Duke had now with him about 75,000 men in all; of whom about 30,000 were English. He formed his first line of the troops on which he could most surely rely--the greater part of the British foot--the men of Brunswick and Nassau, and three corps of Hanoverians and Belgians. Behind this the ground sinks and then rises again. The second line, formed in rear of the first, was composed of the troops whose spirit and discipline were more doubtful--or who had suffered most in the action of Quatre-Bras; and behind these lay all the horse. The position crosses the two highways from Nivelles and Charleroi to Brussels, nearly where they unite: these roads gave every facility for movements from front to rear during the action; and two country roads, running behind and parallel with the first and second lines, favoured equally movements from wing to wing. The line was formed convex, dropping back towards the forest at either extremity; the right to Mark Braine, near Braine-la-Leude; the left to Ter-la-Haye. The chateau and gardens of Hougomont, and the farmhouse and enclosures of La Haye Sainte, about 1500 yards apart, on the slope of the declivity, were strongly occupied, and formed the important out-works of defence. The opening of the country roads leading directly from Wavre to Mont St. Jean, through the wood of Ohain, was guarded by the British left; while those running through Souhain and Frichemont, further in advance, might be expected to bring the first of the Prussians on the right flank of the French, during their expected attack.

The field was open and fair: and in case the enemy should force the Duke from his position, the village of Mont St Jean behind, still further back the town of Waterloo, and lastly the great forest of Soignies--offered successively the means of renewing his defence, and protecting his retreat.--The British front extended, in all, over about a mile. It was Wellington's business to hold the enemy at bay, until the Prussian advance should enable him to charge them with superior numbers: it was Napoleon's to beat the English ere Blucher could disengage himself from Grouchy, and come out of the woods of Ohain; which being accomplished, he doubted not to have easy work with the Prussians amidst that difficult country. He had in the field 75,000 men; all French veterans--each of whom was in his own estimation, worth one Englishman, and two Prussians, Dutch or Belgians. But on the other hand, Wellington's men, all in position over-night, had had, notwithstanding the severe weather, some hours to repose and refresh themselves: whereas the army of Napoleon had been on the march all through the hours of tempestuous darkness, and the greater part of them reached not the heights of Belle Alliance until the morning of the 18th was considerably advanced. The Emperor himself, however, had feared nothing so much as that Wellington would continue his retreat on Brussels and Antwerp--thus deferring the great battle until the Russians should approach the valley of the Rhine; and when, on reaching the eminence of La Belle Alliance, he beheld the army drawn up on the opposite side, his joy was great. "At last, then," he exclaimed, "at last, then, I have these English in my grasp."

The tempest abated in the morning--but the weather all day long was gusty, and the sky lowering. It was about noon that the French opened their cannonade, and Jerome Buonaparte, under cover of its fire, charged impetuously on Hougomont. The Nassau men in the wood about the house were driven before the French; but a party of English guards maintained themselves in the chateau and garden, despite the desperate impetuosity of many repeated assaults. Jerome, masking the post thus resolutely held, pushed on his cavalry and artillery against Wellington's right. The English formed in squares, and defied all their efforts. For some time both parties opposed each other here, without either gaining or losing a foot of ground. At length the English fire forced back the French--and the garrison of Hougomont were relieved and strengthened.

The next attempt was made on the centre of the British line, by a great force of cuirassiers and four columns of infantry. The horse, coming boldly along the causeway of Genappe, were met in the path by the English heavy cavalry, where the road has been cut down deep, leaving high banks on either side. Their meeting was stern: they fought for some time at sword's length; at last the cuirassiers gave way, and fled for the protection of their artillery. The English followed them too far, got amidst the French infantry, and were there charged by fresh cavalry and driven back with much loss.--It was here that Picton died. Meanwhile the infantry of this movement had pushed on beyond La Haye Sainte, and dispersed some Belgian regiments; but being then charged in turn, in front by Pack's brigade of foot, and in flank by a brigade of heavy English horse, were totally routed--losing, besides the slain and wounded, 2000 prisoners and two eagles. The only favourable result of this second grand attempt was the occupation of the farmhouse of La Haye Sainte, which had been garrisoned by Hanoverians. And scarcely had the charge of Pack proved successful, ere the French were again compelled by shells and cannon to evacuate this prize.

The third assault was levelled again on the British right--where the infantry awaited it, formed in a double line of squares, placed chequerwise, and protected in front by a battery of thirty field pieces. The French cuirassiers charged the artillerymen and drove them from their guns; and then rode fiercely on the squares behind. These remained steadfast until the enemy were within ten yards of them, and then fired with deadly effect. The cavalry gave back--rallied again, and renewed their charge: this they did several times--and always with the like result. Sometimes they even rode between the squares, and charged those of the second line. At length protracted exposure to such cross fire completed the ruin of these fearless cavaliers. The far greater part of this magnificent force was annihilated in this part of the battle.

When the relics of the cuirassiers withdrew, the French cannonade opened once more furiously all along the line; and the English were commanded to lie flat on the ground for some space, in order to diminish its effects. Lord Wellington had by this time lost 10,000, Buonaparte at least 15,000 men. It was now half-past six o'clock. The heads of Prussian columns began to be discerned among the woods to the right of the French. It was obvious, that unless a last and decisive onset should drive Wellington from the post which he had continued to hold during near seven hours of unintermitting battle, his allies would come fully into the field, and give him a vast superiority of numbers wherewith to close the work of the day. Napoleon prepared, therefore, for his final struggle. Hitherto he had kept his guard, the flower of his fine army, out of the fray. He now formed them into two columns,-- desired them to charge boldly, for that the Prussians, whom they saw in the wood, were flying before Grouchy--and they doubted not that the Emperor was about to charge in person at their head. He, however, looked on, as they put themselves in motion, and committed them to the guidance of Ney, "the bravest of the brave," whose consciousness of recent treason must have prepared him, even had his temper been less gallant, to set all upon the cast. Four battalions of the Old Guard only remained as a reserve; and were formed in squares to protect the march of the columns.

The English front by this time presented not a convex line, but a concave, either wing having gradually advanced a little in consequence of the repeated repulses of the enemy. They were now formed in an unbroken array, four deep, and poured on the approaching columns (each man firing as often as he could reload) a shower which never intermitted. The wings kept moving on all the while; and when the heads of the French columns approached, they were exposed to such a storm of musketry in front and on either flank, that they in vain endeavoured to deploy into line for the attack. They stopped to make this attempt, reeled, lost order, and fled at last in one mass of confusion.

The Duke of Wellington now dismounted, placed himself at the head of his line, and led them, no longer held to defence, against the four battalions of the Old Guard--the only unbroken troops remaining--behind whom Ney was striving to rally his fugitives.

The Marshal, at Wellington's approach, took post once more in the van, sword in hand, and on foot. But nothing could withstand the impetuous assault of the victorious British. The Old Guard also were shaken. Napoleon had hitherto maintained his usual serenity of aspect on the heights of La Belle Alliance. He watched the English onset with his spy-glass--became suddenly pale as death--exclaimed, "They are mingled together--all is lost for the present," and rode off the field, never stopping for a moment until he reached Charleroi.

Hardly had the English advanced for this fatal charge, when Blucher's columns, emerging from the woods, were at length seen forming on the right of the French, and preparing to take part in the battle. Their cannonade played on the flank of the Old Guard, while the British attack in front was overwhelming them. The fatal cry of sauve qui peut was heard everywhere: the French were now flying pellmell in the most woeful confusion. Blucher and Wellington met at length at the farmhouse of La Belle Alliance; and the Prussian eagerly undertook to continue the pursuit during the night, while the English General halted to refresh his weary men.

The loss of Wellington's army on this great day was terrible: 100 officers slain (many of the first distinction), and 500 wounded, very many mortally; and of rank and file killed and wounded, 15,000. The Duke himself had been, all through the day, wherever the danger was greatest; and he alone, and one gentleman besides, of all a very numerous staff, came off the ground unhurt.

Of the 75,000 men whom Napoleon conducted to this last and severest of his fields, what with the slain and the wounded, and those who, losing heart and hope, deserted and fled separately to their homes, not more than 30,000 were ever again collected in arms. The Prussians followed hard on the miserable fugitives, and in every hamlet and village, for many miles beyond La Belle Alliance, cut down the lingerers without mercy.

Napoleon at length halted at Philippeville: from which point he designed to turn towards Grouchy, and take in person the command of that remaining division, leaving Soult to re-assemble and rally, at Avesnes, the relics of

Waterloo. But hearing that Blucher was already at Charleroi (which was true), and that Grouchy had been overtaken and made prisoner (which was false), the Emperor abandoned his purpose, and continued his journey, travelling post, to Paris.

On the 19th the capital had been greeted with the news of three great victories, at Charleroi, at Ligny, and at Quatre-Bras--100 cannon fired in honour of the Emperor's successes--his partisans proclaimed that the glory of France was secured--and dejection filled the hearts of the royalists. On the morning of the 21st it transpired that Napoleon had arrived the night before, alone, at the Elysees. The secret could no longer be kept. A great, a decisive field had been fought;--and the French army was no more.

[Footnote 72: The fiction of the Duke of Wellington having been surprised on this great occasion has maintained its place in almost all narratives of the war for fifteen years. The Duke's magnanimous silence under such treatment for so long a period will be appreciated by posterity. The facts of the case are now given from the most unquestionable authority.]

[Footnote 73: The fact of Wellington and Blucher having met between the battles of Ligny and Waterloo is well known to many of the superior officers then in the Netherlands; but the writer of this compendium has never happened to see it mentioned in print. The horse that carried the Duke of Wellington through this long night journey, so important to the decisive battle of the 18th, remained till lately, it is understood, if he does not still remain, a free pensioner in the best paddock of Strathfieldsaye.]

CHAPTER XLI

Napoleon appeals in vain to the Chambers--Abdicates for the second time-- Is sent to Malmaison--And then to Rochefort--Negotiates with Capt. Maitland--Embarks in the Bellerophon--Arrives at Torbay--Decision of the English Government--Interview with Lord Keith, &c.--Napoleon on board the Northumberland--Sails for St. Helena.

On how sandy a foundation the exile of Elba had rebuilt the semblance of his ancient authority, a few hours of adversity were more than sufficient to show. He was still consulting with his ministers (even they were not all his friends) on the morning of the 21st, in what manner he ought to inform the Chambers of his great misfortune, and what assistance he should demand, when the news reached the Elysees, that both the assemblies had met as soon as the story of Waterloo transpired, and passed a series of resolutions, one of which declared the state to be in danger--and another, their sittings permanent; in other words, proclaimed his reign to be at an end. If anything could have been wanted to complete Napoleon's conviction that the army had elevated him in opposition to the nation--it must have been found in the fact that the funds rose rapidly from the moment in which it was known in Paris that the army was ruined. They went on to tell him that the Chambers were debating on the means of defending Paris. "Ah," said he--deeply feeling in what loss all had been lost to him--"Ah, could they but defend them like my Old Guard!"

If Napoleon had listened to the advice of his brother Lucien, and the few who really considered their own fortunes as irrevocably bound up with his, he would have instantly put himself at the head of 6000 of the Imperial Guard, who were then in the capital, and dissolved the unfriendly senate of Paris, on the 21st of June, as unceremoniously as he had that of St. Cloud on the 19th of Brumaire. Lucien said ever after, that, "the smoke of Mont St. Jean had turned his brain." He certainly gave what remained of the day to vacillation. Late in the evening he held a council, to which the presidents and vice-presidents of both Chambers were admitted. In their presence La Fayette signified that nothing could be done until a great sacrifice had been made. Maret answered with fierceness; called for severe measures against the royalists and the disaffected. "Had such been resorted to earlier," cried he, "one who hears me would not be smiling at the misfortunes of France, and Wellington would not be marching on Paris." This strong allusion to Fouchesuited not the temper of the moment. Maret was murmured down; and Carnot himself is said to have shed tears, when he perceived that the abdication was judged necessary. That ancient democrat had indeed just consented to be a count; but he enjoys apparently the credit of having acted on this occasion as a good Frenchman. He saw, say even the anti-Buonapartist historians, that France was invaded, and the same feelings which made him offer his own sword in December, 1813, urged him now to oppose any measure which must deprive his country of the military talents of Napoleon. The Emperor heard all in silence--and broke up the meeting without having come to any decision.

Early next morning the Chambers again met, and the necessity of the Emperor's abdication was on the point of being put to the vote--when Foucheappeared, and saved them that trouble by producing the following proclamation. "To the French people ":

Frenchmen! In commencing war for the maintenance of the national independence, I relied on the union of all efforts, all wills, and all authorities. I had reason to hope for success, and I braved all the declarations of the powers against me. Circumstances appear to be changed. I offer myself as a sacrifice to the hatred of the enemies of France. May they prove sincere in their declarations, and to have aimed only at me! My political life is ended; and I proclaim my son, Napoleon II., Emperor of the French. Unite for the public safety, if you would remain an independent nation.--Done at the palace Elysees, June the 22nd,1815.--

NAPOLEON.

The debate which followed the production of this act in either house, but especially in that of the Peers, was violent. In the latter, Carnot, having received some grossly exaggerated accounts of the force and success of Grouchy, endeavoured to persuade the assembly, that that marshal must have ere then added 60,000 men at Laon to Soult and the relics of Waterloo, and so formed an army capable, under fit guidance, of even yet effectually retrieving the affairs of France. But Ney had arrived in Paris the same morning, and this speech called up the man who, if any single energies could have done so, would have saved the day at Waterloo. "Grouchy," said he, "cannot have more than 20--at most 25,000--men; and as to Soult--I myself commanded the guard in the last assault--I did not leave the field until they were exterminated. Be assured there is but one course--negotiate, and recall the Bourbons. In their return I see nothing but the certainty of being shot as a deserter. I shall seek all I have henceforth to hope for in America. Take you the only course that remains for France."

Napoleon, in his bulletins, did not scruple to throw the blame of his discomfiture on the misconduct of his chief officers--particularly of Grouchy-- and even of Ney himself; nor wanted there devoted men, such as Labedoyere, to sustain these most unfounded charges, and all other arguments anywise favouring the cause of the Emperor, in either chamber. But the truth was great, and prevailed. The Senate, no more than the people, could be deceived now; and though a deputation waited on him at the Elysees, and in most respectful terms thanked him for the sacrifice he had made, he in vain endeavoured to extort any direct avowal that, in accepting his abdication, they considered that act as necessarily accompanied with the immediate proclamation of Napoleon II. The Emperor, for the last time clothed in the imperial garb, and surrounded with his great officers of state, received the deputation with calmness and dignity, and dismissed them with courtesy. He perceived clearly that there was no hope for his son.

Thus terminated the second reign--the hundred days of Napoleon.

By this time, however, Labedoyere's violent language in the Senate--his repeated protestations that unless Napoleon II. were recognised, the abdication of his father was null, and that the country which could hesitate about such an act of justice was worthy of nothing but slavery--began to produce a powerful effect among the regular soldiery of Paris. The Senate called on Napoleon himself to signify to the army that he no longer claimed any authority over them; and he complied, though not without mingling many expressions highly offensive to those whose mandate he obeyed. A provisional government, however, consisting of Fouche Carnot, and three more, was forthwith proclaimed; and when the first of these persons conceived that Napoleon's continued presence in the capital might produce disturbances, and accordingly requested him to withdraw to Malmaison, he found himself obliged to do so. This was on the 24th; and no sooner was he established in this villa, than it became obvious to himself that he was in fact a prisoner. Fouches police surrounded him on all sides; and the military duties about Malmaison were discharged by a party of the national guard, attached to Louis XVIII., and commanded by General Beker, an officer well known to be personally hostile to the fallen sovereign. We have seen how the Parisians veered from side to side at every former crisis of his history, according as the wind of fortune happened to blow. To finish the picture it remains to be told that, ere Napoleon had been two days at Malmaison, he was to all appearance, as much forgotten in the neighbouring capital as if he had never returned from Elba.

The relics of Waterloo, and Grouchy's division, having at length been gathered together under Soult at Laon; were now marching towards Paris, and followed hard behind by Wellington and Blucher. The provisional government began to be seriously alarmed lest Buonaparte should, by some desperate effort, escape from Malmaison, and once more place himself at the head of a considerable armed force. He himself, indeed, was continually sending to them, requesting permission to take the field as General for Napoleon II.; and one of the government, Carnot, was heartily desirous that this prayer should be granted. Under such circumstances, Fouche who had, throughout, corresponded with and plotted against all parties, now employed every art to persuade the fallen chief that the only course, whether of safety or of dignity, that remained for him, was to fly immediately to the United States of America; and, that nothing may be wanting to show how the great and the little were perpetually intermingled in the fortunes of Buonaparte, one of the means adopted by this intriguer, and not the least effectual, was that of stimulating the personal creditors of the dethroned Emperor and his family to repair incessantly to Malmaison and torment him with demands of payment. Meantime Fouchesent to the Duke of Wellington, announcing that Napoleon had made up his mind to repair to America, and requesting a safe-conduct for him across the Atlantic. The Duke replied, that he had no authority to grant any passports to Napoleon Buonaparte; and the only consequence (as Fouchehad perhaps anticipated) was, that the English Admiralty quickened their diligence, and stationed no less than thirty cruisers along the western coasts of France, for the purpose of intercepting the disturber of the world in his meditated flight.

Fouche in communicating to Napoleon the refusal of Wellington, took care to signify urgent fears that the English government might adopt such measures as these, and to build on this a new argument for the hastening of his departure from the neighbourhood of Paris. He informed him that two frigates and some smaller vessels awaited his orders at Rochefort, and assured him, that if he repaired thither on the instant, he would still be in time.

Napoleon hesitated at Malmaison, as he had done before at the Kremlin--at Dresden--and at Fontainebleau. The cry of the approaching soldiery of Soult was already in his ear, inviting him to be once more their Emperor. On the other hand, it was now too obvious, that the army alone retained any reverence for him; and, lastly, what after all could he hope to effect with at most 60,000 men, against the victorious hosts of Wellington and Blucher, backed, as they were about to be, by great reinforcements from England and Prussia, and by the whole armies of Spain, Italy, Germany, Austria and the Czar?--Napoleon well knew that ere six weeks more elapsed, 800,000 foreigners would be cantoned within the boundaries of France. He at length yielded; and on the 29th of June left Malmaison, accompanied by Savary, Bertrand, Las Cazes, and others of his attached servants, and attended by a considerable guard.

Napoleon reached Rochefort on the 3rd of July; and took up his residence in the prefect's house, with the view of embarking immediately: but he forthwith was informed, that a British line-of-battle ship (the Bellerophon, Captain Maitland) and some smaller vessels of war were off the roads, and given to understand that the commanders of the squadron at his own disposal showed no disposition to attempt the passage out in face of these watchers. A Danish merchant-ship was then hired, and the Emperor occupied himself with various devices for concealing his person in the hold of this vessel. But the Danish captain convinced him ere long that the British searchers would not be likely to pass him undetected, and this plan too was abandoned. Some young French midshipmen then gallantly offered to act as the crew of a small flat coasting vessel, a chausse-marree, and attempt the escape in this way under cloud of night. But all experienced seamen concurred in representing the imminent hazard of exposing such a vessel to the Atlantic, as well as the numberless chances of its also being detected by the English cruisers. "Where-ever wood can swim," said Napoleon, "there I am sure to find this flag of England."

Meanwhile time passed on; and it became known that the French army had once more retired from before the walls of Paris under a convention: that Wellington and Blucher were about to enter the city, and reseat Louis on his throne; that the royalists were everywhere assuming the decided advantage-- that the white flag was already hoisted in the neighbouring town of Rochelle--and that it would be so at Rochefort itself on the instant, were his person removed. Under such circumstances, to attempt a journey into the interior of France, with the view of rejoining Soult, now marching on the Loire, or with any other purpose, must needs expose Napoleon to every chance of falling into the hands of the Bourbons; and at length, since it was impossible to sail out of Rochefort without the consent of the English, it was resolved to open a negotiation with their commander.

On the 19th of July, Savary and Count Las Cazes came off with a flag of truce, and began their conversation by stating that the Emperor had been promised a safe-conduct for America, and asking if the document were in Captain Maitland's hands? No safe-conduct of any kind had been promised or contemplated by any English authority whatever; and the captain could only answer that, as far as concerned himself, his orders were to make every effort to prevent Buonaparte from escaping, and if so fortunate as to obtain possession of his person, to sail at once with him for England. Savary and Las Cazes made great efforts to persuade Maitland that Napoleon's removal from France was a matter of pure voluntary choice; but this the British officer considered as a question wherewith he had nothing to do. The utmost the Frenchmen could extract from him was, that he, as a private individual, had no reason to doubt but that Buonaparte, if he sailed for England in the Bellerophon, would be well treated there.

The same personages returned on the 14th, and another conversation, longer, but to the same purpose, was held by them with Maitland, in the presence of Captain Sartorius and Captain Gambier, both of the royal navy. These gentlemen have corroborated completely the statement of Maitland, that he, on the second as on the first interview, continued to guard the Frenchmen against the remotest conception of his being entitled to offer any pledge whatever to Napoleon, except that he would convey him in safety off the English coast, there to abide the determination of the English government. Savary and Las Cazes, on the contrary, persisted in asserting that Maitland, on the 14th July, gave a pledge that Napoleon, if he came on board the Bellerophon, should be received there not as a prisoner of war, but as a voluntary guest, and that it was solely in consequence of this pledge that Napoleon finally resolved to embark. But there is one piece of evidence in contradiction of this story, of which even themselves could hardly dispute the weight--to wit, the date of the following letter to the Prince Regent of England, which General Gourgaud brought out the same evening to the Bellerophon, and which clearly proves--that what Napoleon ultimately did on the 15th, depended in nowise on anything that Maitland said on the 14th.

Rochefort, July THE 13TH, 1815

"Royal Highness,

"A victim to the factions which divide my country, and to the hostility of the greatest Powers of Europe, I have terminated my political career, and come, like Themistocles, to seat myself on the hearth of the British people. I put myself under the protection of their laws, which I claim from your Royal Highness as the most powerful, the most constant, and the most generous of my enemies.

NAPOLEON."

Maitland sent on Gourgaud in the Slaney with this letter; and having once more addressed Las Cazes in these words "You will recollect that I am not authorised to stipulate as to the reception of Buonaparte in England, but that he must consider himself as entirely at the disposal of His Royal Highness the Prince Regent"--prepared his ship for the reception of the fallen Emperor.

On the 15th the Epervier brig brought him out of the Aix roads; but wind and tide being unfavourable, Maitland sent the barge of the Bellerophon to transport him to the ship. The officers and most of the crew of the Epervier saw him depart, with tears in their eyes, and continued to cheer him as long as their voices could be heard. Captain Maitland received him respectfully, but without any salute or distinguished honours. Napoleon uncovered himself on reaching the quarter-deck, and said in a firm tone of voice, "I come to place myself under the protection of your prince and laws."

On board the Bellerophon, as before in the Undaunted, Buonaparte made himself very popular among both officers and crew. He examined everything--praised everything--extolled the English nation--above all, the English navy--and even admitted that the Duke of Wellington, "equal to himself in all other military qualities, was superior in prudence." On the 23rd they passed Ushant, and Napoleon gazed long and mournfully--and for the last time--on the coast of France. On the 24th the Bellerophon entered Torbay, and Maitland was instantly admonished to permit no communication of any kind between his ship and the coast. On the 26th Maitland was ordered round to Plymouth Sound: and the arrival of Buonaparte having by this time transpired, the ship was instantly surrounded by swarms of boats, filled with persons whose curiosity nothing could repress. There was considerable difficulty in keeping the ship itself clear of these eager multitudes. Napoleon appeared on the deck, was greeted with huzzas, and bowed and smiled in return.

On the 31st of July, Sir H. Bunbury, under-secretary of state, and Lord Keith, admiral of the Channel fleet, repaired on board the Bellerophon, and announced the final resolution of the British government: namely, 1st, that General Buonaparte should not be landed in England, but removed forthwith to St. Helena, as being the situation in which, more than any other at their command, the government thought security against a second escape, and the indulgence to himself of personal freedom and exercise, might be reconciled; 2ndly, that, with the exception of Savary and L'Allemand, he might take with him any three officers he chose, as also his surgeon, and twelve domestics.

This letter was read in French by Sir Henry Bunbury. Napoleon listened without look or gesture of impatience or surprise. Being then asked if he had anything to reply, he with perfect calmness of voice and manner protested against the orders to which he had been listening, and against the right claimed by the English Government to dispose of him as a prisoner of war. "I came into your ship," said he, "as I would into one of your villages. If I had been told I was to be a prisoner, I would not have come." He then expatiated at great length on the title given him--General Buonaparte--and on the right which he had to be considered as a sovereign prince; he was, he said, three months before, as much Emperor of Elba as Louis was King of France, and, by invading another monarch's dominions, could not have forfeited his own rank as a monarch. He next adverted to the ignoble attitude in which England would place herself in the eyes of the world by abusing his confidence--hinted that either his father-in-law or the Czar would have treated him far differently--and concluded by expressing his belief that the climate and continement of St. Helena would kill him, and his resolution, therefore, not to go to St. Helena. By what means he designed to resist the command of the English government, Napoleon did not say: there can be no doubt he meant Lord Keith and Sir H. Bunbury to understand, that, rather than submit to the voyage in question, he would commit suicide; and what he thus hinted, was soon expressed distinctly, with all the accompaniments of tears and passion, by two French ladies on board the Bellerophon--Madame Bertrand and Madame Montholon. But all this appears to have been set down, from the beginning, exactly for what it was worth. He who had chosen to outlive Krasnoi, and Leipzig, and Montmartre, and Waterloo, was not likely to die by his own hand in the Bellerophon. We desire not to be considered as insinuating, according to the custom of many, that Napoleon ought to have rushed voluntarily on some English bayonet, when the fate of the 18th of June could no longer be doubtful. Laying all religious and moral obligations out of view (as probably he did), Napoleon himself said truly, that "if Marius had fallen on his sword amidst the marches of Minturn? he would never have enjoyed his 7th consulate." No man ever more heartily than Napoleon approved the old maxim, that while there is life there is hope; and, far from thinking seriously at any time of putting an end to his own days, we must doubt if, between his abdication at the Elysees and the time wherein he felt the immediate approach of death, there occurred one day, or even one hour, in which some hope or scheme of recovering his fortunes did not agitate his mind.

 With regard to Napoleon's reclamations against the decision of the English government, it may probably suffice now to observe--1st, that that government had never, at any period, acknowledged him as Emperor of France, and that it refused to be a party to the treaty under which he retired to Elba, simply because it was resolved not to acknowledge him as Emperor of Elba. These things Napoleon well knew; and as to his recent re-exercise of imperial functions in France, he well knew that the English government had continued to acknowledge Louis XVIII. as King all through the hundred days. Upon no principle, therefore, could he have expected beforehand to be treated as Emperor by the ministers of the Prince Regent; nor, even if he had been born a legitimate prince, would it have been in the usual course of things for him, under existing circumstances, to persist in the open retention of his imperial style. By assuming some incognito, as sovereigns when travelling out of their own dominions are accustomed to do, Napoleon might have cut the root away from one long series of his subsequent disputes with the English government and authorities. But in doing as he did, he acted on calculation. He never laid aside the hopes of escape and of empire. It was his business to have complaints. If everything went on quietly and smoothly about him, what was to ensure the keeping up of a lively interest in his fortunes among the faction, to which he still looked as inclined to befriend him, and above all, among the soldiery, of whose personal devotion, even after the fatal catastrophe of Waterloo, he had no reason to doubt? Buonaparte, in his days of success, always attached more importance to etiquette than a prince born to the purple, and not quite a fool, would have been likely to do: but in the obstinacy with which, after his total downfall, he clung to the airy sound of majesty, and such pigmy toys of observance as could be obtained under his circumstances, we cannot persuade ourselves to behold no more than the sickly vanity of a parvenu. The English government acknowledged him by the highest military rank he had held at that time when the treaty of Amiens was concluded with him as First Consul; and the sound of _General Buonaparte_, now so hateful in his ears, who had under that style wielded the destinies of the world, might have been lost, if Napoleon himself had chosen, in some factitious style.

To come to the more serious charges. Napoleon, driven to extremity in 1814 by the united armies of Europe, abdicated his throne, that abdication being the price of peace to France, and to soothe his personal sufferings, obtained the sovereignty of Elba. When he violated the treaty by returning in arms to Provence, the other provisions, which gave peace to France and Elba to him, were annulled of course. When the fortune of Waterloo compelled him to take refuge in the Bellerophon--what was to be done? To replace in Elba, or any similar situation, under some new treaty, the man who had just broken a most solemn one, was out of the question. To let him remain at large in the midst of a country close to France, wherein the press is free to licentiousness, and the popular mind liable to extravagant agitations, would have been to hazard the domestic tranquillity of England, and throw a thousand new difficulties in the way of every attempt to consolidate the social and political system of the French monarchy. In most other times the bullet or the axe would have been the gentlest treatment to be expected by one who had risen so high, and fallen so fatally. This his surrender to Captain Maitland--to say nothing of the temper of the times--put out of the question. It remained to place him in a situation wherein his personal comfort might as far as possible be united with security to the peace of the world; and no one has as yet pretended to point out a situation preferable in this point of view to that remote and rocky island of the Atlantic, on which it was the fortune of the great Napoleon to close his earthly career. The reader cannot require to be reminded that the personage, whose relegation to St. Helena has formed the topic of so many indignant appeals and contemptuous commentaries, was, after all, the same man, who, by an act of utterly wanton and unnecessary violence, seized Pius VII. and detained him a prisoner for nearly four years, and who, having entrapped Ferdinand VII. to Bayonne, and extorted his abdication by the threat of murder, concluded by locking him up during five years at Valeney.

The hints and threats of suicide having failed in producing the desired effect--and a most ridiculous attempt on the part of some crazy persons in England to get possession of Napoleon's person, by citing him to appear as a witness on a case of libel, having been baffled, more formally than was necessary, by the swift sailing of the Bellerophon for the Start--the fallen Emperor at length received in quiet the intimation, that Admiral Sir George Cockburn was ready to receive him on board the Northumberland, and convey him to St. Helena. Savary and L'Allemand were among the few persons omitted by name in King Louis's amnesty on his second restoration, and they were extremely alarmed when they found that the retreat of St. Helena was barred on them by the English government. They even threatened violence--but consulting Sir Samuel Romilly, and thus ascertaining that the government had no thoughts of surrendering them to Louis XVIII., submitted at length with a good grace to the inevitable separation. Napoleon's suite, as finally arranged, consisted of Count Bertrand (grand master of the palace), Count Montholon (one of his council of state), Count Las Cazes, General Gourgaud (his aide-de-camp), and Dr. O'Meara, an Irish naval surgeon, whom he had found in the Bellerophon, and who was now by his desire transferred to the Northumberland. Bertrand and Montholon were accompanied by their respective countesses and some children; and twelve upper domestics of the imperial household followed their master's fortune. Of the money which Napoleon had with him, to the amount of some ?000, the British government took possession, pro tempore, announcing that they charged themselves with providing regularly for all the expenditure of his establishment; but his plate, chiefly gold and of much value, was permitted to remain untouched.

On the 8th of August the Northumberland sailed for St. Helena, and the exile had his first view of his destined retreat on the 15th of October, 1815. During the voyage, Sir George Cockburn departed from some observances of respect into which Captain Maitland had very naturally fallen, under very different circumstances. The admiral, in a word, did not permit Napoleon to assume the first place on board the Northumberland. He did the honours of the table himself; nor did he think it necessary to break up his company immediately after dinner, because the ex-emperor chose to rise then--in adherence to the custom of French society: neither did he man his yards or fire salutes on any occasion, as is done in the case of crowned heads, nor follow the example of the French suite in remaining at all times uncovered in the presence of Napoleon. With these exceptions, General Buonaparte was treated with all the respect which great genius and great misfortunes could claim from a generous mind; nor was he on the whole insensible to the excellent conduct either of Maitland or of Cockburn. Cruelly and most unjustly attacked, as the former had been, by Las Cazes and Savary--and by Napoleon--when the captain of the Bellerophon comes to record his final sentiments towards his prisoner, it is in these affecting words--"It may appear surprising that a possibility should exist of a British officer being prejudiced in favour of one who had caused so many calamities to his country; but to such an extent did he possess the power of pleasing, that there are few people who could have sat at the same table with him for nearly a month, as I did, without feeling a sensation of pity, perhaps allied to regret, that a man possessed of so many fascinating qualities, and who had held so high a station in life, should be reduced to the situation in which I saw him."

To the extraordinary power of fascination which Napoleon had at command, a still more striking testimony occurs in an anecdote, apparently well authenticated, of Lord Keith. When someone alluded in this old admiral's hearing to Buonaparte's repeated request of a personal interview with the Prince Regent, "On my conscience," said Lord Keith, "I believe, if you consent to that, they will be excellent friends within half an hour."

CHAPTER XLII

Napoleon at St. Helena--The Briars--Longwood--Charges against the English Government respecting his accommodations and treatment at St. Helena-- Charges against the Governor, Sir Hudson Lowe--Napoleon's mode of life at Longwood--His Health falls off--His Death and Funeral--Conclusion.

Napoleon was weary of shipboard, and, therefore, landed immediately. Finding the curiosity of the people troublesome, he took up his quarters at The Briars, a small cottage about half a mile from James's Town, during the interval which must needs elapse before the admiral could provide suitable accommodation for his permanent residence. For that purpose Longwood, a villa about six miles from James's Town, was, after an examination of all that the island afforded, determined on; except Plantation House, the country residence of the governor, there was no superior house in St. Helena; and two months having been employed diligently in some additions and repairs, the fallen Emperor took possession of his appointed abode on the 10th of December. The very limited accommodation of the Briars (where, indeed, Napoleon merely occupied a pavilion of two chambers in the garden of a Mr. Balcombe), had hitherto prevented him from having, all his little suite of attendants under the same roof with him. They were now re-assembled at Longwood, with the exception of M. and Mme. Montholon, who occupied a separate house at some little distance from it. While at The Briars, Napoleon made himself eminently agreeable to the family of the Balcombes, particularly the young ladies and children, and submitted on the whole with temper and grace to the inconveniences of narrow accommodation in-doors, and an almost total want of exercise abroad--this last evil occasioned wholly by his own reluctance to ride out in the neighbourhood of the town. He continued also to live on terms of perfect civility with Sir George Cockburn; and, notwithstanding some occasional ebullitions of violence, there seemed to be no reason for doubting that, when fairly established with his suite about him, he would gradually reconcile himself to the situation in which he was likely to remain, and turn his powerful faculties upon some study or pursuit worthy of their energy, and capable of cheating captivity of half its bitterness. These anticipations were not realised.

The accusations brought by the prisoner and his instruments against the government of England, in regard to the accommodations at Longwood, the arrangements concerning the household establishment, and the regulations adopted with a view to the security of his person, have been so often answered in detail, that we may spare ourselves the pain of dwelling on transactions little worthy of filling a large space in the story of Napoleon. It being granted that it was necessary to provide against the evasion of Buonaparte; that the protracted separation from him of his wife and son (not, at any rate, the act of England, but of Austria) was in itself justified by obvious political considerations; and that England would have given good reason of offence to the King of France, had she complied with Napoleon's repeated demands, to be styled and treated as Emperor--if these things be granted, we do not see how even the shadow of blame can attach to the much-abused ministers, on whom fortune threw one of the most delicate and thankless of all offices. His house was, save one (that of the governor), the best on the island: from the beginning it was signified that any alterations or additions, suggested by Napoleon, would be immediately attended to; and the framework of many apartments was actually prepared in England, to be sent out and distributed according to his pleasure. As it was, Napoleon had for his own immediate personal accommodation, a suite of rooms, consisting of a saloon, an eating-room, a library, a billiard-room, a small study, a bedroom, and a bathroom; and various English gentlemen, accustomed to all the appliances of modern luxury, who visited the exile of Longwood, concur in stating that the accommodations around him appeared to them every way complete and unobjectionable. He had a good collection of books, and the means of adding to these as much as he chose. His suite consisted in all of five gentlemen and two ladies: the superior French and Italian domestics about his own person were never fewer than eleven; and the sum allowed for his domestic expenditure was ?2,000 per annum--the governor of St. Helena, moreover, having authority to draw on the treasury for any larger sum, in case he should consider ?2,000 as insufficient. When we consider that wines, and most other articles heavily taxed in England, go duty-free to St. Helena, it is really intolerable to be told that this income was not adequate--nay, that it was not munificent--for a person in Napoleon's situation. It was a larger income than is allotted to the governor of any English colony whatever, except the governor-general of India. It was twice as large as the official income of a British secretary of state has ever been. We decline entering at all into the minor charges connected with this humiliating subject: at least a single example may serve. One of the loudest complaints was about the deficiency and inferior quality of wine: on examination it appeared, that Napoleon's upper domestics were allowed each day, per man, a bottle of claret, costing ? per dozen (without duty) and the lowest menial employed at Longwood a bottle of good Teneriffe wine daily.--That the table of the fallen Emperor himself was always served in a style at least answerable to the dignity of a general officer in the British service--this was never even denied. Passing from the interior--we conceive that we cannot do better than quote the language of one of his casual and impartial visitors, Mr. Ellis. "There never, perhaps," (says this gentleman), "was a prisoner, so much requiring to be watched and guarded, to whom so much liberty and range for exercise was allowed. With an officer he may go over any part of the island: wholly unobserved, his limits extend four miles--partially observed, eight--and overlooked twelve. At night the sentinels certainly close round Longwood itself." It indeed appears impossible to conceive of a prisoner more liberally treated in all these respects. There remains the constantly repeated vituperation of the climate of St. Helena. It appears, however, by tables kept and published by Dr. Arnott, that the sick list of a regiment, stationed close to Buonaparte's residence during his stay, rarely contained more than one name out of forty-five--a proportion which must be admitted to be most remarkably small. In effect, the house of Longwood stands 2000 feet above the level of the sea; the ocean breezes purify the air continually; and within the tropics there is probably no healthier situation whatever. If it be said that Napoleon should not have been confined within the tropics at all--it is answered that it was necessary to remove him from the neighbourhood of the countries in which his name was the watchword of rebellion and discord-- and that, after all, Napoleon was a native of Corsica, one of the hottest climates in Europe, and was at all times, constitutionally, able to endure the extremes of heat much better than of cold--witness Egypt and Russia.

There was a rule that Napoleon's correspondence should all pass through the hands of the governor of St. Helena--and this Sir Walter Scott condemns. Had the English government acted on the Buonapartean model, they would have made no such regulation, but taken the liberty of privately examining his letters, and resealing them, after the fashion of the post-office under Lavalette. It diminishes our regret when we learn from Sir Walter Scott's next page, that, in spite of all laws and severities on this score, Napoleon and the companions of his exile contrived, from the beginning to the end, to communicate with their friends in Europe, without the supervision of any English authorities whatever.

The finishing touch is put to the picture of unworthy duplicity by one of Napoleon's own followers, and most noisy champions, General Gourgaud. This gentleman himself informed the English government, that at the time when Napoleon, in order to create the notion that his supplies were restricted beyond all endurance, sent some plate to James's Town to be broken up and sold, he, Napoleon, had in his strong box at Longwood at least ?0,000 in gold coin.

There is one name which will descend to posterity laden with a tenfold portion of the abuse which Napoleon and his associates lavished on all persons connected in any degree with the superintendence and control of his captive condition--that of Sir Hudson Lowe, a general officer in the English army, who became governor of St. Helena in May, 1816, and continued to hold that situation down to the period of the ex-emperor's death in 1821. The vanity of Napoleon appears to have been wounded from the beginning by this appointment. According to him, no person ought in decency to have been entrusted with the permanent care of his detention, but some English nobleman of the highest rank. The answer is very plain, that the situation was not likely to find favour in the eyes of any such person; and when one considers what the birth and manners of by far the greater number of Buonaparte's own courtiers, peers and princes included, were, it is difficult to repress wonder in listening to this particular subject of complaint. Passing over this original quarrel--it appears that, according to Buonaparte's own admission, Sir H. Lowe endeavoured, when he took his thankless office upon him, to place the intercourse between himself and his prisoner on a footing as gracious as could well be looked for under all the circumstances of the case; and that he, the ex-emperor, ere the governor had been a week at St. Helena, condescended to insult him to his face by language so extravagantly, intolerably, and vulgarly offensive, as never ought, under any circumstances whatever, to have stained the lips of one who made any pretension to the character of a gentleman. Granting that Sir Hudson Lowe was not an officer of the first distinction--it must be admitted that he did no wrong in accepting a duty offered to him by his government; and that Napoleon was guilty, not only of indecorum, but of meanness, in reproaching a man so situated, as he did almost at their first interview, with the circumstances--of which at worst it could but be said that they were not splendid--of his previous life. But this is far too little. Granting that Sir Hudson Lowe had been in history and in conduct, both before he came to St. Helena and during his stay there, all that the most ferocious libels of the Buonapartists have ever dared to say or to insinuate--it would still remain a theme of unmixed wonder and regret, that Napoleon Buonaparte should have stooped to visit on his head the wrongs which, if they were wrongs, proceeded not from the governor of St. Helena, but from the English ministry, whose servant he was. "I can only account," says Mr. Ellis, "for his petulance and unfounded complaints from one of two motives--either he wishes by these means to keep alive an interest in Europe, and more especially in England, where he flatters himself he has a party; or his troubled mind finds an occupation in the tracasseries which his present conduct gives to the governor. If the latter be the case, it is in vain for any governor to unite being on good terms with him to the performance of his duty."

Napoleon did everything he could to irritate this unfortunate governor. He called him scrivener, thieftaker, liar, hangman; rejected all his civilities as insults; encouraged his attendants to rival in these particulars the audacity of his own language and conduct; refused by degrees to take the exercise which his health required, on pretext that it did him more harm than good when he knew himself to be riding within view of English sentinels (which was not necessary at all within four miles of Longwood), or attended by an English officer--which was not necessary unless at the distance of twelve miles from Longwood: above all, opposed every obstacle to the enforcement of that most proper regulation which made it necessary that his person should, once in every twenty-four hours, be visible to some British officer. In a word, Napoleon Buonaparte bent the whole energies of his mighty intellect to the ignoble task of tormenting Sir Hudson Lowe; and the extremities of degradation to which these efforts occasionally reduced himself, in the eyes of his own attendants, are such as we dare not particularise, and as will be guessed by no one who has not read the memoir of his Italian doctor, Antommarchi.

Meantime, the great object was effectually attained. The wrongs of Napoleon, the cold cruelty of the English government, and the pestilent petty tyranny of Sir Hudson Lowe, were the perpetual themes of table-talk all over Europe. There were statesmen of high rank in either house of the British parliament, who periodically descanted on these topics--and the answers as often elicited from the ministers of the crown, only silenced such declamations for the moment, that they might be renewed with increased violence after time had elapsed sufficient to allow the news to come back to England with the comments of Longwood. The utter impossibility of an escape from St. Helena was assumed on all such occasions, with the obvious inference that there could be no use for sentinels and domiciliary visitations at Longwood, except for the gratification of malignant power. But it is now ascertained, that, throughout the whole period of the detention, schemes of evasion were in agitation at St. Helena, and that agents were busy, sometimes in London, more frequently in North America, with preparations which had no other object in view. A steamship, halting just beyond the line of sight, might undoubtedly have received Napoleon at certain seasons of the year without difficulty, could he only contrive to elude the nocturnal vigilance of the sentinels about the house of Longwood: and that this was impossible, or even difficult, General Gourgaud himself does not hesitate to deny. The rumours of these plots reached from time to time Sir Hudson Lowe; and, quickening of course his fears and his circumspection, kept the wounds of jealousy and distrust continually open and angry.

There were moments, however, in which Napoleon appeared, to persons likely to influence public feeling in Europe by their reports, in attitudes of a far different description. When strangers of eminence (generally officers on their way to or from India), halting at St. Helena, requested and obtained permission to pay their respects at Longwood, Napoleon received them, for the most part, with the ease and dignity of a man superior to adversity. It was by these worthier exhibitions that the fallen Emperor earned the lofty eulogy of Byron:

"--Well thy soul hath brooked the turning tide, With that untaught innate philosophy, Which, be it wisdom, coldness, or deep pride, Is gall and wormwood to an enemy. When the whole host of hatred stood hard by, To watch and mock thee shrinking, thou hast smiled With a sedate and all-enduring eye; When Fortune fled her spoiled and favourite child, He stood unbowed beneath the ills upon him piled."

Among the visitors now alluded to was Captain Basil Hall: and he has, perhaps, presented the world with the most graphic sketch of Napoleon as he appeared on such occasions at Longwood. "Buonaparte" (says this traveller) "struck me (Aug. 13, 1817) as differing considerably from all the pictures and busts I had seen of him. His face and figure looked much broader and more square--larger, indeed, in every way, than any representation I had met with. His corpulency, at this time reported to be excessive, was by no means remarkable. His flesh looked, on the contrary, firm and muscular. There was not the least trace of colour in his cheeks; in fact, his skin was more like marble than ordinary flesh. Not the smallest wrinkle was discernible on his brow, nor an approach to a furrow on any part of his countenance. His health and spirits, judging from appearances, were excellent; though, at this period, it was generally believed in England that he was fast sinking under a complication of diseases, and that his spirits were entirely gone. His manner of speaking was rather slow than otherwise, and perfectly distinct: and he waited with great patience and kindness for my answers to his questions. The brilliant and sometimes dazzling expression of his eye could not be overlooked. It was not, however, a permanent lustre, for it was only remarkable when he was excited by some point of particular interest. It is impossible to imagine an expression of more entire mildness, I may almost call it of benignity and kindliness, than that which played over his features during the whole interview. If, therefore, he was at this time out of health and in low spirits, his power of self-command must have been even more extraordinary than is generally supposed; for his whole deportment, his conversation, and the expression of his face, indicated a frame in perfect health, and a mind at ease."

These favourable reports from seemingly impartial witnesses, lent new wings to the tale of Sir Hudson Lowe's oppression; and perhaps the exile of St. Helena continued to fill a larger space in the eye of the world at large, than had ever before fallen to the lot of one removed for ever, to all appearance, from the great theatre of human passions. It was then that Lord Byron thus apostrophised him:

"Conqueror and Captive of the Earth art thou! She trembles at thee still--and thy wild name Was ne'er more bruited in men's minds than now That thou art nothing, save the jest of Fame, Who woo'd thee once, thy vassal and became The flatterer of thy fierceness, till thou wert A god unto thyself--nor less the same To the astounded kingdoms all inert, Who deemed thee for a time whate'er thou didst assert."

And it was then that an English nobleman of high rank, who throughout manifested especial interest in the fortunes of Napoleon, inscribed his statue (in the gardens of Holland House) with the lines of Homer.

In ordinary times, the course of Napoleon's life at Longwood appears to have been as follows. He rose early, and, as soon as he was out of bed, either mounted on horseback, or began to dictate some part of the history of his life to Montholon or Gourgaud. He breakfasted _?la fourchette_, sometimes alone, sometimes with his suite, between 10 and 11 o'clock; read or dictated until between 2 and 3, when he received such visitors as he chose to admit. He then rode out, either on horseback or in his carriage, for a couple of hours, attended generally by all his suite; then read or dictated again until near eight, at which hour dinner was served. He preferred plain food, and ate plentifully. A few glasses of claret, less than an English pint, were taken during dinner; and a cup of coffee concluded the second and last meal of the day, as the first. A single glass of champagne, or any stronger wine, was sufficient to call the blood into his cheek. His constitutional delicacy of stomach, indeed, is said to have been such, that it was at all times actually impossible for him to indulge any of the coarser appetites of our nature to excess. He took, however, great quantities of snuff. A game of chess, a French tragedy read aloud, or conversation, closed the evening. The habits of his life had taught him to need but little sleep, and to take this by starts; and he generally had some one to read to him after he went to bed at night, as is common with those whose pillows are pressed by anxious heads.

Napoleon was elaborately careful of his person. He loved the bath, and took it at least once every day. His dress at St. Helena was generally the same which he had worn at the Tuileries as Emperor--viz. the green uniform, faced with red, of the chasseurs of the guard, with the star and cordon of the Legion of Honour. His suite to the last continued to maintain around him, as far as was possible, the style and circumstance of his court.

As early as the battle of Waterloo, reports were prevalent in France that Napoleon's health was declining; yet we have already seen that, so late as April, 1817, no symptom of bodily illness could be traced in his external appearance. From this time, however, his attendants continued to urge, with increasing vehemence, the necessity of granting more indulgence, in consequence of the shattered condition of his constitution: and, although such suggestions were, for obvious reasons, listened to at first with considerable suspicion, there can be little doubt now, that in this matter the fame of Longwood spake truth.

Dr. Arnott, an English physician, already referred to, who attended on Napoleon's death-bed, has informed us that he himself frequently reverted to the fact, that his father died of scirrhus of the pylorus. "We have high authority" (says this writer) "that this affection of the stomach cannot be produced without a considerable predisposition of the parts to disease. If, then, it should be admitted that a previous disposition of the parts to this disease did exist, might not the depressing passions of the mind act as an exciting cause? It is more than probable that Napoleon Buonaparte's mental sufferings in St. Helena were very poignant. By a man of such unbounded ambition, and who had once aimed at universal dominion, captivity must have been severely felt. I can safely assert, that any one of temperate habits, who is not exposed to much bodily exertion, night air, and atmospherical changes, may have as much immunity from disease in St. Helena as in Europe; and I may, therefore, further assert, that the disease of which Buonaparte died was not the effect of climate."--It is added, that out of all Napoleon's family, which, including English and Chinese servants, amounted to fifty persons, only one individual died during the five years of their stay in St. Helena, and this man, an Italian major-domo, had brought the seeds of consumption with him from Europe.

In March, 1817, Lord Holland made a solemn appeal to the British Parliament on the subject of Napoleon's treatment, and was answered by Lord Bathurst--in such a manner that not one could be found to second him. The intelligence of this appears to have exerted a powerful influence on the spirits of the captive. It was about the 25th of September 1818, that his health began to be affected in a manner sufficient to excite alarm in Dr. O'Meara, who informed him, that unless he took regular exercise out of doors (which of late he had seldom done), the progress of the evil would be rapid. Napoleon declared, in answer, that he would never more take exercise while exposed to the challenge of sentinels. The physician stated, that if he persisted, the end would be fatal. "I shall have this consolation at least," answered he, "that my death will be an eternal dishonour to the English nation, who sent me to this climate to die under the hands of...." O'Meara again represented the consequences of his obstinacy. "That which is written, is written," said Napoleon, looking up, "our days are reckoned."

Shortly after this, O'Meara--being detected in a suspicious correspondence with one Holmes, Napoleon's pecuniary agent in London--was sent home by Sir Hudson Lowe; and, Napoleon declining to receive any physician of the governor's nomination instead, an Italian, by name Antommarchi, was sent out by his sister Pauline. With this doctor there came also two Italian priests, whose presence Napoleon himself had solicited, and selected by his uncle, Cardinal Fesch.

His obstinate refusal to take bodily exercise might have sprung in some measure from internal and indescribable sensations. To all Antommarchi's medical prescriptions, he opposed the like determination. "Doctor," he said (14th October 1820), "no physicking; we are a machine made to live; we are organised for that purpose, and such is our nature; do not counteract the living principle--let it alone--leave it the liberty of self-defence--it will do better than your drugs. Our body is a watch, intended to go for a given time. The watchmaker cannot open it, and must work at random. For once that he relieves or assists it by his crooked instruments, he injured it ten times, and at last destroys it."

With the health of Napoleon his mind sank also. Some fishes in a pond in the garden at Longwood had attracted his notice; a deleterious substance happened to mix with the water--they sickened and died. "Everything I love," said Napoleon, "everything that belongs to me--is stricken. Heaven and mankind unite to afflict me." Fits of long silence and profound melancholy were now frequent. "In those days," he once said aloud, in a reverie, "In those days I was Napoleon. Now I am nothing--my strength, my faculties forsake me--I no longer live, I only exist."

When Sir Hudson Lowe was made aware of the condition of the captive, he informed the government at home; and by his Majesty's desire, authority was immediately given for removing to St. Helena from the Cape, any medical officer on whom Napoleon's choice might fall. This despatch did not, however, reach St. Helena, until Napoleon had breathed his last.

About the middle of April, 1821, the disease assumed such an appearance, that Dr. Antommarchi became very anxious to have the advice of some English physician, and the patient at length consented to admit the visits of Dr. Arnott, already referred to. But this gentleman also was heard in vain urging the necessity of medical applications. "Quod scriptum scriptum," once more answered Napoleon; "our hour is marked, and no one can claim a moment of life beyond what fate has predestined."

From the 15th to the 25th of April, Napoleon occupied himself with drawing up his last will--in which he bequeathed his orders, and a specimen of every article in his wardrobe, to his son. On the 18th he gave directions for opening his body after death, expressing a special desire that his stomach should be scrutinised, and its appearances communicated to his son. "The vomitings," he said, "which succeed one another without interruption, seem to show that of all my organs the stomach is the most diseased. I am inclined to believe it is attacked with the disorder which killed my father--a scirrhus in the pylorus--the physicians of Montpelier prophesied it would be hereditary in our family." He also gave directions to the priest Vignali as to the manner in which he wished his body to be laid out in a chambre ardente (a state-room lighted with torches). "I am neither an atheist," said Napoleon, "nor a rationalist; I believe in God, and am of the religion of my father. I was born a Catholic, and will fulfil all the duties of that church, and receive the assistance which she administers."

On the 3rd of May it became evident that the scene was near its close. The attendants would fain have called in more medical men; but they durst not, knowing his feelings on this head: "Even had he been speechless," said one of them, "we could not have brooked his eye." The last sacraments of the church were now administered by Vignali. He lingered on thenceforth in a delirious stupor. On the 4th the island was swept by a tremendous storm, which tore up almost all the trees about Longwood by the roots. The 5th was another day of tempests; and about six in the evening, Napoleon--having pronounced the words "te d'arm," passed for ever from the dreams of battle.

On the 6th of May the body being opened by Antommarchi, in the presence of five British medical men, and a number of the military officers of the garrison, as well as Bertrand and Montholon, the cause of death was sufficiently manifest. A cancerous ulcer occupied almost the whole of the stomach.

Napoleon desired in his will, that his body should be buried "on the banks of the Seine; among the French people, whom he had loved so well." Sir Hudson Lowe could not, of course, expect the King of France to permit this to take place; and a grave was prepared among some weeping willows beside a fountain, in a small valley called Slane's, very near to Longwood. It was under the shade of these willows that the Exile had had his favourite evening seat; and it was there he had been heard to say, that if he must be interred in St. Helena, he would prefer to lie.

The body of the Emperor, clad in his usual uniform, was now exposed to the public view, and visited accordingly by all the population of the island. The soldiers of the garrison passed the couch slowly, in single file; each officer pausing, in his turn, to press respectfully the frozen hand of the dead. On the 8th, his household, the governor, the admiral, and all the civil and military authorities of the place, attended him to the grave--the pall spread over his coffin being the military cloak which he wore at Marengo. The road not being passable for carriages, a party of English grenadiers bore Napoleon to his tomb. The admiral's ship fired minute guns, while Vignali read the service of his church. The coffin then descended amidst a discharge of three volleys from fifteen cannon; and a huge stone was lowered over the remains of one who needs no epitaph.

* * * * *

Napoleon confessed more than once at Longwood that he owed his downfall to nothing but the extravagance of his own errors. "It must be owned," said he, "that fortune spoiled me. Ere I was thirty years of age, I found myself invested with great power, and the mover of great events." No one, indeed, can hope to judge him fairly, either in the brilliancy of his day or the troubled darkness of his evening, who does not task imagination to conceive the natural effects, on a temperament and genius so fiery and daring, of that almost instantaneous transition from poverty and obscurity to the summit of fame, fortune, and power. The blaze which dazzled other men's eyes, had fatal influence on his. He began to believe that there was something superhuman in his own faculties, and that he was privileged to deny that any laws were made for him. Obligations by which he expected all besides to be fettered, he considered himself entitled to snap and trample. He became a deity to himself; and expected mankind not merely to submit to, but to admire and reverence, the actions of a demon. Well says the Poet,

"O! more or less than man--in high or low, Battling with nations, flying from the field; Now making monarchs' necks thy footstool, now More than thy meanest soldier taught to yield; An empire thou couldst crush, command, rebuild, But govern not thy pettiest passion, nor, However deeply in, men's spirits skilled, Look through thine own--nor curb the lust of war, Nor learn that tempted fate will leave the loftiest star."

His heart was naturally cold. His school-companion, who was afterwards his secretary, confesses that, even in the spring of youth, he was very little disposed to form friendships.[75] To say that he was incapable of such feelings, or that he really never had a friend, would be to deny to him any part in the nature and destiny of his species.--No one ever dared to be altogether alone in the world.--But we doubt if any man ever passed through life, sympathising so slightly with mankind; and the most wonderful part of his story is, the intensity of sway which he exerted over the minds of those in whom he so seldom permitted himself to contemplate anything more than the tools of his own ambition. So great a spirit must have had glimpses of whatever adorns and dignifies the character of man. But with him the feelings which bind love played only on the surface--leaving the abyss of selfishness untouched. His one instrument of power was genius; hence his influence was greatest among those who had little access to observe, closely and leisurely, the minuti?of his personal character and demeanour. The exceptions to this rule were very few.

Pride and vanity were strangely mingled in his composition. Who does not pity the noble chamberlain that confesses his blood to have run cold when he heard Napoleon--seated at dinner at Dresden among a circle of crowned heads--begin a story with, _When I was a lieutenant in the regiment of La Fere_? Who does not pity Napoleon when he is heard speaking of some decorations in the Tuileries, as having taken place "in the time of the king, my uncle?"[76]

This last weakness was the main engine of his overthrow. When he condescended to mimic all the established etiquettes of feudal monarchy--when he coined titles and lavished stars, and sought to melt his family into the small circle of hereditary princes--he adopted the surest means which could have been devised for alienating from himself the affections of all the men of the revolution, the army alone excepted, and for re-animating the hopes and exertions of the Bourbonists. It is clear that thenceforth he leaned almost wholly on the soldiery. No civil changes could after this affect his real position. Oaths and vows, charters and concessions, all were alike in vain. When the army was humbled and weakened in 1814, he fell from his throne, without one voice being lifted up in his favour. The army was no sooner strengthened, and re-encouraged, then it recalled him. He re-ascended the giddy height, with the daring step of a hero, and professed his desire to scatter from it nothing but justice and mercy. But no man trusted his words. His army was ruined at Waterloo; and the brief day of the second reign passed, without a twilight, into midnight.

We are not yet far enough from Buonaparte to estimate the effects of his career. He recast the art of war; and was conquered in the end by men who had caught wisdom and inspiration from his own campaigns. He gave both permanency and breadth to the influence of the French Revolution. His reign, short as it was, was sufficient to make it impossible that the offensive privileges of caste should ever be revived in France; and, this iniquity being once removed, there could be little doubt that such a nation would gradually acquire possession of a body of institutions worthy of its intelligence. Napoleon was as essentially, and irreclaimably, a despot, as a warrior; but his successor, whether a Bourbon or a Buonaparte, was likely to be a constitutional sovereign. The tyranny of a meaner hand would not have been endured after that precedent.

On Europe at large he has left traces of his empire, not less marked or important. He broke down the barriers everywhere of custom and prejudice; and revolutionised the spirit of the Continent. His successes and his double downfall taught absolute princes their weakness and injured nations their strength. Such hurricanes of passion as the French Revolution--such sweeping scourges of mankind as Napoleon Buonaparte, are not permitted but as the avengers of great evils, and the harbingers of great good. Of the influence of both, as regards the continent, it may be safely said--that even now we have seen only "the beginning of the end." The reigning sovereigns of Europe are, with rare exceptions, benevolent and humane men; and their subjects, no less than they, ought to remember the lesson of all history--that violent and sudden changes, in the structure of social and political order, have never yet occurred, without inflicting utter misery upon at least one generation.

It was England that fought the great battle throughout on the same principle, without flinching; and, but for her perseverance, all the rest would have struggled in vain. It is to be hoped that the British nation will continue to see, and to reverence, in the contest and in its result, the immeasurable advantages which the sober strength of a free but fixed constitution possesses over the mad energies of anarchy on the one hand, and, on the other, over all that despotic selfishness can effect, even under the guidance of the most consummate genius.

[Footnote 74:

"The godlike Ulysses is not yet dead upon the earth; He still lingers a living captive within the breadth of ocean, In some unapproachable island, where savage men detain him."

ODYSS. book i. ver. 195.]

[Footnote 75: peu aimant.]

[Footnote 76: Louis XVI.!--married to the aunt of Maria Louisa--See Bourienne.]

Made in the USA
Middletown, DE
02 November 2016